ARCHAEOLOGY
in the GREAT BASIN and SOUTHWEST

FRONTISPIECE. Donald D. and Catherine S. Fowler in the Carson Range, Nevada, about 2008 (photograph by Eugene M. Hattori).

ARCHAEOLOGY
in the GREAT BASIN and SOUTHWEST

Papers in Honor of Don D. Fowler

EDITED BY
Nancy J. Parezo and Joel C. Janetski

THE UNIVERSITY OF UTAH PRESS
Salt Lake City

The Defiance House Man colophon is a registered trademark of the University of Utah Press. It is based on a 4-ft-tall Ancient Puebloan pictograph (late PIII) near Glen Canyon, Utah.

18 17 16 15 14 1 2 3 4 5

LIBRARY OF CONGRESS CATALOGING-IN-PUBLICATION DATA

Archaeology in the Great Basin and Southwest : papers in honor of Don D. Fowler / edited by Nancy J. Parezo and Joel C Janetski.

p. cm.

Includes bibliographical references and index.

ISBN 978-1-60781-282-1 (hardback) — ISBN 978-1-60781-307-1 (paper) — ISBN 978-1-60781-283-8 (ebook)

1. Archaeology—Great Basin. 2. Archaeology—Southwest, New. 3. Indians of North America—Great Basin.—Antiquities. 4. Indians of North America—Southwest, New—Antiquities. 5. Paleo-Indians—Great Basin. 6. Paleo-Indians—Southwest, New. 7. Great Basin—Antiquities. 8. Southwest, New—Antiquities. I. Parezo, Nancy J., author, editor of compilation. II. Janetski, Joel C., author, editor of compilation. III. Fowler, Don D., 1936– honoree.

E78.G67A73 2013

979'.01—dc23

2013030218

Printed and bound by Sheridan Books, Inc., Ann Arbor, Michigan.

Contents

Part III. Specialty Studies in Social and Historical Contexts

Figures

Tables

PART I

Introducing Don D. Fowler

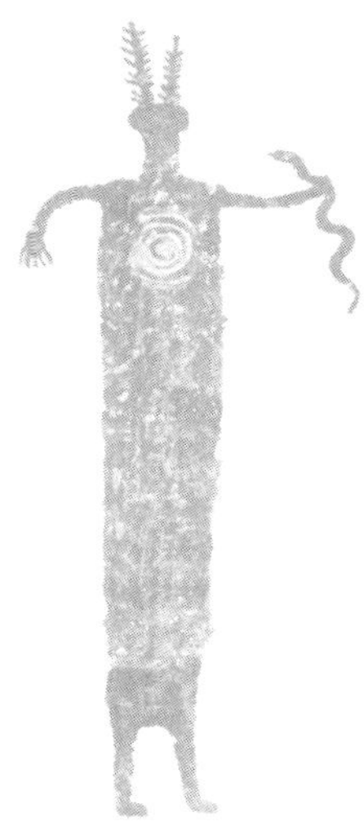

1

Honoring Don D. Fowler

An Introduction

Nancy J. Parezo and Joel C. Janetski

Nineteen thirty-six was an eventful year for American anthropology, especially in the arid Intermountain West. Regional ethnographer and later archaeologist Isabel Kelly was appointed to represent the American Anthropological Association at the Seventh American Scientific Congress in Mexico City. Morris Opler published a summary of Jicarilla Apache culture, while Elsie Clews Parsons analyzed Hopi and Keres relations; Julian Steward summarized Pueblo material culture found in western Utah. Emil Haury proposed the Mogollon Culture concept, Paul Martin published his report on the Lowry Ruin, and L. S. Cressman published his survey of the Guano Valley region in southeastern Oregon. Earl Morris continued to stabilize Mesa Verde ruins, while the Gila Pueblo staff worked at Snaketown. Parsons paid the American Anthropological Association $902.15 to publish Leslie White's Santo Domingo monograph, the final hurdle to his being awarded his doctorate. The inaugural volume of *The Kiva* contained Clara Lee Fraps's short description of the Tanque Verde Ruins. The Society for American Archaeology (SAA) was one year old, and in the first volume of *American Antiquity* practitioners discussed methodology, terminology, the importance of various types of artifacts, the effect of the Great Depression, and the archaeological personality. Much was new and exciting, as men and women dedicated to understanding the history of indigenous peoples of the American West worked at the edges of knowledge, incorporating what was known in new configurations of understanding. Field schools were held throughout the American West, training the next generation of archaeologists, men and women who would spend their lives dedicated to archaeological scholarship. And, finally, in a small town in Utah, Don D. Fowler was born.

This last event, contextualized in terms of what had happened in archaeology in general and archaeology in the Great Basin and American Southwest specifically, is the reason for this volume. *Archaeology in the Great Basin and Southwest* is dedicated to recognizing and honoring Don Fowler's life's work. The volume is based, mostly, on two sessions presented at the 2010 Annual Meeting of the Society for American Archaeology, held in Sacramento, California. It was appropriate to have held these sessions on the seventy-fifth birthday of this eminent anthropologist, who since the late 1950s, when he first set foot in Glen Canyon, has been one of American archaeology's most prolific scholars, noteworthy educators, influential policy makers, skilled interpreters of archaeology to the American public, and inexhaustible institution builders.

The volume pays tribute to the scope and depth of Don Fowler's activities with essays written by his colleagues, students, and friends that reflect and expand on his interests and scholarship. These contributions have been combined into a festschrift organized thematically to serve as a summary of the state of our knowledge in several areas reflective of Don's wide-ranging interests. We asked participants not to honor Don simply by recounting great stories about his life and how he had influenced their careers (though many fine examples were indeed given at the sessions, along with many tantalizing glimpses into his life and past activities) but, rather, by expanding knowledge about their chosen topic. The resulting chapters are thoughtful reflections and summations, calls for future research, discussions of new means to interpret what we know (or think we know) through paradigmatic redirections, and challenges to our current state of understanding. These include challenges to extend our knowledge by asking new questions of archaeology's cumulative "old" curated data and about how archaeology has been and is currently done as a mode of knowledge production and interpreted information dissemination. In short, this is not the usual honoring volume: it is a call for an active archaeology, an archaeology pointed to the future that acknowledges, incorporates, and understands the archaeology of the past. It is archaeology for all times centered on place.

Since Don Fowler's colleagues and students have gone on to influential careers in archaeology and its sister disciplines, and because of the range of Don's scholarship and intellectual interests, a wide variety of themes have emerged in these chapters centering on two regions, the American Southwest and the Great Basin. As a consequence, we have structured the volume in three parts. In brief, Part 1 introduces the reader to Don Fowler, the individual and the archaeologist. Part 2 presents a broad sweep of issues in Great Basin and Southwestern prehistory, with chapters organized, for the most part, and with topics ranging from the Paleoindians in the desert Southwest to insights into Great Basin high-altitude adaptations. Part 3 addresses several themes in Great Basin and Southwestern archaeology, particularly the social and historical factors that play into the practice of archaeology today, from how research questions are posed, to what is considered compelling evidence, to how information is interpreted, to the importance of Native American voices in anthropological interpretation.

Like most of the authors in this volume, Don Fowler spent much of his professional life ensuring that archaeology had the infrastructure to conduct its work and disseminate its understandings and knowledge to the society that supports it. As people noted at the SAA sessions, he worked tirelessly to make sure that the profession's premier association, the Society for American Archaeology, was fiscally healthy and, moreover, that it made a difference. Don also worked Capitol Hill well, helping to develop enforceable antiquities laws and to ensure their passage. As president of the SAA from 1985 to 1987, Don made certain that the perspective of the profession was included in informed federal policy dealing with preservation and stewardship. He did the same at the state and local level, as well as helping to build institutions and organizations to make archaeology a vigorous, active discipline, be it in cultural resource management or conservation and preservation. In short Don has been an institution builder at the local, state, and national level, like John Wesley Powell, the foundational archaeologist and geologist about whom Don has written so insightfully. There is a reason he has been honored by several archaeological associations with lifetime achievement awards. This was a theme expounded upon at length by discussants Linda Cordell, William Lipe, Catherine Fowler, and Jeremy Sabloff, who have also spent many years in similar activities.

We turn now to a more detailed look at the volume. Part 2 initiates the individual thematic contributions beginning with Bruce Huckell's summation of what is known about Paleoindians in the Southwest. Ted Goebel and Joshua Keene offer a critical review of sites, dates, and context for Great Basin Stemmed projectile points, with particular attention to the Clovis–Stemmed temporal relationship. George Jones and Charlotte Beck also deal with rare early sites as they attempt to resolve intriguing questions regarding shifting human strategies and material culture during the transition from the earliest Holocene or Paleoarchaic into the mid-Holocene. The Middle Archaic in the western Great Basin is better known, but the wealth of data is as challenging as is the dearth of data in the earlier periods. Craig Young characterizes this period by looking closely at functionally complementary sites and then relies on diverse theoretical perspectives to understand the social and economic factors at play in the broader settlement and subsistence strategies operating at this time.

Barbara Roth introduces another transition in the region, the acceptance of farming in the southern Southwest. Roth looks specifically at the Tucson Basin, where Middle Archaic foragers integrated maize into their subsistence regimen by 2000 BC. She then explores why maize was accepted and the consequences of that reception. Farming and its consequences are further discussed in Stephen Lekson's stimulating chapter, which looks at the Fremont culture on the interface of the Southwest and the Great Basin, but with a global view. Joel Janetski and Richard Talbot also subscribe to a Southwestern approach in their chapter focused on understanding Fremont material and stylistic variability by introducing a tribal model that predicts such regional differences.

Chapters by David Hurst Thomas and John Ives focus on studies of the more recent past. Thomas asks how and why Great Basin people exploited high altitudes and offers understanding via foraging theory and traditional gender roles. Ives, on the other hand, provides fresh insights into the intriguing Promontory culture of the northeastern Great Basin. His perspective is from the north, the homeland of Athapaskan peoples whom Steward speculated may have spent time in the Promontory Caves.

Polly Schaafsma examines what is perhaps the most intriguing and difficult cumulative archaeological data set of all, rock art, which cannot be preserved and protected in a museum, can be savaged by vandalism, and, from the perspective of research, is difficult to control chronologically. In this chapter she extols the virtues of the ever-growing role of collaborative studies with Native people, as well as more theory-driven approaches to rock art research. This is a topic that reflects the newest interests of Don Fowler's illustrious career: the preservation and study of beauty and the integration of aesthetics and rigorous science.

Finally, Steven Simms, James O'Connell, and Kevin Jones review the impact of their groundbreaking essay from 1982 (see O'Connell et al. 1982), which proposed the use of evolutionary ecology as a theoretical perspective to assist in understanding human behavior in the Great Basin. As attested by this and several other contributions in this volume (those by Thomas, Young, and Jones and Beck), the impact of this approach has been considerable.

Don Fowler has long been noted as a historian of science, an individual who strives to understand how past research has affected what we know and what we think we know. In that vein, Part 3 begins with three chapters that examine how archaeology is both professional work and thrilling adventure and how what researchers have done in the past all too often gets lost as archaeologists practice replaceable rather than cumulative science. David Madsen's chapter on the history of research at the granddaddy of eastern Great Basin archaeological sites, Danger Cave, is a narrative full of insights offered long ago by its first explorers but, unfortunately, long forgotten.

Richard Hughes's contribution relies on sourced obsidian artifacts from Danger Cave to test Jennings's Desert Culture model, which argued for thousands of years of cultural continuity in the Great Basin. By combining materials from museum collections, new technological methodologies to control sourcing, and rigorous methodological controls, Hughes is able to ask new questions of old data, a theme found throughout this volume and an essential methodological aspect of the history of archaeology.

David Rhode's history of the naming of the desert bighorn sheep exposes the role of Shoshone people working with biologist Edward Nelson to find and describe these elusive animals. It is a story, not told elsewhere, that recognizes a truth that is underappreciated in cultural anthropology as well as archaeology: Native Americans taught the scientists who worked in the region, and their work incorporated this knowledge. Americanist theories, descriptions, names, and classifications are as full of Native American knowledge as they are of the theories, knowledge, and heritage of the practitioners.

The next three chapters deal directly with Native American issues, such as the continued consideration of ancestral or contemporary Native peoples as "primitive" or "simple" and the consequences this assumption has for archaeology as a profession, site of engaged social justice, and source of knowledge. Challenging complacency, including unaddressed assumptions that color research designs, interpretations, and conclusions, is a theme that runs through these essays. The first, by Heidi Roberts, is a case study about implementing the Native American Graves Protection and Repatriation Act at the state and federal levels. Roberts argues that archaeologists should listen to descendants for they often have elegant theories of where their ancestors lived that can challenge established assumptions. Nieves Zedeño's chapter extends this argument as an ethical issue that involves Native American rights as well as the value of traditional knowledge. Contemporary scholarship must include multiple voices and perspectives; if it does not, it is simply a tool of those in power—as Don Fowler's many articles on the history and ethics of archaeology eloquently demonstrate. David Wilcox takes archaeologists to task by demanding that they confront their biases, abandon ethnocentric views of Indian people, and recognize the complexity of Native American social, political, and religious lives. As is the case for all the authors in this volume, his goal is to encourage better, more informed archaeology in the future.

The next two chapters of Part 3 reflect on the institutions that make archaeology possible and the history of science and sociology of knowledge perspectives that Don has brought to our understanding of how and why archaeology is what it is today and how past activities affect contemporary science, both practically and philosophically. These essays pay homage to Don's tireless devotion to ensuring that American archaeology has the infrastructure to thrive and function ethically.

William Doelle's piece on the role of nonprofits in archaeological research offers a fascinating temporal perspective on the critical role of these institutions in encouraging and supporting Southwestern archaeology over the last century and a half. Doelle brings to light the evolution of nonprofits and their articulation with antiquities law and the need for modern practitioners to understand and support policy efforts.

In a similar historical vein but on a decidedly different topic is the chapter by Donald Hardesty and Eugene Hattori, which traces the development of historical archaeology from its early roots to a discipline rich with multiple themes and strengths. Southwestern and Great Basin archaeology is not only about indigenous peoples: archaeology in pluralistic societies is about all residents and their descendants.

Part 3 closes with three case studies in dendroarchaeology and material culture studies that demonstrate the fruitfulness of research using existing museum collections and large data sets reflecting the history of specific endeavors in the discipline. Don Fowler has advocated this perspective since his postdoctoral work with the John Wesley Powell collections housed at the Smithsonian Institution. The chapters by Richard Ahlstrom and Christian Downum and by Stephen Nash and Nina Rogers construct and analyze two regional data sets (Flagstaff and Mesa Verde, respectively) and show how their evidential value is a function of their origin. This aspect of methodological rigor, despite "an embarrassment of riches," is a hallmark of good scholarship, especially in issues of chronological control. Improving scholarship so that practitioners can be more certain about their conclusions is an issue that permeates all chapters in this volume.

Museum collections and their associated documents, as well as field notes, are always active data, even if some think of them as "old" because they were collected by someone else at an earlier time. In the third case study, Laurie Webster, Linda Cordell, Kelley Hays-Gilpin, and Ed Jolie prove this point by digging into museum textile collections as they explore the origins of Chacoan ritual behavior. Not only do their investigations lead to convincing conclusions, but in the process they demonstrate the rich research potential of museum holdings, some recovered well over a century ago.

We have left the discussion of Part 1 of this volume for last because it deals with the individual we are honoring, Don Fowler. Two of Don's lifelong friends and colleagues, Melvin Aikens and William Lipe, have penned biographical overviews of Don's life and present personal assessments of him in action, as an individual scholar and friend and as a humanistic scientist, a scholar of world renown.

Don Fowler's career and contributions span several decades and numerous disciplines. He is an esteemed and valued colleague for many in his profession. Don is first and foremost an archaeologist who has concentrated his efforts in the Great Basin and American Southwest. Second, he is an educator and mentor to numerous anthropology students at the University of Nevada, Reno, and elsewhere. Third, Don is a skilled administrator and insightful diplomat whose vision and commitment have played a critical role over the years and, especially, during his tenure as president of the Society for American Archaeology. Specific contributions and biographical highlights including how archaeology entered his life are presented in Mel Aikens's and William Lipe's contributions.

As Bill Lipe notes, in many ways, Don Fowler has emulated his mentor, Jesse D. Jennings, as he has encouraged, supported, and advised promising students and colleagues whom he believed were or would be good scholars. But what makes a good scholar, one worthy of recognition by other scholars? Again, we defer to Aikens's review of Don's life and career for specifics, but we maintain that Don in many ways epitomizes the ideal of an archaeologist. But what is this ideal? To find out we turn to the history of archaeology.

In 1881 an anonymous author wrote a series of articles entitled "A Study of American Archaeology" for the *Universalist Quarterly and General Review*, a Boston-based publication of the Trinitarian Universalist Church. The journal, which ran from 1844 to 1891, was concerned with literature and popular topics, both secular and religious, such as "speculative philosophy," "literary intelligence," "reviews of religious movements and moral enterprises," and "reviews of works that appear to influence or are likely to influence, in any important respect, the public taste, opinions and morals" (Universalist Quarterly and General Review 1848:1). Archaeology fell within at least two of these categories. The author described the ideal archaeologist as an accomplished scholar but skeptical scientist at the beginning of part 3, "Process of Investigation":

> It would be an easy task to construct an ideal archaeologist, and point out the methods he should pursue in order to accomplish his labors. The archaeologist places before himself no set rules or formulas, and yet his labors are systematic, and his methods are easily comprehended. The processes used are not according to mathematical exactions, nor are they based upon his individual inventions; but are the results of long experiment [i.e., experience], and the profound investigations of the most learned authorities. The idea has been promulgated that pre-historic archaeology is a bundle of guess-work. A defense of its principles is not called for by those engaged in the study, and as regards those who would slur its teachings, an exposition of its methods would neither convince nor conciliate [Universalist Quarterly and General Review 1881:281–282].

The wording may have changed over the last century and a half, but the qualities of the ideal archaeologist have not. Don Fowler has represented these qualities throughout his career. We present this portrait because Don Fowler, who has studied the history of science using the sociology of knowledge as his theoretical approach, will recognize the type of scholar being talked about from his own studies and also because we think it is a good portrait of Don.

We also want to call upon the words of another earlier practitioner to fill in this portrait. Don Fowler's career epitomizes Dorothy Keur's ideas about anthropology as a way of life and a worldview:

> When I began anthropology, everyone I knew—friends, relations and even other academicians—thought of anthropology as the study of oddities by eccentrics. And yet, it gave me such a sense of unity with mankind, a reaching out, a feeling of touching other human beings. I gained a feeling of my own insignificance, one tiny being out of all the billions of humans on the earth. I *love* that feeling, and was very stimulated by it, and also by the concept of the relativity of values. I wanted to explore other values, other people's lives, and also to teach that to thousands of others—not that they would ever become professional anthropologists, but that they would have a viewpoint. Anthropology *is* a viewpoint of life. It's a philosophy. It's science. It's humanity [interview, 1985, Daughters of the Desert Project, directed by Barbara A. Babcock and Nancy J. Parezo, Wenner-Gren Foundation for Anthropological Research archives, New York].

Understanding the men and women who hold such a viewpoint is important for understanding cultural anthropology and archaeology. It reflects a passion for archaeology that we hope will come through in this volume, as it has come through in Don Fowler's works.

REFERENCES CITED

O'Connell, James F., Kevin T. Jones, and Steven R. Simms

1982 Some Thoughts on Prehistoric Archaeology in the Great Basin. In *Man and Environment in the Great Basin*, edited by D. B. Madsen and J. F. O'Connell, pp. 227–240. SAA Papers, 2. Society for American Archaeology, Washington, D.C.

Universalist Quarterly and General Review

1848 Introduction. *Universalist Quarterly and General Review* 1(1):1.

1881 A Study of American Archaeology, Pt. III: Process of Investigation. *Universalist Quarterly and General Review* 18, July: 281–294.

2

Don D. Fowler, Archaeologist

C. Melvin Aikens

Don D. Fowler's archaeological career to the time of this writing spans more than 50 years and is still a work in progress. Don's name is known to every North American archaeologist, as well as to others around the world, for his many contributions. From his first field days as an undergraduate research assistant on the Glen Canyon Archaeological Salvage Project in 1957, through his 1985–1987 service as president of the Society for American Archaeology (SAA), and continuing to the present, Don has worked without respite to expand our collective knowledge of the human past. He has been a strong proponent of both national and local regulatory and institutional initiatives to improve the scope and quality of archaeological research in the realm of cultural resource management. He played a key role, as president-elect and president of the SAA during a critical period, helping the premier professional society of American archaeologists recast its organization for a new future after an amicable administrative separation from the American Anthropological Association. Concurrently with his numerous leadership activities, Don has made many scholarly contributions of enduring value through his personal research into the development of anthropology in the American Southwest and the study of ethnohistory and archaeology in the Southwest and Great Basin. He has accomplished this by contextualizing our field within the history of science and the history of American culture and society.

Don was born in 1936 in the remote and tiny central Utah Mormon pioneer community of Torrey. The family moved to Ogden, about 40 mi north of Salt Lake City, where he grew up. Upon graduating from Ogden High School Don entered Weber College, also in Ogden. Weber was a former Church of Jesus Christ of Latter-day Saints academy that had become a public two-year "junior college." Today it is now Weber State University.

At Weber Don came under the energizing influence of Dr. Jennings G. Olson, the college's most charismatic teacher and a broad-gauge scholar who taught across the fields of anthropology, religion, philosophy, and psychology. Drs. Robert Mikkelsen, H. E. D. Redford, and Larry Evans helped Don develop his range of interests and honed his facility with writing and the subtle use of the English language. Prepared by these early scholarly encounters, Don continued on to the University of Utah in Salt Lake City, where he majored in anthropology. There he again had the luck to find outstanding mentors who had broad intellectual range: Professors Jesse D. Jennings, Charles E. Dibble, Robert Anderson, Elmer R. Smith, and Warren L. d'Azevedo. All helped Don prepare for a lifelong career.

Don soon became the trusted and very busy undergraduate assistant of Dr. Jennings, who was just then conceptualizing and preparing for the University of Utah's part in the epic Glen Canyon Project, officially known as the Upper Colorado River Basin Archaeological Salvage Project. The building of a great hydroelectric dam on the Colorado River near the Crossing of the Fathers would ultimately create Lake Powell, which flooded hundreds of miles of the Colorado's and the San Juan's canyons and washes in the Four Corners area of Utah, Arizona, Colorado, and New Mexico, the heartland of Ancestral Puebloan culture. The Glen Canyon Project was to become a major milestone on the path to modern cultural resource management (CRM). Upon this basis Don built the many anthropological, CRM, and leadership contributions of his subsequent career: chair of the American Society for Conservation Archeology Regional Workshop on Cultural Resource Management, Reno; the liaison member of the National Committee on Historic Resources, American Institute of Architects; Nevada director of Preservation Action, Inc.; a member of the U.S. Committee, International Council on Monuments and Sites and the Management Study Team, President's National Commission on Americans Outdoors; science adviser for the Grand Canyon Management Research Center, U.S. Geological Survey; and the national cochair of the Council for the Preservation of Anthropological Records, along with his friend Nancy Parezo. He currently serves on the board of the Center for Desert Archaeology run by William Doelle, one of the volume authors, and has been instrumental in the BSI Foundation and organizations dedicated to the recording, study, and preservation of rock art. He has also been the organizer of numerous workshops and symposia on historic preservation and cultural resource management over the last 40 years and, in 1977, even a consultant to King Abdulaziz University, Jeddah, Saudi Arabia, for research centers for the development of arid lands. Through association leadership and government consultation Don has been instrumental in making conservation and preservation archaeology and CRM the dynamic fields they are today.

Don learned a tremendous amount about the Great Basin and the practice of archaeology—how one surveys, excavates, records, analyzes, and writes up results—in the early 1960s. He also learned how to be a master organizer through years of practice. As Dr. Jennings's man of all work (his general factotum), young Don made endless shopping lists and forays around Salt Lake City, assembling World War II army surplus field gear and other materiel needed to conduct archaeology in the Canyonlands. There were to be a number of crews (we worked together in 1961 for the first time) and long field seasons in the remote and nearly roadless, depopulated landscape, and much logistical preparation was called for. Jennings was ever insistent on thorough planning and preparation and always at pains to see that none of his crews had any "adventures" in the field, which he equated with mishaps caused by inadequate forethought and lack of good sense. But as Don relates in his recent autobiography, *The Glen Canyon Country: A Personal Memoir* (Fowler 2011), adventures and memorable incidents were as inevitable as were the lifelong friendships and collegial associations that have been a hallmark of Don's career. The "daily routines" and "adventures" also provided dozens of good stories that have fascinated students of the history of archaeology and budding archaeologists ever since.

During this period Don had the further good fortune of meeting such legendary archaeologists and Jennings's compatriots as Charlie Steen, Erik K. Reed, Robert C. Lister, and Florence C. Lister and of getting in his personally first archaeological field season—which was also the first season of the Glen Canyon Project—working for James H. Gunnerson at Gates Roost on the Lower Escalante River. As things turned out, Don spent six years in the field on the Glen Canyon Project (1957–1962), more than any other archaeologist or cultural anthropologist who also got started there.

Another portentous Don encounter during the Glen Canyon Project years was with Kay Sweeney, then a bright young undergraduate in cultural anthropology who had impressed Dr. Jennings so much that he offered her a job conducting ethnohistoric and ethnological fieldwork in the Canyonlands with Robert C. Euler as her adviser. Kay was the only woman Jennings ever sent to the field on sustained and self-directed Glen Canyon Project work. He made exception to his rule of archaeology as a male endeavor. He was right about Kay: for over 40 years she has been the well-known Catherine S. Fowler, a distinguished ethnologist, ethnobiologist, museologist, and linguist; graduate of the University of Utah (B.A., 1962) and University of Pittsburgh (Ph.D., 1972); professor emerita of the University of Nevada–Reno; trustee of the Smithsonian Institution's National Museum of the American Indian; and member of both the American Academy of Arts and Sciences and the National Academy of Sciences. She is by far one of the country's most outstanding ethnographers, linguists, and scholars of museology, material culture, and art, as well as a proponent of long-term commitment to work with Native American communities and of conducting fieldwork to ensure dignity and respect for Native collaborators in the way that several authors in this volume have called for. Just as for many Don is the model of what an archaeologist and institution builder should be, so Kay is the model of what an ethnographer should be—and also a walking encyclopedia on flora. (Go for a walk with her sometime.) The careers of Don and Kay have felicitously intertwined in various collaborations ever since the Glen Canyon Project days: since the mid-1960s they have studied John Wesley Powell's journal, manuscripts, and artifact collections; Powell's research in the Grand Canyon and the history of anthropology in the Southwest and Great Basin; Stephen Power's research with the Washoe and Paiute; and the culture history of many Great Basin groups. They have written contributions in scholarly and popular works, from the *Encyclopedia Britannica* to the *Handbook of North American Indians*.

Don completed a B.A. in anthropology at Utah in 1959 and continued on with graduate work in anthropology and American studies until 1962, then matriculating at the University of Pittsburgh. In 1965 he completed a Ph.D. in anthropology under the mentorship of Edward A. Kennard and George Peter Murdock. During these formative years Don's university studies were variously supported by Glen Canyon Project employment and National Defense Education Act, Wenner-Gren, Mellon, National Academy of Science/National Research Council, and Smithsonian fellowships.

The University of Nevada–Reno hired Don in 1964. He quickly climbed the academic ladder there, retiring in 2006 as the Distinguished Mamie Kleberg Professor of Historic Preservation and Anthropology, a title he held since 1978. Over this time he played many leadership roles at the university, including bringing forth modern cultural resource management out of salvage archaeology. One of his most important contributions was education. He was the founding director of the University of Nevada–Reno Continuing Education Program in Heritage Resources Management. In addition to serving his obligatory time as department chair, Don was the executive director of the Sundance Archaeological Research Fund and executive director and research professor of anthropology at the Social Sciences Center, Desert Research Institute, University of Nevada System. Such professional service came easily to Don, and he was good at it. Nationally, he served as president of the American Society for Conservation Archaeology, on two important committees of the Society of Professional Archaeologists, and as chair of the SAA National Archaeological Policy Committee. He was southwest director of the National Council on Preservation Education, coconvener of the SAA/Native American Task Force on Reburial Issues, national cochair of the Council for the Preservation of Anthropological Records, and president of the Society for American Archaeology.

As if Don did not have enough to do, in his spare time, he was a cofounder of the Nevada Archaeological Survey Council, Washoe Heritage Council, Nevada Heritage Council, Truckee Meadows Heritage Trust, and Preserve Nevada and cofounder and president of the Nevada Rock Art Foundation. In the course of these activities Don served as principal investigator on 92 University of Nevada grants and contracts, 1965–2007.

Don has shared his expertise and experience with many publics. He was a traveling lecturer of the Smithsonian Institution National Associates Program for 16 years (1980–1996), making presentations in 30 cities. He was also a University of Nevada and Nevada Humanities Committee traveling speaker, appearing in over 60 Nevada and eastern California communities, and a visiting lecturer for the American Anthropological Association. He has been a consultant and talking head for at least six major television documentaries on the Canyonlands, and there will be more in the future; and he has served his professional colleagues as an Editorial Board member for the *Heritage Management Journal*, the *Journal of California and Great Basin Anthropology*, and *Museum History Journal*.

Over the same period Don has been diligent in the study of archaeology, ethnohistory, and the history of anthropological research in the Southwest and Great Basin. He is the author, coauthor, or editor of 26 books or monographs and 92 journal articles, reviews, and other pieces. Also, over the past 50 years Don has presented some 90 papers of various sorts at professional meetings, many of which subsequently became published works. A short list of personal favorites, some coauthored or coedited, includes the following:

1971 *John Wesley Powell and the Anthropology of the Canyon Country* (with Robert C. Euler and C. S. Fowler)
1971 *Anthropology of the Numa: John Wesley Powell's Manuscripts on the Numic Peoples of Western North America, 1868–1880* (with C. S. Fowler)
1972 *Photographed All the Best Scenery. Jack Hillers' Diary of the Powell Expedition, 1871–75*
1979 *Material Culture of the Numa: The John Wesley Powell Collection, 1867–1880* (with J. F. Matley)
1986 *Anthropology of the Desert West: Essays in Honor of Jesse D. Jennings* (with Carol J. Condie)
1986 *American Archaeology Past and Future: A Celebration of the Society for American Archaeology, 1935–1985* (with David J. Meltzer and Jeremy A. Sabloff)
2000 *A Laboratory for Anthropology: Science and Romanticism in the American Southwest, 1846–1930*
2005 *Southwest Archaeology in the Twentieth Century* (with Linda Cordell)
2007 *Anthropology Goes to the Fair. The Louisiana Purchase Exposition, St. Louis, 1904* (with Nancy J. Parezo)
2008 *The Great Basin. People and Place in Ancient Times* (with C. S. Fowler)
2011 *The Glen Canyon Country: A Personal Memoir*

In his professorial role, Don spent more than 40 years teaching countless undergraduates in the classroom and seeing more hundreds of graduate students down their educational path to archaeological field research and professional careers (he chaired over 40 committees). Several of the authors in this volume gained greatly from his teaching and mentoring. In the process, Don fostered a great deal of cultural resource management and historic preservation work in the Great Basin. Testimonials to the respect with which Don is regarded as a teacher, researcher, and advocate for cultural resources are published in a previous festschrift presented by his students and colleagues (Hockett 2009).

Finally, it is a pleasure to note the many honors bestowed on Don by various bodies of appreciative colleagues. He has received the Award for Excellence and Distinguished Graduate Medal of the University of Pittsburgh, the Society of Professional Archaeologists Special Achievement Award, and the Byron S. Cummings Award of the Arizona Archaeological and Historical Society. He was invited to present the Loren Eiseley Distinguished Lecture of the University of Pennsylvania Museum and the Centennial Lecture of the School of Advanced Research, Santa Fe, New Mexico. Other honors include the Lifetime Achievement Award of the Society for American Archaeology and the McGimsey-Davis Distinguished Service Award of the Register of Professional Archaeologists for a Career Dedicated to Professionalism in Public Archaeology. Closer to home, Don has earned the University of Nevada–Reno Distinguished Faculty and Outstanding Researcher of the Year awards, the Great Basin Anthropological Association's Founders' Award for Lifetime Achievement in Great Basin Anthropology, the City of Reno Historical Resources Commission Distinguished Service Award, and the Lifetime Achievement Award of the Nevada Archaeological Association. And finally, on an international scale Don can be found easily in cyberspace. He even has his own entry on Wikipedia!

References Cited

Condie, Carol J., and D. D. Fowler (editors)
1986 *Anthropology of the Desert West: Essays in Honor of Jesse D. Jennings*. University of Utah Press, Salt Lake City.

Cordell, Linda, and D. D. Fowler (editors)
2005 *Southwest Archaeology in the Twentieth Century*. University of Utah Press, Salt Lake City.

Fowler, Catherine S., and Don D. Fowler (editors)
2008 *The Great Basin. People and Place in Ancient Times*. SAR Press, Santa Fe, New Mexico.

Fowler, Don D.
2010 [2000] *A Laboratory for Anthropology: Science and Romanticism in the American Southwest, 1846–1930*. University of Utah

Press, Salt Lake City. (Originally University of New Mexico Press, Albuquerque.)

2011 *The Glen Canyon Country: A Personal Memoir*. University of Utah Press, Salt Lake City.

Fowler, D. D. (editor)

1972 *Photographed All the Best Scenery. Jack Hillers' Diary of the Powell Expedition, 1871–75*. University of Utah Press, Salt Lake City.

Fowler, D. D., Robert C. Euler, and C. S. Fowler

1971 *John Wesley Powell and the Anthropology of the Canyon Country*. U.S. Geological Survey, Professional Paper No. 670. Washington, D.C.

Fowler, D. D., and C. S. Fowler (editors)

1971 *Anthropology of the Numa: John Wesley Powell's Manuscripts on the Numic Peoples of Western North America, 1868–1880*. Smithsonian Contributions to Anthropology No. 14. Washington, D.C.

Fowler, D. D., and J. F. Matley

1979 *Material Culture of the Numa: The John Wesley Powell Collection, 1867–1880*. Smithsonian Contributions to Anthropology No. 26. Washington, D.C.

Hockett, Bryan (editor)

2009 *Past, Present and Future Issues in Great Basin Archaeology: Papers in Honor of Don D. Fowler*. Cultural Resource Series No. 20. Nevada State Bureau of Land Management, Carson City.

Meltzer, David J., Don D. Fowler, and Jeremy A. Sabloff (editors)

1986 *American Archaeology Past and Future: A Celebration of the Society for American Archaeology, 1935–1985*. Smithsonian Institution Press, Washington, D.C.

Parezo, Nancy J., and Don D. Fowler

2007 *Anthropology Goes to the Fair. The Louisiana Purchase Exposition, St. Louis, 1904*. University of Nebraska Press, Lincoln.

3

Don Fowler and the Glen Canyon Project

Formative Experiences

William D. Lipe

As I was preparing my comments for the 2011 Society for American Archaeology (SAA) symposium that gave rise to this book, I thought back to my first SAA meeting. It was in spring 1959, and Don Fowler and I were both working for Jesse Jennings on the Glen Canyon Project (see Figure 3.1). The University of Utah was the host, and Jennings was the incoming president. It was the largest SAA meeting so far, with over 300 registrants. Don and I were put in charge of projecting slides during the sessions. The revolutionary technology of the Kodak Carousel was still a couple of years away. The speakers, if they had slides, would hand us a bunch when they got up to speak, and we would either drop them one by one into a projector (if it was an old one) or load them into a straight tray (if it was the latest model). For some papers, the order of the slides did not make an appreciable difference. Multiple views of "Another Unusual Artifact from Yoknapatawpha County" do not necessarily demand a particular sequence.

We have come a long way since those days. In addition to being far more numerous, SAA papers now are shorter and almost always better organized and better presented. PowerPoint is a big advance over the ancestors of the Carousel. Papers are more likely to be grouped into symposia. And more of the papers and symposia are planned in advance to be the first runs for eventual publication, as was the case here.

In the over five decades since Don and I showed slides at that SAA meeting, the field of American archaeology has expanded enormously—in numbers of active researchers, in the kinds of questions addressed and the methods used for addressing them, and especially, in detailed knowledge of the archaeological record. We use that last term in two senses—one is for the items and traces that got left in or on the ground by past peoples, but the other is the record we create as a result of observing and analyzing those things. And in turn, our ability to learn from those physical traces of the past is dependent on sets of techniques, methods, and theories.

The archaeological record created by our writings, databases, and conceptual frameworks is vastly larger and more complex than when Don and I entered the field. It provides more evidence on which to base generalizations but makes actually coming up with them harder. It was easier to propose a trend or a big unifying concept when we had only a few data points. Thus, since the 1950s, "doing archaeology" has become an increasingly complicated but increasingly ambitious and productive enterprise.

Essays of the sort included in this volume are invaluable in helping both experienced professionals and incoming students find vantage points from which they can review the large amount of work already done and plot ways forward to accomplish new research. Many of the chapters in this volume review, critically evaluate, and synthesize large amounts of published and unpublished empirical evidence—in some cases, paleoenvironmental and ethnographic as well as archaeological. Several explicitly evaluate and sort out the theoretical and methodological frameworks through which archaeologists attempt to make sense of what happened in the prehistoric Great Basin and Southwest. Still others document aspects of the history of archaeological research, a knowledge of which contributes greatly to understanding why problems and patterns are conceptualized the way they are.

Taken as a group, all the chapters proceed from the assumption that the main goal of archaeology is to provide substantive interpretations of what happened in the past based on empirical evidence. They are successful in helping us navigate portions of the complex landscape of knowledge that archaeology has generated in the decades since that 1959 SAA meeting. That this volume lives up to these standards is a tribute to Don Fowler, who played a role both in the careers of these authors and in varying degrees in the development of the data and the research questions they address in their essays. In fact, the development of the complex and dynamic field that is American archaeology today owes much to Don's work over his career.

In the second chapter of this volume, Mel Aikens does a fine job of reviewing that remarkable career and the quality and diversity of Don's accomplishments. Among other things, he describes Don's early experience working for Jesse Jennings on the

FIGURE 3.1. Glen Canyon crew, July 24, 1960. Back row, left to right: Calvin Porter, Don Fowler, Dan Seurlock, Buddy Thomas, Ed Keane, Bill Lipe, Dick Gould, Frank Weir, Floyd Sharrock; front row, left to right: Robert Cheel, Alex Sharp, Lyle Palmer, Johnny Conway, Keith Rogers, Allen Howard (Archaeology Center Collection, 42Sa00-348; courtesy of Special Collections, Marriott Library, University of Utah).

University of Utah section of the Glen Canyon Archaeological Project (Mel also played a significant role in that work). The "GCP" was the megaproject of its time and one of the largest, if not the largest, of the reservoir salvage era. My comments are designed to complement Mel's and, in particular, to dwell on Don's Glen Canyon experiences and some of the parallels between his career and that of his mentor, Jesse Jennings. (I recently finished a retrospective piece on the GCP [Lipe 2012], so I have just undergone a self-taught refresher course on the way that project was organized and what it did [and did not] accomplish.) In the following pages, I will offer some speculations on how Don's experience on the GCP "preadapted" him to successfully pursue some of the topics and themes that characterize his subsequent career.

I first met Don in June 1958, when I showed up for work as a new crew chief on the GCP. Though still an undergraduate, Don already had one season of fieldwork in the Glen Canyon area under his belt. I put in four field seasons on the project—three on the same crews as Don—but he stayed with it for a total of six—longer than anyone else except Jennings. Don began as an undergraduate assistant to Jennings, helping get equipment and supplies ready to go to the field, but rapidly emerged as a central player in this very large and complex project. Being part of the GCP certainly influenced my subsequent career in many ways, and I think that this experience also gave Don some early opportunities that he later made the most of.

Don of course emerged from the GCP with lots of field experience and his first publications, and the core of his career has been organizing, funding, supervising, and publishing successful research undertakings. Jesse Jennings was a role model for how to effectively administer a very large project (see comments in Lipe 2012), although I think that Don usually found some "kinder and gentler" ways to motivate his people to do what needed to be done.

Several other aspects of Don's remarkably diverse career can perhaps also be traced back to the GCP days. These include building and effectively "working" a large personal network, understanding how to get things done efficiently, actively developing ways to bring the insights of archaeology to a broader public, becoming a leader in the transformation of "salvage" archaeology into modern "cultural resource management," and promoting a professional commitment to preserving archaeological and anthropological collections and records.

Don's early experience in helping Jennings get field projects equipped must have sharpened his intuitive understanding that if you wanted to get something done, you needed to find the person or persons who could best help you do it and then go talk to them. In other words, you needed to develop a network and then make use of it. His role as Jennings's part-time assistant also led to meetings during the academic year with visiting scholars and senior people from academia and the federal agencies involved in implementing this very large project.

I recall that among our 1958 field crew members, Don knew more significant people in archaeology and anthropology than those of us "old-timers" who already had a year or two of graduate work. He has both relied on and contributed to his very large network over the years, and it has included many movers and shakers in the political and business worlds, in addition to professional colleagues. I never saw Don's Rolodex back in the days when that was how you kept track of people, but it must have been a huge one. He has also stayed very loyal to the friends he made along the way. Don is still the guy who keeps in touch with the survivors of the GCP and lets us know what is happening.

The GCP also gave Don the opportunity to develop, display, and be rewarded for his ability to get things done quickly and efficiently. This endeared him to Jesse Jennings, who thought that a lot of academic archaeologists spent too much time wallowing in irrelevant detail but that there was no room for that in a publicly funded salvage project with tight deadlines. (Actually, the opportunity to wallow in irrelevant detail was one of the things that had initially attracted me to the field of archaeology.) But Don learned early to identify the relevant details and not worry about the irrelevant ones. Along with his willingness to work very hard to achieve a goal, this is one of the traits that has made him so productive in so many different areas. We never took classes together, but I am sure that he must have been one of those students who always turn in their term papers a week early.

Another thing that Jennings stressed on the GCP was that salvage archaeology involved a public trust. That is, important evidence about the human past was being destroyed by a publicly financed development project, and public funds were being made available to record that evidence before it was lost. That required a serious commitment to coming up with results that reciprocated the public investment.

Jennings thought that the principal way this responsibility should be met was in the efficient production of timely publications that would increase knowledge of the distant past. However, he was also committed to more direct ways of sharing archaeological findings with a broader public. Shortly after joining the University of Utah faculty, he was involved in the formation of the Utah Statewide Archaeological Society, and he took the lead in organizing a small museum of anthropology. Later, he successfully lobbied (over a period of years) for establishment of the Utah Museum of Natural History (Jennings 1994:175–184).

His (1966) summary of the Glen Canyon Project was intended for an audience of nonspecialists, and he published several other shorter pieces of this sort. He also spent a considerable amount of time producing three educational films on the GCP work. Though somewhat painful to watch in today's media-saturated environment, they nonetheless saw considerable use in classrooms and by avocational groups.

Don has taken to a new level the mission of bringing archaeology and the history of anthropological science directly to the public. Mel Aikens briefly summarizes a very long list of lectureships and speaking engagements, as well as his involvement in producing five major television documentaries—all of the latter having to do with John Wesley Powell and/or the Glen Canyon area. Fowler's recently published book, *The Glen Canyon Country* (2011), is a superb piece of public history—solid scholarship, written to be accessible to a very broad audience.

Throughout most of his career, Jennings was heavily engaged in shaping the field of salvage archaeology—from his early work in the Southeast, as president of the SAA, and through his stance as the director of the very large and highly visible GCP. He (1963) published an influential article analyzing the strengths and weaknesses of salvage work (more of the former than the latter, in his opinion), as well as several less well-known pieces on this topic.

In a similar but even more effective fashion, Don Fowler has helped shape the transformation of salvage archaeology into the more comprehensive and proactive field of cultural resource management (CRM). In the "formative era" of this field, he published a number of seminal essays analyzing its practice and prospects (e.g., Fowler 1982, 1986). As president of the SAA, he continued the efforts begun by C. R. McGimsey to bring CRM and its practitioners into the mainstream of the society's affairs. Through a long string of contracts, he helped make the University of Nevada–Reno a major player in CRM in the Great Basin. Concurrently, he founded or cofounded several broad-based cultural and natural preservation organizations in Nevada. And as founder and director (from 1987 to 2004) of the University of Nevada–Reno Continuing Education Program in Heritage Resources Management, he brought professional-level training and refresher courses to thousands of cultural and natural heritage professionals located across the United States and in its Pacific territories.

In seeking funding for the Glen Canyon Project, Jennings had lobbied very hard and successfully for full financing of the production and publication of basic descriptive reports and for supporting the preparation of all collections and records for permanent curation. In those days, such requirements were often put aside on the frequently unfounded presumption that somehow the academic archaeologists involved—and their institutions—would see that these things happened. As a result of Jennings's foresight and commitment, the collections from the Utah GCP remain in very good order and accessible to researchers at the Utah Museum of Natural History.

Likewise, Don has worked hard and effectively for years to see that archaeological and anthropological records are adequately preserved for posterity (e.g., Fowler and Givens 1992).

This commitment undoubtedly stems in part from his experience working with archival materials in his studies of John Wesley Powell and of the development of anthropological science. On the other hand, those of us who were involved with the GCP came away thinking that proper curation and archiving were the expected standard, which was not generally true at the time and is still not true in some quarters. The efforts of Don and like-minded colleagues have gone a long way toward improving the situation.

Of course, Don's successes over his career have been the product of his own diligence and capabilities, so none of this is intended to diminish his accomplishments. However, having Jesse Jennings as a mentor and literally growing up in the context of a very large, well-organized public archaeological project certainly didn't hurt. The areas of Don's engagement that I have highlighted are all seen today as important parts of American archaeology, and he has played a large role in making that happen.

References Cited

Fowler, Don D.

1982 Cultural Resources Management. *Advances in Archaeological Method and Theory* 5:1–50.

1986 Conserving American Archaeological Resources. In *American Archaeology Past and Future: A Celebration of the Society for American Archaeology 1935–1985*, edited by D. J. Meltzer, D. D. Fowler, and J. A. Sabloff, pp. 135–162. Smithsonian Institution Press, Washington, D.C.

2011 *The Glen Canyon Country: A Personal Memoir*. University of Utah Press, Salt Lake City.

Fowler, Don D., and D. R. Givens

1992 Preserving the Archaeological Record. In *Preserving the Anthropological Record*, edited by S. Silverman and N. J. Parezo, pp. 9–28. Wenner-Gren Foundation, New York.

Jennings, Jesse D.

1963 Administration of Contract Emergency Archaeological Programs. *American Antiquity* 28:282–285.

1966 *Glen Canyon: A Summary*. University of Utah Anthropological Papers No. 81. Salt Lake City.

1994 *Accidental Archaeologist: Memoirs of Jesse D. Jennings*. Foreword by C. Melvin Aikens. University of Utah Press, Salt Lake City.

Lipe, William D.

2012 Why Did We Do It *That* Way? The University of Utah Glen Canyon Project in Retrospect. In *Glen Canyon, Legislative Struggles, and Contract Archaeology: Papers in Honor of Carol J. Condie*, edited by Emily Brown, Carol J. Condie, and Helen K. Crotty, pp. 87–104. Papers of the Archaeological Society of New Mexico No. 38. Albuquerque.

PART II

Case Studies and Regional Syntheses

4

West of the Plains

Paleoindians in the Southwest

Bruce B. Huckell

This chapter is an attempt to create, in a few pages, a brief overview of Paleoindian sites that fall within the limits of the "classic" Southwest. Its principal goals are to draw attention to what we can say about the occupation of this vast region of varied environments between the initial appearance of humans here at the close of the Pleistocene and the economic reorganization known as the Archaic, which was marked by the appearance of ground-stone seed-milling equipment and hot rock roasting/boiling technology. In the western United States this interval roughly corresponds to the Paleoindian period between about 13,200 and 8,500 calibrated years before present (ca. 11,250–7800 ^{14}C yr BP). This 3,000-year-long span incorporates several archaeological cultures, each distinguished primarily by distinctive projectile points and occasionally other flaked-stone artifacts or technologies.

West of the Plains

"Las Vegas, New Mexico, to Las Vegas, Nevada, and Durango, Mexico, to Durango, Colorado" is a fine general description of the limits of the Southwest as they are appropriate for the study of later periods of the region's prehistory after the arrival of ceramics (Cordell 1997:3). For this chapter I use the Rio Grande and the mountains bordering it on the east as an eastern limit for the Southwest. The Virgin River forms the western boundary of the Southwest for this chapter. At the north is that part of Utah southeast of the Colorado River, and southwestern Colorado south of the Dolores River and west of the Rio Grande/San Luis Valley. The southern boundary will not extend to Durango, Mexico, but will correspond with the southern boundaries of the states of Sonora and Chihuahua (Figure 4.1).

Physiographically, this area primarily falls within the Colorado Plateau and Southern Basin and Range provinces, plus a tiny piece of the Southern Rocky Mountains (Huckell 1996:Figure 2). Contemporary biotic provinces associated with the region (from largest to smallest) include the Great Basin, Sonoran, Interior, Chihuahuan, Mohavian, Petran, and Madrean (Huckell 1996:Figure 3, 311–314). The region thus contains considerable physiographic and environmental diversity, much greater than is found farther east or west.

Culture-Historical Systematics

The Paleoindian literature is full of point type names that have in turn come to represent archaeological cultures or complexes. Their names will be familiar to many, but not all, Southwesternists: Clovis and Folsom should hold no mysteries, but Agate Basin, Midland, Plainview/Goshen, Hell Gap, Cody/Firstview/Eden/Scottsbluff, and Allen/Frederick/Angostura are names less frequently encountered. Figure 4.2 illustrates individual examples of these points; larger samples of them are illustrated by Stanford (2005).

Clovis and Folsom, fluted point types that achieve wide distributions across the Plains and Southwest, are well known. However, there is a profusion of point types—and ergo culture-historical complexes—that are laterally thinned, unfluted lanceolate or stemmed forms. For example, Midland, Plainview, and Goshen are morphologically very similar to one another. Plainview is used on the Southern Plains, and Goshen, on the Northern Plains; Midland was defined on the Southern Plains and in the 1960s was applied to points from Hell Gap on the Northern Plains that were subsequently defined as Goshen (Frison et al. 1996:Figure 11.2). In addition, Midland points have been recovered with Folsom points at some Southern Plains sites (Hofman et al. 1990) and found alone at others (Blaine 1968). This has led to the hypothesis that Midland points are technological alternatives for Folsom knappers not wishing to risk raw material in smaller piece sizes or in short supply on the manufacture of fluted points (Amick 1995; Judge 1970). Whether they are separate types or not remains to be ascertained, but their recognition underscores both the variation within this unfluted lanceolate point grouping and how morphology and technology are used in classification (Bousman et al. 2004; Buchanan et al. 2007). Similar debates exist concerning the typological assignment

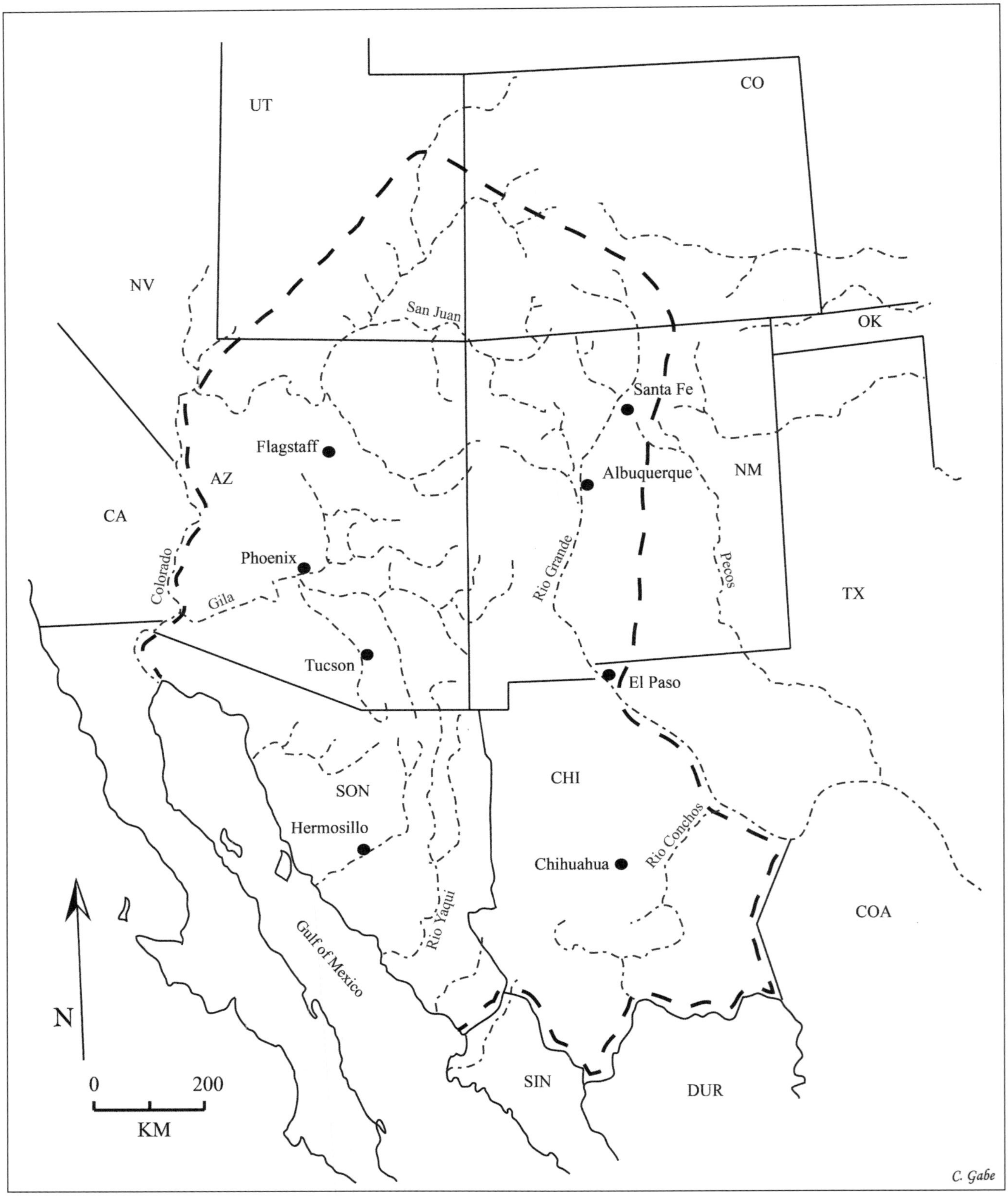

FIGURE 4.1. Map showing the approximate limits of the Southwest.

FIGURE 4.2. Examples of Paleoindian projectile points: (a) Clovis (length = 75.8 mm); (b) Folsom (length = 45.6 mm); (c) Agate Basin (length = 88.9 mm); (d) Midland (length = 22.9 mm); (e) Plainview/Goshen (length = 56.7 mm); (f) Eden (length = 54.9 mm); (g) Scottsbluff (length = 67.7 mm); (h) Allen (length = 26.8 mm) ([a]–[c], [e]–[g], courtesy of Maxwell Museum of Anthropology; [d] from private collection; [h] courtesy of Petroglyph National Monument).

of points representative of the Cody and Firstview complexes (Bradley and Stanford 1987; Wheat 1972, 1979) and the parallel obliquely flaked point types James Allen, Frederick, and Angostura (Hofman 2010). These debates reflect a lack of agreement concerning the ways in which social, raw material, and technological factors contribute to projectile point variation over time and large geographic spaces. This is not the place to delve into, let alone resolve, the debate, particularly inasmuch as this chapter focuses on the Southwest, where very little work has been done with post–fluted point sites or complexes. Therefore, I employ a very general classification to keep the discussion simple; however, readers are urged to bear in mind that this approach may well oversimplify a more complex reality.

Since projectile points are the principal artifacts at Paleoindian sites that show complex manufacture as well as stylistic investment and change, they continue to serve as markers of cultural identity. Temporal control of the ages of these points/complexes is based primarily on radiocarbon dates from Southern and Northern Plains sites (Holliday 2000; Huckell and Judge 2006; Stanford 2005), but these ages can probably be extended into the Southwest (Table 4.1). However, as with matters of point typology, the age ranges for these complexes are by no means fully agreed upon and remain subject to debate (Haynes et al. 2007; Holliday 2000; Waters and Stafford 2007). Ages used in this presentation are in the form of radiocarbon years before present.

TABLE 4.1. Radiocarbon age ranges (in radiocarbon years before the present) for Paleoindian cultural complexes.

Complex	Southern Plains	Northern Plains
Clovis	11,600–11,000	11,200–10,900
Folsom	10,900–10,100	10,900–10,200
Midland	10,900–10,100?	10,900–10,100?
Goshen		11,360–10,100[a]
Plainview	10,000 ± 200[b]	
Agate Basin	10,500–10,000	10,500–10,000
Hell Gap		10,000 ± 500
Alberta		10,200–9400
Cody		9400–8800
Firstview	9400–8200	
Allen/Frederick		9400–7800

Sources: After Holliday 2000 and others.
[a] Haynes et al. 2007.
[b] Also see Holliday et al. 1999.

For many years Paleoindian cultural complexes were viewed as discrete cultural entities following one another in time-sequent fashion (Wormington 1957). This interpretation was based on records of the succession of particular cultural complexes at sites with stratified records of multiple Paleoindian cultural complexes such as Blackwater Draw (Haynes 1995; Hester 1972; Irwin-Williams et al. 1973) in eastern New Mexico and Hell Gap (Irwin 1968; Larson et al. 2009) in eastern Wyoming. More recent investigations at other stratified sites, including Lubbock Lake (Johnson 1987), Carter-Kerr McGee, Wyoming (Frison 1984), and Jake Bluff, Oklahoma (Bement and Carter 2010), have supported aspects of this sequence. However, radiocarbon dating and detailed studies of cultural stratigraphy at sites containing multiple Paleoindian levels suggest a less straightforward picture (Holliday 2000; Sellet 2001). While a general sequence may exist, current interpretations suggest that at least some temporal and spatial overlap may occur between Folsom and Goshen, between Agate Basin and Folsom, between Hell Gap and Goshen, and between Cody and Allen/Frederick (Table 4.1). If such temporal overlap occurs, it may suggest that multiple, coeval Paleoindian cultural groups inhabited the North American Plains and potentially the Southwest as well. Thus, the nature of the relationships among these complexes remains the subject of research, and caution is urged against assuming a simple unilinear evolutionary model of Paleoindian complexes. Finally, as is the case elsewhere in North America, pre- or non-Clovis cultural complexes have been proposed in the Southwest, too, which will be briefly considered.

The remainder of this chapter consists of three sections. The first is a description of the Southwest's principal physiographic and contemporary biotic components and a brief consideration of the general character and dynamics of biotic environments during the Paleoindian period. This is followed by a presentation of the archaeological record as currently understood, organized by cultural complex. The third section offers some fundamental inferences that can be drawn from this record regarding subsistence, mobility, organization.

Late Pleistocene–Early Holocene Environments

Substantial environmental changes have occurred over the past 13,000 years, such that in many parts of the region Paleoindians encountered very different climatic regimes and biotic communities than those of today (Ballenger et al. 2011). Further, the landscapes at the time of their arrival contained lakes that are today ephemeral and rivers with greater volumes of flow. After the Last Glacial Maximum at about 18,000 years ago, rapid climatic warming and wasting of the Laurentide and Cordilleran ice sheets began. In the Southwest, this latest Pleistocene interval was marked by the waning of large lakes such as Lake San Agustin and Lake Cochise as well as the upslope retreat of mountain glaciers. Stratigraphic studies indicate that by approximately 11,000 years ago, Clovis groups in southern Arizona encountered a landscape drier than it had been for several thousand years (Haynes 1991, 2007, 2008). On the Colorado Plateau, pack rat midden studies (Betancourt et al. 1990) suggest that conifer species occurred 700–850 m below modern lower elevational limits, in some places with more xeric species in communities that have no modern analogues (Thompson et al. 1993). Temperatures 3–5°C cooler than modern and precipitation 35–120 percent greater than today have been inferred from these midden assemblages. Similar no-analogue xeric woodlands occupied areas that are now desertscrub; true desertscrub was limited to the Lower Colorado River valley below 350 m elevation.

Shortly after 13,000 years ago, the majority of the genera making up the Pleistocene megafauna were extinct, either with substantial human effects from predation (Alroy 1999, 2001; Barnosky et al. 2004; Haynes 2002; Martin 2005; Surovell et al. 2005) or without them (Grayson 1984, 2001; Grayson and Meltzer 2002, 2003). Clovis overlap with the megafauna, particularly mammoth, is clear, but by Folsom times only bison survived. There is a short-lived climatic reversal toward cooler temperatures during the Younger Dryas (ca. 11,000–10,000 years ago), which correlates with Folsom and perhaps other post-Clovis cultural complexes. The effects of the Younger Dryas on human foragers are debated (Ballenger et al. 2011; Haynes 1991, 2008; Holliday 2000; Meltzer and Holliday 2010). There are suggestions of water table rebound and marsh or wet meadow soil formation at sites across the western United States, although an alternative interpretation of the stratigraphic evidence implies decreasing stream flow. By the end of the Younger Dryas, postglacial warming resumed. Pack rat midden data (Betancourt et al. 1990) suggest that late-glacial woodland species were less abundant or gone at lower elevations, both on the Colorado Plateau and elsewhere in the region. More xeric species such as juniper and oak persisted in the southern Southwest in communities lacking modern analogues, and Sonoran Desertscrub plants such as saguaro were expanding northward and eastward from the Lower Colorado River valley. Climate was characterized by greater-than-modern effective moisture and cooler summers and warmer winters with less frequent freezing temperatures. By the end of the Paleoindian period some 8,000–8,500 years ago, desertscrub communities in the southern Southwest were beginning to assume their modern compositions and distributions, with woodland elements moving upslope and northward.

Within these dynamics of vegetative, landscape, and climatic change, Paleoindian groups appear to have used a wide array of environmental settings. However, indications are that their sites are most abundant in areas where grassland or desert grassland biomes were found, often in proximity to playas, streams, springs, or other water sources.

Sources of Archaeological Information

As for any overview, the published literature and gray literature provide the bulk of the archaeological data used in this study. However, investigations conducted by professional archaeologists specializing in Paleoindian studies in the Southwest have been both few in number and skewed with regard to focus. That is, Southwestern archaeologists have long focused the bulk of their investigations on the ceramic-producing, village-living Ancestral Pueblo, Mogollon, and Hohokam cultural complexes representing the last 1,500 years of prehistory. Investigations of Southwestern Paleoindian (or any other preceramic) sites often have been in response to unsought opportunities, such as reports by public-minded citizens of large bones eroding out of an arroyo or the discovery of projectile points on the surface. This is well illustrated by the fact that of the six major Clovis sites in the San Pedro Valley of southeastern Arizona, only one was discovered by professional archaeologists. A similar situation prevails in New Mexico's Middle Rio Grande Valley. Therefore, the bulk of the available data for Paleoindians in the Southwest are from the surface, not from excavated contexts; fewer than 30 Paleoindian sites have been excavated. While the advent of cultural resource management archaeology has changed this pattern of site discovery, it is still the case that these sites are rare and infrequently encountered by professionals engaged in surveying linear rights-of-way or quadrats of land. The net result of this pattern has been that Paleoindian archaeologists are very dependent on collectors or avocational archaeologists and members of the public for much of their data. This is true not only for the Southwest but for most of North America as well; it is perhaps best illustrated by the online Paleoindian Database of the Americas (http://pidba.utk.edu/), which tracks the distribution of fluted points and fluted point sites across the Americas. The overwhelming majority of points constituting the database are in private collections, and yet the Paleoindian Database of the Americas has been central to professional research into patterns of New World colonization (for an example, see Prasciunas 2011).

Beginning with the investigations of Judge (1973), Southwestern archaeologists focusing on the Paleoindian period have made good research use of both museum and private collections. However, some of these valuable systematic studies have been specifically focused on Folsom (Amick 1994; LeTourneau 2000) or Clovis (Agenbroad 1967; Huckell 1982, 2004; North et al. 2005), with less attention paid to post–fluted point cultural complexes. The result is that our understanding of the distribution of unfluted lanceolate and stemmed points is far less comprehensive across the Southwest, and attention can only be focused on where certain points/complexes have been found. A final consideration: although most archaeologists can recognize Clovis and Folsom points (and generally distinguish the two from one another), no such uniform recognition can be assumed for unfluted points. As a result, reports employ multiple type names for points of similar morphology (Plainview, Belen, Goshen, Midland) or identify specimens as representatives of particular Paleoindian point types that, based on illustrations, are clearly incorrect. I have therefore exercised a certain amount of editorial judgment in compiling this overview, resulting in the elimination of some reported points or cultural complexes. With these caveats in mind, let us turn to the record of Southwestern Paleoindians.

Pre-Clovis?

As elsewhere in North America, possible pre- (that is, antedating Clovis) or non-Clovis (possibly of similar age but culturally unrelated) cultural complexes have been identified. A selected subset is discussed here; all are united by the presence of "primitive" artifacts reminiscent of Old World Lower Paleolithic complexes; their primitive appearance has been hypothesized by some to equate to great age. Included are the Tolchaco focus or complex along the Little Colorado River, Arizona (Bartlett 1943); the New River industry, Arizona (Peru 1984); and the Los Encinos culture, New Mexico (Bryan 1939, 1950). All three comprise surface-collected specimens identified as hand axes, choppers, scrapers, debitage, and cores similar in morphology to Old World Paleolithic specimens. Morphology aside, all three are most probably of Holocene age and reflect palimpsests of rejected products from material quarrying and reduction (Keller and Wilson 1976; Smith and Huckell 2005).

In southwestern Arizona and northwestern Sonora is found the San Dieguito industry of Rogers (1958, 1966) and Hayden (1976). Sites of the San Dieguito complex and its antecedent Malpais complex (Heilen 2003) contain lithic artifacts with variable but often thick coatings of desert varnish associated with boulder-outlined features such as sleeping circles, trails, and shrines, all in areas of desert pavement. One such site is Dateland in southwestern Arizona (Huckell 1998). Although claims for pre-Clovis or Clovis-equivalent radiometric ages on the desert varnish have been made (Whitley and Dorn 1993), recent studies have called the physical basis for such dates into question (Beck et al. 1998; also see Dorn 1998). As is the case for Tolchaco and New River, San Dieguito–Malpais artifacts may also, in part, represent quarry debris because many are located near sources of lithic material. Some Malpais artifacts shown to me by Julian Hayden in 1978 were, in my estimation, not humanly flaked.

Other potential candidates for pre-Clovis Southwestern cultural complexes have been proposed. These include the lowest level or perhaps two levels of Ventana Cave, Arizona, the Conglomerate and the Volcanic Debris, which have been viewed as San Dieguito by Hayden (1976). Objects from the Conglomerate appear to be nonartifactual (Haury 1950:176, Figure 20), and although there is no doubt about the authenticity of the artifacts from the overlying Volcanic Debris layer, radiocarbon dating of this layer suggests that it is more likely late Paleoindian–Early Archaic (10,500–8800 BP [Huckell and Haynes 2003]).

MacNeish (in MacNeish and Libby 2003) has identified multiple pre-Clovis complexes stretching back between 12,000 and perhaps as much as 60,000 years from Pendejo Cave in southern New Mexico. From oldest to youngest they include a pebble tool tradition (the Orogrande complex), a unifacial flake tool complex (McGregor complex), and a "leaf-blade-burin complex." Whether many of the putative flaked-stone objects are of cultural origin is open to debate; many appear to lack diagnostic features of human workmanship. Other cultural data—including fingerprints on clay pellets (see Shaffer and Baker 1999)—upon which these complexes were defined are controversial, as is the degree to which the strata within the cave may have been compromised by bioturbation.

Finally, there is the Sandia complex, represented by Sandia Cave (Haynes and Agogino 1986; Hibben 1941; Thompson et al. 2008) and the Lucy site (Roosa 1956). Controversy has long dogged Sandia (Stevens and Agogino 1975), and most recent treatments do not include it as a valid Paleoindian cultural complex.

Clovis

Clovis manifestations have received more professional investigation and publication than any other aspect of the Paleoindian record of the Southwest. Ten sites—eight in Arizona, one each in New Mexico and Utah—have been excavated (Figure 4.3).

To this list can be added Clovis manifestations in Sonora and Chihuahua, including the Fin del Mundo site, at which a Clovis–gomphothere association has been reported (Sanchez et al. 2009). Most famous are the tightly clustered sites found within the alluvium of the San Pedro River and its tributaries in southeastern Arizona: Naco (Haury 1953), Leikem and Navarette (Haynes and Huckell 2007), Lehner (Haury et al. 1959),

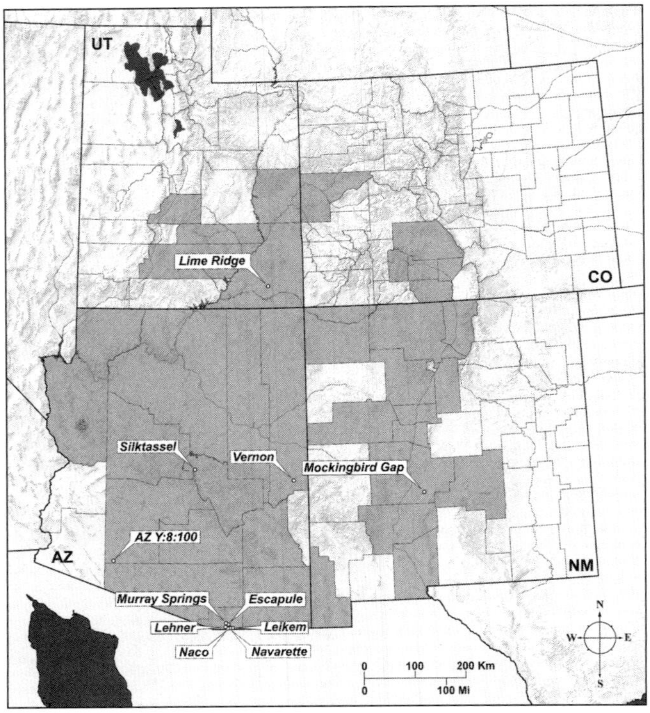

FIGURE 4.3. Investigated Clovis sites and known occurrences of Clovis points (shaded counties contain Clovis points).

Murray Springs (Haynes and Huckell 2007; Hemmings 1970), and Escapule (Hemmings and Haynes 1968). All but Leikem produced Clovis points and other tools in association with mammoth skeletons and together represent about half of all known Clovis mammoth kills. A Clovis point was found at the Leikem mammoth site but not in clear association with the remains of two mammoths. At Murray Springs there is also a multiple bison kill and a short-term camp, the only camp known in the valley (Haynes and Huckell 2007). In addition to finished artifacts, Murray Springs yielded several thousand waste flakes, providing an excellent window into Clovis lithic technology and its clear reliance on the manufacture, transport, and conservative reduction of bifaces, as well as blade and flake tools (Huckell 2007).

Mockingbird Gap, although technically some 30 km east of the eastern boundary used in this chapter, merits mention because of its proximity and the fact that lithic materials from it are derived from sources farther west (Hamilton 2008; Holliday et al. 2009; Huckell et al. 2008; Weber and Agogino 1997). Unlike the southeastern Arizona sites, Mockingbird Gap is huge, extending for approximately 800 m north–south × 80–150 m east–west, and contains a dozen or more small, apparently discrete occupational localities. This suggests repeated occupations by small social units, or perhaps episodic larger aggregations of such groups, or both. Excavations at one locus in 2007 produced probable bison tooth enamel as well as small splinters of large-mammal bone in association with Clovis artifacts (Huckell et al. 2008).

Five other Clovis components at multicomponent surface/shallowly buried sites—Lime Ridge (Utah [Davis 1989]), Dawson (Utah [Byers 2013]), Silktassel (Arizona [Huckell 1978]), Vernon (Arizona [Longacre and Graves 1976]), and AZ Y:8:100 (Arizona [Tucker 2000])—have been investigated. Lime Ridge and Dawson are within what is today Great Basin Desertscrub; Vernon is situated in juniper woodland; Silktassel occurs in a mixed chaparral and pinyon-juniper woodland; and AZ Y:8:100 is within the Lower Sonoran Desertscrub. Artifact assemblages at Silktassel and Lime Ridge contain multiple tool types that can be associated with Clovis points, suggesting that they, and perhaps the other two sites, are camps. The Dawson site is near a spring mound. These sites demonstrate that Clovis groups exploited multiple environmental settings, including upland biomes far from major river valleys.

The distribution of Clovis points in the Southwest has been a topic of interest, and several publications have documented it (Agenbroad 1967; Huckell 1982, 2004; Mabry 1998; North et al. 2005). As shown in Figure 4.3, isolated and other nonsite occurrences of Clovis points are present throughout the region. While most counties contain four or fewer reported Clovis points, Socorro County in south-central New Mexico has produced 75, which is almost completely the product of 50 years of work by a single nonprofessional collector. This suggests that the numbers of Clovis points for many other counties are potentially significantly greater.

In addition, it has recently become clear that Sonora, although long known to have Clovis sites and artifacts (Ortiz and Taylor 1972), is home to numerous Clovis sites and isolated occurrences of Clovis points (Gaines et al. 2009; Sanchez 2001). Although this record is just beginning to be published, indications are that it may exceed in richness the record of Clovis in southeastern Arizona.

Folsom

Indications are that Folsom, which succeeds Clovis, is more ubiquitous in some—but not all—parts of the Southwest than its predecessor. Folsom has received at least as much archaeological attention as Clovis, if not more, but does not achieve the widespread distribution of Clovis. Excavated Folsom sites within the Southwest (Figure 4.4) include three shallowly buried localities in the Middle Rio Grande Valley: Rio Rancho (Dawson and Judge 1969; Huckell and Kilby 2002), Boca Negra Wash (Holliday et al. 2006a; Huckell and Kilby 2000; Huckell et al. 2002; Huckell et al. 2003), and Deann's site (Huckell and Ruth 2004). Rio Rancho is a very large site—340 m east–west × 170 m north–south—containing three spatially discrete camp loci; two are purely Folsom, while the third also contains Cody, Archaic, and younger components (Huckell and Kilby 2002). Large numbers of point bases, preform fragments, and channel flakes show that weaponry repair and replacement was a common task; the abundance of end scrapers implies that hide processing was as well. Whether the three loci are coeval is difficult to establish; this possibility led Hofman (1994) to list Rio Rancho as a possible Folsom aggregation site. Boca Negra Wash and Deann's site

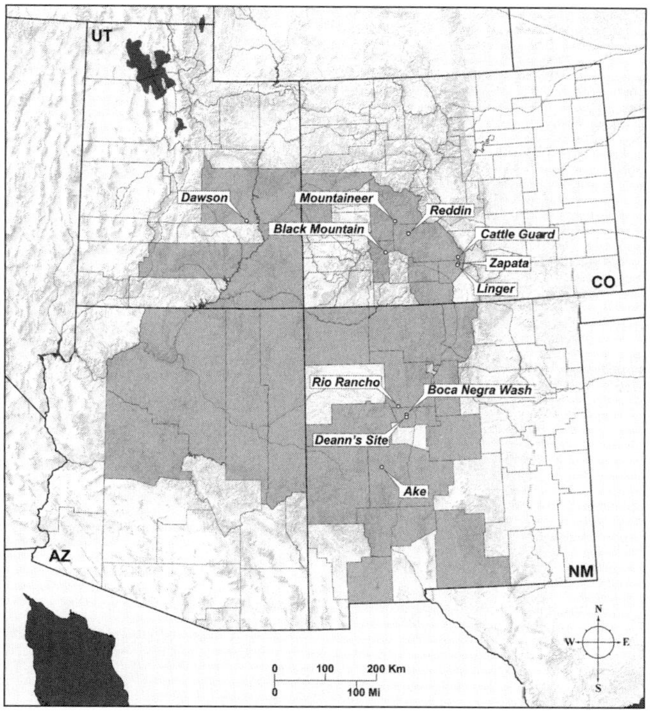

FIGURE 4.4. Investigated Folsom sites and known occurrences of Folsom points (shaded counties contain Folsom points).

are short-term camps that appear to be linked to bison kills made around adjacent playas; both sites yielded hundreds of pieces of tooth enamel morphologically and metrically consistent with bison, as well as occasional small slivers of large-mammal bone. Deann's is a single small locus (ca. 75 m × 60 m), while at Boca Negra Wash two spatially discrete loci (one ca. 80 m × 45 m and the other ca. 25 m × 25 m) were present.

Artifact assemblages suggest that the processing of carcasses, weaponry repair and replacement, and other lithic tool-manufacturing and -maintenance tasks occurred. Small site size and low artifact density led Amick (1999) to interpret Southwestern Folsom sites as the result of patterned residential mobility. To the southwest in the Plains of San Agustin is the multicomponent Archaic and Paleoindian Ake site, which includes a Folsom occupation (Beckett 1980; Holliday et al. 2006b).

In and near the San Luis Valley of Colorado several Folsom sites have been found and investigated to varying degrees, beginning with the Linger site (Hurst 1943; Jodry 1999a:64–73). Other excavated sites include Zapata (Jodry 1999a:73–75), Reddin (a multicomponent site with a substantial Folsom occupation according to Jodry 1999a:76–78), and Stewart's Cattle Guard (Jodry 1999a:78–83, 1999b). These sites all produced bison remains in varying degrees of preservation, and spatially discrete processing and camp areas were identified at Linger and Stewart's Cattle Guard. At the latter a single-event kill of at least 49 bison occurred. All are in eolian dune settings.

Two Folsom sites have been investigated in higher elevations of Colorado: the Black Mountain site is situated above 3,048 m (10,000 ft) in the San Juan Mountains (Jodry 1999a:49–55), and the Mountaineer site, at 2,630 m (8,600 ft) on Tenderfoot Mountain southwest of Gunnison (Stiger 2002, 2006). Black Mountain is some 120 m long × 18 m wide, with at least two areas of concentrated artifacts. Mountaineer is large, extending over an area 300 m × 400 m, and has produced residential structures and a large assemblage of artifacts (Stiger 2002, 2006). Both are camps, and both have produced radiocarbon dates of Folsom age (as well as younger ages), with one assay of ca. 10,600 BP from Black Mountain and four assays on bone at approximately 10,400 BP.

Numerous unexcavated sites and isolated Folsom points are known from across much of the Southwest. By far the bulk of these occurrences were discovered by avocationalists and shared with professionals. Weber (1963) was one of the first to draw attention to Folsom and other Paleoindian sites and artifacts in Socorro County (also see Hill and Holliday 2011); Judge (1973; Dawson and Judge 1969) reported 29 Folsom sites in the central Rio Grande Valley (including Rio Rancho). Amick (1994) and LeTourneau (2000) studied Folsom manifestations in the Southwest and Southern Plains using both avocationalist and museum collections; Figure 4.4 shows the distribution of Folsom points. From the general area considered the Southwest in this chapter, LeTourneau reported a minimum of 139 localities, the bulk of which are concentrated in the west-central portion of New Mexico; an additional eight or nine occur in northeastern Arizona. In the early 1950s, Thomas (1952; Wendorf and Thomas 1951) reported Folsom points from the St. Johns–Concho area of east-central Arizona. I (Huckell 1982:19–24) documented an additional dozen points and preforms collected by a single individual; since that time other collectors have found more Folsom material in that same region. A short distance south of Green River, Utah, 14 Folsom points and preforms, as well as other tool types, have been collected from the multicomponent (Clovis/Folsom/Great Basin Stemmed) Dawson site (Byers 2013). Folsom points are also reported from south-central New Mexico (Wendorf 1959) and northern Chihuahua (Phelps 1990); however, there are at present no published records of Folsom in Sonora.

These data suggest that Folsom hunters in the Southwest, like their counterparts on the Plains, were pursuing bison. While not particularly surprising, and not necessarily indicative of an exclusive economic focus on bison (Amick 1996), these data demonstrate that bison must have been present in the Southwest in sufficient numbers to be attractive to Folsom foragers. Folsom is largely or perhaps completely synchronous with the Younger Dryas, a 1,000-year-long interval of cooler temperatures and potentially more effective precipitation. The effects of the Younger Dryas on biota and Paleoindian cultures in the Southwest continue to be a subject of debate, with perspectives varying between Haynes (2008), who views it as a time of water table rebound from late-glacial lows, to Holliday (2000) and Meltzer (Meltzer and Holliday 2010), who suggest that the Younger Dryas was not particularly noticeable to Paleoindians and was a period of

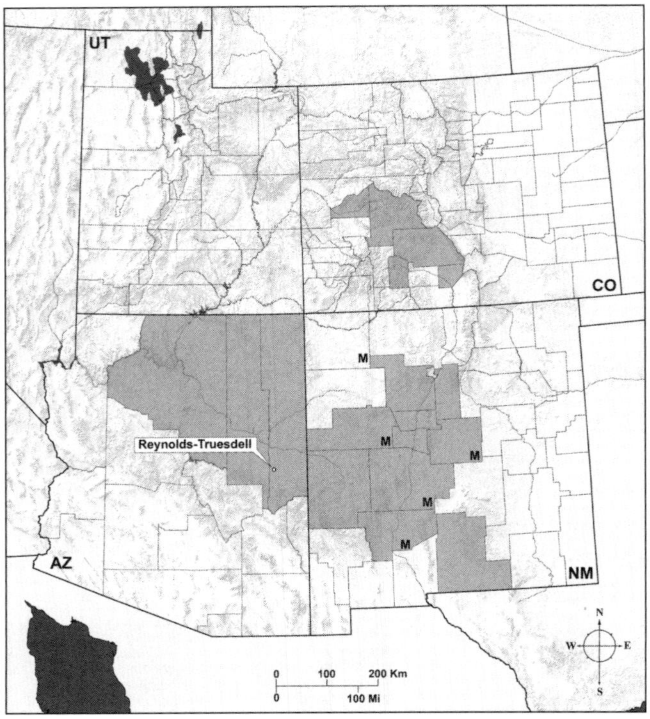

FIGURE 4.5. Investigated Plainview/Goshen site and known occurrences of Plainview/Goshen points (shaded counties contain Plainview/Goshen points; M = Midland point).

lessened surface water availability when compared with Clovis. Southwestern Folsom sites are most common in areas dominated today by grassland or desert grassland and are consistently found close to playas.

Midland

Most recent studies tend to link Folsom and Midland as coeval point styles, with the latter also being referred to as "unfluted Folsom." The co-occurrence of Folsom and Midland at certain sites on the Southern Plains such as Shifting Sands (Hofman et al. 1990) has promoted development of the idea that Midland points are an alternative approach to point manufacture, one that does not entail the risky operation of fluting, and that they do not represent a separate cultural complex. From this perspective, Midland points reflect a tactic to deal with smaller flake blanks (Judge 1970), or to conserve lithic material supplies (Amick 1995; Hofman 1992), or both. Complicating the issue is that Folsom and Midland points do not co-occur on all Folsom sites; purely Folsom sites are known—Rio Rancho is an example—as are occasional pure Midland sites (Winkler-1, just outside the southeast corner of New Mexico [Blaine 1968]). Such sites may reflect sampling issues or patterns of raw material availability and mobility but also signal that other factors may be involved as well. The possibility that Midland points represent a temporally or culturally separate manifestation should remain a hypothesis worthy of testing.

While bearing in mind that the relationship between Folsom and Midland remains unresolved, it is the case that Midland points have been reported from the Southwest, principally from New Mexico (Figure 4.5, "M"). In west-central New Mexico, Weber (1963:Plate 1h–i) and Broster (1981) were the first to report Midland points; they have been reported from the San Juan Basin as well (Vogler et al. 1993). However, Judge (1973) did not identify Midland points per se in his Middle Rio Grande Valley survey, instead suggesting a possible link between Midland and points he classified as Belen (discussed below). LeTourneau (2000:138) analyzed 16 Midland points from portions of his study area that correspond with the Southwest as defined here; this total includes some of those from the Weber collection and Broster's survey and one from northern Arizona.

These reports raise a second issue, which concerns the criteria by which Midland points have been identified. In some cases, these criteria are not explicitly stated, and so the reasons for assigning a particular point to the Midland type (as opposed to other unfluted lanceolate types such as Plainview and Goshen) are unclear. LeTourneau (2000:120–124) summarizes how Midland points may be recognized, but it is unclear to what degree others have used those or similar criteria.

Agate Basin

Although present at Blackwater Draw in eastern New Mexico (Hester 1972:Figure 118j, m), the Agate Basin cultural complex appears to be quite uncommon in the Southwest. Jodry (1999a: 96–97) reports two Agate Basin points from the San Luis Valley. Wendorf and Thomas (1951:Figure 48g) illustrate a possible example of an Agate Basin point from the Concho–St. Johns area of east-central Arizona. I have seen two points that I would classify as Agate Basin, one from the area of Isleta Pueblo just south of Albuquerque and one from the Little Colorado River valley a few kilometers southeast of Winslow. Judge did not report any Agate Basin points from his work in the Middle Rio Grande Valley, and I have not found any others in the literature. Pitblado (1994) reports a few from southwestern Colorado. I suspect that more evidence of this complex may exist in the region, but given the paucity of points of this type thus far reported, it may be that it is uncommon in relation to other Paleoindian cultural complexes.

Hell Gap

Hell Gap points are rare on the Southern Plains, apparently being absent at Blackwater Draw, suggesting that like Agate Basin this Paleoindian complex may also be uncommon in the Southwest. Pitblado (1994) and Jodry (1999a) report them from southwestern and south-central Colorado. Weber (1963:Plate 1c) illustrated a point from west-central New Mexico he labeled as Hell Gap; however, it also resembles a Jay point (defined a decade after Weber's publication), a type believed to be Early Archaic (Irwin-Williams et al. 1973). Many large Jay points resemble Hell Gap points, and as Matson (1991) and Chapin (2005) have pointed out, Jay points are very similar morphologically to Lake Mohave points and some forms of Great Basin Stemmed points as well. Chapin (2005) also notes that Jay points from the Arroyo Cuervo type sites are not well associated with radiocarbon-dated strata, meaning that their hypothesized Early Archaic age is difficult to evaluate. One possibility is that some percentage of points identified as Jay are actually Hell Gap. However, as with Midland points, the specific criteria that would help to distinguish Jay and Hell Gap points remain to be presented. Until these tapering stemmed points can be found in securely dated stratigraphic contexts, it will be challenging to determine with any confidence whether the Hell Gap complex reached the Southwest.

Plainview/Goshen

Debate swirls around the identity and age of Plainview/Goshen unfluted lanceolate points. Plainview was first defined and is most commonly recognized in the Southern Plains (Krieger 1947; Sellards et al. 1947). The type is thought to date to the centuries immediately before and after 10,000 radiocarbon years BP but is very poorly dated (Holliday et al. 1999). Goshen, named from the Hell Gap (Larson et al. 2009) and Mill Iron (Frison et al. 1996) sites on the Northern Plains, may be earlier or of similar age to Plainview; it is the preferred type name in that region. Goshen points are also poorly placed in time—two statistically distinct populations of dates were recovered from Mill Iron, one with a mean of ca. 11,360 radiocarbon years BP and the other with a mean of 10,840 radiocarbon years BP. Contamination from Cretaceous lignite deposits in the area may be the source of the disparity and perhaps generally older ages. Other Goshen point–producing sites have yielded dates of 10,450–10,150 radiocarbon years BP, and at both Hell Gap and the Carter/Kerr-McGee site in Wyoming, Goshen points have been recovered in deposits below Folsom. At the Jim Pitts site in South Dakota Goshen is thought to date to ca. 10,200 radiocarbon years BP (Sellet et al. 2009). Thus, Goshen may either predate or be coeval in part or in whole with Folsom and perhaps Agate Basin.

Belen—a name proposed by avocational archaeologist Ele Baker—is thought to be a local manifestation of Milnesand, or Plainview, or Midland in the Middle Rio Grande Valley (Judge 1973:69–72). Frison et al. (1996:205–208) have shown that Goshen, Plainview, and Midland points are difficult to distinguish when viewed together; I suspect that Belen could also easily be lost among examples of these types. For the purposes of this survey, they are treated as representatives of a single type.

To date, most of the identification of these points has been within New Mexico (Figure 4.5), although no sites have been excavated. Judge (1973) identified 13 Belen sites within the Middle Rio Grande Valley. Weber (1963:Plate 11) illustrated one point he identified as Plainview. Although no systematic inventory of his collection has yet been completed, there are likely to be many more unfluted lanceolate points in it. Broster (1981) reported five Belen points (two definite and three possible) from the Cebolleta Mesa area of the Acoma Indian Reservation west of Albuquerque. In the San Luis Valley, Jodry (1999a:87, 91) has reported three probable and four possible Goshen/Plainvew points; Pitblado (1994) documented them in southwestern Colorado. They also occur in Sonora (Gaines 2006; Gaines et al. 2009) and in Chihuahua (Phelps 1990).

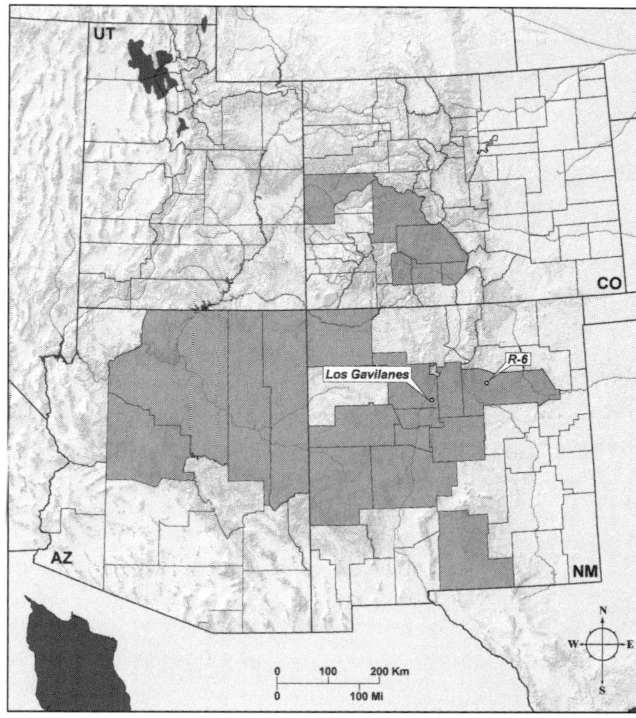

FIGURE 4.6. Investigated Cody sites and known occurrences of Cody points (shaded counties contain Cody points).

There is an apparent concentration of Plainview/Goshen sites and activity in east-central Arizona in the Concho–St. Johns area. In 2004 I was shown and subsequently tested a small (ca. 40-m-×-30-m) site northwest of Concho. The Reynolds-Truesdell site has produced eight fragmentary points of probable Plainview/Goshen/Belen type from the surface of a small dune remnant. Also associated were a few flake tools, debitage, and 30 pieces of probable bison tooth enamel. The severe impact damage seen on several of the point fragments suggests the possibility that this site may be a small, shallowly buried bison kill. In addition, at least a half dozen isolated Plainview points have been recovered in this same general area. Finally, I have also seen a similar quantity of these points from a site on the western Navajo Reservation near Kaibito. Whatever their ultimate age and identity (or identities), these unfluted lanceolate points and their makers had a substantial presence in the Southwest.

Cody

Although it has not been the subject of systematic inquiry within the Southwest, it appears that the Cody complex is widespread across the region (Figure 4.6). "Cody complex" is used here to refer to a suite of square-stemmed points that include such types as Eden, Scottsbluff, and Alberta. *Cody*, as a general term, and more rarely *Eden* and *Scottsbluff* have been used to describe points from sites in the Southwest. It should also be noted that a competing framework—the Firstview complex— was developed

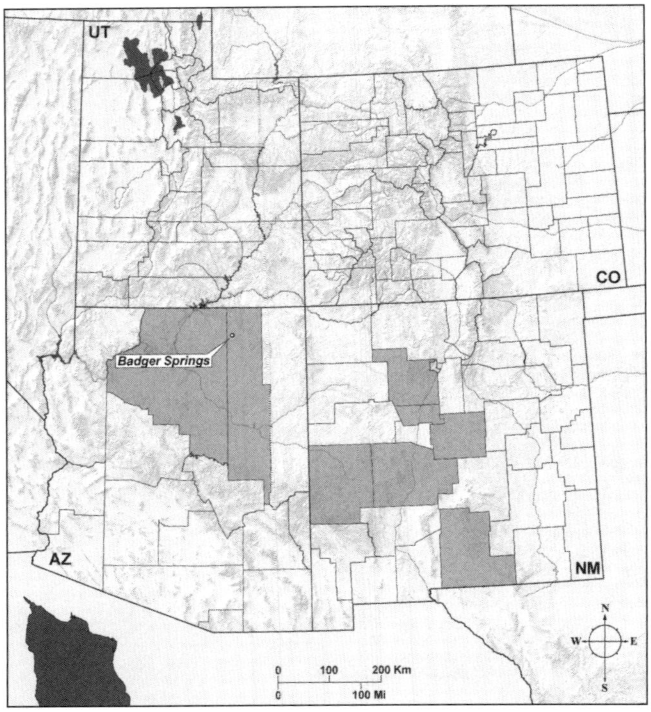

FIGURE 4.7. Investigated Allen site and known occurrences of Allen points (shaded counties contain Allen points).

by Wheat (1972) for the Central and Southern Plains and includes what he (1979) defined as the Firstview, San Jon, and Kersey types. Although Wheat originally proposed that Firstview was older than Cody, subsequent radiocarbon dating has instead suggested that Firstview and Cody are coeval (Holliday 2000). *Cody* is used here. It is worth noting that specific identification of Cody points to type is often challenging due to the fact that the vast majority are short basal fragments (see specimens illustrated in Judge 1973:Figure 9, bottom), which further suggests that use of the more general designation is prudent. Finally, the distinctive Cody knife, which looks like an X-Acto knife blade (Stanford 2005:Figure 33), is also present at a very few Cody sites in Arizona and New Mexico (Vogler et al. 1993:Figure 3.4, lower right).

The first reports of Cody points—not always recognized as such—in the region were from west-central New Mexico (Bryan and Toulouse 1943:Plate XXg; Weber 1963:Plate 1m–o). Subsequent investigations by Judge (1973) in the Middle Rio Grande Valley revealed nine Cody sites. Jodry (1999a:97–102) discusses 14 Cody localities from the uppermost Rio Grande Valley in southern Colorado, including one possible Cody bison kill/processing site. Other isolated occurrences of Cody points have come to attention (for example, Chapin 2005:Figure 4.2m–o). It should be added that Weber's extensive collection from Socorro County holds numerous Cody points, although it has not yet been inventoried systematically. The only excavated Southwestern Cody site is Los Gavilanes in the Middle Rio Grande Valley (Schmader et al. 2006:159–181), a small (ca. 30-m-×-15-m) shallowly buried camp rich in end scrapers and biface reduction debitage, along with two point fragments and portions of two drills remarkably similar to ones illustrated from the Claypool site in Wyoming (Dick and Mountain 1960:Figure 8 MD-1–MD-4).

The Cody complex certainly extends into east-central Arizona; a Cody point was illustrated by Wendorf and Thomas (1951:Figure 48d) from the Concho–St. Johns area. I have seen other Cody points in private collections from this general area, as well as from the Kaibito area of the western Navajo Reservation. To the best of my knowledge, Cody sites and points are absent from Sonora and perhaps from Chihuahua as well. The Cody complex record in the Southwest has yet to see the detailed investigation it merits.

Allen

For many years, the Cody complex was seen as the last "Plains-based" Paleoindian occupation in the Southwest, being replaced by approximately 8500–8000 BP by Early Archaic hunter-gatherer groups such as the Jay phase of the Oshara tradition (Irwin-Williams and Haynes 1970), the Sulphur Spring stage of the Cochise culture (Waters 1986), or the Desha complex (Geib and Ambler 1991; Lindsay et al. 1968). However, evidence of what might be considered terminal Paleoindian occupation in the Southwest has been recognized over the past few years and is the subject of continuing research (Huckell 2011). A growing inventory of occurrences of distinctively lanceolate, concave-based, parallel-obliquely flaked point fragments demonstrates that points most reminiscent of James Allen (Mulloy 1959) or Frederick (Irwin 1968) points (Allen/Frederick for Huckell and Judge 2006) are present in western New Mexico and likely in northeastern Arizona as well (Figure 4.7). The specimens are closely comparable to Allen points from the James Allen site in Wyoming (Mulloy 1959) and the Caribou Lake site west of Boulder, Colorado (Pitblado 1999), and with Frederick points from Hell Gap (Larson et al. 2009).

Thus far they are few and generally found as isolates or specimens within more extensive scatters; midsection and basal fragments are known. In New Mexico, these points have been found within the Valles Caldera in the Jemez Mountains and in the vicinity of Socorro. A single investigated site, Badger Springs near Shonto in northeastern Arizona, produced what were termed Angostura points (Hesse et al. 1999), which is a parallel-obliquely flaked point type reported from South Dakota. *Angostura* has been subsequently used to describe an array of points from other Plains sites but is considered by Hofman (2010) to be synonymous with *Allen*. The Badger Springs points have not been illustrated in the published literature, and only a brief note has been published on this site. Bison and human remains (possibly representing a cremation) are reportedly in association. It is clear that parallel-obliquely flaked points postdating the Cody complex occur in the Southwest. Whether they extend south into Sonora and Chihuahua is unknown.

Discussion

At present, the record of Paleoindians in the Southwest is a thin one and is largely predicated on surface investigations of sites. Aside from Clovis sites in southeastern Arizona and a few Folsom sites in central New Mexico, excavations at single-component Paleoindian sites are few. Still, indications are that Paleoindian sites are widely spread across much of the Southwest, and despite challenges to investigators with respect to sources of data, the region offers much research potential. At this time enough is known to make some observations with respect to the ways in which land-use and subsistence strategies, coupled with environmental change, may have played a role in shaping the pattern of site/isolated artifact distribution. I present these as bullet points first and then discuss subsistence, mobility, and the challenges and opportunities we face in building this record:

- The major Paleoindian cultural complexes present on the Great Plains also occur within the Southwest, although evidence for Agate Basin and Hell Gap is weak.
- Clovis points achieve a nearly ubiquitous distribution across the region, while Folsom and other Paleoindian points and sites tend to be found in a more restricted portion of the Southwest than Clovis.
- When any associated fauna occur with Southwestern Paleoindian sites, bison and mammoth are the two principal species represented.
- Paleoindian site sizes are typically small, with very few large sites (more than 100 m in maximum dimension) that are single-component Paleoindian occupations.
- Lithic material sourcing studies demonstrate primary use of quarries within the Southwest as opposed to outside it, suggesting that Paleoindian land-use patterns involved extended stays in the region.

Sites and points of the Clovis, Folsom, Midland, Plainview/Goshen, Cody, and Allen cultural complexes are present in the Southwest. It is also apparent that Folsom and later Paleoindian complexes are absent from portions of the Southwest where Clovis points and sites have been recovered. This is most apparent in Arizona. If one drew a line along the Mogollon Rim from about Seligman 70 mi west of Flagstaff to Lordsburg in southwestern New Mexico, post-Clovis Paleoindian sites would be absent to the southwest of that line (Ballenger et al. [2011] have independently discovered the same apparent relationship). In essence, this line marks a general contact between the modern Sonoran and Mohave deserts with higher-elevation biomes along the rim escarpment. Folsom and later Paleoindian sites are for the most part found in the Colorado Plateau region above the Mogollon Rim and in the Chihuahuan Desert in New Mexico and Chihuahua. (This is not to say that these deserts were uninhabited—rather, there are indications that other complexes more closely related to subsequent Archaic ones were already in this region by around 9,000–10,000 years ago [Huckell 1996; Huckell and Haynes 2003; Waters 1998].) The reasons for this apparent change in land use are most likely environmental and probably relate to increased summer insolation and greater seasonal variation in temperature and precipitation during the post–Younger Dryas period and its effects on vegetation (Ballenger et al. 2011). Although xeric woodlands persisted in the lower desert mountains, desertscrub vegetation was an increasingly significant component in southern Arizona and southern New Mexico. Extant medium-sized animals (deer, pronghorn) were part of this environment, but whether bison—the sole surviving element of the megafauna—would have been found there as well is questionable. Bison distribution is likely controlled by the presence of sufficient grass and water; grassland replacement by desertscrub probably removed or at least greatly lessened bison populations in significant parts of the southern Southwest.

Because most Southwestern sites are known only from surface collection, it is difficult to discuss artifact assemblage variability and site function. Excavated single-component sites of the Clovis and Folsom periods appear to be kills (Naco, Lehner), dominated by projectile points and butchering tools; short-term camps occupied adjacent to kills, with a more diverse tool assemblage and large quantities of debitage (Murray Springs Areas 6 and 7, Boca Negra Wash); or large camps apparently not near kills, with what is likely nearly the full range of tool types and abundant debitage (Rio Rancho, Mountaineer).

With the exception of Clovis sites in southeastern Arizona, Paleoindian subsistence in the Southwest is not well documented. The presence of five or six mammoth kill sites in the San Pedro Valley, a gomphothere kill in Sonora, and two bison kills—one in the San Pedro and another in central New Mexico—documents Clovis exploitation of these animals, which G. Haynes (2002) has argued were top-ranked prey in the diet. Waguespack and Surovell (2003) have proposed that Clovis hunters found in North America a land of plenty containing abundant faunal resources; however, mammoth and nearly three dozen genera of the late Pleistocene megafauna disappeared by approximately 13,000 years ago, within at most a few centuries of Clovis arrival. If C. V. Haynes (1991, 2008) is correct that Clovis foragers in the western United States encountered environmental conditions more arid than at any time since the last interglacial, it is possible that mammoth and other taxa were in population decline and therefore relatively rare on the landscape. While grassland or desert grassland communities may have been widespread, animal populations may have been few. Under such conditions, Clovis hunters may have spent considerable time searching for mammoth and bison and potentially covering considerable areas in that search. As a species slow to reach sexual maturity and with a low rate of reproduction, proboscideans are particularly susceptible to human hunting pressure. Putting together mammoth distribution and ecology, plus environmental deterioration and Clovis foraging behavior, the cosmopolitan distribution Clovis points and sites in the Southwest may be a reflection of highly mobile, widely ranging hunter-gatherers.

The few post-Clovis sites in the Southwest that have produced fauna have contained bison, including Folsom sites in the San Luis Valley and Middle Rio Grande Valley as well as the mountains (Mountaineer site). While it is probably overly simplistic to consider the distribution of bison as the sole determinant of Folsom and later Paleoindian mobility, current knowledge of Paleoindian technological organization and the location of those sites in grassland or former grassland environments suggest a strong link between them. This is not to argue that Paleoindians only pursued bison; almost certainly other animals and some plant products were significant components of the diet. The degree to which pursuit of these other resources affected foraging strategies and movement among biotic communities is not currently known. Paleoindian sites occur in a wide range of environmental settings, but clearly grasslands/desert grasslands have thus far yielded the greatest numbers of sites. Further, there is a clear tendency for Paleoindian sites to be situated at or near water sources, which may be either at springs or flowing streams, as is the case with Clovis sites in southeastern Arizona and Folsom sites in the San Luis Valley, or near ephemeral playas, as documented for Folsom and later sites in central New Mexico. Judge observed that 75 percent of his Middle Rio Grande Folsom sites were positioned near playas, a location less frequently used in the subsequent "Belen" and Cody periods. Such playas certainly attracted bison and other animals, making them special and to some extent predictable features of the landscape where probabilities increased that animals (and water) could be found.

Attempts to reconstruct Southwestern Paleoindian foraging strategies, mobility, and group organization are few, but variations in site size and content are one avenue of approach (Andrews et al. 2008). Surprisingly few data are available on Southwestern Paleoindian site size, but it is my impression that most sites are small, typically less than 100 m × 50 m in maximum dimension. For example, figures for Albuquerque Basin Folsom sites include Deann's site (75 m × 60 m), Boca Negra Wash Locus A (30 m × >25 m) and Locus B (30 m × 25 m), and Loma Machete (70 m × 30 m); the Los Gavilanes Cody site is of similar size (35 m × 30 m). These small sites appear to be the products of a single occupation or cultural component. There are a few large sites—the Mockingbird Gap Clovis site (800 m × 80–150 m [Huckell et al. 2006]) and two Folsom sites, Rio Rancho (340 m × 170 m) and Los Lunas (150–210 m × 75 m [Dawson and Judge 1969]). Rio Rancho contains two spatially discrete, purely Folsom loci: Locus 4148 (75 m × 30 m) and Locus 4147/AS-2 (80 m × 40 m); the distribution of artifacts within Los Lunas is unknown. Post-Folsom occupations occur at Los Lunas and a third locus at Rio Rancho. A third Folsom "site" reported by Dawson and Judge (1969) is Correo, which is described as five small loci (dimensions not given) scattered over an area some 1,080 m long. The Mountaineer site measures 300 m × 400 m (Stiger 2006) but appears to consist of multiple clusters or loci. Thus, larger sites may be viewed as aggregations of smaller occupational loci, each locus similar in size to the small sites.

Because most sites are known only from surface examination, and their apparent sizes are dependent on exposure by postoccupational geomorphic processes, it is difficult to infer much about social and mobility organization. Further, where multiple, spatially discrete but demonstrably Paleoindian loci are recognized, it is very challenging to determine whether they represent temporally separate reoccupations or coeval but spatially separate groups. The preponderance of small site sizes may suggest that typically coresidential groups were correspondingly small, possibly representing bands comprising a small number of families related consanguineally and/or affinally. Andrews et al. (2008) and LaBelle (2010) have reviewed site size data for the Plains and report a pattern very similar to that described for the Southwest—numerous small sites, fewer large ones, and rare very large ones. LaBelle infers that the predominance of small, single-component sites is a reflection of the interplay of high resource abundance with low resource predictability. Bison are predictably found in grassland and savanna environments but due to climatically related variation in forage production, are renowned for the unpredictability of their location within a particular area from season to season and year to year (Hanson 1984; Roe 1970). Therefore, human foragers may encounter and hunt them in opportunistic fashion, and small groups making small kills may reflect the general strategy adopted by Paleoindians to exploit this animal. A corollary of this pattern might well be that many (most?) small sites are single-component occupations because the odds of repeatedly finding prey at the same place on the landscape are low. Occasional sites with two or more loci (i.e., Boca Negra Wash) or larger areas (Reddin?) may represent separate occasions when hunters discovered bison at the same place. Again, isolated playas may mark the landscape features most likely to have attracted bison and hunters.

Amick (1996) has proposed that Southwestern Folsom groups practiced residential, as opposed to logistical, mobility. This interpretation can perhaps be extended to other Paleoindian groups in the region as well. The presence of larger sites such as Rio Rancho and Los Lunas (Dawson and Judge 1969) or Mountaineer (Stiger 2006) may signal either episodic aggregations of smaller social groups or repeated uses of the same site by small groups over time. If it is the latter, a pattern of fairly regular land use over the course of years may be indicated. The larger Middle Rio Grande Valley Folsom sites are distinguished by locations in proximity to more permanent sources of water (Dawson and Judge 1969), which might make them candidates for repeated occupation over time.

As is true of Paleoindian sites elsewhere in North America, sourcing of lithic artifacts to particular raw material sources can provide valuable insights into Southwestern Paleoindian technological organization and patterns of land use. The Southwest contains numerous, widespread, and diverse lithic sources, as documented by Shackley (2005) for obsidian and other volcanics and LeTourneau (2000), who has inventoried many of the geological formations known or thought to contain toolstone of all kinds suitable for Paleoindian use. This variety and diversity of lithic sources stands in stark contrast to the Southern Plains, where Paleoindian lithic assemblages are dominated by a handful of major sources (sometimes only two or three) such as Edwards chert, Alibates silicified dolomite, and Tecovas jasper (Holliday 1997:244–252; Jodry 1999b:120–138). Southwestern assemblages, in contrast, may have a dozen or more distinct materials (see Huckell and Kilby 2002 for an example); in central New Mexico Folsom sites most materials are from sources in the northwestern quarter of the state (O'Brien et al. 2009). However, significant differences of opinion about whether particular materials are derived from primary as opposed to secondary sources exist among investigators and may result in very different interpretations of patterns of mobility and technological organization.

The studies carried out thus far focus primarily on Folsom and, to a lesser extent, Clovis. Because relatively few Paleoindian sites have been excavated within the region, these studies have relied on the use of surface-collected temporally diagnostic projectile points, preforms, and channel flakes rather than complete lithic artifact assemblages. Using only the weaponry component of these assemblages may yield biased results regarding raw material frequencies and limit inferences about the nature of the exploited sources. Amick (1996, 1999) has argued that the occupants of Rio Grande Valley Folsom sites relied principally on chert, obsidian, and other materials obtained from secondary Pliocene–Pleistocene cobble sources. However LeTourneau (2000) used X-ray fluorescence to demonstrate that a large proportion of the obsidian used at these sites is derived from the Valles Rhyolite (Cerro del Medio) source in the Jemez Mountains, a source that has not been eroded into secondary contexts outside the Valles Caldera. Consequently, travel to the primary source is the only way to obtain it. Subsequent studies (Huckell et al. 2011) have further supported this finding.

From the few excavated single-component sites, the entire excavated Folsom assemblage, all tools and debitage, can be used to examine raw material frequencies and procurement patterns. For example, at the Boca Negra Wash site, two materials—obsidian sourced to Cerro del Medio (Huckell et al. 2011) and Pedernal chert—make up 68 percent of the assemblage (O'Brien et al. 2009). Low frequencies of cortex and particular color characteristics can be used to support an interpretation of direct procurement of Pedernal chert and Cerro del Medio. Conversely, a similar study of tools and debitage from Deann's site (only 4 km to the west of Boca Negra) shows that over one-fourth of the assemblage is cobble chert and chalcedony derived from nearby Pliocene–Pleistocene alluvium (O'Brien et al. 2009). Similarly, the assemblage at Mountaineer is dominated by locally available quartzite (Stiger 2002). While space limits detailed treatment of these investigations, they reveal the existence of a fairly flexible strategy of material procurement and use that includes both long- and short-distance transportation, but a strategy dominated by exploitation of sources located in the Southwest as opposed to ones from outside the region. Other Southwestern Folsom sites share this pattern, including Cattle Guard and other San Luis Valley sites (Jodry 1999a, 1999b). This is likely true for Paleoindian groups other than Folsom as well. Finally, although present in small quantities at some sites, artifacts made of Southern Plains raw materials are not common in the Southwest west of the Rio Grande (Amick 1996; LeTourneau 2000; O'Brien et al. 2009). However, Jodry (1999b:Figure 35) has reported relatively high percentages of Edwards and Alibates at the Zapata and Linger Folsom sites in the San Luis Valley, suggesting that Southern High Plains groups moved occasionally into the Rio Grande headwaters region.

In conclusion, despite a history of research that spans 60 years, Southwestern Paleoindian studies are very much in their infancy. They have already contributed much to broader debates about matters of colonization, subsistence, megafaunal extinction, paleoenvironmental change, mobility, and technological organization. This brief overview has suggested that while the region is best known for its Clovis and Folsom sites, there is considerable evidence to suggest that the record of other Paleoindian cultural complexes has equal potential to contribute important data and ideas to the study of the processes of cultural differentiation and adaptation during the early Holocene. In order to take maximum advantage of the Paleoindian record, archaeologists must not only continue to document and explore the surface record but also continue to find and excavate single-component sites in buried geological contexts. Such an approach will provide complementary data for both broadscale and site-focused treatments of the record of these earliest Southwestern peoples.

Acknowledgments

Thanks first go to Don Fowler for his friendship and exemplary career; his eclectic research interests and desire to make archaeology better than he found it have created a lasting legacy on which we can all build. Among his many accomplishments is his creation with Joe Cramer of the Sundance Archaeological Research Fund, an organization dedicated to the investigation of the Paleoindian record in the Great Basin. It was a great pleasure to be invited to contribute to this volume by Joel Janetski, and I appreciate the chance to shine a little light on the earliest part of the human history of the Southwestern United States. This chapter would have been impossible without the prior contributions and generous support from a great number of colleagues (in no particular order): Pegi Jodry, Bonnie Pitblado, Jim Judge, Joel Janetski, Dave Byers, Vance Holliday, Vance Haynes, Dan Amick, Phil LeTourneau, Steve Shackley, Jason LaBelle, Dennis Stanford, Jesse Ballenger, Ned Gaines, Lupita Sanchez, Matt Schmader, Bob Weber, David Kilby, Marcus Hamilton, Christina Sinkovec, Matt O'Brien, Chris Merriman, and Briggs Buchanan. There are far too many public-spirited folks who have generously shared their Paleoindian discoveries with me to recognize individually here, but I must single out Robert Truesdell, Elizabeth Brawley, Gordon Nelson, Louis Escapule, and Don Formby. Without their contributions, I would have little to use in creating this chapter. I am indebted to Caroline Gabe for the creation of the maps that accompany this chapter and to Catherine Baudoin for the photographs of Paleoindian points.

References Cited

Agenbroad, Larry D.

1967 The Distribution of Fluted Points in Arizona. *Kiva* 32:113–120.

Alroy, John

1999 Putting North America's End-Pleistocene Megafaunal Extinction in Context: Large-Scale Analyses of Spatial Patterns, Extinction Rates, and Size Distributions. In *Extinctions in Near Time: Causes, Contexts, and Consequences*, edited by Ross D. E. MacPhee, pp. 105–143. Plenum, New York.

2001 A Multispecies Overkill Simulation of the End-Pleistocene Megafaunal Mass Extinction. *Science* 292:1893–1896.

Amick, Daniel S.

1994 Technological Organization and the Structure of Inference in Lithic Analysis: An Examination of Folsom Hunting. In *The Organization of North American Prehistoric Chipped Stone Tool Technologies*, edited by Philip J. Carr, pp. 9–34. International Monographs in Prehistory, Archaeological Series, 7. Ann Arbor.

1995 Patterns of Technological Variation Among Folsom and Midland Projectile Points in the American Southwest. *Plains Anthropologist* 40:23–38.

1996 Regional Patterns of Folsom Mobility and Land Use in the American Southwest. *World Archaeology* 27:411–426.

1999 *Folsom Lithic Technology: Explorations in Structure and Variation*. International Monographs in Prehistory, Archaeological Series, 12. Ann Arbor.

Andrews, Brian N., Jason M. Labelle, and John D. Seebach

2008 Spatial Variability in the Folsom Archaeological Record: Multi-Scalar Approach. *American Antiquity* 73:464–490.

Ballenger, Jesse A. M., Vance T. Holliday, Andrew L. Kowler, William T. Reitze, Mary M. Prasciunas, D. Shane Miller, and Jason D. Windingstad

2011 Evidence for Younger Dryas Global Climate Oscillation and Human Response in the American Southwest. *Quaternary International* 242:502–519.

Barnosky, Anthony D., Paul L. Koch, Robert S. Feranec, Scott L. Wing, and Alan B. Shabel

2004 Assessing the Causes of Late Pleistocene Extinctions on the Continents. *Science* 306:70–75.

Bartlett, Katherine

1943 A Primitive Stone Industry of the Little Colorado Valley, Arizona. *American Antiquity* 8:266–268.

Beck, W., D. J. Donahue, A. J. T. Jull, G. Burr, W. S. Broecker, G. Bonani, I. Hajdas, and E. Malotki

1998 Ambiguities in Direct Dating of Rock Surfaces Using Radiocarbon Measurement. *Science* 280:2132–2135.

Beckett, Patrick H.

1980 *The Ake Site: Collection and Excavation of LA 13423, Catron County, New Mexico*. New Mexico State University, Department of Sociology and Anthropology, Cultural Resources Management Division Report, 357. Las Cruces.

Bement, Leland C., and Brian J. Carter

2010 Jake Bluff: Clovis Bison Hunting on the Southern Plains of North America. *American Antiquity* 75:907–933.

Betancourt, Julio L., Thomas R. Van Devender, and Paul S. Martin (editors)

1990 *Packrat Middens*. University of Arizona Press, Tucson.

Blaine, Jay C.

1968 A Preliminary Report on an Early Man Site in West Texas. In *Transactions of the Third Regional Archaeological Symposium for Southeastern New Mexico and Western Texas*, pp. 1–11. El Paso Archaeological Society, El Paso.

Bousman, C. Britt, Barry W. Baker, and Anne C. Kerr

2004 Paleoindian Archaeology in Texas. In *The Prehistory of Texas*, edited by Timothy K. Pertula, pp. 15–97. Texas A&M University Press, College Station.

Bradley, Bruce A., and Dennis J. Stanford

1987 The Claypool Study. In *The Horner Site: The Type Site of the Cody Cultural Complex*, edited by George C. Frison and Lawrence C. Todd, pp. 405–434. Academic Press, Orlando.

Broster, John B.

1981 Paleo-Indian Occupation of the Cebolleta Mesa Region, New Mexico. *Artifact* 19:13–19.

Bryan, Kirk

1939 Stone Cultures near Cerro Pedernal and Their Geological Antiquity. *Bulletin of the Texas Archeological and Paleontological Society* 11:9–46.

1950 *Flint Quarries: The Sources of Tools and, at the Same Time, the Factories of the American Indian; With a Consideration of the Theory of the Blank and Some of the Techniques of Flint Utilization*. Papers of the Peabody Museum of American Archaeology and Ethnology, 17(3). Harvard University, Cambridge.

Bryan, Kirk, and Joseph H. Toulouse

1943 The San Jose Non-Ceramic Culture and Its Relation to a Puebloan Culture in New Mexico. *American Antiquity* 8: 269–280.

Buchanan, Briggs, Eileen Johnson, R. E. Straus, and Patrick J. Lewis

2007 A Morphometric Approach to Assessing Late Paleoindian Projectile Point Variability on the Southern High Plains. *Plains Anthropologist* 52:279–299.

Byers, David A.

2013 The Dawson Site: A Paleoindian Camp in the San Rafael Desert. *Utah Archaeology*, in review.

Chapin, Nicholas M.

2005 Hunter-Gatherer Technological Organization: The Archaic Period in Northern New Mexico. Unpublished Ph.D. dissertation, Department of Anthropology, University of New Mexico, Albuquerque.

Cordell, Linda S.

1997 *Archaeology of the Southwest*. 2nd ed. Academic Press, San Diego.

Davis, William E.

1989 The Lime Ridge Clovis Site. *Utah Archaeology*, 1989: 5–28.

Dawson, Jerry, and W. James Judge

1969 Paleo-Indian Sites and Topography in the Middle Rio Grande Valley of New Mexico. *Plains Anthropologist* 14:149–163.

Dick, Herbert W., and Bert Mountain

1960 The Claypool Site: A Cody Complex Site in Northeastern Colorado. *American Antiquity* 26:223–235.

Dorn, Ronald I.

1998 Response to Beck et al. *Science* 280:2135–2139.

Frison, George C.

1984 The Cater/Kerr-McGee Paleoindian Site: Cultural Resource

Management and Archaeological Research. *American Antiquity* 49:288–314.

Frison, George C., C. Vance Haynes, Jr., and Mary Lou Larson

1996 Discussion and Conclusions. In *The Mill Iron Site*, edited by George C. Frison, pp. 205–216. University of New Mexico Press, Albuquerque.

Gaines, Edmund P.

2006 Paleoindian Geoarchaeology of the Upper San Pedro River Valley, Sonora, Mexico. Unpublished Master's thesis, Department of Anthropology, University of Arizona, Tucson.

Gaines, Edmund P., Guadalupe Sanchez, and Vance T. Holliday

2009 Paleoindian Archaeology in Northern and Central Sonora, Mexico. *Kiva* 74:305–335.

Geib, Phil R., and J. Richard Ambler

1991 Sand Dune Side-Notched: An Early Archaic Projectile Point Type of the Northern Colorado Plateau. *Utah Archaeology* 4:17–23.

Grayson, Donald K.

1984 Explaining Pleistocene Extinctions: Thoughts on the Structure of a Debate. In *Quaternary Extinctions: A Prehistoric Revolution*, edited by Paul S. Martin and Richard G. Klein, pp. 807–823. University of Arizona Press, Tucson.

2001 The Archaeological Record of Human Impacts on Animal Populations. *Journal of World Prehistory* 15:1–68.

Grayson, Donald K., and David J. Meltzer

2002 Clovis Hunting and Large Mammal Extinction: A Critical Review of the Evidence. *Journal of World Prehistory* 16:313–359.

2003 A Requiem for North American Overkill. *Journal of Archaeological Science* 30:585–593.

Hamilton, Marcus J.

2008 Quantifying Clovis Dynamics: Confronting Theory with Models and Data Across Scales. Unpublished Ph.D. dissertation, Department of Anthropology, University of New Mexico, Albuquerque.

Hanson, Jeffrey R.

1984 Bison Ecology on the Northern Plains and a Reconstruction of Bison Patterns for the North Dakota Region. *Plains Anthropologist* 29:93–113.

Haury, Emil W.

1950 *The Stratigraphy and Archaeology of Ventana Cave, Arizona.* University of New Mexico Press, Albuquerque; and University of Arizona Press, Tucson.

1953 Artifacts with Mammoth Remains, Naco, Arizona. *American Antiquity* 19:1–14.

Haury, Emil W., E. B. Sayles, and William W. Wasley

1959 The Lehner Mammoth Site, Southeastern Arizona. *American Antiquity* 25:2–30.

Hayden, Julian D.

1976 Pre-Altithermal Archaeology in the Sierra Pinacate, Sonora, Mexico. *American Antiquity* 41:274–289.

Haynes, C. Vance, Jr.

1991 Geoarchaeological and Paleohydrological Evidence for a Clovis-Age Drought in North America and Its Bearing on Extinction. *Quaternary Research* 35:438–450.

1995 Geochronology of Paleoenvironmental Change, Clovis Type Site, Blackwater Draw, New Mexico. *Geoarchaeology* 10:317–388.

2007 Quaternary Geology of the Murray Springs Clovis Site. In *Murray Springs: A Clovis Site with Multiple Activity Areas in the San Pedro Valley, Arizona*, edited by C. V. Haynes, Jr., and B. B. Huckell, pp. 16–56. Anthropological Papers of the University of Arizona No. 71. University of Arizona Press, Tucson.

2008 Younger Dryas "Black Mats" and the Rancholabrean Termination in North America. *Proceedings of the National Academy of Sciences of the United States of America* 105:6520–6525.

Haynes, C. Vance, Jr., and George A. Agogino

1986 *Geochronology of Sandia Cave.* Contributions to Anthropology No. 32. Smithsonian Institution, Washington, D.C.

Haynes, C. Vance, Jr., and Bruce B. Huckell (editors)

2007 *Murray Springs: A Clovis Site with Multiple Activity Areas in the San Pedro Valley, Arizona.* Anthropological Papers of the University of Arizona No. 71. University of Arizona Press, Tucson.

Haynes, Gary

2002 *The Early Settlement of North America: The Clovis Era.* Cambridge University Press, Cambridge.

Haynes, Gary, David G. Anderson, C. Reid Ferring, Stuart J. Feidel, Don K. Grayson, C. Vance Haynes, Jr., Vance T. Holliday, Bruce B. Huckell, Marcel Kornfeld, David J. Meltzer, Juliet Morrow, Todd Surovell, Nicole M. Waguespack, Peter Wigand, and Robert M. Yohe, II

2007 Comment on "Redefining the Age of Clovis: Implications for the Peopling of the Americas." *Science* 317(320b). DOI 10.1126/science.1141960.

Heilen, Michael P.

2003 Julian Hayden's Malpais Model: A Pre-Clovis Claim from the American Southwest. *Kiva* 69:305–331.

Hemmings, E. Thomas

1970 Early Man in the San Pedro Valley, Arizona. Unpublished Ph.D. dissertation, Department of Anthropology, University of Arizona, Tucson.

Hemmings, E. Thomas, and C. Vance Haynes, Jr.

1968 The Escapule Mammoth and Associated Projectile Points, San Pedro Valley, Arizona. *Journal of the Arizona Academy of Science* 5:184–188.

Hesse, India S., William J. Parry, and Francis E. Smiley

1999 Badger Springs: A Late-Paleoindian Site in Northeastern Arizona. *Current Research in the Pleistocene* 16:27–30.

Hester, James J.

1972 *Blackwater Locality No. 1: A Stratified, Early Man Site in Eastern New Mexico.* Publication of the Fort Burgwin Research Center No. 8. Southern Methodist University, Dallas.

Hibben, Frank C.

1941 *Evidences of Early Occupation in Sandia Cave, New Mexico, and Other Sites in the Sandia-Manzano Region.* Smithsonian Miscellaneous Collections Vol. 99, No. 23. Washington, D.C.

Hill, Matthew E., Jr., and Vance T. Holliday

2011 Paleoindian and Later Occupations Along Ancient Shorelines of the San Agustin Plains, New Mexico. *Journal of Field Archaeology* 36:3–20.

Hofman, Jack L.

1992 Recognition and Interpretation of Folsom Technological Variability on the Southern Plains. In *Ice Age Hunters of the Rockies*, edited by Dennis J. Stanford and Jane S. Day, pp. 193–224. Denver Museum of Natural History and University Press of Colorado, Niwot.

1994 Paleoindian Aggregations on the Great Plains. *Journal of Anthropological Archaeology* 13:341–370.

2010 Allen Complex Behavior and Chronology in the Central Plains. In *Exploring Variability in Early Holocene Hunter-Gatherer Lifeways*, edited by Stance Hurst and Jack L. Hofman, pp. 135–152. University of Kansas Publications in Anthropology, 25. Lawrence.

Hofman, Jack L., Daniel S. Amick, and Richard O. Rose
1990 Shifting Sands: A Folsom-Midland Assemblage from a Campsite in Western Texas. *Plains Anthropologist* 35:221–253.

Holliday, Vance T.
1997 *Paleoindian Geoarchaeology of the Southern High Plains.* University of Texas Press, Austin.
2000 The Evolution of Paleoindian Geochronology and Typology on the Great Plains. *Geoarchaeology* 15:227–290.

Holliday, Vance T., Bruce B. Huckell, James H. Mayer, and Steven L. Forman
2006a Geoarchaeology of the Boca Negra Wash Area, Albuquerque Basin, New Mexico. *Geoarchaeology* 21:765–802.

Holliday, Vance T., Bruce B. Huckell, Robert H. Weber, Marcus J. Hamilton, William T. Reitze, and James H. Mayer
2009 Geoarchaeology of the Mockingbird Gap (Clovis) Site, Jornada del Muerto, New Mexico. *Geoarchaeology* 24:348–370.

Holliday, Vance T., Eileen Johnson, and Thomas W. Stafford
1999 AMS Radiocarbon Dating of the Type Plainview and Firstview (Paleoindian) Assemblages: The Agony and the Ecstasy. *American Antiquity* 64:444–454.

Holliday, Vance T., Robert H. Weber, and James H. Mayer
2006b Geoarchaeological Investigations at the Ake Folsom Site, New Mexico. *Current Research in the Pleistocene* 23:112–114.

Huckell, Bruce B.
1978 AZ O:15:68, the Silktassel Site. In *The Oxbow Hill–Payson Project*, pp. 61–71. Arizona State Museum Contribution to Highway Salvage Archaeology in Arizona No. 48. University of Arizona, Tucson.
1982 *The Distribution of Fluted Points in Arizona: A Review and an Update.* Arizona State Museum Archaeological Series No. 145. University of Arizona, Tucson.
1996 The Archaic Prehistory of the North American Southwest. *Journal of World Prehistory* 10:305–373.
1998 A San Dieguito Site on the Lower Gila River, Southwestern Arizona. *Kiva* 64:145–174.
2004 Clovis in the Southwestern United States. In *New Perspectives on the First Americans*, edited by Bradley T. Lepper and Robson Bonnichsen, pp. 93–101. Center for the Study of the First Americans, Texas A&M University, College Station.
2007 Clovis Lithic Technology: A View from the Upper San Pedro Valley. In *Murray Springs: A Clovis Site with Multiple Activity Areas in the San Pedro Valley, Arizona*, edited by C. V. Haynes, Jr., and B. B. Huckell, pp. 170–213. Anthropological Papers of the University of Arizona No. 71. University of Arizona Press, Tucson.
2011 The End of the Beginning: Late Paleoindian Parallel-Obliquely Flaked Points in the Southwest. Paper presented at the 69th Annual Plains Anthropological Conference, Tucson.

Huckell, Bruce B., and C. Vance Haynes, Jr.
2003 The Ventana Complex: New Dates and New Ideas on Its Place in Early Holocene Western Prehistory. *American Antiquity* 68:353–371.

Huckell, Bruce B., Vance T. Holliday, Marcus J. Hamilton, Christina Sinkovec, Chris W. Merriman, M. Steven Shackley, and Robert H. Weber
2008 The Mockingbird Gap Clovis Site: 2007 Investigations. *Current Research in the Pleistocene* 25:95–97.

Huckell, Bruce B., Vance T. Holliday, Robert H. Weber, and James H. Mayer
2006 Archaeological and Geological Test Investigations at the Mockingbird Gap Clovis Site, Central New Mexico. *Current Research in the Pleistocene* 23:115–116.

Huckell, Bruce B., and W. James Judge
2006 Paleo-Indian: Plains and Southwest. In *Environment, Origins, and Population*, ed. by Douglas H. Ubelaker, pp. 148–170. Handbook of North American Indians Vol. 3. Smithsonian Institution, Washington, D.C.

Huckell, Bruce B., and J. David Kilby
2000 Boca Negra Wash, a New Folsom Site in the Middle Rio Grande Valley, New Mexico. *Current Research in the Pleistocene* 17:45–47.
2002 Folsom Point Production at the Rio Rancho Site, New Mexico. In *Folsom Technology and Lifeways*, edited by John E. Clark and Michael B. Collins, pp. 11–29. Lithic Technology Special Publication No. 4. Department of Anthropology, University of Tulsa, Tulsa.

Huckell, Bruce B., J. David Kilby, Briggs Buchanan, Marcus J. Hamilton, and Susan Ruth
2002 2001 Excavations at the Boca Negra Wash Folsom Site, North-Central New Mexico. *Current Research in the Pleistocene* 19:39–40.

Huckell, Bruce B., J. David Kilby, and Marcus J. Hamilton
2003 2002 Investigations at the Boca Negra Wash Folsom Site, North-Central New Mexico. *Current Research in the Pleistocene* 20:33–35.

Huckell, Bruce B., and Susan Ruth
2004 Test Investigations at Deann's Folsom Site, North-Central New Mexico. *Current Research in the Pleistocene* 21:48–50.

Huckell, Bruce B., M. Steven Shackley, Matthew J. O'Brien, and Christopher W. Merriman
2011 Folsom Obsidian Procurement and Use at the Boca Negra Wash Site, New Mexico. *Current Research in the Pleistocene* 28:49–52.

Hurst, C. T.
1943 A Folsom Site in a Mountain Valley of Colorado. *American Antiquity* 8:250–253.

Irwin, Henry T.
1968 The Itama: Late Pleistocene Inhabitants of the Plains of the United States and Canada and the American Southwest. Unpublished Ph.D. dissertation, Department of Anthropology, Harvard University, Cambridge.

Irwin-Williams, Cynthia, and C. Vance Haynes, Jr.
1970 Climatic Change and Early Population Dynamics in the Southwestern United States. *Quaternary Research* 1:59–71.

Irwin-Williams, Cynthia, Henry T. Irwin, George A. Agogino, and C. Vance Haynes, Jr.
1973 Hell Gap: Paleo-Indian Occupation on the High Plains. *Plains Anthropologist* 18:40–53.

Jodry, Margaret A.
1999a Paleoindian Stage. In *Colorado Prehistory: A Context for the Rio Grande Basin*, by Marilyn A. Martorano, Ted Hoefer, III, Margaret A. Jodry, Vince Spero, and Melissa L. Taylor, pp. 45–114. Colorado Council of Professional Archaeologists, Denver.
1999b Folsom Technological and Economic Strategies: Views from Stewart's Cattle Guard Site and the Upper Rio Grande Basin. Unpublished Ph.D. dissertation, Department of Anthropology, American University, Washington, D.C.

Johnson, Eileen

1987 *Lubbock Lake: Late Quaternary Studies on the Southern High Plains*. Texas A&M University Press, College Station.

Judge, W. James

1970 Systems Analysis and the Folsom-Midland Question. *Southwestern Journal of Anthropology* 26:40–51.

1973 *Paleoindian Occupation of the Central Rio Grande Valley in New Mexico*. University of New Mexico Press, Albuquerque.

Keller, Donald R., and Suzanne M. Wilson

1976 New Light on the Tolchaco Problem. *Kiva* 41:225–239.

Krieger, Alex D.

1947 Artifacts from the Plainview Bison Bed. In "Fossil Bison and Associated Artifacts from Plainview, Texas," by E. H. Sellards, G. L. Evans, and G. E. Meade. *Bulletin of the Geological Society of America* 58:938–954.

LaBelle, Jason M.

2010 *Re*Occupation of Place: Late Paleoindian Land Use Strategies in the Central Plains. In *Exploring Variability in Early Holocene Hunter-Gatherer Lifeways*, edited by Stance Hurst and Jack L. Hofman, pp. 37–72. University of Kansas Publications in Anthropology, 25. Lawrence.

Larson, Mary Lou, Marcel Kornfeld, and George C. Frison (editors)

2009 *Hell Gap: A Stratified Paleoindian Campsite at the Edge of the Rockies*. University of Utah Press, Salt Lake City.

LeTourneau, Philippe D.

2000 Folsom Toolstone Procurement in the Southwest and Southern Plains. Unpublished Ph.D. dissertation, Department of Anthropology, University of New Mexico, Albuquerque.

Lindsay, Alexander J., Jr., J. Richard Ambler, Mary Anne Stein, and Philip M. Hobler

1968 *Excavations North and East of Navajo Mountain, Utah, 1959–1962*. Museum of Northern Arizona Bulletin, 45; Glen Canyon Series, 8. Northern Arizona Society of Science and Art, Flagstaff.

Longacre, William A., and Michael W. Graves

1976 Probability Sampling Applied to an Early Multi-Component Surface Site in East-Central Arizona. *Kiva* 41:277–287.

Mabry, Jonathan B.

1998 *Paleoindian and Archaic Sites in Arizona*. Technical Report No. 97-7. Center for Desert Archaeology, Tucson.

MacNeish, Richard S., and Jane G. Libby (editors)

2003 *Pendejo Cave*. University of New Mexico Press, Albuquerque.

Martin, Paul S.

2005 *Twilight of the Mammoths*. University of California Press, Berkeley.

Matson, R. G.

1991 *The Origins of Southwestern Agriculture*. University of Arizona Press, Tucson.

Meltzer, David J., and Vance T. Holliday

2010 Would North American Paleoindians Have Noticed Younger Dryas Age Climate Changes? *Journal of World Prehistory* 23:1–41.

Mulloy, William T.

1959 The James Allen Site near Laramie, Wyoming. *American Antiquity* 25:112–116.

North, Chris D., Michael S. Foster, John M. Lindly, and Douglas R. Mitchell

2005 A Newly Discovered Clovis Point from the Phoenix Basin and an Update on Arizona Clovis Point Attributes. *Kiva* 70:293–307.

O'Brien, Matthew J., Susan M. Ruth, Chris W. Merriman, and Bruce B. Huckell

2009 Reevaluating Folsom Mobility and Land Use in New Mexico. *Current Research in the Pleistocene* 26:97–100.

Ortiz, Manuel Robles, and Francisco Manzo Taylor

1972 Clovis Fluted Points from Sonora, Mexico. *Kiva* 37:199–206.

Peru, Donald V.

1984 *New River: A Lithic Industry in Maricopa County, Arizona*. Occasional Paper No. 1. Phoenix Chapter, Arizona Archaeological Society, Phoenix.

Phelps, Alan L.

1990 A Paleo-Indian Presence in Northern Chihuahua—El Millon Site. *Artifact* 24:53–59.

Pitblado, Bonnie L.

1994 Paleoindian Presence in Southwest Colorado. *Southwestern Lore* 60:1–20.

1999 New ^{14}C Dates and Obliquely Flaked Points from a High-Altitude Paleoindian Site, Colorado Rocky Mountains. *Current Research in the Pleistocene* 16:65–66.

Prasciunas, Mary M.

2011 Mapping Clovis: Projectile Points, Behavior, and Bias. *American Antiquity* 76:107–126.

Roe, Frank G.

1970 *The North American Buffalo: A Critical Study of the Species in Its Wild State*. 2nd ed. University of Toronto Press, Toronto.

Rogers, Malcolm J.

1958 San Dieguito Implements from the Terraces of the Rincon-Pantano and Rillito Drainage System. *Kiva* 24:1–23.

1966 *Ancient Hunters of the Far West*. Union-Tribune Publishing Company, San Diego.

Roosa, William B.

1956 Preliminary Report on the Lucy Site. *El Palacio* 63:36–49.

Sanchez, Guadalupe

2001 A Synopsis of Paleo-Indian Archaeology in Mexico. *Kiva* 67:119–136.

Sanchez, Guadalupe, Edmund P. Gaines, Vance T. Holliday, and Jose Arroyo-Cabrales

2009 El Fin del Mundo. In *Paleoindians in the American Southwest and Northern Mexico*, by Vance T. Holliday, Michael Bever, and David J. Meltzer, pp. 6–7. Archaeology Southwest, 23. Center for Desert Archaeology, Tucson.

Schmader, Matthew F., Michael J. Dilley, and David Barsanti

2006 *The Hawk Project: Archaeological Data Recovery at Ten Sites in Unit 25, Rio Rancho Estates, N.M.* Rio Grande Consultants, Inc., Albuquerque.

Sellards, E. H., Glen L. Evans, and Grayson E. Meade

1947 Fossil Bison and Associated Artifacts from Plainview, Texas. *Bulletin of the Geological Society of America* 58:927–954.

Sellet, Frederic

2001 A Changing Perspective on Paleoindian Chronology and Typology: A View from the Northwestern Plains. *Arctic Anthropology* 38:48–63.

Sellet, Frederic, James Donohue, and Matthew G. Hill

2009 The Jim Pitts Site: A Stratified Paleoindian Site in the Black Hills of South Dakota. *American Antiquity* 74:735–758.

Shackley, M. Steven

2005 *Obsidian: Geology and Archaeology in the North American Southwest*. University of Arizona Press, Tucson.

Shaffer, Brian S., and Barry W. Baker

1999 How Many Epidermal Ridges per Linear Centimeter?

Comments on Possible Pre-Clovis Human Friction Skin Prints from Pendejo Cave. *American Antiquity* 62:559–560.

Smith, Gary A., and Bruce B. Huckell
2005 The Geological and Geoarchaeological Significance of Cerro Pedernal, Rio Arriba County, New Mexico. In *Geology of the Chama Basin*, edited by S. G. Lucas, K. E. Zeigler, V. W. Lueth, and D. E. Owen, pp. 425–431. 56th Field Conference Guidebook. New Mexico Geological Society, Socorro.

Stanford, Dennis J.
2005 Paleoindian Archaeology and Late Pleistocene Environments in the Plains and Southwestern United States. In *Ice Age Peoples of North America*, 2nd ed., edited by Robson Bonnichsen and Karen L. Turnmire, pp. 281–339. Center for the Study of the First Americans, College Station.

Stevens, Dominique E., and George A. Agogino
1975 *Sandia Cave: A Study in Controversy*. Contributions in Anthropology, 7(1). Eastern New Mexico University, Portales.

Stiger, Mark
2002 The Mountaineer Site, a Large Folsom Camp near Gunnison, Colorado. *Current Research in the Pleistocene* 19:80–81.
2006 A Folsom Structure in the Colorado Mountains. *American Antiquity* 71:321–352.

Surovell, Todd A., Nicole M. Waguespack, and P. Jeffrey Brantingham
2005 Global Archaeological Evidence for Proboscidean Overkill. *Proceedings of the National Academy of Sciences of the USA* 102:6231–6236.

Thomas, Tully H.
1952 The Concho Complex: A Popular Report. *Plateau* 25:1–10.

Thompson, Jessica C., Nawa Sugiyama, and Gary S. Morgan
2008 Taphonomic Analysis of the Mammalian Fauna from Sandia Cave, New Mexico, and the "Sandia Man" Controversy. *American Antiquity* 73:337–360.

Thompson, Robert S., Cathy Whitlock, Patrick J. Bartlein, Sandy P. Harrison, and W. Geoffrey Spaulding
1993 Climatic Changes in the Western United States Since 18,000 yr. BP. In *Global Climates Since the Last Glacial Maximum*, edited by Herbert E. Wright, John E. Kutzbach, Thompson Webb, III, William F. Ruddiman, F. A. Street-Perrott, and Patrick J. Bartlein, pp. 468–513. University of Minnesota Press, Minneapolis.

Tucker, David B.
2000 *Footsteps on the Bajada*, Vol. 1. Cultural Resource Report No. 99-140. SWCA, Inc., Tucson.

Vogler, Larry E., K. Langenfeld, and Dennis Gilpin
1993 *DAA'AK'EH NITSAA: An Overview of the Cultural Resources of the Navajo Indian Irrigation Project, Northwestern New Mexico*. Navajo Nation Papers in Anthropology No. 29. Navajo Nation Archaeology Department, Window Rock, Arizona.

Waguespack, Nicole M., and Todd A. Surovell
2003 Clovis Hunting Strategies, or How to Make Out on Plentiful Resources. *American Antiquity* 68:333–352.

Waters, Michael R.
1986 *The Geoarchaeology of Whitewater Draw, Arizona*. Anthropological Papers of the University of Arizona No. 45. University of Arizona Press, Tucson.
1998 The Sulphur Spring Stage of the Cochise Culture and Its Place in Southwestern Prehistory. *Kiva* 64:115–135.

Waters, Michael R., and Thomas W. Stafford, Jr.
2007 Refining the Age of Clovis: Implications for the Peopling of the Americas. *Science* 315:1122–1126.

Weber, Robert H.
1963 Human Prehistory of Socorro County. In *Socorro Region*, edited by F. J. Kuellmer, pp. 225–233. Fourteenth Field Conference Guidebook. New Mexico Geological Society, [Socorro].

Weber, Robert H., and George A. Agogino
1997 Mockingbird Gap Paleoindian Site: Excavations in 1967. In *Layers of Time: Papers in Honor of Robert H. Weber*, edited by Meliha S. Duran and David T. Kirkpatrick, pp. 123–127. Archaeological Society of New Mexico, 23. Albuquerque.

Wendorf, Fred
1959 Folsom Points from Deming, New Mexico. *El Palacio* 25:109.

Wendorf, Fred, and Tully H. Thomas
1951 Early Man Sites near Concho, Arizona. *American Antiquity* 17:107–114.

Wheat, Joe Ben
1972 *The Olsen-Chubbuck Site: A Paleo-Indian Bison Kill*. Memoirs of the Society for American Archaeology No. 26.Washington, D.C.
1979 *The Jurgens Site*. *Plains Anthropologist* Memoir No. 15. *Plains Anthropologist* 24(84), Pt. 2. Lincoln.

Whitley, David S., and Ronald I. Dorn
1993 New Perspectives on the Clovis vs. Pre-Clovis Controversy. *American Antiquity* 58:626–647.

Wormington, H. M.
1957 *Ancient Man in North America*. 4th ed. Denver Museum of Natural History Popular Series No. 4. Denver.

5

Are Great Basin Stemmed Points as Old as Clovis in the Intermountain West?

A Review of the Geochronological Evidence

Ted Goebel and Joshua L. Keene

The Paleoindian record of the Great Basin, Snake River Plain, and Columbia Plateau—an area making up the Intermountain West of North America—is dominated by large bifacial points with distinctive stems and sometimes shouldered bases. Called Great Basin Stemmed points by many, they come in a variety of forms grouped into types with names such as Parman, Haskett, Cougar Mountain, Windust in the north, and Lake Mojave and Silver Lake in the south. Given that much of the Intermountain West is a cool desert with relatively low precipitation, depositional and erosive processes have led to an elusive Paleoindian record. While numerous surface sites with stemmed points have been found, stratified sites typically occur in very deeply buried, often redeposited alluvial contexts (Beck and Jones 1997) or in caves or rockshelters that record not just human occupations but also stays by ground-burrowing rodents, wood rats, carnivores, and even raptors. Teasing apart geomorphic and biogenic formation processes at archaeological sites in the Intermountain West is more than a menial exercise; it must be a major component of any substantive and successful Paleoindian study. Unfortunately, not all studies in the region have been carried out with the rigor necessary to interpret how early sites formed and hence how old they may be. Even in our own work at Bonneville Estates Rockshelter during the past decade, we learned the hard way how wood rats could move cultural debris into secondary contexts and how old wood burned in young hearths could create aberrant radiocarbon chronologies.

A case in point relates to the age of the earliest stemmed points in the Intermountain West. Are they as old as or older than Clovis, the earliest recognized archaeological complex in North America? In other words, do they date to before or during the Allerød interstadial, ~14,000–13,000 calendar years ago (cal BP), or are they younger than this, dating instead only to the Younger Dryas and post–Younger Dryas periods (12,800–8000 cal BP)? Beck and Jones (2009, 2010), and Bryan (1979, 1988) before them, have argued that the earliest stemmed points are very old, potentially older than Clovis, and therefore possibly represent a separate founding population of early Americans, one that originated in northeast Asia or Alaska separate from ancestors of Clovis. In this chapter, we argue that the "stemmed/Clovis contemporaneity" thesis is severely weakened by reliance on a series of sites with problematic contexts and/or aberrant dates. Adhering to a strict regimen of chronological hygiene, we find that virtually all stemmed point sites in the Intermountain West postdate 12,800 cal BP and therefore likely represent a late Paleoindian phenomenon. Only Smith Creek Cave, Bonneville Estates Rockshelter, and Paisley Caves have yielded evidence that may contradict this pattern, but the evidence from these three sites is still ambiguous, providing only equivocal acceptance for a long chronology.

The Case for Clovis-Aged Stemmed Points

At ~13,000 cal BP, Clovis remains the oldest confirmed Paleoindian complex of sites in North America, and archaeologists traditionally believe that all other Paleoindian point forms followed it in some way (Haynes 2002; Pendleton 1979). Successive Paleoindian complexes include Folsom/Goshen/Plainview in the Great Plains, Gainey/Barnes in the Great Lakes region, and Dalton/Simpson in the Southeast (Meltzer 2009; Stanford et al. 2005). The status of Clovis as the earliest evidence for humans inhabiting temperate North America, however, is potentially changing in light of recent discoveries of possibly earlier occupations at sites such as Paisley Caves (Gilbert et al. 2008; Jenkins et al. 2012), Schaefer/Hebior (Overstreet and Kolb 2003), and Debra L. Friedkin (Waters et al. 2011a). Further, in the far west of temperate North America, many archaeologists argue that stemmed bifacial points could be as old as or older than Clovis, implying that an earlier population ancestral to both must have existed in the Americas. In other words, Clovis was not "first" but instead was only "one of the first."

The notion of early American "co-traditions" is not new; some of the first comprehensive studies of North American prehistory recognized deep technological differences west and east of the Rocky Mountains (Bryan 1965; Wormington 1957). This dichotomy was carefully documented by the mid-1960s, and emergent Paleoindian culture-historical frameworks indicated that Clovis sites were common east of, and rare west of, the Rockies, with the Intermountain West's Paleoindian record being dominated by large stemmed points (e.g., Butler 1961; Cressman 1942; Daugherty 1956, 1962; Davis et al. 1969). Soon, radiocarbon dates confirmed suspicions that stemmed points dated to the terminal Pleistocene and early Holocene (e.g., Cressman 1966; Swanson 1972), and at two sites in particular—Wilson Butte Cave and Fort Rock Cave—archaeologists obtained dates surpassing Clovis in antiquity (Bedwell 1973; Gruhn 1965). Wilson Butte Cave's earliest cultural layers, however, were convincingly reinterpreted to date to only the early Holocene (Haynes 1967), while the dated charcoal and small lithic assemblage from the base of Fort Rock Cave were never demonstrated to be primarily associated (Aikens and Jenkins 1994; Grayson 1993; Haynes 1971; Willig and Aikens 1988). Nonetheless, inferences about the Clovis or pre-Clovis age of Great Basin Stemmed points have continued to be made, partly because of their co-occurrence on fossil shoreline features of ancient lakes (e.g., Davis 1975) or because of obsidian-hydration measurements on artifacts suggesting pre-13,000 cal BP ages (Jenkins et al. 2004).

Perhaps no one has been more outspoken about the existence of coeval late Pleistocene projectile point traditions than A. L. Bryan. He (1978, 1988; Bryan and Tuohy 1999) argued that fluted and stemmed points could represent different components of a synchronous tool kit or, more likely, different cultural traditions that ultimately developed from a common root. Bryan's interpretations were based on findings from Smith Creek Cave, Nevada, where he (1988:67–68) found a stratified assemblage of stemmed points directly associated with a hearth feature dated to 11,140 ± 200 ^{14}C BP and scattered charcoal dated to 11,680 ± 160 ^{14}C BP. Based on these findings, along with an analogous record recovered from Taima-taima, Venezuela (Bryan et al. 1978), Bryan concluded that "refined technological innovations were being made in several widely separated parts of the New World before 11,000 years BP," so that it "seems clear that all of these distinctive technological traditions could not have been derived from the Clovis technological complex, whether or not Clovis technology came directly from the Old World" (1978:307).

The most recent proponents of the co-tradition theory are C. Beck and G. T. Jones (2007, 2009, 2010), who have called attention to a number of stratified stemmed point sites with radiocarbon dates spanning the time of Clovis and beyond (Table 5.1; Beck and Jones 2009:234, 2010:104; see also Beck and Jones 1997; Jones and Beck 1999). They argue that the existing chronology shows that stemmed point industries predate Clovis in the Intermountain West and are noticeably different from Clovis. Stemmed point assemblages lack blade tools favored by Clovis (Beck and Jones 2010:97), while crescents are common in assemblages exclusively containing stemmed points but virtually absent in assemblages exclusively containing fluted points (Beck and Jones 2010:100). Toolstone differences occur as well, with stemmed points typically occurring on obsidian and fine-grained volcanic rocks (e.g., basalt, dacite), even where chert was available, while Clovis points were preferentially produced on chert (Beck and Jones 2009, 2010:99). Further, stemmed point blanks were frequently produced from side-struck flakes, while fluted point blanks were more often produced from end-struck flakes (Beck and Jones 2010:98; see also Pendleton 1979). Another important technological distinction relates to hafting strategies, with large, thick stemmed points (i.e., Haskett, Parman, Cougar Mountain forms) representing a socketed-shaft, thrusting/processing technology and fluted points and square-based stemmed points (i.e., Windust, Scottsbluff forms) representing a split-shaft, projectile-specific throwing technology (Beck and Jones 2009:236; see also Beck and Jones 1997:202–205).

In this chapter, we specifically review the chronological evidence used by Beck and Jones (2009, 2010) to support their hypothesis that stemmed points represent a co-tradition coeval with and possibly earlier than Clovis. We do this by applying a set of chronological-hygiene criteria that has been used, we think quite successfully, to critically evaluate and establish Paleolithic chronologies in the Old World. Through this analysis, we find that the chronological evidence presented by Beck and Jones (2009, 2010) does not adequately support the notion that the earliest stemmed points in the Intermountain West were synchronous with Clovis. Instead, virtually all are post-Clovis in age. Despite this, three cave/rockshelter sites in particular—Smith Creek Cave, Bonneville Estates Rockshelter, and Paisley Caves—may contain evidence of early stemmed points, but the evidence from these sites remains ambiguous.

Contextual and Chronological Hygiene in Paleolithic and Paleoindian Archaeology

Archaeologists must be well versed in geoarchaeological and geochronological methods to successfully unravel the processes through which the prehistoric record formed (Schiffer 1987; Taylor 2009; Waters 1992). Identification of taphonomic agents of accumulation, interpretation of site depositional histories, and application of suitable chronometric techniques to accurately and precisely date archaeological events are perhaps the most important tools through which archaeologists can establish the all-important contexts of their finds. Without a clear understanding of these processes, we should not expect to be able to accurately chronicle events in human prehistory, especially events that occurred many millennia ago. This is definitely the case when dealing with the Paleolithic and Paleoindian periods of the human past. Sites predating the early Holocene often show

TABLE 5.1. Relevant dates from sites presented in Beck and Jones 2010.

Site	Provenience	Material	Age (^{14}C BP)	Lab Number	Reference
Sentinel Gap	Feature 99.1	Charcoal	10,680 ± 190[a]	Beta-133650[b]	1
	Oxidized/artifact concentration	Oxidized staining	10,180 ± 40[a]	Beta-124167[c]	1
	Feature 99.1	Charcoal	10,160 ± 60[a]	Beta-133663[c]	1
	Feature 99.3	Charcoal	10,130 ± 60[a]	Beta-133665[c]	1
	Feature 99.6	Charcoal	10,010 ± 60[a]	Beta-133664[c]	1
Marmes Rockshelter	Base of stratum I	Bird bone	11,230 ± 50	Beta-156698[c,d,e]	2
	Stratum I	Mollusk shell	10,810 ± 300[a]	WSU-363	2
	Stratum I	Mollusk shell	10,750 ± 300[a]	WSU-211	2
	Stratum I	Mollusk shell	10,475 ± 300	WSU-366	2
	Stratum I	Mollusk shell	9610 ± 40	Beta-168491[d,e]	2
	Stratum I	Mollusk shell	7550 ± 300	WSU-120[b]	2
Marmes Floodplain	Below Harrison	Composite charcoal	10,570 ± 70	Beta-156697[c,d]	2
	Harrison	Charcoal	10,130 ± 300	W-2218	2
	Marmes	Mollusk shell	9970 ± 110	Y-2481	2
	Marmes	Bone	9870 ± 50	Beta-120802[c,d]	2
	Harrison	Charcoal	9840 ± 300	W-2212	2
	Marmes	Mollusk shell	9820 ± 300	W-2209	2
	Marmes	Bone	9710 ± 40	Beta-156699[c,d]	2
Hatwai I, Area B	?	Composite charcoal	8660 ± 1612[f]	Tx-3266	3
	Unit 1	Composite charcoal	8796 ± 1272[f]	Tx-3265	3
	Unit 1	Composite charcoal	9155 ± 223[f]	Tx-3265	3
	Unit 7	Composite charcoal	10,816 ± 136[a,f]	Tx-3159	3
Hatwai B/C trenches	Secondary channel	Composite charcoal	7951 ± 87[f]	WSU-1840	3
	Gravel facies	Composite charcoal	8563 ± 505[f]	Tx-3082	3
	Secondary channel	Composite charcoal	9282 ± 107[f]	Tx-3083	3
	Secondary channel	Composite charcoal	9320 ± 1777[f]	Tx-3081	3
	Secondary channel	Composite charcoal	9883 ± 107[f]	WSU-2440	3
	Mid-bar sand foreset	Alluvial wood and charcoal	10,107 ± 699[f]	Tx-3160	3
Coopers Ferry	Top of stratum 3	Dispersed charcoal	11,410 ± 130[a]	TO-7349	4
	Strata 3–4 pit	Dispersed charcoal	11,370 ± 40[a]	Beta-114949	4
	Above cultural strata	Charcoal	8430 ± 70	Beta-114952	4
	Strata 3–4 pit	Bone collagen	12,020 ±- 170	Beta-109971[b,c]	4
	Stratum 3	Bone collagen	10,050 ± 180	TO-7357[b,c]	4
	Strata 3–4 pit	Dispersed charcoal	8710 ± 120	TO-7346[b,c]	4
	Stratum 5	Dispersed charcoal	8410 ± 70	Beta-114951[b,c]	4
	Strata 3–4 pit	Dispersed charcoal	7300 ± 70	Beta-114948[b,c]	4
Wildcat Canyon	Stratum J	Roots	3110 ± 120	GaK-1327[b]	5
	Stratum J	Peat	4480 ± 360	WSU-284[b]	5
	Stratum J (intrusive?)	Wood (artifact?)	5540 ± 440	GaK-1323[b]	5
	Stratum J	Carbon and soil	7370 ± 190	GaK-1326	5
	Stratum J	Organic material	8100 ± 130	GaK-1324	5
	Stratum H?	Organic material	9860 ± 510	GaK-1325	5
	Stratum J	Wood (root?)	10,600 ± 200[a]	GaK-1322	5
Buhl	Main burial	Human remains	10,675 ± 95[a]	Beta-43055/ETH-7729[c]	6
Connley Cave 4B	Stratum 4, level 32	Probably charcoal	11,200 ± 200[a]	GaK-2141	7
	Stratum 4, level 38	Probably charcoal	10,600 ± 190[a]	GaK-2143	7
	Stratum 4, level 34	Probably charcoal	9670 ± 180	GaK-2142	7
Connley Cave 4A	Stratum 4, level 35	Probably charcoal	10,100 ± 400	GaK-1742	7

TABLE 5.1. (cont'd.) Relevant dates from sites presented in Beck and Jones 2010.

Site	Provenience	Material	Age (^{14}C BP)	Lab Number	Reference
Handprint Cave	Main chamber, 10–20 cm	Charcoal	10,740 ± 70[a]	Beta-21885	8
Sunshine	Stratum B	Organic sediment	8120 ± 70	Beta-105660	9
	Stratum C	Organic sediment	8560 ± 100	Beta-69781	9
	Stratum C	Organic sediment	9040 ± 190	Beta-86200	9
	Stratum C	Charred material	9800 ± 60	Beta-69782[c]	9
	Stratum C	Charred material	9900 ± 50	Beta-86202[c]	9
	Stratum C	Organic sediment	9920 ± 50	Beta-86203[c]	9
	Stratum C	Organic sediment	10,000 ± 50	Beta-86204[c]	9
	Stratum D	Organic sediment	7380 ± 60	Beta-86199[b]	9
	Stratum D	Charred material	9840 ± 50	Beta-86201[c]	9
	Stratum D	Charred material	9920 ± 60	Beta-86198[c]	9
	Stratum E	Charred material	9860 ± 50	Beta-86206[c]	9
	Stratum E	Charred material	9860 ± 60	Beta-105659[c]	9
	Stratum E	Charred material	10,240 ± 80	Beta-69779[c]	9
	Stratum E	Charred material	10,240 ± 60	Beta-69780[c]	9
	Stratum E	Charred material	10,300 ± 60	Beta-83090[c]	9
	Stratum E	Charred material	10,300 ± 50	Beta-86205[c]	9
	Stratum E	Charred material	10,690 ± 430[a]	Beta-37515	9
	Stratum E	Charred material	10,640 ± 70	Beta-105658[c]	9
	Stratum E	Charred material	10,930 ± 60	Beta-105657[c]	9
	Stratum E	Camel bone collagen	11,390 ±60	Beta-105662[b,c]	9
	Stratum E	Camel tooth	11,340 ± 50	UCR-3934[b,c]	9
	Stratum E	Camel tooth	11,910 ± 50	UCR-3933[b,c]	9
	Stratum E (base)	Calcic concretion	13,450 ± 70	Beta-105661[b,c]	9
Smith Creek Cave	Pit dug into gray ash	TP8 1st hearth charcoal	11,140 ± 120[a]	Tx-1637	10
	Gray ash	Bovid hair	10,840 ± 250[a]	RIDDL-795	10
	Pit dug into gray ash	TP8 4th hearth charcoal	10,740 ± 130[a]	Birm-702	10
	Pit dug into gray ash	TP8 4th hearth charcoal	10,460 ± 260	GaK-5444b	10
	Average of 2		*10,647 ± 116*		10
	Pit dug into gray ash	TP8 4th hearth charcoal	9800 ± 190	GaK-5444[b]	11
	Gray ash	Wood (cellulose)	10,700 ± 180[a]	Birm-917	10
	Pit dug into gray ash	TP8 2nd hearth charcoal	10,660 ± 220[a]	GaK-5442	10
	Pit dug into gray ash	TP8 3rd hearth charcoal	10,630 ± 190[a]	GaK-5443	10
	Pit dug into gray ash	TP8 3rd hearth charcoal	10,570 ± 160[a]	GaK-5445	10
	Average of 2		*10,590 ± 122*		10
	Pit dug into gray ash	TP8 3rd hearth charcoal	9280 ± 160	GaK-5446[b]	10
	Gray ash and silt	S-twist cordage	10,420 ± 100	TO-1173	10
	Pit dug into gray ash	TP6 12th hearth charcoal	10,330 ± 190	Tx-1638	10
	Pit dug into gray ash	TP6 9th hearth charcoal	9940 ± 160	Tx-1420	10
Bonneville Estates Rockshelter	F05.06, stratum 18b	Hearth charcoal	11,010 ± 40	Beta-207009[c]	10
	F03.15a, stratum 18b	Hearth charcoal	10,800 ± 60	AA-58594[c]	10
	F03.15a, stratum 18b	Hearth charcoal	10,760 ± 70	AA-58592[c]	10
	Average of 2		*10,773 ± 46*		10
	D4-10-C8/C7b, stratum 12	Hearth charcoal	10,560 ± 50[a]	Beta-182931[c]	10
	F04.14, stratum 18b	Hearth charcoal	10,540 ± 40	Beta-195047[c]	10
	F03.14, stratum 18b	Hearth charcoal	10,405 ± 50	AA-58593[c]	10
	E4-12-C5/D3-10-C10, stratum 12	Hearth charcoal	10,380 ± 40	Beta-195013[c]	10
	E4-12-C5/D3-10-C10, stratum 12	Hearth charcoal	10,340 ± 60	Beta-203504[c]	10
	Average of 2		*10,367 ± 33*		10
	E3-13-C4, stratum 12	Hearth charcoal	10,250 ± 50	Beta-206278[c]	10

TABLE 5.1. (cont'd.) Relevant dates from sites presented in Beck and Jones 2010.

Site	Provenience	Material	Age (^{14}C BP)	Lab Number	Reference
	F01.01, stratum 18a	Hearth charcoal	10,130 ± 60	Beta-170444[c]	10
	F01.01, stratum 18a	Hearth charcoal	10,080 ± 50	Beta-164229[c]	10
	F01.01, stratum 18a	Hearth charcoal	10,040 ± 70	Beta-170443[c]	10
	Average of 3		*10,090 ± 34*		10
	D5-10-C8a/C8d, stratum 12	Hearth charcoal	10,050 ± 50	Beta-182935[c]	10
	D4-12-C9b, stratum 12	Hearth charcoal	10,030 ± 50	Beta-182934[c]	10
	D4-10-C8/C7b, stratum 12	Hearth charcoal	9990 ± 50	AA-58598[c]	10
	F05.02, stratum, 18a/17b′	Hearth charcoal	9580 ± 40	Beta-207010[c]	10
	F03.13, stratum, 17b′	Hearth charcoal	9440 ± 50	AA-58589[c]	10
	F03.13, stratum, 17b′	Hearth charcoal	9430 ± 50	AA-58588[c]	10
	Average of 2		*9435 ± 35*		10

Note: 1 = Galm and Gough 2000; 2 = Hicks 2004; 3 = Ames et al. 1980; 4 = Davis and Schweger 2004; 5 = Dumond and Minor 1983; 6 = Green et al. 1998; 7 = Bedwell 1973; 8 = Gruhn and Bryan 1988; 9 = Beck and Jones 2009; 10 = Goebel et al. 2007; 11 = Bryan 1979.
[a] Cited by Beck and Jones (2010).
[b] Rejected by original authors.
[c] Accelerator mass spectrometry date.
[d] New dates acquired by Hicks (2004).
[e] Collected below cultural component at contact between Stratum I and underlying sandy sediment.
[f] Dates converted to 5,568 half-life from 5,730 half-life (5,730 date divided by 1.03, following the style guide for *American Antiquity*).

signs of aging: they occur in less-than-ideal contexts, contain only the most durable materials, and often lack the most suitable resources for dating. As a result, Paleolithic or Paleoindian site excavations that ignore these shortcomings can end up doing more harm than good, often leading to severe critique and reinterpretation based on careful geoarchaeological analysis. Consider, for example, Villa's (1983) analysis of site formation at Terra Amata, a Lower Paleolithic site in southern France once thought to contain the earliest known remnants of artificial human habitations, or the reinterpretation of so-called pre-Clovis "hearths" as natural accumulations of uncharred organics at the Topper (South Carolina) and Tule Springs (Nevada) sites (Shutler 1967; Waters et al. 2008). Put simply, we have to repeatedly ask the question, "How did those artifacts and features get there?" and we must carefully scrutinize contexts and associations to come to the most accurate answer.

Moreover, the interpretation of radiocarbon dates from Paleolithic and Paleoindian settings can be an especially vexing task. This is partly because of contextual issues like those raised above, as well as potential issues with radiocarbon sample size, preservation, and chemistry. Before the development of accelerator mass spectrometry (AMS) in the early 1980s, old sites could only be dated with large samples. Because of this, multiple samples of charcoal were often pooled to obtain single dates or efforts focused on less desirable materials, such as soil organics to produce "ballpark" dates, potentially contaminated bone collagen, and even bone apatite, which if left untreated could cause major headaches. As a result, early radiocarbon dates often had large errors, or multiple dates for early features/occupations often did not overlap even at two sigma. Nowadays, many of these problems can be easily avoided, for example, by dating small samples of decontaminated charcoal through AMS procedures or purifying bone collagen with XAD-2 resin filters. Results are typically much more accurate and precise, with standard errors as low as ±30 years for samples dating in the 13,000- to 11,000-year range.

Even with these higher levels of precision, radiocarbon chronologies continue to confound Great Basin archaeologists. Old conventional dates still exist in the archaeological literature, and they are repeatedly incorporated into our interpretations, despite obvious degrees of imprecision and evidence of inaccuracy. To safeguard against these pitfalls, we argue that it is imperative that archaeologists working in the Intermountain West carefully scrutinize radiocarbon dates from archaeological contexts, following a set of criteria for evaluating radiocarbon dates proposed by Paleolithic archaeologists in Europe and northern Asia (e.g., Graf 2009; Pettitt et al. 2003) and recently applied to American Paleoindian situations (e.g., Erlandson 2009; Erlandson et al. 2008; Waters and Stafford 2007). We summarize these criteria below, following Pettitt et al. (2003:1687–1690) and Graf (2009:700) by defining what a well-dated archaeological event should look like.

A well-dated archaeological occupation should contain the following characteristics to counter potential errors:

1. To avoid contamination by older or younger carbon, the dated sample should be derived from either (a) specific amino acids known to occur only in bone or (b) wood charcoal identified to genus and for which the effects of "old wood" can be eliminated.
2. To ensure that a specific sample material is not affecting results, AMS dates should be obtained using at least two discrete materials, preferably charcoal and bone/antler/ivory; dated samples should be clearly associated and statistically overlap at two sigma.

3. To ensure accuracy, multiple dates should be obtained, and all of them should fit a clear chronological sequence.
4. If different sample materials do not result in overlapping radiocarbon measurements, then to test for contamination different chemical fractions of the same sample material (e.g., wood charcoal and humate fractions of charcoal samples) should be dated, or other tests of contamination should be performed.
5. Dates are published with full sample information, including pretreatment procedures as well as measurement and stable isotope data.
6. There is full certainty that the dated sample is associated with human activity (i.e., the dated sample is itself of anthropogenic origin, or it is directly related either functionally or contextually, for example, identified charcoal from a hearth feature).
7. There is full certainty that the dated sample is related to the *specific* archaeological event of concern, either through dating of the culturally diagnostic sample itself (e.g., a stemmed point) or through dating of materials unequivocally associated with the diagnostic artifact (e.g., a piece of cordage associated with a stemmed point).
8. To date the archaeological event with a measure of statistical confidence, there should be more than five AMS dates that overlap at two sigma.
9. To ensure against postdepositional movement of dated samples, AMS dates should be derived either from bone >10 cm in size or from features >10 cm in size.

Pettitt et al. (2003) and Graf (2009) admit that few archaeological sites meet the criteria for acceptable dating outlined above, and in the Intermountain West if we adhered rigidly to them, we would likely have a regional chronology of stemmed points based on just one or two sites. Nonetheless, these are good rules to develop site chronologies by, and they are certainly worthwhile criteria for evaluating existing records. In the section of the chapter that follows, we attempt to do just this, evaluating each of the presumed early stemmed point occupations that Beck and Jones (2010) present as evidence that these western point forms rival the age of Clovis east of the Rocky Mountains.

The Sample of Early Sites with Stemmed Points

Beck and Jones (2010) present 11 sites from the Intermountain West that they argue potentially overlap in age with Clovis. Six of these—Sentinel Gap, Marmes Rockshelter, Hatwai, Coopers Ferry, Wildcat Canyon, and Buhl—are from the Columbia Plateau, while five—Connley Cave No. 4B, Handprint Cave, Sunshine, Smith Creek Cave, and Bonneville Estates Rockshelter—are from the Great Basin (Figure 5.1). Below we review the geochronology and archaeology of each of these sites. In the process, we define what we think are the most likely ages of the stemmed point components at these sites.

Sentinel Gap

The Sentinel Gap site (45KT1362) was discovered in 1997 just west of the Columbia River in central Washington and was excavated in 1998–2000 by J. Galm and S. Gough. All artifacts came from a single, 8-cm-thick cultural component capped by 1.5 m of loess and containing numerous points and bifaces resembling Haskett forms (Figure 5.2). In addition to collecting over 200,000 artifacts, Galm and Gough (2000, 2008; Gough and Galm 2002) found two burn features that may represent structures, as well as several artifact concentrations directly associated with bone artifacts and charcoal.

Beck and Jones cite five dates for Sentinel Gap (Tables 5.1 and 5.2), with the oldest being 10,680 ± 190 ^{14}C BP (Beta-133650), potentially overlapping the latest ages for Clovis. However, this oldest date is more than 400 years older than the other four dates, which themselves overlap at two sigma. Further, the oldest date is the only date derived from conventional rather than AMS techniques, and as a result it has a much higher standard deviation than the AMS dates. The original excavators of Sentinel Gap dismissed this early date and concluded that the site's stemmed point occupation occurred at about 10,200 ^{14}C BP, not 10,700 ^{14}C BP as implied by Beck and Jones (2010). To conclude, the age of the Sentinel Gap component is about 600 years later than the latest known Clovis occupations.

Marmes Rockshelter

The Marmes Rockshelter site (45FR50) is located in the southern Columbia River basin near the confluence of the Snake and Palouse rivers in southeastern Washington. The original 1962–1964 field seasons were headed by R. Daugherty, though R. Fryxell directed the 1968 excavations, after which the site was inundated following completion of the Lower Monumental Dam. The site was excavated stratigraphically, with the oldest components of the rockshelter and adjacent floodplain containing stemmed points (Hicks 2004; Rice 1972).

Beck and Jones (2010) cite two dates on *Margaritifera falcata* shell found in stratum I of the rockshelter area: 10,810 ± 300 (WSU-363) and 10,750 ± 300 ^{14}C BP (WSU-211). Stratum I is largely colluvial and is associated with four Windust points, two Cascade points, and a possible hearth feature, suggesting an early date on stemmed points potentially overlapping the latest dates for Clovis. However, Beck and Jones neglect to include other ages acquired from the same stratum that, even when discounting an erroneous 7550 ± 300 ^{14}C BP (WSU-120) date, span a range of over 1,000 years (Table 5.1). Hicks (2004) mentions several cases of potential mixing to explain the broad range of dates, but original excavation notes are fragmentary, so details of provenience and associations cannot be reconstructed.

In addition, the dates and standard deviations used by Beck and Jones (2010) reflect those presented in Rice 1972 and do not reflect the updated dates and standard deviations presented in the final site report completed by Hicks (2004). Hicks increased the standard deviations of all shell dates to ±300 (Table 5.1),

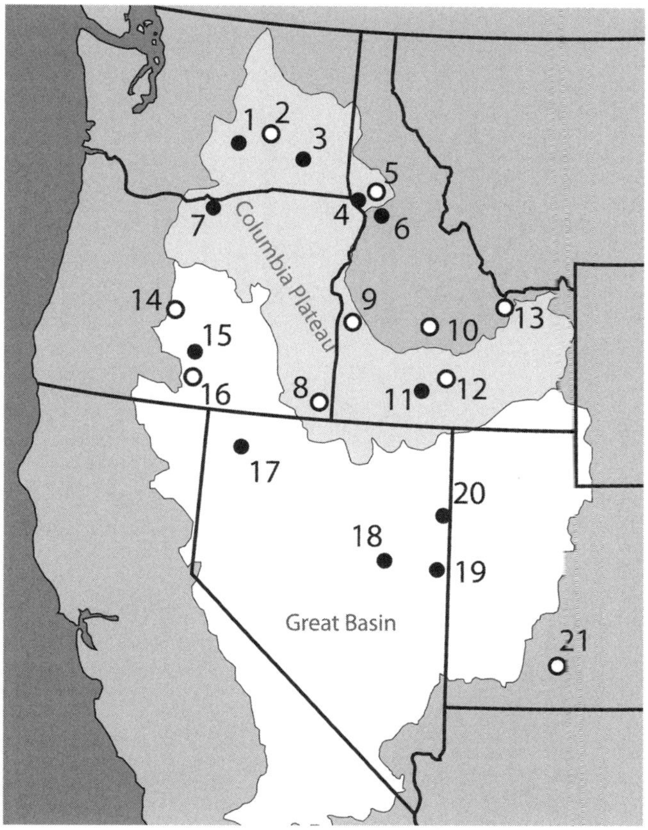

FIGURE 5.1. Stemmed point sites cited in the text (black dots represent sites described by Beck and Jones [2010] as potentially Clovis in age; white dots represent other important early stemmed point sites): (1) Sentinel Gap; (2) Lind Coulee; (3) Marmes Rockshelter; (4) Hatwai; (5) Wewukiyepuh; (6) Coopers Ferry; (7) Wildcat Canyon; (8) Dirty Shame Rockshelter; (9) Hetrick; (10) Redfish Overhang; (11) Buhl burial; (12) Wilson Butte Cave; (13) Bison Rockshelter; (14) Paulina Lake; (15) Connley Caves; (16) Paisley Caves; (17) Handprint Cave; (18) Sunshine Locality; (19) Smith Creek Cave; (20) Bonneville Estates Rockshelter; (21) North Creek Shelter.

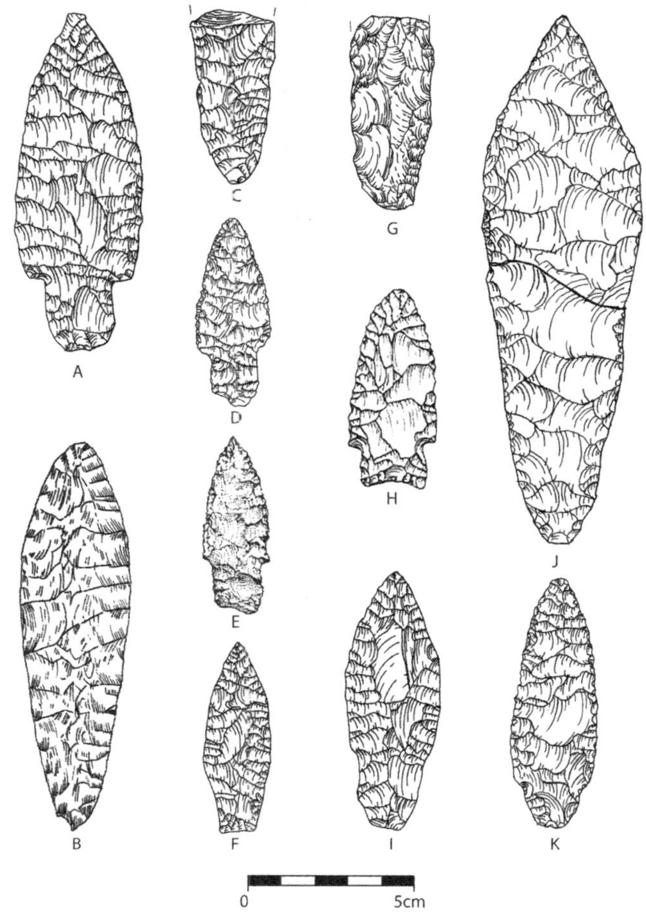

FIGURE 5.2. Stemmed points from the Intermountain West: (A) Buhl (redrawn from Goebel et al. 2011); (B) Connley Cave (Bedwell 1973); (C) Smith Creek Cave (redrawn from Goebel et al. 2011); (D) Marmes (redrawn from http://archaeology.wsu.edu); (E) Coopers Ferry (Davis 2001); (F) Handprint Cave (redrawn from Goebel et al. 2011); (G) Bonneville Estates Rockshelter (drawn from original); (H) Hatwai (Sappington 1994); (I) Sunshine (redrawn from Goebel et al. 2011); (J) Sentinel Gap (redrawn from Galm and Gough 2008); (K) Wildcat Canyon (redrawn from Dumond and Minor 1983).

TABLE 5.2. Accepted early dates from Table 5.1, associated with stemmed points in the Intermountain West.

Site	Age (^{14}C BP)	Cal BP (2σ)	Lab Number	Source
Sentinel Gap	10,180 ± 40	12,043–11,712	Beta-124167	1
	10,160 ± 60	11,430–11,411 (p = .01) 11,530–11,494 (p = .02) 11,544–11,533 (p < .01) 12,072–11,601 (p = .97)	Beta-133663	1
	10,130 ± 60	11,456–11,405 (p = .04) 11,564–11,466 (p = .08) 12,026–11,593 (p = .88)	Beta-133665	1
	10,010 ± 60	11,754–11,267	Beta-133664	1
Marmes Floodplain	10,130 ± 300	10,852–10,794 (p = .01) 10,959–10,862 (p = .02) 11,021–11,007 (p < .1) 12,609–11,067 (p = .97)	W-2218	2
	9840 ± 300	10,453–10,440 (p < .01) 12,229–10,493 (p = .97) 12,385–12,247 (p = .02)	W-2212	2

TABLE 5.2. (cont'd.) Accepted early dates from Table 5.1, associated with stemmed points in the Intermountain West.

SITE	AGE (^{14}C BP)	CAL BP (2σ)	LAB NUMBER	SOURCE
Coopers Ferry	8710 ± 120	9971–9522 (*p* = .85) 10,157–9981 (*p* = .15)	TO-7346	4
	8410 ± 70	9536–9266	Beta-114951	4
Wildcat Canyon	9860 ± 510	10,071–9920 (*p* = .01) 12,693–10,116 (*p* = .99)	GaK-1325	5
Buhl	10,675 ± 95	12,810–12,391	Beta-43055/ETH-7729	6
Connley Cave 4B	10,600 ± 190*	11,892–11,827 (*p* = .01) 11,912–11,907 (*p* < .01) 12,920–11,954 (*p* = .99)	GaK-2143	7
	9670 ± 180	11,613–10,503	GaK-2142	7
Sunshine	9920 ± 60	11,507–11,217 (*p* = .88) 11,610–11,520 (*p* = .12)	Beta-86198	9
	9840 ± 50	11,352–11,181 (*p* > .99) 11,380–11,380 (*p* < .01)	Beta-86201	9
	9800 ± 60	11,337–11,101	Beta-69782	9
Smith Creek Cave	10,660 ± 220*	11,878–11,829 (*p* = .01) 13,095–11,958 (*p* = .99)	GaK-5442	10
	10,647 ± 116	12,195–12,142 (*p* = .02) 12,359–12,207 (*p* = .08) 12,784–12,363 (*p* = .90)	Average of hearth 4	10
	10,590 ± 122	12,710–12,102	Average of hearth 3	10
	10,420 ± 100	12,580–11,994	TO-1173	10
	10,330 ± 190	11,583–11,403 (*p* = .06) 12,594–11,590 (*p* = .94)	Tx-1638	10
	9940 ± 160	10,948–10,871 (*p* = .02) 12,062–11,073 (*p* = .98)	Tx-1420	10
Bonneville Estates Rockshelter	10,540 ± 40	12,600–12,409	Beta-195047	10
	10,405 ± 50	12,430–12,081 (*p* = .94) 12,523–12,469 (*p* = .06)	AA-58593	10
	10,367 ± 33	12,390–12,082	Average of feature E4-12-C5/ D3-10-C10, stratum 12	10
	10,250 ± 50	12,151–11,760 (*p* = .99) 12,212–12,191 (*p* = .01) 12,367–12,358 (*p* < .01)	Beta-206278	10
	10,090 ± 34	11,570–11,404 (*p* = .20) 11,826–11,591 (*p* = .75) 11,906–11,884 (*p* = .01)	Average of F01.01, stratum 18a	10
	10,050 ± 50	11,817–11,320	Beta-182935	10
	10,030 ± 50	11,292–11,289 (*p* < .01) 11,763–11,303 (*p* > .99)	Beta-182934	10
	9990 ± 50	11,646–11,261 (*p* = .96) 11,705–11,666 (*p* = .04)	AA-58598	10
	9580 ± 40	11,107–10,741 (*p* >.99) 11,122–11,117 (*p* < .01)	Beta-207010	10
	9435 ± 35	10,749–10,577	Average of F03.13, stratum 17b'	10

Note: 1 = Galm and Gough 2000; 2 = Hicks 2004; 4 = Davis and Schweger 2004; 5 = Dumond and Minor 1983; 6 = Green et al. 1998; 7 = Bedwell 1973; 9 = Beck and Jones 2009; 10 = Goebel et al. 2007.

presumably to account for the potential reservoir effect inherent when dating shell. As a result, all but one date for stratum I of the rockshelter are from shell with high standard deviations and have the potential to be skewed due to reservoir effect. It is well established that ^{14}C dates on shell from the Columbia River basin often differ by thousands of years when compared with comparable charcoal samples (e.g., Chance 1989; Chatters 1986). Sheppard et al. (1987) accepted the shell chronology, but even in their date list for the middle and late Holocene layers of the site, shell dates consistently were significantly older than charcoal dates when paired. The only date on bone from the rockshelter is 11,230 ± 50 ^{14}C BP (Beta-156698), and this date comes from a bone found on top of a sand component underlying stratum I and can only serve as a lower-limiting date for the stemmed point–bearing cultural occupation. It should also be noted that a mussel shell acquired from the same context as this bone dated to only 9610 ± 40 ^{14}C BP, which is over 1,600 years younger. Given that both are conventional dates on nonpurified materials, we place little faith in either.

The adjacent floodplain has two cultural components in low-energy alluvial deposits associated with stratum I in the rockshelter, called the Marmes component and the underlying Harrison component. Of these two horizons, only the Harrison component has a single Windust point associated with it. This stratum has dates on charcoal ranging from 10,130 ± 300 (W-2218) to 9840 ± 300 ^{14}C BP (W-2212), which postdate the supposedly older dates found in the rockshelter by approximately 800 years (Table 5.1). As in the rockshelter, a lower-limiting age of 10,570 ± 70 ^{14}C BP on charcoal was acquired by Hicks (2004), again suggesting that the stemmed points at Marmes postdate this time.

In summary, the older dates obtained from the stemmed point components at Marmes Rockshelter are unreliable due to the almost exclusive use of *Margaritifera falcata* shell for radiocarbon dating of the earliest component, causing large standard deviations and potentially aberrant ages due to reservoir effects and possible insufficient sample pretreatment procedures (Hicks 2004). In addition, conflicting and reversed dates suggest likely mixing of materials from multiple layers, further confusing the Marmes chronology. The earliest reliable ages are the charcoal dates associated with the Harrison horizon in the floodplain, which provide an age of approximately 10,000 ^{14}C BP; this may reflect the actual age of the earliest stemmed points from inside the rockshelter.

Hatwai

The Hatwai site (10NP143), located on the northern bank of the Clearwater River in the Idaho panhandle, was excavated in 1977–1978 by K. Ames (Ames et al. 1980). The site consists primarily of a large Late Archaic village underlain by deeper gravel bar strata containing evidence for a Paleoindian component characterized by numerous Windust points and a few Cascade points. This component is referred to as the "Hatwai I" cultural component (Ames et al. 1980; Sanders 1982) and was almost exclusively recovered from 3- to 4-m-deep sediments from "Area B" excavated in 1978. Sanders (1982) subsequently divided Hatwai I Area B into seven stratigraphic units ranging from stratum 1 at the top (upper gravels) to stratum 7 at the bottom (lower gravels), all of which contain Windust points.

Beck and Jones (2010) cite two "pooled mean" dates from the Windust component of this site: 10,796 ± 138 ("5500-year half life") and 11,120 ± 138 ^{14}C BP ("5730-year half life").[1] However, radiocarbon dates provided by Ames et al. (1980) for the lower Hatwai I component at Area B are shown in Table 5.1 and cover a range of 10,816 to 8408 ^{14}C BP. The date in question is sample TX-3159, reported by Ames et al. (1980) in two ways. On the one hand, they calculated the date using a 5,730-year half-life resulting in an age of 11,140 ± 120 ^{14}C BP, and on the other hand, they calculated the date using a "5,570-year" half-life resulting in an age of 10,820 ± 140 ^{14}C BP. Stuiver and Polach reported long ago, however, that only the 5,568-year half-life should be used in chronological studies "where the measurement of age is the most important aspect," while the 5,730-year half-life should be used for "geochemical samples, dendrochronological samples, reservoir equilibria, and diffusion models" (1977:362–363). Convention among archaeological and geological studies has been to use the 5,568-year half-life to date archaeological and geological events; thus, for consistency the date obtained from the 5,730-year half-life should not be used here but, instead, converted using 5,568. This means that at face value, the earliest the stemmed points from Hatwai could be is 10,816 ± 136 ^{14}C BP. Ames et al. (1980) also list a number of other dates from the lower gravel bar strata from other parts of the site, but these dates are not described, and their exact provenience is unclear (Table 5.1).

While it would appear that the 10,816 ± 136 date reflects the earliest Windust component at the site (Unit 7), Ames et al. mentioned that Sanders "was unable to prove, to his satisfaction, that all the material was indeed *in situ*" (1980:96–101), due to possible alluvial redeposition. After analyzing edge damage and refitting 127 artifacts, Sanders (1982) concluded that minimal damage and a large number of refits indicated alluvial transportation, but over short distances. However, Sanders went on to write that excavators had difficulty identifying stratigraphic boundaries and that

> a detailed analysis of the artifacts from each stratigraphic unit is discouraged on the basis of the lack of precision in the boundaries of those units. It is therefore argued that the analysis consider the gravel bar as a single unit with the exception of the most general questions [1982:54].

This lack of stratigraphic control, combined with acquiring dates from composite, scattered charcoal samples rather than directly from cultural contexts, makes the association between the dates and the Windust points unreliable. To further blur the exact age of this component, many of the dates provided have very high standard deviations.

In conclusion, we find it difficult to estimate the actual age of the stemmed point component at Hatwai due to questionable associations and the possibility of artifacts being in a secondary fluvial context. The oldest date of 10,816 ± 136 ^{14}C BP is from a composite charcoal sample that could have washed in from another context and is not corroborated by multiple dates. If one treats all units within the Hatwai I gravel bar as a single unit, as suggested by Sanders (1982), the average age is about 9300 ^{14}C BP; however, none of the dates are reliable.

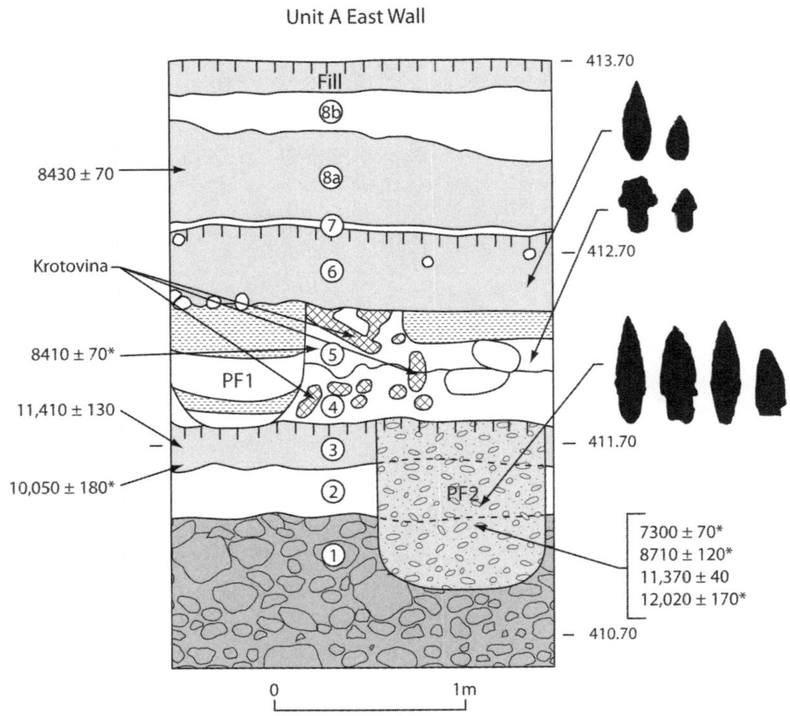

FIGURE 5.3. Coopers Ferry stratigraphic profile (redrawn from Davis and Schweger 2004). Ages considered suspect by Davis and Schweger (2004) are designated with an asterisk.

Coopers Ferry

Coopers Ferry (10IH73) is a multicomponent site located in the Lower Salmon River canyon of west-central Idaho. Investigations there in the late 1990s yielded an assemblage of stemmed points from a buried, stratified context (Davis and Schweger 2004; Davis and Sisson 1998). The site's main cultural component occurs about 2 m below the modern surface. Site stratigraphy is complex, primarily because of pervasive rodent burrowing and Archaic pit digging (Davis and Schweger 2004). Stemmed points were recovered from strata 4–5 and in a pit feature associated with the contact of strata 3 and 4 (Figure 5.3).

Beck and Jones (2010) cite two dates from Coopers Ferry that are contemporaneous with, possibly older than, Clovis. These dates' association with the stemmed point assemblage, however, is less than clear, and understanding of the site's chronology requires careful review. The original excavators obtained eight ^{14}C dates from the site but accepted only three of them. Accepted were a date of 11,410 ± 130 ^{14}C BP (TO-7349) on dispersed charcoal from the top of stratum 3, a date of 11,370 ± 40 ^{14}C BP (Beta-114949) on dispersed charcoal from within the pit associated with the strata 3–4 contact, and a date of 8430 ± 70 ^{14}C BP (Beta-114952) on charcoal from deposits overlying the site's cultural layers. Rejected were five dates: 12,020 ± 170 ^{14}C BP (Beta-109971) on bone from the pit, 10,050 ± 180 ^{14}C BP (TO-7357) on bone from stratum 3 (underlying the site's cultural components), 8710 ± 120 ^{14}C BP (TO-7346) on dispersed charcoal from the pit, 8410 ± 70 ^{14}C BP (Beta-114951) on dispersed charcoal from stratum 5, and 7300 ± 70 ^{14}C BP (Beta-114948) on dispersed charcoal from within the pit. The earlier dates of 12,200 and 10,050 ^{14}C BP were rejected because they were on bone and potentially not properly pretreated (Davis and Schweger 2004), while the dates of 8710, 8410, and 7300 ^{14}C BP were rejected because they seemed out of sequence with the remaining accepted dates. Davis and Schweger (2004:699) cite bioturbation as the prime cause of the problematic radiocarbon sequence, and their reasoning for accepting the early dates and rejecting the late dates involved the presumed age of stemmed points in the Columbia Plateau region and the observation that the Rock Creek soil, at Coopers Ferry thought to be represented by layer 3, had been independently dated to before 11,000 ^{14}C BP at other localities in the region.

However, there are some issues with the long chronology presented by Davis and Schweger (2004), suggesting to us that the stemmed point occupation at the site may actually postdate 10,000 ^{14}C BP. First, the 11,410 ± 130 date came from the top of stratum 3, while stemmed points were reportedly not from stratum 3 but instead from higher in the stratigraphic profile, in stratum 4. Second, the date of 11,370 ± 40 came from the pit feature that prehistorically had been dug into strata 3, 2, and 1 and thus could be from redeposited charcoal. Third, by our reasoning, the bioturbation that reportedly displaced the ~8000 and ~7000 ^{14}C BP dates could instead have displaced the ~11,000 ^{14}C BP dates, meaning that the pit dug into stratum 3 could actually have been dug around 9000–8000 ^{14}C BP. By accepting the

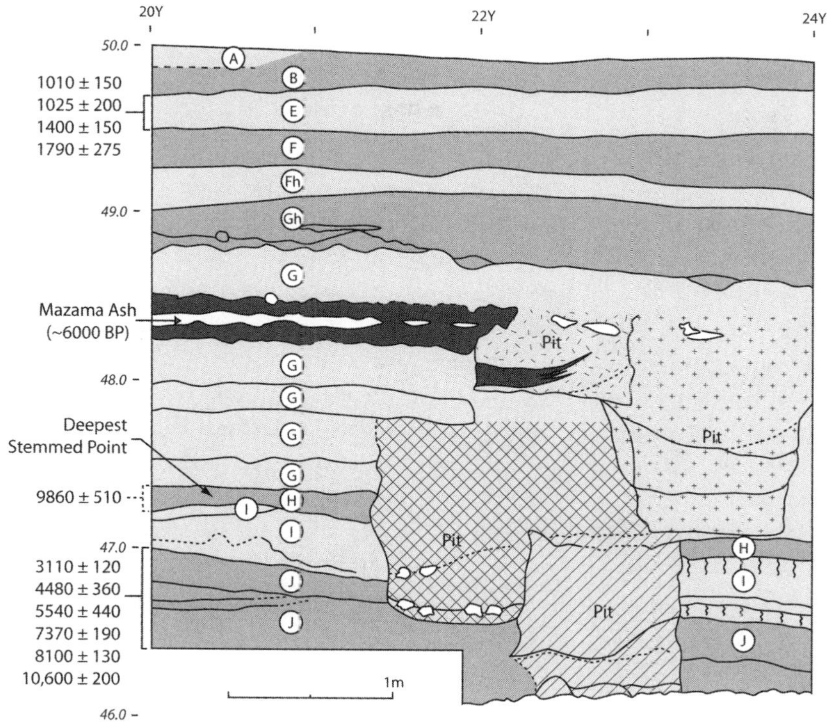

FIGURE 5.4. Wildcat Canyon stratigraphic profile (redrawn from Dumond and Minor 1983).

8710 ^{14}C BP date from the pit instead of the 11,370 ^{14}C BP date, the 8410 and 8430 dates from higher in the profile seem less out of place. Fourth, the Rock Creek soil, represented at Coopers Ferry by stratum 3, has been regionally dated to only 13,000–10,740 ^{14}C BP, and no artifacts were found at the site within it (i.e., outside of the pit feature [Davis and Schweger 2004]); to us this suggests that the cultural occupation at Coopers Ferry must postdate 10,740 ^{14}C BP because all of the recovered artifacts are from above the Rock Creek soil or in the pit that is dug into it from above. Finally, fifth, we must acknowledge that stemmed points across the Intermountain West have been found in numerous contexts dating to 10,000–8000 ^{14}C BP (e.g., Paulina Lake, Dirty Shame Rockshelter, as discussed below [Beck and Jones 1997; Connolly and Jenkins 1999]).

In sum, the problem with Coopers Ferry is the pervasive bioturbation that seems to have riddled the site's sediments. In developing the long chronology for the site—that its earliest stemmed points date to about 11,300 ^{14}C BP—Davis and Schweger (2004) seem to have ignored their own dating of the Rock Creek soil to as late as 10,740 ^{14}C BP. The stemmed points from Coopers Ferry occur above this stratum or in a pit feature that has been dug into it, implying to us that they have to be younger than this lower-limiting age. Until a more refined chronology is developed for the site, one built on dated material from clear hearth features and unequivocally associated with stemmed points, we conclude conservatively that the stemmed point occupation more likely dates to 9000–8000 ^{14}C BP than to the Clovis era. Davis is currently reexcavating Coopers Ferry, and we look forward to his results, which will undoubtedly permit testing of our hypothesis.

Wildcat Canyon

The Wildcat Canyon site (35GM9) lies along the middle Columbia River in northern Oregon and was excavated extensively between 1959 and 1968 by D. L. Cole and L. S. Cressman. Six areas were excavated; we focus attention here on area 5, where 11 strata composed of fine-grained overbank floodplain deposits (A–K) were identified and excavated stratigraphically. During excavations, however, identification of strata was made difficult by the presence of numerous prehistoric pit features (Figure 5.4; Dumond and Minor 1983).

Beck and Jones (2010) cite a date of 10,600 ± 200 ^{14}C BP (GaK-1322) that they infer was from a stratum that yielded a single contracting stemmed projectile point, likely a Parman or Windust form. However, this point was found within stratum H, underlying stratum G and a layer of Mazama tephra, while the 10,600 ^{14}C BP date was from two layers deeper, in stratum J (Figure 5.4). Dumond and Minor (1983) point out that this date was from noncultural wood suspected to be a root. Furthermore, the other three accepted dates from strata J and H (Table 5.1) are all from questionable, noncultural contexts and may not even be from the specific stratum indicated, as the original records of sample provenience were spotty or missing when the site report was completed 15 years later. According to Dumond and Minor, rather than providing dates for specific cultural horizons, these four accepted ^{14}C measurements "together provide a battery of dates that relate to the deposition of the strata (H, I, and J) underlying" the volcanic ash and stratum G (1983:128).

In summary, the single date of 10,600 ± 200 ^{14}C BP from Wildcat Canyon is from noncultural root material from a stratum not associated with stemmed points—or any other cultural material for that matter. Additionally, other dates from the same stratum have reversals and range from 10,600 to 7370 ^{14}C BP. The actual age of the Windust point from Wildcat Canyon remains unclear. The single date apparently acquired from the same stratum (H) suggests an age of about 10,000 ^{14}C BP, and this is supported by the point's stratigraphic position below the Mazama ash, which provides an upper-limiting age of about 6750 ^{14}C BP.

Buhl Burial

The Buhl burial (10TF1019) was located along the Snake River, near Twin Falls, southern Idaho. It was accidentally discovered in 1989 in an active gravel quarry and consisted of a nearly complete, very well-preserved skull and postcranium (Green et al. 1998).

Direct AMS dating of a sample of human bone produced a date of 10,675 ± 95 ^{14}C BP (Beta-43055), and we have no reason to question this date except that it would have been helpful to corroborate it with a second date before the skeleton's reburial. Four artifacts and a badger (*Taxidea taxus*) baculum were associated with the burial. The artifacts included a fragment of an eyed bone needle, two fragments of an incised bone pin or awl, and an obsidian stemmed point. The point showed no signs of having been used, suggesting that it may have served as a grave offering. It had well-defined shoulders and a square-shaped, edge-ground stem—morphologically a Windust point (Figure 5.2A).

At ~10,700 ^{14}C BP, the stemmed point from Buhl likely represents one of the earliest stemmed points in the Intermountain West. The point was from a human burial that was directly AMS dated, and it appears to have been intentionally placed in the grave with the deceased.

Connley Cave 4B

The Connley Caves (35LK50) are located in Fort Rock Valley, central Oregon, and were excavated by S. Bedwell in 1967 (see Bedwell 1973) and more recently by the University of Oregon in 1999–2001 (Beck et al. 2004). Here we call attention to Connley Cave 4B, a wave-cut rockshelter containing materials thought to span the latest Pleistocene and early Holocene. Bedwell excavated Cave 4B following arbitrary levels of an unreported thickness, and his description of the recovered assemblage is vague (see Goebel et al. 2011 for a more thorough review). This makes any specific interpretations of Cave 4B's record tenuous.

Beck and Jones (2010) cite two radiocarbon dates from Bedwell's excavation of stratum 4 in Cave 4B that overlap the Clovis era, 11,200 ± 200 (GaK-2141) and 10,600 ± 190 ^{14}C BP (GaK-2143 [Bedwell 1973:35]). At face value, these two dates suggest that stratum 4 represents a Clovis-aged cultural occupation; however, these two dates are stratigraphically reversed—the older 11,200 ^{14}C BP date was from level 32, while the younger 10,600 ^{14}C BP date was from level 38, six levels down. Further, Bedwell (1973:35) reported a third date that came from the intervening level 34—9670 ± 180 ^{14}C BP (GaK-2142). All three of the stratum 4 dates cannot be correct, and we prefer the two younger dates, which are in stratigraphic concordance with one another. This would make the assemblage no older than about 10,600 ± 190 ^{14}C BP. Further, there is reason to hypothesize that the earliest occupation at Connley Cave 4B may date to even later than this, given dates from the adjoining Cave 4A as well as more recent work in Connley Caves 5 and 6 by University of Oregon archaeologists, which together suggest that the earliest human occupations of the caves date to 10,500–10,000 ^{14}C BP (Beck et al. 2004). Bedwell himself noted that evidence for the utilization of the caves during the period represented by stratum 4 "gradually increased, reaching a high point toward the middle of the period" (1973:143), ~9500–9000 ^{14}C BP.

The lithic assemblage from Connley Cave 4B was not reported adequately enough for us to ascertain how the early radiocarbon dates from the cave were associated with stemmed points. Bedwell (1973) did not present a complete list of artifacts from stratum 4 or other strata, and in his report he did not clearly distinguish between stratum 4 assemblages from Cave 4A and Cave 4B. In fact, the only described artifacts that he clearly states came from stratum 4 in Cave 4B are two possible gravers (from levels 35 and 37 [1973:117]) and a core (level 37 [1973:120]). Nonetheless, Bedwell (1973:141–146) did note that "stemless" Haskett-like points and other lanceolate-shaped points (a few of them with concave bases; Figure 5.2B) were most common in stratum 4 of "Cave 4," and by this we figure that he meant both Cave 4A and Cave 4B.

Therefore, we conclude that at Connley Cave 4B, even though Haskett stemmed points occur in the early assemblage, they likely postdate the time of Clovis by at least several centuries. Renewed studies of the site will be required to demonstrate a Clovis-aged stemmed point occupation there.

Handprint Cave

Handprint Cave (26HU1836) is located in the Black Rock Desert of northwest Nevada. Gruhn and Bryan (1988) excavated three areas of the cave in 1987, two in its well-lit entrance chamber and a third in its dark main chamber, adjacent to some red handprints painted on a stalagmitic column.

Beck and Jones (2010) cite a date of 10,740 ± 70 ^{14}C BP (Beta-21885) for Handprint Cave. This date is from a sample of charcoal recovered from the test pit in the main chamber of the cave, specifically from the test pit's "10–20 cm level" (Gruhn and Bryan 1988:12). According to the test pit's stratigraphic profile, this would suggest that the charcoal came from the top of a soft buff silt unit, very close to the modern surface of the cave (Gruhn and Bryan 1988:6). Unfortunately, details on the date were not provided in the report—whether it was a conventional or AMS date, whether it was from a single lump of charcoal, grab-bag sample, or cultural feature. Gruhn and Bryan, however, report that the soft buff silt unit did contain much "charred wood" (1988:7).

Gruhn and Bryan (1988:7; see also Bryan 1988:55) reported that a stemmed bifacial point and retouched blade came from the same test pit as the radiocarbon date and that the artifacts were associated with several bovid hairs and a single strand of human hair. The point came from the same stratigraphic unit as the dated charcoal sample, except higher in the profile, from a depth of 0–10 cm (Gruhn and Bryan 1988:9). The point was "exceptionally fine" and made on white agate (Gruhn and Bryan 1988:7), "lanceolate and symmetrical, with excurvate edges, slight bilateral shoulders, and a slightly concave base," shaped by "very fine lateral pressure flaking" but no basal grinding (Gruhn and Bryan 1988:9; Figure 5.2F). It is also quite small, 54 mm long, 20 mm wide at its widest point, and 6 mm thick (Gruhn and Bryan 1988:10); its base is ~11 mm wide. Bryan described the point as a "square-based shouldered point" (1988:55) and compared it with Windust and Firstview/Scottsbluff/Alberta forms from the northern Great Basin and Great Plains, respectively. However, some might take issue with this characterization because the point's proximal lateral margins are not square but, instead, contracting, its shoulders are very weak, and its base is concave (Figure 5.2F). Windust points, further, typically have edge-ground stems, while this point shows no signs of grinding. The morphology, size, and "very fine pressure flaking" noted may be an indication that this is not a stemmed point at all but, instead, a middle Holocene Humboldt point, examples of which were recovered from Gruhn and Bryan's (1988:8–9) excavations in the entrance cavern of the cave.

The preliminary nature of the test excavations inside Handprint Cave makes the dating of the artifacts tenuous (Adams et al. 2008:618); the most we can say for certain is that the date of 10,740 ± 70 ^{14}C BP should be treated as a lower-limiting age for the point. It could certainly date to the terminal Pleistocene–early Holocene, but the size, shape, and flaking quality of the point may indicate that it instead dates to the middle Holocene. This large cave deserves more attention to ascertain whether an early stemmed point occupation is indeed represented in its deposits.

Sunshine Locality

Sunshine (26WP various) is located in southern Long Valley, east-central Nevada. Excavations were carried out there in 1989 and between 1992 and 1997, ultimately under the direction of Beck and Jones (2009). Their final report on the excavations presents details on site stratigraphy, dating, and assemblages (Cannon et al. 2009; Holmes and Huckleberry 2009; Jones and Beck 2009), and Goebel et al. (2011) present a recent critique. Here we present details only on the site's radiocarbon chronology and excavated sample of stemmed points.

Beck and Jones (2010:104) report a single date from Sunshine, 10,700 ± 180 ^{14}C BP, citing Huckleberry et al. 2001. However, this date is not reported in either that article or Beck and Jones's (2009) monograph on Sunshine. There is a similar date, though, 10,690 ± 430 ^{14}C BP (Beta-37515), which is a conventional date on pooled charcoal from various depths within stratum E near the base of the site's stratigraphic profile. Beck and Jones (2009:18–19) report that no diagnostic artifacts were directly associated with this date, and instead it was associated with "several lithic flakes" (2009:19). Elsewhere in the site (ST3), Beck and Jones report a "stemmed preform" (2009:74) and biface from stratum E, near a camel bone directly dated to 11,390 ± 60 ^{14}C BP (Beta-105662), but they conclude that these bones were likely redeposited. Stratum E consists of coarse alluvial gravels, so that any associations between its dated samples and artifacts cannot be trusted (Beck and Jones 2009). Further up the profile of this excavation, more secure dates are from the fine-grained alluvium of stratum D, 9920 ± 60 and 9840 ± 50 ^{14}C BP (Beta-86198 and Beta-86201). While no stemmed points were found associated with these dates, they provide an upper-limiting age for the stemmed biface found within stratum E. Besides this, in all the excavations at Sunshine, only one finished stemmed point was found in situ in close association with a ^{14}C date, and it came from stratum C and was associated with an AMS date on charcoal of 9800 ± 60 ^{14}C BP (Beta-69782).

Certainly stratum E at Sunshine, which has yielded at least a stemmed biface, seems to date to between about 10,640 ± 70 ^{14}C BP (Beta-105658) and 9900 ^{14}C BP; however, not all of the bifacial points from this stratum are stemmed—at least one concave-based point was recovered from stratum E. Possibly some of the materials recovered from this stratum are associated with this point form and not the stemmed forms, suggesting that we should be careful not to assume that all of the cultural materials from the Sunshine excavations were produced by stemmed point makers. Conservatively, the earliest stemmed point at the site dates to only 9900–9700 ^{14}C BP; however, possibly they are as early as 10,700 ^{14}C BP.

Smith Creek Cave

Smith Creek Cave (26WP46) is a large rockshelter located in the uplands of the Snake Range, east-central Nevada. Bryan excavated the mouth area of the rockshelter between 1968 and 1974 (see Bryan 1979, 1988), finding a well-preserved cultural component containing several stemmed point fragments associated with hearth features, faunal remains, and perishable artifacts including cordage.

Beck and Jones (2010) cite seven radiocarbon dates from the Smith Creek Cave cultural layer that range from 11,140 ± 120 (Tx-1637) to 10,570 ± 160 ^{14}C BP (GaK-5445), presumably singling out these from the entire date series because they overlap the Clovis interval at two sigma. The dating of Smith Creek Cave, however, has been controversial (Goebel et al. 2007; Goebel et al. 2011; Thompson 1985), and there are four reasons why we think that its stemmed point occupation postdates the time of Clovis by a few centuries. First, all of the dates on charcoal were obtained using conventional ^{14}C methods, so that large bulk samples were needed to obtain dates. The problem with this is that Bryan could not date individual charred lumps of short-lived shrub species such as sagebrush or rabbitbrush; instead, his samples may have contained large amounts of pine, potentially creating an "old wood" problem (see Graf 2007 for a discussion of this in relation to the early layers at Bonneville Estates Rockshelter). Second, when we consider the Smith Creek Cave dates in terms of the six hearths from which they came, it becomes clear that all but one likely postdate Clovis—hearth 2 dates to 10,660 ± 220 (GaK-5442), hearth 3 dates to 10,590 ± 122 (average of two), hearth 4 dates to 10,647 ± 116 (average of two), hearth 9 dates to 9940 ± 160 (Tx-1420), and hearth 12 dates to 10,330 ± 190 (Tx-1638 [Goebel et al. 2007]). Third, the single date that Beck and Jones cite that completely overlaps (i.e., within one sigma) the Clovis era—11,140 ± 120 ^{14}C BP—came from a small hearth (hearth 1) that intruded from the upper part of the stemmed point component (the "dung, rubble, and silt" layer) into its lower part (the "gray ash and silt" layer). Stratigraphically underlying it in the gray ash layer was a fragment of S-twist cordage that yielded a date of 10,420 ± 100 ^{14}C BP (TO-1173). The cordage's position in the lower part of the cultural layer makes us wonder again whether old wood was a culprit in producing the 11,140 ^{14}C BP date. Until this presumed old hearth of the upper part of the cultural layer is AMS ^{14}C dated using charcoal of a short-lived species, we conservatively conclude that the stemmed point occupation at Smith Creek dates to no earlier than 10,700 ^{14}C BP, following Thompson (1985:117). We cannot unequivocally accept it as evidence that makers of stemmed points occupied Smith Creek Cave during the Clovis era; however, additional dating of the hearth in question, and additional excavations at the site, may eventually demonstrate otherwise.

Bonneville Estates Rockshelter

Bonneville Estates Rockshelter (26EK3682) is located in the Lead Mine Hills of northeast Nevada, along the western margin of the Bonneville Basin. The shelter was the focus of a decade-long field project directed by Goebel, K. Graf, B. Hockett, and D. Rhode, between 2000 and 2010. Preliminary results of the excavation, focusing primarily on the terminal Pleistocene and early Holocene layers in the west and east excavation blocks, have been presented in a series of recent publications (Goebel 2007; Goebel et al. 2007; Goebel et al. 2011; Graf 2007; Hockett 2007; Hockett et al. 2008; Rhode and Louderback 2007; Rhode et al. 2005).

Beck and Jones (2010) cite one radiocarbon date from Bonneville Estates Rockshelter (10,560 ± 50 ^{14}C BP [Beta-182931]); however, Graf (2007) reports 26 additional ^{14}C ages on hearth charcoal that help date the terminal Pleistocene–early Holocene cultural occupations represented in strata 18b, 18a, and 17b' of the rockshelter's deposits (Table 5.1). More recently, Goebel et al. (2011) have presented 50 accepted ^{14}C ages dating 41 hearth features from the early layers preserved at Bonneville Estates. In the west excavation block, stratum 18b constitutes the earliest unequivocal cultural component; its hearths span from 11,010 ± 40 (Beta-207009) to 10,405 ± 50 ^{14}C BP (AA-58593). Stratum 18a dates from 10,130 ± 60 (Beta-170444) to 10,040 ± 70 ^{14}C BP (Beta-170443), while stratum 17b' dates from 9580 ± 40 (Beta-207010) to 9430 ± 50 ^{14}C BP (AA-58588 [Graf 2007:95]). In some areas within the west block, these strata could not be conveniently separated, so they were grouped into the more general designation "stratum 18." Graf concludes that stratum 18b accumulated within a 1,100-year span, between about 13,100 and 12,000 cal BP, and that it "likely represents a series of short-term human occupations during that time" (2007:97). In the east block, 13 ^{14}C ages from a series of hearth features in strata 12 and 10 span from 10,560 ± 50 (Beta-182931) to 8830 ± 60 ^{14}C BP (Beta-203507 [Graf 2007:100]).

Eight fragments of stemmed points and one complete stemmed point have been recovered from Bonneville Estates Rockshelter, six within strata 18b, 18a, and 17b' of the west excavation block (Goebel 2007:163) and two within strata 12 and 10 in the east block (Goebel 2007:160). Among the west block points, three are unidentifiable stemmed point fragments (from stratum 18), two are Haskett point fragments (from strata 18b and 17b'), one is a Parman point fragment (from stratum 18a), and one is a Windust point fragment (from stratum 17b'). The Haskett point from stratum 18b (Figure 5.2G) came from excavation square N5W21 and was closest to hearth feature 04.14 (about 2 m to the south, in N7W21), dating to 10,540 ± 40 ^{14}C BP (Beta-195047). Other nearby hearths from stratum 18b, including features 03.14 and 03.15a (both from N8W20, about 3 m south of the Haskett point), date to 10,405 ± 50 (AA-58593) and 10,787 ± 46 ^{14}C BP (average of two), respectively. The oldest-dated hearth feature from the west block at Bonneville Estates, feature 05.06 at 11,010 ± 40 ^{14}C BP (Beta-207009), was from square N6W16, about 5 m east of the Haskett point. Only debitage was recovered from around this feature. In the east block, the oldest hearth potentially associated with a stemmed point yielded a date of 10,380 ± 40 ^{14}C BP (Beta-195013 [Goebel 2007; Graf 2007]), but the point could be considerably younger, closer to 10,000 ^{14}C BP, because of its proximity to several different hearth features in a very rubbly layer of silt. This artifact is the distal fragment of a stemmed point, likely a Parman point, broken below the shoulder.

Thus, even though the recent excavations at Bonneville Estates uncovered at least one Clovis-aged hearth feature, no diagnostic stemmed points can be unequivocally tied to it. On the age for the earliest stemmed point in the shelter, we agree with Graf that both "horizontal and vertical placement of the Haskett point, coupled with radiocarbon assays, suggest that it dates to between 10,800 and 10,400 ^{14}C BP (12,900 and 12,000 cal BP)" (2007:97), perhaps 10,500–10,400 ^{14}C BP. The rockshelter's earliest unequivocally dated hearth feature, at 11,010 ^{14}C BP (~13,120–12,720 cal BP), "falls into the established time of Clovis; however, to date no diagnostic projectile points have been found associated with the feature that produced this date" (Graf 2007:103). In fact, the only Clovis point fragment recovered from the excavation came from the rockshelter's historic-period occupation near the top of the stratigraphic column (Goebel 2007:157).

Discussion

The Radiocarbon Age of Early Stemmed Points in the Intermountain West

Do any of the stemmed point occupations discussed above meet Pettitt et al.'s (2003) criteria for a well-dated cultural occupation? The answer is certainly not a resounding yes, but two or three sites come close. As a result, to keep from "throwing out the baby with the bathwater," so to speak, essentially discarding every dated site from the region, we need to loosen our standards a bit, like Graf (2009) did for the Siberian Upper Paleolithic, carefully defining good, bad, and ugly dated sequences—saving the good, discarding the bad, and provisionally accepting, with conditions, the ugly. By doing this, we can develop a tentative chronology for early stemmed points in the Intermountain West. Dates associated with stemmed points from the above sites that are acceptable to us are shown in Table 5.2.

Sentinel Gap may be the best-dated stemmed point occupation in the region, but even it has its problems. It has one conventional date of 10,680 ± 190 ^{14}C BP and four AMS dates on wood charcoal from features that cluster around 10,100 ^{14}C BP and average 10,108 ± 26 ^{14}C BP. We agree with the original excavators that the AMS chronology more accurately defines the age of the site.

The stemmed point occupation at Marmes Rockshelter remains poorly dated. Its assignment to the Clovis era is based on a pair of conventional dates derived from shell, a material notoriously difficult to accurately date and often requiring a reservoir correction, which is not available for the Marmes area. Other conventional shell dates from the lower strata in the shelter are much younger than the Clovis-aged dates, and in the shelter's later deposits when shell dates are paired with charcoal dates, the shell dates are consistently older. Two charcoal dates from floodplain deposits outside the shelter, still loosely associated with stemmed points, are also much younger and average 9985 ± 212 ^{14}C BP. To us, this is the best approximation of the stemmed point occupation's age at Marmes.

Hatwai has two major problems. First, its cultural remains come from a secondary, high-energy fluvial context, so any association of stemmed points and ^{14}C dates is suspect. Second, its early date of 10,820 ± 140 ^{14}C BP was based on a conventionally dated composite sample of charcoal. We concur with the original excavators that the occupation probably dates to much later than the Clovis era, perhaps around 9500 ^{14}C BP. However, the site's context makes this interpretation as tenuous as Beck and Jones's (2010) suggestion that the site dates to Clovis times.

The stemmed points from Coopers Ferry may date to the Clovis era, but we are not yet convinced. The site has two sets of dates, some around 11,000 ^{14}C BP and others around 9000–8000 ^{14}C BP. The early dates are either from below the stemmed point–bearing horizon or from a pit that has been dug into the underlying deposit. According to the original excavators' published descriptions and profiles, stemmed points in a primary context are from the same deposits as some of the younger dates. To us, the site's "young" chronology has fewer reversals and is hence more parsimonious, and this suggests that the stemmed point occupation at Coopers Ferry could be 2,000–3,000 ^{14}C years younger than Clovis. Given the significant bioturbation evident in the site's deposits, however, we have to admit that our interpretation is just as equivocal as the original excavators' interpretation. We await the reporting of results from the ongoing excavation at the site, with the hope that the chronological inconsistencies can be cleared up.

Wildcat Canyon's single stemmed point is not at all associated with the early date cited by Beck and Jones (2010). Instead, the early date of 10,600 ± 200 ^{14}C BP is from two strata below, and the stratum that yielded the stemmed point has a single date of 9860 ± 510 ^{14}C BP. This artifact is more than a millennium younger than the Clovis era.

The shallowly buried cultural occupation at Handprint Cave could date to 10,740 ± 70 ^{14}C BP, but we are not convinced that the bifacial point loosely associated with this date is an early-period stemmed point. It could be a Middle Archaic Humboldt point, and if so, the old conventional date on charcoal, which came from below the point, would serve only as a lower-limiting age.

The Buhl burial is dated with a single, relatively reliable AMS date on human bone of 10,675 ± 95 ^{14}C BP directly associated with a Windust point. However, this age is not corroborated with any other dates, and even if it was, its age range postdates the time of Clovis.

Connley Cave 4B stratum 4 seems to contain stemmed points and radiocarbon dates ranging from 11,200 to 9670 ^{14}C BP; however, the associations between stemmed points and dated samples are suspect. In addition, the dates acquired were done using conventional means and are reversed stratigraphically. This, combined with more recent work at Connley Caves 5 and 6, suggests a younger age of 10,500–10,000 ^{14}C BP.

Sunshine has several Clovis-era dates, but none of these are clearly associated with stemmed points. Perhaps Sunshine's stemmed points date to as early as 10,760 ± 70 ^{14}C BP, but this and other early dates could just as likely be associated with concave-based points recovered from the site's early deposits. The earliest clear association of a stemmed point and a ^{14}C age dates to 9800 ± 60 ^{14}C BP, from stratum C. Because a stemmed biface was found below this in stratum E, however, our interpretation of the results of the Sunshine excavations is that early stemmed points there could date anywhere from 10,760 to 9900 ^{14}C BP.

Smith Creek Cave has a fairly uniform series of conventional ^{14}C dates on charcoal from hearths and an AMS date on cordage, with one of the charcoal dates overlapping the Clovis era (11,140

± 200 ^{14}C BP). Unfortunately this old date has not been replicated by AMS dating charcoal from the same hearth feature, so we cannot rule out the possibility that it represents the burning of old wood. Other hearth features with multiple conventional charcoal dates are not all synchronous (e.g., 10,740, 10,460, and 9800 ^{14}C BP for hearth 5; 10,630, 10,570, and 9280 ^{14}C BP for hearth 3), heightening our fears that if the old hearth was AMS dated using charcoal from short-lived woody shrubs, it too could turn out to be significantly younger. We tentatively conclude that the earliest unequivocal age of the stemmed point occupation dates to no earlier than 10,647 ± 116 ^{14}C BP, the average of two concordant dates from hearth 4. This date overlaps nearly all of the dated hearths from the upper part of the stemmed point occupation at Smith Creek Cave, as well as the date on cordage that came from the lower part of the occupation. Rejection of the 11,140 ± 200 ^{14}C BP date is further justified because it is stratigraphically reversed from a date of 10,420 ± 100 ^{14}C BP on cordage found lower in the profile, a date that overlaps (at two sigma) with the 10,647 average date for hearth 4. For now, this discussion needs to be left open, until more dates can be obtained on the Smith Creek Cave hearths or additional excavations are undertaken there.

Bonneville Estates Rockshelter, finally, has a relatively consistent series of AMS dates on wood charcoal from hearth features, but as at Smith Creek Cave, there are some issues. The oldest hearth dates to 11,010 ± 40 ^{14}C BP, but this is a single date that has not been replicated, and no stemmed points were directly associated with it. Instead the closest association between a dated hearth and a stemmed point is several centuries younger, 10,540 ± 40 ^{14}C BP. To us, this is the earliest clear age for a stemmed point in the rockshelter, although we admit that some or even all of the earlier hearths could have been ignited by people accustomed to manufacturing stemmed points. We need more dates on Bonneville Estates' earliest hearths and renewed excavations in the vicinity of the oldest hearth, to determine whether diagnostic bifacial points are associated with it.

Beyond the sites presented by Beck and Jones (2010) and reviewed in detail here, there are at least 10 additional Intermountain West archaeological sites that contain stemmed points in relatively early contexts (Table 5.3); however, only one may be as early as Clovis. Five of these sites are in Idaho: Bison Rockshelter, Wilson Butte Cave, Wewukiyepuh, Redfish Overhang, and Hetrick. Bison Rockshelter may contain stemmed points dating to as early as 10,340 ± 830 ^{14}C BP (WSU-760 [Swanson 1972:51]), but this was a conventional date on bison bone from stratum 32b, and even though it was from just above a tephra identified as Glacier Peak ash, it needs to be replicated using modern AMS technology. Wilson Butte Cave yielded an AMS age estimate of 10,230 ± 90 ^{14}C BP (TO-1485) on charcoal from stratum C (Gruhn 2006:20), which Gruhn (2006) concludes represents the earliest human occupation in the cave, seemingly in direct association with stemmed points. The Wewukiyepuh site contained a well-preserved living floor in an open-air context. Two concordant AMS dates on charcoal (one from a hearth feature) average 10,350 ± 31 ^{14}C BP; these were found with remains of elk and grizzly bear and two stemmed points, one nearly complete and Haskett-like (Sappington and Schuknecht-McDaniel 2001). Redfish Overhang yielded a Haskett point fragment from a cultural layer dating to 10,100 ± 330 ^{14}C BP (WSU-1396), as well as a cache of Haskett points and preforms dating to 9860 ± 300 ^{14}C BP (WSU-1395 [Reid 2011; Yohe and Woods 2002]). At the Hetrick site, finally, the earliest occupations date from 9850 ± 110 to 9730 ± 60 ^{14}C BP. Related artifacts include Windust stemmed points found with hearth features and a variety of fauna including lagomorphs, artiodactyls, fish, and waterfowl (Reid 2011; Yohe and Woods 2002).

Farther west in Washington, the stemmed point occupation at the Lind Coulee site has yielded AMS dates on bone of 10,250 ± 45 (CAMS-94857), 10,060 ± 45 (CAMS-94856), and 9810 ± 40 ^{14}C BP (CAMS-95524 [Craven 2004:29]). Together these dates suggest a late or post–Younger Dryas age for the Lind Coulee occupation.

In the northwestern Great Basin, additional sites with early stemmed points and directly associated ^{14}C chronologies are rare. Most important are the newly reported materials from Paisley Cave 5, where four stemmed points were recovered from deposits dating to the terminal Pleistocene (Jenkins et al. 2012). Three of these were from the screen and not in situ, so that bracketing dates were used to determine their ages. According to D. Jenkins and his team, the first *ex situ* stemmed point appears to date from 10,855 ± 30 to 10,200 ± 35 ^{14}C BP (artifact number 1961-PC-5/18a-10-1); the second, from 12,260 ± 60 to 10,050 ± 50 ^{14}C BP (1294-PC-5/6D-47-1); and the third, from 11,070 ± 25 to 10,855 ± 30 ^{14}C BP (1895-PC-5/16A-23-6A [Jenkins et al. 2012:226, Table 1]). The fourth point was recovered in situ (1895-PC-5/16A-24) in a thin lens of silt, and its proposed age is reported to be from 11,340 ± 50 to 11,070 ± 25 ^{14}C BP (Jenkins et al. 2012:226, Table 1). Based on these interpretations, Jenkins et al. (2012) conclude that while point 18a-10-1 is post-Clovis in age, the other three (6D-47-1, 16A-23-6A, and 16A-24) are at least coeval with Clovis.

Although at face value the dates presented by Jenkins et al. (2012) support a Clovis age (and possibly a pre-Clovis age depending on the Clovis chronology used) for stemmed points at Paisley Caves, the evidence is less than secure, largely because of contextual issues and problematic associations. The terminal Pleistocene sediments of Cave 5, which produced the four stemmed points, contained many signs of contemporaneous pack rat (*Neotoma* sp.) activity (pellets and burrows), and sediment deposition in the cave was laterally interrupted by boulder- and cobble-sized rocks, complicating associations between excavated artifacts and dated materials. The stemmed points do not appear to have come from an intact living floor with hearth features, leading us to query whether the remains were in a secondary context, having been transported from elsewhere in the cave by pack rats. These problems are compounded by contextual

TABLE 5.3. Relevant dates from other early stemmed point sites in the Intermountain West, not cited in Beck and Jones 2010.

Site	Provenience	Material	Age (^{14}C BP)	Cal BP (2σ)	Lab Number	Source
Bison Rockshelter	Period IIb, level 32b	Bison bone collagen	10,340 ± 830	11,938–11,824 (*p* = .06) 12,438–11,942 (*p* = .89) 12,528–12,459 (*p* = .04)	WSU-760	1
Wilson Butte Cave	Stratum C, unit C8	Charcoal	10,230 ± 90	11,421–11,419 (*p* < .01) 11,526–11,501 (*p* = .01) 12,391–11,605 (*p* = .99)	TO-1485	2
Wewukiyepuh	Cultural layer	Hearth charcoal	10,270 ± 50	11,863–11,839 (*p* = .95) 12,318–12,274 (*p* = .03) 12,377–12,347 (*p* = .02)	Beta-124446	3
	Cultural layer	Dispersed charcoal	10,390 ± 40	12,417–12,082	Beta-124447	4
Hetrick	Stratum IIId	Bone collagen	9730 ± 60	10,847–10,800 (*p* = .03) 10,954–10,865 (*p* = .13) 11,015–11,012 (*p* < .01) 11,251–11,068 (*p* = .84)	Beta-78722	4
	Stratum IIIc	Bone collagen	9850 ± 110	10,841–10,821 (*p* < .01) 10,952–10,861 (*p* = .03) 11,756–11,070 (*p* = .96)	Beta-78880	4
	Stratum IIIe	Bone collagen	9830 ± 30	11,265–11,200	UCIAMS-907	4
Redfish Overhang	Unsorted colluvium	Charcoal	10,100 ± 100	11,293–11,288 (*p* < .01) 12,046–11,303 (*p* > .99)	WSU-1396	5
	Layers 3/4 contact	Hearth charcoal	9860 ± 300	12,389–10,510	WSU-1395	5
Lind Coulee	Cultural layer, .20–.25 m B.D.	Elk/bison bone collagen	10,250 ± 40	12,132–11,818	CAMS-94857	6
	Cultural layer, .29–.39 m B.D.	Elk/bison bone collagen	10,060 ± 45	11,820–11,338	CAMS-94856	6
	Cultural layer, .30–.40 m B.D.	Elk/bison bone collagen	9810 ± 40	11,267–11,178	CAMS-95524	6
Paisley Cave 5	LU2	Macerated plant material	10,855 ± 30	12,879–12,611	UCIAMS-98932	7
	LU2	*Artemisia* twig	11,070 ± 25	13,102–12,770	UCIAMS-80378	7
Paulina Lake	82134EBB13/3F9	Charcoal	9920 ± 470	12,677–10,202	Beta-56722	8
Dirty Shame Rockshelter	Charcoal	Charcoal	9500 ± 95	11,159–10,557	SI-1774	9
North Creek Rockshelter	IIa	Charcoal	9960 ± 30	11,602–11,259	PRI-07-102-3716	10
	IIa	Charcoal	9800 ± 50	11,306–11,149	Beta-239022	10
Average of Two			*9880 ± 26*	*11,325–11,224*		

Note: 1 = Swanson 1972; 2 = Gruhn 2006; 3 = Sappington and Schuknecht-McDaniel 2001; 4 = Reid 2011; 5 = Sargeant 1973; 6 = Craven 2004; 7 = Jenkins et al. 2012; 8 = Connolly and Jenkins 1999; 9 = Hanes 1988; 10 = Bodily 2009.

issues with the stemmed points themselves. Three of the four stemmed points were recovered *ex situ* in the screen, making associations with radiocarbon samples difficult to document fully. The context for point 6D-47-1, for example, is described as a vertical zone of sediment spanning ~50 cm elevationally and more than 2,000 years temporally. The authors calculate a depositional rate implying an age of 11,600 ^{14}C BP, but this was based on a uniform rate of deposition, arguably an oversimplification given the complex depositional history of the site, potential variability in pack rat activity and rock fall within the cave, and the variable stratigraphic dip of the cave's early deposits. Arguably, this point could be pre-Clovis, Clovis, or post-Clovis in age. Moreover, the single stemmed point (16A-24) recovered in situ in the silt lens is reported to have been associated with dates of 11,070, 11,165, 11,295, and 11,340 ^{14}C BP (the latter three on coprolites); however, these associations are less than clear. Multiple discontinuous silt bands occurred in stratum LU2, and the silt lens shown in Profile III of Cave 5 (Jenkins et al. 2012:Figures 2b and 3b) may or may not have been the one that produced the stemmed point. If it was, as Jenkins and colleagues posit, then all four of these dates should be treated as lower-limiting ages for the artifact, instead of part of its age range, because they were collected from below the silt lens preserved in Profile III. Even the youngest of the four dates, obtained from a small sagebrush (*Artemisia* sp.) twig, came from the basal contact of the silt lens (Jenkins et al. 2012:Figure S4), about 40 cm away from and stratigraphically under the stemmed point (which came from 2 cm below the top of the silt lens [Jenkins et al. 2012:S16]). Jenkins et al. state that the in situ point was the "stratigraphically deepest" (2012: S16) of the four stemmed points, and if this is indeed the case, then all likely postdate 11,070 ^{14}C BP.[2] An upper-limiting age for this stemmed point definitely would help establish its age, but unfortunately there are only two such dates available, 10,855 ± 30 and 10,000 ± 25 ^{14}C BP, respectively, ~8 cm and ~10 cm above the silt lens on Profile III, both on macerated plant remains. Additional dates are obviously needed from just above the

TABLE 5.4. Accepted dates from North American Clovis sites.

SITE	AGE (^{14}C BP)	CAL BP (2σ)	SOURCE(S)
Lange-Ferguson	11,080 ± 40	13,112–12,766	1
Sloth Hole	11,050 ± 50	13,093–12,733	1
Anzick	11,040 ± 35	13,103–12,731	1, 2
Dent	10,990 ± 25	12,981–12,677 (*p* = .96) 13,063–13,015 (*p* = .04)	1
Paleo Crossing	10,980 ± 75	13,082–12,669	1, 3
Domebo	10,960 ± 30	12,957–12,659	1
Lehner	10,950 ± 40	12,964–12,648	1, 4
Shawnee-Minisink	10,935 ± 15	12,920–12,663	1, 5
Blackwater Draw	10,914 ± 72	12,973–12,611 (*p* = .98) 13,056–13,026 (*p* = .02)	6
Colby	10,870 ± 20	12,886–12,624	1
Jake Bluff	10,765 ± 25	12,750–12,573	1, 7

Note: 1 = Waters and Stafford 2007; 2 = Morrow and Fiedel 2006; 3 = Brose 1994; 4 = Haynes 1992; 5 = Gingerich 2007; 6 = Haynes 2008; 7 = Bement and Carter 2003.
Sources: Following Haynes 2002; Waters and Stafford 2007.

point to clarify its potential age range. To us, this combination of issues—lack of explanation of how artifacts and dated materials became incorporated into Cave 5's sediments, absence of cultural features such as hearths in the cave's lower deposit, and inclusion of dates from underlying strata to define the age range of the single stemmed point recovered in situ—clouds Jenkins et al.'s (2012) interpretation of the ages of the early stemmed points at Paisley Caves. Humans seemingly occupied the site during and before Clovis times (Gilbert et al. 2008; Jenkins et al. 2012), but whether humans produced stemmed points throughout the early occupation remains an open question to us.

Other early stemmed points in Oregon are significantly younger, dating to the earliest Holocene or later. Paulina Lake's earliest cultural occupation, called component 1, yielded an AMS date on charcoal of 9920 ± 470 ^{14}C BP (Beta-56722); the dated sample was from a charcoal-rich feature, and two stemmed points came from the component (Connolly and Jenkins 1999). Similarly, Dirty Shame Rockshelter's earliest stemmed point may date to just 9500 ± 95 ^{14}C BP (Hanes 1988). Other early radiocarbon-dated sites in eastern Oregon, for example, Connley Cave 5 and Tucker, did not yield stemmed points from clearly dated contexts (Beck et al. 2004; Pinson 2004).

Farther south in Nevada and eastern California, additional early sites are difficult to find. Several have early dates but no reported stemmed points in clear association (e.g., Tule Lake Rockshelter, Fishbone Cave, Wizards Beach, Spirit Cave, Elephant Mountain Cave, Panamint Valley [Adams et al. 2008; Connolly and Barker 2004; Dansie and Jerrems 2005; Davis et al. 1969; Tuohy 1988; Tuohy and Dansie 1997]), while sites with stemmed points typically remain undated because of poor contexts. Exceptions include Last Supper Cave, Rogers Ridge, and Henwood, all presumably postdating 9000 ^{14}C BP (Douglas et al. 1988; Grayson 1988). In the eastern Great Basin, after Bonneville Estates Rockshelter, Smith Creek Cave, and Sunshine, stemmed points from dated contexts are rare. They have not yet been recovered from the well-dated lowest layers at Danger Cave, and at nearby Hogup Cave they appear to date to just the early to mid-Holocene (Aikens 1970; Rhode et al. 2005). North Creek Rockshelter, located in the Upper Escalante River basin of south-central Utah, recently yielded stemmed points in association with a cultural feature radiocarbon dated to the earliest Holocene (a split charcoal sample produced dates of 9960 ± 30 [PRI-07-102-3716] and 9800 ± 50 ^{14}C BP [Beta-239022; Bodily 2009]).

Thus, as with the stemmed point occupations reviewed in detail earlier in this chapter, virtually all of the additional cases of early stemmed points presented above postdate the Clovis interval by centuries, if not millennia. Only Paisley Cave 5 presents possible evidence contradicting this pattern.

The Age of Clovis in the Intermountain West

Across North America, Clovis, where it has been found in stratified and datable contexts, repeatedly dates to between about 11,050 and 10,800 ^{14}C BP (Waters and Stafford 2007), although it has been argued recently that some earlier Clovis ages should not be rejected (Beck and Jones 2010; Haynes 2002; Haynes et al. 2007). When Clovis dates are calibrated using the IntCal09 curve (Stuiver and Reimer 1993), it becomes apparent that the bulk of Clovis sites range in age from 13,200 to 12,700 cal BP, and only one (Jakes Bluff, Oklahoma), seems to be younger, ca. 12,650 cal BP (Table 5.4).

In the Intermountain West, radiocarbon ages clearly associated with Clovis fluted points are still lacking. Most Clovis sites occur in surface or near-surface contexts, so they cannot be reliably dated; such examples include the Simon cache in Idaho, Dietz and Sage Hen Gap in Oregon, Jakes Depression in Nevada, and Hell'n Moriah in Utah (Davis et al. 1996; Kohntopp 2010; O'Grady et al. 2008; Rondeau et al. 2007; Willig 1988). Other Clovis sites occur in more deeply buried contexts but either still have not been radiocarbon dated (e.g., the Clovis cache from East Wenatchee, Washington [Mehringer and Foit 1990]) or occur in unusually young contexts, perhaps where they were recycled and incorporated into later cultural occupations (e.g., Bonneville Estates Rockshelter, Henwood, and Rogers Ridge [Goebel 2007; Warren and Phagan 1988]). At Sunshine in Nevada, fluted points that are not Clovis forms have been recovered in buried and dated contexts, but again these presumably date to later than the Clovis era (Beck and Jones 2009, 2010). At Heil Pond, southern Idaho, K. Murphey (1985) found Clovis fluted points and fluting debitage in a disturbed setting loosely associated with a possible hearth feature that yielded a radiocarbon age of 10,880 ± 260 ^{14}C BP (Beta-10069; 13,293–12,121 cal BP [Reid 2011]). The fluted points, though, were not from a controlled excavation, and the material dated was recorded by Beta Analytic to be "soil 0.2% carbon" (Reid 2011:26), not necessarily charcoal. Nonetheless, the tenuous evidence from Heil Pond suggests that in the northern Intermountain West, Clovis possibly dates to the same interval as it does elsewhere in temperate North America—13,200–12,700 cal BP, but excavations are needed there to investigate this possibility.

Calibration Analysis of Stemmed Point and Clovis Occupations

Given the above review, we conclude that there are two alternative chronologies—both currently defensible—that potentially define the age range and significance of early stemmed points in the Intermountain West. We refer to these as the "short" and "long" chronologies for stemmed points (Figures 5.5 and 5.6).

The Short Chronology

In Figure 5.5 we present a short chronology for stemmed points, the result of the above critical review and calibration analysis (following Stuiver and Reimer 1993) of ^{14}C dates found most suitable for defining the age range of stemmed points in the Intermountain West (Tables 5.2 and 5.3). In the chart we compare these dates with calibrated ages for Clovis (Table 5.4). To recap, the analysis did not include the conventional 10,680 ^{14}C BP age from Sentinel Gap, questionable shell dates from Marmes Rockshelter, any of the dates from Hatwai I (because its stemmed point occupation is in a high-energy secondary context), dates from the presumed 11,370 ^{14}C BP pit dug at Coopers Ferry, the 11,200 ^{14}C BP reversed age from Connley Cave 4B, the 11,140 ^{14}C BP hearth 2 from Smith Creek Cave (because it is inconsistent with other geochronological data from the same and lower-lying strata), or the 10,600 ^{14}C BP date from Wildcat Canyon (because it was not associated with any stemmed points). In addition, from this analysis we excluded the earliest two dates on hearths from Bonneville Estates Rockshelter because stemmed points were not directly associated with these features, as well as the earliest acceptable dates of 10,855 and 11,070 ^{14}C BP from Paisley Cave 5 because both were on natural materials (macerated plant material and a twig, respectively), not from a hearth feature or artifact of obvious human manufacture, and because the association of these materials and the in situ stemmed point is ambiguous.

The trend in the resulting data is clear. Modes of the calibrated Clovis ages fall within the range of 13,200–12,650 cal BP, while virtually all modes of calibrated age ranges for stemmed point sites postdate this interval of time. Admittedly, the two-sigma ranges for acceptable dates from Buhl, Smith Creek Cave, Connley Caves, Bonneville Estate Rockshelter, Marmes (floodplain), Paulina Lake, and Wildcat Canyon minimally overlap the Clovis interval, but none have modes that fall within it. To us, these results strongly suggest that stemmed points and Clovis points may not be coeval and, instead, that stemmed point technologies are later.

The Long Chronology

The alternative long chronology presented in Figure 5.6 includes the early dates from Smith Creek Cave, Bonneville Estates Rockshelter, and Paisley Cave 5. These were excluded from the first analysis because of contextual ambiguities or internal inconsistencies or simply because they need to be replicated by additional testing. In these cases, however, equivocality should not equal automatic rejection. We acknowledge that the early dates from these sites could be correct, and as a result they need to be part of our continuing dialogue regarding Paleoindian chronology in the Intermountain West. We justify tentative acceptance of these dates in the following ways. The series of hearths preserved in the early layers at Smith Creek Cave and Bonneville Estates Rockshelter were likely produced by repeated short-term occupations by small groups of people (Goebel et al. 2007), not single occupations by large multifamily groups. The full range of dates and full set of hearths, therefore, could indeed represent occupations by stemmed point makers spanning many centuries. Similarly, despite our hesitancy in accepting the Paisley Cave 5 dates without reservation, we feel that they cannot be rejected until archaeologists in the region have had ample opportunity to replicate Jenkins et al.'s (2012) results, either through renewed excavations at Paisley or by new discoveries at some other archaeological site in eastern Oregon.

Considered accordingly, Smith Creek Cave's earliest stemmed points could be associated with an age of 13,268–12,719 cal BP, while Bonneville Estates Rockshelter's stemmed points could be associated with ages of 12,965–12,750 and 12,792–12,566 cal BP. The three hearths that produced these dates could therefore overlap Clovis in time (Figure 5.6). The age of Paisley Cave 5's in situ stemmed point could range from 12,611–12,879 to 12,770–13,102 cal BP, based on the dates of 10,855 and 11,070 ^{14}C BP seemingly bracketing the in situ point linked to Profile III (Jenkins et al. 2012). These data suggest that at these three sites at least, human occupations by makers of stemmed points could be synchronous with Clovis elsewhere in western North America; however, we caution readers once again that these dating results should be considered provisional until they can be replicated or shown to be unequivocally tied to stemmed points.

Conclusions

Our conclusion here is that when geochronological evidence is carefully weighed, unequivocal support for Clovis-aged stemmed points has not yet been found in the Intermountain West. Instead, the bulk of the evidence suggests that stemmed points in the region are a late Paleoindian phenomenon. However, three sites—Smith Creek Cave, Bonneville Estates Rockshelter, and Paisley Cave 5—may contain evidence of Clovis-aged stemmed points. If this is the case, then stemmed points could have been the projectile technology of choice for the earliest peoples of the Intermountain West. Continued work at these three sites will undoubtedly clarify their earliest records, and we look forward

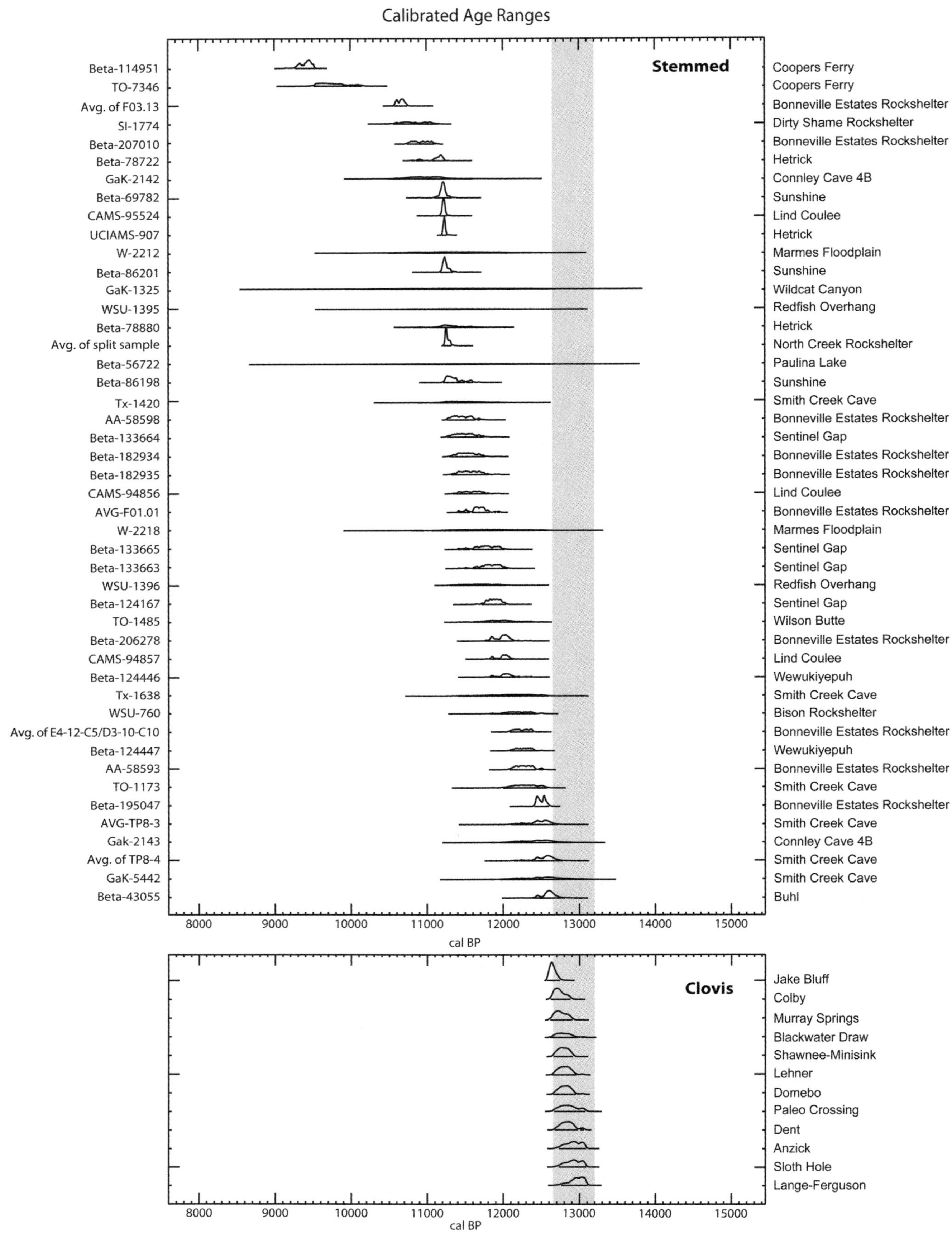

FIGURE 5.5. Calibrated (IntCal09) date ranges at two sigma from Intermountain West stemmed point sites and Clovis sites (data from Tables 5.2, 5.3, and 5.4). Shaded area represents the calibrated range of the Clovis era (13,200–12,650 cal BP).

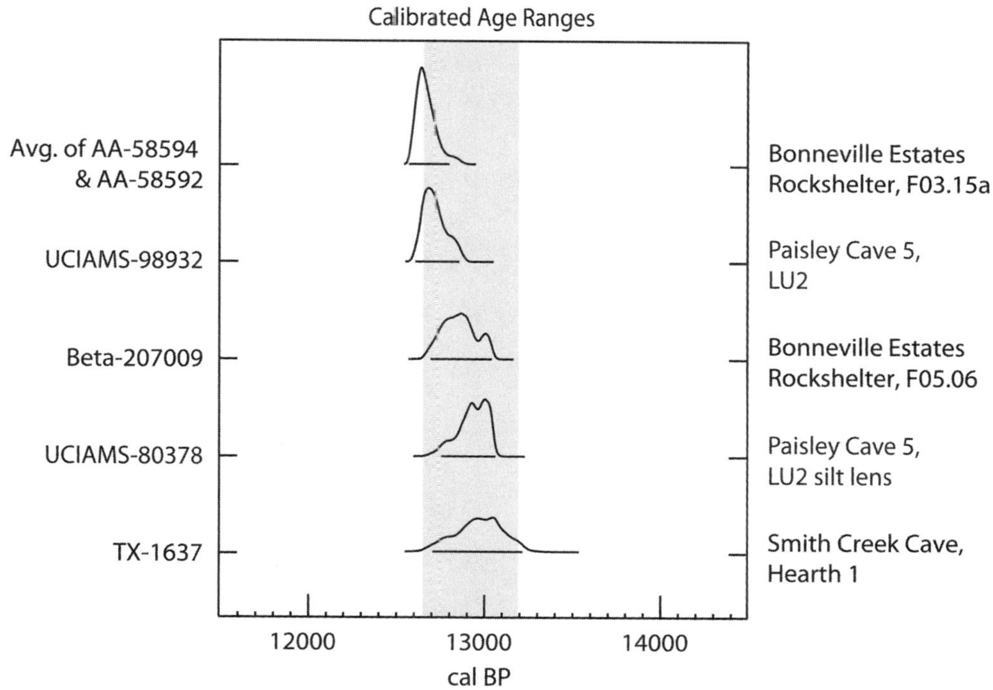

FIGURE 5.6. Calibrated (IntCal09) date ranges at two sigma tentatively associated with stemmed points, including three samples of charcoal from hearth features at Smith Creek Cave and Bonneville Estates Rockshelter and noncultural plant material from LU2 at Paisley Cave 5, compared with date ranges from Clovis sites (from Table 5.4). Shaded area represents the calibrated range of the Clovis era (13,200–12,650 cal BP). See the text for detailed discussions about these dates.

to continued discussion about them. Questions about hearth 1 at Smith Creek Cave can only be addressed through renewed excavation because no charcoal from this hearth is available in the curated collection at the Nevada State Museum. The oldest hearth at Bonneville Estates Rockshelter should and will be redated, and work at Bonneville Estates should be renewed to expose the unexcavated area immediately east of this hearth. At Paisley Cave 5, we challenge the investigators to confirm the age of the deposit immediately overlying the silt lens containing the in situ point, clarify the positions of the silt lens and ^{14}C dates associated with Profile III, and provide more details about the site-formation processes operating inside the cave, specifically the processes that led to the accumulation of the terminal Pleistocene archaeological record there. This as well as renewed excavations to look for intact living floors with preserved hearths will be key for testing the initial results.

The implications of the discovery of stemmed points synchronous with Clovis are clear. It would mean that stemmed point technology did not emerge from a Clovis antecedent but, instead, potentially represents a separate, possibly coastal, migration from Beringia into temperate western North America. If confirmed, such findings would support the emerging interpretation that the late Pleistocene peopling of the Americas was a much more complicated process than traditionally thought, as recent pre-Clovis discoveries in the western United States also seem to imply (Gilbert et al. 2008; Jenkins 2007; Jenkins et al. 2012; Waters et al. 2011b). Because a new paradigm is being developed based on this evidence, we need to carefully scrutinize and ensure the soundness of new results and not retract from potentially difficult dialogues. When we first set out to review the evidence for early stemmed points in the Intermountain West, our goal was not to prove that these artifacts always postdated the time of Clovis. After all, our own results at Bonneville Estates Rockshelter potentially suggested otherwise. Instead, our objective simply was to carefully weigh the geochronological evidence being used to promote a new theory explaining the origins of the first Americans west of the Rocky Mountains. Even if readers are not convinced by our arguments that stemmed points presently cannot be unequivocally shown to date to the same time as Clovis in the Intermountain West, we hope that all will agree that when evaluating radiocarbon dates to make interpretations regarding early cultural chronology, attention to good contextual and chronological hygiene is a must. Dates should not be treated simply as data.

Certainly, the interpretations presented here do not represent the endgame for dating early stemmed point occupations; instead they represent an effort to call attention to the fact that more rigorous chronology-building must be accomplished in the future if we are ever to understand the origins of stemmed point technologies and their significance to the late-glacial peopling of the Americas. Numerous sites that were dated decades ago need to be reanalyzed, either by directly dating curated specimens or by returning to old sites and conducting new excavations using modern geoarchaeological techniques. This is what is happening currently at Coopers Ferry, and it needs to happen, too, at places like the Bison/Veratic rockshelters, Smith Creek Cave, and Handprint Cave. In the end, we may find that the earliest stemmed points at Paisley Caves, Smith Creek Cave, Bonneville Estates Rockshelter, and Coopers Ferry really are as old as Clovis, but at the same time, we may find that they are not.

NOTES

1. Both of the dates cited by Beck and Jones (2010) for Hatwai are from a single combined sample of charcoal from two separate, nonadjacent units. The "11,120 ± 138" date probably refers to a date of "11,140 ± 140" (5,730-year half-life) provided by Ames et al. (1980), while the "10,796 ± 138" date seems to be a conversion of 11,120 to the standard 5,568-year half-life. Actual ^{14}C ages converted by dividing by 1.03 (following the style guide for *American Antiquity*) using a 5,568-year half-life are provided in Table 5.1. The date cited by Beck and Jones (2010) refers to TX-3159 (10,816 ± 136).
2. Even if the in situ point came from a lower silt lens not represented on Profile III, relating it to one of these ^{14}C dates would be problematic because Cave 5's early deposits dip 5–7 degrees toward the mouth of the cave, a 4- to 5-cm vertical drop per 50 cm horizontally. Using a sedimentation rate of 1 cm per 80–100 years (based on dates from LU2 in Profile III), such a drop represents ~400 ^{14}C years of offset. The smallest error in stratigraphic correlation could cause significant age discrepancy, with a 10,800 ^{14}C BP artifact date being interpreted as 11,000 ^{14}C BP or vice versa.

REFERENCES CITED

Adams, Kenneth D., Ted Goebel, Kelly Graf, Geoffrey M. Smith, Anna J. Camp, Richard W. Briggs, and David Rhode

2008 Late Pleistocene and Early Holocene Lake-Level Fluctuations in the Lahontan Basin, Nevada: Implications for the Distribution of Archaeological Sites. *Geoarchaeology* 23:608–643.

Aikens, C. Melvin

1970 *Hogup Cave*. University of Utah Anthropological Papers No. 93. Salt Lake City.

Aikens, C. Melvin, and Dennis L. Jenkins

1994 Environment, Climate, Subsistence, and Settlement: 11,000 Years of Change in the Fort Rock Basin, Oregon. In *Archaeological Researches in the Northern Great Basin: Fort Rock Archaeology Since Cressman*, edited by C. M. Aikens and D. L. Jenkins, pp. 1–20. University of Oregon Anthropological Papers, 50. Department of Anthropology and State Museum of Anthropology, University of Oregon, Eugene.

Ames, Kenneth M., James P. Green, and Margaret Pfoertner

1980 *Hatwai (10NP143): Interim Report*. Boise State University Archaeological Reports No. 9. Boise State University, Boise.

Beck, Charlotte, and George T. Jones

1997 The Terminal Pleistocene/Early Holocene Archaeology of the Great Basin. *Journal of World Prehistory* 11(2):161–236.

2007 Early Paleoarchaic Point Morphology and Chronology. In *Paleoindian or Paleoarchaic? Great Basin Human Ecology at the Pleistocene–Holocene Transition*, edited by Kelly E. Graf and Dave N. Schmitt, pp. 23–41. University of Utah Press, Salt Lake City.

2009 *The Archaeology of the Eastern Nevada Paleoarchaic, Pt. 1: The Sunshine Locality*. University of Utah Anthropological Papers No. 126. University of Utah Press, Salt Lake City.

2010 Clovis and Western Stemmed: Population Migration and the Meeting of Two Technologies in the Intermountain West. *American Antiquity* 75(1):81–116.

Beck, Charlotte, George T. Jones, Dennis L. Jenkins, Craig E. Skinner, and Jennifer J. Thatcher

2004 Fluted or Basally-Thinned? Re-Examination of a Lanceolate Point from the Connley Caves in the Fort Rock Basin. In *Early and Middle Holocene Archaeology of the Northern Great Basin*, edited by D. L. Jenkins, T. J. Connolly, and C. M. Aikens, pp. 281–294. University of Oregon Anthropological Papers, 62. Eugene.

Bedwell, Stephen F.

1973 *Fort Rock Basin: Prehistory and Environment*. University of Oregon Books, Eugene.

Bement, L. C., and B. J. Carter

2003 Clovis Bison Hunting at the Jake Bluff Site, NW Oklahoma. *Current Research in the Pleistocene* 20:5–7.

Bodily, Mark L.

2009 Residential Mobility of Paleoarchaic and Early Archaic Occupants at North Creek Shelter (42GA5863): An Analysis of Chipped Stone Artifacts. Unpublished Master's thesis, Department of Anthropology, Brigham Young University, Provo.

Brose, D. S.

1994 *The First Discovery of America: Archaeological Evidence of the Early Inhabitants of the Ohio Area*, edited by W. S. Dancey, pp. 61–76. Ohio Archaeological Council, Columbus.

Bryan, Alan L.

1965 *Paleo-American Prehistory*. Occasional Papers of the Idaho State University Museum No. 16. Idaho State University, Pocatello.

1978 An Overview of Paleo-American Prehistory from a Circum-Pacific Perspective. In *Early Man in America from a Circum-Pacific Perspective*, edited by A. L. Bryan, pp. 306–327. Occasional Papers No. 1. Department of Anthropology, University of Alberta, Archaeological Researches International, Edmonton.

1979 Smith Creek Cave. In *The Archaeology of Smith Creek Canyon, Eastern Nevada*, edited by D. R. Tuohy and D. L. Rendall, pp. 162–253. Nevada State Museum Anthropological Papers No. 17. Carson City.

1988 The Relationship of the Stemmed Point and Fluted Point Traditions in the Great Basin. In *Early Occupation in Far Western North America: The Clovis–Archaic Interface*, edited by J. A. Willig, C. M. Aikens, and J. L. Fagan, pp. 53–74. Nevada State Museum Anthropological Papers No. 21. Carson City.

Bryan, Alan L., R. Casamiquela, J. Cruxent, R. Gruhn, and C. Ochsenius

1978 An El Jobo Mastodon Kill at Taima-taima, Venezuela. *Science* 200:1275–1277.

Bryan, Alan L., and Donald R. Tuohy

1999 Prehistory of the Great Basin/Snake River Plain to About 8,500 Years Ago. In *Ice Age Peoples of North America: Environ-*

ments, Origins, and Adaptations, edited by Robson Bonnichsen and Karen L. Turnmire, pp. 249–263. Center for the Study of the First Americans, Texas A&M University, College Station.

Butler, B. Robert

1961 *The Old Cordilleran Culture in the Pacific Northwest*. Occasional Papers of the Idaho State College Museum No. 5. Idaho State College, Pocatello.

Cannon, Michael D., Stephanie D. Livingston, and Jack M. Broughton

2009 Faunal Remains from the Sunshine Locality. In *The Archaeology of the Eastern Nevada Paleoarchaic, Pt. I: The Sunshine Locality*, by Charlotte Beck and George T. Jones, pp. 218–228. University of Utah Anthropological Papers No. 126. Salt Lake City.

Chance, D. H.

1989 *Archaeology of the Hatiuhpuh Village*. Alfred W. Bowers Laboratory of Anthropology, U.S. Army Corps of Engineers, Walla Walla District, University of Idaho, Moscow.

Chatters, J. C.

1986 *The Wells Reservoir Archaeological Project, Washington, Vol. 1: Summary of Findings*. Central Washington Archaeological Survey Archaeological Report, 86-6. Central Washington University, Ellensburg.

Connolly, T. J., and P. Barker

2004 Basketry Chronology of the Early Holocene in the Northern Great Basin. In *Early and Middle Holocene Archaeology of the Northern Great Basin*, edited by T. J. Connolly, pp. 86–130. University of Oregon Anthropological Papers, 62. Eugene.

Connolly, Thomas J., and Dennis L. Jenkins

1999 The Paulina Lake Site (35DS34). In *Newberry Crater: A Ten-Thousand-Year Record of Human Occupation and Environmental Change in the Basin–Plateau Borderlands*, edited by Thomas J. Connolly, pp. 86–127. University of Utah Anthropological Papers No. 121. Salt Lake City.

Craven, Sloan L.

2004 New Dates for the Lind Coulee Site (45GR97), Washington. *Current Research in the Pleistocene* 21:28–30.

Cressman, L. S.

1942 Archaeological Researches in the Northern Great Basin. *Carnegie Institution of Washington Year Book* 39:300–306. Washington, D.C.

1966 *The Sandal and the Cave: The Indians of Oregon*. Oregon State University Press, Corvallis.

Dansie, A. J., and W. J. Jerrems

2005 More Bits and Pieces: A New Look at Lahontan Chronology and Human Occupation. In *Paleoamerican Origins: Beyond Clovis*, edited by R. Bonnichsen, B. T. Lepper, D. Stanford, and M. R. Waters, pp. 51–79. Center for the Study of the First Americans, Texas A&M University, College Station.

Daugherty, Richard D.

1956 Archaeology of the Lind Coulee Site, Washington. *Proceedings of the American Philosophical Society* 100(3):223–278.

1962 The Intermontane Western Tradition. *American Antiquity* 28:144–150.

Davis, Emma Lou

1975 The "Exposed Archaeology" of China Lake, California. *American Antiquity* 40:39–53.

Davis, E. L., C. W. Brott, and D. L. Weide

1969 *The Western Lithic Co-Tradition*. San Diego Museum Papers No. 6. San Diego Museum of Man, San Diego.

Davis, Loren G., and Charles E. Schweger

2004 Geoarchaeological Context of Late Pleistocene and Early Holocene Occupation at the Cooper's Ferry Site, Western Idaho, USA. *Geoarchaeology: An International Journal* 19:685–704.

Davis, Loren G., and David A. Sisson

1998 An Early Stemmed Point Cache from the Lower Salmon River Canyon of West-Central Idaho. *Current Research in the Pleistocene* 15:12–14.

Davis, William E., Dorothy Sack, and Nancy Shearin

1996 The Hell'n Moriah Clovis Site. *Utah Archaeology* 9(1):55–70.

Douglas, Charles L., Dennis L. Jenkins, and Claude N. Warren

1988 Spatial and Temporal Variability in Faunal Remains from Four Lake Mojave–Pinto Period Sites in the Mojave Desert. In *Early Human Occupation in Far Western North America: The Clovis–Archaic Interface*, edited by Judith A. Willig, C. Melvin Aikens, and John L. Fagan, pp. 131–151. Nevada State Museum Anthropological Papers No. 21. Carson City.

Dumond, Don E., and Rick Minor

1983 *Archaeology in the John Day Reservoir: The Wildcat Canyon Site 35-GM-9*. Anthropological Papers No. 30. University of Oregon, Eugene.

Erlandson, Jon M.

2009 Contextual and Chronological Hygiene in Interpreting Paleocoastal Sites of North America's Pacific Coast. *Quaternary Science Reviews* 28:2539–2541.

Erlandson, J. M., M. L. Moss, and M. Des Lauriers

2008 Life on the Edge: Early Maritime Cultures of the Pacific Coast of North America. *Quaternary Science Reviews* 27:2232–2245.

Galm, Jerry R., and Stan Gough

2000 Site 45KT1362, a c. 10,000 yr BP. Occupation in Central Washington. *Current Research in the Pleistocene* 17:29–31.

2008 The Projectile Point/Knife Sample from the Sentinel Gap Site. In *Projectile Point Sequences in Northwestern North America*, edited by Roy L. Carlson and Martin P. R. Magne, pp. 209–220. Archaeology Press, Simon Fraser University, Burnaby.

Gilbert, M. T. P., D. L. Jenkins, A. Götherstrom, N. Naveran, J. J. Sanchez, M. Hofreiter, P. F. Thomsen, J. Binladen, T. F. G. Higham, R. M. Yohe, II, R. Parr, L. S. Cummings, and E. Willerslev

2008 DNA from Pre-Clovis Human Coprolites in Oregon, North America. *Science* 320:786–789.

Gingerich, Joseph A. M.

2007 Picking Up the Pieces: New Paleoindian Research in the Upper Delaware Valley. *Archaeology of Eastern North America* 35:117–124.

Goebel, Ted

2007 Pre-Archaic and Early Archaic Technological Activities at Bonneville Estates Rockshelter: A First Look at the Lithic Artifact Record. In *Paleoindian or Paleoarchaic? Great Basin Human Ecology at the Pleistocene–Holocene Transition*, edited by Kelly E. Graf and Dave N. Schmitt, pp. 156–184. University of Utah Press, Salt Lake City.

Goebel, T., K. Graf, B. Hockett, and D. Rhode

2007 The Paleoindian Occupations at Bonneville Estates Rockshelter, Danger Cave, and Smith Creek Cave (Eastern Great Basin, U.S.A.): Interpreting Their Radiocarbon Chronologies. In *On Shelter's Ledge: Histories, Theories and Methods of Rockshelter Research*, edited by M. Kornfeld, S. Vasil'ev, and L. Miotti, pp. 147–161. BAR International Series, Oxford.

Goebel, T., B. Hockett, K. D. Adams, D. Rhode, and K. Graf

2011 Climate, Environment, and Humans in North America's Great Basin During the Younger Dryas, 12,900–11,600 Calendar Years Ago. *Quaternary International* 242:479–501.

Gough, Stan, and Jerry R. Galm
2002 Bone Technology at the Sentinel Gap Site. *Current Research in the Pleistocene* 19:27–29.
Graf, Kelly E.
2007 Stratigraphy and Chronology of the Pleistocene to Holocene Transition at Bonneville Estates Rockshelter, Eastern Great Basin. In *Paleoindian or Paleoarchaic? Great Basin Human Ecology at the Pleistocene–Holocene Transition*, edited by K. E. Graf and D. N. Schmitt, pp. 82–104. University of Utah Press, Salt Lake City.
2009 "The Good, the Bad, and the Ugly": Evaluating the Radiocarbon Chronology of the Middle and Late Upper Paleolithic in the Enisei River Valley, South-Central Siberia. *Journal of Archaeological Science* 36:694–707.
Grayson, Donald K.
1988 *Danger Cave, Last Supper Cave, and Hanging Rock Shelter: The Faunas*. Anthropological Papers of the American Museum of Natural History Vol. 66, Pt. 1. New York.
1993 *The Desert's Past: A Natural Prehistory of the Great Basin*. Smithsonian Institution Press, Washington, D.C.
Green, T. J., B. Cochran, T. W. Fenton, J. C. Woods, G. L. O. Titmus, L. Tieszen, M. A. Davis, and S. J. Miller
1998 The Buhl Burial: A Paleoindian Woman from Southern Idaho. *American Antiquity* 63:437–456.
Gruhn, Ruth
1965 Two Early Radiocarbon Dates from the Lower Levels of Wilson Butte Cave, South-Central Idaho. *Tebiwa* 8(2):57.
2006 *New Excavations at Wilson Butte Cave, South-Central Idaho*. Occasional Papers of the Idaho Museum of Natural History No. 38. Idaho Museum of Natural History, Pocatello.
Gruhn, Ruth, and Alan L. Bryan
1988 The 1987 Archaeological Fieldwork at Handprint Cave, Nevada. *Nevada Archaeologist* 6(2):1–13.
Hanes, Richard C.
1988 Early Cultural Traditions of the Owyhee Uplands as Seen from Dirty Shame Rockshelter. In *Early Human Occupation in Far Western North America: The Clovis–Archaic Interface*, edited by Judith A. Willig, C. Melvin Aikens, and John L. Fagan, pp. 361–372. Nevada State Museum Anthropological Papers No. 21. Carson City.
Haynes, C. Vance, Jr.
1967 Carbon-14 Dates and Early Man in the New World. In *Pleistocene Extinctions: The Search for a Cause*, edited by P. S. Martin and H. E. Wright, Jr., pp. 267–268. Yale University Press, New Haven.
1971 Time, Environment, and Early Man. *Arctic Anthropology* 8(2):3–14.
1992 Contributions of Radiocarbon Dating to the Geochronology of the Peopling of the New World. In *Radiocarbon Dating After Four Decades*, edited by R. F. Taylor, A. Long, and R. S. Kra, pp. 355–374. Springer-Verlag, New York.
2008 Younger Dryas "Black Mats" and the Rancholabrean Termination in North America. *Proceedings of the National Academy of Sciences* 105(18):6520–6525.
Haynes, Gary A.
2002 *Early Settlement of North America: The Clovis Era*. Cambridge University Press, Cambridge.
Haynes, Gary, David G. Anderson, C. Reid Ferring, Stuart J. Fiedel, Donald K. Grayson, C. Vance Haynes, Jr., Vance T. Holliday, Bruce B. Huckell, Marcel Kornfeld, David J. Meltzer, Julie Morrow, Todd Surovell, Nicole M. Waguespack, Peter Wigand, and Robert M. Yohe, II
2007 Comment on "Redefining the Age of Clovis: Implications for the Peopling of the Americas." *Science* 317:320b.
Hicks, Brent A.
2004 *Marmes Rockshelter, a Final Report on 11,000 Years of Cultural Use*. Washington State University Press, Pullman.
Hockett, Bryan
2007 Nutritional Ecology of Late Pleistocene to Middle Holocene Subsistence in the Great Basin: Zooarchaeological Evidence from Bonneville Estates Rockshelter. In *Paleoindian or Paleoarchaic? Great Basin Human Ecology at the Pleistocene–Holocene Transition*, edited by K. E. Graf and D. N. Schmitt, pp. 204–230. University of Utah Press, Salt Lake City.
Hockett, Bryan, Ted Goebel, and Kelly Graf
2008 The Early Peopling of the Great Basin. In *The Great Basin: People and Place in Ancient Times*, edited by Catherine S. Fowler and Don D. Fowler, pp. 61–68. SAR Press, Santa Fe, New Mexico.
Holmes, A. M., and G. A. Huckleberry
2009 Stratigraphy and Paleoenvironment. In *The Archaeology of the Eastern Nevada Paleoarchaic, Pt. I: The Sunshine Locality*, by C. Beck and G. Jones, pp. 67–76. University of Utah Anthropological Papers No. 126. Salt Lake City.
Huckleberry, G. A., C. Beck, G. T. Jones, A. M. Holmes, M. D. Cannon, S. D. Livingston, and J. M. Broughton
2001 Terminal Pleistocene/Early Holocene Environmental Change at the Sunshine Locality, North-Central Nevada, U.S.A. *Quaternary Research* 55:303–312.
Jenkins, Dennis L.
2007 Distribution and Dating of Cultural and Paleontological Remains at the Paisley Five Mile Point Caves in the Northern Great Basin: An Early Assessment. In *Paleoindian or Paleoarchaic? Great Basin Human Ecology at the Pleistocene–Holocene Transition*, edited by K. E. Graf and D. N. Schmitt, pp. 57–81. University of Utah Press, Salt Lake City.
Jenkins, Dennis L., Thomas J. Connolly, and C. Melvin Aikens
2004 Early and Middle Holocene Archaeology in the Northern Great Basin: Dynamic Natural and Cultural Ecologies. In *Early and Middle Holocene Archaeology of the Northern Great Basin*, edited by D. L. Jenkins, T. J. Connolly, and C. M. Aikens, pp. 1–20. University of Oregon Anthropological Papers, 62. Eugene.
Jenkins, Dennis L., Loren G. Davis, Thomas W. Stafford, Jr., Paula F. Campos, Bryan Hockett, George T. Jones, Linda Scott Cummings, Chad Yost, Thomas J. Connolly, Robert M. Yohe, II, Summer C. Gibbons, Maanasa Raghavan, Morten Rasmussen, Johanna L. A. Paijmans, Michael Hofreiter, Brian M. Kemp, Jodi Lynn Barta, Cara Monroe, M. Thomas P. Gilbert, and Eske Willerslev
2012 Clovis Age Western Stemmed Projectile Points and Human Coprolites at the Paisley Caves. *Science* 337:223–228.
Jones, G. T., and C. Beck
1999 Paleoarchaic Archaeology in the Great Basin. In *Models for the Millennium: Great Basin Anthropology Today*, edited by C. Beck, pp. 83–95. University of Utah Press, Salt Lake City.
2009 The Hamilton College Excavations, 1992–1997. In *The Archaeology of the Eastern Nevada Paleoarchaic, Pt. I: The Sunshine Locality*, by C. Beck and G. Jones, pp. 25–66. University of Utah Anthropological Papers No. 126. Salt Lake City.

Kohntopp, Steve W.
2010 *The Simon Clovis Cache: One of the Oldest Archaeological Sites in Idaho*. Center for the Study of the First Americans, Texas A&M University, College Station.

Mehringer, Peter J., Jr., and Franklin F. Foit, Jr.
1990 Volcanic Ash Dating of the Clovis Cache at East Wenatchee, Washington. *National Geographic Research* 6:495–503.

Meltzer, David J.
2009 *First Peoples in a New World*. University of California Press, Berkeley.

Morrow, J. E., and S. J. Fiedel
2006 New Radiocarbon Dates for the Clovis Component of the Anzick Site, Park County, Montana. In *Paleoindian Archaeology: A Hemispheric Perspective*, edited by J. E. Morrow and G. Gnecco, pp. 123–138. University Press of Florida, Tallahassee.

Murphey, Kelly
1985 Native American Settlement and Subsistence in Devil's Creek: Twin Falls and Owyhee Counties, Idaho. Unpublished Master's thesis, University of Idaho, Moscow.

O'Grady, P., S. P. Thomas, and M. F. Rondeau
2008 The Sage Hen Gap Fluted Point Site, Harney County, Oregon. *Current Research in the Pleistocene* 25:127–130.

Overstreet, D. F., and M. F. Kolb
2003 Geoarchaeological Contexts for Late Pleistocene Archaeological Sites with Human-Modified Woolly Mammoth Remains in Southeastern Wisconsin. *Geoarchaeology: An International Journal* 18(1):91–114.

Pendleton, Lorrane S.
1979 Lithic Technology in Early Nevada Assemblages. Unpublished Master's thesis, Department of Anthropology, California State University, Long Beach.

Pettitt, P. B., W. Davies, C. S. Gamble, and M. B. Richards
2003 Palaeolithic Radiocarbon Chronology: Quantifying Our Confidence Beyond Two Half-Lives. *Journal of Archaeological Science* 30:1685–1693.

Pinson, Ariane Oberling
2004 Of Lakeshores and Dry Basin Floors: A Regional Perspective on the Early Holocene Record of Environmental Change and Human Adaptation at the Tucker Site. In *Early and Middle Holocene Archaeology of the Northern Great Basin*, edited by D. L. Jenkins, T. J. Connolly, and C. M. Aikens, pp. 53–76. University of Oregon Anthropological Papers, 62. Eugene.

Reid, Kenneth C.
2011 Updating the Age of the Clovis Culture and Western Stemmed Tradition in Idaho. *IPAC News: The Newsletter of the Idaho Professional Archaeological Council* 4(1):24–38.

Rhode, D., T. Goebel, K. E. Graf, B. S. Hockett, K. T. Jones, D. B. Madsen, C. G. Oviatt, and D. N. Schmitt
2005 Latest Pleistocene–Early Holocene Human Occupation and Paleoenvironmental Change in the Bonneville Basin, Utah–Nevada. In *Interior Western United States*, edited by J. Pederson and C. M. Dehler, pp. 211–230. Geological Society of America Field Guide, 6. Boulder.

Rhode, D., and L. A. Louderback
2007 Dietary Plant Use in the Bonneville Basin During the Terminal Pleistocene/Early Holocene Transition. In *Paleoindian or Paleoarchaic? Great Basin Human Ecology at the Pleistocene–Holocene Transition*, edited by K. E. Graf and D. N. Schmitt, pp. 204–230. University of Utah Press, Salt Lake City.

Rice, David G.
1972 *The Windust Phase in Lower Snake River Region Prehistory*. Report of Investigations No. 50. Washington State University Laboratory of Anthropology, Pullman.

Rondeau, Michael F., Ted Goebel, and Mark B. Estes
2007 Fluted-Point Variability in the Central Great Basin. *Current Research in the Pleistocene* 24:138–141.

Sanders, Paul H.
1982 A Lithic Analysis of the Windust Phase Component, Hatwai Site (10NP143), Nez Perce County, Idaho. Unpublished Master's thesis, University of Wyoming, Laramie.

Sappington, R. L., and S. Schuknecht-McDaniel
2001 Wewukiyepuh (10-NP-336): Contributions of an Early Holocene Windust Phase Site to Lower Snake River Prehistory. *North American Archaeologist* 22(4):353–370.

Sargeant, Katheryne
1973 *Final Report on the Archaeology of the Redfish Overhang, 10-CR-121, Sawtooth National Forest, Custer County, Idaho*. Report on file at the Idaho State Historic Preservation Office, Boise.

Schiffer, Michael B.
1987 *Formation Processes of the Archaeological Record*. University of New Mexico Press, Albuquerque.

Sheppard, J. C., P. E. Wigand, C. E. Gustafson, and M. Rubin
1987 A Reevaluation of the Marmes Rockshelter Radiocarbon Chronology. *American Antiquity* 52(1):118–125.

Shutler, Richard, Jr.
1967 Archaeology of Tule Springs. In *Pleistocene Studies in Southern Nevada*, edited by H. M. Wormington and D. Ellis, pp. 297–303. Nevada State Museum Anthropological Papers No. 13. Carson City.

Stanford, Dennis, Robson Bonnichsen, Betty Meggers, and D. Gentry Steele
2005 Paleoamerican Origins: Models, Evidence, and Future Directions. In *Paleoamerican Origins: Beyond Clovis*, edited by R. Bonnichsen, B. T. Lepper, D. Stanford, and M. R. Waters, pp. 313–354. Center for the Study of the First Americans, Texas A&M University, College Station.

Stuiver, M., and Henry A. Polach
1977 Discussion: Reporting of ^{14}C Data. *Radiocarbon* 19(3):355–363.

Stuiver, M., and P. J. Reimer
1993 Extended ^{14}C Data Base and Revised CALIB 3.0 ^{14}C Age Calibration Program. *Radiocarbon* 35(1):215–230.

Swanson, Earl H., Jr.
1972 *Birch Creek: Human Ecology in the Cool Desert of the Northern Rocky Mountains 9000 BC–AD 1850*. Idaho State University Press, Pocatello.

Taylor, R. E.
2009 Six Decades of Radiocarbon Dating in New World Archaeology. *Radiocarbon* 51(1):173–212.

Thompson, R. S.
1985 The Age and Environment of the Mount Moriah (Lake Mohave) Occupation at Smith Creek Cave, Nevada. In *Environments and Extinctions: Man in Late Glacial North America*, edited by J. I. Mead and D. J. Meltzer, pp. 111–119. Center for the Study of Early Man, University of Maine, Orono.

Tuohy, D. R.
1988 Artifacts from the Northwestern Pyramid Lake Shoreline. In *Early Human Occupation in Far Western North America*,

edited by J. A. Willig, C. M. Aikens, and J. L. Fagan, pp. 201–216. Nevada State Museum Anthropological Papers No. 15. Carson City.

Tuohy, D. R., and A. J. Dansie
1997 New Information Regarding Early Holocene Manifestations in the Western Great Basin. *Nevada Historical Society Quarterly* 40:24–53.

Villa, Paola
1983 *Terra Amata and the Middle Pleistocene Archaeological Record of Southern France*. University of California Press, Berkeley.

Warren, Claude N., and Carl Phagan
1988 Fluted Points in the Mojave Desert: Their Technology and Cultural Context. In *Early Human Occupation in Far Western North America*, edited by J. A. Willig, C. M. Aikens, and J. L. Fagan, pp. 121–130. Nevada State Museum Anthropological Papers No. 15. Carson City.

Waters, Michael R.
1992 *Principles of Geoarchaeology: A North American Perspective*. University of Arizona Press, Tucson.

Waters, Michael R., Steven L. Forman, Thomas A. Jennings, Lee C. Nordt, Steven G. Driese, Joshua M. Feinberg, Joshua L. Keene, Jessi Halligan, Anna Lindquist, James Pierson, Charles T. Hallmark, Michael B. Collins, and James E. Wiederhold
2011a The Buttermilk Creek Complex and the Origins of Clovis at the Debra L. Friedkin Site, Texas. *Science* 331:1559–1603.

Waters, Michael R., Steven L. Forman, Thomas W. Stafford, Jr., and John Foss
2008 Geoarchaeological Investigations at the Topper and Big Pine Tree Sites, Allendale County, South Carolina. *Journal of Archaeological Science* 36:1300–1311.

Waters, Michael R., and Thomas W. Stafford, Jr.
2007 Redefining the Age of Clovis: Implications for the Peopling of the Americas. *Science* 315:1122–1126.

Waters, Michael R., Thomas W. Stafford, Jr., H. Gregory McDonald, Carl Gustafson, Morten Rasmussen, Enrico Cappellini, Jesper V. Olsen, Damian Szklarczyk, Lars Juhl Jensen, M. Thomas P. Gilbert, and Eske Willerslev
2011b Pre-Clovis Mastodon Hunting 13,800 Years Ago at the Manis Site, Washington. *Science* 334:351–353.

Willig, Judith A.
1988 Paleo-Archaic Adaptations and Lakeside Settlement Patterns in the Northern Alkali Basin, Oregon. In *Early Occupation in Far Western North America: The Clovis–Archaic Interface*, edited by J. A. Willig, C. M. Aikens, and J. L. Fagan, pp. 417–482. Nevada State Museum Anthropological Papers No. 21. Carson City.

Willig, Judith A., and C. Melvin Aikens
1988 The Clovis–Archaic Interface in Far Western North America. In *Early Occupation in Far Western North America: The Clovis–Archaic Interface*, edited by J. A. Willig, C. M. Aikens, and J. L. Fagan, pp. 1–40. Nevada State Museum Anthropological Papers No. 21. Carson City.

Wormington, H. M.
1957 *Ancient Man in North America*. Denver Museum of Natural History, Popular Series No. 4. Denver.

Yohe, R. M., II, and J. C. Woods
2002 *The First Idahoans: A Paleoindian Context for Idaho*. State Historic Preservation Office, Idaho State Historical Society, Boise.

6

Moving into the Mid-Holocene

The Paleoarchaic/Archaic Transition in the Intermountain West

George T. Jones and Charlotte Beck

In his 1978 survey of Great Basin archaeology, Aikens remarks that the "origins of the Great Basin Desert Culture have long been obscure" (1978:74). Thirty years of research focusing on terminal Pleistocene/early Holocene technology and adaptation has done much to correct this deficiency. From this work it is clear that many elements of the Desert Culture had beginnings in the Paleoarchaic and are ancient, just as Jennings (1957) had surmised from his stratigraphic investigations of Danger Cave. Yet subsequent cultural achievements, perhaps encompassing the crystallization of the Desert Culture, or Desert Archaic, as Jennings (1968) later referred to it, remain elusive.

The beginning of the Desert Archaic (or Early Archaic), broadly speaking, encompasses the latter part of the early Holocene and beginning of the middle Holocene, a period marked by significant climatic and environmental change. Since before the middle of the last century, archaeologists have given more than a little causal weight to climate change for cultural events in this period, and no event has been accorded more importance than the early–middle Holocene transition. Antevs (1948, 1955), to name a familiar proponent of climate–culture correlation, believed that middle Holocene warming was so severe as to make large sections of the province uninhabitable to humans. Contemporary researchers may not hold quite so strong a view as Antevs, but there is little doubt that the synchrony of environmental and cultural change at the early–middle Holocene transition is much more than coincidence (Grayson 2011).

There is no consensus among Great Basin archaeologists as to the precise timing of the Paleoarchaic–Archaic transition. In their 1986 surveys for the *Handbook of North American Indians*, Cressman (1986) and Elston (1986), for example, agree on an approximate age of 8000 rcy BP in the northern and western Great Basin, while Jennings (1986) and Aikens and Madsen (1986) place the transition in the eastern Great Basin a millennium earlier. Similarly, in his recent synthesis Simms (2008) suggests an approximate age of 8500 rcy BP for this boundary. Disagreements as to timing—if they can be called that—acknowledge, of course, that the evolution of cultural patterns was not contemporaneous everywhere but also that the timing of the appearance and the subsequent widespread use of diagnostic technologies are not equally well resolved in all parts of the province. Owing to the "thinness" of this record in some places, archaeologists continue to question if technologies such as milling tools and coiled basketry, which rise in frequency during the transition, represent fundamental reorganizations of Native lifeways or if they mark elaborations of economic trends toward subsistence diversification well under way during Paleoarchaic times. Moreover, the paucity of remains in some areas also leaves open the question as to the nature of demographic trends during the transitional period, including the possibility raised by Antevs (1948, 1955) that some sections of the province witnessed significant declines—even the extirpation—of human populations.

This chapter examines several lines of evidence relating to adaptive trends prior to and during the early–middle Holocene (EMH). As in most work that concerns the early cultural record of the Great Basin, our empirical focus will be on technologies of adaptation, and for methodological perspective we lean on precepts of human behavioral ecology. The chapter reviews three broad topics: early–middle Holocene environment, technology, and adaptive strategies. Before we take up these matters, however, we might first ask why the archaeological record of the EMH is less well known and what factors might account for the dearth of archaeological evidence.

An Absence of Data?

Does our limited understanding of the transition from the Paleoarchaic to the Early Archaic arise from a paucity of remains from this time? For many years, archaeologists have targeted rockshelters containing deeply stratified deposits for their potential to yield detailed sequences of cultural remains, and consequently, most radiocarbon assays of this age come from rockshelters (see the Appendix). Yet these excavations appear to have yielded fewer cultural sequences of EMH age than of earlier or later age (Jones and Beck 2012). Louderback et al. (2011) have made a careful study of the radiocarbon record in order to assess whether prehistoric population sizes shifted through time in three distinct regions of the Great Basin. Although the number of radiocarbon dates may not be a perfect population proxy (see discussions in Louderback et al. 2011), at a more basic level the record effectively expresses the frequency of buried cultural deposits of various ages. Louderback et al. find a substantial decline in radiocarbon dates beginning around 8000 rcy BP in each of the regions they studied.

These results suggest that disproportionately fewer sites of EMH age have been studied. This is apparently not due to a disinterest on the part of archaeologists but, rather, to the paucity of sites of this age. If EMH sites are indeed rare, we may ask if this reflects lower rates of site formation during that time period, presumably because of low population sizes, as Louderback et al. (2011) suggest, or if it relates to the inability of archaeologists to find these sites. As to the latter point, Eerkens et al. (2007) point out that a geomorphic bias may be at work. They note that during this period channel incision may be responsible for destruction of some cultural deposits and deep burial of others. One has only to gaze upon the many extensive Holocene alluvial fans in the Great Basin to wonder how deeply we need to excavate to expose early Holocene sites. It has been our experience in research in more northern sections of the Great Basin that mid-Holocene marker beds like the Mazama ash are often exposed well down in stratigraphic columns, suggesting that their deposition followed an interval of alluvial entrenchment, which left early and middle Holocene surfaces "out of view."

This situation contrasts sharply with the earlier Paleoarchaic record precisely because earlier folk sought out elevated landforms adjacent to, rather than in, active floodplains at which to carry out activities. It has been the accessibility of this surface record, in part, that has fueled a two-decade-long renaissance in Paleoarchaic research; indeed, the geographic coverage made possible by a rich surface record has enabled archaeologists to develop syntheses of broad distributional patterns such as stone tool conveyance (Jones et al. 2003; Jones et al. 2012; Smith 2010). Still, as Basgall (1993) points out, the Paleoarchaic record may, itself, present us with a biased view of early land use because of our inability to sample from terminal Pleistocene surfaces outside particular contexts and the tendency on the part of researchers to limit searches to those landforms where Paleoarchaic remains are expected. There are exceptions in the occasional open site, such as the Sunshine Locality in eastern Nevada (Beck and Jones 2009) and several sites at Ft. Irwin and China Lake in the central Mojave Desert (Basgall and Hall 1994; Hall 1993; Jenkins 1985), but these have thus far yielded only the rare primary depositional context.

Another possible explanation for a modest EMH record in some areas is substantive demographic change from the preceding period. We know that the northern half of the Great Basin was significantly warmer and drier by ca. 8300 rcy BP (Grayson 2000; Louderback and Rhode 2009), which reduced, or at least altered, the subsistence resource potential of many lowland areas, and these conditions may have been met with changes in the distribution of human populations (Grayson 2011; Louderback et al. 2011). In a related fashion, foragers may have adapted to changes in resources by substantially reorganizing settlement and subsistence, employing new modes of task organization and changing how social/economic units were deployed over landscapes (Elston and Zeanah 2002; Schmitt and Madsen 2005). As a result, if, as we suspect, people extended their subsistence to include more kinds of resource patches, they might have left far more ephemeral records that contain fewer artifacts of clear chronological-diagnostic value (Basgall and Delacorte 2006).

A third factor relates to the difficulty we have in identifying artifacts of diagnostic value for this period. The early Holocene projectile point chronology of many parts of the province has not received the same systematic attention from archaeologists as those of the preceding or subsequent periods. Consequently, we may not know if a small stemmed point or an oddly shaped notched point represents a transitional phase or comes from a later period.

A final issue concerns how we conceive of the transition. The Paleoarchaic and Early Archaic are generally distinguished in culture-historical summaries by attributes of technology and subsistence that are intended to emphasize difference as much as possible. Sometimes criticized as a normative view, this approach organizes chronological sequences using diagnostic traits and leaves the impression of abrupt changes between cultural periods. As a consequence, the Paleoarchaic–Archaic transition is sometimes represented as one of "adaptive discontinuity" (e.g., Pinson 2007); that is, viewed in this way the archaeological record appears to suggest major differences in diet breadth and diversity, stone tool technology, and settlement strategy between the Paleoarchaic and Early Archaic (see Simms 1988). The reality, however, may be that change was gradual and space- and time-transgressive, and most of the hallmarks of the Archaic (reduced mobility, expanded diet breadth, heavy reliance on seeds and other plant foods, simplification of the flaked-stone technology, and wide use of ground-stone tools) see their beginnings sometime before the EMH (Jones and Beck 2012). As useful as the terms *Paleoarchaic* and *Archaic* are, they obscure the gradual nature of change. For example, the Paleoarchaic, as defined primarily by technology—the Western Stemmed Tradition—is dated between ca. 11,000 rcy BP (or earlier) and ca. 7500–7000 rcy BP (Beck and Jones 1997, 2010). These dates relate to the persistence of projectile points of the Great Basin Stemmed Series. As will be discussed below, however, a number of new smaller stemmed forms appear during the early Holocene, including Pinto, along with several other lesser-known forms, which are considered to be neither Paleoarchaic nor Archaic, yet they occur during the latter part of the Paleoarchaic period. In addition, notched forms, which *are* considered Archaic, occur as early as 8500 rcy BP at Danger Cave (Jennings 1957) and even earlier on the Colorado Plateau (Janetski et al. 2012). With these thoughts in mind, we turn our attention to aspects of environment, technology, and adaptive strategy that constitute dimensions of the early–middle Holocene transition.

To accompany our discussions we have compiled a list of sites with radiocarbon dates between ca. 10,000 and 6000 rcy BP (Appendix). We note that many of these sites also have earlier components (Beck and Jones 1997), but only components relevant to the EMH are listed. Associated stratigraphic components are listed, but direct relationships between dates and material culture items cannot be assumed. Also included in the Appendix are associations with projectile points of the Great Basin Stemmed Series, other stemmed points (such as Pinto), Archaic notched points, and ground stone. Great Basin Stemmed Series points and ground stone are identified only as being present, while other stemmed and Archaic points are noted by type. Other types of artifacts, such as textiles and shell beads, are not included.

Environmental Setting

Modern Great Basin valleys are distinguished by biotic associations adapted to salty substrates and low moisture conditions. Surface waters tend to be localized in springs and seeps, and stream-supported wet prairies/marshes and lakes are less common. In contrast, under a cooler climate regime during the Younger Dryas, higher effective moisture induced lake transgressions in some valleys and the expansion of wetlands in nearly every valley. The largest of these lakes, like Lake Gilbert, persisted until about 10,000 rcy BP (Benson et al. 2011). Although warmer conditions followed lake recession, a moister-than-modern precipitation regime persisted until about 8500 ^{14}C BP and supported streams, springs, and extensive marshes in many valleys (e.g., Huckleberry et al. 2001; Oviatt et al. 2003; Quade et al. 1998; Wells et al. 2003). A significant interval of warming and drying followed, and the biotic changes at this time are believed by many archaeologists (see reviews in Grayson 2011; Simms 2008) to have significantly influenced human adaptations in the region.

In many sections of the Great Basin the early Holocene paleoenvironmental record is less well resolved than that of the terminal Pleistocene (but see Benson et al. 2002). Recent studies in the Bonneville Basin provide one of the most complete records of this time period (e.g., Louderback and Rhode 2009; Oviatt et al. 2003). With the recession of Lake Bonneville from the Gilbert level shortly before 10,000 rcy BP, large marshes formed at the termini of major rivers entering the basin, and smaller wetlands occurred at springs along the valley aprons. A large marsh formed where the Old River discharged into the Great Salt Lake Desert. Until about 8800 rcy BP, this wetland was fed by meandering distributaries and afforded a rich habitat for human exploitation (Madsen et al. 2005; Madsen et al. 2013). At Blue Lake, situated along the western edge of the Great Salt Lake Desert, the relative abundances of pollen of plants such as limber pine (*Pinus flexilis*) and big sagebrush (*Artemesia* sp.) were displaced by increases in Cheno-ams pollen soon after the drying of Lake Gilbert (Louderback and Rhode 2009). The expansion of a xeric shrub flora consisting of plants such as shad scale (*Atriplex*) and rabbitbrush (*Chrysothamnus* [Rhode and Madsen 1995; Wigand and Rhode 2002]) reflects both a warming trend and an expansion of the alkaline substrate on which these plants thrive. This warming trend, which may have begun rather abruptly (Madsen et al. 2005), corresponds to significant changes in animal taxa at Homestead Cave (Grayson 2000, 2002) and Camels Back Cave (Schmitt and Madsen 2005). In the highly resolved Homestead Cave sequence occurrences of several small mammal species with preferences for relatively cool and moist conditions drop significantly about 8300 rcy BP; some of these taxa were extirpated by 8000 rcy BP and were replaced by a xeric fauna (Grayson 2000).

Records from other parts of the Great Basin indicate that drying conditions probably began slightly earlier in the Mojave Desert section, between 9000 and 8600 rcy BP. Spaulding (1990) reports that succulent plant taxa, which make up about 50 percent of the macrofossils in wood rat middens prior to 9000 rcy BP, drop to just 10 percent of the macrofossil record during the next millennium. They are replaced by desert thermophiles, which dominate the modern flora. Farther to the north in the western Lahontan Basin, the upslope retreat of Utah juniper took place before 9500 rcy BP, and a transition to a more xeric lowland flora occurred between 9000 and 8000 rcy BP (Nowak et al. 1994a, 1994b). During the same period at Hidden Cave, also in the Lahontan Basin, a significant increase in greasewood pollen and other desert shrubs reflects the effects of regional desiccation (Wigand and Mehringer 1985; Wigand and Rhode 2002). Expansion of xeric plants begins by 8800 rcy BP in the northern Great Basin (Mehringer 1986).

Generally drier-than-modern conditions persisted throughout the Great Basin until 6000–5500 rcy BP (Wigand and Rhode 2002). Although the 8500–5500 rcy BP interval almost certainly was punctuated by periods of greater moisture, its arid aspect is indisputable. Of course, a warm, dry middle Holocene was the centerpiece of Antevs's (1955) Neothermal climate sequence, although his reconstruction favored a slightly different chronology. He argued that the initial phases of marked aridity began about 7500 rcy BP; the "Long Drought," or Altithermal period, that followed lasted until about 4000 rcy BP. We can appreciate that some of the disparity between Antevs's and contemporary climate sequences reflects the relative paucity of paleoenvironmental and radiocarbon records in Antevs's era. Nevertheless, Antevs's ideas influenced some Great Basin archaeologists trying to understand why the middle Holocene archaeological record was so much more ephemeral than records before and after this period (e.g., Baumhoff and Heizer 1965).

The Material Culture Record

Jennings (1957) observed that the twin markers of Desert Culture are the milling stone and the basket. As he suspected, both classes of artifacts were in use prior to the EMH, but their predominance in the material culture record becomes evident soon after 8500 rcy BP. In addition, several other classes of artifacts,

FIGURE 6.1. Examples of Paleoarchaic projectile points. The Haskett point is from the Old River Bed in the Bonneville Basin; others are from the Sunshine Locality in eastern Nevada.

both persistent and perishable, underwent changes. Among these changes was the disappearance of a suite of formal tools, including several projectile point types that distinguish Paleoarchaic technology. Following ca. 8500 rcy BP a new projectile point hafting technology, notching, became widespread. Last, there appear to have been shifts in patterns of lithic raw material use. We discuss each of these in turn.

Changes in Projectile Point Form

Several projectile point morphologies are characteristic of the Paleoarchaic, including both fluted and unfluted lanceolates and large stemmed forms (Figure 6.1; Beck and Jones 1997). The timing of the appearance of Clovis technology in the region and its technological affinities with stemmed points of the Western Stemmed Tradition are subjects of debate (e.g., Beck and Jones 2010, 2012; Fiedel and Morrow 2012; Goebel and Keene, this volume). Nevertheless, it is clear that Clovis points (in the strict morphological sense) were succeeded by at least one later fluted variant and one or more unfluted forms (Beck and Jones 2009, 2010; Bryan 1980, 1988). Fluting may not have persisted well beyond the terminal Pleistocene–early Holocene, but unfluted lanceolates are found commonly in Western Stemmed Tradition assemblages, and their use may persist as long as stemmed points.

The Great Basin Stemmed Series (GBSS [Tuohy and Layton 1977]) subsumes a number of distinct morphological types (Figure 6.1). With the exception of Silver Lake, all of these types are large and have parallel or slightly contracting stems of long to medium length; this morphology may have been designed for hafting in socketed rather than split foreshafts (Musil 1988; but see Galm and Gough 2008). Although they are referred to as "projectile points," their exclusive use as armatures is uncertain. Occurrences of abraded edge damage on many Cougar Mountain, Parman, Lake Mohave, and Silver Lake specimens in our

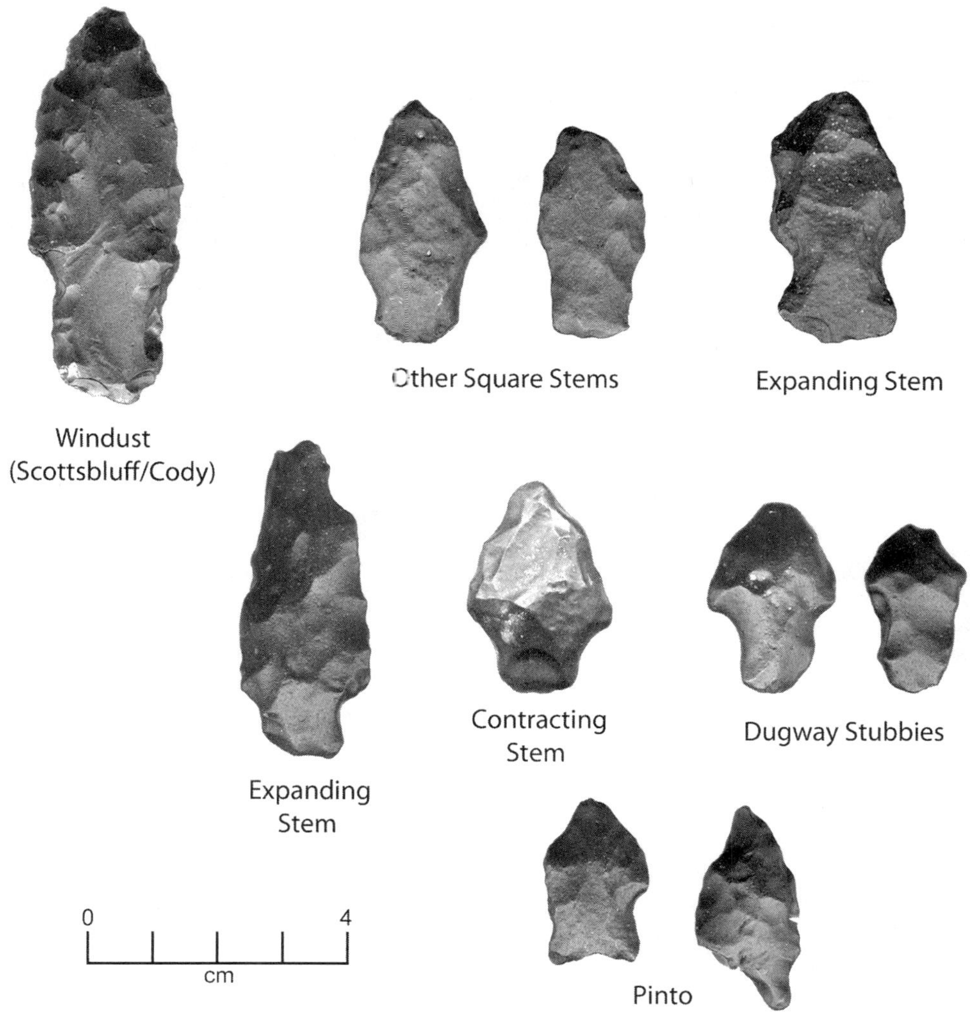

FIGURE 6.2. Examples of early Holocene stemmed points from the Old River Bed in the Bonneville Basin.

eastern Nevada research sample, for example, indicate that these points often performed cutting functions. On the other hand, Lafayette (2006) analyzed Cougar Mountain, Haskett, Parman, and Windust points from the northern Great Basin and suggests that all of these types were used frequently as projectiles as well as for other purposes. The differences in these results may be due to different material use in these areas or different dietary requirements, but this is difficult to know from the data at hand.

If a full understanding of the evolution of GBSS projectile points and their spatial distributions has not been achieved, technological developments across the EMH are even less securely known. But two important developments are notable. One is a significant reduction in the size of projectile points. The other is the appearance of notching.

Smaller stemmed morphologies begin to appear at least by 9000 rcy BP in most areas of the Great Basin (Appendix). Among these are points attributed to the Pinto series (Figure 6.2), which was originally identified in Mojave Desert assemblages (Amsden 1935; Campbell et al. 1937). Radiocarbon dates associated with Pinto points in this region fall across a range between 9800 and 6400 rcy BP (see the Appendix). The deep antiquity of some of these dates challenges traditional interpretations (see discussion of the Pinto controversy in Beck and Jones 2009:206–208), but Sutton et al. (2007) conclude that they are accurate, indicating that the Pinto Complex developed during the early Holocene and was a contemporary, at least for a time, of the Lake Mojave Complex. Sutton et al. (2007) remark that many of these points appear to have tipped thrusting spears.

Early Pinto points also are found in the east-central and eastern Great Basin, at the Sunshine Locality (Beck and Jones 2009) and the Butte Valley sites in eastern Nevada (Beck and Jones 1990), and at Danger Cave (Jennings 1957) and the Old River Bed (Beck and Jones 2013; Duke 2011; Schmitt et al. 2007) in western Utah (Figure 6.3). In addition to Pinto, several other short-stemmed types, including one similar to Windust, are present in these assemblages. These points are particularly prevalent in the Old River Bed assemblage and have been categorized as Square Stem, Expanding Stem, and Contracting Stem forms (Beck and Jones 2013; Figure 6.2).

In contrast to Sutton et al. (2007), Schmitt and Madsen (2005) suggest that the diminished size of Pinto and other contemporaneous forms may be an accommodation to a new

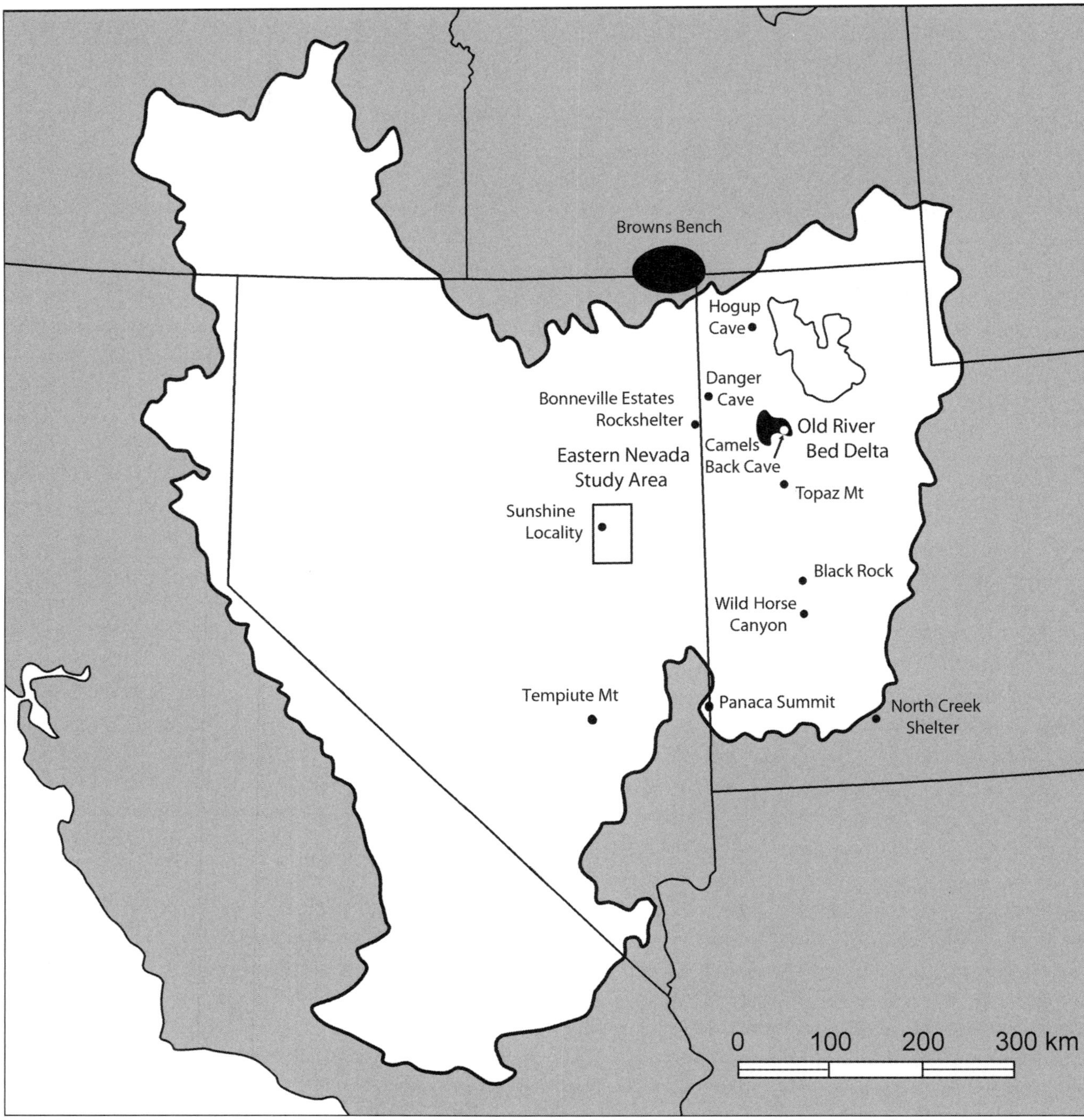

FIGURE 6.3. Locations discussed in the text.

propulsion technology, the atlatl, which, they argue, is an important technological advance over the javelin in accuracy and propulsive force (see also Hughes 1998). Although archaeologists debate whether concave-based points tipped atlatl darts, this argument is difficult to make for GBSS points because of their large size and, often, asymmetrical shape. Smaller, more symmetrical forms such as Pinto make better candidates for dart points. The earliest date for the atlatl in the Great Basin comes from one of the Nicolarsen caches in western Nevada that dates to 7980 ± 610 rcy BP (Hester 1974:2; see the Appendix), but the large standard deviation of this date makes it difficult to interpret. If the appearance of the atlatl did occur during the early Holocene, it would coincide with a peculiar feature of the subsistence record noted by several researchers (e.g., Hockett 2007; Pinson 2007)—that large game constituted a more significant component of the Early Archaic diet than of the Paleoarchaic. If Paleoarchaic hunters were limited to hand-propelled weapons, success in taking large prey may have been relatively modest. With the advent of atlatl and dart technology, however, return rates for artiodactyls may have been altered appreciably, resulting

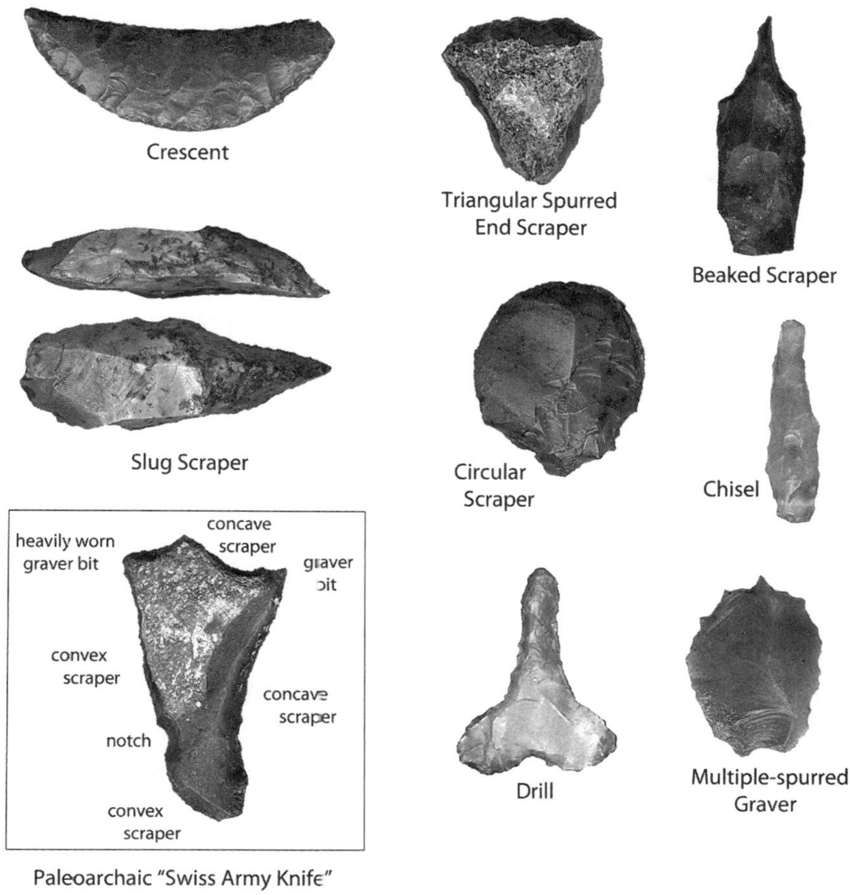

FIGURE 6.4. Other Paleoarchaic formal tools from the Old River Bed in the Bonneville Basin.

in their relative increase in the Early Archaic record. We discuss this further below.

The introduction of notching probably increased the effectiveness of this weapon system by providing a superior way of attaching a weapon tip (Hughes 1998). The timing of notching, however, varies considerably across the basin. The earliest record of this innovation in the region is in the Bonneville Basin, where both corner-notched and side-notched points are present at Danger Cave at ca. 8500 rcy BP (Jennings 1957). However, Janetski et al. (2012) report corner-notched points in ca. 9000 rcy BP deposits at North Creek Shelter in the south-central Utah section of the Colorado Plateau (Figure 6.3). In the northern Great Basin notching appears at least 1,000 years before the Mt. Mazama eruption, about 8000 rcy BP and possibly earlier (see Jenkins 2004; Appendix); GBSS points occur with foliate points until that time, and foliate points persist until ca. 6000 rcy BP (Jenkins et al. 2004). In the central, western, and southwestern Great Basin the appearance of notching is relatively late, ca. 5000 rcy BP (Sutton et al. 2007). Again, this could reflect decreased population densities at different times during the middle Holocene (e.g., Louderback et al. 2011) or another recovery bias.

This temporal gradient is evident in other technologies as well. In view of the long span of time entailed, it is difficult to explain this pattern as resulting simply from the slow pace of diffusion or from the resistance of some local populations to technological innovations. Again, this temporal patterning may reflect substantially lower populations in some areas with commensurately rare records or some other agent preventing our sampling from this time period.

Other Formal Tools

Crescents (Figure 6.4) occur in many, but certainly not all, assemblages containing GBSS projectile points. For example, 245 crescents were collected from the Sunshine Locality in Long Valley of eastern Nevada. In adjacent Butte Valley, by way of contrast, 10 Paleoarchaic sites yielded just three fragmentary specimens (Beck and Jones 2009). The contexts of the sites in both valleys are similar, but clearly, environmental association at this level of specificity is not sufficient to predict crescent occurrence. Although they are associated with few radiocarbon dates, they appear to span a period of at least 3,500 radiocarbon years, from nearly 11,000 rcy BP in the California Channel Islands (Erlandson et al. 2011) to ca. 8500 rcy BP at the C.W. Harris site in the Mojave Desert (Warren 1967). They are not found with Pinto or Windust points (except when these types co-occur with GBSS forms) and so were probably gone by the EMH transition.

Because their function remains elusive, whether other kinds of tools were substituted for crescents or their functions became extinct is not known.

Less well known are other components of Paleoarchaic lithic technology, although just like stemmed projectile points and crescents, they disappear by the close of the early Holocene. These tools—including end, side, circular, concave, and beaked scrapers; single- and multiple-spurred gravers; compass gravers; notches; chisels; and drills—mirror formal types known from Paleoindian assemblages elsewhere in North America (see, for example, Gramly 1990). Nearly always made from chert (Figure 6.4), these tools often occur in combination on the same artifact, representing multifunctional tools—the Swiss Army knives of the Paleoarchaic. Along with stemmed points and crescents, these diagnostic tools made up a mobile tool kit. The almost exclusive use of chert to make all but projectile points indicates efforts to optimize the durability of the tools and to permit their resharpening or recycling. At the Old River Bed (Figure 6.3), simplification of the flaked-stone technology appears to be under way well before 8500 rcy BP. Duke (2011) attributes these technological changes to diminished mobility and a corresponding shift in lithic procurement strategies. As we discuss below, the disappearance of the Paleoarchaic tool kit and substitution of more expediently manufactured alternatives coincide with changes in raw material selection patterns.

Raw Material Use for Flaked-Stone Tools

Basgall (1993) reports that in the Mojave Desert the patterns of lithic material selection of the Lake Mohave Complex carry over into the Pinto Complex. Among the notable features of these complexes is the considerable use of less tractable toolstones such as andesite for biface manufacture. This is a common pattern in Paleoarchaic assemblages in other sections of the Great Basin, especially in areas where sources of large nodular obsidian are uncommon. But in contrast to the Mojave Desert record, the early Holocene record of eastern Nevada and western Utah underwent shifts in material use patterns. Specifically, there was an increasing reliance on obsidian and chert and a decreasing use of fine-grained volcanic (FGV) toolstone. Eastern Nevada assemblages record much greater chert frequencies among early Holocene and Archaic projectile points.

The choice of raw material appears, in some part, then, to reflect where lithic sources occurred within foraging territories. The manufacture of GBSS points, however, placed constraints on which raw material sources could be used, regardless of quality, because cobbles of suitable size were required (Jones and Beck 1999). The shift to smaller weapon tips lifted this constraint. It meant that lithic sources of good quality but smaller package size were as viable as large-package sources. In addition, with the development of broader land-use practices, opportunities for use of upland lithic sources would have increased. All in all, access and package size limitations appear to have lessened, and with that, the emphasis on costly tool production diminished. As a result, tool production was more opportunistic, with less attention to the manufacture of standardized forms.

Ground Stone

One of Jennings's (1957) hallmarks of the Early Archaic is the use of ground stone, which he argues reflects the regular milling of small seeds. Dates for its earliest appearance vary across different sections of the province, and it is clear that in some areas ground stone constitutes a small component of late Paleoarchaic tool assemblages (Appendix). Ground stone in the form of mauls, handstones, and grinding slabs, for example, appears at the Tucker site in the northern Great Basin as early as 9400 rcy BP (Pinson 2008; Appendix). Milling stones and handstones "comprise a regular, if minimal constituent" of most Paleoarchaic Lake Mohave components in the Nelson Basin of the Mojave Desert (Basgall 1993:347; see also Sutton et al. 2007). This appears to be the case in the Coso Basin as well (e.g., Eerkens et al. 2007). By about 8500 rcy BP, ground-stone tools are represented in most regional records, and their use continues into the historic era.

In the Bonneville Basin, ground stone use most likely dates later than ca. 8750 rcy BP, when milling stones first appear at Danger Cave (Rhode et al. 2006); ground stone is present at Hogup Cave shortly thereafter (Aikens 1970). To the south at North Creek Shelter, just outside the Great Basin, ground stone occurs earlier than 9000 rcy BP (Yoder et al. 2010). We note that the earliest use of ground stone does not necessarily indicate seed grinding. This technology simply allows for the processing of resistant materials, whether or not they are food items. In some cases early ground stone is believed to have been used to process ochre (see, for example, Connolly and Jenkins 1999:125). In other early cases it may have been used to enhance the palatability of tough dried meat or plant foods. In fact, at Bonneville Estates Rockshelter, terminal Pleistocene strata contain examples of burnt and unburnt seeds of potential economic plants, which may provide evidence for seed consumption without an associated record of ground-stone tools (Rhode and Louderback 2007). This suggests that the increased investment in ground-stone technology during the EMH coincided not with the first use of tough plant foods, including seeds, but with an upsurge in their use as the availability of lower-cost alternative food types diminished.

Textiles

Tools woven from plant fibers along with hide and sinew artifacts have a long history of use in the Great Basin (Adovasio 1970, 1986; Connolly and Barker 2004; Cressman et al. 1942; Fowler and Hattori 2009). Textile artifacts produced by a twining construction technique, including sandals, bags, mats, and trays, have been recovered from dry rockshelters in the northern and western Great Basin in pre-9,000-year-old contexts (see reviews in Adovasio 1986; Beck and Jones 1997; Fowler and Hattori 2009). Although many textile artifacts are fragmentary and thus resist precise functional interpretation, the technology suggests a range of uses relating to processing, transport, and storage.

Important changes in textile manufacture appear to have occurred during the EMH transition. The coiling construction technique is unknown in Paleoarchaic contexts. It is represented along with new types of plant fibers in the earliest cultural stratum at Hogup Cave, which dates to about 8500 rcy BP (Aikens 1970). Adovasio draws a specific linkage between coiled baskets and the demands of emerging subsistence practices involving the "collection, parching, and consumption of chenopods and their floral allies" (1986:203). He notes that twined basketry is ill-suited to parching. The development of coiled construction techniques "would seem to reflect a functional necessity arising from a specialized economic adaptation predicated around the parching of very small seeds such as pickleweed" (Adovasio 1986: 203). Coiling was originally used to construct trays but was increasingly applied to bowl construction. Tightly woven coiled baskets can be caulked and made relatively watertight. As Madsen et al. (2005) argue, such vessels may have been used as water containers and for stone boiling, the latter an important adjunct for processing small seed foods.

Adaptive Strategies

The changes in material culture we have discussed can best be understood in the context of evolving patterns of subsistence, mobility, and land use that took place during the EMH period. These time- and spatially transgressive changes coincide with the long episode of warming climate that began after the end of the Younger Dryas and culminated in the hot and dry middle Holocene (Broughton et al. 2008). We examine these adaptive responses in the following section, selecting illustrations from the archaeological record of eastern Nevada and the Bonneville Basin where we have conducted field research.

Mobility and Land-Use Patterns

Mobility Patterns in Eastern Nevada

For most of the Paleoarchaic period groups of foragers traversed large subsistence territories (Jones et al. 2003; Smith 2010). Two kinds of evidence figure centrally in this interpretation. First, most assemblages contain stone tools obtained from distant geologic sources, often indicating conveyance across several hundred kilometers. Whether directly acquired or obtained via exchange, for example, between trading partners, exotic raw materials were never so common or from such distant sources in subsequent time periods. Second, the design of formal stone tools shows concern for reliability and portability. Individual artifacts often comprise more than one tool; many are made to be hafted, they tend to be large, and they often show evidence of resharpening. By contrast, the lithic record of the transitional period exhibits a simplified stone tool inventory, containing fewer standardized tool forms and comparatively lower representations of tools made of raw material from distant sources. Together these shifts suggest that EMH foragers were operating in more circumscribed territories, perhaps acting more logistically, as Elston and Zeanah (2002) and Schmitt and Madsen (2005) hypothesize. We return to this point shortly.

The obsidian and FGV provenance records in eastern Nevada represent more than 30 Paleoarchaic assemblages in four valleys. Patterns of source representation are quite uniform among these assemblages and indicate that tool material was conveyed from geologic sources as much as 250 km away (Estes 2009; Jones et al. 2003, Jones et al. 2012). Based on source representation and coordinated technological patterning we have hypothesized that exotic lithic materials circulated in a conveyance zone measuring roughly 500 × 200 km during the Paleoarchaic period. This zone, which was oriented on a north–south axis, was centered on the east-central section of the Great Basin. The precise behavioral correlate of this zone—whether it represents a foraging territory (Jones et al. 2003), overlapping territories of related groups (Jones et al. 2012; Madsen 2007), or a zone of exchange (Beck and Jones 2011; Newlander 2011a, 2011b)—is a matter of current debate. Nonetheless, the axis of material movements remains north–south until the early Holocene, when a shift in source representation took place that persisted through the early–middle Holocene transition (Jones et al. 2003). The representation of Browns Bench obsidian (Figure 6.3), a northern source that constitutes 60 percent of the GBSS projectile points in the assemblages studied, decreases by one-half among early Holocene and Archaic projectile points. Similarly, there is a substantial drop in the representation of Panaca Summit obsidian (Figure 6.3), formerly a dominant southern source. These deficits are made up by western Utah obsidian sources, particularly Topaz Mountain and Wild Horse Canyon (Figure 6.3). This shift represents a different axis of material conveyance.

It is not apparent that any of the Utah obsidians offered technological advantages that would explain their adoption. They neither knap better nor occur in larger package sizes. In fact, Topaz Mountain yields smaller cobbles than Browns Bench. Still, it seems unlikely that the use of either Browns Bench or Panaca Summit obsidian by Paleoarchaic folk was strictly dictated by a need for obsidian of sufficient nodule size, though for the manufacture of bifaces from which GBSS points were fashioned this must have been a consideration. This is because there were many FGV sources in the intervening areas that could be (and were) substituted for obsidian. Rather, the appearance of Utah obsidian is consistent with a change in movement patterns encompassing foraging destinations to the east. We suspect that this is a reflection of a geographic reconfiguration of populations, a response to diminished numbers and foraging potential of wetlands in the eastern Nevada region. As wetlands grew scarcer, alternative foraging destinations, such as the large, productive wetlands at the terminus of the Old River in the Bonneville Basin (see Beck and Jones 2013; Duke 2011; Madsen et al. 2013), may have attracted increasing numbers of foraging groups.

In addition to shifts in lithic source representation, the early Holocene assemblages of the eastern Nevada sample exhibit a decrease in source variety. This trend is suggestive but cannot be fully resolved since shifts in sample size may bear some influence on source representation. This trend in richness, nevertheless, is precisely what would be expected if the length of residence time shifted from brief site visits to longer spans of occupation. In a parallel fashion, the frequency of exotic raw materials declined, and local raw material sources grew more common. This shift is evident at Bonneville Estates Rockshelter (Figure 6.3), where, following a long span of disuse, occupation resumes in the middle Holocene. In contrast to terminal Pleistocene assemblages at the site, these later assemblages contain very few artifacts made from distant source material (Goebel 2007). At Camels Back Cave (Figure 6.3), where roughly contemporaneous middle Holocene assemblages are preserved, lithic assemblages contain few artifacts of distant obsidian. In contrast, early Holocene assemblages from the nearby Old River Bed (Figure 6.3) exhibit much higher frequencies of artifacts made from exotic toolstone. (See Duke 2011 for a discussion of variation across the early Holocene.)

These lines of evidence indicate a reorientation of EMH foragers to the lithic landscape. Decreasing frequencies of distant toolstone suggest a contraction of the territories over which foragers traveled. Changes in the relative frequencies of exotic source material imply shifts in the configurations of territories. Such trends in lithic conveyance are entirely consistent with shifting subsistence practices involving increased investment in procuring higher-cost subsistence items. To use a distinction favored by Bettinger (1991, 1999), the foragers of the EMH transition increasingly acted like "processors," leaving behind a "traveler" pose. As they invested more effort in recovering food energy from higher-cost sources, divisions of labor and logistical organization grew (Elston and Zeanah 2002). Foragers may not have grown less mobile in the absolute sense (Schmitt and Madsen 2005) but, rather, confined their moves to smaller territories, probably more fully exploiting the vertical landscape for subsistence opportunities (Simms 2008).

Land-Use Patterns in the Old River Bed Marsh

Until ca. 8800 rcy BP an extensive network of distributary channels emptied waters of the Old River into a vast wetland in the southeastern Great Salt Lake Basin (Figure 6.3; Madsen et al. 2013; Schmitt et al. 2007). During the early Holocene Paleoarchaic foragers moved into these wetlands along narrow fingers of alluvium left standing above ponds and deflating mudflats. They left behind a considerable stone tool record containing many projectile points and some formal, but many more opportunistically fashioned, tools (Beck and Jones 2013; Duke 2011; Duke and Young 2007). Precisely what food sources were sought by these foragers is unknown, although they probably included a mix of fish, birds, mollusks, and mammals as well as plants such as cattail and bulrush. Even plants with small seeds may have been harvested, although there is no milling equipment in the record to suggest such a focus. After ca. 8800 rcy BP the Old River Bed marshes were gone, and so too were its human occupants. While the desiccation of the Old River Bed marshes was the single greatest loss of wetland habitat in the eastern Great Basin, this pattern of desertification seems to have played out in many other valleys and basins. In Long Valley, for instance, the stream system supporting Sunshine Wash shifted from perennial to ephemeral conditions before ca. 8500 rcy BP (Holmes and Huckleberry 2009; Huckleberry et al. 2001). The final occupation phase at Sunshine Wash was coterminous with the formation of marls and peats, indicating ponded water of varying depths. This is succeeded by a pattern of periodic stream flow and sheet flood deposition and by a shift in land-use patterns away from Sunshine Wash. Similarly, the Ruby marshes may have contained a deep lake until about 8000 rcy BP, but higher frequencies of desert shrub pollen indicate a strong drying trend following that time (Thompson 1992). As stated earlier, we suspect that a reorganization of lithic conveyance across parts of the eastern Great Basin was brought about as a result of the growing importance of the Old River Bed as a subsistence destination, which supplanted other wetland resource areas as their productivity diminished in the wake of early Holocene drying and biotic reorganization.

The sheer scale of the Old River Bed archaeological record is certainly noteworthy, but it exhibits other distinctive features that shed light on shifts in land-use patterns at the close of the Paleoarchaic period. We briefly consider two of these characteristics: the diminutive nature of much of the tool assemblage and the high levels of expedient tool manufacture. Arkush and Pitblado (2000) were the first to draw attention to the unusually high frequencies of small, often recycled stone tools in the Old River Bed assemblages. They argue that Old River Bed occupants were inadequately provisioned with toolstone, staying in the marshes for longer periods than they had planned for. Thus, as toolstone supplies were depleted, they increasingly recycled exhausted tools, many scavenged from scatters left by earlier visitors to the marshes. Such behavior unquestionably accounts for the high levels of reuse and repurposing of tools, particularly projectile points. Within this class of tools the largest fraction are small projectile points, some looking like small versions of GBSS types. There are unique morphologies as well, such as the Dugway Stubby (see Figure 6.2), so named for its small size and abbreviated blade segment. Like other small projectile points, Stubbies were typically made from recycled bifacial tools and occasionally from modified flakes. Some are quite delicately flaked, having been made on thin bifacial preforms. But most necessitated accommodating the morphology of the recycled object, including its original flaking pattern and broken facets, which were the likely reason for the discard of the original tool.

A more complete look at the Old River Bed record (Beck and Jones 2013; Duke 2011) shows that many assemblages are made up of artifacts that compare favorably with Paleoarchaic technology across the wider region. That is, they contain large projectile points and other formal tools, often made from exotic obsidian. They exhibit the hallmarks of a mobile tool kit, designed with attention to long use lives and multipurpose usage (Duke and Young 2007). In this sense, the Old River Bed was one of many stops across a large subsistence territory. A significant share of the assemblages, however, notably those dating to the latest phase of occupation, reflect a different set of design priorities (Duke 2011). In these assemblages a far greater share of tools are made on small flake blanks, using lithic materials of poorer quality. Duke (2011) suggests that these assemblages reflect more targeted and predictable subsistence activities. Rather than designing for multiple eventualities, the Old River Bed foragers knew what resources they would be harvesting and fine-tuned their lithic tool inventory to meet these goals. Curiously, this does not mean that Old River Bed foragers assembled tools of particular design. Rather, they maximized the quantities of raw material taken into the marshes, provisioning their foraging locales with numerous small flakes rather than cores. These tools were equally capable as cutting edges or for additional shaping.

Summary

The evidence for changes in technology and patterns of raw material selection indicates that Paleoarchaic foragers grew less mobile as the early Holocene advanced. These changes parallel shifts toward more diversified subsistence practices, which we believe have been properly attributed to the reduction in both the number and the quality of wetlands where the majority of subsistence activities took place. Very soon after the desiccation of the Old River Bed marshes, rockshelters in the Bonneville Basin record important shifts in subsistence practices. At Danger Cave, for example, milling tools and substantial quantities of iodine bush (*Allenrolfea occidentalis*) chaff co-occur in deposits dating to ca. 8600 rcy BP (Rhode et al. 2006). This association coincides with the expansion of dry-loving, salt-tolerant plants over the valley floor. But it would be a mistake to assume that the use of iodine bush seeds and other plant resources was because of their greater abundance or higher productivity. In fact, experimental harvesting and processing of its small seeds indicate that iodine bush is no great shakes as a food resource (Simms 1987). Rather, its prevalence in the Danger and Hogup cave records shows just how uncommon better food alternatives had become in the area. Indeed, this pattern is evident throughout the Great Basin. These effects were not felt equally in every sector of the province or at precisely the same time. Nevertheless, the cumulative effect of EMH environmental change throughout the province was to alter the balance between sources of food energy and human foragers.

Subsistence Change

Although sporadically represented in Paleoarchaic records in various parts of the Great Basin, ground-stone tools become common elements of artifact assemblages after the early–middle Holocene transition (Appendix). Ground-stone tools recovered in Paleoarchaic contexts often appear to have been made more expediently and used less intensively, although at North Creek Shelter, just outside the Great Basin (Figure 6.3), intensive use of formal ground stone begins by at least 9000 rcy BP (Yoder et al. 2010). The growth in the numbers and kinds of ground-stone tools has been interpreted as marking a substantial shift toward the use of vegetal foods, particularly hard seeds, which archaeologists have explained as relating to a downturn in the efficiency of using preferred food types when their abundance diminished in response to the growing dryness of the EMH transition.

There seems to be little dispute about these facts. But a question remains: Among the food types preferred by Paleoarchaic foragers, which grew less common? Most probably all grew rarer, but the general consensus suggests that hunting, especially of larger game such as antelope, mountain sheep, and deer, grew less successful (e.g., Elston and Zeanah 2002). Yet it is a curious fact that artiodactyls are poorly represented in terminal Pleistocene/early Holocene faunas. In fact, as Schmitt and Madsen (2005:237) point out, there is little evidence that Paleoarchaic foragers depended heavily on any high-ranked resources. As noted earlier, both Pinson (2007) and Hockett (2007) argue that artiodactyl use increases *after* ca. 8000 rcy BP. The association of Paleoarchaic sites with wetlands strongly suggests that subsistence resources were derived from these settings (Grayson 2011). Yet, as Schmitt and Madsen (2005:237) also point out, marsh resources generally have low to medium return rates. The importance of these settings, they argue, is that so many different kinds of resources occur in close proximity, certainly lessening the costs of searching for them.

Then how do we reconcile the abundant artifact record of hunting with the dearth of large game in the Paleoarchaic faunal record? The traditional model of terminal Pleistocene occupation in the Great Basin identifies the first occupants as Clovis, and Clovis hunting is still believed by many to have focused on large game for the reasons explored by Kelly and Todd (1988; but see Cannon and Meltzer 2004). The scenario continues that the Western Stemmed Tradition grew out of Clovis, and although their diet broadened to include some marsh resources, hunting was still focused on large game. Therefore, terminal Pleistocene/early Holocene lithic assemblages were assumed to reflect the hunting and processing of large animals. Regardless of the status of the Clovis-to-Western Stemmed scenario (e.g., Beck and Jones 2010), the evidence does not support Paleoarchaic dependence on large game. The Paleoarchaic faunal remains from sites across the Great Basin do, in fact, contain artiodactyls, but they also contain rabbits, jackrabbits, sage grouse, small rodents, mollusks, fish, and lizards (Beck and Jones 1997; Grayson 2011). In fact, there is evidence that mass-capture techniques for the taking of small animals such as jackrabbits were already being used in the northern Great Basin by ca. 9000–8500 rcy BP (Oetting 1994).

At this point Paleoarchaic hunting strategies are still poorly understood. The non–projectile point component of these assemblages that reflects hunting mirrors that of other Paleoindian assemblages across the continent, but the projectile point component does not. As discussed earlier, there is some doubt that the large stemmed points associated with the Western Stemmed Tradition were used exclusively as projectile points. It is just as likely that concave-based points, and subsequently early small stemmed points such as Pinto, served this purpose.

Regarding the Paleoarchaic artiodactyl record, however, we return to those patterns noted by Pinson (2007) and Hockett (2007), that use of these animals was lowest during the Paleoarchaic and increased sometime after 8000 rcy BP. Byers and Broughton (2004) have noted that in making the assumption that Paleoarchaic foragers depended heavily upon large game, archaeologists have not paid careful attention to the actual variation in the size of artiodactyl populations across the Holocene, despite using shifts in their abundances at archaeological sites to develop interpretations. Based on their analysis of several well-resolved faunal sequences from the Bonneville Basin, Byers and Broughton argue that the number of artiodactyls was much higher in the late Holocene (post-4000 rcy BP) than in preceding periods, dating back to ca. 9500 rcy BP.

They extend this analysis in more recent work (e.g., Broughton et al. 2008; Broughton et al. 2011) to illuminate these relationships for the EMH transition. Artiodactyl population sizes, generally speaking, are sensitive to the quality of forage and the availability of water (see references in Byers and Broughton 2004). To the degree that both factors are highly correlated with effective precipitation, a decreasing trend in moisture through the early Holocene and especially after the EMH transition would be expected to significantly decrease herd sizes and consequently decrease foraging efficiency (by increasing the costs associated with finding prey) as it relates to these taxa. Byers and Broughton argue that until the late Holocene, artiodactyls were rarely taken despite ranking highly among subsistence alternatives, and this apparent paradox probably relates to their paucity even during the moister terminal Pleistocene and early Holocene (Broughton et al. 2008). Small population sizes, Broughton et al. (2008) argue, are a consequence of a pattern of heightened seasonality that sets in during the terminal Pleistocene. From an equable regime during the late glacial marked by cooler, moister but less extreme summer and winter conditions, a pattern of winter precipitation and summer drought intensified in the Younger Dryas and lasted into the middle Holocene.

So, it remains a puzzle as to why Paleoarchaic lithic assemblages suggest a strong hunting focus, while Pinson's (2007) and Hockett's (2007) analyses of the faunal record indicate stronger evidence of hunting after the EMH transition. As to the first point, the answer may be quite simple. First, because hunting technologies contain elements made from durable stone, they can be expected to be better represented than such artifacts as netting and woven articles that do not preserve as well. Further, the processes of subtractive knapping used to make hunting implements will accentuate the hunting signal relative to other modes of subsistence. Second, hunted game always ranks among the most efficient sources of food energy. Thus, for foragers who make regular moves between subsistence patches and, consequently, are in a position to actively or passively search for large animals, it is an expectable practice to have equipment ready for their capture. And so, even while large game apparently was not the principal focus of Paleoarchaic subsistence, Paleoarchaic foragers were always ready to pursue such resources.

On the second point we return to the observations of several researchers that the atlatl and dart may not have constituted an important weapon technology until the latter part of the early Holocene. The advantages usually ascribed to this delivery system—greater propulsive force and penetrating capability and great accuracy at a distance—would not necessarily enhance capture efficiency at close quarters, as, for example, when taking fish or small mammals in a marsh. A leister might be optimal for fishing or procuring muskrats, while a well-aimed throwing-stick might achieve better results than a dart or spear in rabbit or hare hunting. The atlatl and dart, however, are likely to have enhanced capture efficiency when applied to artiodactyls, especially in circumstances aided by blinds or natural features that provided hunters with cover. These sorts of subsistence forays are more easily envisioned as part of expeditions into upland areas and as part of a general diversifying pattern of patch and resource use in motion at the early–middle Holocene transition.

Summary and Conclusions

The Paleoarchaic/Desert Archaic transition in the Great Basin coincides with important shifts in resource structure brought on by increasingly warm and dry climatic conditions. This episode is conventionally placed at between 8500 and 8000 rcy BP, although encompassed within the transition are technological and organizational changes under way in some parts of the province at least a millennium earlier. While mesic conditions prevailed, foragers focused on a suite of animal and plant resources associated with shallow water habitats. With the expansion of Holocene plants and animal associations and the diminished productivity of wetlands, foragers began to use a wider set of food resources. These circumstances favored the adoption or intensification of technologies that increased the efficiency of the capture, processing, and transport of lower-ranking food resources.

Evidence of adaptive changes during this interval includes changes in lithic tool assemblages. For example, local sources of stone material came to replace more distant sources in tool inventories, suggesting a reduction in the size of foraging ranges, increased residence time, and reconfigurations of territory. Many components of technology, such as ground stone, atlatl and dart weapons, and some woven tools, which appear well before the end of the Paleoarchaic period, point to an expanding diet breadth. With the numbers and quality of wetlands on the wane, Great Basin foragers shifted effort into procuring a wider range of food items and relying less on extensive mobility practices. The efficient capture, storage, and consumption of these resources required investment in weaving and milling technologies, probably at the expense of flaked-stone technology.

In summary, the Paleoarchaic/Early Archaic transition was part of a long process of adaptive change reflecting adjustments by humans to environmental change, technological innovation, and population fluctuations. The early–middle Holocene saw the use of a broader array of food resources with attending shifts to longer in-patch residence time, reduced mobility ranges, increasing use of mass-capture techniques, tool caching in rockshelters, and probably realigned divisions of labor. These innovations were adopted across the region, coalescing to form the Desert Archaic.

References Cited

Adovasio, James M

1970 Textiles. In *Hogup Cave*, by C. Melvin Aikens, pp. 133–153. University of Utah Anthropological Papers No. 93. Salt Lake City.

1986 Prehistoric Basketry. In *Great Basin*, edited by Warren L. d'Azevedo, pp. 194–205. Handbook of North American Indians, Vol. 11, Smithsonian Institution Press, Washington, D.C.

Aikens, C. Melvin

1970 *Hogup Cave*. University of Utah Anthropological Papers, 93. Salt Lake City.

1978 Archaeology of the Great Basin. In *Annual Review of Anthropology*, edited by B. J. Siegel, pp. 71–87. Annual Reviews, Inc., Palo Alto.

Aikens, C. M., D. L. Cole, and Robert Stuckenrath

1977 *Excavations at Dirty Shame Rockshelter, Southeastern Oregon*. Tebiwa Miscellaneous Papers No. 4. Pocatello.

Aikens, C. Melvin, and David B. Madsen

1986 Prehistory of the Eastern Area. In *Handbook of North American Indians, Vol. 11: Great Basin*, edited by Warren L. d'Azevedo, pp. 149–160. Smithsonian Institution, Washington, D.C.

Amsden, Charles A.

1935 The Pinto Basin Artifacts. In *The Pinto Basin Site*, by Elizabeth W. C. Campbell and William H. Campbell, pp. 33–51. Southwest Museum Papers No. 9. Los Angeles.

Antevs, Ernst

1948 Climate Changes and Pre-White Man. In "The Great Basin, with Emphasis on Glacial and Postglacial Times," *Bulletin of the University of Utah* 38(20):167–191.

1955 Geologic-Climatic Dating in the West. *American Antiquity* 20:317–335.

Arkush, B. S., and B. L. Pitblado

2000 Paleoarchaic Surface Assemblages in the Great Salt Lake Desert, Northwestern Utah. *Journal of California and Great Basin Anthropology* 22:12–42.

Arnold, J. R., and W. F. Libby

1950 *Radiocarbon Dates (September 1, 1950)*. Institute for Nuclear Studies, University of Chicago, Chicago.

Basgall, Mark E.

1993 Early Holocene Prehistory of the North-Central Mojave Desert. Unpublished Ph.D. dissertation, Department of Anthropology, University of California, Davis.

2003 *Further Archaeological Assessments in Deadman Lake Basin, Marine Corps Air Ground Combat Center, Twentynine Palms, California*. Report submitted to the Department of the Army Corps of Engineers, Sacramento.

Basgall, Mark E., and Michael G. Delacorte

2006 Trends in Occupational Intensity Across the Southwestern Great Basin over the Holocene: The Obsidian Hydration Evidence. Paper presented at the 30th Great Basin Anthropological Conference, Las Vegas.

Basgall, Mark E., and Mark A. Giambastiani

2000 *An Archaeological Evaluation of 13 Locations in the Deadman Basin, Marine Corps Ground Combat Center, Twentynine Palms, California*. Report submitted to the Department of the Army, Corps of Engineers, Los Angeles.

Basgall, Mark E., and M. C. Hall

1993 *Archaeology of the Awl Site, CA-SBR-4562, Fort Irwin, San Bernadino County, California*. Report prepared for the U.S. Army Corps of Engineers, Los Angeles District. Far Western Anthropological Research Group, Davis.

1994 *Archaeological Investigations at Golstone (CA-SBR-2348): A Middle Holocene Occupation Complex in the North-Central Mojave Desert, California*. Report submitted to the Department of the Army, National Training Center, Fort Irwin, California.

Basgall, Mark E. and D. M. Jurich

2006 Archaeological Investigations at Nine Prehistoric Sites in the Emerson Lake Training Area, Marine Corps Air Ground Combat Center, Twentynine Palms, California. ARC Technical Report 05-100. Submitted to U. S. Marine Corps, Twentynine Palms.

Basgall, Mark E., and W. Pierce

2004 *Archaeological Assessment of Four Prehistoric Sites in the Acorn Training Area, Marine Corps Air Ground Combat Center, Twentynine Palms, California*. Report submitted to the Department of the Army, Corps of Engineers, Fort Worth.

Baumhoff, Martin A., and Robert F. Heizer

1965 Postglacial Climate and Archaeology of the Desert West. In *The Quaternary of the United States*, edited by Henry E. Wright, Jr., and D. G. Frey, pp. 697–708. Princeton University Press, Princeton.

Beck, Charlotte, and George T. Jones

1990 Late Pleistocene/Early Holocene Occupation in Butte Valley, Eastern Nevada. *Journal of California and Great Basin Anthropology* 12:231–261.

1997 The Terminal Pleistocene/Early Holocene Archaeology of the Great Basin. *Journal of World Prehistory* 11:161–235.

2009 *The Archaeology of the Eastern Nevada Paleoarchaic, Pt. 1: The Sunshine Locality*. With contributions by G. Huckleberry, M. Cannon, A. Holmes, S. Livingston, J. Broughton, D. Tuohy, P. Hutchinson, G. Noyes, and A. Dansie. University of Utah Anthropology Papers No. 126. University of Utah Press, Salt Lake City.

2010 Clovis and Western Stemmed: Population Migration and the Meeting of Two Technologies in the Intermountain West. *American Antiquity* 75:81–116.

2011 The Role of Mobility and Exchange in the Conveyance of Toolstone During the Great Basin Paleoarchaic. In *Perspectives on Prehistoric Trade and Exchange in California and the Great Basin*, edited by Richard E. Hughes, pp. 55–82. University of Utah Press, Salt Lake City.

2012 Clovis and Western Stemmed Again: Reply to Fiedel and Morrow. *American Antiquity* 77:386–397.

2013 Artifact Analysis. In *The Paleoarchaic Occupation of the Old River Bed Delta*, by David B. Madsen, Dave Schmitt, and David Page, with contributions by Charlotte Beck, Daron Duke, George T. Jones, Lisbeth Louderback, Charles G. Oviatt, David Rhode, and D. Craig Young, in preparation.

Bedwell, Stephen E.

1973 *Fort Rock Basin: Prehistory and Environment*. University of Oregon Books, Eugene.

Bedwell, Stephen E., and Luther S. Cressman

1971 Fort Rock Report: Prehistory and Environment of the Pluvial Fort Rock Area of South-Central Oregon. In *Great Basin Anthropological Conference 1970: Selected Papers*, edited by C. Melvin Aikens, pp. 1–26. University of Oregon Anthropological Papers No. 1. Eugene.

Benson, L., M. Kashgarian, R. Rye, S. Lund, F. Paillet, J. Smoot, C. Kester, S. Mensing, D. Meko, and S. Lindstrom

2002 Holocene Multidecadal and Multicentennial Droughts Affecting Northern California and Nevada. *Quaternary Science Reviews* 21:659–682.

Benson, L. V., S. P. Lund, J. P. Smoot, D. E. Rhode, R. J. Spencer, K. L. Verosub, L. A. Louderback, C. A. Johnson, R. O. Rye, and R. M. Negrini

2011 The Rise and Fall of Lake Bonneville Between 45 and 10.5 ka. *Quaternary International* 235:57–69.

Bettinger, Robert L.

1991 *Hunter-Gatherers. Archaeological and Evolutionary Theory*. Plenum Press, New York.

1999 What Happened in the Medithermal? In *Models for the Millennium: Great Basin Anthropology Today*, edited by Charlotte Beck, pp. 62–74. University of Utah Press, Salt Lake City.

Broughton, Jack M., David A. Byers, Reid A. Bryson, William Eckerle, and David B. Madsen

2008 Did Climatic Seasonality Control Late Quaternary Artiodactyl Densities in Western North America? *Quaternary Science Reviews* 27:1916–1937.

Broughton, Jack M., Michael D. Cannon, Frank E. Bayham, and David A. Byers

2011 Prey Body Size and Ranking in Zooarchaeology: Theory, Empirical Evidence, and Applications from the Northern Great Basin. *American Antiquity* 76:403–428.

Bryan, Alan L.

1980 The Stemmed Point Tradition: An Early Technological Tradition in Western North America. In *Anthropological Papers in Memory of Earl H. Swanson, Jr.*, edited by L. B. Harten, Claude N. Warren, and Donald R. Tuohy, pp. 77–107. Special Publication of the Idaho State Museum of Natural History, Pocatello.

1988 The Relationship of the Stemmed Point and Fluted Point Traditions in the Great Basin. In *Early Human Occupation in Far Western North America: The Clovis–Archaic Interface*, edited by Judith A. Willig, C. Melvin Aikens, and John L. Fagan, pp. 53–74. Nevada State Museum Anthropological Papers No. 21. Carson City.

Byers, David A., and Jack M. Broughton

2004 Holocene Environmental Change, Artiodactyl Abundances, and Human Hunting Strategies in the Great Basin. *American Antiquity* 69:235–255.

Campbell, Elizabeth W. C., W. H. Campbell, Ernst Antevs, Charles A. Amsden, J. A. Barbieri, and F. D. Bode

1937 *The Archaeology of Pleistocene Lake Mohave: A Symposium*. Southwest Museum Papers, 11. Los Angeles.

Cannon, Michael D., and David J. Meltzer

2004 Early Paleoindian Foraging: Examining the Faunal Evidence for Large Mammal Specialization and Regional Variability in Prey Choice. *Quaternary Science Reviews* 23:1955–1987.

Connolly, Thomas J., and Pat Barker

2004 Basketry Chronology of the Early Holocene in the Northern Great Basin. In *Early and Middle Holocene Archaeology of the Northern Great Basin*, edited by Dennis L. Jenkins, Thomas J. Connolly, and C. Melvin Aikens, pp. 241–250. University of Oregon Anthropological Papers, 62. Eugene.

Connolly, Thomas J., and Dennis L. Jenkins

1999 *Newberry Crater. A Ten-Thousand-Year Record of Human Occupation and Environmental Change in the Basin–Plateau Borderlands*. University of Utah Anthropological Papers No. 121. Salt Lake City.

Cressman, Luther S.

1986 Prehistory of the Northern Area. In *Handbook of North American Indians, Vol. 11: Great Basin*, edited by Warren L. d'Azevedo, pp. 120–126. Smithsonian Institution, Washington, D.C.

Cressman, Luther S., F. C. Baker, Henry P. Hansen, P. Conger, and Robert F. Heizer

1942 *Archaeological Researches in the Northern Great Basin*. Carnegie Institution of Washington Publications, 538. Washington, D.C.

Douglas, Charles L., Dennis L. Jenkins, and Claude N. Warren

1988 Spatial and Temporal Variability in Faunal Remains from Four Lake Mojave–Pinto Period Sites in the Mojave Desert. In *Early Human Occupation in Far Western North America: The Clovis–Archaic Interface*, edited by Judith A. Willig, C. Melvin Aikens, and John L. Fagan, pp. 273–301. Anthropology Papers, 21. Nevada State Museum, Carson City.

Duke, Daron

2011 If the Desert Blooms: A Technological Perspective on Paleoindian Ecology in the Great Basin from the Old River Bed, Utah. Unpublished Ph.D. dissertation, Department of Anthropology, University of Nevada, Reno.

Duke, Daron, and D. Craig Young

2007 Episodic Permanence in Paleoarchaic Basin and Settlement. In *Paleoindian or Paleoarchaic? Great Basin Human Ecology at the Pleistocene–Holocene Transition*, edited by Kelly E. Graf and Dave N. Schmitt, pp. 123–138. University of Utah Press, Salt Lake City.

Eerkens, Jelmer W., Jeffrey S. Rosenthal, D. Craig Young, and Jay King

2007 Early Holocene Landscape Archaeology in the Coso Basin, Northwestern Mojave Desert, California. *North American Archaeologist* 28:87–112.

Elston, Robert B.

1986 Prehistory of the Western Area. In *Handbook of North American Indians, Vol. 11: Great Basin*, edited by Warren L. d'Azevedo, pp. 135–148. Smithsonian Institution, Washington, D.C.

Elston, Robert G., and David W. Zeanah
2002 Thinking Outside the Box: A New Perspective on Diet Breadth and Sexual Division of Labor in the Prearchaic Great Basin. *World Archaeology* 34(1):103–130.
Erlandson, Jon M., Torben C. Rick, Todd J. Braje, Molly Casperson, Brendon Culleton, Brian Fulfrost, Tracy Garcia, Daniel A. Guthrie, Nicholas Jew, Douglas J. Kennett, Madonna L. Moss, Leslie Reeder, Craig Skinner, Jack Watts, and Lauren Willis
2011 Paleoindian Seafaring, Maritime Technologies, and Coastal Foraging on California's Channel Islands. *Science* 331:1181–1185.
Estes, Mark B.
2009 Paleoindian Occupations in the Great Basin: A Comparative Study of Lithic Technological Organization, Mobility, and Landscape Use from Jakes Valley, Nevada. Unpublished Master's thesis, Department of Anthropology, University of Nevada, Reno.
Ferguson, G. J., and W. F. Libby
1962 UCLA Radiocarbon Dates, I. *Radiocarbon* 4:109–114.
Fiedel, Stuart J., and Juliet E. Morrow
2012 Comment on "Clovis and Western Stemmed Population Migration and the Meeting of Two Technologies in the Intermountain West" by Charlotte Beck and George T. Jones. *American Antiquity* 77:376–385.
Fowler, Catherine, and Eugene M. Hattori
2009 Recent Advances in Great Basin Textile Research. In *Past, Present, and Future Issues in Great Basin Archaeology: Papers in Honor of Don D. Fowler*, edited by Bryan Hockett, pp. 103–124. Bureau of Land Management Cultural Resource Series, 20. Reno.
Galm, Jerry R., and Stan Gough
2008 The Projectile Point/Knife Sample from the Sentinel Gap Site. In *Projectile Point Sequences in Northwestern North America*, edited by Roy L. Carlson and Martin P. R. Magne, pp. 209–220. Archaeology Press, Simon Fraser University, Burnaby.
Gardner, Jill K., S. F. McGill, and Mark Q. Sutton
2002 Early and Middle Holocene Hearth Features Along the Garlock Fault, Western Fremont Valley, California. *Pacific Coast Archaeological Society Quarterly* 38(4):45–59.
Goebel, Ted
2007 Pre-Archaic and Early Archaic Technological Activities at Bonneville Estates Rockshelter: A First Look at the Lithic Artifact Record. In *Paleoindian or Paleoarchaic? Great Basin Human Ecology at the Pleistocene–Holocene Transition*, edited by Kelly E. Graf and Dave N. Schmitt, pp. 156–184. University of Utah Press, Salt Lake City.
Graf, Kelly E.
2007 Stratigraphy and Chronology of the Pleistocene to Holocene Transition at Bonneville Estates Rockshelter, Eastern Great Basin. In *Paleoindian or Paleoarchaic? Great Basin Human Ecology at the Pleistocene–Holocene Transition*, edited by Kelly E. Graf and Dave N. Schmitt, pp. 82–104. University of Utah Press, Salt Lake City.
Gramly, Richard M.
1990 *Guide to the Paleo-Indian Artifacts of North America*. Persimmon Press, Buffalo.
Grayson, Donald K.
2000 The Homestead Cave Mammals. In *Late Quaternary Paleoecology in the Bonneville Basin*, edited by David B. Madsen, pp. 67–89. Utah Geological Survey Bulletin, 130. Salt Lake City.
2002 Great Basin Mammals and Late Quaternary Climate History. In *Great Basin Aquatic Systems History*, edited by R. Hershler, David B. Madsen, and Donald R. Currey, pp. 369–385. Smithsonian Contributions to the Earth Sciences No. 33. Washington, D.C.
2011 *The Great Basin: A Natural Prehistory*. Rev. and expanded ed. University of California Press, Berkeley.
Hall, M. C.
1993 *Archaeology of Seven Prehistoric Sites in Tiefort Basin, Fort Irwin, San Bernardino County, California*. Report prepared for the U.S. Army Corps of Engineers, Los Angeles District. Far Western Anthropological Group, Inc., Davis.
Hanes, Richard C.
1988 *Lithic Assemblages of Dirty Shame Rockshelter: Changing Traditions in the Northern Intermontane*. University of Oregon Anthropological Papers No. 40. Eugene.
Hattori, Eugene M.
1982 *The Archaeology of Falcon Hill, Winnemucca Lake, Washoe County, Nevada*. Ph.D. dissertation, University Microfilms, Ann Arbor.
Heizer, Robert F.
1951 Preliminary Report on the Leonard Rockshelter Site, Pershing County, Nevada. *American Antiquity* 18:89–98.
Hester, Thomas R.
1974 Archaeological Materials from Site NV-Wa-197, Western Nevada: Atlatls and Animal Skin Pouches. *University of California Archaeological Research Facility* 21:1–36. Berkeley.
Hockett, Bryan
2007 Nutritional Ecology of Late Pleistocene to Middle Holocene Subsistence in the Great Basin. Zoological Evidence from Bonneville Estates Rockshelter. In *Paleoindian or Paleoarchaic? Great Basin Human Ecology at the Pleistocene–Holocene Transition*, edited by Kelly E. Graf and Dave N. Schmitt, pp. 204–230. University of Utah Press, Salt Lake City.
Holmes, Amy M., and Gary A. Huckleberry
2009 Stratigraphy and Paleoenvironment. In *The Archaeology of the Eastern Nevada Paleoarchaic, Pt. 1: The Sunshine Locality*, by Charlotte Beck and George T. Jones, pp. 67–76. University of Utah Anthropology Papers No. 126. University of Utah Press, Salt Lake City.
Huckleberry, Gary, Charlotte Beck, George T. Jones, Amy Holmes, Michael Cannon, Stephanie Livingston, and Jack Broughton
2001 The Geoarchaeology of the Sunshine Locality, a Terminal Pleistocene/Early Holocene Archaeological Site in Eastern Nevada. *Quaternary Research* 55(3):303–312.
Hughes, Susan S.
1998 Getting to the Point: Evolutionary Change in Prehistoric Weaponry. *Journal of Archaeological Method and Theory* 5:345–408.
Janetski, Joel C., Mark L. Bodily, Bradley A. Newbold, and David T. Yoder
2012 Paleoarchaic to Early Archaic Transition on the Colorado Plateau: The Archaeology of North Creek Shelter. *American Antiquity* 77:125–159.
Jenkins, Dennis L.
1985 Dating the Pinto Occupation at Rogers Ridge: A Fossil Spring Site in the Mojave Desert, California. *Journal of California and Great Basin Anthropology* 9:303–318.
2000 Project Summary and Conclusions. In *Human Adaptations in*

Drews Valley: A Mid-Elevation Setting on the Northern Great Basin Periphery, South-Central Oregon, edited by Dennis L. Jenkins, pp. 335–376. Report 2000-3. State Museum of Anthropology, University of Oregon, Eugene.

2004 The Grasshopper and the Ant: Middle Holocene Occupations and Storage Behavior at the Bowling Dune Site in the Fort Rock Basin, Oregon. In *Early and Middle Holocene Archaeology of the Northern Great Basin*, edited by Dennis L. Jenkins, Thomas J. Connolly, and C. Melvin Aikens, pp. 123–155. University of Oregon Anthropological Papers, 62. Eugene.

Jenkins, Dennis L., Thomas J. Connolly, and C. Melvin Aikens

2004 Early and Middle Holocene Archaeology in the Northern Great Basin: Dynamic Natural and Cultural Ecologies. In *Early and Middle Holocene Archaeology of the Northern Great Basin*, edited by Dennis L. Jenkins, Thomas J. Connolly, and C. Melvin Aikens, pp. 1–20. University of Oregon Anthropological Papers, 62. Eugene.

Jennings, Jesse D.

1957 *Danger Cave*. University of Utah Anthropological Papers, 27. Salt Lake City.

1968 *Prehistory of North America*. McGraw-Hill, New York.

1986 Prehistory: Introduction. In *Handbook of North American Indians, Vol. 11: Great Basin*, edited by Warren L. d'Azevedo, pp. 113–119. Smithsonian Institution, Washington, D.C.

Jennings, Jesse D., Alan R. Schroedl, and Richard N. Holmer

1980 *Sudden Shelter*. University of Utah Anthropology Papers No. 103. University of Utah Press, Salt Lake City.

Jones, George T., and Charlotte Beck

1999 Paleoarchaic Archaeology in the Great Basin. In *Models for the Millennium: Great Basin Anthropology Today*, edited by Charlotte Beck, pp. 83–95. University of Utah Press, Salt Lake City.

2012 The Emergence of the Desert Archaic in the Great Basin. In *The Paleoindian–Archaic Transition*, edited by B. Bousman and B. Vierra. Texas A&M University Press, in press.

Jones, George T., Charlotte Beck, Eric E. Jones, and Richard E. Hughes

2003 Lithic Source Use and Paleoarchaic Foraging Territories in the Great Basin. *American Antiquity* 68:5–38.

Jones, George T., Lisa M. Fontes, Rachel A. Horowitz, Charlotte Beck, and David C. Bailey

2012 Reconsidering Paleoarchaic Mobility in the Central Great Basin. *American Antiquity* 77:351–367.

Kelly, Robert L., and Larry C. Todd

1988 Coming into the Country: Early Paleoindian Hunting and Mobility. *American Antiquity* 53:231–244.

Lafayette, Linsie M.

2006 Use-Wear Analysis of Great Basin Stemmed Points. Unpublished Master's thesis, Department of Anthropology, University of Nevada, Reno.

Layton, Thomas N.

1979 Archaeology and Paleo-Ecology of Pluvial Lake Parman, Northwestern Great Basin. *Journal of New World Archaeology* 3:41–56.

Louderback, Lisbeth A., Donald K. Grayson, and Marcos Llobera

2011 Middle-Holocene Climates and Human Population Densities in the Great Basin, Western USA. *Holocene* 21:366–373.

Louderback, Lisbeth A., and David E. Rhode

2009 15,000 Years of Vegetation Change in the Bonneville Basin: The Blue Lake Pollen Record. *Quaternary Science Reviews* 28:308–326.

Madsen, David B.

2007 The Paleoarchaic to Archaic Transition in the Great Basin. In *Paleoindian or Paleoarchaic? Great Basin Human Ecology at the Pleistocene–Holocene Transition*, edited by Kelly E. Graf and Dave N. Schmitt, pp. 3–20. University of Utah Press, Salt Lake City.

Madsen, David B., Charles G. Oviatt, and Dave N. Schmitt

2005 A Geomorphic, Environmental, and Cultural History of the Camels Back Cave Region. In *Camels Back Cave*, edited by Dave N. Schmitt and David B. Madsen, pp. 20–45. University of Utah Anthropological Papers, 125. Salt Lake City.

Madsen, David B., Charles G. Oviatt, D. Craig Young, and David Page

2013 Old River Bed Geomorphology and Chronology. In *The Paleoarchaic Occupation of the Old River Bed Delta*, by David B. Madsen, Dave Schmitt, and David Page, with contributions by Charlotte Beck, Daron Duke, George T. Jones, Lisbeth Louderback, Charles G. Oviatt, David Rhode, and D. Craig Young, in preparation.

Madsen, David B., and David Rhode

1990 Early Holocene Pinyon (*Pinus monophylla*) in the Northeastern Great Basin. *Quaternary Research* 33:94–101.

Mehringer, Peter J., Jr.

1986 Prehistoric Environments. In *Handbook of North American Indians, Vol. 11: Great Basin*, edited by Warren L. d'Azevedo, pp. 31–50. Smithsonian Institution, Washington, D.C.

Mehringer, Peter J., Jr., and William J. Cannon

1994 Volcaniclastic Dunes of the Fort Rock Valley, Oregon: Stratigraphy, Chronology, and Archaeology. In *Archaeological Researches in the Northern Great Basin: Fort Rock Archaeology Since Cressman*, edited by C. Melvin Aikens and Dennis L. Jenkins, pp. 283–327. University of Oregon Papers No. 50. Eugene.

Musil, Robert R.

1988 Functional Efficiency and Technological Change: A Hafting Tradition Model for Prehistoric North America. In *Early Human Occupation in Far Western North America: The Clovis–Archaic Interface*, edited by Judith A. Willig, C. Melvin Aikens, and John L. Fagan, pp. 373–389. Anthropology Papers, 21. Nevada State Museum, Carson City.

Newlander, Khori S.

2011a Exchange, Embedded Procurement, and Hunter-Gatherer Mobility: A Case Study from the North American Great Basin. Unpublished Ph.D. dissertation, Department of Anthropology, University of Michigan, Ann Arbor.

2011b Reconsidering the Lithic Landscape of East-Central Nevada During the Terminal Pleistocene/Early Holocene. Paper presented at the 76th Annual Meeting of the Society for American Archaeology, Sacramento.

Nowak, C. L., R. S. Nowak, R. J. Tausch, and P. E. Wigand

1994a A 30,000 Year Record of Vegetation Dynamics at a Semi-Arid Locale in the Great Basin. *Journal of Vegetation Science* 5:579–590.

1994b Tree and Shrub Dynamics in Northwestern Great Basin Woodland and Shrub Steppe During the Late-Pleistocene and Holocene. *American Journal of Botany* 81(3):265–277.

Oetting, Albert C.

1994 Early Holocene Rabbit Drives and Prehistoric Land-Use Patterns on Buffalo Flat, Christmas Lake Valley, Oregon. In *Archaeological Researches in the Northern Great Basin: Fort Rock Archaeology Since Cressman*, edited by C. Melvin Aikens and Dennis L. Jenkins, pp. 155–169. University of Oregon Papers No. 50. Eugene.

Oviatt, Charles G., David B. Madsen, and Dave N. Schmitt

2003 Late Pleistocene and Early Holocene Rivers and Wetlands in the Bonneville Basin of Western North America. *Quaternary Research* 60:200–210.

Pinson, Ariane

2007 Artiodactyl Use and Adaptive Discontinuity Across the Paleo-archaic/Archaic Transition in the Northern Great Basin. In *Paleoindian or Paleoarchaic? Great Basin Human Ecology at the Pleistocene–Holocene Transition*, edited by Kelly E. Graf and Dave N. Schmitt, pp. 187–203. University of Utah Press, Salt Lake City.

2008 Geoarchaeological Context of Clovis and Western Stemmed Tradition Sites in the Dietz Basin, Lake County, Oregon. *Geoarchaeology: An International Journal* 23:63–106.

Quade, Jay, Richard M. Forester, William L. Pratt, and Claire Carter

1998 Black Mats, Spring-Fed Streams, and Late-Glacial-Age Recharge in the Southern Great Basin. *Quaternary Research* 49:129–148.

Rhode, David, and Lisbeth A. Louderback

2007 Dietary Plant Use in the Bonneville Basin During the Terminal Pleistocene/Early Holocene Transition. In *Paleoindian or Paleoarchaic? Great Basin Human Ecology at the Pleistocene–Holocene Transition*, edited by Kelly E. Graf and Dave N. Schmitt, pp. 231–247. University of Utah Press, Salt Lake City.

Rhode, David, and David B. Madsen

1995 Late Wisconsin/Early Holocene Vegetation in the Bonneville Basin. *Quaternary Research* 44(2):246–256.

Rhode, David, David B. Madsen, and Kevin T. Jones

2006 Antiquity of Early Holocene Small-Seed Consumption and Processing at Danger Cave. *Antiquity* 80:328–339.

Schmitt, Dave N., and David B. Madsen

2005 *Camels Back Cave*. University of Utah Anthropological Papers No. 125. Salt Lake City.

Schmitt, Dave N., David B. Madsen, Charles G. Oviatt, and Rachel Quist

2007 Late Pleistocene/Early Holocene Geomorphology and Human Occupation of the Old River Bed Delta, Western Utah. In *Paleoindian or Paleoarchaic? Great Basin Human Ecology at the Pleistocene–Holocene Transition*, edited by Kelly E. Graf and Dave N. Schmitt, pp. 105–119. University of Utah Press, Salt Lake City.

Schroth, Adella B.

1994 *The Pinto Controversy in the Western United States*. Ph.D. dissertation, University of Michigan. University Microfilms, Ann Arbor.

Simms, Steven R.

1987 *Behavioral Ecology and Hunter-Gatherer Foraging: An Example from the Great Basin*. BAR International Series, 381. Oxford.

1988 Conceptualizing the Paleoindian and Archaic in the Great Basin. In *Early Human Occupation in Far Western North America: The Clovis–Archaic Interface*, edited by Judith A. Willig, C. Melvin Aikens, and John L. Fagan, pp. 41–52. Anthropology Papers, 21. Nevada State Museum, Carson City.

2008 *Ancient Peoples of the Great Basin and Colorado Plateau*. Left Coast Press, Walnut Creek.

Smith, Geoff M.

2010 Footprints Across the Black Rock: Temporal Variability in Prehistoric Foraging Territories and Toolstone Procurement Strategies in the Western Great Basin. *American Antiquity* 75:865–885.

Spaulding, W. Geoffrey

1990 Vegetation and Climatic Development of the Mojave Desert: The Last Glacial Maximum to the Present. In *Packrat Middens—The Last 40,000 Years of Biotic Change*, edited by Julio L. Betancourt, T. R. Van Defender, and Paul S. Martin, pp. 59–85. University of Arizona Press, Tucson.

Sutton, Mark Q., Mark E. Basgall, Jill K. Gardner, and M. W. Allen

2007 Advances in Understanding Mojave Desert Prehistory. In *California Prehistory: Colonization, Culture, and Complexity*, edited by Terry L. Jones and K. A. Klar, pp. 229–245. AltaMira Press, Lanham, Maryland.

Thompson, Robert S.

1992 Late Quaternary Environments in Ruby Valley, Nevada. *Quaternary Research* 37:1–15.

Tuohy, Donald R.

1988 Artifacts from the Northwestern Pyramid Lake Shoreline. In *Early Human Occupation in Far Western North America: The Clovis–Archaic Interface*, edited by Judith A. Willig, C. Melvin Aikens, and John L. Fagan, pp. 201–216. Anthropology Papers, 21. Nevada State Museum, Carson City.

Tuohy, Donald R., and Amy Dansie

1997 New Information Regarding Early Holocene Manifestations in the Western Great Basin. *Nevada Historical Society Quarterly* 40:24–53.

Tuohy, Donald R., and Thomas N. Layton

1977 Towards the Establishment of a New Series of Great Basin Projectile Points. *Nevada Archaeological Survey Reporter* 10(6):1–5.

Warren, Claude N.

1967 The San Dieguito Complex: A Review and Hypothesis. *American Antiquity* 32:168–185.

Wells, Stephen G., William J. Brown, Yehouda Enzel, Roger Y. Anderson, and Leslie D. McFadden

2003 Late Quaternary Geology and Paleohydrology of Pluvial Lake Mojave, Southern California. In *Paleoenvironments and Paleohydrology of the Mojave and Southern Great Basin Deserts*, edited by Yehouda Enzel, Stephen G. Wells, and Nicholas Lancaster, pp. 79–114. Geological Society of America Special Paper, 368. Washington, D.C.

Wigand, Peter E., and Peter J. Mehringer, Jr.

1985 Pollen and Seed Analyses. In *The Archaeology of Hidden Cave*, edited by David H. Thomas, pp. 108–124. Anthropological Papers of the American Museum of Natural History, 61(1). New York.

Wigand, Peter E., and David Rhode

2002 Great Basin Vegetation History and Aquatic Systems: The Last 150,000 Years. In *Great Basin Aquatic Systems History*, edited by R. Hershler, David B. Madsen, and Donald R. Currey, pp. 309–367. Smithsonian Contributions to the Earth Sciences No. 33. Washington, D.C.

Yoder, David T., Mark L. Bodily, Sara Hill, Joel Janetski, and Bradley A. Newbold

2010 The Onset of Small Seed Processing on the Colorado Plateau. *Kiva: The Journal of Southwestern Anthropology and History* 75:425–446.

Appendix: Sites with Cultural Radiocarbon Dates Ranging Between 10,000 and 6000 rcy BP

Region and Site	Unit/ Depth	Lab Number	Material Dated[a]	^{14}C Age (BP)	Reference(s)	Great Basin Stemmed Series[b]	Other Stemmed Types[c]	Archaic Types[d]	Ground Stone
Northern Great Basin									
Fort Rock Cave	Str2, L6	GaK-2146	C	8550 ± 150	Bedwell 1973	x			x?
	NG	C-428a	UA	9188 ± 480	Arnold and Libby 1950	NI	NI	NI	NI
	NG	C-428b	UA	8916 ± 540	Bedwell and Cressman 1971	NI	NI	NI	NI
	NG	GaK-2146	C	8550 ± 150	Bedwell and Cressman 1971	NI	NI	NI	NI
	NG	I-1917	UA	8500 ± 140	Bedwell and Cressman 1971	x	NI	NI	NI
Cougar Mt. Cave No. 1	NG	UCLA-112	UA	8510 ± 250	Ferguson and Libby 1962	x?	WD?		NG
Connley Cave No. 3	L24	GaK-1739	C	8290 ± 310	Bedwell 1973				NG
Connley Cave No. 4A	U2, L28	GaK-1741	C	7900 ± 170	Bedwell 1973				NG
	U3, L31	GaK-2136	C	9150 ± 150	Bedwell 1973	x			
	U3, L35	GaK-1742	C	10,100 ± 400	Bedwell 1973				
Connley Cave No. 4B	U3, L30	GaK-2140	C	7240 ± 150	Bedwell 1973				NG
	U3, L32	GaK-2141	C	11,200 ± 200	Bedwell 1973	x			
	U3, L34	GaK-2142	C	9670 ± 180	Bedwell 1973				
	U3, L35	GaK-2143	C	10,600 ± 190	Bedwell 1973				
Connley Cave No. 5A	U3, L27	GaK-1743	C	9800 ± 250	Bedwell 1973	x		E	NG
Connley Cave No. 5B	U2, L27	GaK-2135	C	7430 ± 140	Bedwell 1973	x		E, GSS	NG
	U3, L33	GaK-1744	C	9540 ± 260	Bedwell 1973				NG
Connley Cave No. 6	U3, L22	GaK-1745	C	9710 ± 880	Bedwell 1973	x			NG
Locality III	Comp 2	WSU-4867	OM	5550 ± 180	Jenkins 2000	x		NSN, E	x
	Comp 2	WSU-4861	OM	6120 ± 180	Jenkins 2000	x		NSN, E	x
	Comp 2	Beta-99003	OM	6140 ± 80	Jenkins 2000	x		NSN, E	x
	Comp 2	WSU-4868	OM	6200 ± 70	Jenkins 2000	x		NSN, E	x
	Comp 2	WSU-4864	OM	6370 ± 190	Jenkins 2000	x		NSN, E	x
	Comp 2	WSU-4865	OM	6530 ± 80	Jenkins 2000	x		NSN, E	x
	Comp 2	Beta-85685	OM	6900 ± 120	Jenkins 2000	x		NSN, E	x
	Comp 2	Beta-99002	OM	7010 ± 90	Jenkins 2000	x		NSN, E	x
	Comp 2	WSU-4866	C	7040 ± 135	Jenkins 2000	x		NSN, E	x
	Comp 2	WSU-2859	C	7280 ± 70	Mehringer and Cannon 1994	x		NSN, E	x
	Comp 2	WSU-4860	C	7350 ± 130	Jenkins 2000	x		NSN, E	x
	Comp 2	WSU-4863	OM	7445 ± 190	Jenkins 2000	x		NSN, E	x
	Comp 2	Beta-85686	C	7670 ± 230	Jenkins 2000	x		NSN, E	x
	Comp 1	WSU-4862	C	7880 ± 240	Jenkins 2000				
		Beta-85687	OM	8940 ± 130	Jenkins 2000				
		WSU-3499	C	9400 ± 270	Mehringer and Cannon 1994				
	Comp 1	Beta-85688	OM	10,170 ± 230	Jenkins 2000				
Kelly's Site	50-65cm	NG	C	6550 ± 90	Mehringer and Cannon 1994			NSN?	

Region and Site	Unit/ Depth	Lab Number	Material Dated[a]	^{14}C Age (BP)	Reference(s)	Great Basin Stemmed Series[b]	Other Stemmed Types[c]	Archaic Types[d]	Ground Stone
Buffalo Flat Sites									
35-LK-1180	NG	Beta-23351	NG	8220 ± 430	Oetting 1994	x		HCB	
	NG	Beta-26024	NG	9880 ± 360	Oetting 1994	x			
35-LK-1881	NG	Beta-22579	C	8080 ± 120	Oetting 1994	x			
	NG	Beta-34209	C	8710 ± 140	Oetting 1994	x			
	NG	Beta-30340	C	8880 ± 120	Oetting 1994	x			
	NG	Beta-30342	C	8950 ± 120	Oetting 1994	x			
	NG	Beta-30341	C	9120 ± 120	Oetting 1994	x			
35-LK-2076	NG	Beta-22580	C	8780 ± 120	Oetting 1994	x			
	NG	Beta-26026	C	8870 ± 200	Oetting 1994	x			
	NG	Beta-26025	C	10,020 ± 370	Oetting 1994	x			
35-LK-2095	NG	Beta-17754	C	10,800 ± 600	Oetting 1994	x			
	NG	Beta-23593	C	9130 ± 130	Oetting 1994	x			
Bowling Dune	F3			8080 ± 90	Jenkins 2004			NSN	
	F12	Beta-75080	C	6040 ± 120	Jenkins 2004	x		NSN, E	
	F17	Beta-75082	C	6420 ± 230	Jenkins 2004				
Paulina Lake	Comp 3	Beta-56721	NG	6540 ± 150	Connolly and Jenkins 1999	x	WD		x
	Comp 3	Beta-40027	OM	7080 ± 150	Connolly and Jenkins 1999	x	WD		x
	Comp 3	Beta-57732	NG	7560 ± 190	Connolly and Jenkins 1999	x	WD		x
	Comp 2	Beta-56724	C	7930 ± 80	Connolly and Jenkins 1999	x	WD		x
	Comp 2	Beta-24298	NG	8210 ± 60	Connolly and Jenkins 1999	x	WD		x
	Comp 2	Beta-59315	UA	8460 ± 110	Connolly and Jenkins 1999	x	WD		x
	Comp 2	Beta-59316	UA	8540 ± 90	Connolly and Jenkins 1999	x	WD		x
	Comp 2	Beta-57733	UA	8670 ± 110	Connolly and Jenkins 1999	x	WD		x
	Comp 2	Beta-56723	C	8680 ± 70	Connolly and Jenkins 1999	x	WD		x
	Comp 2	Beta-60883	C	8880 ± 110	Connolly and Jenkins 1999	x	WD		x
	Comp 2	Beta-60884	NG	8980 ± 190	Connolly and Jenkins 1999	x	WD		x
	Comp 2	Beta-56725	C	9060 ± 80	Connolly and Jenkins 1999	x	WD		x
	Comp 1	Beta-56722	C	9920 ± 470	Connolly and Jenkins 1999	x	WD		x
Dirty Shame Rockshelter	Zone III	SI-2267	UO	5855 ± 125	Aikens et al. 1977; Hanes 1988			NSN, E, GSS	x
	Zone III	SI-1769	C	6210 ± 65	Aikens et al. 1977; Hanes 1988			NSN, E, GSS	x
	Zone III	SI-2269	UO	6315 ± 195	Aikens et al. 1977; Hanes 1988			NSN, E, GSS	x
	Zone III	SI-2266	UO	7100 ± 85	Aikens et al. 1977; Hanes 1988			NSN, E, GSS	x
	Zone IV	SI-1770	C	6845 ± 85	Aikens et al. 1977; Hanes 1988		P?	GSS?	x
	Zone V	SI-1768	UO	7925 ± 80	Aikens et al. 1977; Hanes 1988	x	WD, SS	NSN, E	x
	Zone V	SI-1773	C	7880 ± 100	Aikens et al. 1977; Hanes 1988	x	WD, SS		x
	Zone V	SI-1771	C	7850 ± 120	Aikens et al. 1977; Hanes 1988	x	WD, SS		x
	Zone V	SI-1772	C	6535 ± 100	Aikens et al. 1977; Hanes 1988	x	WD, SS		x
	Zone V	SI-1774	C	9500 ± 95	Aikens et al. 1977; Hanes 1988	x	WD, SS		x
	Zone VI	SI-1775	C	8905 ± 75	Aikens et al. 1977; Hanes 1988	x	WD	NSN, HCB, E	x
	Zone VI	SI-2265	C	8865 ± 95	Aikens et al. 1977; Hanes 1988	x	WD	NSN, HCB, E	x

Region and Site	Unit/ Depth	Lab Number	Material Dated[a]	^{14}C Age (BP)	Reference(s)	Great Basin Stemmed Series[b]	Other Stemmed Types[c]	Archaic Types[d]	Ground Stone
	Zone VI	SI-2268	UO	8850 ± 75	Aikens et al. 1977; Hanes 1988	x	WD	NSN, HCB, E	x
Western Great Basin									
Last Supper Cave	NG	LSU-73-120	S	8790 ± 350	Layton 1979	x			
	NG	WSU-1431	S	8630 ± 195	Layton 1979	x			
	NG	TX-2541	C	8960 ± 190	Layton 1979	x			
	NG	WSU-1706	C	8260 ± 90	Layton 1979	x			
Shiners Site A	NG	UCLA-672	UA	8380 ± 120	Hattori 1982		SS		
	NG	UCLA-675	UA	9540 ± 120	Hattori 1982		SS		
Nicolarsen	NA	I-6873	UA	7980 ± 610	Hester 1974				
Leonard Rockshelter	NG	C-281a	UO	8820 ± 400	Heizer 1951	x			
	NG	C-281b	UO	8443 ± 510	Heizer 1951	x			
	NG	C-298	UA	7038 ± 350	Heizer 1951	x			
Grimes Point Burial Cave	NG	UCR-3477	UA	9470 ± 60	Tuohy and Dansie 1997				
Crypt Cave	NG	UCR-3483	UA	9120 ± 60	Tuohy and Dansie 1997				
North Side Pyramid Lake	NG	GX-13744	UA	9660 ± 170	Tuohy 1988				
Wizards Bch, Pyramid Lake	NG	UCR-3445	HB	9225 ± 60	Tuohy and Dansie 1997				
Spirit Cave	NG	UCR-3230	HB	9430 ± 60	Tuohy and Dansie 1997				
	NG	UCR-3261-2	HH	9360 ± 60	Tuohy and Dansie 1997				
	NG	UCR-3261-3	HH	9440 ± 60	Tuohy and Dansie 1997				
	NG	UCR-3261-4	HH	9350 ± 60					
	NG	UCR-3323	UA	9430 ± 70	Tuohy and Dansie 1997				
	NG	UCR-3324-1	UA	9410 ± 60	Tuohy and Dansie 1997				
	NG	UCR-3324-2	UA	9460 ± 60	Tuohy and Dansie 1997				
	NG	UCR-3478	UA	9040 ± 50	Tuohy and Dansie 1997				
	NG	UCR-3480	UA	9270 ± 60	Tuohy and Dansie 1997				
	NG	UCR-3475	HB	9300 ± 70	Tuohy and Dansie 1997				
Central Great Basin									
Sunshine Locality	B	Beta-105660	OM	8120 ± 70	Beck and Jones 2009	x			
	C	Beta-69781	OM	8560 ± 100	Beck and Jones 2009	x			
	C	Beta-86200	OM	9040 ± 190	Beck and Jones 2009	x			
	C	Beta-69782	C	9820 ± 60	Beck and Jones 2009	x			
	C	Beta-86202	C	9910 ± 50	Beck and Jones 2009	x			
	C	Beta-86203	OM	9940 ± 50	Beck and Jones 2009	x			
	C	Beta-86204	OM	10,060 ± 50	Beck and Jones 2009	x			
	D	Beta-86198	C	9920± 60	Beck and Jones 2009	x			
	D	Beta-86199	OM	7420 ± 60	Beck and Jones 2009	x			
	D	Beta-86201	C	9880 ± 50	Beck and Jones 2009	x			
Eastern Great Basin									
Danger Cave	DII	Beta-187451	C	5030 ± 40	Rhode et al. 2006		SS, ES, P, US, DS	NSN, LSN, E, HCB, GSS	
	DII	Beta-187451	C	5060 ± 40	Rhode et al. 2006		SS, ES, P, US, DS	NSN, LSN, E, HCB, GSS	
	DII	Beta-187452	C	6020 ± 50	Rhode et al. 2006		SS, ES, P, US, DS	NSN, LSN, E, HCB, GSS	

Region and Site	Unit/ Depth	Lab Number	Material Dated[a]	^{14}C Age (BP)	Reference(s)	Great Basin Stemmed Series[b]	Other Stemmed Types[c]	Archaic Types[d]	Ground Stone
	DII	Beta-187453	C	8100 ± 40	Rhode et al. 2006		SS, ES, P, US, DS	NSN, LSN, E, HCB, GSS	
	DII	Beta-187454	C	8100 ± 40	Rhode et al. 2006		SS, ES, P, US, DS	NSN, LSN, E, HCB, GSS	
	DII	Beta-187447	C	8130 ± 50	Rhode et al. 2006		SS, ES, P, US, DS	NSN, LSN, E, HCB, GSS	
	DII	Beta-189084	C	8160 ± 40	Rhode et al. 2006		SS, ES, P, US, DS	NSN, LSN, E, HCB, GSS	x
	DII	Beta-187450	C	8300 ± 40	Rhode et al. 2006		SS, ES, P, US, DS	NSN, LSN, E, HCB, GSS	x
	DII	Beta-187449	C	8380 ± 40	Rhode et al. 2006		SS, ES, P, US, DS	NSN, LSN, E, HCB, GSS	x
	DIIup	AA-3623	UO	7410 ± 120	Madsen and Rhode 1990		NG	NG	NG
	DIIup	Beta-23653	NR	7920 ± 80	Madsen and Rhode 1990		NG	NG	NG
	DIIup		UO	8370 ± 60	Rhode et al. 2006		NG	NG	NG
	DIIup	Beta-168857	UO	8270 ± 40	Rhode et al. 2006		NG	NG	NG
	DIIup	NSRL-11436	C?	8410 ± 50	Rhode et al. 2006		NG	NG	NG
	DIIup		UO	8570 ± 40	Rhode et al. 2006		NG	NG	NG
	DIIu/m	Beta-187448	C	8190 ± 50	Rhode et al. 2006		NG	NG	NG
	DIIm/u	C-11	C	9784 ± 630	Jennings 1957		NG	NG	NG
	DIImid	Beta-190887	C?	8440 ± 50	Rhode et al. 2006		NG	NG	NG
	DIImid	Beta-193124	UO	8380 ± 60	Rhode et al. 2006		NG	NG	NG
	DIIlow	Beta-169848	C	10,050 ± 50	Rhode et al. 2006		NG	NG	NG
	DI	Beta-187446	C	8680 ± 50	Rhode et al. 2006		US		x
	DI	Beta-19336	NG	9780 ± 210	Madsen and Rhode 1990		US		x
	DI	Beta-196611	UO	9920 ± 185	Rhode et al. 2006		US		x
	DI	Beta-158549	C	10,270 ± 50	Rhode et al. 2006		US		x
	DI	Beta-168656	C	10,310 ± 40	Rhode et al. 2006		US		x
Bonneville Estates Rockshelter									
West Block	Str 14	Beta-29542	C	6040 ± 80	Goebel 2007; Graf 2007			NSN, HCB	x
	Str 14	Beta-16224	UA	6100 ± 50	Goebel 2007; Graf 2007			NSN, HCB	x
	Str 14	Beta-164226	C	6100 ± 80	Goebel 2007; Graf 2007			NSN, HCB	x
	Str 14	Beta-164227	C	6280 ± 40	Goebel 2007; Graf 2007			NSN, HCB	x
	Str 14	AA-58591	C	6315 ± 40	Goebel 2007; Graf 2007			NSN, HCB	x
	Str 16	Beta-164230	UA	7190 ± 50	Goebel 2007; Graf 2007				x
	Str 16	CAMS-73252	C	7280 ± 50	Goebel 2007; Graf 2007				x
	Str 17a	CAMS-72351	C	7420 ±50	Goebel 2007; Graf 2007				
	Str 17b	AA-58589	C	9430 ± 50	Goebel 2007; Graf 2007	x	WD		
	Str 17b	Beta-207010	C	9440 ± 50	Goebel 2007; Graf 2007	x	WD		
East Block	Str 10	Beta-195042	C	9580 ± 40	Goebel 2007; Graf 2007	NI	NI	NI	NI
	Str 10	Beta-195044	C	9570 ± 40	Goebel 2007; Graf 2007	NI	NI	NI	NI
	Str 10	Beta-161891	C	9520 ± 60	Goebel 2007; Graf 2007	NI	NI	NI	NI
	Str 10	AA-58599	C	9440 ± 80	Goebel 2007; Graf 2007	NI	NI	NI	NI
	Str 10	Beta-203507	C	8830 ± 60	Goebel 2007; Graf 2007	NI	NI	NI	NI
	Str 9b	AA-58596		7240 ± 50	Goebel 2007; Graf 2007	NI	NI	NI	
Hogup Cave	1	GaK-1569	C	8350 ± 160	Aikens 1970		WD	E	x
	1	GaK-2086	UO	7860 ± 160	Aikens 1970		WD	E	x

Region and Site	Unit/ Depth	Lab Number	Material Dated[a]	^{14}C Age (BP)	Reference(s)	Great Basin Stemmed Series[b]	Other Stemmed Types[c]	Archaic Types[d]	Ground Stone
	2	GaK-1570		3970 ± 100*	Aikens 1970				x
	3	GaK-2083	UO	8800 ± 200	Aikens 1970		P	NSN, E	x
	3	GX-1288	C	6820 ± 380*	Aikens 1970		P	NSN, E	x
	4	GX-1287	UO	7815 ± 350	Aikens 1970		P	NSN, E	x
	5	GaK-2082	UO	7250 ± 100	Aikens 1970		P	NSN, E, HCB	x
	5	GX-1288	UO	5795 ± 160	Aikens 1970		P	NSN, E, HCB	x
	6	GaK-1563	C	6400 ± 100	Aikens 1970		P	NSN, E, HCB	x
	6	GaK-1567	C	5950 ± 100	Aikens 1970		P	NSN, E, HCB	x
	7	GaK-2084	C	6190 ± 110	Aikens 1970		P	NSN, E, HCB, RG	x
Camels Back Cave	VIII	Beta-63481	C	6110 ± 90	Schmitt and Madsen 2005			LSN	x
	VI	Beta-122775	C	6430 ± 60	Schmitt and Madsen 2005			NSN, E	x
	V	Beta-122774	C	6390 ± 70	Schmitt and Madsen 2005			NSN, E	x
	V	Beta-122776	C	6550 ± 130	Schmitt and Madsen 2005				x
	V	Beta-122777	C	6550 ± 50	Schmitt and Madsen 2005				x
	V	Beta-122778	C	7230 ± 160	Schmitt and Madsen 2005				x
	IV	Beta-64369	C	7350 ± 220	Schmitt and Madsen 2005			GSS, E	x
	III	Beta-118937	C	7530 ± 50	Schmitt and Madsen 2005			NSN	x
Sudden Shelter	Str 8	UGa-906	C	6310 ± 240	Jennings et al. 1980			E	x
	Str 5	RL-422	C	6670 ± 180	Jennings et al. 1980		P	NSN, E, RSN, HCB	x
	Str 4	UGa-859	C	7090 ± 85	Jennings et al. 1980		P	E	x
	Str 4	RL-476	C	7900 ± 190	Jennings et al. 1980		P	E	x
	Str 2	UGa-903	C	7565 ± 115	Jennings et al. 1980		P		x
	Str 2	RL-474	C	7840 ± 330	Jennings et al. 1980		P		x
Mojave Desert									
Ft. Irwin Sites									
SBR-2348, Locus G	TU-1, 30–40 cm	AA-12403	SA	9125 ± 80	Basgall and Hall 1994		P		x
SBR-4562, Locus A	F1, S50/W65, 90–100 cm	Beta-16100	C	9410 ± 115	Basgall and Hall 1993		P		x
	F4,S49/W64, 80–90 cm	Beta-16313	C	9470 ± 115	Basgall and Hall 1993		P		x
	S60/W72, 130–140 cm	AA-12404	SA	9450 ± 110	Basgall and Hall 1994		P		x
SBR-5250, Locus H	S122/W2, 0–5 cm	AA12405	SA	10,495 ± 85	Basgall and Hall 1994	x			
SBR-5251, Locus A	F2,S43/E3, 30–40 cm	Beta-45611	C	6640 ± 65	Hall 1993		P		
Locus C	F2,S44/E4, 10–20 cm	AA-12406	SA	9340 ± 85	Basgall and Hall 1994		P		x
Owens Lake INY-4454, Locus 1	N2/E10, 80–83 cm	Beta-63637	C	6740 ± 70	Gilreath and Holanda 2000	x			
	Trench 14, 75–100 cm	Beta-132585	OM	7780 ± 90	Gilreath and Holanda 2000	x			
	Trench 16, 75–100 cm	Beta-132586	OM	7010 ± 100	Gilreath and Holanda 2000	x			

Region and Site	Unit/ Depth	Lab Number	Material Dated[a]	^{14}C Age (BP)	Reference(s)	Great Basin Stemmed Series[b]	Other Stemmed Types[c]	Archaic Types[d]	Ground Stone
Lake China INY-5825	S48/W, 30.5, 2–6 cm	Beta-170208	P	10,010 ± 110	Basgall 2003	x			
	S48/W, 30.5, 37–47 cm	Beta-170210	OM	9870 ± 50	Basgall 2003	x			x
	S50/W17, 35–45 cm	Beta-170209	OM	8390 ± 130	Basgall 2003	x			x
Garlock Fault	NI	Beta-74108	C	7170 ± 140	Gardner et al. 2002		P		NI
	NI	AA-14553	C	6968 ± 109	Gardner et al. 2002		P		x
Twenty-Nine Palms Sites									
SBR-3632, Locus A	F1 S45/E139, 8–10 cm	Beta-103975	C	8030 ± 50	Basgall and Giambastiani 2000		P		x
SBR-3632, Locus I	S1/W16, 50–60 cm	Beta-136533	C	7970 ± 70	Basgall 2003		DL		x
	N2/E18, 112–125 cm	Beta-136534	OM	6760 ± 80	Basgall 2003		DL		x
	N2/E18, 110–120 cm	Beta-183170	SA	7560 ± 40	Basgall and Pierce 2004		DL		x
SBR-8959, Locus B	N86/W11, 20–30 cm	Beta-183171	C	6410 ± 80	Basgall and Jurich 2006		DL		x
SBR-9415	S15/E0, surface	Beta-175147	SA	8570 ± 50	Basgall and Pierce 2004		P		x
SBR-9727	N65/E0, surface	Beta-183173	C	7620 ± 40	Basgall and Pierce 2004		DL		x
Awl									
Locus A, A5	80–90 cm	Beta-16313	C	9470 ± 115	Basgall and Hall 1993	x	P		x
	90–100 cm	Beta-16100	C	9410 ± 115	Basgall and Hall 1993	x	P		x
		AA-12404	SA	9860 ± 110	Basgall and Hall 1994				
C. W. Harris[e]	NG	A-724	C	8540 ± 400	Warren 1967	x			
	NG	A-725	C	8540 ± 400	Warren 1967	x			
	NG	A-722A	C	9080 ± 350	Warren 1967	x			
Rogers Ridge	F2	Beta-10790	OM	7910 ± 420	Jenkins 1985	x			
	F4	Beta-13463	C	8180 ± 150	Jenkins 1985	x	P		
	F4	Beta-12843	OM	8300 ± 110	Jenkins 1985	x	P		
	F3	Beta-12840	OM	8410 ± 140	Jenkins 1985	x	P		
	F2	Beta-12844	OM	8410 ± 210	Jenkins 1985	x			
	NI	AA-12405	SA	10,085 ± 85	Basgall and Hall 1994	x	P		NI
Henwood	Loc H	AA-405	OM	7140 ± 290	Douglas et al. 1988	x	P		
	C2	AA-800	OM	7400 ± 280	Douglas et al. 1988	x	P		
	C2	AA-649	OM	7150 ± 290	Douglas et al. 1988	x	P		
	C1	AA-648	OM	8470 ± 370	Douglas et al. 1988	x	P		
	C1	AA-798	OM	4360 ± 280	Douglas et al. 1988	x	P		
Pinto Basin	U3, 100-110	AA-8615	SA	7225 ± 85	Schroth 1994				
	U3, 120-130	AA-8617	SA	7730 ± 85	Schroth 1994				x
	U4, 40-50	AA-8614	SA	7920 ± 85	Schroth 1994				
	U8, 25-35	AA-8613	SA	9330 ± 90	Schroth 1994				x
	U10, 10-30	UCR-2621	OM	7520 ± 120	Schroth 1994				
	Surface	AA-8618	BA	7820 ± 80	Schroth 1994				
Stahl Trench 20	U 1&2, L8	AA-10537	OM	7060 ±60	Schroth 1994		P		NI
	U6, L16	AA-8622	SA	8400 ± 85	Schroth 1994				NI
	U9, L 110	AA-8621	SA	8625 ± 110	Schroth 1994		P		NI

Region and Site	Unit/ Depth	Lab Number	Material Dated[a]	^{14}C Age (BP)	Reference(s)	Great Basin Stemmed Series[b]	Other Stemmed Types[c]	Archaic Types[d]	Ground Stone
	U4, L7	AA-8620	SA	8670 ± 85	Schroth 1994		P		NI
	U1&2, L5	AA-10536	CO	8900 ± 65	Schroth 1994		P	HCB	NI
Stahl Trench 21	U1, L9	AA-10535	OM	8625 ± 60	Schroth 1994			HCB	NI

Note: NG = not given; NI = no information.

[a] BA = uncharred bone artifact; C = charcoal; CO = charred nonartifactual organic; HB = human bone; HH = human hair; OM = bulk organic material; P = peat; S = nonartifactual shell; SA = shell artifact; UA = uncharred organic artifact; UO = uncharred nonartifactual organic; NR = not recorded.

[b] Great Basin Stemmed Series types include Haskett, Cougar Mountain, Parman, Lake Mohave, and Silver Lake (Foliate from northern Great Basin also included; Windust not included).

[c] Other Stemmed types include Windust (WD), Pinto (P), Deadman Lake (DL—see Sutton et al. 2007), Old River Bed Stemmed types (Square Stem [SS], Expanding Stem [ES], Dugway Stubby [DS]—see Figure 2), and unknown Stemmed (US).

[d] Archaic types include Elko (E), Gatecliff Split Stem (GSS), Humboldt Concave Base (HCB), other large side-notched (LSN), Northern Side-notched (NSN), Rocker Side-notched (RSN), and Rosegate (RG).

[e] Although the C. W. Harris site is not in the Mojave section but, rather, in San Diego County, it is included here because of its proximity to the Mojave section and because of the similarity of its assemblage to those in the Mojave section.

7

Points on the Continuum

Three Sites in a Middle Archaic Settlement System in the Western Great Basin

D. Craig Young

A simple axiom in Great Basin prehistory is this: Either foragers moved people to resources, or collectors moved resources to people (Binford 1980; Kelly 1992). Archaeologists have mulled over sites and their assemblages in search of patterns indicative of one or the other and, ultimately, have searched high and low (macro and micro) for theoretical frameworks that best suited their observations. The Middle Archaic of the western Great Basin is interesting because of its rich archaeological record and a diversity of site types, some of which contain datable assemblages in spatially organized patterns (O'Connell 1975; Riddell 1960; Smith and Ruest 1995; Young et al. 2009). The goal of this essay is to illustrate, using a series of archetypical sites, an elaborated pattern in regional prehistory—a pattern in which the interplay among provisioning behavior, social organization, and reduced residential mobility is relatively clear.

Prior to 4,000 years ago, it appears that Great Basin hunter-gatherers lived in relatively small groups that practiced an adaptive strategy characterized by a high degree of residential mobility (Simms 2008). Seasonal changes in the geographic distribution of important subsistence resources were dealt with by moving the entire group from places with declining productivity to locations where economic returns were enhanced. It has been suggested that sometime around 4,000 years ago this "forager" adaptation was generally replaced by a "collector" system with higher residential stability (Delacorte 1999; Elston et al. 1994; Hildebrandt and McGuire 2002; Madsen and Simms 1998; McGuire and Hildebrandt 2005). As Kelly (1992:51) points out, however, the appearance of villages or residential bases is not a cessation of movement; it is simply a change in movement. If we can isolate specific points on the continuum of movement, what might those places have looked like?

This chapter presents an analysis of three sites located between the Honey Lake Basin and the Truckee Meadows on the borderlands of Nevada and California, at the western edge of the Great Basin (Figure 7.1). The well-dated sites present a series of *poses*, or site types resulting from structural roles (Gearing 1958) within or along a varying continuum that comprises a complex Middle Archaic settlement-subsistence system in full elaboration. I present these sites because they provide a clear look at how gender-based behavioral differentiation, observed via site structure, had developed to a level that facilitated residential and logistical organization that, when conditions permitted, allowed economic shifts away from maximizing energetics toward political and social returns.

Each site presentation begins with a discussion of temporal data derived from radiocarbon dates, obsidian hydration, and projectile point types. After establishing the contemporaneity of the assemblages, the unique structural features of each site are presented to illustrate the settlement position or pose (e.g., base–camp–station [sensu Binford 1980:12]) within the Middle Archaic system. The site discussion concludes by describing the pattern of resource use indicated by toolstone acquisition and subsistence targets presented in each site assemblage. Full site descriptions along with site-specific excavation methods and laboratory analyses are presented in a series of reports and publications (Pendleton and Thomas 1983; Young and Garner 2009; Young et al. 2009). A discussion of the Middle Archaic settlement system and its implications for a clear framework regarding the provisioning–prestige continuum (Winterhalder and Bettinger 2010) exposed in the western Great Basin closes this chapter.

A Middle Archaic Base— Tufa Village (26Wa2460)

Tufa Village is a moderately sized, multicomponent site on the southern margin of Honey Lake (Figure 7.2). It was originally recorded as a small lithic scatter in the 1970s (Dunbar 1976); archaeological excavations in 2006 and 2007 revealed discrete loci spread across a sandy landform surrounding a set of dramatic tufa outcrops. Loci 1 and 3 comprise segregated activity areas

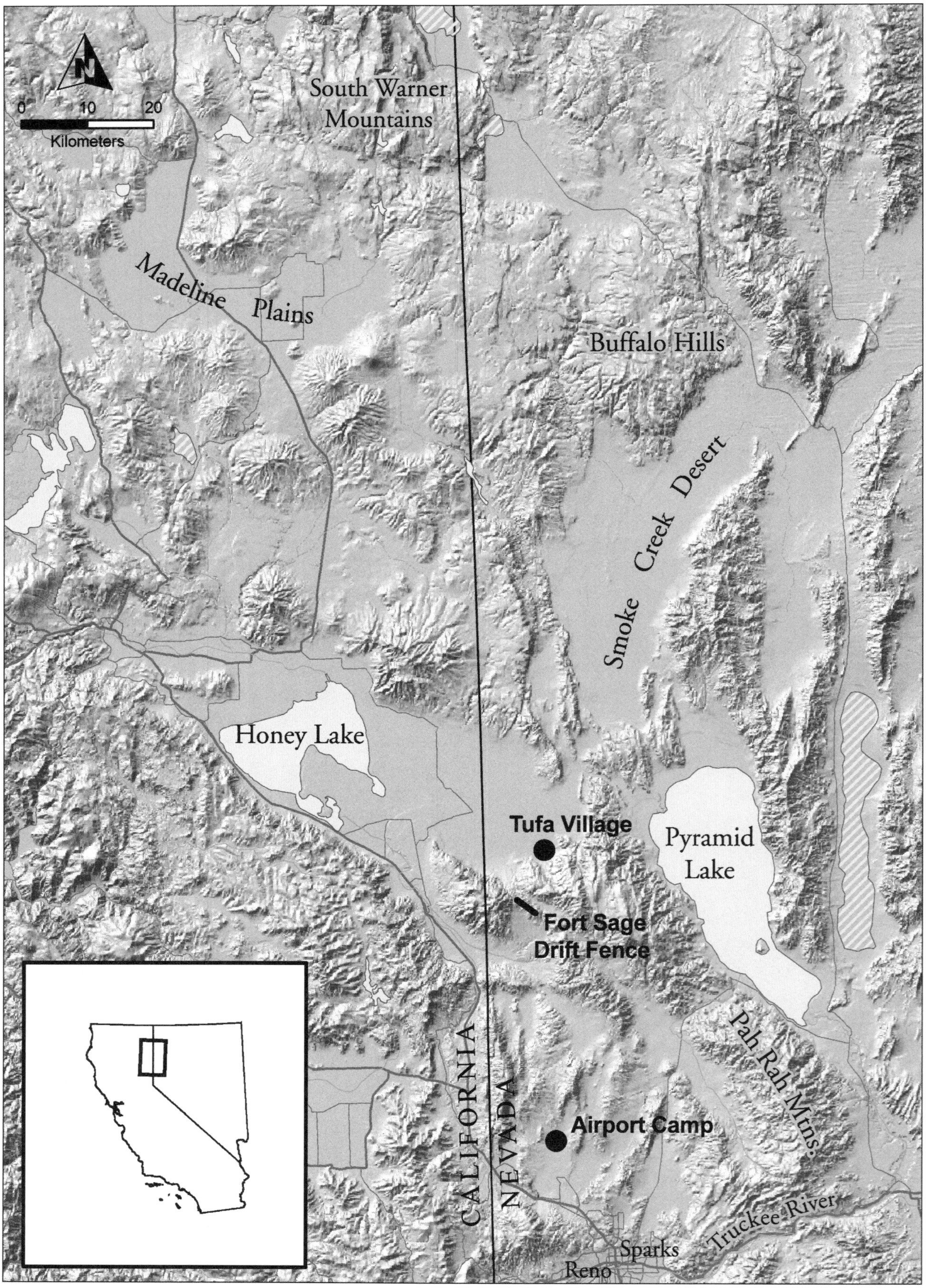

FIGURE 7.1. Poses of the western Great Basin Middle Archaic.

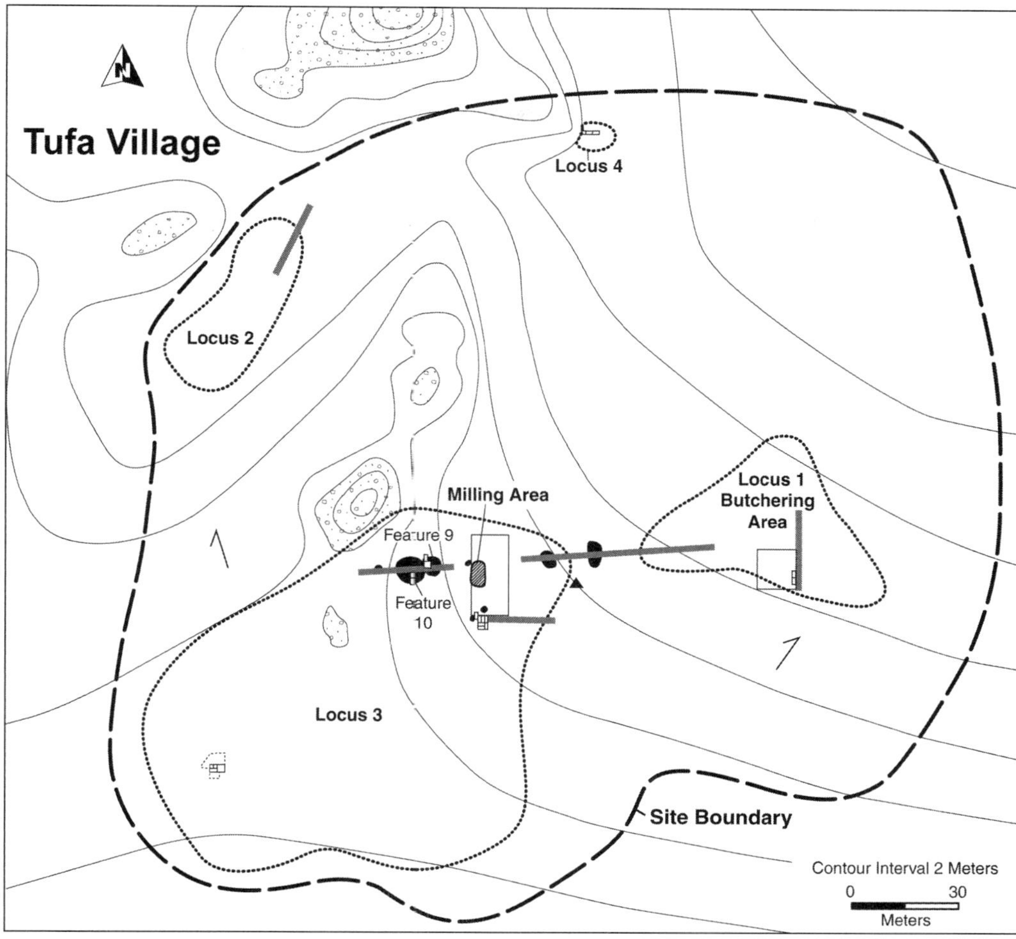

FIGURE 7.2. Tufa Village site map.

TABLE 7.1. Chronometric radiocarbon data from Tufa Village.

Provenience	Material	Lab No.	Conventional Age	Calibration 2σ	Calibration Intercept (cal BP)
Locus 1 (N1-E54)	Charcoal	Beta-230707	3503 ± 40	3910–3700	3830
Feature 3 Floor	Charcoal	Beta-230702	3260 ± 40	3570–2940	3470
Feature 4 Floor	Charcoal	Beta-230703	2910 ± 40	3210–2940	3060
Feature 9 Floor	Charcoal	Beta-236439	2700 ± 40	2870–2750	2780
Feature 10 Hearth (F15)	Bone	Beta-230705	3430 ± 40	3830–3580	3690
Feature 10 Floor	Charcoal	Beta-230706	3170 ± 40	3460–3340	3390
Feature 1 Hearth	Charcoal	Beta-230701	1590 ± 40	1560–1390	1520
Feature 8 Stain	Charcoal	Beta-230704	960 ± 40	940–780	920

(other loci, a small late-component rockshelter and a historic- to modern-era trash dump, are stratigraphically and spatially separate from the Middle Archaic component). The site sits well above the level of Holocene-age lake stands in the basin and does not appear to be positioned to take direct advantage of fringing wetland resources, though resources from the lake and its margins, including trout, suckers, and chub, were processed and used at the site (Young et al. 2009:71).

A narrow temporal resolution across the site shows that the segregated activity areas were in use at the same time (Figure 7.3; Tables 7.1–7.3). Radiocarbon dates, hydration readings, and point typology show tight clustering across the loci at Tufa Village. With the exception of one late radiocarbon date from the upper portion of the site's stratigraphy, samples drawn from each area cluster around 3,300 calendar years ago. Obsidian hydration on points, tools, and debitage from each area is similarly grouped. At first glance the distribution of hydration readings in Figure 7.3 appears rather broad, but each source has a slight, relative offset such that the plot reveals variation in hydration rates across the sources. It is clear that Buffalo Hills hydrates slower

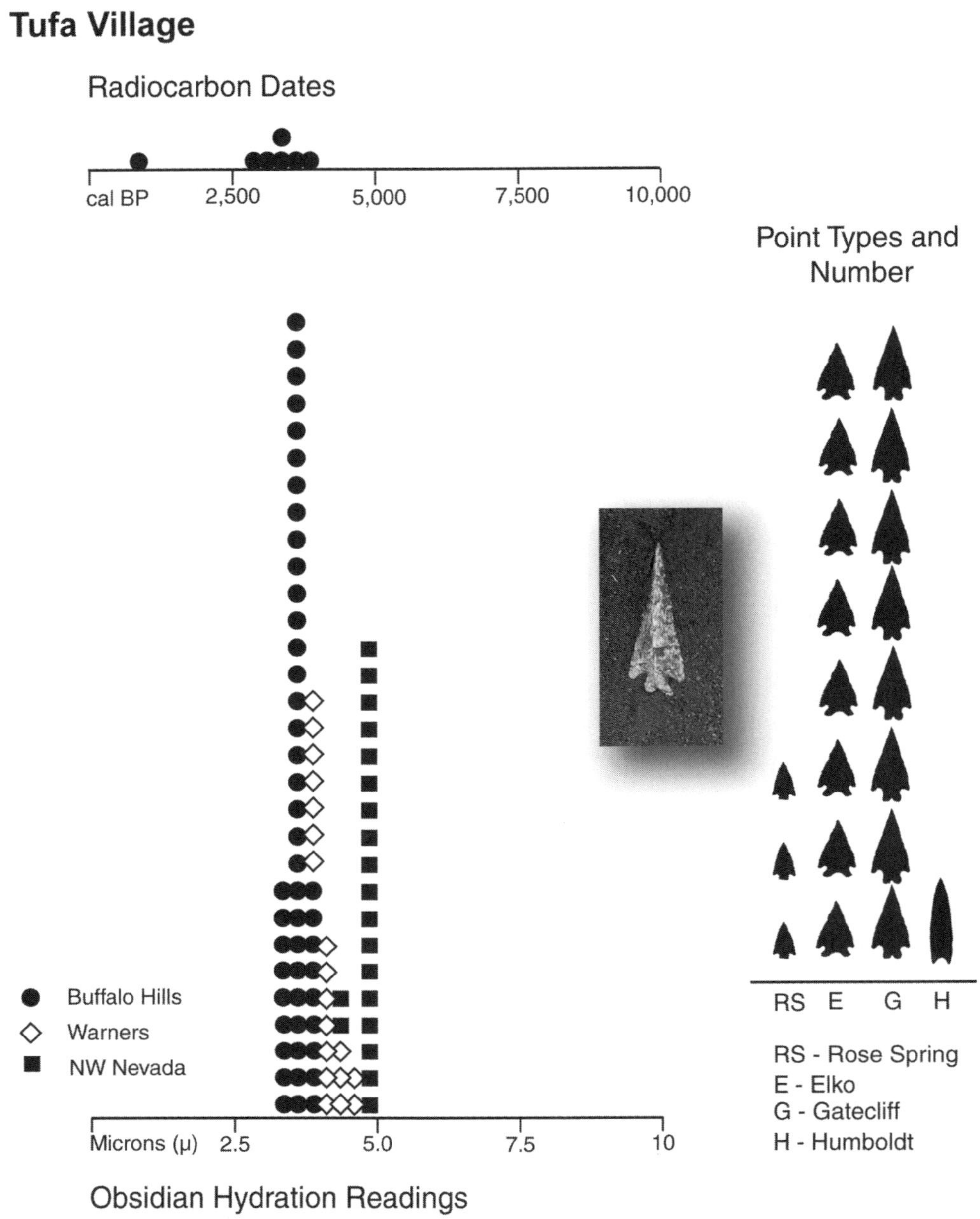

FIGURE 7.3. Temporal indicators at Tufa Village; inset: Gatecliff point.

than Warners, which hydrates slower than northwestern Nevada obsidians (see also Hildebrandt and King 2002). At the most general temporal resolution, the point assemblage from Loci 1 and 3 at Tufa Village still shows a distinct clustering of dart-sized Elko and Gatecliff series projectile points. All in all, it is relatively clear that site occupation, resulting in the formation of distinct organization patterning, falls within a narrow temporal range of the Great Basin Middle Archaic, with only minor revisits during more recent times.

Excavations using mechanical means for profile and broad surface exposures, along with focused hand excavations of over 20 m^3 of cultural deposits, revealed three discrete activity areas. Locus 1 contained primarily flaked-stone tools and debitage within a midden deposit containing a faunal assemblage with equal proportions of artiodactyl and leporid bones and minor amounts of bird and fish (Table 7.4). Locus 3 revealed two activity areas, a discrete milling area surrounded by a variety of midden-filled house depressions and processing features. The milling area contained numerous shaped and polished groundstone tools, including handstone and milling slab pairs. Handstones were also recycled as boiling rocks and cached within the milling area. Flaked-stone tools and some debitage were present in the milling area but in proportionally much lower numbers. Faunal elements in the milling area were predominantly rabbit remains.

The house features of Locus 3 surround the milling area. Hand excavations focused on four of the six large features exposed within the locus. Buried by recent alluvium and eolian re-

TABLE 7.2. Chronometric obsidian-hydration and sourcing data from Tufa Village.

PROVENIENCE	COUNT	SOURCE	MEAN (μm)	S D.	C.V.
Locus 1	9	Buffalo Hills	3.9	5	.13
	1	South Warners	4.3	—	—
Locus 3: Milling Area	16	Buffalo Hills	3.6	.5	.14
	6	South Warners	3.8	.5	.13
	6	NW Nevada	4.8	.3	.06
Locus 3: Feature 3	5	Buffalo Hills	3.7	.7	.19
	2	South Warners	4.4	—	—
	3	NW Nevada	4.9	.9	.18
Locus 3: Feature 4	7	Buffalo Hills	3.7	.6	.16
	2	South Warners	4.4	—	—
	1	NW Nevada	4.4	—	—
Locus 3: Feature 9	6	Buffalo Hills	3.4	.9	.26
	3	South Warners	4.3	.5	.12
	1	NW Nevada	4.3	—	—
Locus 3: Feature 10	4	Buffalo Hills	3.6	.3	.08
	9	NW Nevada	4.8	.3	.06

TABLE 7.3. Chronometric projectile point data from Tufa Village.

TYPE	COUNT	PROVENIENCE
Great Basin Stemmed	2	Locus 3
Humboldt Series	1	Locus 3
Gatecliff Series	8	Locus 1 (1), Locus 3 (7)
Elko Series	8	Locus 1 (1), Locus 3 (7)
Dart-Sized	3	Locus 3
Rose Spring Series	3	Locus 3
Nondiagnostic	7	Locus 1 (1), Locus 3 (6)

TABLE 7.4. Faunal assemblage by locus at Tufa Village.

		LOCUS 3			
FAUNA	LOCUS 1	FEATURE 3	FEATURE 9	MILLING AREA	TOTAL
Artiodactyl	47	10	46	15	118
Mountain Sheep		2	32	2	36
Deer	11		9	1	21
Subtotal	53	12	87	18	175
Lagomorph	65	184	127	66	443
Jackrabbit		5	15	3	23
Cottontail	2	15	8	2	27
Subtotal	63	204	150	71	493
Dog/Coyote			3		3
Bird	22		4	1	27
Duck			1	1	2
Subtotal	22		5	2	29
Fish	8	12	1	2	23
Minnows/Suckers	1	8			9
Cut Throat Trout/Trout		1	3		4
Tui Chub		1	2		3
Subtotal	9	22	6	2	39
Reptiles	1	29	64	4	98
Rodents/Insectivores	4	23	10	2	39
Total	162	290	325	99	876

working, the features lack modern surface expression, but, once exposed, the midden-filled matrix in the sandy parent material made documentation and excavation of the features straightforward. The features are generally circular depressions with steep to moderately sloping margins; they vary from 3 to 6 m in maximum diameter and can be as much as 70 cm deep.

Archaeological sampling of the features provided a relatively clear look at feature structure and variability. The large features are circular house-like structures and refuse areas for faunal debris; abandoned houses were filled with discarded faunal elements and other organic residues following shifts in house position. Features 9 and 10 are particularly interesting. Feature 9 had an even mix of flaked- and ground-stone implements and a relatively even mix of small and large faunal elements. Flotation revealed abundant *Typha* seeds and fragments in Feature 9, likely remnants of building material or matting. Excavations in

FIGURE 7.4. Bone bed within Feature 10 at Tufa Village.

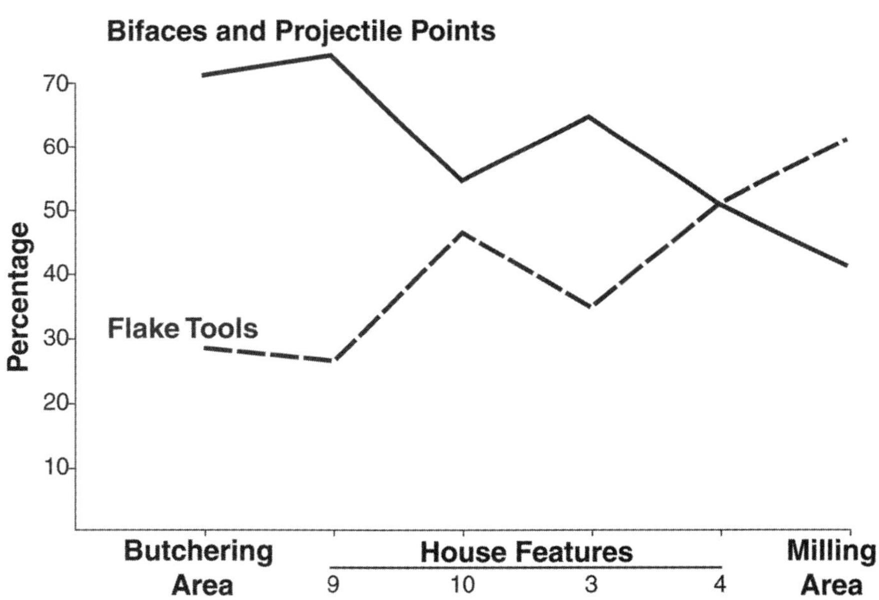

FIGURE 7.5. Hunting vs. processing equipment: bifaces/points to flaked tools.

Feature 10 revealed internal hearths with articulated and semi-articulated artiodactyl bones in a midden overlying the hearths (Figure 7.4). Similarly large, complete faunal remains were absent from Feature 9, but this relatively clean structure contained a bighorn ram skull and Gatecliff series projectile points resting on the floor.

The intrasite patterning at Tufa Village is well preserved. Along with the spatial segregation of features and processing areas, assemblage analyses revealed a distribution of artifact types mirroring the overall site pattern. Across the loci, there is a relatively linear transition between hunting equipment and processing tools (Figure 7.5) and even greater shifts in the distribution of tool types (Figure 7.6). Flaked-stone tools dominated the butchering area and were less important in the milling area. Bone tool use was centered on the domestic or storage areas of the house features. In sum, the segregation of the butchering area of Locus 1, the milling area, and surrounding house features of Locus 3 reveals clear patterns of site organization that likely

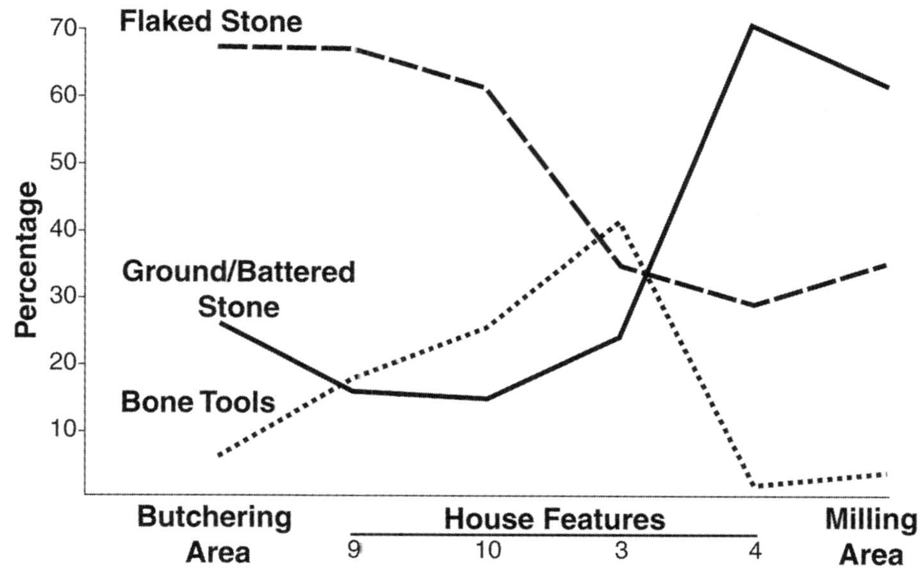

FIGURE 7.6. Hunting vs. processing equipment: tool type indexes.

TABLE 7.5. Chronometric radiocarbon data from Airport Camp.

Provenience	Material	Lab Number	Conventional Age	Calibration	
				2σ	Intercept (cal BP)
Feature 2	Charcoal	Beta-250583	2980 ± 40	3350–3080	3230
Feature 3	Charcoal	Beta-250584	3030 ± 40	3320–3030	3170, 3190, 3200
Feature 4	Charcoal	Beta-250582	3020 ± 40	3350–3090	3250

developed within a structure of distinct gender-differentiated work patterns.

A Middle Archaic Camp: Airport Camp (26Wa3227)

Airport Camp is a small site on the northwestern margin of the broad basin occupied by the Silver Lake and Lemmon Valley marshes, northwest of the Truckee Meadows (Figure 7.7). As with Tufa Village, the site's landform position allowed quick, postoccupation burial by alluvium and eolian sands.

The camp's chronology and obsidian source profile, though derived from a much smaller sample across a much simpler space, mirror those of Tufa Village (Figure 7.8). Three radiocarbon dates from the sealed occupation cluster tightly at about 3,000 years ago (Table 7.5). As at Tufa Village, the obsidian-hydration readings from across the site show a tight grouping, with inter-source differences due to slightly different hydration rates (Table 7.6). The obsidian sources show a distinct northern (i.e., Buffalo Hills and Warners) emphasis, also mirroring that from Tufa Village. Elko series dart points dominate the point assemblage (Table 7.7).

The site consists of a small midden adjacent to a single house floor with milling gear and an exterior hearth. The count of milling artifacts, handstones and slabs, equals the number of points

TABLE 7.6. Chronometric obsidian-hydration and sourcing data from Airport Camp.

Provenience	Count	Source	Mean (μm)	S.D.	C.V.
Feature 2	1	Bodie Hills	3.8	—	—
	4	Buffalo Hills	3.0	—	—
	1	South Warners	3.5	—	—
Feature 3	2	Buffalo Hills	3.3	—	—
	3	South Warners	3.9	.05	.01
Feature 4	4	Buffalo Hills	3.3	.5	.15
	1	South Warners	3.7	—	—

TABLE 7.7. Chronometric projectile point data from Airport Camp.

Type	Count	Provenience
Elko Series	6	Feature 2 (2); Site (4)
Nondiagnostic	1	Site

recovered at the site, yet the entire tool assemblage consists of fewer than 30 items. Milling gear includes large slabs retrieved from nearby hills that show shaping and incipient strong polishing. Local milling of fall-season seeds, augmented by acorns transported from the Sierran foothills nearby, appears to have been the focus of site use (Table 7.8). The degree of midden development and use-wear on the milling gear suggests site

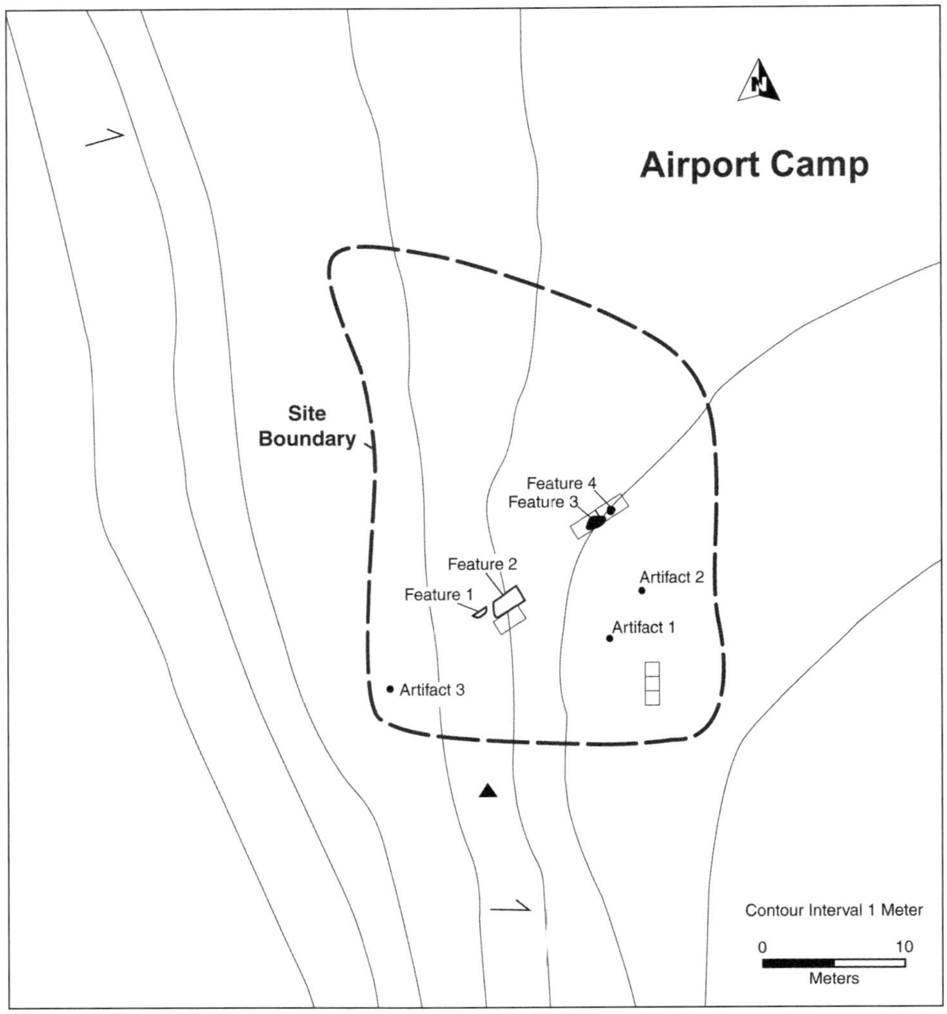

FIGURE 7.7. Airport Camp site map.

TABLE 7.8. Floral assemblage at Airport Camp: botanical attributes and cultural uses.

Taxon	Common Name	Growth	Habitat(s)	Part Eaten	Seasonal Availability
Atriplex spp.	Saltbush	Shrub	Saline flats	Seed	Fall
Chenopodium spp.	Goosefoot	Herb	Varied; often disturbed places	Seed	Summer and fall
Mentzelia spp.	Blazing star	Herb	Dry well-drained soils	Seed	Late spring
Pinus spp.	Pine	Tree	Varied	Nut	Fall
Quercus spp.	Oak	Tree	Eastern Sierra front	Nut	Fall

occupation of some duration, but feature number and size suggest little reuse of this camp locale. Hunters accompanied the camp, adding dart points to the assemblage.

Airport Camp functioned as a camp (sensu Binford 1980:10) within the regional Middle Archaic settlement and subsistence system. The low-diversity artifact assemblage marks a small field camp positioned near seed and plant resources on the dry margins of Lemmon Valley. Site structure and assemblage composition suggest that Airport Camp may have been a short-term, family-occupied, logistical camp, possibly with ties to Tufa Village, along the eastern front of the northern Sierra.

The camp is a pose within a Honey Lake (northern) pattern without significant connections to the Truckee Meadows. Truckee Meadows sites tend to have a relatively even distribution of obsidian toolstones (Stoner et al. 2006) and often have very little northwestern Nevada obsidian at all (Kautz 1999). A field camp (or other site type) tethered to a residential base in the Truckee Meadows should retain an obsidian profile similar to that observed at the base. The Airport Camp obsidian profile is very different than the sources found at the winter base at 26Wa7522 in the Truckee Meadows, which includes a well-preserved Middle Archaic (Early Martis) component (Stoner et al. 2006). When compared with the base of Tufa Village, however, the radiocarbon dates are basically the same, and the obsid-

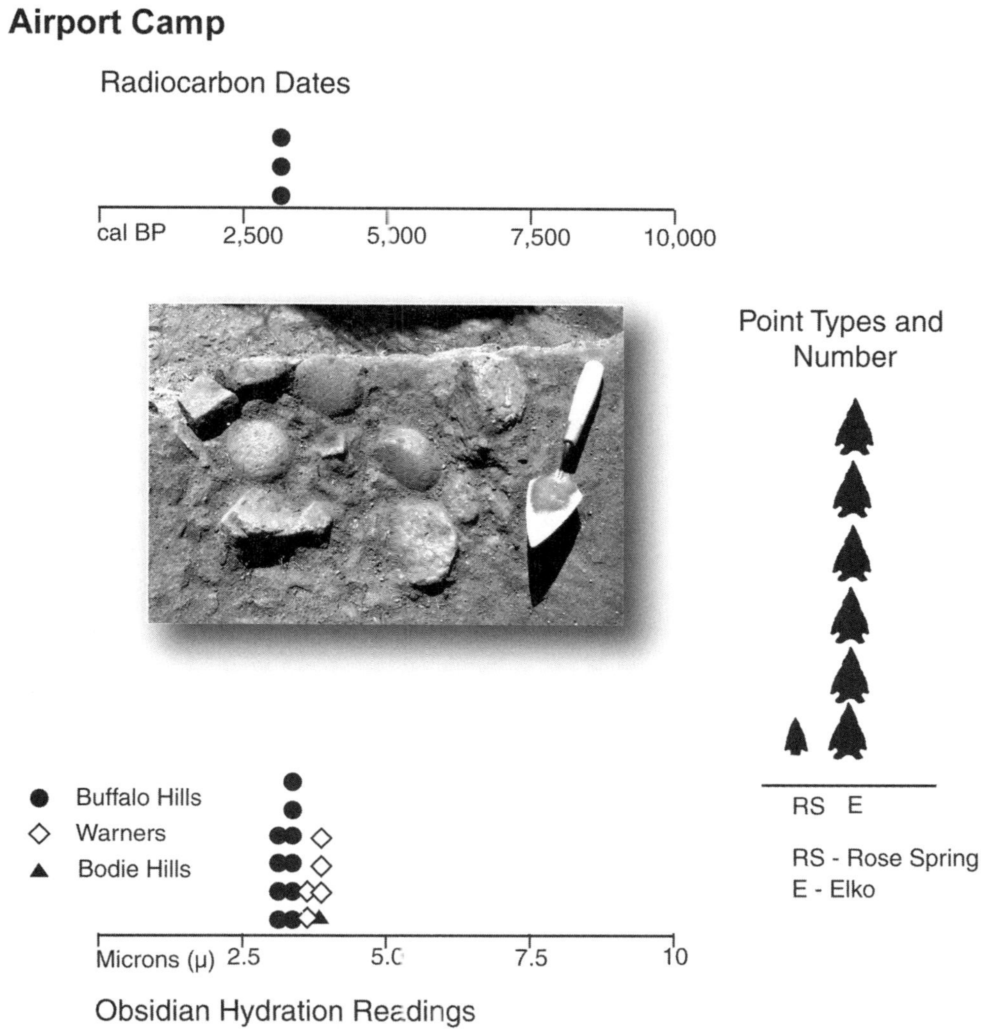

FIGURE 7.8. Temporal indicators at Airport Camp; inset: hearth (F1).

ian profiles are almost identical. It is almost a luxury to have two capped and contemporaneous, single-component sites marking different poses along the settlement continuum.

A Middle Archaic Location: The Fort Sage Drift Fence

For a third pose, the dramatic, large-scale features of the Fort Sage Drift Fence in the low mountain range between Tufa Village and Airport Camp stand out. Documented by Pendleton and Thomas (1983), the Drift Fence is one of the largest prehistoric rock features in the Great Basin (Figure 7.9). It stretches with purposeful gaps across almost 2,200 m of the south-facing slopes of the Fort Sage Mountains. The substantial, well-built walls commonly approach a meter in height, and in places the walls exceed this dimension in width. Clast sizes vary from large boulders to small cobbles, and many of the placed boulders certainly required several people to move. Bedrock outcrops and massive boulders were incorporated in the structure's position and alignment. The pattern of construction is relatively consistent across the extent of the fence complex, an indication that it was likely built over a relatively short period of time. As Pendleton and Thomas (1983) point out, this is clearly a labor-intensive feature.

Pendleton and Thomas's (1983) summary of diagnostic artifacts associated with the Drift Fence and similar large, permanent facilities across the Great Basin revealed that the construction and use of these features began and were regularized in the Middle Archaic. The collection is small, but dart points collected by Pendleton and Thomas (1983:14–15) dominate the Fort Sage point assemblage (Figure 7.10). The leaf-shaped points are not temporally diagnostic, but those from the fence are in the same size range as Gatecliff and Elko series points in the collection.

With the assistance of the American Museum of Natural History, I was able to analyze all of the obsidian debitage and a sample of the obsidian tools surface-collected by Pendleton and Thomas during their inventory of the Drift Fence (Tables 7.9 and 7.10). Sourcing data provided by Richard Hughes show a distinct prevalence of northwestern Nevada sources including Bordwell Springs and Buffalo Hills. A single obsidian flake originated from a Truckee Meadows–area source (Sutro Springs) to the

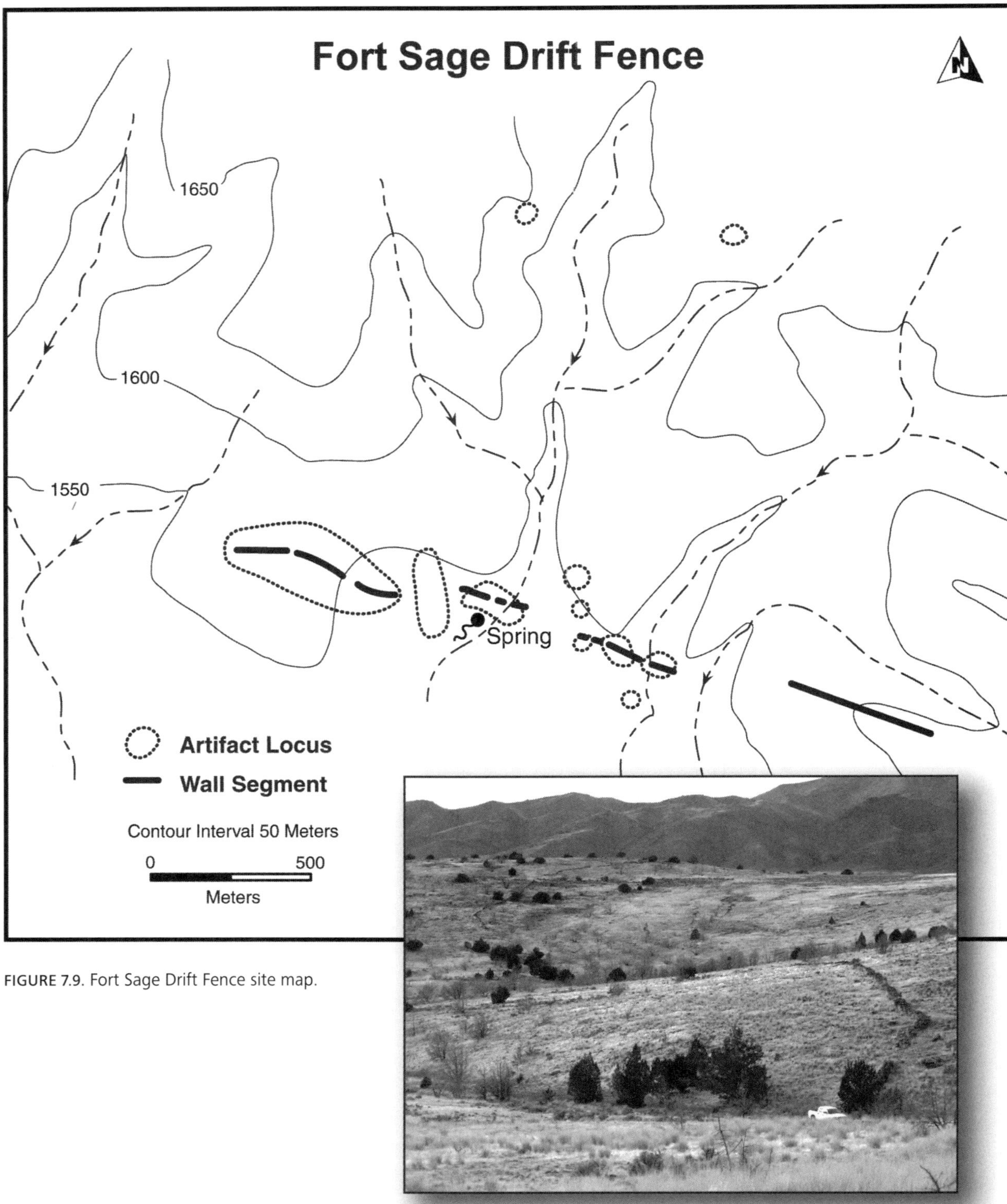

FIGURE 7.9. Fort Sage Drift Fence site map.

south. The hydration data, produced by Tim Carpenter, reveal a wide distribution of rind thickness, with many pieces heavily weathered such that readings were difficult. This preliminary information supports the hypothesis (Pendleton and Thomas 1983) that the fence was first established several thousand years ago within a Middle Archaic pattern. In general, the hydration rinds are larger than expected for direct association with either Tufa Village or Airport Camp, but it is clear that the Drift Fence was in use within the temporal range of occupation at the two sites. And based on the faunal assemblage and projectile point similarities observed at Tufa Village, a patterned connection between the base and the location is suggested. The lakeside Tufa

FIGURE 7.10. Temporal indicators at Fort Sage Drift Fence.

Village is only separated from the dry-land Drift Fence by one low pass and a few miles.

At the time, Pendleton and Thomas (1983) stressed that interpretation of the Drift Fence was problematic because of a general lack of subsistence and assemblage information available at a logistical location (Binford 1980:9). And yet, they successfully looked across the Great Basin to provide the facility with a general interpretive context. It is clear that this logistical location required group cooperation and a large time and energy investment. These social and energetic investments reveal, at a minimum, Middle Archaic expectations of significant and predictable returns. Today, the features and assemblages at Tufa Village and, by extension, Airport Camp provide a contextual backdrop for viewing the Fort Sage Drift Fence as a third pose within an elaborate Middle Archaic system.

Discussion: An Elaborate Middle Archaic System and the Provisioning–Prestige Continuum

At first glance, archaeologists have recently focused on a theoretical dichotomy to explain the apparent patterning in hunter-gatherer behavior in prehistoric California and the Great Basin, in general, and during the Middle Archaic, in particular (Broughton and Bayham 2003; Codding and Jones 2007; Hildebrandt and McGuire 2002; McGuire and Hildebrandt 2005; see also papers from the "Human Behavioral Ecology and California Archaeology" symposium reviewed by Winterhalder and Bettinger [2010]). Although it is termed the *provisioning vs. prestige* debate by Winterhalder and Bettinger (2010:96), a closer look reveals that these seemingly polarized arguments have produced a better understanding of the complexities along the broad continuum of hunter-gatherer behavior. It is unlikely that this fact is lost on any of the debate participants.

TABLE 7.9. Chronometric obsidian-hydration and sourcing data from Fort Sage Drift Fence.

Provenience	Count	Source	Mean (μm)	S.D.	C.V.
Site	2	Majuba—Seven Troughs	14.0	.2	.02
Site	10	Northwest Nevada	5.3	1.7	.33
Site	4	Buffalo Hills	4.6	2.4	.52
Site	1	Sutro Springs	4.2	—	—
Site	2	South Warners	3.7	.3	.08

TABLE 7.10. Chronometric projectile point data from Fort Sage Drift Fence.

Type	Count	Provenience
Leaf-Shaped	5	Locus 1, Locus 7, Locus 9 (2), Locus 11
Gatecliff Series	3	Locus 3 (2), Locus 9
Elko Series	3	Locus 1 (2), Locus 11
Rose Spring Series	2	Locus 1, Locus 3
Desert Series	1	Locus 5

Regardless of one's entry point along the "debate" continuum, it is clear that site structure, social organization, and assemblage composition, that is, the myriad of things we have come to call Middle Archaic, experienced fundamental changes across the middle to late Holocene, reaching full elaboration in and around Honey Lake at about 3,000 years ago. Prior to this time, prehistoric people were relatively dispersed, relying on a "mapping-on" strategy to resolve seasonal or environmental changes in resources (Hildebrandt and McGuire 2002; Simms 2008). Provisioning theory, including diet breadth and central place foraging models, may best predict the mobility changes as hunter-gatherers transitioned from foragers to collectors. These changes may be induced by environmental stress, resource abundance, or local demographic shifts (Bayham et al. 2012; Broughton and Bayham 2003). As people adapted to local environments, activity differentiation, especially along gender lines, and social interactions took precedence; this may have occurred seasonally or as resource conditions allowed. While female provisioning underwrote male behavior, activities such as hunting and toolstone acquisition became increasingly imbued with social and political meaning (McGuire and Hildebrandt 2005). For example, Morgan (2009) has shown that activities predicted by diet breadth and central place foraging theory likely supported relatively circumscribed but influential elaborations in behavior. Elaborations likely included growing sociopolitical agendas and prestige-seeking behavior. Prestige theory, or costly signaling theory, may better explain the rise of inefficient provisioning (McGuire and Hildebrandt 2005) and better predict the structure of the archaeological record as social feedback strengthened under appropriate conditions.

In looking at this admittedly small, though highly resolved sample of sites, or discrete poses within the settlement pattern of the western Great Basin, it is possible to view some characteristics of the Middle Archaic in full elaboration. Tufa Village, Airport Camp, and the Fort Sage Drift Fence are simply three sites illustrative of the elaborated pattern; each site has a relatively clear and contemporaneous temporal context and well-preserved social space.

Tufa Village may have been first occupied as a lakeside camp where a variety of resource patches—fish, rabbits, seeds, and, increasingly, artiodactyls—were in close proximity on the broad fans and lacustrine benches of the Honey Lake basin. Female and male provisioning activities influenced camp formation, as might be predicted by central place foraging. At the same time or earlier, use of the Fort Sage Drift Fence became regular (Pendleton and Thomas 1983), and big-game deposition, important because of high caloric rank and prestige potential (Bayham et al. 2012; Hildebrandt and McGuire 2002), increased at Tufa Village. The village retained spatial segregation of milling and processing areas as local provisioning continued; but game was brought to camp via targeted logistical trips. A ram's skull was given prominence in the center of a house floor (Feature 9), accompanied by complete Gatecliff series projectile points. Social organization in the form of gender-differentiated work space and signaling behavior (e.g., the displayed trophy or icon?) was evident within the village. Male activities included many trips to the Drift Fence, while other logistical forays targeted toolstone sources at Buffalo Hills (the rarity of other sources reinforces the reliance on specifically targeted resources). Signaling required an audience (McGuire and Hildebrandt 2005), so settlement aggregations, such as Tufa Village, were necessary for the social feedback to become established. However, a game-acquisition location of the scale of the Fort Sage Drift Fence requires cooperation for construction and use, so political necessities were also important. Construction and drive activities may have benefited from leadership positions garnered through sharing and political reinforcement of intragroup relations.

Based on its obsidian profile and contemporary age, Airport Camp may have had a role in the targeted logistics emanating from Tufa Village. At times, small family groups may have separated from the aggregate to monitor resources or take advantage of local abundance some distance from the village. Although Airport Camp is in relatively close proximity to the fishery and relative resource abundance of the Truckee Meadows, the camp relied on Buffalo Hills obsidian and lacks toolstone commonly found in Truckee Meadows (Stoner et al. 2006). The site was connected to a northern Honey Lake settlement system. Quite possibly, Airport Camp was a satellite, short-term camp used by a family or other small group familiar with Tufa Village and the Drift Fence. Provisioning theory may best explain and predict the location, assemblage structure, and resource targets for sites, such as Airport Camp, tethered to village or base locations, while prestige theory may be useful for investigating the interactions (e.g., retrieved resources) and overall organization within the system (Grimstead and Bayham 2010).

In sum, the three sites (Tufa Village, Airport Camp, and the Fort Sage Drift Fence) provide archetypical settings, or poses, illustrative of a formalized settlement system we can identify as the regional Middle Archaic. The elaborated pattern may also be evident in assemblages from well-known Middle Archaic components from the Karlo site (Riddell 1960), with its formalized and socially stratified burials, to the storage facilities and resource targets in the decoys and textiles of Lovelock Cave (Fowler and Fowler 1990:8; Heizer and Napton 1970). These sites and many others reveal that environmental and social conditions facilitated residential and logistical organizations unprecedented in Great Basin prehistory. If we recognizing the possibilities, the Middle Archaic of the Great Basin provides a rich laboratory for archaeological investigation, where robust discussion from a variety of theoretical perspectives will continue to progress and thrive.

Acknowledgments

In the more than 20 years since I first met Don Fowler, on my first encounter with the archaeologist and the Great Basin, I have been attracted to and challenged by the archaeological record of the region. In Warner Valley, Oregon, we shared that wonder with groups of students during the University of Nevada's annual field school. In that great landscape below Hart Mountain, Dr. Fowler presented me with many opportunities and introduced me to mentors, colleagues, and friends who continue to influence me. Thank you, Don.

I am honored that Joel Janetski asked that I be a small part of this esteemed collection. Tammara Norton kindly produced all the graphics. Jim Carter and the Carson City Bureau of Land Management provided the opportunity to work on these wonderful sites. My consideration of Tufa Village has benefited from many conversations with Bill Hildebrandt. Thanks go to each of you.

References Cited

Bayham, Frank E., R. Kelly Beck, and Kimberley L. Carpenter

2012 Large Game Exploitation and Intertribal Boundaries on the Fringe of the Western Great Basin. In *Meetings at the Margins: Prehistoric Cultural Interactions in the Intermountain West*, edited by David Rhode, pp. 103–123. University of Utah Press, Salt Lake City.

Binford, Lewis R.

1980 Willow Smoke and Dogs' Tails: Hunter-Gatherer Settlement Systems and Archaeological Site Formation. *American Antiquity* 45:4–20.

Broughton, Jack M., and Frank E. Bayham

2003 Showing Off, Foraging Models, and the Ascendance of Large-Game Hunting in the California Middle Archaic. *American Antiquity* 68:783–789.

Delacorte, Michael G.
1999 The Changing Role of Riverine Environments in the Prehistory of the Central-Western Great Basin: Data Recovery Excavations at Six Prehistoric Sites in Owens Valley, California. Report submitted to the California Department of Transportation, District 9, Bishop. Far Western Anthropological Research Group, Inc., Davis.

Dunbar, Helen R.
1976 ArNV-31-59 Short Form, Cultural Resources Inventory Record. Bureau of Land Management, Carson City.

Elston, Robert G., Susan Stornetta, Daniel P. Dugas, and Peter Mires
1994 *Beyond the Blue Roof: An Archaeological Survey on Mt. Rose Fan and Northern Steamboat Hills*. Report submitted to Toiyabe National Forest, Reno. Intermountain Research, Silver City, Nevada.

Fowler, Catherine S., and Don D. Fowler
1990 A History of Wetlands Anthropology in the Great Basin. In *Wetlands Adaptations in the Great Basin*, edited by Joel C. Janetski and David B. Madsen, pp. 5–16. Occasional Papers No. 1. Museum of Peoples and Cultures, Brigham Young University, Provo.

Gearing, Fred
1958 The Structural Poses of 18th Century Cherokee Villages. *American Anthropologist* 60:1148–1157.

Grimstead, Deanna N., and Frank E. Bayham
2010 Evolutionary Ecology, Elite Feasting, and the Hohokam: A Case Study from a Southern Arizona Platform Mound. *American Antiquity* 75:841–864.

Heizer, Robert F., and Kyle L. Napton
1970 *Archaeological Investigations in Lovelock Cave, Nevada*. University of California Archaeological Research Facility Contributions, 10. Berkeley.

Hildebrandt, William R., and Jerome H. King
2002 Projectile Point Variability Along the Northern California–Great Basin Interface: Results from the Tuscarora-Alturas Projects. In *Boundary Lands: Archaeological Investigations Along the California–Great Basin Interface*, edited by Kelly R. McGuire, pp. 5–28. Anthropological Papers No. 24. Nevada State Museum, Carson City.

Hildebrandt, William R., and Kelly R. McGuire
2002 The Ascendance of Hunting During the California Middle Archaic: An Evolutionary Perspective. *American Antiquity* 67:231–256.

Kautz, Robert R.
1999 Modeling Precontact Lifeways in the Truckee Meadows. Paper presented at the 28th Annual Conference of the Nevada Archaeological Association, Reno.

Kelly, Robert L.
1992 Mobility/Sedentism: Concepts, Archaeological Measures, and Effects. *Annual Review of Anthropology* 21:43–66.

Madsen, David B., and Steven R. Simms
1998 The Fremont Complex: A Behavioral Perspective. *Journal of World Prehistory* 12:255–336.

McGuire, Kelly R., and William R. Hildebrandt
2005 Re-Thinking Great Basin Foragers: Prestige Hunting and Costly Signaling During the Middle Archaic Period. *American Antiquity* 70:693–710.

Morgan, Christopher
2009 Optimal Foraging Patterns in the Sierra Nevada, Alta California. *California Archaeology* 1:205–226.

O'Connell, James F.
1975 *The Prehistory of Surprise Valley*. Anthropological Papers Vol. 4. Ballena Press, Ramona, California.

Pendleton, Lorann S. A., and David H. Thomas
1983 *The Fort Sage Drift Fence, Washoe County, Nevada*. Anthropological Papers Vol. 58, Pt. 2. American Museum of Natural History, New York.

Riddell, Francis A.
1960 *The Archaeology of the Karlo Site (Las-7), California*. Reports of the University of California Archaeological Survey Vol. 53. Department of Anthropology, University of California, Berkeley.

Simms, Steven R.
2008 Ancient Peoples of the Great Basin and the Colorado Plateau. Left Coast Press, Walnut Creek.

Stoner, Edward J., Mary C. Ringhoff, Robert R. Peterson, and Jennifer Sigler
2006 The Archaeology of "The Biggest Little City in the World," the ReTrac Project, Reno, Washoe County, Nevada: Prehistoric Resources, Vol. 1. Report submitted to the Federal Highway Administration, Carson City. Western Cultural Resources Management, Sparks.

Winterhalder, Bruce, and Robert L. Bettinger
2010 Nutritional and Social Benefits of Foraging in Ancient California. *California Archaeology* 2:93–110.

Young, D. Craig, and Albert R. Garner
2009 Archaeological Data Recovery at 26Wa3227: A Middle Archaic Logistical Camp near the Reno/Stead Airport in Lemmon Valley, Washoe County, Nevada. Report No. CRR3-3113-7. Submitted to the Carson City District Office, Bureau of Land Management. Far Western Anthropological Research Group, Inc., Davis.

Young, D. Craig, William R. Hildebrandt, Steven D. Neidig, and Sharon A. Waechter
2009 *From Fish Springs to Dry Valley: Archaeological Investigations on the Vidler Water Project Corridor, Washoe County, Nevada*. Report No. CRR3-2237-8. Submitted to the Carson City District Office, Bureau of Land Management. Far Western Anthropological Research Group, Inc., Davis.

8

Foragers, Farmers, and In Between

Variability in the Late Archaic in the Southern Southwest

Barbara J. Roth

Don Fowler has written numerous essays in which he discusses variability in the archaeological record and how important it is to look for patterns in that record. He has also talked about how archaeologists use data to reconstruct social categories in the past. The goal of this chapter is to present a summary of the Late Archaic in the southern Southwest, so I use Don's work as a starting point to discuss the variability that we see during this period. I argue that part of the difficulty that researchers have in accepting this variability and incorporating it into their interpretations is tied to the way that they view projectile points. Despite the fact that most researchers today grew up in the era of processual or postprocessual archaeology, the approach taken by Archaic period researchers is often very traditional, classifying "cultures" based on the projectile points that groups used. One of the major problems with this emphasis on typology is that it results in an artificial portrayal of homogeneity during the Archaic period. There has been a lack of concern with the way differences in both economic and social strategies are reflected in site location and site contents, despite the fact that these are often apparent in the archaeological record. I argue that we should study the Late Archaic period by focusing on settlement and subsistence strategies and social organization across the region, seeking to document both similarities and differences between groups. This approach provides a different view of southern Late Archaic populations, one that reflects variation and flexibility rather than uniform adaptation.

The Late Archaic Period in the Southern Southwest

Several key issues frame our understanding of the Late Archaic period in the southern Southwest, defined here as encompassing the portion of southern Arizona south of the Mogollon Rim and east of the Papagueria, southwestern New Mexico, and portions of northern Mexico (Figure 8.1). This chapter focuses on the Middle-to-Late Archaic transition and the earliest part of the Late Archaic period, the San Pedro phase (1200–800 BC). The succeeding Cienega phase (800 BC–AD 200) witnessed some substantial changes in economic and social organization, and its classification as part of the Late Archaic period has been debated (Huckell 1995), so it is not included in this discussion. Huckell (1995) has encouraged classifying both the San Pedro and Cienega phases within the "Early Agricultural period" in the southern deserts. However, because of the variability discussed below, classifying all of these groups under this rubric may not be valid. As a result, many researchers, including me, have continued to refer to the San Pedro phase as falling within the Late Archaic period.

The Middle Archaic period (ca. 4000–1500 BC) in the southern Southwest is represented by a number of campsites and resource-procurement sites located in a range of environmental zones but generally concentrated in areas with reliable water sources and high resource density (Agenbroad 1970; Chavarria 1996; Dart 1986; Douglas and Craig 1986; Downum et al. 1986; Gregory 1999; Kaldahl 2001; Roth 1995, 1996; Simpson and Wells 1983; Slawson 1987; Whalen 1971). The available data suggest that Middle Archaic groups were mobile foragers moving within specific territories, with some evidence of prolonged and/or repeated occupation in resource-rich zones such as river floodplains and mountain foothills. Recent research documents the presence of maize at several different sites across southern Arizona dating to 2000 BC, during the latter part of the Middle Archaic period, and a number of sites in the northern Southwest also have maize dating within this time frame (Table 8.1). For the southern Southwest, Freeman and I (Roth and Freeman 2008) have argued that certain Middle Archaic period foraging behaviors facilitated the adoption of maize agriculture, including the repetitive use of the floodplain, a seasonal focus on annual grasses, and the availability of ground-stone technology for processing maize. Patterns in the northern Southwest appear to be different, with maize added as a supplement to facilitate foraging behaviors (Huber 2005; Wills 1992).

The San Pedro phase (1200–800 BC) witnessed some sub-

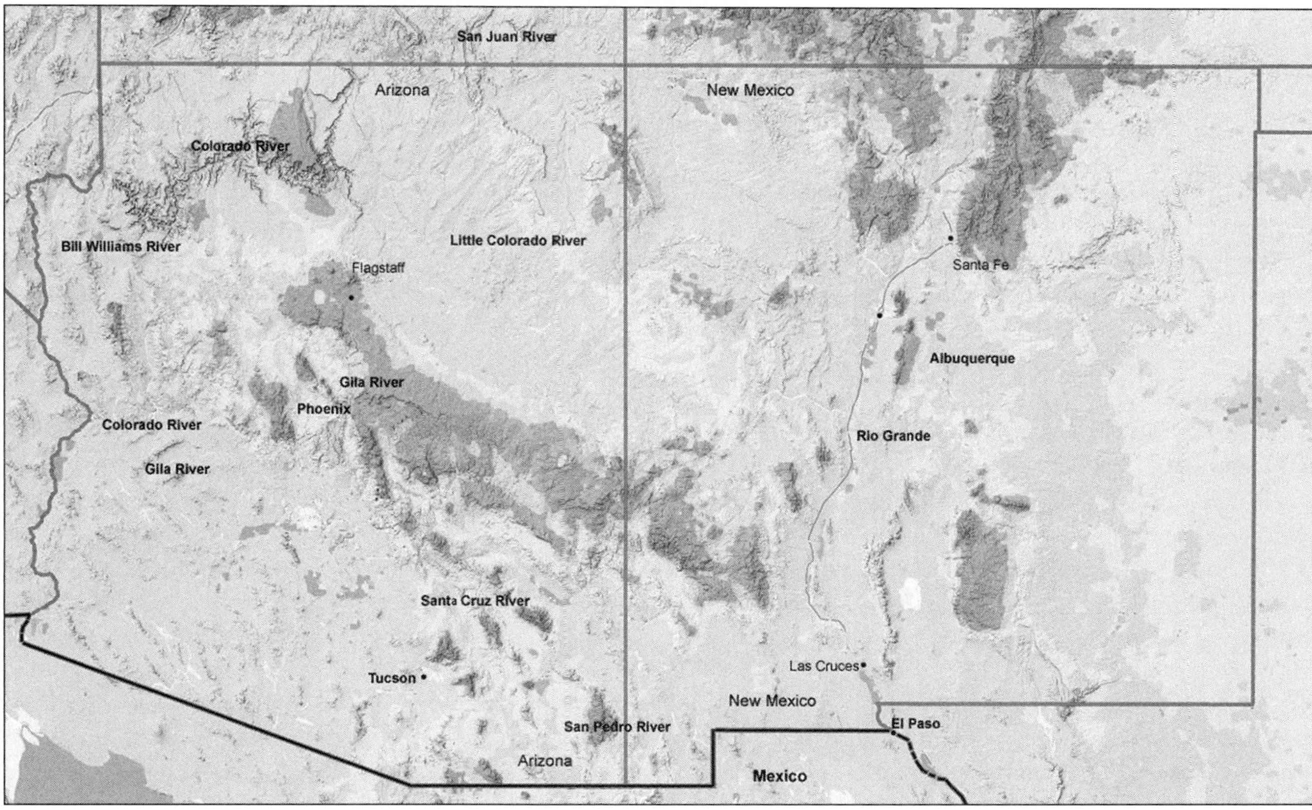

FIGURE 8.1. Map of the southern Southwest.

stantial changes in occupation, tied primarily to the integration of maize into the diet. Diehl (2005) has emphasized that although maize became an important resource, San Pedro phase groups still maintained a focus on wild resource procurement and refers to these groups as "farmagers" to illustrate this point. Other material culture changes documented at some sites during the San Pedro phase include the use of pit structures, usually shallow round or oval structures with bent-pole construction (Gregory and Huckell 1998); a plethora of pits, including hearths, roasting pits, conical pits, and large bell-shaped storage pits; shell jewelry (suggesting shell exchange); ceramic figurines; ceramic sherds that represent what Heidke et al. (1998) refer to as "incipient plainware"; and San Pedro points (Huckell 1995; Mabry 2005a, 2008). Some sites in the Tucson Basin contain extensive irrigation systems (Mabry 2008). As will be discussed in more detail below, not all of these traits appear at the same time in all portions of the southern Southwest.

TABLE 8.1. Early dates on maize in the southern Southwest.

Site	Location	Date(s)	Reference
Las Capas	Tucson Basin	3670 ± 40 BP (2100 BC)	Whittlesey et al. 2007
Los Pozos	Tucson Basin	4050 ± 50 BP[a] 3340 ± 60 BP 3300 ± 80 BP 3230 ± 50 BP 3140 ± 50 BP (2500–1500 BC)	Gregory 2001
Clearwater Site	Tucson Basin	3690 ± 40 BP 3650 ± 40 BP (2100 BC)	Thiel and Mabry 2006
McEuen Cave	Gila Mountains, southern Arizona	3690 ± 50 BP (2100 BC)	Huckell et al. 1999

[a] The excavator argues that this could be an anomalous date.

Early Maize in the Southern Southwest

The introduction of maize agriculture is a key trait associated with the Middle-to-Late Archaic transition in the southern Southwest. The central question is no longer *when* it arrived, as numerous dates from well-defined contexts place its presence in the southern Southwest at 2000 BC, but has now moved to a focus on *how* it arrived and the relationship between Middle Archaic foragers and Late Archaic farmers. Was it brought in by migrant farmers from Mexico (Carpenter et al. 2002; Huckell 1995; Matson 2002)? Or was it adopted by indigenous Middle Archaic hunter-gatherer groups who were already seasonally occupying the riverine floodplains where it first occurs (Roth and Freeman 2008; Wills 1995)?

Early maize has been recovered from surprisingly variable contexts across the Greater Southwest (Table 8.1). Both Wills (1992; Wills and Huckell 1994) and Vierra (2008) have stressed the flexibility in the adaptations of early farmers in the northern Southwest and Mogollon regions, and Wills (1992) has noted that this was due in part to the fact that early maize was not particularly productive. Varying techniques for agricultural production have been documented for these early farmers (Mabry 2005b; Mabry and Doolittle 2008). The earliest techniques include dry faming, runoff farming, floodwater farming, water table farming, and irrigation and vary based on the environmental setting. Mabry (2005b) has emphasized that these techniques also differed in terms of productivity, risks, and labor requirements.

Despite this documented variability in contexts and techniques for growing maize across the Greater Southwest, the introduction of agriculture to the southern Southwest is often treated as a singular process. This has become manifest in the questions that are asked of the data. Many of the recent publications on the Late Archaic period have focused on linguistics, with an attempt to infer how the archaeology supports linguistic models (Carpenter et al. 2002; Hill 2001, 2002; LeBlanc 2008; Merrill et al. 2009). The two current linguistic debates center on Uto-Aztecan speakers and their role in the introduction of maize agriculture to the region. One model proposed by Merrill et al. (2009) posits that Proto-Uto-Aztecan speakers migrated into the southern deserts from the Great Basin at the end of the Early Archaic period, approximately 6900 BC, in response to climate change. These foragers later adopted maize from farming groups in Mexico. The second model, proposed by Bellwood (2001), Hill (2001, 2002), and others (Carpenter et al. 2002; LeBlanc 2008), posits that maize agriculture entered the region via a migration of Uto-Aztecan speakers from Mexico during the Late Archaic period. Hill (2001) has argued that maize was cultivated by Proto-Uto-Aztecan speakers in Mexico who then moved north. She bases this on the presence of shared vocabulary words for maize cultivation and processing across Mesoamerica and the Southwest, arguing that maize was cultivated before Uto-Aztecan languages began to diverge. A similar debate based on linguistic data has been of concern to Great Basin researchers dealing with the concept of the Numic Spread, with equally differing opinions on the timing and modes of change (Bettinger and Baumhoff 1982; Madsen and Rhode 1994). For the Southwest, this linguistic issue has of late in some ways transcended the archaeological data.

A second related question associated with the introduction of maize agriculture to the region concerns why agriculture was introduced or adopted in the first place. This can be dealt with easily if the migration model is accepted, although the question then becomes why groups migrated. It is more difficult to explain if hunter-gatherers were adopting cultigens. Wills (1988, 1992) and Diehl (1997, 2005) have cogently argued that the adoption of agriculture by Southwestern hunter-gatherers is related to two specific factors: control and predictability. Maize would have enhanced the predictability of the resources base; hence it was adopted for just that purpose. Most researchers working in the region who argue for an indigenous adoption maintain the view that maize was adopted because of these factors.

The final issue faced by researchers working on the Late Archaic period in the southern Southwest concerns the consequences of the introduction of cultigens. Throughout the Greater Southwest we see very different responses to this introduction that lead to very different archaeological records, and this is the case for the southern Southwest as well. In some areas such as the Tucson Basin, maize became an integral part of the diet, with irrigation networks and extensive storage as the archaeological signatures of this increasing focus on cultivation (Gregory 2001; Mabry 1998, 2008; Thiel and Mabry 2006; Whittlesey et al. 2007). These groups apparently integrated maize into the diet quickly and employed a range of technologies to support their efforts. The consequences of this emphasis on maize and irrigation resulted in increased sedentism and associated economic and social changes, including discrete burial areas, the use of ceramic technology (primarily figurines), the expansion of trade networks, and more formal ritual activities (Mabry 2005c). In other portions of the southern Southwest, maize was present but appears, at least archaeologically, to have had very little impact until later (Gilman 1997; Whalen 1971). San Pedro groups in these areas, such as the San Simon region of southeastern Arizona, continued to practice seasonal rounds and lack evidence of extensive storage, irrigation, or any of the other material items related to sedentism and agricultural production observed along the Santa Cruz and San Pedro rivers. Despite these substantial differences in response to the introduction of agriculture, many models posited for the southern Southwest seek to explain a uniform adaptation.

Projectile Points Redux

The reliance on projectile points for defining Late Archaic "groups" may be masking some of the variability present across the region. The use of projectile points as proxies for prehistoric Southwestern groups dates back to the original definition of the San Pedro Cochise by Sayles and Antevs (1941). When the Cochise Culture was defined, interpretations of the Southwest Archaic derived from the identification and description of lithic assemblages at certain "type" sites. Sayles and Antevs divided the Cochise into three stages (Sulphur Springs, Chiricahua, San Pedro) using geologic contexts of several excavated sites in alluvial settings in southeastern Arizona. They recognized that substantial changes in adaptation occurred during the San Pedro stage, including the adoption of agriculture and a reduction in residential mobility. The conceptual frameworks used by Sayles and Antevs (1941) in defining the Cochise Culture linked groups occupying diverse settings based on their possession of similar artifact assemblages. A range of artifacts was used to define the San Pedro Cochise, including deep-basin metates, manos, the mortar and pestle, various scrapers and other unifacially flaked tools, and San Pedro points. However, despite the list of other artifacts and features, most San Pedro phase occupations were defined based on the presence of San Pedro points.

Today researchers studying the Archaic period in the southern Southwest do not treat projectile points as people, but they have a tendency to treat points as representative of specific adap-

FIGURE 8.2. San Pedro and Cortaro points.

tations (cf. Huckell 1995; Mabry 1998; Roth and Huckell 1992; Shackley 1996; Whittlesey et al. 2007). This is not necessarily a problem in and of itself—but it becomes a problem when the adaptation becomes a proxy for a social group and all of the individuals within that group. The sharing of an adaptation is often taken a step further, in that, if the adaptations are deemed similar, then the groups are viewed as *somehow* related—culturally, linguistically, ideologically, or all of the above.

Middle Archaic Projectile Point Styles

Distinct forms of Middle Archaic projectile points have been found throughout the southern Southwest in a wide variety of settings, and in general researchers have been satisfied with arguing that the Middle Archaic period was characterized by relatively mobile hunter-gatherers who operated within large-scale fluid territories (Huckell 1984; Roth 1995, 1996; Wills 1988). Projectile point variability is viewed as part of this generalized adaptation, with groups adapting technologically, economically, and socially to their particular circumstances (Wills 1988).

A study of Middle Archaic foraging adaptations in the Picacho Dune region north of the Tucson Basin identified distinct point styles associated with different forms of subsistence-settlement systems (Bayham et al. 1986). San Jose/Pinto points were found on the Buried Dune site, representing a short-term task-oriented occupation with a narrow range of specialized tool types focused on plant processing and evidence of the use of distant raw material sources. Radiocarbon dates place its occupation at 3000 BC. In contrast, Chiricahua points were found at the Arroyo site, which contained evidence of a more substantial residential occupation including a midden and a possible pithouse, a diverse tool assemblage, and an emphasis on local raw material use. Radiocarbon dates place its occupation at 3200 BC. The temporal overlap of the sites led Bayham et al. (1986) to argue that the two occupations represented separate cultural groups moving into the region. The occupation of the Arroyo site was inferred to be locally based, with groups using the Picacho dunes seasonally on a relatively intensive basis, while the Buried Dune site was viewed as representing a more mobile occupation based farther north. In this case, Bayham et al. (1986) did not rely solely on the presence of different point styles in inferring the distinctions between the two groups but instead used a plethora of other data, including settlement type, tool assemblage data, and raw material sourcing to infer these differences. They make a good argument that these are separate adaptations, but not based on the presence of distinct point styles alone.

The use of projectile points as proxies for adaptations has been employed to support the idea of a migration of farmers bearing Cortaro points into southern Arizona during the latter portion of the Middle Archaic period (Carpenter et al. 2002). Cortaro points (Figure 8.2) have now been found associated with the earliest occupations with maize in the southern Southwest, at McEuen Cave, Los Pozos, Las Capas, and Clearwater (Table 8.1). The association of Cortaro points with these early occupations is solid, although the current data are from small exposures of deeply buried sites.

The problem is that archaeologically these sites do not look like the remains of migrating farmers, and recent DNA and other archaeological data do not support the movement of Uto-Aztecan speakers north (Merrill et al. 2009). The sites in the Tucson Basin (Los Pozos, Las Capas, Clearwater) contain the remains of ephemeral houses, thermal features (roasting pits and hearths), and an associated stone tool assemblage that looks very much like the preceding Middle Archaic assemblage (Sliva 1999). Even more vexing is the variability within Cortaro points themselves and the fact that they are used into the Late Archaic period (although their function may have changed to the role of bifacial knives). Cortaro points are distinct to the southern deserts and thus can be linked very generally to an adaptation to these desert settings (Roth and Huckell 1992). But they have been recovered from both the Sonoran and Chihuahuan deserts, from uplands, and adjacent to large rivers that crosscut the desert. They have been recovered from small sites and large ones; although as Huckell and I (Roth and Huckell 1992) noted when we first defined them, the bulk of the data are from undated surface finds. They have been found at sites associated with other Middle and Late Archaic point styles, including Pinto, Chiricahua, Gypsum, and San Pedro points. This does not indicate that they represent a uniform adaptation, and their recovery at a large number of sites with material remains suggestive of generalized hunting and gathering activities strongly suggests that they are not associated with a singular adaptation to early farming.

San Pedro Points and the San Pedro Phase

San Pedro points (included here are the earlier Empire points [Stevens and Sliva 2002]) pose yet another problem when examining Late Archaic period prehistory in the southern Southwest. San Pedro points are easily recognized because their morphology is distinct and their distribution is therefore well documented (Figure 8.2). They are found across a large portion of the Southwest, including northern Mexico and into the northern Southwest, where they are often found with San Jose/Pinto and Basketmaker points. As noted earlier, they were the hallmarks of the San Pedro stage of the Cochise Culture (Sayles and Antevs 1941). The San Pedro *phase* (1200–800 BC) was initially defined by Huckell (1995), with the definition more recently expanded by Mabry (2008). It is characterized by the suite of material culture remains noted earlier, including small circular structures, large bell-shaped storage pits, a range of other pit features, ceramic figurines, shell jewelry, and San Pedro points. San Pedro phase sites exhibiting these characteristics have been found in alluvial settings along the San Pedro and Santa Cruz rivers and their tributaries (Ezzo and Deaver 1998; Huckell 1995; Mabry 2008; Sayles 1983; Wellman 2008; Whittlesey et al. 2007). Although most sites found on the floodplains exhibit this suite of features and artifacts, the degree to which they are present varies. For example, at Las Capas, located on the floodplain of the Santa Cruz River near its confluence with the Cañada del Oro, excavations have documented a substantial San Pedro phase occupation, with numerous houses, literally hundreds of pits, an extensive canal system, burials, and a diverse artifact assemblage dating to 1200–900 BC (Mabry 2008; Whittlesey et al. 2007). However, the nearby and contemporaneous Costello-King (Ezzo and Deaver 1998) and Valley Farms (Wellman 2008) sites exhibit much less intensity of occupation. Valley Farms had one house and many pits that were both horizontally and vertically separated. Wellman and I (Roth and Wellman 2001) interpret this site as representing the repeated use of this portion of the floodplain by family groups during the San Pedro phase for farming and processing. Costello-King had primarily pits associated with irrigation canals, and the excavators interpret it as representing a short-term occupation, perhaps a field house or processing area (Ezzo and Deaver 1998). The importance of this variability for this chapter is that these sites share the distinct traits of the San Pedro phase—structures, bell-shaped storage pits, processing pits, similar artifacts—yet the nature of their occupation is clearly *not* the same.

Also in the Tucson Basin, San Pedro points have been found at campsites in the upper bajada of the foothills surrounding the basin (Roth 1992). These sites do not exhibit the suite of features and artifacts seen at the floodplain sites and instead reflect the continuation of a degree of residential mobility. They represent the use of the foothills for seasonal hunting and gathering and are therefore associated with a logistical mobility strategy (Roth 1995, 1996).

Sites with San Pedro points have also been found in a range of other settings throughout the southern deserts. Three finds can be used to illustrate that San Pedro points are not indicative of a uniform, region-wide adaptation. San Pedro points have been found at Cerro Juanaqueña, a large *cerro de trincheras* site located along the Rio Casas Grandes in Chihuahua dating to 1200 BC (Hard and Roney 1998, 2004; Roney and Hard 2002). The site was apparently a planned village, with hundreds of rock rings and terraces used for habitation. It represents a degree of labor investment and sedentism not seen elsewhere in the Southwest. While at a very general level Cerro Juanaqueña represents an early farming adaptation coeval with the southern Arizona sites, it is substantially different in its layout, architecture, and intensity of occupation. The sharing of San Pedro points and maize farming cannot overshadow the tremendous cultural differences apparent between these Chihuahuan *trincheras* sites and their Sonoran Desert counterparts. Interestingly Beale (2007) did a detailed comparison of San Pedro points from the Tucson Basin, the San Simon region (see below), and Cerro Juanaqueña and found that the points from Cerro Juanaqueña differed from those in the other two regions in size and raw material. He interprets these differences as tied to the degree of sedentism exhibited at Cerro Juanaqueña and the fact that the occupants consequently had less contact with other groups in southern Arizona.

The second find illustrating the degree of variability in San Pedro phase occupations is the Coffee Camp site, located on an alluvial fan north of Tucson near the Santa Cruz flats (Halbirt and Henderson 1993). The site was one of the first large-scale Late Archaic occupations to be found, yielding pithouses, large storage pits, hundreds of other pits, burials, and an oversized structure that was possibly ceremonial in nature. Dates from Coffee Camp place its occupation within the Cienega phase, with the majority of the dates falling within the 400–200 BC range. The recovery of a large number of San Pedro points and some Cienega points has linked this site closely with the early agricultural sites found on the floodplain of the Santa Cruz River in the Tucson Basin. Yet, in 90 flotation and 75 pollen samples, no evidence of maize was found, indicating that the site was occupied by groups who maintained a foraging adaptation for at least part of the year, focusing on wild plants such as mesquite and cacti. The absence of agriculture coincident with the presence of San Pedro points and the later date of occupation of the site again call into question the idea of a uniform early farming adaptation.

Finally, work in southeastern Arizona has documented the presence of San Pedro points associated with campsites and evidence of higher levels of mobility than that seen in the Tucson Basin (Gilman 1997; Whalen 1971). Gilman's (1997) work in the San Simon region of southeastern Arizona, located on the edge of the Sonoran and Chihuahuan deserts, has documented camps and resource-procurement sites with San Pedro points tied to seasonal resource procurement and perhaps an emphasis on hunting. Beale's (2007) analysis of San Pedro points from sites in the San Simon region supports the inference of higher levels of mobility and a focus on hunting.

The variability documented in these sites raises important questions concerning the relationship between San Pedro points and the San Pedro phase and challenges the assumption that possession of San Pedro points automatically means that groups were farmers with a specific suite of material culture traits. Should these sites be classified as San Pedro phase because of the presence of San Pedro points and radiocarbon dates that fall within that time frame? And if these points are characteristic of a specific adaptation associated with early farming on alluvial floodplains, then why are they found in such variable settings and associated with such variable occupations?

Embracing Diversity

When we put aside the notion that these projectile point styles are related to specific adaptations and move toward looking at other data that reflect behavior, such as feature types, settlement locations, and artifact assemblages, a different picture of the Late Archaic period emerges, one that is more flexible and dynamic than the projectile point typological view allows. Variability in adaptation is present across time and space. Wills (1988, 1995) has stressed the flexibility of adaptations represented in early farming groups in the Mogollon highlands, and this same kind of flexibility can and should be considered for the southern deserts. It appears that this variation in adaptation occurred within small areas and that these groups were sometimes foragers, sometimes farmers, and sometimes both.

Simms (1986, 1999) has documented similarly diverse subsistence practices for Fremont groups in the Great Basin. He argues that the Fremont varied their reliance on farming and wild resources both regionally and temporally, yet they were linked by shared material culture traits such as basketry and rock art. Madsen and Simms (1998) note that the Fremont ranged from full-time farmers and full-time foragers to part-time farmers and foragers, stressing that this flexibility in adaptation was essential given the arid and unpredictable climate of the eastern Great Basin.

This variability in adaptation also mirrors the flexibility seen in many ethnographic hunter-gatherers and farmers in the Great Basin and Southwest. These groups varied their subsistence and mobility strategies depending on a variety of environmental, economic, and social factors. For hunter-gatherers such as the Paiute, resource density and availability influenced the kinds of resources that were exploited, the timing of exploitation, and group size (Fowler 1992; Kelly 1932; Steward 1933). This same kind of flexibility is observed in ethnographic farmers in the Southwest. Varying levels of agricultural dependence were observed between the Pima and Tohono O'odham in the Sonoran Desert and Yuman groups along the Colorado River. These groups were all farmers, but all still used a wide variety of wild resources and maintained complex schedules and divisions of labor for planting, gathering, hunting, and fishing. Trading expeditions were also important components of resource exchange. Castetter and Bell noted that the dependence on wild resources by the Pima and Tohono O'odham varied based on local geography but stressed that for the Tohono O'odham, wild plants were a "larger and more dependable fraction of the food supply than cultivated plants" (1942:45). The Pima were more dependent on agriculture and practiced irrigation agriculture along the Gila River. However, Russell (1908) noted that the river failed midwinter one out of every five years, so the Pima retained flexibility in the amount of wild resources in their diet. Castetter and Bell (1951) noted that Yuman groups varied their dependence on agriculture during the course of a single year, with some groups heavily dependent during the growing season and post-harvest but much less dependent during the late winter and early spring, when wild resources became the major dietary source. The Cocopa were located in a lush portion of the Colorado River with abundant arable land, and yet they maintained a mixed subsistence strategy focused on mesquite procurement rather than agriculture, something that appears to have been vexing to Kelly (1977), who noted their lack of dependence on agriculture despite the fact that they lived in an area that was well suited to crop production.

While Late Archaic groups are clearly not analogous to these nineteenth-century farmers, the key point of this discussion is that these ethnographic groups maintained a level of flexibility in adaptation despite the use of a range of cultigens. I argue that this same kind of flexibility would have been critical to the success of these early farmers in the southern Southwest. As maize was a new resource and foragers are generally risk-adverse (Cashdan 1990), they would have been cautious in their approach to it, and it is unlikely that they would have immediately changed their subsistence regime to accommodate it. It is probable that Late Archaic groups were already manipulating plants, as has been documented for foragers in other regions (Fowler 1996; Shipek 1989; Winter and Hogan 1986), and through communication with others using this new resource and cooperation, maize was integrated into the diet. It is most likely that this integration varied based on local geography, as Castetter and Bell (1942) noted for the Pima and Tohono O'odham and Kelly (1964) documented for the Southern Paiute in the St. George Basin. The archaeological record of Late Archaic groups in the southern Southwest reflects this varying degree of integration and the flexibility inherent in the response to the introduction of maize.

Future Directions

The Late Archaic period in the southern Southwest was a dynamic period, and a tremendous amount of work remains to be done before the variability discussed here can be fully documented and understood. Although currently linguistics remains a popular venue for addressing this variability (Hill 2001, 2002; LeBlanc 2008; Merrill et al. 2009), it is unlikely that linguistic data will provide the kinds of information needed to document and explain the changes that occurred across the Middle-to-Late Archaic period. It is perhaps time to return to the archaeological record for these answers. We can take heed of the generations of archaeologists in the Great Basin who have debated the Numic Spread and have had, in turn, to return to the archaeological record for their answers. We can then start asking questions of the wealth of data from Late Archaic sites across the Southwest.

What Is the Meaning of These Shared Projectile Point Styles?

It is clear that the prevalence of shared styles across broad areas indicates some kind of social network. It is not clear, however, how these networks formed or what their role was in the economic and social systems of Archaic groups. Wiessner's (1983) now classic study of San projectile points indicated that projectile point styles coincide with large-scale social boundaries such as language groups. McBrinn's (2005) recent work on social identity during the Archaic period in the Mogollon highlands indicates that shared point styles were tied to exchange networks. Several researchers (e.g., LeBlanc 2008; Shackley 1996) have lamented the lack of quantitative data on projectile point differences, and this may be an important starting point for addressing the causes of similarities and differences in point styles. Beale's (2007) study shows that even broadly shared styles exhibit variability when more fine-grained quantitative analyses are done. Further studies along these lines may help researchers tease out this variability and may be able to contribute to our understanding of the meaning of shared styles.

How Can We Look at Identity in Late Archaic Groups?

Much of the important work on identity in the Archaic during recent years has been done using perishable artifacts (Geib 2000; McBrinn 2005), which are unfortunately lacking at most Late Archaic sites in the southern Southwest. Many researchers studying identity have focused on technological style to look at traits that are important indicators of learning styles and enculturation. The wealth of artifacts (such as chipped-stone tools, debitage, ground stone) and the range of feature types found at Late Archaic sites could be studied under the rubric of technological style, which may aid in reconstructing social boundaries. For example, the similarity between Middle Archaic lithic technology and the technology of early farming sites such as Las Capas and Los Pozos has been discussed by Sliva (1999). These similarities suggest continuity between the two time periods, and this concept challenges the idea of a migration. Continued efforts focused on technological attributes and raw material use should further enable researchers to address the relationships between occupations, over both time and space. Vierra's (2005) study of the surface lithic assemblage from Cerro Juanaqueña indicates that although the assemblage reflects multiple technologies used for core reduction, as observed at Archaic sites across the region, there was a greater emphasis on biface technology at Cerro Juanaqueña than at San Pedro and Cienega phase sites along the Santa Cruz River. These kinds of studies could also shed light on the relationship between groups possessing San Pedro points and yet occupying distinct settings and lacking the suite of features characteristic of the San Pedro phase.

The concept of identity can then be expanded to look at group dynamics during the Archaic period to address issues of gender, social organization, and interaction. For example, I compared artifacts and features recovered at Late Archaic sites in the Tucson Basin with ethnographically documented activities to argue that women were responsible for the adoption of agriculture in the region, in large part due to the association of gendered activities ethnographically with particular forms of material culture that could be linked to these Archaic sites (Roth 2006). These kinds of studies have important implications for reconstructing social activities and social relationships in the past but have been rare in Southwestern Archaic studies.

What Is the Role of Demography in the Variability That We See in the Late Archaic Across the Southern Southwest?

Researchers often discuss "groups" and "migrants," but few Archaic period archaeologists have tried to link demographic trends with the changes observed during the Late Archaic period. Population density most likely had a tremendous impact on the variability observed in the Late Archaic archaeological record. It is not surprising that the most substantial changes occurred in areas with dense resources and abundant arable land and in areas where Middle Archaic foragers appear to have been reoccupying these same kinds of niches. It appears that these areas have the highest population densities, and that population density may have led to the development of social boundaries observed in architecture, feature types, and artifact types. In some regions such as the San Simon area where we see evidence of higher mobility and more fluid social boundaries, population density may have remained low until agriculture became fully entrenched. Population density needs to be addressed as part of any study of the development of social boundaries, as it may account for many of the observed differences between groups and likely influenced how and when maize was accepted and integrated into the diet. It also very likely influenced the speed and extent of the integration of cultigens.

What Is the Regional Context of These Late Archaic Occupations?

In order to fully understand what was going on during the Late Archaic period in the southern Southwest, it is critical that regional data are used to place Late Archaic sites in context (Roth 1992). Much of the recent data on the Late Archaic period comes from alluvial settings; although this has greatly expanded our knowledge of these groups, it is important that researchers realize that this is only providing part of the picture and that an understanding of the overall adaptation to this region cannot be attained until all portions of the settlement system are documented. These contextual data will greatly enhance our understanding of the economic and social circumstances within which these groups operated and may help us further define the pace of and reasons for the changes observed in these aspects.

Conclusion

Despite great strides in our understanding of the Late Archaic period in the southern Southwest in the last decades, much remains to be learned about this period and the transitions that occurred within it. If we begin to view the archaeological record of this period with the expectation of observing and accounting for variability, and look for patterns within that variability, we will find a more meaningful and perhaps more accurate view of this dynamic and important time.

Acknowledgments

Many thanks go to Joel Janetski, Nancy Parezo, and James Snead for the invitation to participate in the symposium. Thanks also go to Joel Janetski and Chip Wills for their helpful comments on a previous draft of this chapter. This chapter has also benefited from discussions with Nick Beale and Bernard Schriever.

References Cited

Agenbroad, Larry D.
1970 Cultural Implications from the Statistical Analysis of a Prehistoric Lithic Site in Arizona. Unpublished Master's thesis, Department of Anthropology, University of Arizona, Tucson.

Bayham, Frank E., Donald H. Morris, and M. Steven Shackley
1986 *Prehistoric Hunter-Gatherers of South Central Arizona: The Picacho Reservoir Archaic Project.* Anthropological Field Studies No. 13. Department of Anthropology, Office of Cultural Resource Management, Arizona State University, Tempe.

Beale, Nicholas H.
2007 Archaic Projectile Points and Cultural Differences in the Southern Southwest. Unpublished Master's thesis, Department of Anthropology, University of Oklahoma, Norman.

Bellwood, Peter
2001 Early Agriculturalist Population Diasporas? Farming, Languages, and Genes. *Annual Review of Anthropology* 30:181–207.

Bettinger, Robert L., and Mark A. Baumhoff
1982 The Numic Spread: Great Basin Cultures in Competition. *American Antiquity* 47:485–503.

Carpenter, John P., Guadalupe Sanchez, and Elisa Villalpando C.
2002 Of Maize and Migration: Mode and Tempo in the Diffusion of *Zea mays* in Northwest Mexico and the American Southwest. In *Traditions, Transitions, and Technologies*, edited by Sarah H. Schlanger, pp. 245–258. University Press of Colorado, Boulder.

Cashdan, Elizabeth A. (editor)
1990 *Risk and Uncertainty in Tribal and Peasant Economies.* Westview Press, Boulder.

Castetter, Edward F., and Willis H. Bell
1942 *Pima and Papago Indian Agriculture.* University of New Mexico Press, Albuquerque.
1951 *Yuman Indian Agriculture.* University of New Mexico Press, Albuquerque.

Chavarria, Sara P.
1996 *Archaeological Investigations at the Summit at Alvernon Site, AZ BB:9:280 (ASM).* Old Pueblo Archaeology Center Report No. 4. Tucson.

Dart, Alan
1986 *Archaeological Investigations at La Paloma: Archaic and Hohokam Occupations at Three Sites in the Northeastern Tucson Basin, Arizona.* Institute for American Research Anthropological Papers, 4. Tucson.

Diehl, Michael
1997 Rational Behavior, the Adoption of Agriculture, and the Organization of Subsistence During the Late Archaic Period in the Greater Tucson Basin. In *Rediscovering Darwin: Evolutionary Theory and Archaeological Explanation*, edited by C. Michael Barton and Geoffrey A. Clark, pp. 251–265. Archaeological Papers of the American Anthropological Association No. 7. Arlington, Virginia.
2005 *Subsistence and Resource Use Strategies of Early Agricultural Communities in Southern Arizona.* Center for Desert Archaeological Anthropological Papers No. 34. Tucson.

Douglas, John E., and Douglas B. Craig
1986 *Investigations of Archaic and Hohokam Sites on the Flying V Ranch, Tucson, Arizona.* Pima Community College Archaeological Report No. 13. Tucson.

Downum, Christian E., Adrianne G. Rankin, and Jon S. Czaplicki
1986 *A Class III Archaeological Survey of the Phase B Corridor, Tucson Aqueduct, Central Arizona Project.* Arizona State Museum Archaeological Series, 168. Tucson.

Ezzo, Joseph A., and William L. Deaver
1998 *Watering the Desert: Late Archaic Farming at the Costello-King Site.* Statistical Research Technical Series No. 68. Tucson.

Fowler, Catherine S.
1992 *In the Shadow of Fox Peak: An Ethnography of the Cattail-Eastern Northern Paiute People of Stillwater Marsh.* Cultural Resource Series No. 5. Fish and Wildlife Service, Stillwater National Wildlife Refuge, Stillwater.
1996 Historical Perspectives on Timbish Shoshone Land Management Practices, Death Valley, California. In *Case Studies in Environmental Archaeology*, edited by E. J. Reitz, L. A. Newsom, and S. J. Scudder, pp. 87–102. Plenum Press, New York.

Geib, Phil R.

2000 Sandal Types and Archaic Prehistory on the Colorado Plateau. *American Antiquity* 65:509–524.

Gilman, Patricia A.

1997 *Wandering Villagers: Pit Structures, Mobility and Agriculture in Southeastern Arizona.* Arizona State University Anthropological Research Papers No. 49. Tempe.

Gregory, David A. (editor)

1999 *Excavations in the Santa Cruz River Floodplain: The Middle Archaic Period Component at Los Pozos.* Center for Desert Archaeology Anthropological Papers No. 20. Tucson.

2001 *Excavations in the Santa Cruz River Floodplain: The Early Agricultural Occupation at Los Pozos (AZ AA:12:91, ASM).* Center for Desert Archaeology Anthropological Papers No. 21. Tucson.

Gregory, David A., and Bruce B. Huckell

1998 Small, Round, and Stable: Early Agricultural Period Pithouse Architecture and Its Implications for the Rise of Long-Term Settlements in Southeastern Arizona. Paper presented at the 63rd Annual Meeting of the Society for American Archaeology, Seattle.

Halbirt, Carl D., and T. Kathleen Henderson (editors)

1993 *Archaic Occupation on the Santa Cruz Flats: The Tator Hills Archaeological Project.* Report submitted to the U.S. Department of the Interior, Bureau of Reclamation, Arizona Projects Office, Contract No. 3-PA-30-00740. Northland Research, Inc., Flagstaff.

Hard, Robert J., and John R. Roney

1998 A Massive Terraced Village Complex in Chihuahua, Mexico, 3000 Years Before Present. *Science* 279:1661–1664.

2004 Late Archaic Period Hilltop Settlements in Northwestern Chihuahua, Mexico. In *Identity, Feasting, and the Archaeology of the Greater Southwest*, edited by B. J. Mills, pp. 276–294. University Press of Colorado, Boulder.

Heidke, James, Elizabeth J. Misksa, and Michael K. Wiley

1998 Ceramic Artifacts. In *Archaeological Investigations of Early Village Sites in the Middle Santa Cruz River Valley: Analysis and Synthesis Pt. II*, edited by J. B. Mabry, pp. 471–544. Center for Desert Archaeological Anthropological Papers No. 19. Tucson.

Hill, Jane H.

2001 Proto-Uto-Aztecan: A Community of Cultivators in Central Mexico? *American Anthropologist* 103:913–934.

2002 Toward a Linguistic Prehistory of the Southwest: "Azteco-Tanoan" and the Arrival of Maize Cultivation. *Journal of Anthropological Research* 58:457–475.

Huber, Edgar

2005 Early Maize at the Old Corn Site (LA 137258). In *Fence Lake Project: Archaeological Data Recovery in the New Mexico Transportation Corridor and First Five-Year Permit Area, Fence Lake Coal Mine Project, Catron County, New Mexico*, edited by Edgar K. Huber and Carla R. Van West, pp. 36.1–36.33. Statistical Research Inc. Technical Series, 84. Tucson.

Huckell, Bruce B.

1984 *The Archaic Occupation of the Rosemont Area, Northern Santa Rita Mountains, Southeastern Arizona.* Arizona State Museum Archaeological Series No. 147, Vol. 1. Tucson.

1995 *Of Marshes and Maize: Preceramic Agricultural Settlements in the Cienega Valley, Southeastern Arizona.* University of Arizona Anthropological Papers No. 59. University of Arizona Press, Tucson.

Kaldahl, Eric J.

2001 *The Rosetta Site: Archaic Occupations in the Southern Santa Catalina Foothills.* Old Pueblo Archaeology Center Report No. 22. Tucson.

Kelly, Isabel T.

1932 *Ethnography of the Surprise Valley Paiute.* University of California Publications in American Archaeology and Ethnology Vol. XXXI. University of California Press, Berkeley.

1964 *Southern Paiute Ethnography.* University of Utah Anthropological Papers No. 69. Salt Lake City.

Kelly, William H.

1977 *Cocopa Ethnography.* Anthropological Papers of the University of Arizona No. 29. University of Arizona Press, Tucson.

LeBlanc, Steven A.

2008 The Case for an Early Farmer Migration into the Greater American Southwest. In *Archaeology Without Borders*, edited by Laurie D. Webster and Maxine E. McBrinn, pp. 107–142. University Press of Colorado, Boulder.

Mabry, Jonathan

1998 *Archaeological Investigations of Early Village Sites in the Middle Santa Cruz Valley: Analysis and Synthesis.* Center for Desert Archaeology Anthropological Papers No. 19. Tucson.

2005a Changing Knowledge and Ideas About the First Farmers in Southeastern Arizona. In *The Late Archaic Across the Borderlands: From Foraging to Farming*, edited by Bradley J. Vierra, pp. 41–82. University of Texas Press, Austin.

2005b Diversity in Early Southwestern Farming and Optimization Models of Transitions to Agriculture. In *Subsistence and Resource Use Strategies of Early Agricultural Communities in Southern Arizona*, edited by Michael W. Diehl, pp. 113–152. Center for Desert Archaeology Anthropological Papers No. 34. Tucson.

2005c The Material Culture of Rituals in Early Farming Communities in the Desert Southwest. In *Material Cultures and Lifeways of Early Agricultural Communities in Southern Arizona*, edited by R. Jane Sliva, pp. 217–238. Center for Desert Archaeology Anthropological Papers No. 35. Tucson.

2008 *Las Capas: Early Irrigation and Sedentism in a Southwestern Floodplain.* Center for Desert Archaeology Anthropological Papers No. 28. Tucson.

Mabry, Jonathan B., and William E. Doolittle

2008 Modeling the Early Agricultural Frontier in the Desert Borderlands. In *Archaeology Without Borders*, edited by Laurie D. Webster and Maxine E. McBrinn, pp. 55–70. University Press of Colorado, Boulder.

Madsen, David B., and David Rhode (editors)

1994 *Across the West: Human Population Movement and the Expansion of the Numa.* University of Utah Press, Salt Lake City.

Madsen, David B., and Steven R. Simms

1998 The Fremont Complex: A Behavioral Perspective. *Journal of World Prehistory* 12:255–336.

Matson, R. G.

2002 The Spread of Maize Agriculture in the U.S. Southwest. In *Examining the Farming/Language Dispersal Hypothesis*, edited by P. Bellwood and C. Renfrew, pp. 341–356. McDonald Institute for Archaeological Research, University of Cambridge, Cambridge.

McBrinn, Maxine
2005 *Social Identities Among Archaic Mobile Hunters and Gatherers in the American Southwest*. Arizona State Museum Archaeological Series, 197. University of Arizona, Tucson.
Merrill, William L., Robert J. Hard, Jonathan B. Mabry, Gayle J. Fritz, Karen R. Adams, John R. Roney, and A. C. MacWilliams
2009 The Diffusion of Maize to the Southwestern United States and Its Impact. *Proceedings of the National Academy of Science* 106:21019–21026.
Roney, John R., and Robert J. Hard
2002 Early Agriculture in Northwestern Chihuahua. In *Traditions, Transitions, and Technologies: Themes in Southwestern Archaeology*, edited by S. H. Schlanger, pp. 160–177. University Press of Colorado, Boulder.
Roth, Barbara J.
1992 Sedentary Agriculturalists or Mobile Hunter-Gatherers? Evidence on the Late Archaic Occupation of the Northern Tucson Basin. *Kiva* 57:291–314.
1995 Late Archaic Occupation of the Upper Bajada: Excavations at AZ AA:12:84 (ASM). *Kiva* 61:189–207.
1996 Regional Land Use in the Late Archaic of the Tucson Basin. In *Early Formative Adaptations in the Southern Southwest*, edited by Barbara J. Roth, pp. 37–48. Monographs in World Archaeology No. 25. Prehistory Press, Madison, Wisconsin.
2006 The Role of Gender in the Adoption of Agriculture in the Southern Southwest. *Journal of Anthropological Research* 62:513–538.
Roth, Barbara J., and Andrea K. Freeman
2008 The Middle Archaic Period and the Transition to Agriculture in the Sonoran Desert of Southern Arizona. *Kiva* 73:321–353.
Roth, Barbara J., and Bruce B. Huckell
1992 Cortaro Points and the Archaic of Southern Arizona. *Kiva* 57:353–370.
Roth, Barbara J., and Kevin Wellman
2001 New Insights into the Early Agricultural Period in the Tucson Basin: Excavations at the Valley Farms Site (AZ AA:12:736). *Kiva* 67:59–79.
Russell, Frank
1908 *The Pima Indians*. Twenty-Sixth Annual Report of the Bureau of American Ethnology. Washington, D.C.
Sayles, E. B.
1983 *The Cochise Cultural Sequence in Southeastern Arizona*. Anthropological Papers of the University of Arizona No. 42. University of Arizona Press, Tucson.
Sayles, E. B., and Ernst Antevs
1941 *The Cochise Culture*. Medallion Papers No. 29. Gila Pueblo, Globe, Arizona.
Shackley, M. Steven
1996 Elko or San Pedro? Inferences from a Quantitative Analysis of Late Archaic Period Projectile Points from White Tanks, Yuma County, Arizona. *Kiva* 61:413–432.
Shipek, Florence C.
1989 An Example of Intensive Plant Husbandry: The Kumeyaay of Southern California. In *Foraging and Farming: The Evolution of Plant Exploitation*, edited by D. R. Harris and G. C. Hillman, pp. 159–170. Unwin Hyman, London.
Simms, Steven R.
1986 New Evidence for Fremont Adaptive Diversity. *Journal of California and Great Basin Anthropology* 8:204–216.
1999 Farmers, Foragers, and Adaptive Diversity: The Great Salt Lake Wetlands Project. In *Prehistoric Lifeways in the Great Basin Wetlands: Bioarchaeological Reconstruction and Interpretation*, edited by B. E. Hemphill and C. S. Larsen, pp. 21–54. University of Utah Press, Salt Lake City.
Simpson, Kay, and Susan J. Wells
1983 *Archaeological Survey in the Eastern Tucson Basin, Rincon Mountain Unit, Cactus Forest Area*. Western Archaeological and Conservation Center Publications in Anthropology, 22(1). Tucson.
Slawson, Laurie V.
1987 *Archaic and Hohokam Land Use in the Santa Catalina Mountains: The Excavation of the Kolb Road Site*. Southwest Cultural Series No. 6. Cultural and Environmental Systems, Inc., Tucson.
Sliva, R. Jane
1999 Archaic Settlement, Subsistence, and Lithic Technology in the Southern Southwest. Paper presented at the 64th Annual Meeting of the Society for American Archaeology, Chicago.
Stevens, Michelle N., and R. Jane Sliva
2002 Empire Points: An Addition to the San Pedro Phase Lithic Assemblage. *Kiva* 67:297–326.
Steward, Julian
1933 *Ethnography of the Owen's Valley Paiute*. University of California Publications in American Archaeology and Ethnology Vol. 33. University of California Press, Berkeley.
Thiel, J. Homer, and Jonathan B. Mabry (editors)
2006 *Rio Nuevo Archaeology, 2000–2003: Investigations at the San Agustin Mission and Mission Gardens, Tucson Presidio, Tucson Pressed Brick Company, and Clearwater Site*. Desert Archaeology, Inc. Technical Report No. 2004-11. Tucson.
Vierra, Bradley J.
2005 Late Archaic Stone Tool Technology Across the Borderlands. In *The Late Archaic Across the Borderlands: From Foraging to Farming*, edited by Bradley J. Vierra, pp. 187–218. University of Texas Press, Austin.
2008 Early Agriculture on the Southeastern Periphery of the Colorado Plateau: Diversity in Tactics. In *Archaeology Without Borders*, edited by Laurie D. Webster and Maxine E. McBrinn, pp. 71–88. University Press of Colorado, Boulder.
Wellman, Kevin D. (editor)
2008 *The Valley Farms Sites: Prehistoric Floodplain Agriculture on the Santa Cruz River in Southern Arizona*. SWCA Anthropological Research Paper No. 11. Tucson.
Whalen, Norman M.
1971 Cochise Culture Sites in the Central San Pedro Drainage, Arizona. Unpublished Ph.D. dissertation, Department of Anthropology, University of Arizona, Tucson.
Whittlesey, Stephanie M., S. Jerome Hesse, and Michael S. Foster (editors)
2007 *Recurrent Sedentism and the Making of Place: Archaeological Investigations at Las Capas, a Preceramic Period Farming Community in the Tucson Basin, Southern Arizona*. SWCA Cultural Resources Report No. 07-556. Tucson.
Wiessner, Polly
1983 Style and Social Information in Kalahari San Projectile Points. *American Antiquity* 48:253–276.
Wills, Wirt H., III
1988 *Early Prehistoric Agriculture in the American Southwest*. School of American Research Books, Santa Fe, New Mexico.

1992 Plant Cultivation and the Evolution of Risk-Prone Economies in the Prehistoric American Southwest. In *Transitions to Agriculture in Prehistory*, edited by Anne B. Gebauer and T. Douglas Price, pp. 153–176. Monographs in World Archaeology No. 4. Prehistory Press, Madison, Wisconsin.

1995 Archaic Foraging and the Beginning of Food Production in the American Southwest. In *Last Hunters, First Farmers*, edited by T. D. Price and A. B. Gebauer, pp. 215–242. School of American Research Press, Santa Fe, New Mexico.

Wills, W. H., and Bruce E. Huckell

1994 Economic Implications of Changing Land-Use Patterns in the Late Archaic. In *Themes in Southwest Prehistory*, edited by George Gummerman, pp. 33–52. School of American Research Press, Santa Fe, New Mexico.

Winter, Joseph C., and Patrick F. Hogan

1986 Plant Husbandry in the Great Basin and Adjacent Northern Colorado Plateau. In *Anthropology of the Desert West: Essays in Honor of Jesse D. Jennings*, edited by Carol J. Condie and Don D. Fowler, pp. 117–144. University of Utah Anthropological Papers No. 110. Salt Lake City.

9

Thinking About Fremont

The Later Prehistory of the Great Basin and the Southwest

Stephen H. Lekson

Don D. Fowler is a major player in the archaeologies of both the Southwest and the Great Basin—among other places. That combination suggested a theme for this chapter: archaeology at the interface of the Southwest and the Great Basin, namely, Fremont.

"Fremont" has been with us for a long time (at least since the late 1920s), but it remains a nebulous creature. To an interested outsider, Fremont appears to be a trait-list package of basketry types, pottery types, moccasin types, rock art styles, pueblo-esque architecture, maize farming, and so forth at sites on the northwestern edge of the Southwest (recent summaries: Janetski 2008; Simms 2008:Chapter 5, 2010; see also syntheses of Fremont architecture in Talbot 2000a and of basketry in Adovasio et al. 2002). Early interpretations made Fremont a periphery of Anasazi (e.g., Gunnerson 1969; Morss 1931; and in dissent, Wormington 1955). (I use the unpopular term *Anasazi* in its original, technical, archaeology jargon application: ancient societies of the Four Corners region.) David Madsen complained that "the Fremont have always been considered to be some sort of poor, out-back Anasazi described by terms like 'Puebloan,' 'Puebloid,' or 'Northern Periphery' of the Anasazi" (1989:21). Culture historians such as Jesse Jennings and Marie Wormington were not satisfied with peripheral status for Fremont, but the final break came in the 1970s, a revolutionary time marked by the secession of several previously peripheral districts from the thrall of the Four Corners—and the "San Juan Hypothesis" that everything of interest in the region oozed out from Mesa Verde. Mimbres, for example, declared independence from Anasazi (LeBlanc 1983, 1986)—a case with intriguing parallels to Fremont. I will revisit Mimbres, below.

Fremont's independence was affirmed, perhaps in the breach, by the small scales of New and Processual archaeologies. As in the adjacent Southwest (Lekson 2009:110–111), the new archaeologies favored relatively small scales, studying local adaptations and local evolutions; seldom did those studies exceed (or even question) the scale of cultural units inherited from culture history days. (The Southwest snapped out of it: entities such as Chaco and Hohokam exceeded the scales of New Archaeology; indeed in Chaco's case, I will argue below that it exceeded the Southwest itself.) Fremont became a stand-alone "culture"–and nobody's periphery, thank you very much. Steven Simms discusses the history of comparisons of Fremont and Anasazi: "Despite that obvious [Anasazi] heritage, most such comparisons in the past forty years have emphasized the distinctiveness of the Fremont—an almost nationalistic exercise" (2010:12; see also Madsen and Simms 1998).

What, then, is Fremont supposed to be? A culture? A culture area? A geographic region? On most maps (see, for example, the historical series presented in Madsen 1989), Fremont conforms rather closely to the outline of the state of Utah (minus the Beehive State's famously Anasazi southeast corner)—even sliding the famous "Fremont" site of Mantle's Cave from northwesternmost Colorado into northeasternmost Utah! This curious coincidence of ancient culture and modern political unit will surface again, below.

It is hard for an outsider (such as me) to get a handle on Fremont as a "stand-alone" entity: "There are four relatively distinct artifact categories which do distinguish the Fremont from other prehistoric [Anasazi] societies. Unfortunately, they are only rarely found together" (Madsen 1989:9; see also Madsen 1979). Fremont's most notable, distinctive elements appear sometimes together, more often separately, and occasionally not at all on sites deemed Fremont because they are in Fremont territory. Perhaps it boils down to basketry:

> Whereas the extant lithic and ceramic evidence does not lend itself individually or collectively to the recognition of a Fremont culture distinctive from and basically unrelated to contemporary groups like the Anasazi...this is not the case with the basketry data that is of, in, and by itself conclusive [Adovasio 1979:729; see also Adovasio et al. 2002].

Fremont basketry differs indeed from conventional Anasazi basketry and harks back to local Archaic fiber traditions. But does that mean that Fremont was a separate entity, isolated from the alarums and excursions of its world? I am willing to toss Mimbres Mogollon back into Chaco's Anasazi world (below) despite the substantial material differences of, for example, square Mimbres great kivas and round Chaco great kivas. Fremont's distinctive fiber traditions indicate a degree of continuity in place, but continuity in place may not insulate Fremont from larger regional dynamics, most particularly the unsettling developments of its neighbor to the south, Anasazi (Lekson 2009). Pueblos, for example, are famous for continuity in place; yet they have been battered and hammered and shaped by storms brewed in other people's worlds—both before and after Columbus.

Turn the problem on its head: instead of promoting a stand-alone Fremont, let us pretend that the Southwest wants Fremont back—a sort of reconstruction of Fremont. Looking covetously at Fremont from the Southwest, it seems that Fremont's southwestern Anasazi-like elements have been steamrolled by Great Basin methodologies. Several years ago, James Allison published an insightful essay, "Human Ecology and Social Theory in Utah Archaeology" (2008), in which he traces the divergent archaeologies of the Great Basin vs. the Southwest. Those differences, today, are significant. Allison argues that they reflect different social and intellectual histories of the two fields or subfields. For the question at hand—Fremont—Allison says:

> Archaeologists studying the Fremont have too often relied on theoretical concepts and assumptions rooted in Great Basin hunter-gatherer studies. Fremont archaeologists would benefit from increased awareness and use of the theoretical approaches prevalent among those who specialize in the archaeology of Southwestern farmers [2008:57].

By a happy coincidence, I specialize in the archaeology of Southwestern farmers, although I may not be precisely the tonic Dr. Allison ordered. Indeed, we are already seeing the things Allison wants by scholars far better versed in Fremont, in recent works by Steve Simms (2010), Joel Janetski (e.g., 2000, 2002), of course Allison (2008) himself, and others. But I shall add my two Southwestern bits on Fremont, from the perspective of a Southwestern archaeologist who sees the ancient Southwest as something more than farmers (Lekson 2009).

By a less happy coincidence, I have lately had to think—a lot—about Fremont, in my role as curator of archaeology, doing the work of the Native American Graves Protection and Repatriation Act (NAGPRA). A short digression: the University of Colorado Museum holds collections from putatively Fremont sites in western Colorado (including Mantle's Cave). Some of these sites produced human remains, and it was my responsibility to determine their "cultural affiliation." I typically do that by reading a lot of local archaeology, talking to local archaeologists, and reviewing past NAGPRA determinations. And, perhaps most important, I do this by consulting with Native nations.

Several of the human remains came from what is now Dinosaur National Monument (at the time of excavation, private lands). Dinosaur National Monument also has human remains from National Park Service (NPS) lands that fell under NAGPRA. Both the University Museum and NPS consulted with tribes, independently. The University Museum consulted with Ute, Paiute, Shoshone, and other tribes from the west and north, plus the Ute tribes of Colorado and the Kiowa Tribe. NPS consulted mainly with Pueblos, plus the nearby Ute tribes. Awkward: there was little overlap between our two lists. However, both NPS and the University Museum (i.e., me) determined, independently, that the remains were "culturally unidentifiable": the remains were Native American, but we could not trace a "shared group identity" between the remains and any modern group. So we reached the same agreeable conclusion.

Why unidentifiable? Very little is straightforward in NAGPRA, but Fremont is particularly sticky. For one thing, it covers a very large area, which (as noted above) corresponds almost exactly to Utah. I am not sure if that is a happy coincidence; it is certainly a *strange* coincidence. I worry about archaeological taxa that conform to modern political boundaries. It happens, but we should be wary, especially since one of those ecotones that actually matter—between the Great Basin and Colorado Plateau—slices right through the middle of the Beehive State—and Fremont (Figure 9.1). Obviously that great divide was noted by Fremont researchers from very early on (for a review, see Madsen 1979); but somehow Fremont survives that ecological draw-and-quartering.

In the Southwest, our major culture areas conventionally are bound by major ecotones: The Mogollon Rim (separating plateau and deserts) marks a line between Anasazi and Hohokam; the Continental Divide (separating the Sonoran and Chihuahuan deserts) marks a rough (and variably porous) boundary between Hohokam and Mogollon. In the Southwest if scenery changes, so should the archaeology. Thus, we might assume, the Great Basin–Plateau ecotone should mean something to Fremont—it cuts it right in two. How could there be a single, unitary taxon that straddles both sides of the dramatic Basin–Plateau boundary?

Of course, Fremont is not unitary and homogeneous over its vast area (e.g., Madsen 1979; Madsen and Simms 1998:259). It is splintered and divided into numerous regional districts that are not immediately obvious to an outsider—and those divisions seem to change, markedly, from map to map (again, see the series of maps presented in Madsen 1989:Figures 15, 21–22). Even someone who specializes in Southwestern farmers begins to realize that Fremont may be complicated. There is spatial variation, and there is also time: history. Is "Fremont" anything that happened within the territory archaeologists have staked out as "Fremont"? Or was "Fremont" an event or events, specific to a time and played out mainly in Utah?

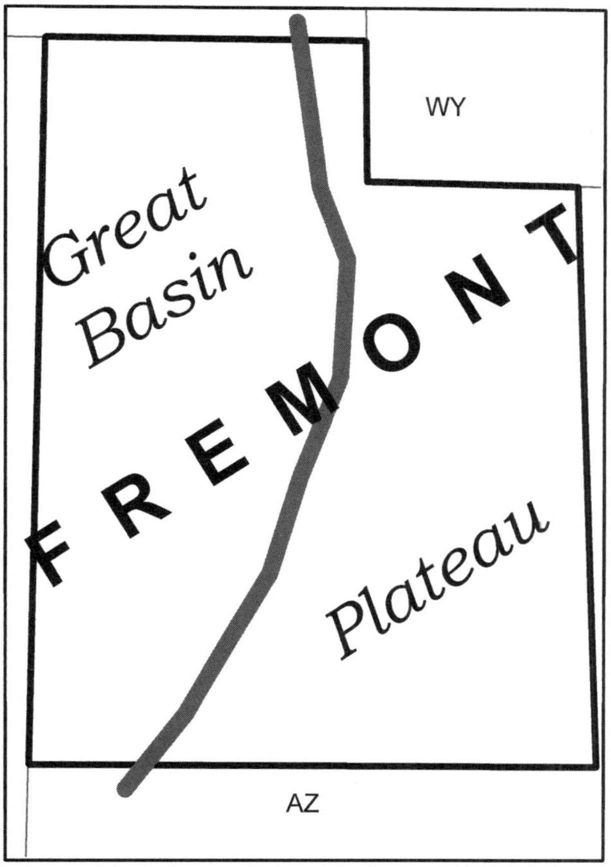

FIGURE 9.1. Ecotone separating the Great Basin and Colorado Plateau, slicing right down the middle of Fremont.

Archaeologists have a parallel problem with Southwestern farmers: Hohokam. *Hohokam* means a geographic region defined and controlled by sunburned archaeologists of Phoenix and Tucson—dust stormy, scorchy, sprawling, cities of broad hat brims. "Hohokam" is their home turf, the south half of Arizona. On another level, *Hohokam* refers to a historical event or phenomenon that burst out of the Colonial period (AD 700–900) in the Phoenix Basin, spread and peaked across most of southern Arizona in the Sedentary period (AD 900–1150), and then fell back in on its Phoenix core in the misnamed Classic period (AD 1150–1450). "Hohokam" was an event—or series of events—in history (Lekson 2009:80–89). In terms of archaeological geographies, *Hohokam* also means the entire area before, during, and after that event. *Hohokam* conflates a region and an event: so too, perhaps, *Fremont*.

Many archaeologists are content to have Fremont be a region and to have "Fremont" (the phenomenon) be a process within a region sufficiently large that all elements required for the process/phenomenon were surely contained within it. For processes, we can stipulate test criteria, calibrate trajectories, and predict outcomes. As Allison notes, that kind of archaeology works fairly well for Great Basin hunter-gatherers. But with farmers, after a certain point, it is history. Stuff happens. One thing leads to another. People obtain power and make decisions, and some of the decisions are not very smart. That is not process: that is human history. And, as Allison notes, a bit of history might go a long way for understanding Fremont.

Perhaps "Fremont" was an event, like the historical (not territorial) use of *Hohokam*: a history or histories. From a slightly facetious historical perspective, it seems that for centuries Fremont people were happy living in pithouses, hunting, gathering, and growing a bit of corn when the fancy took them. Then on a morning sometime around AD 1000, they woke up and for some reason said: "Let's build pueblos, paint black-on-white (or black-on-gray) pottery, and really commit to corn!" (Corn they already had [Coltrain et al. 2007]; but the settled farming life was, perhaps, something new.) Then for one brief shining moment, the Fremont *were* Southwestern farmers. They were no longer merely a process; they were a part of history.

History comes hard to the Southwest (Lekson 2009). For most of my time in Southwestern archaeology, we rejected or even denigrated history as "just-so stories" or background noise cluttering up our study of process. Yet, like all evolutionary sciences (astronomy or cosmology), archaeology is fundamentally a *historical* science, if it is to be any kind of science at all. "Natural history" disciplines are necessarily historical. But human history is a somewhat different critter than historical geology or astronomical cosmology or biological evolution, which is why we have an immense, time-honored discipline in the humanities called "history." I think that archaeologists need to *think like* historians (and borrow historical chops) to define the phenomena of interest, that is, the things we wish to study. Once we understand what happened historically, we can do all the science the law allows on that history (Lekson 2012).

History is nothing to be ashamed of. Every Americanist archaeologist would do well to read Stephen Jay Gould's articulate defense of history in the historical sciences, and their necessary difference and distance from "real" or "hard" sciences, in the second half of his 1989 book *Wonderful Life: The Burgess Shale and the Nature of History*. A short quote, in which Gould contrasts history and the procedures of the experimental scientific method:

> These procedures [of experimental sciences] are powerful but they do not encompass all of nature's variety. How should scientists operate when they must try to explain the results of history, those inordinately complex events that can occur but once in detailed glory?... The appropriate methods focus on narrative, not experiment as usually conceived.... The resolution of history must be rooted in the reconstruction of past events themselves—in their own terms—based on narrative evidence of their own unique phenomenon [1989:277–278].

If archaeologists want to do science, we first have to do history. In the Southwest, our search for processes absent history led us for many decades to ask the wrong questions, expensively. Great amounts of time, energy, funding, and brainpower were spent on projects that produced useful data, to be sure, but which ultimately *missed the point*. We asked the wrong questions because in our attempts to mimic experimental sciences, we ignored history—and convinced ourselves that ahistorical studies were "good science." Thanks to NAGPRA and intellectual winds from across the seas, history has been revalued as integral to Southwestern research, scientific or humanist.

But how to "do" history? Many processualists (plus processualist-plusists) hope to deal with history scientifically using contingencies, path dependence, and those sorts of things. I am not aware of any scientific discipline the purports to write narrative human history. Science lacks the tools for narrative history—cliometrics and psychohistory (for those of a certain age and reading habit) are still a long way off. When scientists such as Jarred Diamond and Peter Turchin tackle history, they use the history historians give them and then put some science on it.

Science does not "do" history—because human narrative history cannot be assessed with "scientific certainty." (Try that on a historian, and watch him or her laugh.) Science cannot interpret intention and cause. That is why there is a separate discipline called history, over in the humanities or in some cases wedded to colleges of social sciences. For now, at least, the best tools we have for human history are those of disciplinary history—narrative. But without written documents and historiographical methods of memory, evaluating archaeological narratives is hard to do, though not impossible. Lack of documents does not preclude narrative history; this lack simply means that we have had to develop our own methods and protocols for writing prehistory. New methods are coming. I am working on it (see my feeble first efforts: Lekson 2009:8–14), and I know of several others who are addressing this brave new methodological world, hopefully with more success than I. Importantly, archaeological narrative histories, for the present at least, are necessarily arguments, predictions, or attempts at recognizing universal processes. They are *not* experiments, *not* demonstrations, *not* hypothesis testing. Remember Gould! Sufficient unto the problem the methodologies thereof: for history, use history—not science. But still analyze and seek context.

I am aware of only two attempts to write narrative histories of the Southwest. The first was over 50 years ago (Gladwin 1957); it was little noted and not long remembered. The second one (Lekson 2009) came out a few years ago and may suffer the same fate as Gladwin's. I took the plunge and essayed a regional narrative: put it out there for all to see. Perhaps that was rash and unwise; time will tell. But I suggest that we all—scientist and humanist—operate with individual, unspoken narratives as subtexts for our particular areas and interests: our ideas about what happened when and by whom and why, back then. We all frame our thinking about the past in narrative, even if implicit and unstated.

One particularly strong cycle of silent subtexts for Fremont concerns its relationship to Anasazi, or Ancestral Pueblo. A leitmotif of Fremont studies is *no*: Fremont was no stinkin' periphery! Nobody wants to work in a periphery (I have worked in several). The term itself seems impolite and intentionally marginalizing or dismissive. But we do need these relational concepts, cores and peripheries; they, or something like them, are central to the kind of history we can hope to write. Not every historical development evinces cores and peripheries, but many do.

Take Mimbres, for example. The archaeology of this ancient society in southwestern New Mexico (e.g., Anyon and LeBlanc 1984; LeBlanc 1983; Lekson 2006; Shafer 2003) exemplifies the role of personality and place (to borrow the title and insights of Reid and Whittlesey 2010) in perceptions of the past, with some obvious (even heavy-handed) implications for Fremont. Reading about Fremont reminded me immediately of Mimbres; and for the remainder of this essay I will spin off from Utah, 500 km to southwestern New Mexico.

Mimbres, like Fremont, is both place and phenomenon: for Mimbres, the southwest corner of New Mexico and a remarkable cultural development (an event) of the tenth through twelfth centuries. For Fremont, the place was most of Utah, and the event was the appearance of Pueblo- or Anasazi-like settlements, again in the tenth through twelfth centuries. Mimbres (the event) was roughly contemporary with Fremont (the event). I will argue that co-incidence was *not* a coincidence.

Mimbres trod a parallel path. For centuries, Mimbres people apparently were happy living in pithouses, hunting, gathering, and growing a bit of corn when the fancy took them. Then one day sometime after AD 900, they woke up and said: "Let's build pueblos, paint black-on-white pottery, and really commit to corn!" And the rest is history—mostly art history.

What is up with Mimbres? Where did it come from? What was its history? I consider myself a Mimbres archaeologist. The Membership Committee is reviewing my credentials, in part because I argue that Mimbres was a periphery, first to Hohokam and then (after AD 950) to Chaco Anasazi (Lekson 2006, 2009). The suggestion of Hohokam interests in Mimbres prior to AD 950 is fairly recent (Creel 1989; Lekson 1993). Anasazi claims have greater antiquity: Emil Haury (1986) and Joe Ben Wheat (1955) long ago espoused "Anasazi swamping" of Mimbres after AD 1000. Mimbres, in my view, was a weather vane pointing toward the Southwest's maximum bluster: Hohokam until AD 1000, Chaco thereafter.

These views, of course, are not shared by many modern Mimbres archaeologists (e.g., Hegmon and Nelson 2007 on Hohokam; LeBlanc 1983, 1986, on Anasazi; see also Shafer 2003). Just as Fremont archaeologists of the late 1960s and 1970s rejected peripheral status, so too did the Mimbres archaeologists of those decades (e.g., LeBlanc 1986). Mimbres was local! No periphery, no swamping! Mimbres was first and foremost a local process. Of course (in part) that is correct: there is a lot that is local about Mimbres (and Fremont). How could there not be? I insist, however, that many key Mimbres (and Fremont) elements

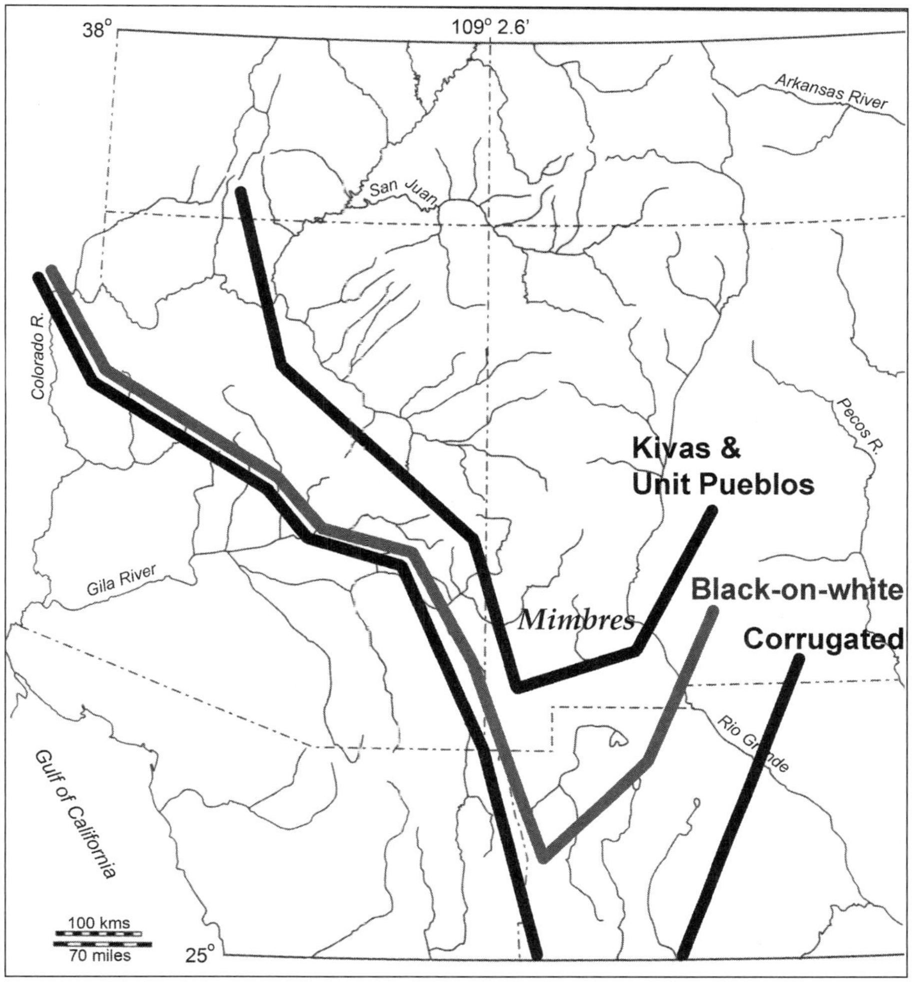

FIGURE 9.2. Anasazi sagging south, around AD 1000, into Mimbres.

(objects, events, social developments both major and minor) can only be understood in the context of regional histories. Mimbres was indeed peripheral, but "peripheral" in the best possible way!

Consider Mimbres and Anasazi. If we were to stereotype Anasazi about AD 1000, when Mimbres was really picking up speed (that is, painting pottery and building pueblos), Anasazi would be unit pueblos and black-on-white and corrugated pottery. If you look at the distribution of those traits, they slide south, curiously, right into Mimbres (Figure 9.2). Mimbres built unit pueblos, painted black-on-white pottery, and indented their corrugated pottery. Before AD 1000, they did not do those things.

Something happened, something that can best (and perhaps only) be understood historically. What happened was Chaco. Mimbres had its own story of course; it was local, much as Fremont was local. But Mimbres was also and importantly part of its larger world. Before AD 950 or 1000 (that is, before Chaco), Mimbres paid close attention to Hohokam, to the west (Lekson 2006, 2009; contra Hegmon and Nelson 2007). Hohokam (as noted above) exploded outward around AD 700, peaked around AD 1050, and, by AD 1150, shrank back into the Phoenix Basin. Mimbres communities dropped Hohokam like a bad habit and turned their attention north toward the explosion that was under way in eleventh-century Chaco (Lekson 2006:vii–xxi, 2009:133–137; contra LeBlanc 1986, among many others). Mimbres was (mostly) local, but after AD 1000 Mimbres looked Anasazi.

The result for Mimbres was a string of large, very interesting pueblo-like towns along the interface of the outermost Mogollon Rim (the southern edge of the Colorado Plateau, at least biotically) and the Chihuahuan Desert. It was an ecotone that mattered! Big sites popped up where the steady streams of the Mogollon highlands flowed out into the Chihuahuan Desert. It was an ideal setting: mountains at communities' backs, lots of water, and plenty of sunshine. It was rather like the trans-Fremontane ecotone shown in Figure 9.1. Starting about that same time in Fremont, a string of large, very interesting, relatively pueblo-like towns popped up along the interface of the Wasatch Range, the west edge of the Colorado Plateau, at least biotically, and the Great Basin (Talbot 2000b:Figure 11.8; reproduced here as Figure 9.3).

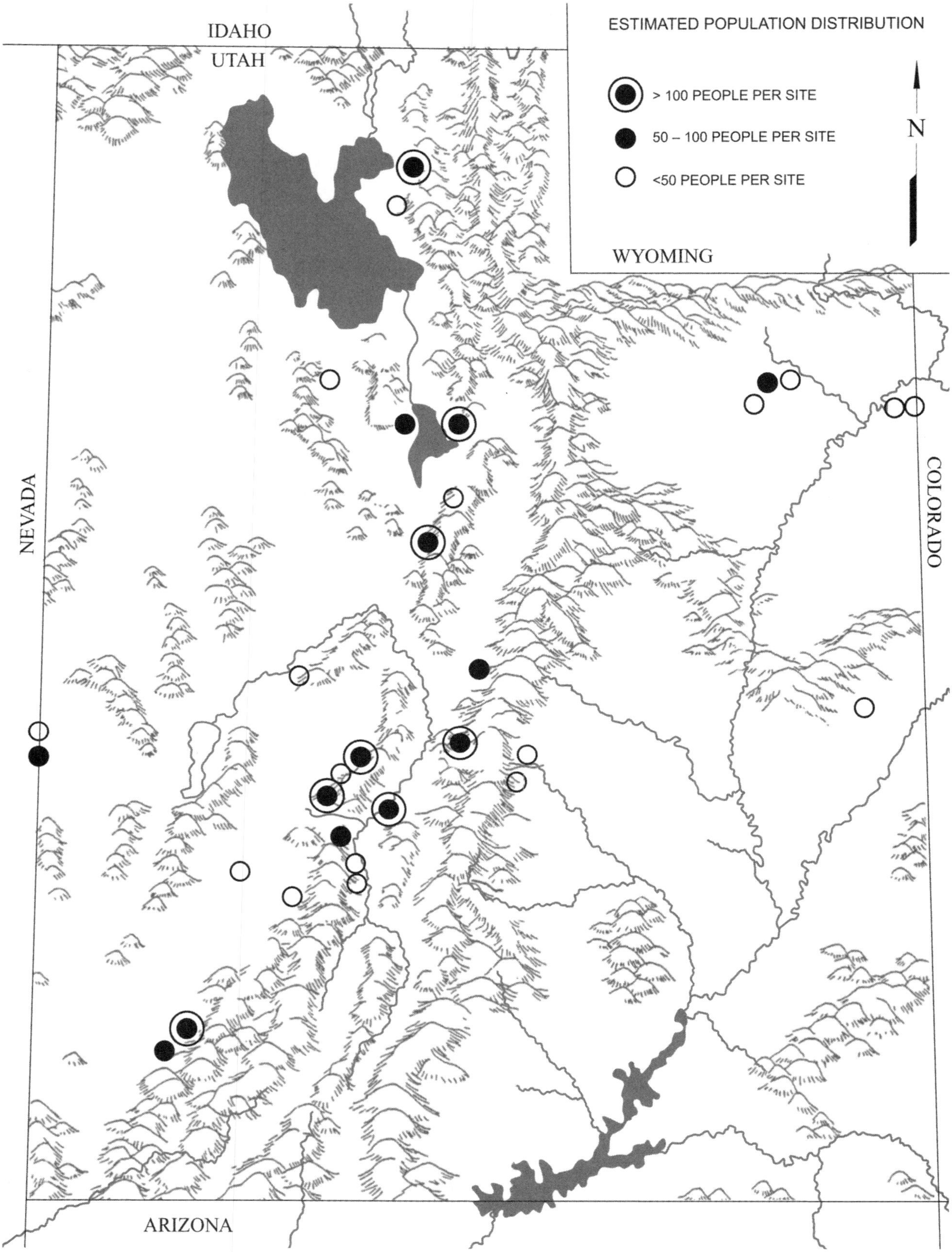

FIGURE 9.3. "A synchronic view of Fremont population concentrations, primarily AD 900–1350" (from "Fremont Settlement Patterns and Demography" by Richard K. Talbot [2000b:Figure 11.8]).

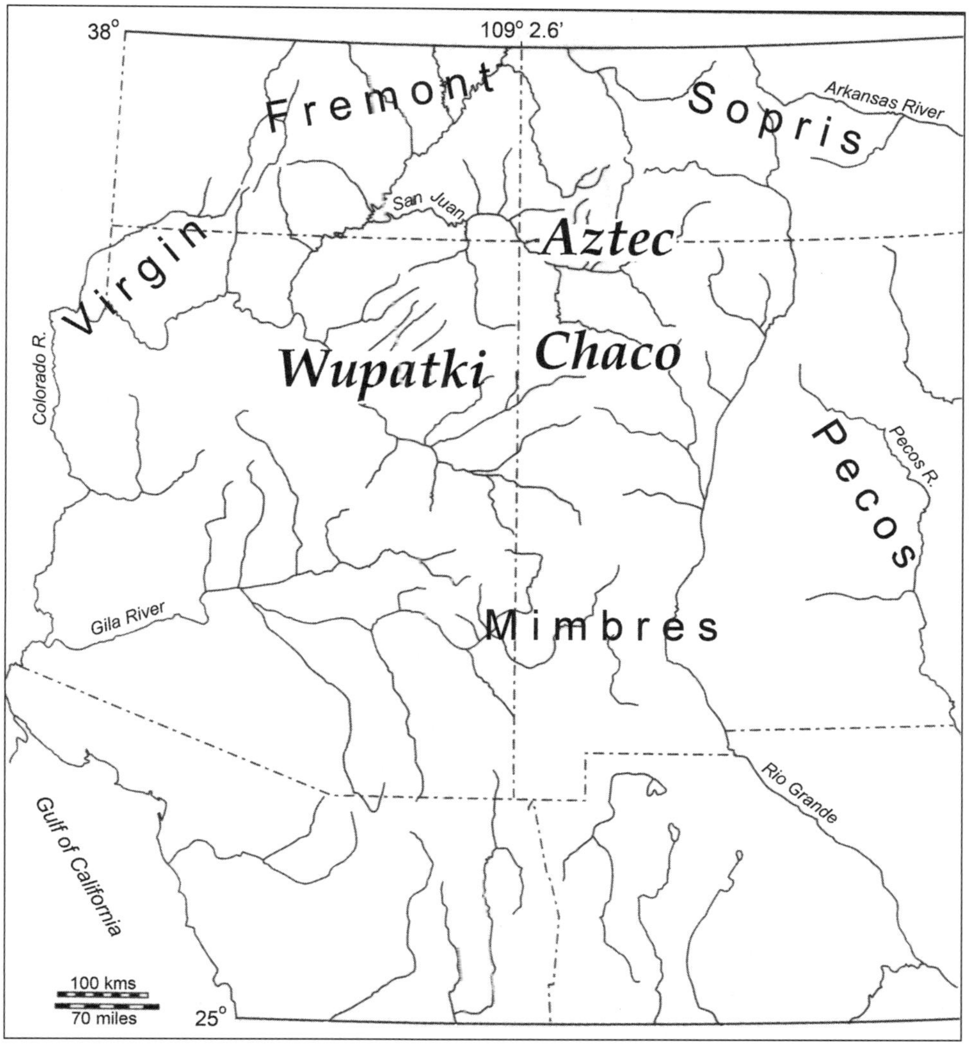

FIGURE 9.4. Chaco, Aztec, Wupatki, and surroundir g events.

Coincidence? I think not. Fremont and Mimbres experienced the same motors: a nice wet period for farming and, more important, the political explosion at Chaco, radiating out in all directions. Chaco's direct impacts reached at least 250 km from Chaco Canyon (Lekson 2009:132–133). Its indirect impacts reached into Mimbres and—I argue—into Fremont. Chaco was the key historical context for both Fremont and Mimbres.

It is all about context, a central contention in history. In archaeology, context is everything; but we typically apply that slogan to the smallest possible individual proveniences and too often forget that there is a great big wonderful world out there, perhaps the most important context of all, of which Mimbres and Fremont were a part. Five hundred kilometers apart, at opposite ends of the Colorado Plateau (biotically defined), at the opposite edges of Anasazi and Chaco (which were pretty much the same thing [Lekson 2009:130–133]), Mimbres and Fremont were arcs on a circle of ancient events, ancient societies, which at slightly different times and with slightly different local histories ringed Chaco's core, the place where history was really happening (Figure 9.4).

Big things happened in Anasazi, hurling energy and ideas and people out in all directions like a blender when the lid flies off or a reactor when the core melts down. Chaco (from AD 850 to 1125), Wupatki (in the middle twelfth century), and Aztec Ruins were in like a lion at AD 1110 and out like a very sick lamb by 1280 (Lekson 2009). Now we can be sure that Mimbres, Virgin Anasazi, Middle Pecos, Sopris, and Fremont all have lovely, logical, local adaptations, in situ processes that explain them neatly—but perhaps not correctly. Local adaptations describe local economies, not regional social and political dynamics. Purely local explanations are more or less bunk: Mimbres and Fremont and the rest *must* be understood in the context of all that larger regional history. Contrary to the man who gave our great-grandparents the Model T: history is *not* bunk.

To my colleagues around the outer edges of the ancient Southwest: do not fear the periphery! Because there, out on the edges, lies a means for writing prehistory, for developing that difficult methodology for addressing hard problems: comparisons at multiple scales, in expanding contexts, on a single observational plane, within a single observational space. Always recall

Gould: we will write history as "the reconstruction of past events themselves—in their own terms—based on narrative evidence of their own unique phenomenon." We could do this by comparing and contrasting Fremont, Mimbres, Virgin Anasazi, Sopris, and the Middle Pecos Valley, early and late, and after that move on to Chaco, to Chumash, to Cahoki, and to Cholula. Then sighting back from those more distant points to the phenomenon of interest, we can return to our case study or local problem.

I call this triangulation, but not in the sense of Patrick Kirch (Kirch and Green 2001), who uses the term *triangulation* for multiple, independent lines of evidence. *Triangulation* for me works in its geodetic sense, as a mesh or nexus of comparisons, observations of the same target from many different angles: contemporary, pre-, and post-peers, but all focused on the phenomenon in question, be it Fremont, Chaco, or Mimbres. Fremont and Mimbres are fascinating in their own right; but they are also useful as triangulation stations for understanding Anasazi and Chaco.

This paradigmatic perspective, I believe, is how we might write history without written documents: relentless, progressive comparisons, *understanding past events in their own terms and in a series of small to large social contexts*. Certainly this will not be by "upstreaming," a pernicious and illogical strategy much loved in the Southwest (and a topic for other essays). And it will probably not be accomplished by cross-cultural calibrations, in the old Michigan sense; these are useful, perhaps even necessary, but not sufficient for what I have in mind: understanding events in their own terms, their contexts, "rooted in the reconstruction of past events themselves—in their own terms—based on narrative evidence of their own unique phenomenon."

Archaeological "cultures" are necessarily things of shreds and patches, archaeological remains being notoriously shreddy and patchy, to borrow Robert Lowie's phrase about cultural research. And those shreds and patches are (or were) in motion, like fallen leaves in a breeze. Everything we know about North America's prehistory—from first peoplings to colonial wars—suggests movement, fluidity, change, and adaptation. Yet archaeological regions, once defined, become fixed and inflexible, their boundaries nonnegotiable, frozen in time and space. Hohokam is Hohokam, and Anasazi is Anasazi. Bad things happen if you cross that line (e.g., Berry 1982—a brilliant book wrecked by regional barriers).

The Southwest and Fremont are firmly held to be two separate areas. Those regions structure our thinking about the past. They structure the practice and profession of archaeology: as noted above, Great Basin and Southwestern archaeologies have differing intellectual histories and consequently differing conventions, methods, and theories. This does disservice to the ancient people we study. It is hard enough to know the past without stumbling over obstacles of our own making.

This essay may be the first (and may well be the last) to consider Mimbres and Fremont as part of the same historic event: the explosive geopolitics of the eleventh century, the era of Chaco Canyon and its successors. By focusing on Mimbres and Fremont separately but simultaneously, I generate new ideas about Chaco. I hope that Mimbres and Fremont archaeologists might consider a similar approach. Were Mimbres and Fremont regions separate entities about which we debate degrees of interaction with Anasazi? Perhaps, but surely they were something more: the entire corn-growing world of western North America can and should be seen as a whole, interconnected in a deep, dense nexus of historical causes and effects.

Acknowledgments

My sincere thanks go to the Society for American Archaeology session organizers and volume editors for the invitation to participate in the celebration of Dr. Don D. Fowler. I greatly admire Don Fowler: a man who thinks big and thinks well and who values history. I have come to rely on his histories of Southwestern archaeology, as I have come to realize that intellectual history is fundamental to our understanding of the ancient Southwest—or any other archaeological region. Particular thanks go to Joel Janetski and Steven Simms for leading me through the basics of Fremont 101 and to Simms for a close and careful reading of this chapter. They are not responsible for my misunderstandings or misuse of the references they sent me or the good advice they gave me. As always, my errors are my own.

References Cited

Adovasio, James M.
1979 Comment by Adovasio. *American Antiquity* 44(4):723–731.
Adovasio, James M., David R. Pedlere, and Jeffrey S. Illingworth
2002 Fremont Basketry. *Utah Archaeology* 15(1):1–47.
Allison, James R.
2008 Human Ecology and Social Theory in Utah Archaeology. *Utah Archaeology* 21(1):57–88.
Anyon, Roger, and Steven A. LeBlanc
1984 *The Galaz Ruin*. University of New Mexico Press, Albuquerque.
Berry, Michael S.
1982 *Time, Space, and Transition in Anasazi Prehistory*. University of Utah Press, Salt Lake City.
Coltrain, Joan B., Joel C. Janetski, and Shawn W. Carlyle
2007 The Stable- and Radio-Isotope Chemistry of Western Basketmaker Burials: Implications for Early Puebloan Diets and Origins. *American Antiquity* 72:301–321.
Creel, Darrell
1989 A Primary Cremation at the NAN Ranch Ruin. *Journal of Field Archaeology* 16:309–329.
Gladwin, Harold S.
1957 *A History of the Ancient Southwest*. Bond Wheelright, Portland, Maine.
Gould, Stephen Jay
1989 *Wonderful Life: The Burgess Shale and the Nature of History*. W. W. Norton, New York.
Gunnerson, James H.
1969 *The Fremont Culture*. Papers of the Peabody Museum of Amer-

ican Archaeology and Ethnology, 59(2). Peabody Museum, Cambridge, Massachusetts.

Haury, Emil W.

1986 Thoughts After Sixty Years as a Southwest Archaeologist. In *Emil W. Haury's Prehistory of the American Southwest*, edited by J. Jefferson Reid and David E. Doyel, pp. 435–464. University of Arizona Press, Tucson.

Hegmon, Michelle, and Margaret C. Nelson

2007 In Sync, but Barely in Touch: Relations Between the Mimbres Region and the Hohokam Regional System. In *Hinterlands and Regional Dynamics in the Ancient Southwest*, edited by Alan P. Sullivan and James M. Bayman, pp. 70–96. University of Arizona Press, Tucson.

Janetski, Joel C.

2000 Fremont External Relations. In *Clear Creek Canyon Archaeological Project: Results and Synthesis*, by Joel C. Janetski, Richard K. Talbot, Deborah E. Newman, Lane D. Richens, and James D. Wilde, pp. 231–240. Occasional Papers No. 7. Museum of Peoples and Cultures, Brigham Young University, Provo.

2002 Trade in Fremont Society: Contexts and Contrasts. *Journal of Anthropological Archaeology* 21:344–370.

2008 The Enigmatic Fremont. In *The Great Basin*, edited by Catherine S. Fowler and Don D. Fowler, pp. 105–116. SAR Press, Santa Fe, New Mexico.

Kirch, Patrick V., and Roger C. Green

2001 *Hawaiki, Ancestral Polynesia: An Essay in Historical Anthropology*. Cambridge University Press, Cambridge.

LeBlanc, Steven A.

1983 *The Mimbres People*. Thames and Hudson, London.

1986 Development of Archaeological Thought on the Mimbres Mogollon. In *Emil W. Haury's Prehistory of the American Southwest*, edited by J. Jefferson Reid and David E. Doyel, pp. 297–304. University of Arizona Press, Tucson.

Lekson, Stephen H.

1993 Chaco, Hohokam, and Mimbres: The 11th and 12th Centuries in the American Southwest. *Expedition* 35(1):44–52.

2006 *The Archaeology of the Mimbres Region*. BAR International Series, 1466. Archaeopress, Oxford.

2009 *A History of the Ancient Southwest*. SAR Press, Santa Fe, New Mexico.

2012 *The Southwest in the World*. Blog, http://stevelekson.com/.

Madsen, David B.

1979 New Views on the Fremont: The Fremont and the Sevier: Defining Prehistoric Agriculturalists North of the Anasazi. *American Antiquity* 44(4):711–772.

1989 *Exploring the Fremont*. University of Utah Occasional Publication, 8. Utah Museum of Natural History, Salt Lake City.

Madsen, David B., and Steven R. Simms

1998 The Fremont Complex: A Behavioral Perspective. *Journal of World Prehistory* 12(3):255–336.

Morss, Noel

1931 *The Ancient Culture of the Fremont River, Utah*. Papers of the Peabody Museum of American Archaeology and Ethnology, 12(3). Peabody Museum, Cambridge, Massachusetts.

Reid, Jefferson, and Stephanie Whittlesey

2010 *Prehistory, Personality, and Place: Emil W. Haury and the Mogollon Controversy*. University of Arizona Press, Tucson.

Shafer, Harry J.

2003 *Mimbres Archaeology at the NAN Ranch Ruin*. University of New Mexico Press, Albuquerque.

Simms, Steven R.

2008 *Ancient Peoples of the Great Basin and Colorado Plateau*. Left Coast Press, Walnut Creek.

2010 *Traces of Fremont*. University of Utah Press, Salt Lake City.

Talbot, Richard K.

2000a Fremont Architecture. In *Clear Creek Canyon Archaeological Project: Results and Synthesis*, by Joel C. Janetski, Richard K. Talbot, Deborah E. Newman, Lane D. Richens, and James D. Wilde, pp. 131–184. Occasional Papers No. 7. Museum of Peoples and Cultures, Brigham Young University, Provo.

2000b Fremont Settlement Patterns and Demography. In *Clear Creek Canyon Archaeological Project: Results and Synthesis*, by Joel C. Janetski, Richard K. Talbot, Deborah E. Newman, Lane D. Richens, and James D. Wilde, pp. 201–230. Occasional Papers No. 7. Museum of Peoples and Cultures, Brigham Young University, Provo.

Wheat, Joe Ben

1955 *Mogollon Culture Prior to AD 1000*. Memoir 82. American Anthropological Association, Washington, D.C.

Wormington, H. Marie

1955 *A Reappraisal of the Fremont Culture with a Summary of the Archaeology of the Northern Periphery*. Proceedings 1. Denver Museum of Natural History, Denver.

10

Fremont Social Organization

A Southwestern Perspective

Joel C. Janetski and Richard K. Talbot

Social organization in small-scale agriculturalists has persisted as a topic of interest in the American Southwest and beyond for decades (Adler 2002; Lipe and Hegmon 1989; Longacre 1970; Neitzel 1999). Insights often rely heavily on ethnographic analogy for obvious reasons; that is, historic pueblos at Hopi, at Zuni, and along the Rio Grande are remarkable for their visual and presumably structural similarity to ancient ruins in the Four Corners region. Assuming ancestral Anasazi connections for these communities is common despite the pitfalls of such an assumption (Wobst 1977). Here we focus on the societal structure of the Fremont, an archaeologically defined culture in the northern Southwest for which analogy is geographically discontinuous (see Gould 1980), as no comparable societies existed in the Fremont geographic homeland at the time of European arrival.

The Fremont flourished between 2,000 and 700 years ago north of the Virgin and Colorado rivers (Figure 10.1). Traditional literature describes Fremont as semisedentary farmers living in small communities close to arable land but who supplemented their diet with wild foods (Jennings 1978; Marwitt 1986; Morss 1931). Beginning with the work of Morss (1931) and Judd (1926), scholars have recognized diversity in portable artifacts (temper in ceramics, stone tool morphology, etc.), as well as architecture and subsistence strategies (see Janetski et al. 2000; Madsen and Simms 1998 for recent reviews). This diversity led to the development of regional variant models to reflect differences across space (Marwitt 1970; Wormington 1955; and others; but see Madsen and Simms 1998 for a different view). In the 1980s and 1990s researchers were less interested in material traits and more focused on dietary differences, which were explained as behavioral responses to temporal and spatial shifts in ecological factors favorable or unfavorable for farming (Barlow 2002; Madsen and Simms 1998; Simms 1986). More recently interest in exchange and social structure has increased (Janetski and Talbot 2000; Simms and Gohier 2010; Watkins 2006).

Few Fremont scholars have braved the muddy waters of Fremont social structure. We note first the work of Julian Steward, who excavated several mound sites in Utah during his tenure at the University of Utah. Included were sites at Provo, Grantsville, and Kanosh and in the Uinta Basin, among others. Based on this work Steward characterized Fremont occupations as Basketmaker III or "Developmental Pueblo" in form and artifact content (1941:281). He (1955:162) later concluded that small Basketmaker III settlements of up to 10 houses or so consisted of kin-related families or lineages that valued agricultural lands more than foraging territories. Those lineages retained their integrity as communal living became common due to population increase during the late Pueblo I period, roughly AD 800 into the early AD 900s. Lineage growth and communal living resulted in the emergence of exogamous clans, a characteristic of a segmented society. But when considering Fremont social structure, Steward states: "The haphazard arrangement of pit lodges in the Great Salt Lake and the adobe Pueblo houses in the Sevier Desert and of Utah [Valley]...indicates a similar lack of the San Juan type of social unit" (1955:169). He (1955:169) proposes that the absence of kivas or other obvious integrating architecture and site planning suggests that clans were absent.

Steward's (1955) conclusions regarding the lack of clan development in the Fremont area may be explained by the absence of community-focused excavations, although Judd's (1919, 1926) work in Parowan Valley and elsewhere had been published for some time. Steward's own work, including his excavations at one of the many mounds at Kanosh (see Steward 1936), represents this lack of expansive excavation. This topic is revisited below.

James Gunnerson (1969:156) also pondered Fremont social structure. He described Colorado Plateau Fremont villages and houses as small, with scant evidence to suggest the existence of permanent social groupings beyond the household unit. Despite that view he concluded that dispersed communities existed, stating that "evidence for social groups larger than extended families can also be found. The clustering of many small villages along a single stream suggests some social interaction took place between communities" (1969:157).

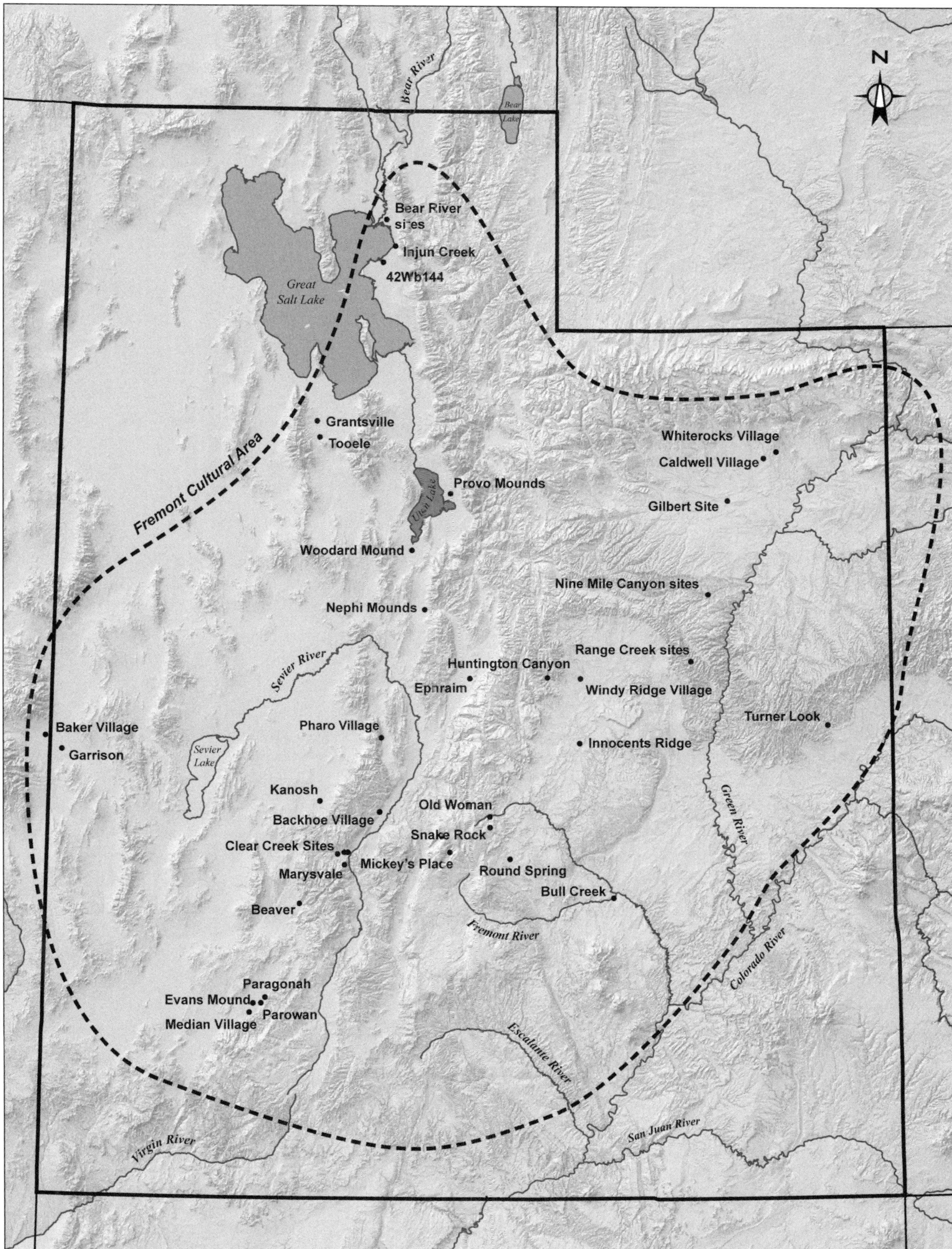

FIGURE 10.1. Fremont culture area with selected sites.

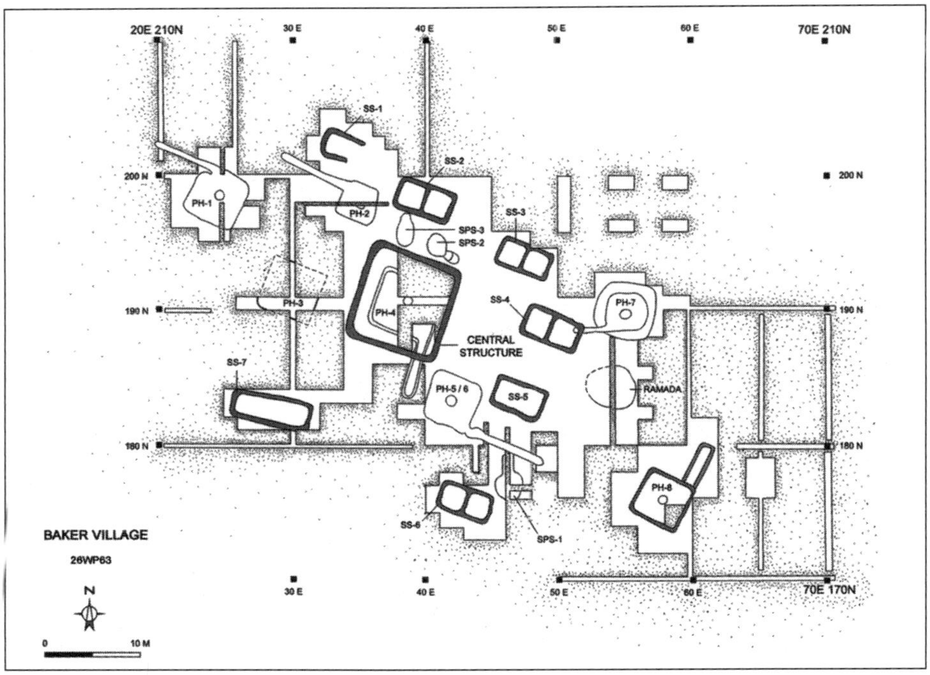

FIGURE 10.2. Plan map of Baker Village.

Gunnerson went on to note evidence for irrigation and the existence of larger-than-average pithouses in some sites "that could have served as a meeting place or club house in addition to being a dwelling," "possible dance plazas," and "large, defensible [storage] structures" (1969:157), all of which could suggest cooperative activities of groups larger than families. These and other factors, especially a farming-focused subsistence strategy, led Gunnerson (1969:162) to conclude that Fremont social structure was basically Puebloan. This somewhat vague reference we take to invoke a western rather than eastern Puebloan lifeway. Further insights into Gunnerson's thinking on this point come from his belief that the origin of the distinctive Fremont culture was to be traced to the Puebloan expansion in the mid–AD 900s, with migrants from the Virgin branch of the Anasazi becoming Proto-Fremont.

Although Jennings largely ignored Fremont social issues, one of his students, Dorothy Sammons-Lohse (1981), explicitly confronted the topic of Fremont villages and communities, and by extension social organization, in a section of the Bull Creek report (Jennings and Sammons-Lohse 1981). Her geographical scope broadened Gunnerson's by including both the eastern Great Basin and the Colorado Plateau, although her conclusions were similar:

> In terms of numbers of structures, no one occupation at any (Fremont) site is significantly different, statistically, from any occupation at any other site. This implies that, despite reoccupation and continuous building at some optimal locations, the self-sufficient, somewhat isolated homestead is the recurrent Fremont community pattern. There is no indication of community organization above the household level. The household and not some wider community appears to be the economically self-sufficient, politically independent corporate unit [1981:134].

Madsen and Simms (1998:310–312) briefly consider Fremont social complexity in the context of their much broader discussion of subsistence diversity. They recognize the existence of what may have been communal efforts at constructing "big houses" and irrigation systems but suggest that these are rare and, in the case of big houses, functionally problematic. Janetski and Talbot (2000) offer a more systematic assessment of Fremont society in their synthesis of the Clear Creek Canyon research. Relying on Wenke's (1990) approach to complexity in the Near East and Lightfoot and Feinman's (1982) model developed for the Mogollon, they found evidence for emerging complexity at the Late Fremont (post–AD 900) Five Finger Ridge site. Of particular note were two architecturally unique structures discussed in more detail later on, one that may have been the home of a community leader and the other a large jacal surface "central structure" that probably functioned as a community or dispersed community integrative facility (Janetski and Talbot 2000; Talbot 2000a, 2000b). Both have parallels in contemporaneous Southwest farming societies (e.g., Kamp and Whittaker 1999).

Intriguing insights into Fremont social life come from research at Baker Village on the Utah–Nevada border (Wilde and Soper 1999), which was occupied ca. AD 1000–1300. Large-scale horizontal exposure here revealed evidence of community planning in the form of architectural alignments (Figure 10.2; Wilde and Soper 1999). Also, Bryan Hockett's (1998) analysis of faunal remains from the site focused on the central structure and suggested that the massive quantities of leporid remains there evidenced communal feasting.

Given the presence of farming, village or community life, pithouse and above ground architecture, high-volume storage facilities, and ceramic styles reminiscent of Anasazi traditions found in Fremont sites, invoking a Puebloan analogue for post–AD 900/1000 Fremont seems appropriate. We recognize that *Puebloan* is vague at best, as there is much diversity in Puebloan strategies and material culture over time and across the region. Still, the above-mentioned parallels follow contemporary Puebloan groups in areas of southern Utah and northern Arizona.

Proposed Model

In our attempt to model Fremont social organization we turn first to Service's (1962) oft-cited typology of human social organization involving bands, tribes, chiefdoms, and states. Herein Service presents Puebloan peoples as premier examples of a tribal or segmentary society. Certainly many have pointed to the ambiguity of Service's scheme, in particular the tribe label (Carneiro 2002:34; Herr and Clark 2002:123); nonetheless, the term *tribe* is common to the literature and therefore hard to ignore. For the Southwest, it is a convenient and apt descriptor of clan-based Puebloan societies, and the term is central to a wide range of literature, both ethnographic and archaeological (e.g., Fried 1966; Hodder 1982; various in Parkinson 2002; Sahlins 1968; Service 1962). The emergence of segmented societies among Ancestral Puebloans is hinted at in Steward's comments above; that is, such structures arose as populations aggregated into villages. The timing of those changes would have varied across the Puebloan world since that vast region was certainly not in lockstep (Cordell 1997; Doyel and Dean 2006; Mills 2000).

Turning away from Southwest studies for a moment, we note the utility of Hodder's (1982) ethnographic work with three tribal groups in the Baringo District of Kenya in understanding how tribal societies use material goods to maintain internal cohesion as well as reconcile internal tensions. Hodder notes, for example, the "clear homogeneity in material culture within tribes" (1982:25) and goes on to state, "In their various ways, the pots, stools, and hearth positions all exemplify the remarkable extent to which the inhabitants of Baringo continually reinforce and repeat the same regional patterning of material symbols" (1982:56). He also notes that material homogeneity is strongest "in the border areas where there is greatest tension and competition, [and] material culture of many forms is used to justify between-group negative reciprocity and to support the social and economic dependencies within groups" (1982:56). Importantly, despite these means of maintaining group unity, there are "many other forces [that] are concerned to deny or disrupt the clear material culture distinctions" (Hodder 1982:57). Nonetheless, it is clear that group members use material culture symbolically as a means to set themselves in contrast to members of other groups (Hodder 1982:95).

John O'Shea and Claire Milner (2002) offer excellent insights into understanding the social structure of past small-scale agriculturalists or tribes and note challenges similar to those described by Hodder, although they focus on intratribal challenges rather than those between tribes. In essence, they recognize two opposing problems: "large-scale integration and local differentiation" (2002:201). Archaeologists studying such nonliterate societies face the task of recognizing the mechanisms that hold tribes together, on the one hand, and those that allow local groups to maintain identity, on the other. In their study of the Juntunen phase in the Great Lakes region, O'Shea and Milner (2002:207) identify three social and spatial scales: (1) the territory occupied by the tribe as a whole, (2) macroregions within the tribal area, and (3) band territories. The tribal level is marked by style expressed in material goods, especially ceramics, while macroregions are integrated by aggregation sites located in areas with abundant resources to support large gatherings. Smaller band territories are marked by natural features and built structures. Juntunen ceramics varied subtly within regions depending on traditional patterns of interaction, although always expressing the Juntunen style. Variation in resource productivity within band territories or larger regions encouraged social ties to "level out shortages" in crop production and other resource scarcities.

We maintain that the O'Shea and Milner (2002) scenario and the work of Hodder (1982) provide a basis for framing or conceptualizing Fremont as a tribal society and provide understanding of the much modeled regional variability. First, it is widely recognized that a pan-regional style expressed in various media, such as rock art, ceramics, figurines, and ornaments, existed during the Fremont period (Marwitt 1986; Figure 10.3). The meaning of this style beyond a kind of shared symbolism is unclear (Madsen and Simms 1998); nonetheless, it is this style, along with a core farming strategy (Talbot 2000b), that defines Fremont (Janetski et al. 2011; but see Madsen and Simms 1998: 283). There is no implication here of a shared language. We need only reference Puebloan peoples who share numerous material, subsistence, ceremonial, and social similarities yet speak very different languages to demonstrate this point (various in Ortiz 1983). We suggest that regular gatherings such as trade fairs or similar social gatherings maintained networks and influenced subtle changes in the Fremont style through interaction among disparate groups. Although it is probable that Fremont households saw to their own needs and villages were in large part autonomous, it is becoming increasingly clear that exchange played an important economic role in Fremont society (Janetski 2002; Janetski et al. 2011). The work of Watkins (2006) and Cole (2010, 2012) has demonstrated that communities were linked by ceramic exchange, and the existence of ceramic production zones from which unique wares moved into neighboring areas is now apparent. Such linkages would have been social as well as economic in providing mates, foodstuffs, and goods in addition to ceramics (e.g., Lyneis 1996:16).

Second, aggregated sites emerge in the Fremont area possibly as early as AD 900 but surely by AD 1000 and coincident with the

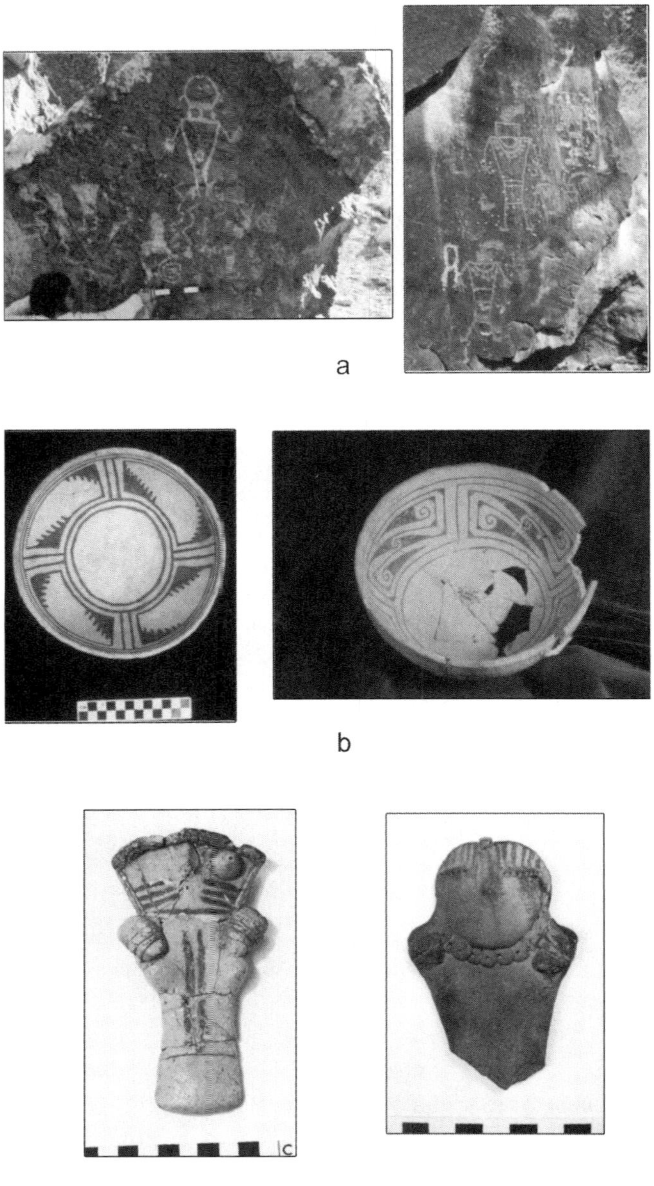

FIGURE 10.3. Examples of Fremont regional styles. (a) Rock art: left, Clear Creek Canyon; right, Capital Reef National Park. (b) Painted bowls: left, Five Finger Ridge; right, Coombs Village (Archaeology Center Collection, 42Ga34-490; courtesy of Special Collections, Marriott Library, University of Utah). (c) Clay figurines: left, Evans Mound (courtesy of Southern Utah University); right, Nine Mile Canyon (courtesy of the Museum of Peoples and Cultures, Brigham Young University).

Chaco phenomenon, the influence of which spread across the Four Corners region and farther (Cordell 1997; Neitzel 1999, 2000; Wills 2000; see Lekson, this volume). This aggregation is most pronounced in the Great Basin–Colorado Plateau Transition Zone (Stokes 1986) or eastern Great Basin rim (Figure 10.4). This zone might be appropriately subdivided into several subregions comparable to O'Shea and Milner's (2002) macroregions. We suggest northern, central, and southern areas along with the southern base of the Uinta Mountains and the western edge of Snake Valley on the Utah–Nevada border. These are areas of higher resource abundance, which is consistent with expectations derived from the work of O'Shea and Milner. All include the rich valley-edge settings where abundant water and replenished soils promoted farming, but which also placed aggregated populations in close proximity to both upland and lowland natural resources (Lindsay 1986). It is within these macroregions that subtle material and strategy differences emerged after aggregation occurred, again as predicted by the O'Shea and Milner model for the Juntunen region. Those differences are also in large measure what led early scholars to identify regional variants based on material traits (e.g., Ambler 1966; Madsen 1979; Marwitt 1970; Steward 1933; Wormington 1955). Most variant schemes relied predominantly on ceramic expression (Berry and Berry 2003; Madsen 1977) and secondarily on architecture (see Lohse 1980; Talbot 2000b). Additional differences included regional contrasts in settlement and subsistence strategies (Jennings 1978; Madsen 1979) and stylistic variability in rock art and figurines (e.g., Baker and Billat 1999; Castleton and Madsen 1981). We suggest that these variants may simply be regional expressions of identity to set groups apart from neighbors. We expect identity to be expressed particularly in terms of active style (Sackett 1982, 1985; Wiessner 1983, 1985); therefore, we should see those expressions in more visible media such as rock art, figurines, arrows, clothing, ornaments, and body adornment. However, we also expect regional variability in a passive style, such as in architecture and culinary ceramics, to develop over time.

The third-level band territories within macroregions are more difficult to see or define archaeologically, but we suggest that they existed at the valley or neighboring valleys level. For example, within the northern macroregion Fremont population aggregations occurred east of the Great Salt Lake and Utah valleys (Figure 10.4). Valleys within this region have unique physiographic boundaries and contrasting resource suites that may have encouraged the movement of goods both within and between valleys. We would expect social and economic networks within valleys or between proximal valleys to be stronger than those with more distant valleys. In the case of Utah Valley, known population aggregations existed along the eastern and southern shores of Utah Lake. Fremont populations were especially abundant on the Lower Provo River delta, as evidenced by the findings of avocational archaeologists, who documented over 100 mounds here during the 1930s despite 75 years of mound leveling and development (Janetski 1990). Other communities were likely present along the American Fork and Spanish Fork rivers, which drain into the eastern shore of the lake, although development has obscured past use. Surveys in less developed Goshen Valley to the south have found numerous Fremont residential sites, some with long-term occupations (Gilsen 1968; Janetski 2004). The rich flatlands to the east of the Great Salt Lake were also heavily occupied during the Fremont era, with site concentrations along the Lower Bear River and the Weber

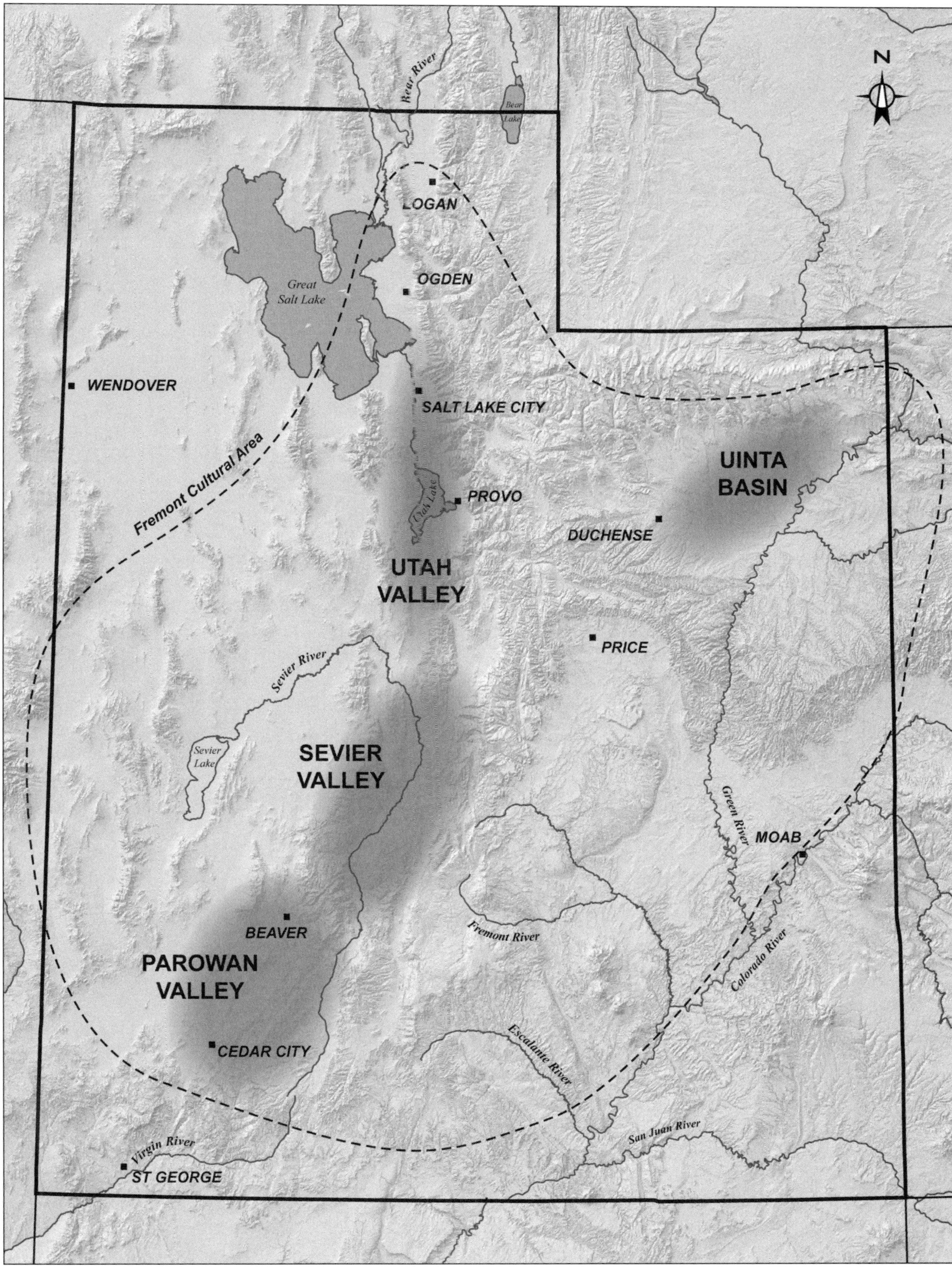

FIGURE 10.4. Late Fremont centers of influence.

River drainages (Aikens 1967; Simms 1999). Less is known in Salt Lake Valley proper due to extensive development, although recent fortuitous discoveries and subsequent excavations hint that a considerable population was present here as well (Talbot et al. 2004). These valleys making up the northern or Wasatch Front macroregion likely contained local bands with intravalley subdivisions. Local band territories would have been intricately interconnected by kinship ties and by fluid membership.

Parowan Valley is perhaps the best-known population aggregation in the Fremont region and constitutes an important component of the southern macroregion. At least three massive sites existed here: Summit, Parowan, and Paragonah, with the latter consisting of over a hundred mounds (Berry 1972, 1974; Judd 1926; Marwitt 1970; Meighan et al. 1956). We know that large sites existed in Cedar Valley just to the south and in Beaver Valley to the north as well. Although little is known of the site in Cedar Valley, the Parowan Valley sites, and perhaps the Beaver mounds, seem somewhat united in styles of material goods including ceramics, residential architecture, gaming bones (Hall 2008), and projectile points (Woods 2009). We say more about these Parowan Valley occupations below.

The Sevier River and its tributaries contain evidence for perhaps even greater sum population aggregations than the macroregions described above. These make up the central macroregion. From Marysvale (Gillin 1941) and Clear Creek Canyon (Janetski et al. 2000) on the south, and through the long Sevier Valley (various but especially Madsen and Lindsay 1977; Talbot and Richens 1993), numerous village sites are spread out across some of the best-watered farmlands in Utah (see Talbot 2000b).

Discussion

To return to Steward's (1955) conditions for clan development and his conclusion that clans were absent in the Fremont area, we suggest that the scarcity of community-focused excavations at the time influenced his thoughts, although Judd's (1919, 1926) work in Parowan Valley and elsewhere had been published for some time. Steward's own work, including his excavations in a single mound rather than exposing more broadly at Kanosh (see Steward 1936), represents this lack of expansive excavation.

In fact, data that bear directly on this issue were largely lacking until the work at Five Finger Ridge in Clear Creek Canyon (Talbot et al. 2000) and Baker Village discussed earlier (Wilde and Soper 1999). In both cases, the research design called for more than the sampling so common in Fremont excavations; consequently, in both cases excavators discovered public architecture and evidence of site planning. At Five Finger Ridge two structures are unique in the context of the site architecture, one a public central structure and the other a pithouse that was nearly twice as large as any other. Both were located adjacent to a central area that may have served as a plaza or similar gathering space. Planning is more apparent at Baker Village, where all excavated contemporary structures, including a large public building, are aligned, demonstrating planning for some purpose, perhaps relating to seasonal solstices and planting/ceremonial cycles.

Additional evidence of site planning and communal space, built and cleared, is present in the massive sites in Parowan Valley. Neil Judd's (1919) map of his 1917 excavations on the accretional "Big Mound" reveals a linear room block alignment around what Judd called a "central court" (1919:Plate 10 caption; Figure 10.5), a pattern described earlier by Montgomery (1894) and which has now been recognized at several other Fremont village sites (Talbot 2000c; Wilde and Soper 1999). Two or possibly three central structures were directly associated with the room block alignment, although it is unknown if these structures are contemporary. This arrangement clearly suggests site planning, although several occupation levels were noted and the arrangement probably grew in stages. Judd also excavated portions of other accretional mounds at Paragonah (see Judd 1926), and a compilation of excavation maps generated by the University of California, Los Angeles, work in the 1950s and 1960s (Hall 2008; Jardine 2007; Meighan et al. 1956) to the north and west of Judd's excavations hints at extensive residential architecture around an area that appears to be a large mound, although it was not excavated (Figure 10.6). This is similar to the case at the Evans site, a large accretional mound ~10 mi to the southwest of Paragonah that has evidence of linear and contiguous storage rooms surrounded by residential architecture.

The north–south architectural alignment evident at Paragonah and probably at Evans Mound resembles the Baker Village pattern and may mark a move toward more communal living, as noted by Steward. The highly formalized pithouses with plastered walls and floors present at these three sites and the presence of Snake Valley ceramics at Baker made in Parowan Valley suggest considerable interaction between Baker and Parowan Valley sites (Cole 2012). Although true communal living as seen in Pueblo II Anasazi sites to the south did not develop, it seems logical that the architectural segments visible at these larger sites were composed of lineages that aggregated in the later period. And at locales such as Paragonah and Summit, lineages may have experienced growth leading to clan formation.

Summary

We have proposed a model for Fremont social organization that recognizes a pan-regional style and a general strategy but which allows for and attempts to explain regional differences relying on both ethnographic and archaeological tribal studies. These regional differences occur in material goods—ceramics, architecture, figurines, and others—a pattern expected in tribal societies. We believe that this model offers understanding of the several variant models posed by Fremont scholars from Morss (1931) to Madsen (1979). We have said little about variability in subsistence strategies (e.g., Madsen 1982; Madsen and Simms 1998; Simms 1986), as we agree that climatic shifts and the spatial distribution of resources altered dietary emphases and strate-

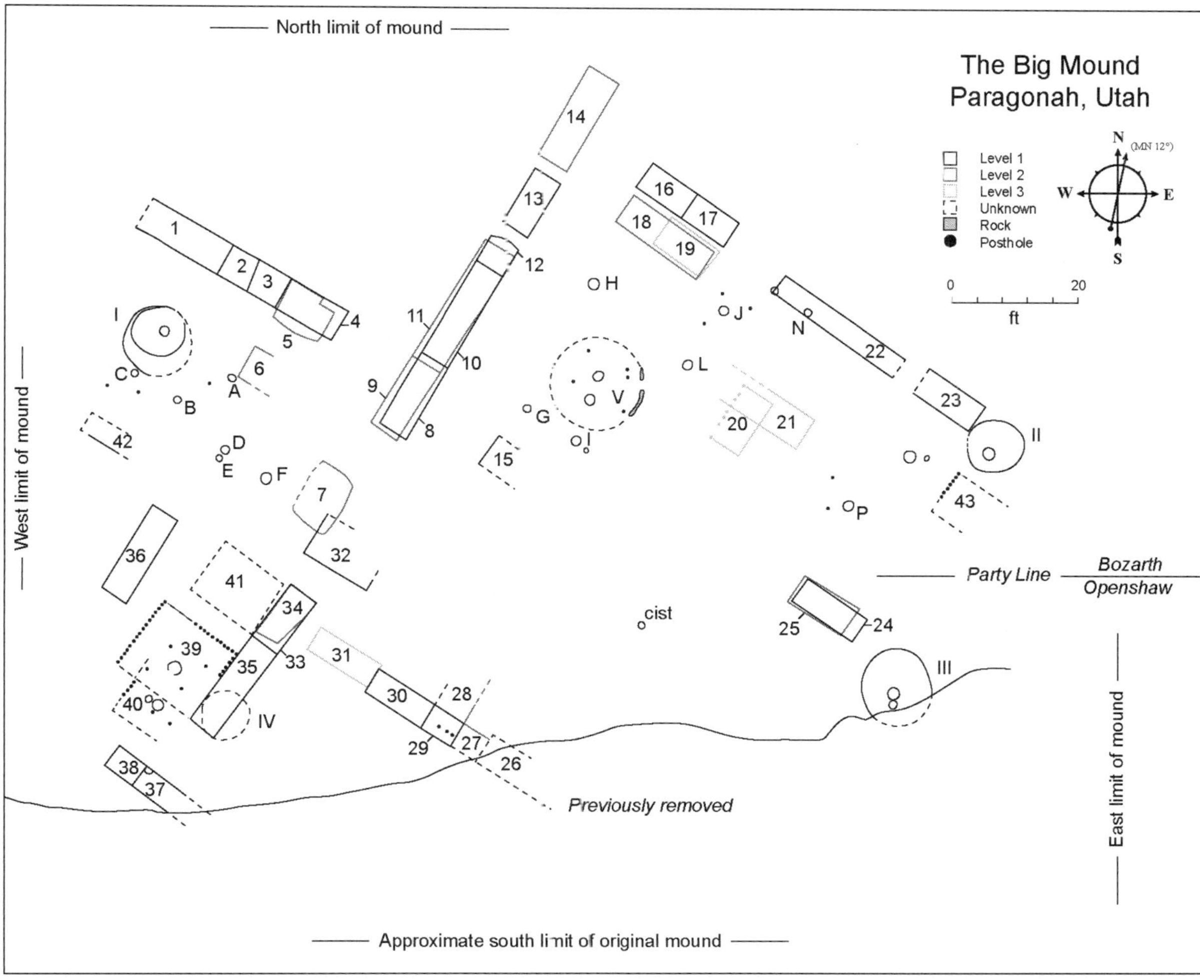

FIGURE 10.5. Plan map of Paragonah excavations (after Judd 1919).

gies. We maintain, however, that social tensions and trials pushed Fremont people to express identities via material goods, a move that more readily accommodates the numerous variant models proposed in the past.

The Fremont case offers considerable potential for understanding the development of social organization in small-scale agricultural societies. To increase understanding of Fremont social structure, however, we need more community-focused research in the Fremont region with explicit interest in social structure. The broad horizontal exposures required to reveal communities are costly and require longitudinal commitments to sites and specific regions if we are to answer such questions. Bruce Trigger said this very well in a talk some years back at Brigham Young University: "The long-term, intensive research on particular cultures, peoples, or regions that most archaeologists enjoy carrying out provides the most valuable data for understanding the forces that have shaped the archaeological record" (2003).

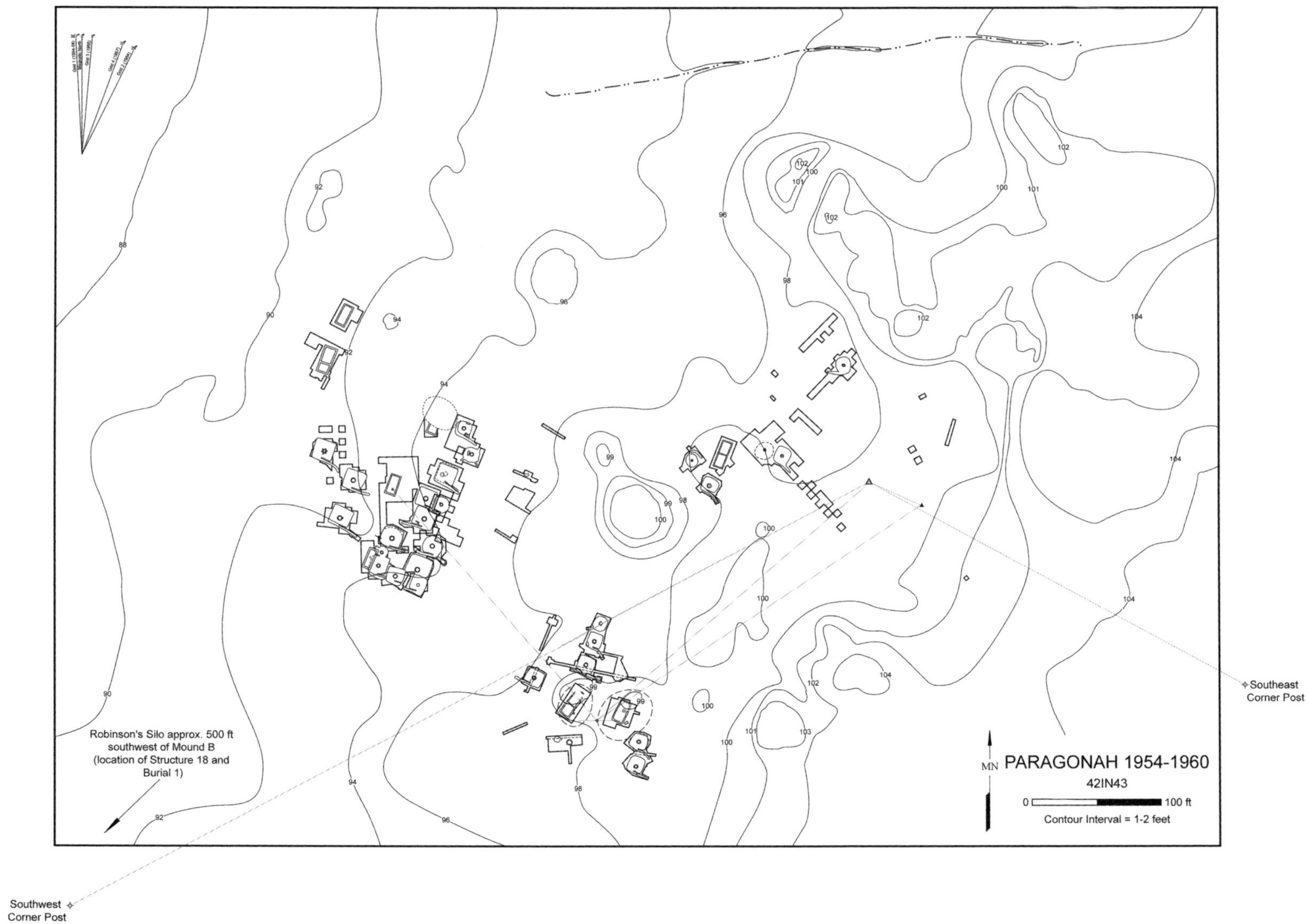

FIGURE 10.6. Plan map of the University of California, Los Angeles, excavations at Paragonah (drafted from University of California, Los Angeles, excavation notes).

Acknowledgments

We thank Scott Ure for the excellent graphics used herein. Thanks are also due to Steve Lekson and Phil Geib as well as the volume reviewers for their comments on an earlier draft of this chapter.

References Cited

Adler, Michael
2002 Building Consensus: Tribes, Architecture, and Typology in the American Southwest. In *The Archaeology of Tribal Societies*, edited by William A. Parkinson, pp. 155–172. Archaeological Series, 15. International Monographs in Prehistory, Ann Arbor.

Aikens, C. Melvin
1967 *Excavations at Snakerock Village and the Bear River No. 2 Site.* Anthropological Papers No. 87. University of Utah Press, Salt Lake City.

Ambler, Richard
1966 Caldwell Village and Fremont Prehistory. Unpublished Ph.D. dissertation, Department of Anthropology, University of Colorado, Boulder.

Baker, Shane A., and Scott E. Billat
1999 *Rock Art of Clear Creek Canyon in Central Utah.* Museum of Peoples and Cultures Occasional Paper No. 6. Brigham Young University, Provo.

Barlow, K. Renee
2002 Predicting Maize Agriculture Among the Fremont: An Economic Comparison of Farming and Foraging in the American Southwest. *American Antiquity* 67(1):65–88.

Berry, Michael S.
1972 *The Evans Site.* Special report, Department of Anthropology, University of Utah, Salt Lake City.
1974 The Evans Mound: Cultural Adaptation in Southwestern Utah. Unpublished Master's thesis, Department of Anthropology, University of Utah, Salt Lake City.

Berry, Michael S., and Claudia F. Berry
2003 An Archaeological Analysis of the Prehistoric Fremont Culture for the Purpose of Assessing Cultural Affiliation with Ten Claimant Tribes. Submitted to the U.S. Department of the Interior Bureau of Reclamation. Manuscript on file, Bureau of Reclamation, Upper Colorado Regional Office, Salt Lake City.

Carneiro, Robert L.
2002 The Tribal Village and Its Culture: An Evolutionary Stage in the History of Human Society. In *The Archaeology of Tribal Societies*, edited by William A. Parkinson, pp. 34–52. Archaeological Series, 15. International Monographs in Prehistory, Ann Arbor.

Castleton, Kenneth B., and David B. Madsen
1981 The Distribution of Rock Art Elements and Styles in Utah. *Journal of California and Great Basin Anthropology* 3(2): 163–175.

Cole, Clint R.
2010 The Fremont Frontier in North Meadow Valley Wash, Eastern Nevada. Paper presented at the 32nd Biannual Great Basin Anthropological Conference, Layton.
2012 Prehistoric Archaeology and the Fremont Frontier at North Meadow Valley Wash, Eastern Nevada. Unpublished Ph.D. dissertation, Department of Anthropology, University of California, Davis.

Cordell, Linda
1997 *Archaeology of the Southwest.* 2nd ed. Academic Press, Inc., San Diego.

Doyel, David E., and Jeffrey S. Dean (editors)
2006 *Environmental Change and Human Adaptation in the Ancient American Southwest.* University of Utah Press, Salt Lake City.

Fried, Morton
1966 On the Concept of "Tribe" and Tribal Society. *Transactions of the New York Academy of Sciences* (Series II) 26:527–540.

Gillin, John
1941 *Archaeological Excavations in Central Utah.* Papers of the Peabody Museum of Archaeology and Ethnology, 17(2). Cambridge, Massachusetts.

Gilsen, Leland
1968 An Archaeological Survey of Goshen Valley, Utah County, Central Utah. Unpublished Master's thesis, Department of Anthropology, Brigham Young University, Provo.

Gould, Richard A.
1980 *Living Archaeology.* Cambridge University Press, Cambridge.

Gunnerson, James H.
1969 *The Fremont Culture: A Study in Culture Dynamics on the Northern Anasazi Frontier.* Papers of the Peabody Museum of Archaeology and Ethnology, 59(2). Cambridge, Massachusetts.

Hall, Molly J.
2008 Parowan Valley Gaming Pieces and Insights into Fremont Social Organization. Unpublished Master's thesis, Department of Anthropology, Brigham Young University, Provo.

Herr, Sarah A., and Jeffery J. Clark
2002 Mobility and the Organization of Prehispanic Southwest Communities. In *The Archaeology of Tribal Societies*, edited by William A. Parkinson, pp. 123–154. Archaeological Series, 15. International Monographs in Prehistory, Ann Arbor.

Hockett, Bryan S.
1998 Sociopolitical Meaning of Faunal Remains from Baker Village. *American Antiquity* 63:289–302.

Hodder, Ian
1982 *Symbols in Action: Ethnoarchaeological Studies of Material Culture.* Cambridge University Press, Cambridge.

Janetski, Joel C.
1990 Utah Lake: Its Role in the Prehistory of Utah Valley. *Utah Historical Quarterly* 58(1):5–31.
2002 Trade in Fremont Society: Contexts and Contrasts. *Journal of Anthropological Archaeology* 21(3):344–370.
2004 *Archaeological Survey and Limited Excavations in Utah Valley.* Museum of Peoples and Cultures Technical Series, 04-19. Brigham Young University, Provo.

Janetski, Joel C., Cady B. Jardine, and Christopher N. Watkins
2011 Interaction and Exchange in Fremont Society. In *Perspectives on Prehistoric Trade and Exchange in California and the Great Basin*, edited by Richard E. Hughes, pp. 22–54. University of Utah Press, Salt Lake City.

Janetski, Joel C., and Richard K. Talbot
2000 Social and Community Organization. In *Clear Creek Canyon Archaeological Project: Results and Synthesis*, by J. C. Janetski, R. K. Talbot, L. D. Richens, D. E. Newman, and J. D. Wilde, pp. 247–262. Occasional Papers No. 7. Museum of Peoples and Cultures, Brigham Young University, Provo.

Janetski, Joel C., Richard K. Talbot, Lane D. Richens, Deborah E. Newman, and James D. Wilde
2000 *Clear Creek Canyon Archaeological Project: Results and Synthesis.* Museum of Peoples and Cultures Occasional Papers No. 7. Brigham Young University, Provo.

Jardine, Cady B.
2007 Fremont Finery: Exchange and Distribution of Turquoise

and *Olivella* Ornaments in the Parowan Valley and Beyond. Unpublished Master's thesis, Department of Anthropology, Brigham Young University, Provo.

Jennings, Jesse D.
1978 *Prehistory of Utah and the Eastern Great Basin*. Anthropological Papers No. 98. University of Utah Press, Salt Lake City.

Jennings, Jesse D., and Dorothy Sammons-Lohse
1981 *Bull Creek*. University of Utah Anthropological Papers No. 105. Salt Lake City.

Judd, Neil M.
1919 *Archaeological Investigations at Paragonah, Utah*. Smithsonian Miscellaneous Collections Vol. 70, No. 3. Washington, D.C.
1926 *Archeological Observations North of the Rio Colorado*. Bulletin No. 82. Bureau of American Ethnology, Smithsonian Institution, Washington, D.C.

Kamp, Kathryn A., and John C. Whittaker
1999 *Surviving Adversity: The Sinagua of Lizard Man Village*. Anthropological Papers No. 120. University of Utah Press, Salt Lake City.

Lightfoot, Kent G., and Gary M. Feinman
1982 Social Differentiation and Leadership Development in Early Pithouse Villages in the Mogollon Region of the American Southwest. *American Antiquity* 47:64–86.

Lindsay, La Mar W.
1986 Fremont Fragmentation. In *Anthropology of the Desert West: Essays in Honor of Jesse D. Jennings*, edited by Carol J. Condie and Don D. Fowler, pp. 229–251. Anthropological Papers No. 110. University of Utah Press, Salt Lake City.

Lipe, William D., and Michelle Hegmon (editors)
1989 *The Architecture of Social Integration in Prehistoric Pueblos*. Occasional Paper No. 1. Crow Canyon Archaeological Center, Cortez, Colorado.

Lohse, Ernest L.
1980 Fremont Settlement Pattern and Architectural Variation. In *Fremont Perspectives*, edited by David B. Madsen, pp. 41–54. Antiquities Section Selected Papers No. 16. Utah State Historical Society, Salt Lake City.

Longacre, William A. (editor)
1970 *Reconstructing Prehistoric Pueblo Societies*. School of American Research and University of New Mexico Press, Santa Fe.

Lyneis, Margaret M.
1996 Pueblo II–Pueblo III Change in Southwestern Utah, the Arizona Strip, and Southern Nevada. In *The Prehistoric Pueblo World AD 150–1350*, edited by Michael A. Adler, pp. 11–18. University of Arizona Press, Tucson.

Madsen, David B.
1979 The Fremont and the Sevier: Defining Prehistoric Agriculturalists North of the Anasazi. *American Antiquity* 44(4):711–722.
1982 Get It Where the Gettin's Good: A Variable Model of Great Basin Subsistence and Settlement Based on Data from the Eastern Great Basin. In *Man and Environment in the Great Basin*, edited by David B. Madsen and James F. O'Connell, pp. 207–226. SAA Papers No. 2. Society for American Archaeology, Washington, D.C.

Madsen, David B., and LaMar W. Lindsay
1977 *Backhoe Village*. Antiquities Section Selected Papers, 4(12). Utah Division of State History, Salt Lake City.

Madsen, David B., and Steven R. Simms
1998 The Fremont Complex: A Behavioral Perspective. *Journal of World Prehistory* 12:255–336.

Madsen, Rex E.
1977 *Prehistoric Ceramics of the Fremont*. Ceramic Series No. 6. Museum of Northern Arizona, Flagstaff.

Marwitt, John
1970 *Median Village and Fremont Culture Regional Variation*. Anthropological Papers No. 95. University of Utah, Salt Lake City.
1986 Fremont Cultures. In *Great Basin*, edited by Warren L. d'Azevedo, pp. 161–172. Handbook of North American Indians, Vol. 11, William Sturtevant, general editor, Smithsonian Institution, Washington, D.C.

Meighan, Clement W., Norman E. Coles, Frank D. Davis, Geraldine M. Greenwood, William M. Harrison, and E. Heath MacBain
1956 *Archaeological Excavations in Iron County, Utah*. Anthropological Papers No. 25. University of Utah Press, Salt Lake City.

Mills, Barbara J. (editor)
2000 *Alternative Leadership Strategies in the Prehispanic Southwest*. University of Arizona Press, Tucson.

Montgomery, Henry
1894 Prehistoric Man in Utah. *Archaeologist* 2(8):227–342.

Morss, Noel
1931 *The Ancient Culture of the Fremont River in Utah*. Papers of the Peabody Museum of American Archaeology and Ethnology Vol. 12, No. 2. Harvard University, Cambridge.

Neitzel, Jill E.
2000 What Is a Regional System? Issues of Scale and Interaction in the Prehistoric Southwest. In *The Archaeology of Regional Interaction: Religion, Warfare, and Exchange Across the American Southwest and Beyond*, edited by Michelle Hegmon, pp. 25–40. University Press of Colorado, Boulder.

Neitzel, Jill E. (editor)
1999 *Great Towns and Regional Polities in the Prehistoric American Southwest and Southeast*. University of New Mexico Press, Albuquerque.

Ortiz, Alfonso (editor)
1983 *Southwest*. Handbook of North American Indians, Vol. 10, William C. Sturtevant, general editor, Smithsonian Institution, Washington, D.C.

O'Shea, John M., and Claire M. Milner
2002 Material Indicators of Territory, Identity, and Interaction in a Prehistoric Tribal System. In *The Archaeology of Tribal Societies*, edited by William A. Parkinson, pp. 200–226. Archaeological Series, 15. International Monographs in Prehistory, Ann Arbor.

Parkinson, William A. (editor)
2002 *The Archaeology of Tribal Societies*. International Monographs in Prehistory, Archaeological Series, 15. Ann Arbor.

Sackett, James
1982 Approaches to Style in Lithic Archaeology. *Journal of Anthropological Archaeology* 1:59–112.
1985 Style and Ethnicity in the Kalahari: A Reply to Wiessner. *American Antiquity* 50:154–159.

Sahlins, Marshall D.
1968 *Tribesmen*. Prentice-Hall, Englewood Cliffs, New Jersey.

Sammons-Lohse, Dorothy
1981 Households and Communities. In *Bull Creek*, by Jesse D. Jennings and Dorothy Sammons-Lohse, pp. 111–135. University of Utah Anthropological Papers No. 105. Salt Lake City.

Service, Elman R.
1962 *Primitive Social Organization: An Evolutionary Perspective*. 1st ed. Random House, New York.

Simms, Steven R.

1986 New Evidence for Fremont Adaptive Diversity. *Journal of California and Great Basin Anthropology* 8(2):204–216.

1999 Farmers, Foragers, and Adaptive Diversity: The Great Salt Lake Wetlands Project. In *Prehistoric Lifeways in the Great Basin Wetlands: Bioarchaeological Reconstruction and Interpretation*, edited by Brian E. Hemphill and Clark S. Larsen, pp. 21–54. University of Utah Press, Salt Lake City.

Simms, Steven R., and Grancois Gohier

2010 *Traces of Fremont: Society and Rock Art in Ancient Utah*. University of Utah Press, Salt Lake City.

Steward, Julian H.

1933 Archaeological Problems of the Northern Periphery of the Southwest. *El Palacio* 30(8):121–130.

1936 *Pueblo Material Culture in Western Utah*. University of New Mexico Bulletin No. 287. Albuquerque.

1941 *Archaeological Reconnaissance of Southern Utah*. Anthropological Papers No. 18; Bureau of American Ethnology Bulletin No. 128. Smithsonian Institution, Washington, D.C.

1955 Lineage to Clan: Ecological Aspects of Southwestern Society. In *Theory of Culture Change: The Methodology of Multilineal Evolution*, pp. 151–172. University of Illinois Press, Urbana.

Stokes, William L.

1986 *Geology of Utah*. Occasional Paper No. 6. Utah Museum of Natural History, Salt Lake City.

Talbot, Richard K.

2000a Fremont Architecture. In *Clear Creek Canyon Archaeological Project: Results and Synthesis*, by Joel C. Janetski, Richard K. Talbot, Lane D. Richens, Deborah E. Newman, and James D. Wilde, pp. 131–184. Occasional Papers No. 7. Museum of Peoples and Cultures, Brigham Young University, Provo.

2000b Fremont Settlement Patterns and Demography. In *Clear Creek Canyon Archaeological Project: Results and Synthesis*, by Joel C. Janetski, Richard K. Talbot, Lane D. Richens, Deborah E. Newman, and James D. Wilde, pp. 201–230. Occasional Papers No. 7. Museum of Peoples and Cultures, Brigham Young University, Provo.

2000c Fremont Farmers: The Search for Context. In *The Archaeology of Regional Interaction: Religion, Warfare, and Exchange Across the American Southwest and Beyond*, edited by Michelle Hegmon, pp. 275–293. University Press of Colorado, Boulder.

Talbot, Richard K., Shane A. Baker, and Lane D. Richens

2004 *The Right Place—Fremont and Early Pioneer Archaeology in Salt Lake City*. Technical Series No. 03-07. Museum of Peoples and Cultures, Brigham Young University, Provo.

Talbot, Richard K., and Lane D. Richens

1993 *Archaeological Excavations in Richfield and Vicinity*. Technical Series, 93-15. Museum of Peoples and Cultures, Brigham Young University, Provo.

Talbot, Richard K., Lane D. Richens, James D. Wilde, Joel C. Janetski, and Deborah E. Newman

2000 *Excavations at Five Finger Ridge, Clear Creek Canyon, Central Utah*. Occasional Papers No. 5. Museum of Peoples and Cultures, Brigham Young University, Provo.

Trigger, Bruce

2003 Archaeological Theory: The Big Picture. Shallit Lecture presented at Brigham Young University, Provo.

Watkins, Christopher

2006 Parowan Pottery and Fremont Complexity: Late Formative Ceramic Production and Exchange. Unpublished Master's thesis, Department of Anthropology, Brigham Young University, Provo.

Wenke, Robert J.

1990 *Patterns in Prehistory: Mankind's First Three Million Years*. 3rd ed. Oxford University Press, New York.

Wiessner, Polly

1983 Style and Social Information in Kalahari San Projectile Points. *American Antiquity* 48:253–276.

1985 Style or Isochristic Variation? A Reply to Sackett. *American Antiquity* 50:160–166.

Wilde, James D., and Reed Soper

1999 *Baker Village Excavations*. Technical Series. Museum of Peoples and Cultures, Brigham Young University, Provo.

Wills, W. H.

2000 Political Leadership and the Construction of Chacoan Great Houses, AD 1020–1140. In *Alternative Leadership Strategies in the Prehispanic Southwest*, edited by Barbara J. Mills, pp. 19–44. University of Arizona Press, Tucson.

Wobst, Martin

1977 Stylistic Behavior and Information Exchange. In *For the Director: Research Essays in Honor of James B. Griffin*, edited by C. Cleland, pp. 317–342. Anthropological Papers, University of Michigan Museum of Anthropology, Ann Arbor.

Woods, Aaron

2009 Distribution, Function, and Value of Parowan Valley Projectile Points. Unpublished Master's thesis, Department of Anthropology, Brigham Young University, Provo.

Wormington, H. Marie

1955 *A Reappraisal of the Fremont Culture*. Proceedings No. 1. Denver Museum of Natural History, Denver.

11

Alta Toquima

Why Did Foraging Families Spend Summers at 11,000 Feet?

David Hurst Thomas

Why would Great Basin foraging families elect to spend their summers atop the very highest place in their world? This question first arose in the 1920s, when Julian Steward was told of ancient house foundations between 10,000 and 13,000 ft in California's White Mountains. None of the Paiute and Shoshone elders apparently mentioned these alpine houses in their interviews, and Steward puzzled over "why houses were so often built above the piñon zone" (1938:58; see Steward 1941:233 n. 43, 335 n. 653). An experienced backpacker, Steward was well aware that extreme cold and deep snow eliminated the possibility of overwintering at that elevation. While he thought it likely that these house foundations resulted from family residential occupations in the summertime, he also left the door open for all-male bighorn hunting parties. To my knowledge, Steward never mentioned the alpine houses again after the early 1940s. As it turns out, then, Steward knew about Great Basin alpine villages all along—he just did not know what to do with them.

These same questions popped up again with the modern discovery of Alta Toquima in 1978 (Thomas 1982, 1994; Figure 11.1). A few years later, Bettinger (1991, 1999a, 1999b, 2008) found several surprisingly similar residential villages in California's White Mountains, some at nearly 13,000 ft (Grayson 1991).[1] As part of a large-scale survey for alpine residences, Canaday (1997) found three solitary alpine structures between 10,920 and 11,200 ft in the Toiyabe Range (Nevada), overlooking the Reese River valley. In Utah's Fish Lake Valley, Janetski (2010) has excavated three high-elevation, apparently residential components at roughly 8,900 ft. Ongoing research at High Rise Village in Wyoming's Wind River Range further begs the question of why *families* chose to live at such extreme elevations in North America (Adams 2010; Koenig 2010; Morgan et al. 2012; see also Wingerson 2010). Here, I will address only part of the larger issues raised by these alpine residential sites, focusing on a single, deceptively simple question: *Why did foraging families elect to live at 11,000 ft in Monitor Valley, Nevada?*

History of Monitor Valley Archaeology

I started doing archaeology in Monitor Valley in 1970 as a direct outgrowth of my doctoral research in the nearby Reese River valley.[2] The Reese River research design was a systematic, probabilistic regional sample, involving strictly surface material culture (Thomas 1971, 1973; Thomas and Bettinger 1976). Given the total lack of paleobiological evidence in surface archaeology, such regional sampling programs depend heavily upon a couple of key assumptions—especially regarding cultural chronology and environmental change. Understanding that our surface-based research designs cried out for solid stratigraphic backup, we were drawn to nearby Monitor Valley, where we would spend a dozen years excavating several caves and rockshelters, conducting a variety of systematic regional surveys, and exploring the Mt. Jefferson tablelands (Nevada's third-highest spot). This research generated parallel 7,000-year-old archaeological and paleoenvironmental sequences, today grounded in more than 200 cultural radiocarbon dates (Thomas 1982, 1983a, 1983b, 1988, 2013a).

For six field seasons we excavated at Gatecliff Shelter, exposing a 40-ft profile of extraordinarily well-stratified deposits (divided into 56 distinct geological strata and 16 cultural horizons [Thomas 1983b]). Most of this stratigraphic column was deposited by sediment-laden, turbulent water, filtered from debris flowing downslope. The chronology is today supported by more than 75 radiocarbon dates. The basal layer contains a lens of 6,900-year-old volcanic ash blown in from the exploding Mt. Mazama more than 400 mi to the northwest. More than 51,000 identifiable animal bones were recovered from these deposits; over 90 percent (by weight) are bighorn sheep. Beginning about 4300 cal BC, Gatecliff was apparently an exclusive, all-male logistic hunting camp, a staging area for hunting bighorn sheep in the surrounding mountains. The pattern shifted about 2,000 years ago at Gatecliff, with hunters camping there only sporadically and female foragers often using the place while procuring

FIGURE 11.1. Alta Toquima (center), located on top of Mt. Jefferson, the third-highest spot in Nevada. The 31 aboriginal pithouses are carved into the rocky summit at the head of Barker Creek, the springy place near the snow patches. Another alpine village site, Alta Toquima East, appears in the foreground. In the middle distance is Big Smoky Valley, with the crest of the Toiyabe Range on the skyline. The Reese River valley lies just beyond, and on a clear day, you can see the White Mountains and sometimes even the snowcapped Sierra Nevada, more than 150 mi away.

pine nuts and basketry supplies nearby and probably also when preparing bighorn hides.

The initial systematic surveys in Reese River valley established, for the first time, that the piñon ecotone settlements remembered by Shoshone elders and mapped by Julian Steward (1938) extended well back before European contact. The abundant time-marker artifacts, milling stones, and house foundations showed that some sites dated back to the beginning of the late Holocene. Without detailed excavations, these temporal estimates remain seriously coarse-grained, but we think that the first campsites were constructed shortly after single-leaf piñon arrived into the Reese River valley, perhaps as early as 6,000 years ago.

Subsequent archaeological surveys and excavations revealed similar patterns in Monitor Valley, about 15–20 mi to the east of Reese River. But there are major differences because Monitor Valley always had lower effective moisture levels and a less productive piñon-juniper forest than Reese River valley. Comparable piñon ecotone surveys demonstrated a considerably less intensive archaeological occupation of Monitor Valley, with markedly fewer sites, fewer time-markers, and fewer houses (Thomas 1983b:514, 1988). Taken together, these diverse and independent measures defined the relatively more verdant, more populous Reese River valley as a heartland, with neighboring valleys—east and west—functioning mostly as hinterlands, consistent with Steward's (1938) previous population estimates.

As part of the Monitor Valley regional survey, we recorded and subsequently excavated Alta Toquima (26Ny920), the most significant of several alpine settlements overlooking Monitor Valley (Figure 11.1).[3] Located 15 mi southwest of Gatecliff Shelter, Alta Toquima is perched atop Mt. Jefferson at almost exactly 11,000 ft. This unusual alpine residential site was built on the highest peak in the Toquima Range, a huge table-like plateau that varies in elevation from about 10,000 ft to 11,949 ft (Thomas 1982, 2012, 2013a, 2013b). More than 600 time-diagnostic projectile points were recovered by surface collection and stratigraphic excavation, which also produced a large sample of ceramics and milling stones. The chronology of Alta Toquima is today anchored in a suite of 70 radiocarbon dates.[4]

We excavated 18 of the Alta Toquima houses, and the radiocarbon dates indicate that summertime residential usage was well under way during the late Reveille phase (about 750 cal BC through cal AD 570), when Houses I-F, II-D, and II-E were constructed and numerous milling implements were deposited within the Terrace Midden strata F and G (see Figure 11.2). The occupation of Alta Toquima apparently ceased briefly during the ninth and tenth centuries AD and then picked up again shortly after AD 1000, when several houses were occupied and reoccupied into the late precontact and protohistoric periods.

Alta Toquima was built on an isolated spur adjacent to the expansive Mt. Jefferson tableland, where, over the millennia,

FIGURE 11.2. Archaeologists digging House II-I at Alta Toquima. The perspective is looking north across the Mt. Jefferson tablelands. Two other residential sites can be seen: North Flats (Ny2731) in the middle background and the 11,215 Peak site (Ny2729) in the extreme center background.

scores of bighorn hunters set up blinds, rock cairns, and walls. Systematic archaeological surveys recovered an additional 450 time-sensitive projectile points, demonstrating that alpine hunting began toward the end of the middle Holocene, when sheep hunters started working the very highest reaches of the Toiyabe, Toquima, and Monitor mountains.

Explaining Alta Toquima

While digging Alta Toquima and Gatecliff Shelter, we simultaneously struggled to find a workable epistemological framework for understanding Monitor Valley archaeology. At the time, we were heavily invested in Lewis Binford's (1980) forager-collector model: while it was clear that Binford's approach helped capture broadscale patterns of adaptive diversity, the forager–collector continuum completely failed to explain the surprisingly variable adaptations within the bounds of the Great Basin. At the time, I lamented that "we currently lack the theoretical models to explain that variability" (Thomas 1983a:39) and (optimistically) suggested that such a general theory would likely evolve through the interplay of innovative archaeological fieldwork and continued research in midrange theory building (Binford 1980).

Simultaneously, a cadre of scholars was developing a broad-based *optimal foraging* approach, applying the principles of natural selection within the general paradigm of human behavioral ecology (O'Connell et al. 1982; see also Simms et al., this volume). Optimal foraging advocates attempted to identify models general enough to apply to a broad range of animal species, yet sufficiently rigorous to explain the behavior exhibited by an individual forager.

Although admitting some potential for bridging the gap between archaeological data and general theory, I was quite skeptical of how early applications of optimal foraging theory (mis) treated the archaeological data (Thomas 1986). In fact, I might have been one of their most vocal critics, arguing that better general theoretical grounding would evolve through an intensive focus on building midrange archaeological theory (to attribute meaning to our empirical observations [Thomas 1983a:18, 1986]). As it turns out, I was wrong.

Particularly over the past two decades, research into human behavior ecology has achieved a remarkable symbiosis that effectively articulates general evolutionary theory with high-quality archaeological data (see the discussion in Simms et al., this volume). Today, I believe strongly that human behavioral ecology does indeed provide a workable general theoretical framework for the practice of contemporary archaeology. In the Monitor Valley research (and elsewhere), I have wholeheartedly embraced this overarching theoretical umbrella as a means for generating testable hypotheses about human foraging patterns of the past (see also Thomas 2008 for a similar application in a vastly different setting). Here, I will attempt to situate the empirical trends evident at Alta Toquima and the rest of Monitor Valley in larger contexts combining both the models of human behavioral ecology and the realities of the fine-grained archaeological and paleoenvironmental records today available for the central Great Basin.

Traveler and Processor Strategies

To date, alpine residences in the Great Basin have been explained as an outcome of processors outcompeting travelers, effectively triggering the expansion of Numic-speaking people across the Great Basin (Bettinger 1991, 1999a). I think it useful to examine the alpine archaeology of Mt. Jefferson and the rest of Monitor Valley through the lens of the traveler–processor model.

Robert Bettinger and Martin Baumhoff (1982:485, 1983) drew upon optimal foraging models to generate expectations about how prey and patch choice decisions should play out in long-term settlement and mobility patterning. They wrote of "travelers" pursuing a relatively narrow diet breath with a high average foraging return from individual investments, restricting their diet to rare resources with high caloric returns and low encounter rates. Travelers pay high search costs but enjoy low handling costs, encouraging a mobile strategy that favors foragers who search for high-ranked resources and move frequently to the most productive resource patches.

Bettinger and Baumhoff also wrote of "processors," who, by contrast, tolerate lower average foraging returns to pursue a wider diet breadth and exploit many resources with higher encounter rates and handling costs. Processors spend less time searching for things (cutting down their travel expenses) but expend more effort handling and processing what they find. This means that they occupy fewer resource patches for longer times.

Over the past two decades, the Bettinger and Baumhoff (1982, 1983) model has been both criticized and expanded. Simms et al. (this volume) critique the traveler–processor model for reliance on essentialist/normative categories, either/or adaptive strategies that direct attention away from investigating the circumstances that would select for trends in the mix of behaviors over time (for additional critical consideration of the traveler–processor model, see also Grayson 1991; Madsen 1993; Simms 1983).

Proponents have enlarged the conversation beyond microeconomics to emphasize the transition from traveler to processor strategies in the Great Basin—framing a shift from band-like organizations living in large centralized villages to small, household-size groups that exploit resources more efficiently because they shift residences among numerous short-term generalized encampments (Basgall and Delacorte 2011; Delacorte 1997:16–17; Hildebrandt and McGuire 2002; McGuire 2002a; McGuire and Hildebrandt 2005; Zeanah 2000; Zeanah and Leigh 2002:37). Historic-period Owens Valley Paiute families, one such processor society, spent much of the year in multihousehold villages but at other times established satellite camps (such as piñon and alpine settlements) where a few related families worked and lived independently (Basgall et al. 2003:360; Bettinger 1989, 1991; Steward 1933, 1938).

Although costly, the processor strategy was seen as providing certain competitive advantages. The argument goes that small household-size groups placed the returns of increasingly intense foraging efforts under the control of one (or a few) senior family members, providing both economic and adaptive incentive to individuals who could allocate these recourses as they saw fit. This rarely happens in bands, where there is little incentive for individuals to produce more than is required to meet immediate needs. Expressed as Darwinian fitness, the advantages of independent foraging households and the privatization of food are straightforward. By allocating at will, families enjoyed an economic and adaptive incentive to produce more food (and presumably more offspring). Competition between households contributed to a more intensive, albeit costly food-procurement strategy (resource intensification) and growing population—as individuals vied for resources (Zeanah and Leigh 2002:41).

The rest of this chapter examines the archaeological evidence from Alta Toquima (and elsewhere in the central Great Basin) in light of the traveler–processor models. I am specifically interested in clarifying the role of paleoclimatic change in the rise and demise of logistic hunting and the origins of alpine residential lifeways.

Sexual Division of Labor

Julian Steward (1938, 1955) recognized the sexual division of labor as a fundamental organizing principle among foraging people. Pioneering applications of optimal foraging models in the Great Basin treated men's and women's foraging strategies collectively, under the implicit assumption that both sexes worked for the "common good." Echoing in some ways Steward's earliest Basin research, these models assumed that men's subsistence choices either implicitly or explicitly drove the prehistoric subsistence-settlement strategies (e.g., Bettinger 1999a; Bettinger and Baumhoff 1982, 1983; Kelly 1995; O'Connell et al. 1982; see also Zeanah 2004:26).

More recent applications question the degree to which subsistence is a shared strategy and emphasize the different goals pursued by male and female foragers in the Great Basin. Investigators have recently explored how men and women might have reconciled these conflicting foraging objectives, given the probable abundance of resources, post-encounter return rates, and transport costs (Raven and Elston 1989; Zeanah 2004:5; Zeanah and Simms 1999; see also Hildebrand and McGuire 2002; McGuire and Hildebrandt 2005).

Male Hunting Behaviors

Human behavioral ecology emphasizes that throughout their lifetime, males enjoy many more mating opportunities than females, each bearing lower costs and fewer risks. For a settlement pattern to be driven by the needs of hunting, the benefits must be sufficiently productive and reliable to overcome women's provisioning concerns; should this happen, then families would

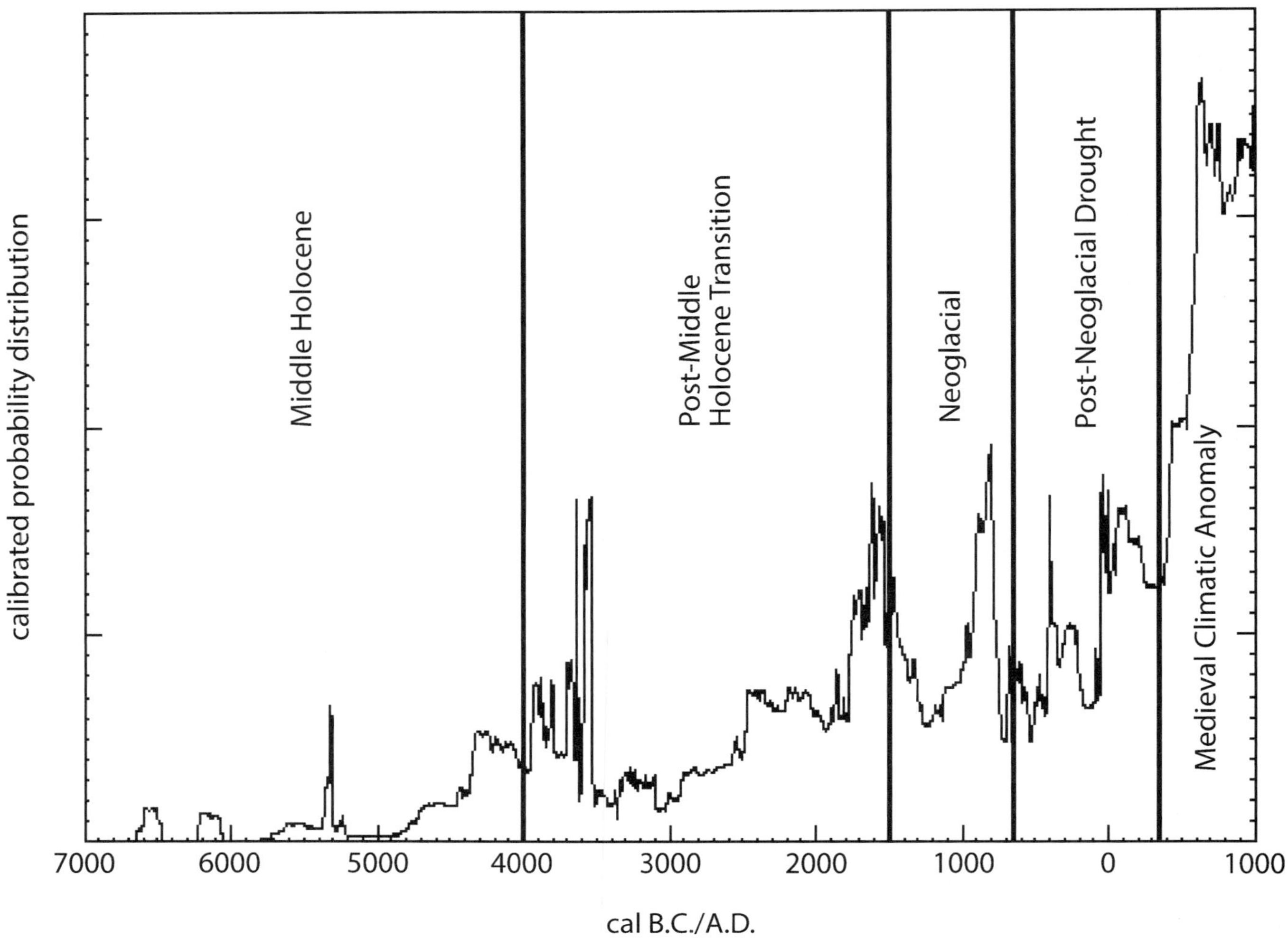

FIGURE 11.3. Calibrated probability distribution of 517 cultural ^{14}C dates from the central Great Basin (based on data presented in Thomas 2013a).

live near the best hunting patches, and male hunting return rates should be sufficiently high to reliably provision the children. But if men cannot do that on a consistent basis, then they should hunt logistically, working from residential base camps positioned according to women's foraging decisions.

So what determined the rates of Great Basin hunting successes over time? Elsewhere, I have discussed the controversial hypothesis by Broughton et al. (2008) linking the seasonality of temperature and precipitation with artiodactyl population densities across western North America (see also Broughton et al. 2011:411–413; Byers and Broughton 2004; Hockett 2005). This argument holds that the highest-quality forage is typically most abundant in wetter conditions early in the springtime and during the early-summer growing season, in turn influencing artiodactyl survival, birth weight, resistance to disease, and, ultimately, herd size. Bighorn living in arid settings require free drinking water in close proximity to the summer range. Spring and summer droughts have demonstrable negative impacts on a wide variety of artiodactyls across western North America. They conclude, then, that some climatic conditions will be more favorable than others for enhanced artiodactyl densities.

A broad range of paleoclimatic data document that seasonal extremes in temperature peaked during the terminal Pleistocene and early Holocene intervals, followed by a winter-wet, summer-dry pattern that prevailed during the early and middle Holocene—and these conditions depressed artiodactyl densities. Thus, they argue that a shift to summer-wet conditions strongly favored artiodactyl populations. Broughton et al. (2008) conclude that whereas overall effective precipitation is not correlated with artiodactyl indexes, the strong influence of seasonality has a demonstrable positive relationship to artiodactyl abundances in the middle and late Holocene.

Models derived from human behavioral ecology suggest that such high-return prey types would have attracted foragers to the greater hunting efficiency. Although both male and female foragers benefited from the onset of summer-wet conditions at the end of the middle Holocene, Zeanah (2004:10) argues that intensified logistic hunting of artiodactyls—especially bighorn—should take place during such favorable climatic intervals (see also Kelly 2001).

Whereas the Broughton et al. (2008) hypothesis provides a potentially fruitful approach for unpacking changes in Great

Basin hunting practices, the underlying model and the empirical proxies have been criticized on a number of levels (Grayson 2011:235–238; see also Thomas 2013b). By employing multiscalar approaches to archaeological chronology, I will explore the Broughton et al. (2008) hypothesis relative to the most recent evidence charting the spatial distribution of time-diagnostic projectile points with a data set of 498 cultural radiocarbon dates from the central Great Basin (Figure 11.3). In this way, it is possible to explore whether summer-wet conditions fostered increases in artiodactyl densities and an upswing in hunting practices in the terminal middle Holocene and late Holocene periods.

Female Foraging Behaviors

Female foraging needs presumably conditioned the location of the residential bases. Enjoying relatively fewer reproductive opportunities than males, women are likely to benefit most, in a fitness sense, from the economics of caring for their own offspring (Raven and Elston 1989; Zeanah 2004:5; Zeanah and Simms 1999). Because child rearing tends to constrain female mobility, women typically pursue foraging strategies that emphasize parental investment, commonly dealing with smaller resource "packages"—gathering seeds and nuts, digging roots, and taking smaller animals closer to home—and prey items that can generally be collected by any individual and are commonly distributed to children and other family members. This is why, I think, during the earliest human use of Monitor Valley (and throughout much of the contemporary central Great Basin), the critical factor conditioning the location of central place residence must have been the female imperative to feed her children, with logistic male hunters ranging far afield.

Excavations at Alta Toquima, Gatecliff Shelter, and many other central Great Basin sites demonstrate that this pattern changed dramatically when logistic hunters ceased hunting the alpine landscape and family households moved up there instead. Why should crying babies and aging elders now be living in places formerly considered to be prime hunting territory for elite hunting bands?

To understand the alpine residences at Alta Toquima, we must privilege the role of female foragers. The sheer number of milling stones recovered here strongly suggests an intensive, onsite processing of plant foods. To me, the most obvious candidate on the alpine tableland is limber pine nuts, today available right next to Alta Toquima houses (and likely never far away over the past couple of millennia). Although some investigators have promoted limber pine as a worthwhile subsistence item (e.g., Frison 1992:333; Grayson 1991:504–505; Steward 1938:28; Thomas 1983a:151), limber pine nuts have also been dismissed as "a marginal resource at best" (Bettinger 2000:189; see also Scharf 2009:21)—considered to be vastly inferior to piñon because limber pine nuts are more difficult to harvest and have fewer nuts per cone, with a thicker hull and smaller nutmeat.

David Rhode (2010) has recently clarified this issue with a simple optimal foraging experiment (see also Rhode and Madsen 1998). After harvesting and processing limber pine nuts in Nevada's Wassuk Range, Rhode learned from nutritional analysis that limber pine nuts are fat- and protein-rich, much more energetic than piñon nuts. While it is true that hulling limber pine nuts is considerably more difficult than shelling the larger, thin-shell piñon nuts, the problem disappears if limber pine nuts are eaten whole or ground into flour. The return rate is a quite respectable 13,437 kcal/hr—comparable to rabbits, better than small game, and an order of magnitude greater than piñon nuts.

This suggests that female foragers could indeed have relied heavily on limber pine nuts as a late-summertime alpine staple—a hypothesis that is currently being tested by conducting starch residue analysis on the ground-stone assemblage recovered at Alta Toquima (and the several additional alpine residential sites now known on Mt. Jefferson).[5]

Paleoclimatic Change and Observed Behavioral Responses

The relationship between climatic and cultural change in the Great Basin has been hotly debated of late, particularly in the context of events that transpired roughly cal AD 350–1350 during the so-called Medieval Climatic Anomaly (MCA). Jones et al. (1999) and Stine (1994) argue that abrupt climate change was so severe and so unprecedented as to precipitate immediate cultural instability, manifested as wholesale settlement shifts, regional abandonments, increased interpersonal violence, and the deterioration of long-distance trade. Speaking of the same period, Benson et al. (2007) concur, offering some "broad-brush explanations" about the widespread correlations connecting persistent multidecadal droughts and demographic disasters among some Native American populations in the American West—including parts of the western Great Basin.

Others feel that the impact of the MCA in the Great Basin has been overrated and lacks support by convincing evidence from the archaeological record (e.g., Basgall 2008; Basgall and Delacorte 2011:13; Basgall et al. 2003:352; Bettinger 1991, 1999a; Zeanah and Leigh 2002). Specifically addressing the traveler–processor transformation, investigators working in the Inyo-Mono area have minimized the role of environmental change. Zeanah and Leigh (2002:42) interpret pack rat and other paleoclimatic evidence as showing little significant change in Owens Valley vegetation over the last 8,000 years. While admitting that "it can hardly be doubted that [MCA] conditions sometimes caused extreme hardships," Bettinger argues that "*humans in the Inyo-Mono region can be thought of as operating under effectively uniform climatic constraints during much of the Holocene, and certainly during the latter half of it*" (1999a:41; emphasis added).

I read the central Great Basin evidence quite differently. To paraphrase my good friend Bob Bettinger, I think that *major climatic change can indeed be demonstrated throughout the Holocene and certainly during the latter half of it—with a major corresponding impact on human behavior*. Here is why I think that.

Late Pleistocene and Early Holocene (pre-7000 cal BC)

The late Pleistocene and early Holocene were characterized by an overall warming trend that shifted subalpine woodland communities to semiarid woodlands dominated by Utah juniper on the lower and middle slopes. The central Great Basin experienced an overall drying trend, interrupted by a two-century wet oscillation centered at 8300 cal BC. The process of aridification resulted in lower lake levels, the retreat of subalpine conifers, and an increase of arid-climate shrubs. The last part of the early Holocene (9550—6940 cal BC) experienced relatively wet conditions.

There is a dearth of evidence for early Holocene occupations in the central Great Basin (Thomas 1982); not a single cultural radiocarbon date has been recorded during this interval. Elsewhere (Thomas 2013a, 2013b) I have plotted the distribution of roughly 22,600 late Pleistocene and early Holocene diagnostics (stemmed and fluted projectile points) across the central and western Great Basin.[6] Not surprisingly, early Holocene diagnostics cluster along a western arc running from southeastern Oregon, across the Black Rock Desert, through the Tonopah floristic zone, into the northern Mojave. A second arc of early Holocene diagnostics begins in the Calcareous Mountains (including Railroad Valley, the Sunshine Locality, and Butte Valley) and joins the northeastern Bonneville Basin. Diagnostic Paleoindian/Paleoarchaic projectile points are found here and there in the central Great Basin, but in vastly diminished numbers compared with surrounding areas. There is an almost complete absence of Paleoindian and Paleoarchaic diagnostics in the mountainous central Great Basin.[7]

The central Great Basin was virtually uninhabited during the early Holocene because the first foragers lived between the mountains, not among them. Mountain glaciers still capped the highest ranges—the Ruby Mountains and the East Humboldt Range along the northern tier, the White Mountains to the west, and the Egan and Schell Creek mountains to the east. The first intermountain foragers were not mountain people. They stayed away from the stormy, dark, and forested uplands that fringed their wetland ecosystems. They avoided the uplifted Great Basin heartland because mountains must have been viewed as obstacles back then, not destinations. The mountainous central Great Basin would be significantly occupied for the first time only after the onset of dramatic and fairly rapid paleoclimatic events.

Middle Holocene (7000–4000 cal BC)
Entrada into the Central Great Basin Core

Much of western North America experienced higher temperatures and lower precipitation during the middle Holocene. The Great Basin was much hotter and drier than today, with lake levels lowering and tree lines moving higher; floral and faunal communities responded significantly. Kennett et al. (2007:531) argue that "severe and prolonged" drought conditions directly triggered population dispersals as people from the desert interior moved into coastal and aquatic habitats to escape the ameliorated effects of drought conditions (see also Louderback et al. 2010).

The middle Holocene drought ended with a dramatic increase in annual rainfall, in the Great Basin and beyond. Single-leaf piñon expanded its range, perhaps in response to an increased growing season due to precipitation from summer monsoons. Piñon pine arrived in the Schell Creek and northern Snake ranges by at least 5400 BC (Wigand 2010).

The central Great Basin was first significantly occupied under these summer-wet conditions, which likely favored dramatic increases in artiodactyl densities. We can now compare and contrast the most recent archaeological evidence of this entrada by charting the spatial distribution of time-diagnostic projectile points with the 517 cultural radiocarbon dates that are available from the central Great Basin (Figure 11.3).[8]

Twenty cultural radiocarbon dates define the first significant occupation of the central Great Basin (Figure 11.3). Three-quarters of these dates come from Monitor Valley (Gatecliff and Triple T shelters), with others from Pine Valley, the Diamond Mountains, and Upper South Fork Shelter. This evidence is entirely consistent with multiple paleoenvironmental proxies from the central Great Basin documenting the onset of summer-wet conditions that ended middle Holocene aridity.[9]

The earliest datable presence in Monitor Valley is Horizon 16 at Gatecliff Shelter (4350–4100 cal BC), and Triple T Shelter was occupied about the same time (Figure 11.3). Subsequent middle Holocene occupations at Gatecliff Shelter (Horizons 14 and 15) document the beginning of a long-term pattern of sheep hunters visiting it as a logistic camp to work the remote uplands of the Toquima Range, especially the Mt. Jefferson tablelands. These alpine hunters seem to be "travelers" (in the sense of Bettinger and Baumhoff 1982), operating some distance from their residential bases.

These first foragers engineered Gatecliff Shelter (and several other central Basin caves and shelters) to suit their high-mobility hunting lifestyle. These south-facing shelters are huge lithic heat sinks, remaining fairly cool in the summertime and holding heat in the wintertime. Alpine hunters crafted their personal space in repetitious and redundant ways, building fire hearths in exactly the same places, sleeping in the same spaces, reworking their gear while sitting in the same spots through time. They carried field-dressed bighorn into Gatecliff Shelter, where they lightened the load by discarding waste and drying the meat for transport. They painted the walls with red, yellow, black, and white pictographs. Eventually, the hunters picked through their gear—carrying some and caching other things for later—and then headed home. This logistic pattern would persist throughout the post–middle Holocene transition and into the Neoglacial periods; as noted below, there is considerable evidence of hunting losses throughout the highest reaches of the Toquima Range and elsewhere in the central Great Basin.

Very similar logistic hunting patterns are evident at a number of caves and rockshelters throughout the central Great Basin—

the Man Caves—including James Creek Shelter (Elston and Budy 1990), South Fork Shelter (Heizer et al. 1968; Spencer et al. 1987), Bronco Charlie Cave (Casjens 1974), Ruby Cave (Garcia 2006), Deer Creek Cave (Shutler and Shutler 1963), and, to a somewhat lesser extent, Pie Creek Shelter (McGuire et al. 2004). The genesis of logistic bighorn procurement (clearly evident in the hunting camps discussed above) is likewise overwhelmingly confirmed by the distribution of diagnostic projectile points demarcating the hunting catchments that spanned out around the Man Caves. Elsewhere (Thomas 2013b), I have tracked the distribution of Northern Side-notched points, generally considered to be time-diagnostic for the middle Holocene. A number of investigators have observed that Northern Side-notched points are distributed in an "arc" across the northern Great Basin, generally north of the Humboldt River (Delacorte 1997; Hildebrandt and King 2002; Layton 1985; O'Connell 1975). McGuire et al. suggest that the Northern Side-notched type constitutes "a marker for a uniquely northern population that inhabited this region more than 4,500 years ago" (2004:58; see also Delacorte and Basgall 2012).

I agree with this argument, but more recent evidence (summarized in Thomas 2013b) defines not so much a fan-shaped distribution as a spotty, yet mostly contiguous spread of Northern Side-notched points throughout the Reese River and Monitor valleys northward. In particular, I note a cluster of Northern Side-notched points recovered in the central Great Basin—in exactly the same area conspicuously lacking in early Holocene occupational diagnostics. Northern Side-notched points mark the initial entrada into the mountainous heartland of the Intermountain West.

Numerous systematic archaeological surveys amplify these results. By controlling for elevation, it is possible to test and expand the evidence from Gatecliff Shelter and the other bighorn hunting camps into the hunting catchments in the mountains of Monitor Valley, the Clan Alpine Range, and elsewhere across the central Great Basin (McGuire and Hatoff 1991:101–102; Thomas 1988, 2013a).

Diagnostic projectile point distributions likewise track the introduction of pronghorn procurement toward the end of the middle Holocene. Evidence for central Great Basin pronghorn hunting is best preserved at the Spruce Mountain Trap Complex of northeastern Nevada (Hockett 2005; Hockett and Murphy 2009), where Northern Side-notched points were recovered from Cobre Trap, Trap Hill, and Storey Trap. The recurrent and redundant use of these facilities began in the middle Holocene and continued throughout the late Holocene (as is also witnessed by the concentration of projectile points on most valley floors covered in the systematic surveys).

Post–Middle Holocene Transition (4000–1500 cal BC)

This interval begins with a spike of 11 ^{14}C dates from Monitor Valley (eight from Gatecliff Shelter and three from Triple T Shelter, with a pooled two-sigma mean of 3970–3780 cal BC), probably reflecting a carry-over of summer-wet conditions from the terminal middle Holocene. The 3900–2900 cal BC sediments at Gatecliff and Triple T shelters record decreasing overall precipitation but increasingly winter-wet conditions (Davis 1983:84; Melhorn and Trexler 1983:93). Despite this shift—which should certainly have a significant impact on artiodactyl population densities—the cultural radiocarbon record contains 21 radiocarbon determinations across this millennium. Two-thirds of the dates come from Gatecliff and Triple T shelters, with additional determinations from Pie Creek Shelter, South Fork Shelter, Deer Creek Cave, and Tosawihi Quarries. The ^{14}C evidence demonstrates that logistic hunting camps thrived during this era, despite the adverse winter-wet conditions in the central Great Basin.

The next spike in the cultural radiocarbon record is consistent with a return to summer-wet precipitation patterns beginning 2900 cal BC—and likely an attendant increase in artiodactyl densities—with a significant cluster of three dozen dates from Monitor Valley, Tosawihi Quarries, Pie Creek Shelter, Ruby Cave, South Fork Shelter, James Creek Shelter, and the Spruce Mountain Trap Complex.[10] Surface projectile point distributions confirm the intensification of high-elevation bighorn hunting during the post–middle Holocene transition, with a major proportion of Gatecliff series points recovered high in the mountains of the central Great Basin. This is certainly true for Monitor Valley, where nearly one-third of Gatecliff series points were found well above the modern piñon-juniper woodland; an equal proportion was found on the valley floor, suggesting both bighorn and pronghorn hunting during this interval (Thomas 1988:409–412, Table 71). Similar patterns characterize both the Reese River valley (Thomas 1971) and the Cortez Mountains/Sulphur Springs Range bordering Pine Valley (Brian Hatoff, personal communication 2000), where one-quarter of the Gatecliff (and to a lesser extent, Elko) series hunting losses took place above the contemporary piñon-juniper zone.

A probabilistic survey of Crescent Valley (Delacorte et al. 1992:Map 2) documents that half of the recovered Gatecliff series points came from the mountain domain (above 6,500 ft)—a considerably higher proportion than later types. Delacorte et al. (1992) think that this pattern reflects a more extended foraging radius from residential bases, almost certainly in search of bighorn. Systematic surveys of Whirlwind Valley and Mule Canyon (Ataman et al. 1994:24; Elston and Bullock 1994) likewise demonstrate that Gatecliff (and Elko) diagnostics were "by far the most frequent" point forms recovered above 6,000 ft, concentrated along Mule and Deer canyons draining the highest part of the Shoshone Range. Available archaeological data thus reflect a sudden and rapidly spreading pattern of logistic hunting throughout the central Great Basin, with intensive hunting in lowland areas (likely for pronghorn) and bighorn procurement in the upland and alpine reaches, often associated with rock walls, cairns, and hunting blinds (Hockett 2005; Hockett and Murphy 2009; McGuire and Hildebrandt 2005; Pendleton and Thomas 1983; Thomas 2013a).

Neoglacial (1500–650 cal BC)

The Neoglacial generally marks the cessation of summer storm activities and a return to much cooler temperatures with winter-dominated precipitation—climatic conditions posited by Broughton et al. (2008; see also Broughton et al. 2011; Byers and Broughton 2004) to be quite unfavorable for maintaining artiodactyl densities at previously high levels. Although the timing of the Neoglacial varies considerably across the western Intermountain West, in the central and western Great Basin, these cool, moist climatic conditions likely persisted until cal AD 1 or so.

The cultural radiocarbon record supports this contention (Figure 11.3), trailing off notably from the preceding summer-wet period. During the first half of the Reveille phase, Monitor Valley continued to function as a logistic hinterland for more densely populated places, such as the Reese River valley. Gatecliff and Triple T shelters were still used as field camps, and temporal diagnostics recovered in numerous highland surveys across Monitor Valley confirm that bighorn hunting continued at the most remote elevations.

There is a significant spike in ^{14}C dates at 1070–760 cal BC, with 19 dates from 11 central Basin sites. Several systematic archaeological surveys from this area likewise demonstrate a significant drop in the proportion of Elko points found at high elevations. But the projectile point data become difficult to interpret because the Elko series spans the Neoglacial, Post-Neoglacial Drought, and early Medieval Climatic Anomaly—an interval during which significant demographic and social changes transpired.

Post-Neoglacial Drought (650 cal BC–cal AD 350)

The best paleoclimatic evidence in the central Great Basin comes from the uplands of the Toquima, Toiyabe, and Monitor ranges (Miller et al. 2001; Miller et al. 2004; Tausch et al. 2004). Post-Neoglacial precipitation declined significantly, triggering decreased vegetation cover, a notable increase in hillside erosion, the growth of alluvial fans, and sediment deposition in channel and valley bottoms throughout most of the upland drainages. Toquima Range wood rat middens show a drop in the number of plant taxa from a Neoglacial high (Chambers et al. 1998; Miller et al. 2001; Tausch et al. 2004:35), and a wet-meadow pollen core in the Toiyabe Range confirms a major drought during this period.

The drought cycles dating ca. 600 cal BC–cal AD 300 across interior western North America were interrupted by a "dramatic winter wet event" centered between about 100 cal BC and cal AD 100 (Wigand 2006:2776). Correlative radiocarbon dates derived from the mountains of central Nevada confirm that fan building and valley aggradation declined dramatically after cal AD 50. Wood rat middens from the Toiyabe Range also show the local extinction of riparian species during an apparently severe drought, when sedge meadows converted to dry grassy flats, around 150 cal BC, with drought conditions lasting until about cal AD 710 (Tausch et al. 2004).

These climatic events had a direct and significant impact on terrestrial ecosystems and the organisms living there, with decreased discharge from mountain streams into wetlands and reduced primary production (and thus harvestable biomass of wetland plants in the floodplains). There was considerably less available drinking water, with mountain springs experiencing decreased moisture flux and many ceasing to flow, at least during the autumn months. Increased salinity in playa lakes made them unfit for human consumption (Benson et al. 2007:345). Wood rat middens and correlative palynology demonstrate that plant diversity decreased dramatically in the Toiyabe Range after 800 cal BC (Chambers et al. 1998; Smith 2003:49). Fire intensity increased across the central Great Basin between 800 cal BC and cal AD 1, "cleaning out diseased and insect-ridden vegetation communities weakened by a shift to drier conditions. These, most likely diseased and probably insect-ridden, plant communities were then replaced by drier climate adapted vegetation assemblages more attuned to the new climate regime" (Wigand 2010:111). This must have been a time of considerable stress on artiodactyl populations in the central Great Basin.

The correlative cultural radiocarbon record (Figure 11.3) shows only 22 dates recorded during a seven-century gap (760–50 cal BC). Significantly, several of these ^{14}C determinations come from the alpine residences at Alta Toquima—clearly not logistic hunting sites.

Figure 11.4 demonstrates the dramatically differing radiocarbon trajectories of Gatecliff Shelter and Alta Toquima during the late Holocene. For millennia, Gatecliff Shelter functioned as a camp for logistic hunters pursuing bighorn in the upland Toquima Range catchment. But Gatecliff Shelter was abandoned during the Post-Neoglacial Drought, as were virtually all of the Man Caves of the central Great Basin. Logistic bighorn hunting—a pattern that had persisted for nearly 4,000 years—had effectively died out by about 200 cal BC. Setting aside Alta Toquima for the moment, the high-impact Post-Neoglacial Drought correlates with a distinct hiatus in cultural ^{14}C evidence from 800 cal BC to about cal AD 10. The radiocarbon record further demonstrates that with the onset of the Post-Neoglacial Drought, the mountainous core of the central Great Basin was virtually depopulated as well, with a couple of very significant exceptions.

For one thing, Figure 11.4 demonstrates that families began to live at Alta Toquima during the early Post-Neoglacial Drought (as early as 780–541 cal BC); these are the earliest documented alpine residences in the Great Basin. Foragers returned to Gatecliff Shelter sometime between 200 cal BC and cal AD 1, but it was no longer a logistical hunting camp. Instead, Horizons 4–6 and subsequent occupations reflect a complex interplay of male and female maintenance, extraction, and fabrication activities. The multiple usages of Gatecliff Shelter (and several other caves and shelters in the central Great Basin) document this distinctive change in settlement pattern—they simply were no longer Man Caves.

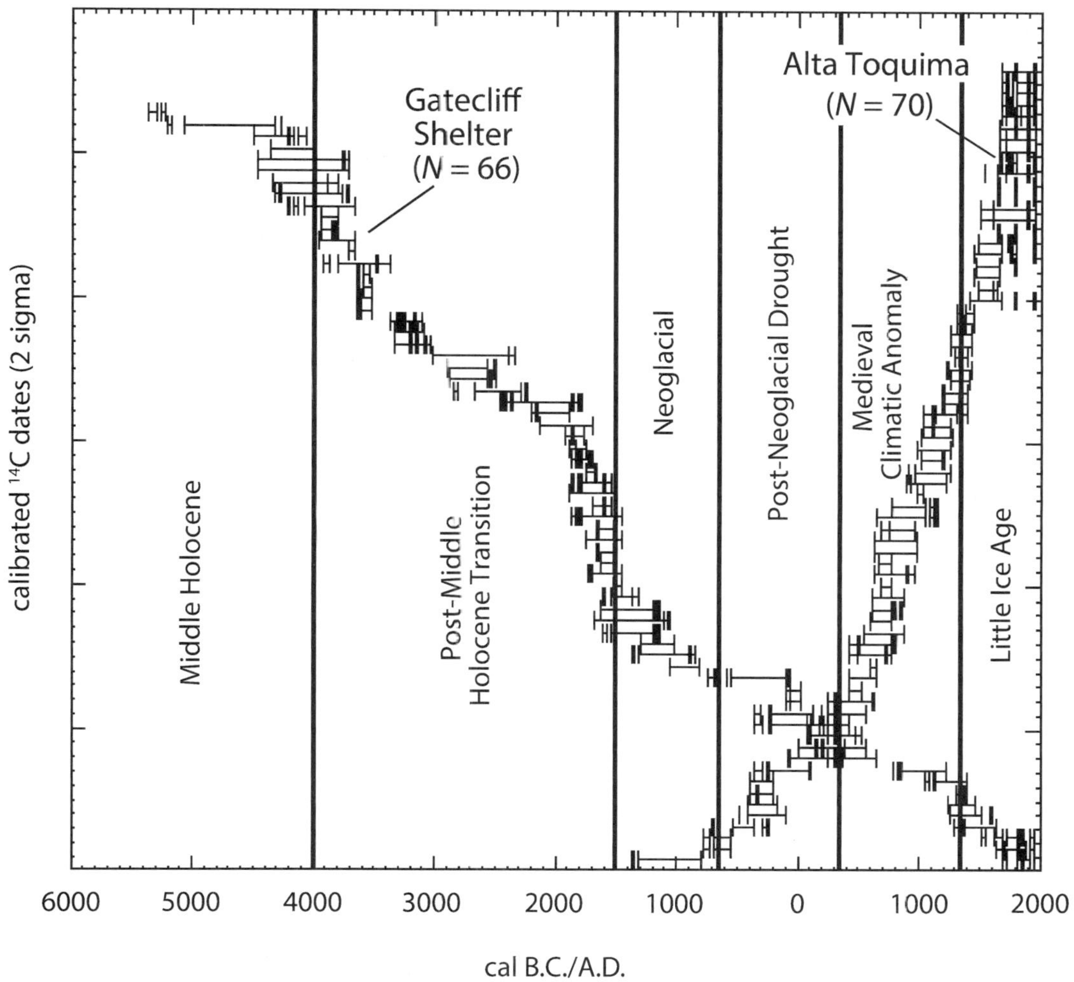

FIGURE 11.4. Probabilistic distribution profile for the 120 most recent radiocarbon dates from Monitor Valley.

The Little Boulder Basin is a second major exception—a notable cluster of sites along the Middle and Upper Humboldt River, where an apparently continuous human occupation can be documented from the middle Neoglacial period (roughly 1200 cal BC) through the latest prehistoric period. Cannon concludes that

> all sites, from all time periods [in the Little Boulder Basin], appear to represent the remains left by small groups of highly mobile hunters and gatherers who occupied sites for short periods of time. Overall, site structure is extremely simple. No residential structures have been identified on any sites of any time period in the [Little Boulder Basin] area, numbers of other types of features on sites are generally low and the features are relatively simple, and no secondary refuse areas have been identified [2010:ii, see also 306].

This evidence is most consistent with expectations for residential foragers who moved from one resource patch to another within a generally large annual range.

The abundant archaeological evidence amassed in the Little Boulder Basin is supported by more limited ^{14}C data from Marys River (Hockett 2007:Table 31), the Franklin Delta in northern Ruby Valley (King 1994:Table 24), and Maggie Creek (Rusco et al. 1979:Table 66). Each of these Upper Humboldt River drainages shows virtually no evidence of occupation during the preceding Neoglacial period, but beginning with the onset of the Post-Neoglacial Drought, each demonstrates an occupational pattern that continues throughout the MCA (and in the case of Marys River and the Franklin Delta, into the Little Ice Age as well).

In light of the near-total abandonment of the central Great Basin during the post-Neoglacial interval, one must ask why people came to the Little Boulder Basin (and parts of the Upper Humboldt River drainage) throughout this time interval. I believe that this shift reflects the occupation of the Little Boulder Basin by locally organized family bands—these were not logistically organized foragers—and the timing corresponds almost precisely to parallel developments at Alta Toquima.

The demise in summer-wet precipitation patterns and the onset of drought conditions had a direct and significant impact on people living in the central Great Basin. Beyond the obvious impact of extreme climatic stress, the Post-Neoglacial Drought likewise marks the shift from logistic, band-like foragers to small, independent household-size groups. Alpine and upland hunting was totally abandoned (in Monitor Valley and elsewhere across the central Great Basin), replaced by a more widespread utilization of the piñon-juniper woodland for both male and female foraging. Alpine residences were constructed at Alta Toquima and several other sites on Mt. Jefferson. The Post-Neoglacial Drought ends with a huge spike of 28 cultural ^{14}C dates from multiple central Basin localities (cal AD 1–350; see Figure 11.3). In the terminology of Bettinger and Baumhoff (1982, 1983), this is the traveler–processor transition—apparently happening simultaneously across nearly all of the central Great Basin.

Medieval Climatic Anomaly (cal AD 350–1350) and Later

Cook et al. term the Medieval Climatic Anomaly a time of "epoch megadroughts" (2004:1018), and beyond the obvious, Great Basin climates were generally becoming warmer and drier, with a seasonal shift in precipitation to the early summer (Davis 1982; Wigand 1987; Wigand and Nowak 1992; Wigand and Rhode 2002:328; Wigand and Rose 1990). Milder winters reduced the snowpack, and lower lake levels were evident in the western Great Basin. In central Nevada, the total number of plant taxa began to increase in upland areas (Miller et al. 2001:386, Figure 11). Bison appear in the eastern and western Great Basin during part of this interval (Schroedl 1973; Wigand and Rhode 2002). Despite the drought intervals, these would seem to be auspicious conditions favoring increased artiodactyl densities (Broughton et al. 2011), and considerable bighorn hunting was staged out of residentially mobile base camps (witness the major "bone bed" with at least two dozen bighorn on Horizon 2 [cal AD 1250] at Gatecliff Shelter).

Alpine residences continued at Alta Toquima throughout the MCA (which largely corresponds to the Underdown phase, cal AD 750–1300; see Figure 11.4). Although more than 400 Rosegate and Desert series projectile points were recovered from the alpine residences at Alta Toquima, both types are virtually absent as hunting losses above the piñon-juniper zone in the Toquima Range (Thomas 2013a), reflecting a significant downhill shift in bighorn hunting in Monitor Valley and elsewhere in the central Great Basin.

In the Crescent Valley systematic survey, for instance, Delacorte et al. found a high proportion of isolated Rosegate series points, indicating a "general pattern wherein hunting seems to have been most intensively pursued in the piñon-juniper woodland during this interval" (1992:66). Noting the parallel with Monitor Valley, Delacorte et al. record that Desert series points were mostly recovered from the lowland slopes: "The reason for this difference is unclear and somewhat puzzling since the uplands are generally a better place to hunt, supporting larger populations of most ungulates" (1992:65).

Similar systematic surveys universally demonstrate the near total absence of Rosegate and Desert diagnostics above the piñon-juniper in the Reese River, Pine Valley, Ruby Valley, Owens Valley, and Stillwater mountains (Bettinger 1975; Casjens 1974; Delacorte 1990; Hatoff, personal communication 2000; Kelly 2001; Thomas 1971). Delacorte's (1990) Deep Springs survey did recover a significant number of Rosegate points at some elevation, but virtually no Desert series diagnostics were recovered here. Similarly, the Mt. Augusta hunting complex had only two associated Rosegate points and no Desert series points (McGuire and Hatoff 1991).

Cooler Little Ice Age conditions prevailed ca. cal AD 1450–1850, with Great Basin vegetation patterns differing significantly between then and now (Tausch et al. 2004:38). Piñon-juniper woodlands became more spatially variable than before, with trees typically located in large savannas or higher-density locales confined to fire-protected sites. In the western and central Great Basin, piñon pine (which benefited more from the shift toward a mesic climate) expanded dramatically northward and downward in elevation (Wigand and Nowak 1992).

There is an intensive Yankee Blade phase (cal AD 1300–1850) residential occupation of Alta Toquima, but calibration distortion effects make the radiocarbon record difficult to interpret. Except for a single glass trade bead, there is no evidence of postcontact usage of Alta Toquima.

Travelers to Foragers: Invasion and Population Replacement?

At a very minimum, then, archaeological evidence from the White Mountains and Toquima Range reflects a major theme in the Bettinger and Baumhoff (1982, 1983) travel-to-forager model—namely, a significant shift from the logistic pursuit of high-return resources (such as bighorn sheep) to alpine village life. In these two widely separated mountain ranges, this shift seems to signal a transition from band-like villages with logistic outposts to household groups living in largely independent family camps.

More difficult is identifying the catalyst that triggered this strategic shift. Could that mechanism be a response to climate change? Could this shift in gender-differentiated labor organization arise from increased competition spurred by localized population growth? Or was this shift tied into a massive invasion and population replacement?

The temporal implications of the Bettinger and Baumhoff model were clearly spelled out two decades ago: the traveler–processor model

> predicts alpine village occupation later in central Nevada than in the White Mountains. The lag, however, might not have been great and might be invisible archaeologically; the entire Numic spread from eastern California to Idaho, Utah, and Oregon is regarded as having required no less than perhaps five, nor any more than perhaps seven, centuries [Bettinger 1991:675].

This sequence was justified by the frequencies of diagnostic projectile points (specifically Rose Spring points), apparently more prevalent in the White Mountain houses than in the Mt. Jefferson villages, leading to the conclusion that "the oldest of the White Mountain villages are older than Alta Toquima" (Bettinger 1991:673).

I found this chronology to be problematic at the time and tested this prediction against then-available radiocarbon dates from both areas (Thomas 1994). There was relatively little overlap between the Alta Toquima and White Mountains village dates because virtually all of the Mt. Jefferson radiocarbon dates are older than those from the White Mountain houses. The median (uncalibrated) age for the Alta Toquima houses for that sample of ^{14}C dates was 940 BP, as compared with 345 BP for the White Mountain villages. The statistical difference of nearly 600 radiocarbon years is highly significant.

My previous discussion concluded by asking:

> What does this all mean? If one insists on relating these high-elevation sites to population movements—which I do not—this would be a clear contradiction of the Numic spread hypothesis. If migrations are involved, then the [radiocarbon] evidence strongly suggests the Numics spread in a direction opposite to the one suggested in Lamb's model.... [S]ome authors, such as Aikens and Witherspoon (1986) may welcome such results as support for their own models. To me, these findings demonstrate something else. I think that the presence (and absence) of high-altitude residential sites in the Great Basin must be explained by causes other than population movement. *I think that hypothesized migrations of Numic-speaking people had nothing to do with it* [Thomas 1994:60; emphasis added].

I still think this and point up the considerable new evidence relative to the traveler–processor transition(s). For one thing, we have recently completed a high-precision reanalysis of the Alta Toquima house sequence, doubling the number of ^{14}C dates (Figure 11.4) and establishing that alpine residences were first built on Mt. Jefferson ca. 780–540 cal BC (considerably earlier than indicated in Thomas 1994). Unless the previous Owens Valley chronology was seriously flawed, and it is significantly revamped with *considerable* more time depth, one simply cannot argue that the White Mountain villages are more ancient than Alta Toquima.

There is also compelling new evidence raising the possibility of multiple transitions between the traveler and processor archetypes in the Great Basin. As detailed above, I see the most significant change taking place in the central Great Basin with the onset of the Post-Neoglacial Drought (650 cal BC–cal AD 350), when a vast area of more than 30,000 mi^2 was virtually abandoned—except for the first alpine residences then being established at Alta Toquima, signaling the beginning of a family-based pattern of foraging in the central Basin.

By contrast, Zeanah and Leigh note that the introduction of bow and arrow technology at 1300 BP in the Inyo-Mono area "coincides perfectly with the purported change to household economies" shifting away from the highly mobile Newberry (and slightly later) large house structures in Owens Valley (2002:42; see also Bettinger 1999a; Delacorte 1999). Basgall and Delacorte (2011:363) date the shift slightly later, about 1,000 years ago. The timing is critical given the role of bow and arrow technology in the Numic expansion model.

This shift is even more dramatic in the archaeology of the Truckee and Humboldt River drainages, where a significant degree of residential stability (and attendant logistic hunting) is evident about 2,000 years ago (Delacorte 1999; Hildebrandt and McGuire 2002; McGuire and Hildebrandt 2005).[11] These major villages composed of multiple structures disappear entirely sometime within the last 1,500 years (Delacorte 1997), a time of severe drought, population increase in some places, technological changes, and social conflict (McGuire 2002a). Not only do these new data sets suggest considerable temporal variability in the traveler–processor transition, they show that the most critical changes in subsistence, technology, social organization, use of landscape, and climate tend to transpire *within* rather than *between* cultural phases based on conventional projectile point typology (see also Thomas 2013b).

I have already argued that in the central Great Basin, the traveler–processor shift took place *in the middle of* the Reveille phase—meaning that travelers living in logistic hunting camps at Gatecliff and elsewhere were manufacturing "diagnostic" Elko series projectile points just as alpine processors living at Alta Toquima were. Similarly, Basgall and Delacorte (2011:21) suggest that the most significant changes in Owens Valley residential strategies took place not at Newberry–Haiwee or Haiwee–Marana transitions but, rather, *midway through* these respective periods. Along the Sierra/Cascade Front, where phase-defining Rosegate/Rose Spring projectile points are "diagnostic" of the cal AD 650–1300 interval, the most significant changes along the western fringe of the Great Basin take place *in mid–Rose Spring times*, about cal AD 1000 (Young et al. 2009:21; see also Hildebrandt and King 2002; Milliken and Hildebrandt 1997). Each of these findings points up the multiscalar problems inherent in projectile point chronology and underscores the importance of establishing the fine-grained chronologies necessary to evaluate the relationship between climate and culture change in Great Basin prehistory (Thomas 2011, 2013b).

Travelers to Foragers: Responding to Climate Change?

Julian Steward warned of the perils inherent in any form of "environmental determinism" (1955:35–36). Today, with the allure of high-precision records and models charting abrupt and short-term climate change, it is true that we must be equally wary of any seductive *paleoenvironmental determinism* that suggests any direct, one-to-one relationships between environmental and cultural change (see also Bettinger 2008:92–93). But Steward also cautioned that environment and geography must never be "relegated to a purely secondary or passive role" (1955:35), and I agree with that.

I see a strong paleoclimatic signal in the shifting settlement patterns of the Toquima Range, the rest of Monitor Valley, and the central Great Basin. This is not merely a "response to megadroughts" but, rather, a considered assessment of detailed ^{14}C paleoclimatic and cultural chronologies and broadscale settlement shifts tracked at multiple levels. Compelling new evidence links specific climatic conditions with changes in artiodactyl densities during the Holocene. Models derived from human behavioral ecology predict that such high-return prey types would have attracted foragers during key moments of positive climatic conditions. Although this chapter has focused on evidence from the central Great Basin, much broader, larger regional comparisons demonstrate an astonishing degree of paleoclimatic variability across the Intermountain West and a remarkable range of behavioral responses to these sometimes rapidly changing conditions (Thomas 2013a).

Other investigators have minimized the role of environmental change in explaining the evolution of the White Mountains alpine villages. Instead, the traveler–processor transformation and the appearance of alpine villages in both the White Mountains and the Toquima Range have been explained by a resource intensification and population replacement model—specifically invoking the spread of Numic-speaking people from southeastern California northward and then eastward into the Great Basin (Bettinger 1991, 1993:46; Bettinger and Baumhoff 1982; Delacorte 1997; McGuire 2002a).

Basgall et al. suggest that the climate–culture conversation "has in many cases devolved to an argument of faith and epistemology" (2003:352). Basgall cautions that

> simple correlative claims of the sort attending much of the MCA debate remain little different than arguments forwarded by Baumhoff and Heizer some 40-years ago. Deja vu all over again. It is certainly useful to identify evident correspondences between time, environment, and culture, but this is only a first step and a far cry from explaining why those coincidences exist [2008:265].

Zeanah and Leigh similarly emphasize "the importance of gauging the effects of general paleoenvironmental change on micro habitat structure and foraging choices, rather than making broad brush generalizations about good and bad climatic periods and their effects on hunter-gatherers" (2002:638).

This is all good advice—particularly regarding the importance of avoiding broad-brush generalization when evaluating cultural and paleoclimatic change. But given the massive scale of the invasion and population replacements required to drive the traveler–processor model, I must confess some impatience when reading that "the history of Numic is fairly well understood, at least in general outline" (Sutton et al. 2010:243). I do not believe this to be true at all.

The problem is not the innovative hypothesis of Bettinger and Baumhoff (1982, 1983), who linked linguistic and optimal foraging modeling. This was pioneering thinking that has transformed Great Basin archaeology. The problem is the regrettable more recent tendency to view Great Basin archaeology through Numic-colored glasses—reflecting a remarkable diffidence to the critical testing of these compelling hypotheses.

These would seem to be some (probable) facts:

- Post-Pleistocene human (biological) populations certainly moved across the Great Basin landscape, probably multiple times—sometimes colonizing habitats anew and other times, perhaps, outcompeting those already living there.
- Multiple manifestations of cultural practice—foraging strategies, sociopolitical organization, projectile point stylistics, bow and arrow technology, and various basketry formats—were doubtless transmitted across the Desert West.
- At some point(s) in time, Proto-Numic and Numic languages expanded across the Intermountain West (and beyond).

Whatever happened to the age-old Boasian premise—the heart of modern anthropology—insisting that language, biology, and culture be addressed as independent variables? Why must these events be confounded into a single, Great Basin–wide "Numic expansion"?

Why are broad-brush generalizations suspect only when evaluating paleoclimatic–cultural correlations, yet they still rule the road when evaluating the Numic expansion model? Where are the fine-grained comparative studies that convincingly link the current archaeological evidence with proposed causal mechanisms involving such linguistic and/or ethnic migrations, invasions, and population replacement?

In my view, understanding the Numic expansion remains a goal, not an achievement. With the accumulation of massive sets of relevant archaeological data over the past two decades, the recent advancements in chronometrics, the development of century-scale and localized paleoenvironmental reconstructions, and the advances in toolstone sourcing, we stand in a perfect position to refine independent regional sequences, local adaptations, and interactions over large-scale Great Basin landscapes. This, to me, is the path to understanding the nature of the Numic expansion, with the fine-grained precision necessary and appropriate for evaluating this complex model. This will not happen if we continue to assume our conclusions.

Conclusions

This chapter began with a deceptively simple question: *Why did foraging families decide to live at 11,000 ft in Monitor Valley, Nevada?* But this conversation will not conclude with a simple answer.

At the most basic level, we know this: the earliest detectable occupation of this upland valley took place at 4350–4100 cal BC, a time when summer-wet climatic conditions may have helped foster dramatic increases in artiodactyl densities, particularly in the extreme alpine reaches. Logistic bighorn hunters operating some distance from their residential bases engineered multiple field camps and hunted the mountains, including the alpine Mt. Jefferson tablelands (between 11,000 and 12,000 ft above sea level). They built hundreds, perhaps thousands, of traps, blinds, and rock walls to increase their hunting success. They discarded thousands, perhaps tens of thousands, of diagnostic projectile points as hunting losses. This pattern of logistic hunting far away from lowland village settlements seems to have operated throughout much of the central and western Great Basin during the post–middle Holocene transition and early Neoglacial periods.

The probable combination of overhunting and the Neoglacial shift to much cooler temperatures and winter-dominated precipitation perhaps stressed artiodactyl populations—particularly in the highest elevations of their range. When severe drought conditions gripped the mountains of central Nevada about 800–650 cal BC, not only did logistic bighorn hunting cease in Monitor Valley, but most of the central Great Basin was virtually depopulated for centuries.

At the beginning of the Post-Neoglacial Drought (780–540 cal BC), independent household-size groups were living in Monitor Valley, converting places such as Gatecliff Shelter from logistic hunting camps into multipurpose locations used by both male and female foragers. These same families also began building summertime residential houses at Alta Toquima and elsewhere on the Mt. Jefferson tableland—apparently the earliest alpine residences in the Great Basin. There is little evidence of alpine hunting in Monitor Valley (or anywhere else in the central Great Basin) after the Post-Neoglacial Drought. Families continued to return sporadically to Alta Toquima during the Medieval Climatic Anomaly; these occupations may or may not correlate with specific drought events. Several of the Alta Toquima houses were occupied during the Little Ice Age and then abandoned during European contact or perhaps slightly before.

This simple scenario reflects what we now know about the archaeology of Monitor Valley and the rest of the central Great Basin. It relies heavily on fine-grained dating techniques and detailed comparison of regional sequences, both cultural and paleoclimatic. We also can draw upon models grounded in human behavioral ecology to address the shift from band-like travelers to processors living in dispersed household clusters. But we are still unable to define a specific catalyst that triggered the strategic shift from traveler to processor.

I do not believe that any single explanation can (or will) account for alpine residences across the American West. Previously, some investigators (myself included) have argued that the alpine residential pattern and associated change in the Great Basin must be seen in manifestly local terms, addressing issues of intensified use of marginal resources in the face of local population increase, climatic instability, or perhaps both (Grayson 1991; Madsen 1993; Thomas 1982; see also Bettinger 1991:672). Although the White Mountains and Alta Toquima complexes both involved summer residential living at extreme elevation (as does the High Rise Village complex in Wyoming's Wind River Range), my guess is that a unique mix of environmental, ecological, social, demographic, technological, ideological, and historical factors likely played out in each case. When it comes to alpine residences, one size decidedly does not fit all.

Acknowledgments

I gratefully acknowledge the assistance of Lorann S. A. Pendleton and Diana Rosenthal in preparing this chapter and Catherine Fowler for indispensable conversation. Dennis O'Brien took the photographs.

Notes

1. These are quite likely some of the very same sites mentioned by Steward more than 50 years before.
2. Several archaeologists worked in Monitor Valley before I got there. On May 20, 1937, Robert F. Heizer and R. K. Beardsley conducted limited excavations at "Potts Cave" (26La1l). Sometime in the early 1950s, Margaret Wheat and Phil Orr dug another test pit at the site, but I can find no additional information on what they found. Today, the site is known as "Toquima Cave," and I first visited there in 1967. In 1955, as part of the Nevada State Museum studies, Dick Shutler (1956) visited Stone Cabin Canyon, on the southwestern edge of Monitor Valley, where Mr. Albert Hooper, a Paiute Indian living nearby, showed him a piñon cache inside an iron pot with a stone cover sealed with pitch.
3. Roughly a dozen alpine residential sites have been recorded in the Mt. Jefferson area. In addition to Alta Toquima, we recorded five more residential sites during the 1981 survey. During a 2008 revisit to Alta Toquima, we located and recorded Dakabah, named by Maurice Frank-Churchill, who used a Shoshone word meaning "Snow Water" (his reference to the nearby glacial tarn and cirque that define the eastern margin of Mt. Jefferson). Archaeologists working with the U.S. Forest Service have since identified and mapped several other residential sites nearby (Mark Bodily, Luke Trout, and Fred Frampton, personal communication 2008–10).
4. I am extremely grateful to Douglas Kennett and Bryant Culleton (Penn State University) for their assistance in obtaining new high-precision radiocarbon dates from both Alta Toquima and Gatecliff Shelter.
5. In this chapter, I argue that local histories of paleoclimatic conditions, resource depletion, social setting, and changing demographic conditions differ dramatically between the Toquima Range and the White Mountains of California. While I believe that limber pine processing was a key resource strategy at Alta Toquima (and likely other alpine residential sites as well), I agree completely with Robert Bettinger's (2000; personal communication) conclusion that limber pine processing was totally irrelevant to the alpine villages in the White Mountains.

6. These data are drawn from a database of more than 49,000 projectile points from 247 sites and localities (described in detail in Thomas 2013a).
7. Note the small concentration of stemmed points along the Middle Humboldt River (at Treaty Hill, Whirlwind Valley, and Tosawihi Quarries); an early Holocene presence is also known from Grass Valley (Beck and Jones 2002; Jones et al. 2003:28) and Fire Creek, just south of Beowawe (Estes et al. 2011).
8. In an attempt to place Alta Toquima and the Mt. Jefferson tablelands in a much larger context, Lorann Pendleton and I assembled a database of 3,200 cultural radiocarbon dates, including 517 ^{14}C determinations from the central Great Basin. Elsewhere (Thomas 2013a) I have dissected these data in much greater detail, but for the present purposes, I find it useful to highlight the relationship between these multiscalar chronologies and the paleoclimatic model of projected artiodactyl densities.
9. At 5500–4500 cal BC, summer-wet conditions triggered recurrent floods and debris flows that repeatedly swept into Gatecliff Shelter at intervals of 150 to 250 years (Davis 1983:84; Melhorn and Trexler 1983:95–97). Decreasing pika frequencies at Gatecliff Shelter after 4350 cal BC are consistent with the establishment of a summer-wet climatic regimen (Grayson 2011:258). This trend is confirmed by numerous independent proxies from Ruby Marsh (Thompson 1990, 1992), Kingston Canyon (Smith 2003), and a host of other localities (Tausch et al. 2004; Wigand 2010; Wigand and Rhode 2002; Wigand et al. 1995).
10. Post-2900 cal BC, both Gatecliff and Triple T shelters return to more fluvial conditions, with voluminous debris flows taking place every 150 to 300 years. This was an interval of increased summer-wet precipitation, perhaps in about the same amount as the present (see also Kautz 1988:251).
11. These large settlements from between about 1500 cal BC through cal AD 650 are known to exist throughout the western Great Basin, including Pyramid Lake (Tuohy and Clark 1979), Bordertown (Elston 1979) and the Truckee Meadows–Steamboat area (Elston and Davis 1968), Stillwater Marsh (Kelly 2001; Raven and Elston 1989), Humboldt Sink (Livingston 1988), and the Honey Lake area (McGuire 2000, 2002b).

References Cited

Adams, Richard

2010 Archaeology with Altitude: Late Prehistoric Settlement and Subsistence in the Northern Wind River Range, Wyoming. Unpublished Ph.D. dissertation, Department of Anthropology, University of Wyoming, Laramie.

Aikens, C. Melvin, and Y. T. Witherspoon

1986 Great Basin Numic Prehistory: Linguistics, Archaeology, and Environment. In *Anthropology of the Desert West: Essays in Honor of Jesse D. Jennings*, edited by C. Condie and D. D. Fowler, pp. 7–20. University of Utah Anthropological Papers, 110. Salt Lake City.

Ataman, Katheryn, Margaret Bullock, James A. Carter, Daniel P. Dugas, Robert G. Elston, Julie E. Hammett, Eric E. Ingbar, Christopher Raven, and Susan Stornetta

1994 *Patterns of Prehistoric Activity in a Changing Landscape: An Archaeological Survey in Whirlwind Valley.* Report prepared for Santa Fe Pacific Gold Corporation. Intermountain Research, Silver City, Nevada.

Basgall, Mark E.

2008 An Archaeological Assessment of Late-Holocene Environmental Change in the Southwestern Great Basin. In *From Avocados to Millingstones: Papers in Honor of D. L. True*, edited by M. G. Waugh and M. E. Basgall, pp. 251–267. Monographs in California and Great Basin Anthropology, Davis.

Basgall, Mark E., and Michael G. Delacorte

2011 *Data Recovery Investigations at Six Archaeological Sites in South-Central Owens Valley, Inyo County, California.* Archaeological Research Center, Technical Report, 11-131. California State University, Sacramento; and California Department of Transportation, Bishop.

Basgall, Mark E., M. G. Delacorte, and D. W. Zeanah

2003 *An Archaeological Evaluation of Five Prehistoric Sites near Bishop, Inyo County, California.* Report submitted to the California Department of Transportation. Southern Sierra Analysis Branch, Fresno.

Beck, Charlotte, and George T. Jones

2002 Rocks Are Heavy: Transport Costs and Paleoarchaic Quarry Behavior in the Great Basin. *Journal of Anthropological Archaeology* 21:481–507.

Benson, L. V., M. S. Berry, E. A. Jolie, J. D. Spangler, D. W. Stahle, and Eugene M. Hattori

2007 Possible Impacts of Early-11th-, Middle-12th-, and Late-13th-Century Droughts on Western Native Americans and the Mississippian Cahokians. *Quaternary Science Reviews* 26:336–350.

Bettinger, Robert L.

1975 The Surface Archaeology of Owens Valley: Prehistoric Man–Land Relationships in the Great Basin. Unpublished Ph.D. dissertation, Department of Anthropology, University of California, Riverside.

1989 *The Archaeology of Pinyon House, Two Eagles, and Crater Midden: Three Residential Sites in Owens Valley, Eastern California.* Anthropological Papers of the American Museum of Natural History, 67. New York.

1991 Aboriginal Occupation at Altitude: Alpine Villages in the White Mountains of Eastern California. *American Anthropologist* 93:656–679.

1993 Doing Great Basin Archaeology Recently: Coping with Variability. *Journal of Archaeological Research* 1(1):43–66.

1999a From Traveler to Processor: Regional Trajectories of Hunter-Gatherer Sedentism in the Inyo-Mono Region, California. In *Fifty Years Since Veru: Theoretical Advances and Contributions of Settlement Pattern Studies in the Americas*, edited by B. R. Billman and G. M. Feinman, pp. 39–55. Smithsonian Institution Press, Washington, D.C.

1999b What Happened in the Medithermal. In *Models for the Millennium: Great Basin Anthropology Today*, edited by C. Beck, pp. 62–74. University of Utah Press, Salt Lake City.

2000 Comment. In *Intermountain Archaeology*, edited by D. B. Madsen and D. Metcalfe, pp. 189–193. University of Utah Anthropological Papers, 122. Salt Lake City.

2008 High Altitude Sites in the Great Basin. In *The Great Basin: People and Place in Ancient Times*, edited by C. S. Fowler and D. D. Fowler, pp. 87–94. SAR Press, Santa Fe, New Mexico.

Bettinger, Robert L., and Martin A. Baumhoff

1982 The Numic Spread: Great Basin Cultures in Competition. *American Antiquity* 47(3):485–503.

1983 Return Rates and the Intensity of Resource Use in Numic and Prenumic Adaptive Strategies. *American Antiquity* 48(4): 830–834.

Binford, Lewis R.
1980 Willow Smoke and Dogs' Tails: Hunter-Gatherer Settlement Systems and Archaeological Site Formation. *American Antiquity* 45(1):5–31.

Broughton, J. M., D. A. Byers, R. A. Bryson, W. Eckerle, and David B. Madsen
2008 Did Climatic Seasonality Control Late Quaternary Artiodactyl Densities in Western North America? *Quaternary Science Reviews* 27:1916–1937.

Broughton, J. M., M. D. Cannon, Frank E. Bayham, and Douglas A. Byers
2011 Prey Body Size and Ranking in Zooarchaeology: Theory, Empirical Evidence, and Applications from the Northern Great Basin. *American Antiquity* 76(3):403–428.

Byers, Douglas A., and J. M. Broughton
2004 Holocene Environmental Change, Artiodactyl Abundances, and Human Hunting Strategies in the Great Basin. *American Antiquity* 69(2):235–255.

Canaday, Timothy W.
1997 *Prehistoric Alpine Hunting Patterns in the Great Basin.* Ph.D. dissertation, University of Washington. University Microfilms, Ann Arbor.

Cannon, Michael D.
2010 *A Revised Research Context for the Prehistoric Archaeology of the Little Boulder Basin Area, North-Central Nevada.* Prepared for Barrick Goldstrike Mines, Inc., by SWCA Environmental Consultants. Submitted to the Bureau of Land Management, Elko District.

Casjens, Laurel
1974 The Prehistoric Human Ecology of Southern Ruby Valley, Nevada. Unpublished Ph.D. dissertation, Department of Anthropology, Harvard University.

Chambers, J. C., K. Farleigh, R. J. Tausch, J. R. Miller, D. Germanoski, D. Martin, and C. Nowak
1998 Understanding Long- and Short-Term Changes in Vegetation and Geomorphic Processes: The Key to Riparian Restoration. In *Proceedings of Rangeland Management and Water Resources,* edited by D. F. Potts, pp. 101–110. American Water Resource Association and Society for Range Management, Herndon, Virginia.

Cook, E. R., C. A. Woodhouse, C. M. Eakin, D. M. Meko, and D. W. Stahle
2004 Long-Term Aridity Changes in the Western United States. *Science* 306:1015–1018.

Davis, Jonathan O.
1982 Bits and Pieces: The Last 35,000 Years in the Lahontan Area. In *Man and Environment in the Great Basin,* edited by D. B. Madsen and J. F. O'Connell, pp. 53–75. Society for American Archaeology Papers, 2. Washington, D.C.
1983 Geology of Gatecliff Shelter: Sedimentary Facies and Holocene Climate. In *The Archaeology of Monitor Valley, 2: Gatecliff Shelter,* by David Hurst Thomas, pp. 64–84. Anthropological Papers of the American Museum of Natural History 59(1). New York.

Delacorte, Michael G.
1990 The Prehistory of Deep Springs Valley, Eastern California: Adaptive Variation in the Western Great Basin. Unpublished Ph.D. dissertation, Department of Anthropology, University of California, Davis.
1997 *Culture Change Along the Eastern Sierra Nevada/Cascade Front, Vol. VII: Pah Rah Uplands.* Report prepared for Tuscarora Gas Transmission Company. Far Western Anthropological Research Group, Davis.
1999 *The Changing Role of Riverine Environments in the Prehistory of the Central-Western Great Basin: Data Recovery Excavations at Six Prehistoric Sites in Owens Valley, California.* Report prepared for Caltrans District 9. Far Western Anthropological Research Group, Davis.

Delacorte, Michael G., and Mark E. Basgall
2012 Great Basin–California/Plateau Interactions Along the Western Front. In *Meeting at the Margins: Prehistoric Cultural Interactions in the Intermountain West,* edited by David Rhode, pp. 65–92. University of Utah Press, Salt Lake City.

Delacorte, Michael G., Amy Gilreath, and M. C. Hall
1992 *A Class II Sample Survey for the Cortez Cumulative Effects Study Area, Lander and Eureka Counties, Nevada.* Report prepared for Cortez Gold Mine. Far Western Anthropological Research Group, Davis.

Elston, Robert G.
1979 *The Archaeology of U.S. 395 Right-of-Way Between Stead, Nevada and Hallelujah Junction, California.* Nevada Archaeological Survey, Reno.

Elston, Robert G., and Elizabeth E. Budy (editors)
1990 *The Archaeology of James Creek Shelter.* University of Utah Anthropological Papers, 115. Salt Lake City.

Elston, Robert G., and M. Bullock (editors)
1994 *Behind the Argenta Rim: Prehistoric Land Use in Whirlwind Valley and the Northern Shoshone Range.* Intermountain Research, Silver City, Nevada.

Elston, Robert G., and Jonathan O. Davis
1968 An Archaeological Investigation of the Steamboat Hot Springs Locality, Washoe County, Nevada. *Nevada Archeological Survey Reporter* 6(1):9–14.

Estes, Mark B., Edward J. Stoner, and Geoffrey Cunnar
2011 Preliminary Use-Wear Results from a Concentration of Western Stemmed Points in the Fire Creek Archaeological District, Central Great Basin. Paper presented at the Annual Meeting of the Society for American Archaeology, Memphis.

Frison, George C.
1992 The Foothills-Mountains and the Open Plains: The Dichotomy in Paleoindian Subsistence Strategies Between Two Ecosystems. In *Ice Age Hunters of the Rockies,* edited by D. J. Stanford and J. S. Day, pp. 323–342. University Press of Colorado, Boulder.

Garcia, M.
2006 Ruby Cave. Manuscript on file at the Department of Anthropology Museum, University of California, Davis.

Grayson, Donald K.
1991 Alpine Faunas from the White Mountains, California: Adaptive Change in the Late Prehistoric Great Basin? *Journal of Archaeological Science* 18:483–506.
2011 *The Great Basin: A Natural Prehistory.* Rev. and expanded ed. University of California Press, Berkeley.

Heizer, Robert F., Martin A. Baumhoff, and C. William Clewlow, Jr.
1968 Archaeology of South Fork Shelter (Nv-El-11), Elko County, Nevada. *University of California Archaeological Survey Reports* 71:1–58.

Hildebrandt, William R., and Jerome H. King
2002 Projectile Point Variability Along the Northern California–Great Basin Interface: Results from the Tuscarora-Alturas Projects. In *Boundary Lands: Archaeological Investigations*

Along the California–Great Basin Interface, edited by K. R. McGuire, pp. 15–28. Nevada State Museum Anthropological Papers, 24. Carson City.

Hildebrandt, William R., and Kelly R. McGuire
2002 The Ascendance of Hunting During the California Middle Archaic: An Evolutionary Perspective. *American Antiquity* 76(2):231–256.

Hockett, Bryan S.
2005 Middle and Late Holocene Hunting in the Great Basin: A Critical Review of the Debate and Future Prospects. *American Antiquity* 70(4):713–731.
2007 The Testing of 14 Prehistoric Sites Associated with the Marys River Reverse Land Exchange: A Preliminary Report. Manuscript on file, Bureau of Land Management, District.

Hockett, Bryan S., and T. W. Murphy
2009 Antiquity of Communal Pronghorn Hunting in the North-Central Great Basin. *American Antiquity* 74(4):708–734.

Janetski, Joel C.
2010 *Archaeology and the Native American History of Fish Lake, Central Utah*. Museum of Peoples and Cultures, Brigham Young University, Occasional Paper, 16. Provo.

Jones, George T., Charlotte Beck, E. E. Jones, and Richard E. Hughes
2003 Lithic Source Use and Paleoarchaic Foraging Territories in the Great Basin. *American Antiquity* 68(1):5–38.

Jones, Terry L., G. M. Brown, L. M. Raab, Janet L. McVickar, W. G. Spaulding, Douglas J. Kennett, A. York, and Phillip L. Walker
1999 Environmental Imperatives Reconsidered: Demographic Crisis in Western North America During the Medieval Climatic Anomaly. *Current Anthropology* 40:137–170.

Kautz, Robert R.
1988 Palynology. In *The Archaeology of Monitor Valley, 3: Survey and Additional Excavations*, by David Hurst Thomas, pp. 249–251. Anthropological Papers of the American Museum of Natural History, 66(2). New York.

Kelly, Robert L.
1995 Hunter-Gatherer Lifeways in the Carson Desert: A Context for Bioarchaeology. In *Bioarchaeology of the Stillwater Marsh: Prehistoric Human Adaptation in the Western Great Basin*, edited by C. S. Larsen and R. L. Kelly, pp. 12–32. Anthropological Papers of the American Museum of Natural History, 77. New York.
2001 *Prehistory of the Carson Desert and Stillwater Mountains: Environment, Mobility, and Subsistence in a Great Basin Wetland*. University of Utah Anthropological Papers, 123. Salt Lake City.

Kennett, Douglas J., Brendan J. Culleton, James P. Kennett, Jon M. Erlandson, and Kevin G. Cannariato
2007 Middle Holocene Climatic Change and Human Population Dispersal in Western North America. In *Climate Change and Cultural Dynamics: A Global Perspective on Mid-Holocene Transitions*, edited by D. A. Anderson, K. A. Maasch, and D. H. Sandweiss, pp. 531–557. Academic Press, Amsterdam.

King, Ronald F.
1994 The Franklin Delta Project: Archaeological Investigations in Northern Ruby Valley, Nevada. Manuscript on file, Bureau of Land Management, District.

Koenig, Orrin R.
2010 Does This Hearth Have a Home? A Hearth Centered Spatial Analysis. Unpublished Master's thesis, Department of Anthropology, University of Wyoming, Laramie.

Layton, Thomas N.
1985 Invaders from the South? Archaeological Discontinuities in the Northwestern Great Basin. *Journal of California and Great Basin Anthropology* 7(2):183–201.

Livingston, Stephanie D.
1988 The Avian and Mammalian Faunas from Lovelock Cave and the Humboldt Lakebed Site. Unpublished Ph.D. dissertation, University of Washington.

Louderback, L. A., Donald K. Grayson, and M. Llobera
2010 Middle-Holocene Climates and Human Population Densities in the Great Basin, Western USA. *Holocene* 21(2):366–373.

Madsen, David B.
1993 Testing Diet Breadth Models: Examining Adaptive Change in the Late Prehistoric Great Basin. *Journal of Archaeological Science* 20:321–329.

McGuire, Kelly R.
2002a The Evolution of Prehistoric Domestic Facilities and Community Structure in the Northwestern Great Basin. In *Boundary Lands: Archaeological Investigations Along the California–Great Basin Interface*, edited by K. R. McGuire, pp. 29–40. Nevada State Museum Anthropological Papers No. 24. Carson City.

McGuire, Kelly R. (editor)
2000 *Archaeological Investigations Along the California–Great Basin Interface: The Alturas Transmission Line Project, Vol. I: Prehistoric Archaeological Studies: The Pit River Uplands, Madeline Plains, Honey Lake and Secret Valley, and Sierran Front Project Segments*. Report prepared for Sierra Pacific Power Company. Far Western Anthropological Research Group, Davis.
2002b *Boundary Lands: Archaeological Investigations Along the California–Great Basin Interface*. Nevada State Museum Anthropological Papers No. 24. Carson City.

McGuire, Kelly R., Michael G. Delacorte, and K. Carpenter
2004 *Archaeological Excavations at Pie Creek and Tule Valley Shelters, Elko County, Nevada*. Nevada State Museum Anthropological Papers, 25. Carson City.

McGuire, Kelly R., and Brian W. Hatoff
1991 A Prehistoric Bighorn Sheep Drive Complex, Clan Alpine Mountains, Central Nevada. *Journal of California and Great Basin Anthropology* 13(1):95–109.

McGuire, Kelly R., and W. R. Hildebrandt
2005 Re-Thinking Great Basin Foragers: Prestige Hunting and Costly Signaling During the Middle Archaic Period. *American Antiquity* 70(4):695–712.

Melhorn, Wilton N., and Dennis T. Trexler
1983 Geology of Gatecliff Shelter: Stratigraphic and Climatic Interpretations. In *The Archaeology of Monitor Valley, 2: Gatecliff Shelter*, by David Hurst Thomas, pp. 88–98. Anthropological Papers of the American Museum of Natural History, 59(1). New York.

Miller, J., D. Germanoski, K. Waltman, R. Tausch, and J. Chambers
2001 Influence of Late Holocene Hillslope Processes and Landforms on Modern Channel Dynamics in Upland Watersheds of Central Nevada. *Geomorphology* 38:373–391.

Miller, J., K. House, D. Germanoski, J. J. Tausch, and J. C. Chambers
2004 Fluvial Geomorphic Responses to Holocene Climate Change. In *Great Basin Riparian Ecosystems*, edited by J. C. Chambers and J. R. Miller, pp. 49–87. Island Press, Covelo, California.

Milliken, R., and William R. Hildebrandt
1997 *Culture Change Along the Eastern Sierra Nevada/Cascade*

Front, Vol. V: Honey Lake Basin. Report prepared for the Tuscarora Gas Transmission Company. Far Western Anthropological Research Group, Davis.

Morgan, Christopher, Ashley Losey, and Richard Adams

2012 High-Altitude Hunter-Gatherer Residential Occupations in Wyoming's Wind River Range. *North American Archaeologist* 33(1):35–79.

O'Connell, James F.

1975 *The Prehistory of Surprise Valley*. Ballena Press Archaeological Papers, 4. Ramona, California.

O'Connell, James F., Kevin T. Jones, and Stephen R. Simms

1982 Some Thoughts on Prehistoric Archaeology in the Great Basin. In *Man and Environment in the Great Basin*, edited by D. B. Madsen and J. F. O'Connell, pp. 227–240. Society for American Archaeology Papers, 2. Washington, D.C.

Pendleton, Lorann S. A., and David Hurst Thomas

1983 The Fort Sage Drift Fence Washoe County, Nevada. *Anthropological Papers of the American Museum of Natural History* 58(2):1–38.

Raven, Christopher, and Robert G. Elston

1989 *Prehistoric Human Geography in the Carson Desert, Pt. 1: A Predictive Model of Land-Use in the Stillwater Wildlife Management Area*. Cultural Resources Series No. 3. U.S. Fish and Wildlife Service, Region 1, Portland, Oregon.

Rhode, David

2010 Food Values and Return Rates for Limber Pine (*Pinus flexilis*). Poster presented at the Great Basin Anthropological Conference, Layton.

Rhode, David, and David B. Madsen

1998 Pine Nut Use in the Early Holocene and Beyond: The Danger Cave Archaeobotanical Record. *Journal of Archaeological Science* 25(12):1199–1210.

Rusco, M. K., J. O. Davis, and A. Jensen

1979 *Archaeological Investigations near Carlin, Elko County, Nevada*. Nevada State Museum Archaeological Services Report.

Scharf, E. A.

2009 Foraging and Prehistoric Use of High Elevations in the Western Great Basin: Evidence from Seed Assemblages at Midway (CA-MNO-2196), California. *Journal of California and Great Basin Anthropology* 29(1):11–27.

Schroedl, Gerald F.

1973 *The Archaeological Occurrence of Bison in the Southern Plateau*. Reports of Investigations, 52. Laboratory of Anthropology, Washington State University, Pullman.

Shutler, Elizabeth, and Richard M. Shutler, Jr.

1963 *Deer Creek Cave, Elko County, Nevada*. Anthropological Papers of the Nevada State Museum No. 11. Carson City.

Shutler, Richard S., Jr.

1956 A Piñon Nut Cache near Tonopah, Nevada. *Plateau* 28: 70–71.

Simms, Steven R.

1983 Comments on Bettinger and Baumhoff's Explanation of the "Numic Spread" in the Great Basin. *American Antiquity* 48(4):825–830.

Smith, J. M.

2003 A 6,500 Year Pollen Record from a Wet Meadow Site in Central Nevada. Unpublished Master's thesis, University of Nevada, Reno.

Spencer, L., Richard C. Hanes, Catherine S. Fowler, and S. Jaynes

1987 *The South Fork Shelter Site Revisited: Excavation at Upper Shelter, Elko County, Nevada*. Bureau of Land Management, Nevada, Cultural Resources Series, 11. Reno.

Steward, Julian H.

1933 Ethnography of the Owens Valley Paiute. *University of California Publications in American Archaeology and Ethnology* 33:233–350.

1938 *Basin–Plateau Aboriginal Sociopolitical Groups*. Bureau of American Ethnology Bulletin, 120. Washington, D.C.

1941 *Culture Element Distributions, XIII: Nevada Shoshoni*. University of California Anthropological Records, 4(2). Berkeley.

1955 *Theory of Culture Change*. University of Illinois Press, Urbana.

Stine, Scott

1994 Extreme and Persistent Drought in California and Patagonia During Medieval Time. *Nature* 369:546–549.

Sutton, Mark Q., Mark E. Basgall, Jill K. Gardner, and Mark W. Allen

2010 Advances in Understanding Mojave Desert Prehistory. In *California Prehistory: Colonization, Culture, and Complexity*, edited by T. L. Jones and K. A. Klar, pp. 229–245. AltaMira Press, Walnut Creek.

Tausch, R., C. Nowak, and S. Mensing

2004 Climate Change and Associated Vegetation Dynamics During the Holocene: The Paleoecological Record. In *Great Basin Riparian Ecosystems: Ecology, Management and Restoration*, edited by Jeanne C. Chambers and Jerry R. Millers, pp. 24–48. Island Press, Covelo, California.

Thomas, David Hurst

1971 Prehistoric Subsistence-Settlement Patterns of the Reese River Valley, Nevada. Unpublished Ph.D. dissertation, Department of Anthropology, University of California, Davis.

1973 An Empirical Test for Steward's Model of Great Basin Settlement Patterns. *American Antiquity* 38:155–176.

1982 *The 1981 Alta Toquima Village Project: A Preliminary Report*. Desert Research Institute, Social Sciences Center, Technical Report Series, 27. Reno.

1983a *The Archaeology of Monitor Valley, 1: Epistemology*. Anthropological Papers of the American Museum of Natural History, 58(1). New York.

1983b *The Archaeology of Monitor Valley, 2: Gatecliff Shelter*. Anthropological Papers of the American Museum of Natural History, 59(1). New York.

1986 Contemporary Hunter-Gatherer Archaeology in America. In *American Archaeology: Past and Present*, edited by D. J. Meltzer, D. D. Fowler, and J. A. Sabloff, pp. 237–276. Smithsonian Institution Press, Washington, D.C.

1988 *The Archaeology of Monitor Valley, 3: Survey and Additional Excavations*. Anthropological Papers of the American Museum of Natural History, 66(2). New York.

1994 Chronology and the Numic Expansion. In *Across the West: Human Population Movement and the Expansion of the Numa*, edited by D. B. Madsen and D. Rhode, pp. 56–68. University of Utah Press, Salt Lake City.

2008 *Native American Landscapes of St. Catherines Island, Georgia*. Anthropological Papers of the American Museum of Natural History, 88(1–3). New York.

2011 Multiscalar Perspectives on Trade and Exchange in the Great Basin: A Critical Discussion. In *Perspectives on Prehistoric Trade and Exchange in California and the Great Basin*, edited by R. E. Hughes, pp. 253–265. University of Utah Press, Salt Lake City.

2012 The Chert Core and the Obsidian Rim: Some Long-Term

Implications for the Central Great Basin. In *Meeting at the Margins: Prehistoric Cultural Interactions in the Intermountain West*, edited by David Rhode, pp. 254–270. University of Utah Press, Salt Lake City.

2013a *Alpine Archaeology of Alta Toquima and the Mt. Jefferson Tablelands*. Anthropological Papers of the American Museum of Natural History, in preparation.

2013b Great Basin Projectile Point Typology: Still Relevant? *Journal of California and Great Basin Anthropology*, under review.

Thomas, David Hurst, and Robert L. Bettinger

1976 Prehistoric Piñon Ecotone Settlements of the Upper Reese River Valley, Central Nevada. *Anthropological Papers of the American Museum of Natural History* 53(3):263–366.

Thompson, Robert S.

1990 Late Quaternary Vegetation and Climate in the Great Basin. In *Packrat Middens: The Last 40,000 Years of Biotic Change*, edited by J. L. Betancourt, R. R. van Devender, and P. S. Martin, pp. 200–239. University of Arizona Press, Tucson.

1992 Late Quaternary Environments in Ruby Valley, Nevada. *Quaternary Research* 37:1–15.

Tuohy, Donald R., and David T. Clark

1979 *Excavations at Marble Bluff Dam and Pyramid Lake Fishway, Nevada, Pts. I–VI*. Contract C2520. U.S. Department of the Interior, Heritage Conservation and Recreation Service, Interagency Archaeological Services, San Francisco.

Wigand, Peter E.

1987 Diamond Pond, Harney County, Oregon: Vegetation History and Water Table in the Eastern Oregon Desert. *Great Basin Naturalist* 47(3):427–458.

2006 Postglacial Pollen Records of Southwestern North America. In *Encyclopedia of Quaternary Science*, edited by S. A. Elias, Vols. 1–4:2773–2783. Elsevier, London.

2010 The Environmental Context for Human Occupation in the Central Great Basin. In *The Sierra Pacific Falcon Project: Archaeological Excavations in Central and Eastern Nevada*, edited by K. Ataman and A. Quinlan, pp. 85–114. Summit Envirosolutions, Inc. BLM Report No. BLM1-2229g. Reno.

Wigand, Peter, M. L. Hemphill, S. E. Sharpe, and S. Patra

1995 Great Basin Woodland Dynamics During the Holocene. In *Proceedings of the Workshop—Climate Change in the Four Corners and Adjacent Regions: Implications for Environmental Restoration and Land-Use Planning*, edited by W. J. Waugh, pp. 51–69. U.S. Department of Energy, Grand Junction.

Wigand, Peter E., and Cheryl L. Nowak

1992 Dynamics of Northwest Nevada Plant Communities During the Last 30,000 Years. In *The History of Water: Eastern Sierra Nevada, Owens Valley, White-Inyo Mountains*, edited by C. A. Hall, V. Doyle-Jones, and B. Widawski, pp. 40–62. White Mountain Research Station Symposium Vol. 4. University of California, Los Angeles.

Wigand, Peter E., and David Rhode

2002 Great Basin Vegetation History and Aquatic Systems: The Last 150,000 Years. In *Great Basin Aquatic Systems History*, edited by R. Herschler, D. B. Madsen, and D. R. Currey, pp. 309–368. Smithsonian Contributions to the Earth Sciences, 33. Washington, D.C.

Wigand, Peter E., and Martin A. Rose

1990 Calibration of High Frequency Pollen Sequences and Tree-Ring Records. In *High-Level Radioactive Waste Management: Proceedings of the International Conference Topical Meeting, Sponsored by the American Society of Civil Engineers and the American Nuclear Society; Co-Sponsored by the American Chemical Society*, Vol. 2:1240–1250. La Grange Park, Illinois.

Wingerson, Lois

2010 High Life in the High Mountains? Newfound High Elevation Prehistoric Villages in Wyoming Challenge Old Assumptions About the Shoshone. *American Archaeology* 13(4):12–18.

Young, D. Craig, William R. Hildebrandt, Steven D. Neidig, and Sharon A. Waechter

2009 *From Fish Springs to Dry Valley: Archaeological Investigations on the Vidler Water Project Corridor, Washoe County, Nevada*. Report submitted to the Carson City Field Office, Bureau of Land Management. Far Western Anthropological Research Group, Davis.

Zeanah, David W.

2000 Transport Costs, Central Place Foraging, and Hunter-Gatherer Alpine Land Use Strategies. In *Intermountain Archaeology*, edited by D. B. Madsen and D. Metcalfe, pp. 130–157. University of Utah Anthropological Papers, 122. Salt Lake City.

2004 Sexual Division of Labor and Central Place Foraging: A Model for the Carson Desert of Western Nevada. *Journal of Anthropological Archaeology* 23:1–32.

Zeanah, David W., and A. T. Leigh

2002 *Final Report on Phase II Investigations at 26 Archaeological Sites for the Aberdeen–Black Rock Four-Lane Project on Highway 395, Inyo County, California*. Report prepared for the Department of Transportation, Bishop, California. Archaeological Research Center, Technical Report. California State University, Sacramento.

Zeanah, David W., and Steve R. Simms

1999 Modeling the Gastric: Great Basin Subsistence Studies Since 1982 and the Evolution of General Theory. In *Models for the Millennium: Great Basin Anthropology Today*, edited by C. Beck, pp. 118–140. University of Utah Press, Salt Lake City.

12

Resolving the Promontory Culture Enigma

John W. Ives

Though delighted to be asked to take part in this volume, I freely confess to being a Subarctic and Plains specialist with limited expertise in the two areas of particular interest to Don Fowler, the Southwest and the Great Basin. Both Don and Kay Fowler have, however, been particularly welcoming as I have explored a specific interest that has implications for the prehistory of western North America more generally—the vast extent of Dene or Athapaskan presence from Alaska to the Sierra Madres. For some years now, I have been assessing views concerning Apachean migration expressed by both Julian Steward and Edward Sapir in their thought-provoking work during the 1930s.

Julian Steward undertook intensive archaeological research during his appointment at the University of Utah, including excavation of Promontory Caves 1 and 2 along the north shore of Great Salt Lake in 1930 and 1931. From his correspondence to A. L. Kroeber, it is clear that Steward regarded the late-period deposits in the Promontory Caves as unusual from the outset.[1] With the publication of *Ancient Caves of the Great Salt Lake Region*, Steward described the late-period Promontory Culture as "basically one of a northern hunting people...that...existed in northern Utah sufficiently long to acquire southern and local traits" (1937:86). He went on to suggest that "we may have remains left by one of the Athapascan-speaking tribes...during their southward migrations" (1937:87).

Steward's view of the Promontory Culture laid the basis for what came to be known as the "Promontory Problem," an interpretive divide that has occupied Great Basin archaeologists over a number of decades (Forsyth 1986). In contrast to Steward, some archaeologists came to see the Promontory Culture as an economic variant that was nevertheless an integral part of Fremont (e.g., Aikens 1966, 1967; Simms 1986, 2008). Other archaeologists continued to see important discontinuities concerning the Promontory Culture that set it apart from Fremont, often believing that the Promontory Culture had replaced the earlier Fremont expression (e.g., Janetski 1994; Janetski and Smith 2007; Madsen 1989).

This debate might remain of interest largely to Great Basin practitioners but for the fact that Steward made explicit his suspicions on the Apachean identity of the Promontory Culture. Yet subsequent researchers have been reluctant to even mention this aspect of Steward's perspective. The late Promontory assemblages hover in a time range close to recorded history. They feature such astonishing preservation that it is truly difficult to imagine a hunter-gatherer archaeological record of greater fidelity. It would thus at least *seem* that we should be able to detect some sure signs of cultural identity for the Promontory Culture. I begin that task here.

From Problem to Enigma

Steward did not abandon but, rather, reiterated his sentiments in *Basin–Plateau Aboriginal Sociopolitical Groups* (1938) and again in 1940, saying that the Promontory Culture "appears to have been abruptly intrusive in the area, and one gets the impression that it is of northern origin" (1940:473). He recognized that Promontory hunters arrived in the Salt Lake region while it was still occupied by Pueblo farmers (we would today say "Fremont"), and they "remained there an undetermined length of time after the latter had disappeared." He continued to entertain the "possibility that the Promontory people were Athapaskans" and saw verification or rejection of this hypothesis as an outstanding research need (1940:474).

Steward had made a preliminary but lucid assessment of the Promontory Culture, one he was well qualified to make. Throughout the period in which he worked with these materials, he was engaged either in comprehensive culture element studies for Kroeber (e.g., Steward 1943) or in laying the foundation for his massive comparative work, *Basin–Plateau Aboriginal Sociopolitical Groups* (1938). These activities provided him with significant firsthand experience in evaluating Great Basin material culture, past and present. His 1937 conclusions can readily be confirmed by looking at Driver and Massey's (1957) distribution maps for elements of material culture that Steward keyed upon (e.g., footwear, quillwork, mittens). Steward also had a precise grasp of the ages of the assemblages involved in the Promontory

Point vicinity—decades in advance of the common application of radiocarbon dating.

The publication of *Ancient Caves* came during the point of inflection in Steward's career at which he turned toward a cultural ecological perspective. Kerns (2003) has pointed out that Steward had a strong empirical bent to his work and that he was willing to revisit core ideas, such as his belief that irrigation was a motive force in cultural evolution. While Steward's conclusions could hardly be described as pivotal to his research agenda, in the very year that *Theory of Culture Change* appeared, he made a terse review of Rudy's *Archeological Survey of Western Utah*. He was puzzled that the distinctive Promontory Culture could be regarded as Shoshonean, repeating that

> the pottery is unique, the moccasins are wholly unlike any Shoshonean type but identical with a Canadian style, basketry is unimportant, and the people seem to have been primarily bison hunters and not gatherers. The culture is definitely not "proto-modern" Shoshone [1955:89].

Steward (1955:89) felt that no new evidence had been offered to change his earlier hypothesis that this culture entered from the north and might represent Athapaskans who moved into the Southwest before the Shoshone entered Utah. Still, whether in literature designed for public or professional consumption, it became increasingly common to characterize the Promontory Culture as a hunter-gatherer variant of Fremont Culture, with no indication that other interpretations might be viable (most particularly those of the site's excavator [e.g., Fagan 2005; Madsen 1989]). Many authors—whether they favored continuity or discontinuity—became decidedly oblique in discussing Steward's perception that the Promontory Culture was different from both Fremont and later Numic materials, failing even to mention his proposal that the Promontory Culture might represent migrating Apachean ancestors (e.g., Forsyth 1986; Simms 2008; Simms et al. 1997).

To the eyes of a Great Basin outsider such as myself, this appears to be an odd state of affairs. No other twentieth-century cultural anthropologist had a greater impact on the subdiscipline of archaeology. At least from a theoretical perspective, many practicing archaeologists have an abiding respect for Steward's conception of cultural ecology. They do not defer to his considered judgment in the Promontory case, however, and it seems almost as though Steward may be thought to have committed a serious youthful indiscretion in his Promontory Culture conclusions, before a maturation of his deeper theoretical interests.

Most participants in this volume are better qualified to evaluate why such an enigmatic situation might exist. Perhaps it has in part to do with long-standing notions of continuity in Great Basin archaeological records and an unwillingness for the Great Basin to be perceived as a northern periphery of the Puebloan world. Both Gunnerson (1956) and Aikens (1966, 1967) clearly saw important elements of Steward's conclusions, but their earlier efforts in this regard required revision. Gunnerson found connections with the Dismal River Aspect but initially thought that Dismal River was a protohistoric thrust of Apachean ancestors across the Wasatch Range that had *preceded* the Promontory Culture.[2] Aikens saw the Promontory Culture as a Fremont variant (an aspect of his work that remained influential): he initially construed both as Plains-influenced and of Apachean origin, with Promontory remaining closer to its Plains roots. Neither of these formulations proved to be correct (e.g., Aikens 1972), and it could be that relatively early recognition of these difficulties muted interest in pursuing an Apachean connection for Promontory materials.

Ironically, in more recent decades, it was probably Steward's own impact on archaeological theory that inhibited serious consideration of his Promontory work. Migration had been used to explain anything and everything in much of earlier twentieth-century archaeology. As interest in cultural ecology and processualist approaches grew, any explanation involving migration increasingly became an anathema. Widespread application of cultural ecology eventually led to the advent of evolutionary ecological approaches, with yet more deeply entrenched emphases on adaptive shifts and demographic continuities. The historical idiosyncrasies of Apachean migration have seemed very much of "out of bounds" in most recent approaches to Great Basin prehistory. It is precisely the vast extent of Dene migration in western North America, however, that requires us to expand our horizons.[3]

A Scenario for Apachean Migration

Steward (1960) would later work with other Dene people in British Columbia, but this did not elicit curiosity on his part regarding the broader history of the language family. It was actually Sapir (1936) who articulated a larger scheme for Apachean origins, suggesting that four "strata" should exist in Navajo culture: a fundamental northern layer, similar to that of Dene in the Mackenzie Basin; a pre-equestrian Plains adaptation; an initial Southwestern influence, from relatively simple non-Puebloan cultures of the Southwest; and a second, strongly Puebloan influence. Much more can be said of the incisive brilliance of Sapir's remarks than can be expressed here. For the moment, I ask the reader's forbearance in using Sapir's framework to organize the following remarks.

Scholars generally agree that Apachean ancestors migrated from the Canadian Subarctic in the recent past (e.g., Ives 2010; Krauss and Golla 1981; Magne and Matson 2010; Matson and Magne 2007). The nature and causes of this population movement are debated, but a number of researchers believe that the East Lobe White River eruption (which deposited massive quantities of volcanic ash over much of the Yukon and Northwest Territories) had a ripple effect among northern Dene populations at roughly AD 800 (Ives 1990, 2003; Matson and Magne 2007; Workman 1979). This ecological catastrophe over a vast region of the western Subarctic, when coupled with the highly attractive nature of the Plains bison-hunting lifestyle, very likely encouraged Navajo and Apache ancestors to move from the Peace River country of northeastern British Columbia and northwestern Alberta southward along Alberta's Eastern Slopes and northern Plains regions.[4]

Less subject to debate are certain characteristics of the ancestral Apachean population. Several independent lines of genetic evidence (including sequence variation in mtDNA haplotypes and Y chromosome data) reveal that the initial Apachean population went through a founder effect (Holve et al. 2003; Li et al. 1998; Li et al. 2002; Malhi et al. 2003; Malhi et al. 2008). Yet, by historic times, the various Apachean populations had engaged in significant interaction with other southern societies and had grown dramatically (Brugge 1994). Apachean oral traditions and genetic data further reinforce the idea that many non-Dene people joined the emergent, more westerly Apachean societies. Brugge (2003, 2006; see also Reichard 1928; Wilshusen 2010) has shown that Navajo clans were likely adopted from Puebloan societies, that many clan ancestresses were Puebloan women from specific Puebloan sites, and that early Navajo society was highly incorporative of others. Both mtDNA and Y chromosome data show that population admixture between Apachean and neighboring peoples was the norm (Malhi et al. 2003; Malhi et al. 2008).

My colleagues and I (Ives et al. 2002) gathered Apachean neologisms for unfamiliar species and objects that people leaving the Subarctic would inevitably encounter and for which they would require names (e.g., maize, lizard, turtle, wild turkey, and tobacco). A large and dispersed ancestral Apachean population could be expected to yield notable variation in forming such terms, particularly where geographic barriers intervened. Instead, we find a pattern in which one term will commonly be applied, also suggesting that the original Apachean population was relatively small and cohesive.

Golla and de Reuse have concluded that the most comfortable structural fit for the Apachean languages is with Dene speech communities east of the Rockies (Golla 2008). They postulate that a relatively undifferentiated Proto-Apachean group took up residence on the High Plains, eventually extending over a considerable area. Early differentiation in the Proto-Apachean speech community led to a dialect chain running from Navajo through Plains Apache. At one end of this chain, some Proto-Apachean populations had a long involvement with the Plains that would ultimately lead to the Plains Apache association with the Kiowa. At the other end of the chain, there was an earlier movement westward, into contact with Puebloan society, leading to the emergence of the Navajo in Dinétah.

Consequently, if the inhabitants of the Promontory Caves really did have an Apachean heritage, we would expect them to reflect a small population aggregate situated along the western edge of a diverging Apachean speech community. Recognizing their material culture identity will be complicated by a powerful Dene proclivity to adopt material and ceremonial culture from neighboring societies (e.g., Honigmann 1975). Moreover, this locus would represent Apachean material culture at an approximate midpoint of its transit. We should not expect that assemblages should simply be Subarctic, Plains, or Southwestern in their appearance; they should instead have important intermediate qualities. Wherever Apachean ancestors came to reside after leaving present-day Canada, the cultural entities we are familiar with today (Navajo and Apache groups) had yet to come into existence. We cannot expect predecessor populations to have been exactly like them or, correlatively, just like populations in homeland regions (Brugge 2006).

Empirical Dimensions of the Promontory Cave Occupations

If there has seldom been discussion of Steward's views concerning an Apachean presence in the Promontory Caves, it is equally true that there has been rather little consideration of what he encountered. Because of the pioneering nature of his work, Steward could not apprehend how different the Cave 1 occupations would be from those of other major caves in western North America. Large habitable caves (e.g., Danger, Hogup, Mummy, Spirit) in this general region all had extensive occupations throughout the Holocene.

Promontory Cave 1 does not. It has only a rich Promontory phase occupation: however the subsistence-settlement systems of regional populations had been configured prior to this late-period occupation, they failed to include this largest Promontory Cave in a discernible way. The next-largest cave, Cave 2, also has Promontory phase deposits, though these are preceded by weaker mid-Holocene occupations. Steward thought that the Promontory phase occupations took place in winter. The nearest freshwater source was more than 2 km distant, a factor that could be mitigated by occupation when there was winter snow.

Nor were these Promontory phase occupations modest. Steward (1937) found abundant and diverse materials from all phases of domestic life, much of this organized around a large central hearth in Cave 1 in a layer some 50 cm thick (Figure 12.1). These materials included hunting paraphernalia (Desert series arrowpoints, cane arrow shafts, hardwood foreshafts, and bow fragments). There were several knife handles, including one that served as the base for a fire kit. Intensive hide preparation and sewing activities took place, as revealed by scrapers, bone fleshers, bone awls, and many scraps of hide and leather. Other items involved slate knives, basketry, cordage, and matting of various plant materials, including the use of juniper bark for bedding. Gaming pieces and etched slate were also present. There was no supporting evidence for horticulture or intensive plant food use, and there were few indications of ground-stone technology. The remaining bones in Steward's faunal sample represent more antelope, deer, and sheep, but there can be little doubt from Steward's description that bison remains were abundant. Copious bison hide, fur, leather, bones, and even an articulated lower limb and hoof remain visible in Promontory Cave 1 today. Perhaps this

FIGURE 12.1. Main habitation area of Promontory Cave 1 during new excavations in April 2011. The depression to the right resulted from Steward's main excavation unit. The inset shows the wealth of perishable material (including hide, leather, fur, and dense plant fibers) in remaining deposits being excavated. Note the braided cattail (being held) and the remnant outer perimeter of a stretched bison hide (at trowel tip).

economic focus provides part of the explanation for the sudden occupation of Cave 1, but whatever the cause, a different dynamic came into play in the twelfth and thirteenth centuries.

Despite the intensity of occupation, neither Cave 1 nor Cave 2 has a large habitable space. Steward's data are best interpreted as reflecting small residential bases from which other activities were conducted. Men, women, and children were present. The discarded moccasins come in many sizes, for example, including those for small children. Just how large would these residential groups be? Judging from Steward's diagrams, the habitable space in Cave 1 would be unlikely to exceed 200–300 m^2, while for Cave 2, the habitable space would be roughly 100 m^2. If we allot 2–3 m^2 of space for each person, the two caves could accommodate no more than 150–200 persons at any one time; in reality, this figure may have been considerably less. Considered from the perspective of Dene principles of group formation, it was most likely a moderate-sized local group or microband that created the Cave 1 and Cave 2 occupations (Ives 1990, 1998). The Promontory phase habitation of Promontory Point is not consistent with a population as large as a regional marriage isolate (400–500 persons).

With regard to the timing of the Promontory phase occupation of Caves 1 and 2, Aikens (1966:4) reported a radiocarbon date of 840 ± 75 years BP for a Cave 1 moccasin. Marwitt (1973) recorded a leather date from Promontory Cave 1 of 320 ± 80 years BP. Smith (2004) reports a date of 330 ± 40 on residue from a pottery sherd in Promontory Cave 1, and J. Janetski (personal communication 2010) has provided two additional ceramic residue dates of 360 ± 40 and 610 ± 40 BP (B-286892 and B-286893). Kankainen has reported accelerator mass spectrometry (AMS) dates of 725 ± 35 BP, 755 ± 40 BP, and 785 ± 40 BP for three Promontory moccasins (CAMS 112638, CAMS 112639, CAMS 112640 [see Janetski and Smith 2007:332]).

The perishables in Steward's Promontory Cave collections are currently the subject of an AMS radiocarbon-dating program to be reported in greater detail elsewhere. Another 39 AMS dates (primarily for moccasins but including netting, one-rod-and-bundle basketry, matting, gaming pieces, a bow fragment, and a cane arrow fragment) all cluster tightly, with a range of 826–662 radiocarbon years BP (yielding a two-sigma calendrical range of as much as AD 1167–1395, but with much narrower central tendencies in the thirteenth century: OxA 18156-62, OxA 18460-69, OxA 23853-57, OxA 23882-90, OxA 23917-21, OxA 24002-04). The single exception to this pattern, a date of 165 ± 25(OxA 18463), was for a Shoshone-style winnowing basket (C. Fowler, personal communication March 20, 2011, regarding basket fragment 42BO1 10409.1, Promontory Cave 1), a finding consistent with Steward's (1938) information that there was a nineteenth-century Shoshone presence in the Promontory Point caves.

In terms of the organization of subsistence-settlement systems on Promontory Point, then, something significantly different does seem to have happened in the Promontory Caves. Cave 1 was suddenly and intensively occupied for the first time during the twelfth and thirteenth centuries AD, with much fainter indications of later occupation, while Cave 2 was more heavily occupied than in any preceding Holocene use episodes. The Promontory phase population was likely in the larger micro-band size range (50–100 individuals), carrying out a full range of domestic activities, but with a strong focus on bison and antelope hunting.

Promontory Pottery

Steward (1955) headed his critique of Rudy by saying that Promontory pottery was unique. Promontory pottery has been a prime topic of debate in Promontory discussions: in some quarters, Promontory pottery has simply been regarded as one late-period Great Basin grayware among others. Other analyses (Simms et al. 1997) have focused on the behavioral dimensions of ceramic production and mobility at the expense of cultural affiliation. Recent, comprehensive analyses of Promontory pottery demonstrate that it is distinctive.

Forsyth (1986), Smith (2004), and Janetski and Smith (2007) have clarified that while some Promontory pottery came in the form of smaller bowls, vessels typically resemble large-mouthed jars with thick walls; flattened, everted lips; and rough, undulating surfaces. These vessels were made of iron-rich clays, with coarse, poorly sorted temper. For Utah Valley, Janetski and Smith found that Promontory pottery was fashioned through poorly bound coiling and hand smoothing with some scraping. Firing temperatures for Promontory pottery were notably lower than for Fremont wares (the latter being thinner walled); moreover, Fremont pottery came in a broader variety of vessel forms and generally was more finely made. Promontory vessels frequently have internal residues and external soot. In terms of the mobility distinctions made regarding Great Basin ceramics by Simms et al. (1997), many of these attributes favor a characterization of Promontory pottery as expedient, with a limited investment in construction, as one might associate with more highly mobile hunter-gatherers. Although hunter-gatherers were clearly making Promontory pottery, many of the Utah Valley vessels were large and heavy. They were not readily amenable to transport and are restricted to lower-altitude marsh and lakeshore settings. Interestingly, the Promontory Cave sherds reflect smaller vessels with thinner walls, perhaps serving a somewhat different purpose (Janetski and Smith 2007:336–337).

Discerning the precise nature of Promontory pottery is a topic of more than passing interest. While it has internal variability, it is generally more poorly made than Fremont pottery. It first appears in the thirteenth century, with use continuing over the next two centuries, in a range extending from southern Idaho along the eastern shore of Great Salt Lake and along the Utah Valley.

One can legitimately ask, Who made this pottery? If there were Apachean ancestors in the Promontory Caves, it could have been traded to them by surrounding peoples who began to make it as part of the shifting material culture accompanying the dissolution of Fremont. We know from the prehistoric record of western Subarctic Canada that Proto-Apachean populations did *not* make pottery in that region, even though they did make pottery once they entered the Southwest and southern Plains (Ives 2003). It could be that the expedient qualities of Promontory pottery arose because the Promontory Caves provided one locus (among others) at which Apachean ancestors had begun to assimilate a pottery-making tradition under stimulus from surrounding peoples (Ives 2007; cf. Baugh and Eddy 1987:797; Wilson 1996). Or it could be that both Proto-Apachean and descendant Fremont populations came to make Promontory pottery, which does exhibit internal variability. For the present purposes, it is sufficient to say that Steward was correct: Promontory pottery is a distinctly recognizable ceramic type.

It's the Moccasins, You Ceramicists!

Steward recovered *250* moccasins from caves publicly known in the region for decades (*Box Elder News* 1913). In 1930, he feared that the caves would be looted in their entirety. More than 50 other instances of Promontory-style moccasins are known to be at other institutions or in collectors' hands.[5] Given that Promontory Caves 1 and 2 were not totally excavated, and that more than 300 moccasin instances are already known, it is not far-fetched to think that the Promontory Caves may have held several hundred moccasins.

For those instances where accurate determinations could be made, 73.1 percent of the moccasins had been mended (58 not repaired and 158 with heel, half-sole, or whole-sole repairs). Thus, the large number of moccasins seems to have resulted primarily from discard late in their use life. Many scraps of leather and fur were present in the deposits; parts of moccasins such as ankle wraps were "scavenged," leaving no doubt about the intensive manufacture and repair of clothing, footwear, and other perishables.

Regarding manufacture, hock, Fremont, and Hogup moccasins are fundamentally different from Promontory moccasins (Aikens 1970:97–109; Jennings 1957:221–223; Figure 12.2). The patterns from which the former kinds were sewn differed radically from those used for Promontory moccasins. Hock moccasins rely upon the tubular nature of the lower ungulate limb, while Fremont moccasins are, as Aikens said, fashioned "from the top downward" (Figure 12.3). He indicated that neither the hock nor the more numerous Fremont moccasins at Hogup Cave were well tanned (as in Figure 12.2). Most hock and Fremont moccasins at Hogup came from Stratum 12, where Aikens

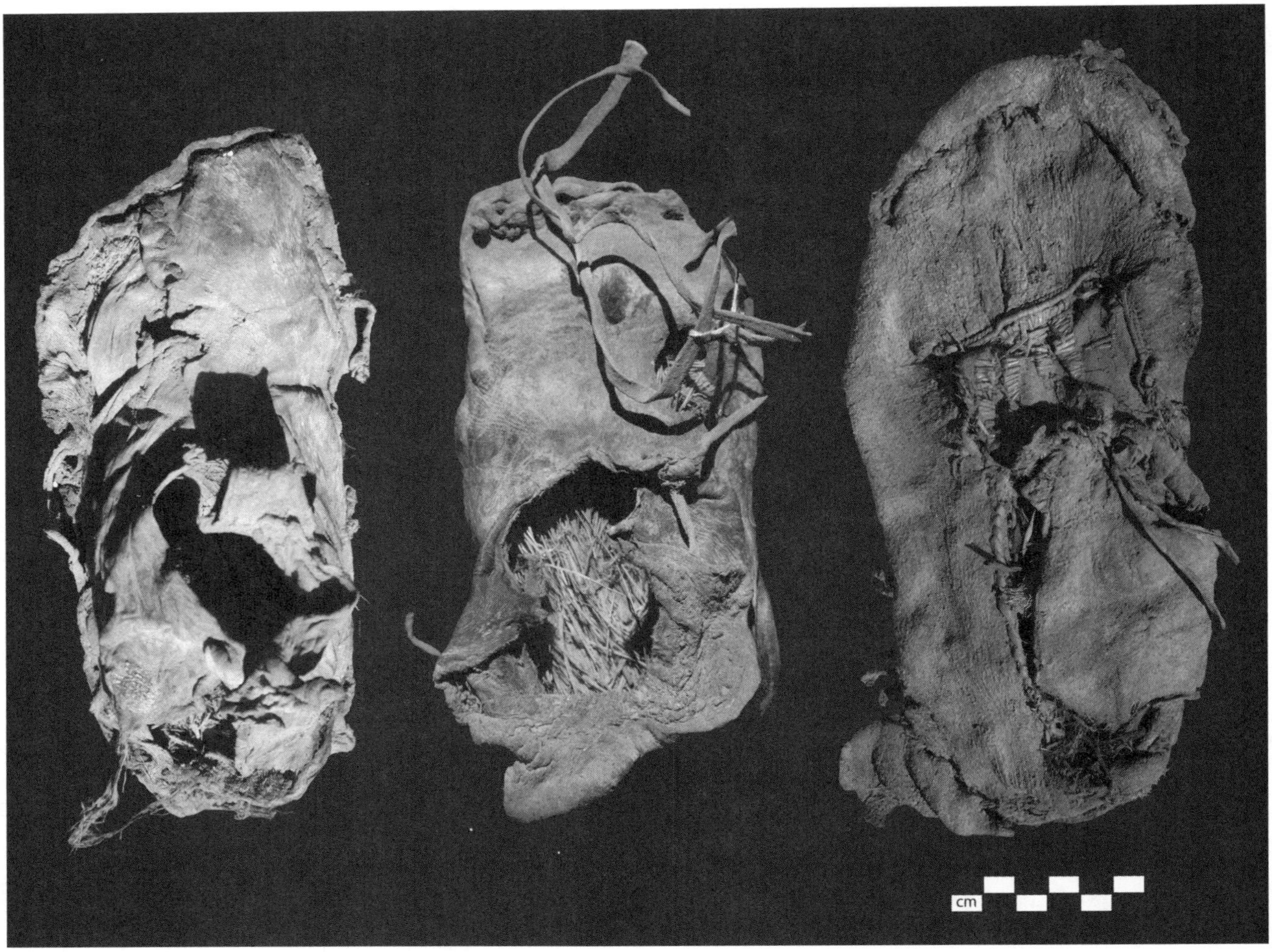

FIGURE 12.2. Left, Fremont moccasin from Hogup Cave (42BO36 FS 47.7 UMNH.AR.12459); center, hock moccasin from Hogup Cave (42BO36 FS 47.7 UMNH.AR.12456); right, moccasin from Promontory Cave 1 (42BO1 10241 UMNH.AR.53760; photograph by the author; courtesy of the Utah Museum of Natural History). The Fremont and hock moccasins are enlarged to facilitate comparison of patterns and sewing details.

preferred a date of ca. 1530 ± 80 BP (AD 420). There is variability in the refinement of the sewing on the Promontory moccasins, but on the whole, the quality of their leather and their construction far exceeds that of previous Great Basin moccasins. Promontory moccasins are fashioned "from the bottom up" and feature sewing as fine as seven–eight stitches per centimeter, whereas stitching on hock and Fremont moccasins is coarse (one stitch per centimeter or less). Although some Promontory moccasins were made of antelope or deer, most are made of bison leather, often with the bison fur turned inward. Despite the thicker hide and fur, Promontory craftspersons were adept at finely gathering this material into a rounded toe. A marked discontinuity for footwear is evident moving from Fremont to Promontory phase times.

Steward (1937), aware of Hatt's (1916) pioneering work on moccasins, was quite correct to point out that the Promontory moccasins were typical of the Canadian north. Today we have better knowledge of the historic distributions of moccasin styles, most notably from Thompson's (1990, 1994) comprehensive studies, records of the global census of Subarctic Canadian clothing gathered for the 1988 *The Spirit Sings* Olympic exhibition (maintained in duplicate by the Canadian Museum of Civilization and the Glenbow Museum), and greater access to historic art depicting clothing in the early nineteenth century.

Specialists working in this area now use the Bata Shoe Museum (BSM) typology for moccasin construction templates (Webber 1989). Moccasins in the BSM 2(Ab) style dominated mid-nineteenth-century Dene and Algonquian ethnological collections. These are two-piece, soft-soled moccasins with an apron or vamp over the arch; the apron meets a front seam that runs toward a somewhat more pointed toe; there is a T-seam at the heel. In the early twentieth century, the BSM 2(Bb) style appears to have swept from the eastern Subarctic northwestward through Mackenzie Basin Dene communities. This style differs from BSM 2(Ab) in that it lacks the center toe seam: the apron meets directly with a single, lower edge of the moccasin, creating a more rounded and puckered toe.

Most Promontory moccasins (237) were sewn in variations of the BSM 2(Bb) moccasin type (variations consisting of features such as the presence or absence of an ankle wrap). Steward

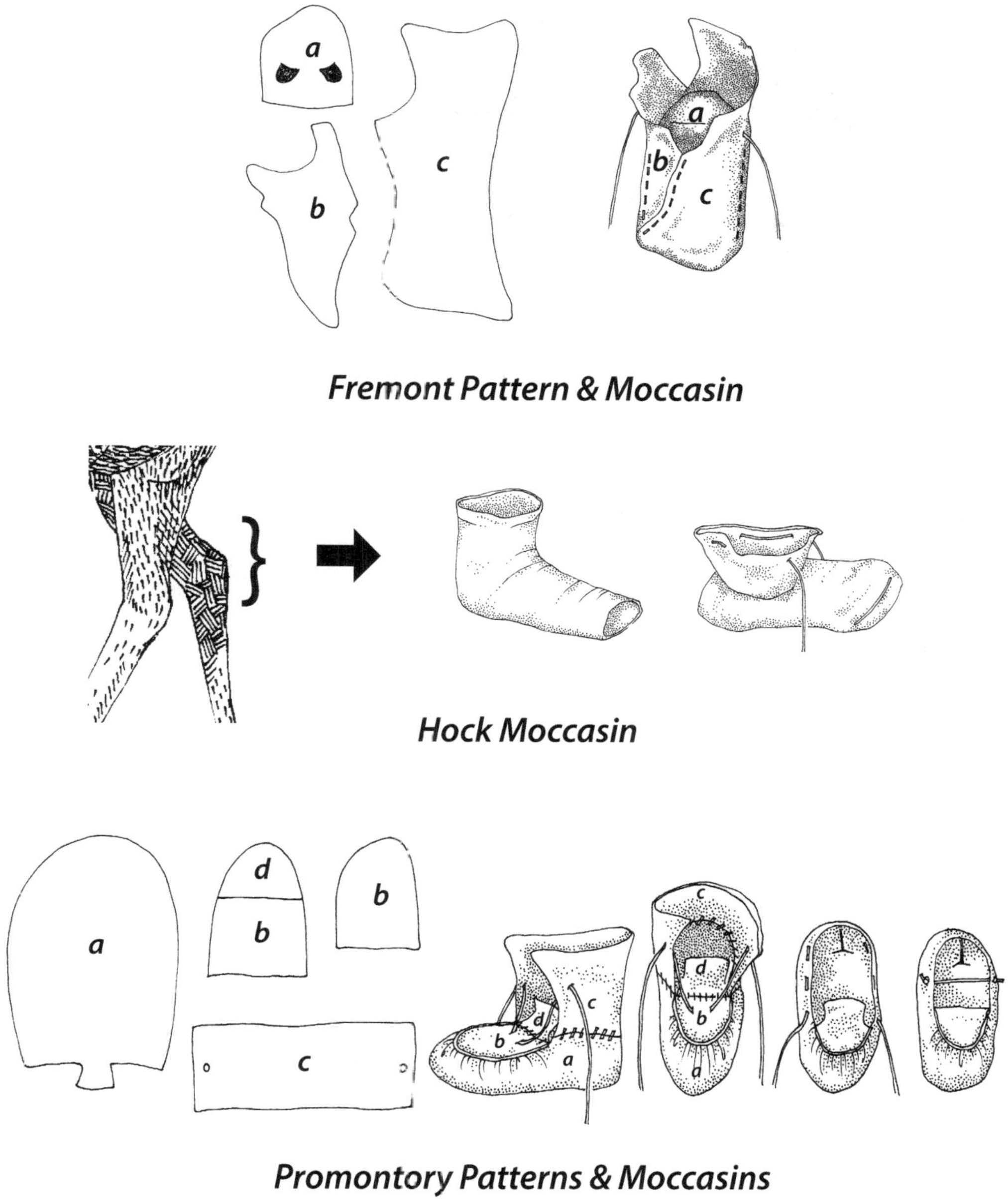

FIGURE 12.3. Fremont, hock, and Promontory moccasin patterns (redrawn from Aikens 1970:103, Figures 63–64; Steward 1937:51, Figure 21). Corresponding letters on the patterns and the moccasins show how the pattern pieces were assembled in the finished moccasin.

did not mention the different construction of 42Bo2 10070 from Cave 2, in BSM style 2(Ab), with a center toe seam. This moccasin is significant in that it means Promontory populations knew both common Subarctic variants from the historic period. Relying upon Hatt, Steward drew his comparisons with northern British Columbia, where Tsimshian, Tlingit, and Tahltan peoples also used BSM 2(Ab), BSM 2(Bb), and BSM 2(Ad) styles early in the twentieth century.[6] The Tlingit and Tsimshian are Northwest Coast peoples who often received moccasins and leggings from inland trade partners such as the Dene Tahltan that Steward mentioned (e.g., Teit 1956).

Compelling prehistoric evidence emerged with the recovery of a low-cut moccasin from the Yukon ice patches (Greer 2005; Hare et al. 2004). This moccasin was left behind during high-altitude hunting on ice patches that are now retreating with climatic change. It has been AMS radiocarbon dated to 1430 ± 40 radiocarbon years BP (Hare et al. 2004). The apron extends farther toward the toe than is typical of most Promontory moccasins, but it remains round-toed, with no center seam, and has a slight gathering or puckering of folds at the toe. The back has a straight seam, but much of the heel is missing. It appears that there is a single stitch at the base of the heel, resembling a T-seam, but which conforms to the BSM 2(Ba) type (a straight seam at the heel). BSM 2(Ab), 2(Bb), and 2(Ba) are all minor variants on one basic plan for making a soft-soled moccasin. Detached moccasins fashioned in the same way as the Promontory moccasins

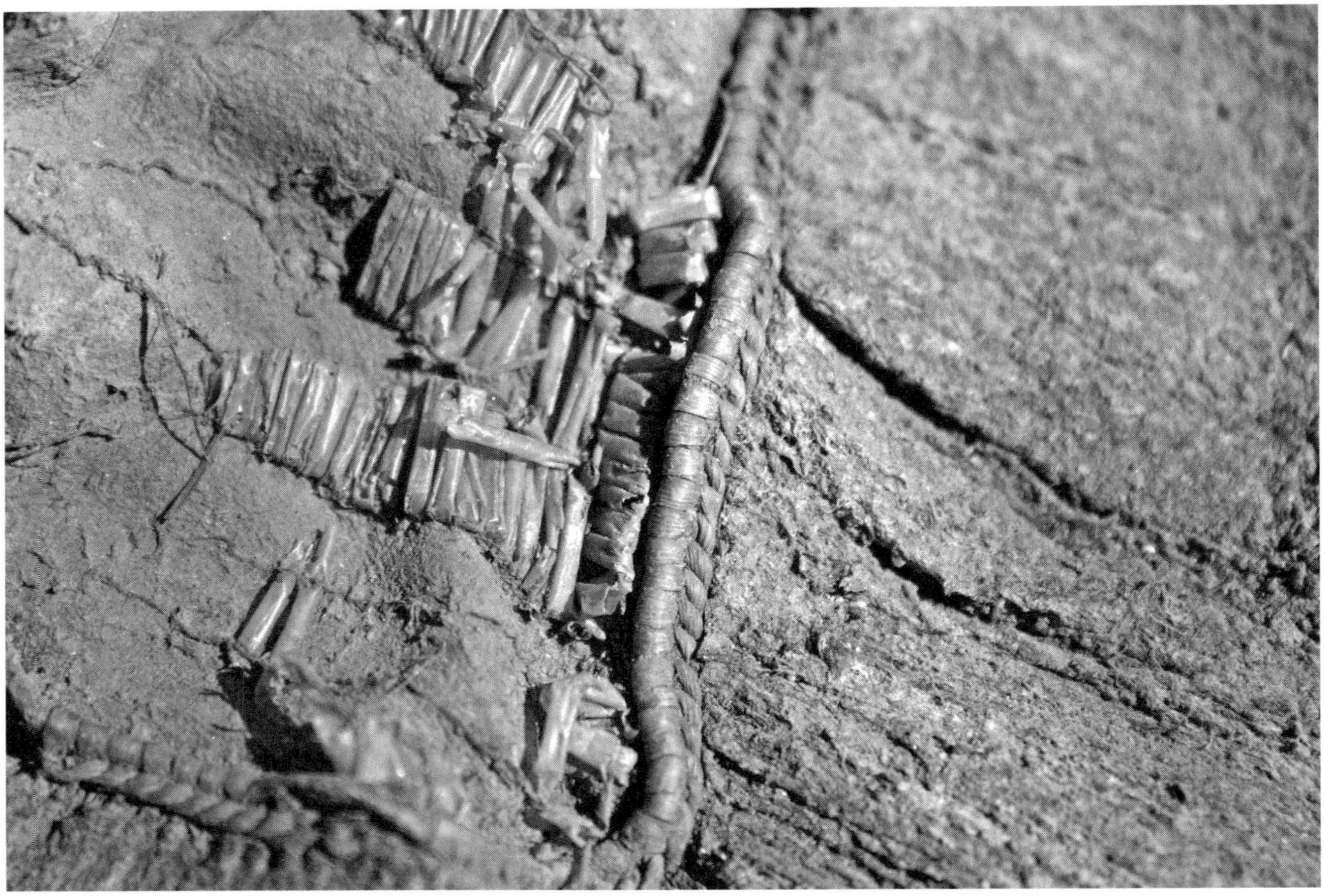

FIGURE 12.4. Sewing details on moccasin 42Bo1 10241 (center of Figure 12.2), Promontory Cave 1 (photograph by the author; courtesy of the Utah Museum of Natural History). Note the delicate fashion in which the sinew catches the leather surface and the manner in which each separate quill segment is individually stitched with sinew. The leather thong piping to the right has been wrapped in basketry material. The person who made this moccasin had consummate sewing skills.

were therefore being made in the Proto-Dene homeland roughly seven centuries prior to the onset of Promontory phase occupation in Caves 1 and 2.

Promontory moccasin decoration is even more intriguing. The Cave 1 moccasin in Figure 12.2 (42Bo1 10241) features exquisite sewing along with porcupine quill appliqué on the apron or vamp (Figure 12.4). There are three remnant, reddish "battleship-shaped" designs on a cream background of eight vertical columns over one horizontal row. The manner of attaching quills, using parallel rows of sinew, is almost identical to that applied by Dene Sųłiné women today in northern Saskatchewan (Reynolds 1977). Yet the overall effect is rather Plains-like and is strongly reminiscent of an early Blackfoot moccasin example from the 1840s, which has similar colors and design (though made in the typical Plains BSM 4 "fold-over" style of construction).[7] This same Promontory moccasin uses a thin cord of leather or welt wrapped in basketry material as piping to cover the seam at the apron, a decorative device characteristic of the Canadian Subarctic (Turner 1976). Piping, involving sinew, basketry material, or quill, was used on nearly half the Promontory moccasins. For this and other Promontory moccasins, the construction template is typical of the Subarctic (most Plains moccasins are of BSM type 4 construction), but the design elements combine Subarctic and Plains decorative ideas.

Steward's recovery of so many moccasins is singular in several ways. The large number of moccasins is highly suggestive of sustained activity from a population with a refined sewing tradition, not the stray deposition of an occasional item of footwear. One could hardly choose a better medium for the expression of ethnicity: in many Subarctic and Plains communities, moccasins are highly visible means for women to show both skill levels and the degree of care they provide for family members. Advanced use of moccasin patterns and decorative motifs requires lengthy apprenticeship; refined sewing reflects highly specific applications of fine motor skills little susceptible to diffusion (cf. Adovasio and Pedler's [1994] views on the diagnostic value of basketry). The moccasins speak unequivocally of northern origins. They are situated in a geographic locale and time frame where we have every expectation that Apachean ancestors could be present and, correspondingly, little realistic expectation that Plains or Subarctic Algonquians would be present.

Future research concerning our large AMS sample for moccasins will allow evaluation of key trends including age structure (using the precise relationships among moccasin size, foot size,

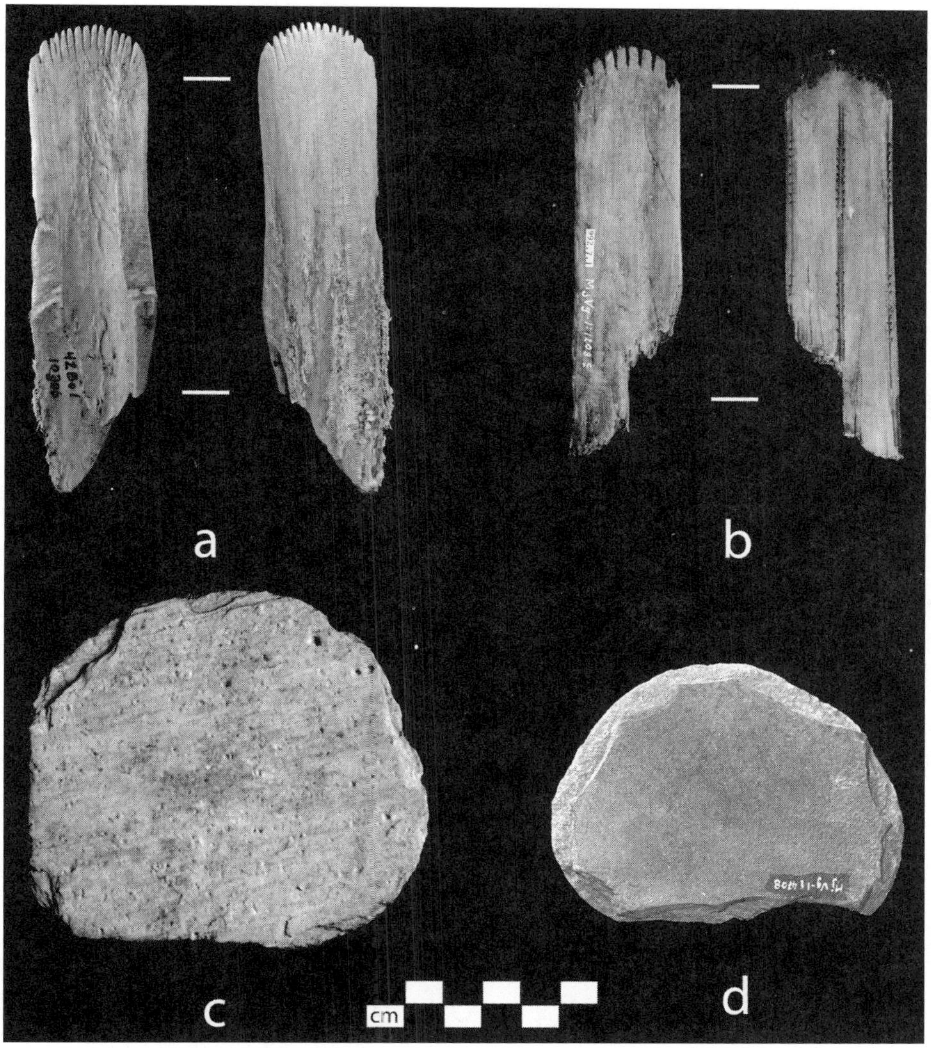

FIGURE 12.5. Hide-working implements from the Promontory Caves and the Yukon, Canada: (a) both faces of a bone flesher from Promontory Cave 1 (photograph by the author; courtesy of the Utah Museum of Natural History); (b) both faces of a bone flesher from the Rat Indian Creek site, Yukon Territory, Canada; (c) a D-shaped *chi-tho* or tabular scraper from Promontory Cave 5; (d) a D-shaped tabular scraper from the Rat Indian Creek site (MjVg-1) in present-day Vuntut Gwich'in country ([d] courtesy of Raymond Le Blanc). These implements "bracket" the hide production process, from the initial preparation of green hides (fleshers) to the final softening of high-quality leather resembling suede (tabular scrapers).

stature, and age) and refinement in sewing technique (as measured through indexes such as stitches per centimeter). Simple inspection of the collections, along with Steward's own table of moccasin dimensions, makes it clear that subadults and children had worn a majority of the moccasins in the caves. This (and the sometimes elaborate nature of the sewing and decoration) suggests that those living in the Promontory Caves were thriving. Yet more detailed hypothesis testing of predictions based on hunter-gatherer group-forming principles and better-developed models of the migration process will be possible (e.g., Anthony 1997; Ives 1998).

The moccasins are not the only northern influences in the Promontory assemblages that we can identify today. D-shaped, bifacially blunted tabular scrapers, sometimes referred to as *chi-thos* by Subarctic archaeologists, also occur in the Promontory phase assemblages (Figure 12.5). Similar implements occur widely in earlier temporal horizons in western North America, including the Great Basin. As far as I know, however, they are not typical of Fremont assemblages. At major sites such as Danger and Hogup caves, they seem to be absent from assemblages for two or more millennia preceding the Promontory phase era. They remain in use in the Canadian Subarctic even today (where they are closely associated with the final softening of high-quality leather) and are known from intervening northern Plains sites (Aikens 1970; Baillargeon 2010; Dyck and Morlan 1995; Jennings 1957; Thompson 1994). Steward's (1937:34) diagram of a piece of netting also shows a pattern of knotless weaving identical to that applied in unique Dene hunting bags (Marie and

Thompson 2004). It is quite likely that continued attention to the Promontory collections will result in other insights linking the two regions.

External Evidence of Long-Range Contacts

We should also consider external dimensions of the Promontory phenomenon that one would expect to exist if it did represent a migrating Dene population. Rock art and obsidian source data each provide fruitful areas of inquiry.

Steward illustrated a series of images from within Promontory Cave 1. These included distinctive triangular-bodied figures with diminished legs (in one case holding ritual paraphernalia) and headdresses. Such figures are common in Fremont-aged rock art in Utah (e.g., Schaafsma 1971). There are virtually identical pictographs (an individual figure and line of dancers, co-occurring with a flute player figure) at Grotto Canyon in southwestern Alberta (Magne and Klassen 2002). Such figures are unique in Alberta rock art. The individuals who made the Grotto Canyon art knew exactly how such art was being made in Utah. The conclusion that those individuals either came from the south or had visited Utah is difficult to avoid. Magne and Klassen (2002) prefer as an explanation Hopi oral traditions of a visit to the land of ice and snow by ancestral beings. More direct Fremont connections—possibly through Dene intermediaries—would provide equally (if not more) plausible interpretations. However we interpret the reasons for the presence of this rock art in Alberta, it definitely shows that links existed between geographic areas likely to have been involved in Apachean migration, at a time when Apachean presence is predicted.

Promontory phase obsidian use is also consonant with both a discontinuity in the archaeological record and the geography of Apachean migration. Janetski (1994:172–173) has shown that obsidian sources used in Fremont times in eastern Utah were typically situated to the south (Mineral Mountain and Black Rock). Obsidian found at Promontory phase sites in Utah Valley and southern Great Salt Lake locations involved a striking shift to primarily northern sources, particularly Malad. Malad is the predominant Late Prehistoric obsidian and has a source area roughly 80 km north of Promontory Point. The five flakes and one Desert Side-notched point from Promontory Cave 1 recently analyzed also all come from the Malad source (J. Janetski, personal communication 2011). This suggests that Promontory phase peoples had either northern socioeconomic connections or an intimate knowledge of resources in those regions, patterns consistent with an argument that Apachean ancestors moved into the northern Wasatch Front from the north. Arkush (2010) has reported late-period bison kill and processing sites in Curlew National Grassland, where Promontory pottery is present, immediately to the north of Promontory Point and west of the Malad obsidian source in south-central Idaho.

Malad obsidian also occurs on the central and southern Plains, where it has a strong north–south orientation through most of the Holocene (Baugh and Nelson 1987; Thompson 2004). Texas occurrences of Malad obsidian peak in the fourteenth century but are absent after AD 1450, when east–west interaction with New Mexico obsidian sources dominated (Hester 2007). Population movement, down-the-line trade, and trade involving more distant redistributive centers could all have created the multimodal fall-off curve Thompson (2004) illustrates for Malad obsidian. Whichever alternatives were involved, the late-period Malad distribution shows that Promontory phase communities participated in interaction spheres that extended both to the north and far to the south.

Recasting the Promontory Evidence

Steward's suspicion that the Promontory Cave assemblages could be of Dene origin remains as well warranted today as it was in the 1930s. There are clear signs of discontinuity between Fremont and Promontory phase assemblages. These involve clothing, ceramics, lithics, and a number of other areas not considered here, such as burial traditions (Janetski 1994). Specific characteristics of the Promontory phase assemblage do have links to the Subarctic and northern Plains world, just as we would expect for a segment of the migrating Apachean population. And just as Sapir (1936) suggested, the Promontory Caves provide abundant evidence for assimilation of a regional material culture prior to Apachean arrival in the Southwest.

Drawing together these empirical threads to interpret the thirteenth-century world of the northeastern Great Basin, then, there would seem to be considerable impetus to think along the following lines. Small bands from the southwestern edge of an expanding Proto-Apachean population, long adept at communal bison hunting from their Subarctic roots and a northern Plains sojourn, probed toward the Great Salt Lake area prior to AD 1200. Obsidian and other evidence suggest that they engaged in bison hunting in Idaho, in valley systems north of Promontory Point, and in Great Salt Lake environs. At Promontory Point, they established themselves in caves seldom used or even uninhabited in previous eras, where they carried out all facets of a domestic winter life, which included hunting, gaming, ceremonies, and intensive hide preparation and sewing, most especially of moccasins. There is every reason to suspect that they interacted with transitional Fremont populations, intermarrying as well as receiving in trade or taking up elements of surrounding material culture in the course of the thirteenth century. If early Spanish contact literature of the sixteenth century is any guide, Dene inhabitants of Promontory Point very likely traded bison products (including robes, hide, leather, sewn garments, and dried meat provisions). There they left abundant traces of successful hunting; their population grew with children and subadults; and there was time for gaming and intricate sewing.

Their Fremont neighbors, a polyethnic community sharing elements of a material culture sphere, were experiencing a different series of events. Paleoenvironmental data strongly suggest that each of the eleventh, twelfth, and thirteenth centuries saw profound episodes of drought (Benson et al. 2007). By AD 1150 maize horticulture had ceased to be important for Fremont population diets; just after AD 1300 Fremont material culture would cease to exist (Coltrain and Leavitt 2002). In more southerly Fremont areas, some populations withdrew deeper into the retracting Puebloan world. In the northeastern quadrant of the Great Basin, always a region with variant subsistence in which hunting and gathering had a larger role, different choices became necessary. If Fremont populations did not simply vanish at the farthest edge of the periphery Lekson (this volume) considers, they may have had to become Great Basin hunter-gatherers. Other options nevertheless existed; among them are the deliberate adoption of a communal bison-hunting lifestyle and movement out of the northeastern Great Basin (cf. Butler 1983:1; Ives 1990:67, 351, 2003; Mooney 1898; Ortman 2009, 2010).

Conclusions

The archaeological evidence suggests that an extraordinary degree of socioeconomic fluidity affected the eastern edge of the Great Basin for the AD 1100–1600 interval. Anthony's (1997) admonition—that cultures do not migrate, but, rather, people do—may provide considerable help in penetrating the enigma that has surrounded the Promontory Culture or phase. One-to-one "mapping" of archaeological units and cultural identities, resulting in the exclusion of one perspective in favor of another, will not serve us well in understanding this fateful period. Thus, the discovery of "one-rod-and-bundle" basketry in Promontory Cave 1 need not mean that the Promontory phase there is Fremont but, rather, that a Fremont trade item entered the cave or a person familiar with Fremont basketry made and used that object in the cave. Similarly, the evocative evidence provided by the Promontory moccasins does not mean that a purely Dene population resided there: given the asymmetries Anthony (1990) described for initial migratory populations (a greater predominance of young males), one would expect that young women from other societies might well have been incorporated in this population, much as the language, genetic, and oral tradition evidence tells us, and especially given the state of flux we anticipate as the Fremont Culture disintegrated.

While the balance of evidence from the Promontory Caves does suggest that it may have involved a predominantly Proto-Apachean population, the Promontory phase itself has a greater geographic spread. The Promontory Cave materials *can* sustain sophisticated hypothesis testing regarding migration, but where preservation is poorer, the discovery of Promontory pottery is the most reliable means to identify this phase. Just as many of our larger archaeological phase or complex constructs may actually have been polyethnic in reality, so too may this have been true of the Promontory phase. This key ceramic diagnostic might also have been made by a variety of ethnicities, some Apachean and some of Fremont or other heritages, encouraging us to focus not purely on cultural identities but on their interaction. Whether one agrees with these ideas or not, by *directly* engaging with Steward's proposition that the Promontory Caves were inhabited by ancestral Apacheans, we may shed further light on a period of fascinating change in the larger region.

Acknowledgments

I thank Joel Janetski for his invitation to participate in this volume. Staff members of the Utah Museum of Natural History, most particularly Michelle Knoll, Kathy Kankainen, Glenna Nielsen-Grimm and Duncan Metcalfe, provided a warm welcome and much-valued assistance. Duane Froese and Sally Rice, Michael Billinger, Fiona Brock, Christopher Ramsey, Beth Shapiro, David Rhode, Brooke Arkush, Lindsay Johansson, Grant Smith, and Joel Janetski are part of a larger Promontory research project that has shaped my views. We are most grateful to George and Kumeroa Chournos for providing access to the Promontory Caves and their many kindnesses. Virginia Kerns directed me to correspondence regarding Steward's Promontory work; Raymond Le Blanc kindly provided the Yukon *chi-tho* image. Justina Smith made the moccasin pattern drawings. Sunday Eiselt and Tom Rocek provided excellent editorial suggestions. I thank the Archaeological Survey of Alberta, Duane Froese, and Sally Rice for significant support for the early stages of this project; the Social Sciences and Humanities Research Council of Canada (Standard Research Grant 410-2010-0480) funded our recent efforts.

Notes

1. Julian Steward to A. L. Kroeber, 8 October and 10 December 1930, A. L. Kroeber Papers, MSS C-B 925, accession 139, Bancroft Library, University of California, Berkeley.
2. The dates Gunnerson reported for Dismal River sites in Nebraska are later than both Promontory Point perishables and ceramic residues I mention in the section following. Gilmore and Larmore (2005) report dates for Dismal River ceramics at Eureka Ridge in Colorado that are contemporaneous with residue dates from Promontory pottery in Caves 1 and 2 but two to three centuries younger than Promontory phase perishables in these caves. The idea that at least some facets of the Dismal River Aspect could flow from Promontory antecedents is worth further evaluation.
3. In deference to expressed wishes of a number of Canadian Dene, Navajo, and Apache individuals, I will use the term *Dene* in reference to all members of the languages that have typically been referred to as "Athapaskan."
4. This would happen later with Tsuu T'ina (Sarsi) people and in fact took place repeatedly for all language families that came into contact with the Plains periphery.
5. There are other Promontory-style moccasins in the Harvard Peabody collections, in the Brigham Young University collections, and in private hands. We found 10 additional moccasins in the 2011 excavations in Cave 1; remaining deposits there will hold yet more moccasins.
6. The 2(Ad) style has the same construction but with a T-shaped center seam at the toe as well.
7. Records of *The Spirit Sings International Exhibition*, 1988, Glenbow Museum, Calgary, item QA85AM33 (P3205-192), from the British Museum: Museum of Mankind, Burlington Gardens, London.

References Cited

Adovasio, J. M., and David R. Pedler

1994 A Tisket, a Tasket: Looking at the Numic Speakers Through the "Lens" of a Basket. In *Across the Desert West: Human Population Movement and the Expansion of the Numa*, edited by David B. Madsen and David Rhode, pp. 114–123. University of Utah Press, Salt Lake City.

Aikens, C. Melvin

1966 *Fremont–Promontory–Plains Relationships, Including a Report of Excavations at the Injun Creek and Bear River No. 1 Sites, Northern Utah*. University of Utah Anthropological Papers No. 82. University of Utah Press, Salt Lake City.

1967 Plains Relationships of the Fremont Culture: A Hypothesis. *American Antiquity* 32(2):198–209.

1970 *Hogup Cave*. University of Utah Anthropological Papers No. 93. University of Utah Press, Salt Lake City.

1972 Fremont Culture: Restatement of Some Problems. *American Antiquity* 37(1):61–66.

Anthony, David W.

1990 Migration in Archaeology: The Baby and the Bathwater. *American Anthropologist* 92(4):895–916.

1997 Prehistoric Migration as Social Process. *BAR International Series* 664:21–32.

Arkush, B. S.

2010 Recent Excavations at 10Oa275: A Big-Game Processing Camp on the Curlew National Grassland, Southeastern Idaho. Paper presented at the 32nd Biennial Great Basin Anthropological Conference, October, Layton.

Baillargeon, Morgan

2010 *North American Aboriginal Hide Tanning. The Act of Transformation and Revival*. Canadian Museum of Civilization, Mercury Series, Ethnology, 146. Hull.

Baugh, Timothy G., and Frank W. Eddy

1987 Rethinking Apachean Ceramics: The 1985 Southern Athapaskan Ceramics Conference. *American Antiquity* 52(4):793–799.

Baugh, Timothy G., and Fred Nelson, Jr.

1987 New Mexico Obsidian Sources and Exchange on the Southern Plains. *Journal of Field Archaeology* 14(3):313–329.

Benson, Larry V., Michael S. Berry, Edward A. Jolie, Jerry D. Spangler, David W. Stahlee, and Eugene M. Hattori

2007 Possible Impacts of Early-11th-, Middle-12th-, and Late-13th-Century Droughts on Western Native Americans and the Mississippian Cahokians. *Quaternary Science Review* 26:336–350.

Box Elder News

1913 Cummings Tells of Great Cave at Promontory Point. 1 May.

Brugge, David M.

1994 Post-Contact Demographic Trends in New Mexico. Special issue, "Artifacts, Shrines and Pueblos: Papers in Honor of Gordon Page," edited by Meliha S. Duran and David T. Kirkpatrick. *Archaeological Society of New Mexico* 20:49–60.

2003 DNA and Ancient Demography. Special issue, "Climbing the Rocks: Papers in Honor of Helen and Jay Croty," edited by Regge N. Wiseman, Thomas C. O'Laughlin, and Cordelia T. Snow. *Archaeological Society of New Mexico* 29:49–56.

2006 When Were the Navajos? Special issue, "Southwestern Interludes: Papers in Honor of Charlotte J. and Theodore R. Frisbe," edited by Regge N. Wiseman, Thomas C. O'Laughlin, and Cordelia T. Snow. *Archaeological Society of New Mexico* 32:45–52.

Butler, B. Robert

1983 *The Quest for the Historic Fremont and a Guide to the Prehistoric Pottery of Southern Idaho*. Occasional Papers of the Idaho Museum of Natural History No. 33. Pocatello.

Coltrain, Joan B., and Steven W. Leavitt

2002 Climate and Diet in Fremont Prehistory: Economic Variability and Abandonment of Maize Agriculture in the Great Salt Lake Basin. *American Antiquity* 67:453–485.

Driver, Harold R., and William C. Massey

1957 Comparative Studies of North American Indians. *Transactions of the American Philosophical Society* (N.S.) 47(2):165–456.

Dyck, Ian, and Richard G. Morlan

1995 *The Sjovold Site. A River Crossing Campsite in the Northern Plains*. Archaeological Survey of Canada Mercury Series Paper, 151. Canadian Museum of Civilization, Hull.

Fagan, Brian M.

2005 *Ancient North America. The Archaeology of a Continent*. Thames and Hudson, London.

Forsyth, Donald W.

1986 Post-Formative Ceramics in the Eastern Great Basin. *Journal of California and Great Basin Anthropology* 8(2):180–203.

Gilmore, Kevin P., and Sean Larmore

2005 *Archaeological Investigations at Eureka Ridge (5TL3296), Teller County, Colorado*. Report prepared for the Colorado Historical Society and the U.S. Department of Agriculture Forest Service. Site Assessment Grant Project No. 2004-AS-010. RMC Consultants Inc., Lakewood, Colorado.

Golla, Victor

2008 Discussant remarks at "Ways of Becoming: Dynamic Processes in the Creation of Athapaskan Identities and Landscapes" Symposium, 73rd Annual Meeting of the Society for American Archaeology, March 26–30, Vancouver, Canada.

Greer, Sheila

2005 *Ice Patch 2*. Carcross/Tagish First Nation, Champagne and Aishihik First Nations, Kluane First Nation, Kwanlin Dun First Nation, Ta'an Kwach'an Council, and Teslin Tlingit Council. Unpaginated pamphlet.

Gunnerson, James H.

1956 Plains–Promontory Relationships. *American Antiquity* 22(1): 69–72.

Hare, P. Gregory, Sheila Greer, Ruth Gotthardt, Richard Farnell, Vandy Bowyer, Charles Schweger, and Diane Strand

2004 Ethnographic and Archaeological Investigations of Alpine Ice Patches in Southwest Yukon, Canada. *Arctic* 57(3):260–272.

Hatt, Gudmund

1916 Moccasins and Their Relation to Arctic Footwear. *Memoirs of the American Anthropological Association* 3(3):149–250.

Hester, Thomas R.

2007 Archeological Roots. Discovery: Research and Scholarship at the University of Texas at Austin. Electronic document, http://www.utexas.edu/opa/pubs/discovery/ disc2000v15n3 /disc_archeology.html, accessed April 2007.

Holve, Steve, Barbara Friedman, H. Eugene Hoyme, Theodore J. Tarby, Sharon J. Johnstone, Robert P. Erickson, Carol L. Clericuzio, and Christopher Cunniff

2003 Athabascan Brainstem Dysgenesis Syndrome. *American Journal of Medical Genetics* 120A:169–173.

Honigmann, John J.

1975 Psychological Traits in Athapaskan Culture. In *Proceedings: Northern Athapaskan Conference, 1971*, pp. 545–576. National

Museum of Man Mercury Series, Canadian Ethnology Service Vol. 2. Ottawa.

Ives, John W.

1990 *A Theory of Northern Athapaskan Prehistory*. Westview Press, Boulder; and University of Calgary Press, Calgary.

1998 Developmental Processes in the Pre-Contact History of Athapaskan, Algonquian and Numic Kin Systems. In *Transformations of Kinship, the Round Table: Dravidian, Iroquois and Crow-Omaha Kinship Systems*, edited by Maurice Godelier, Thomas R. Trautmann, and Franklin Tjon Sie Fat, pp. 94–139. Smithsonian Institution Press, Washington, D.C.

2003 Alberta, Athapaskans and Apachean Origins. In *Archaeology in Alberta: A View from the New Millennium*, edited by Jack W. Brink and John F. Dormaar, pp. 256–289. Archaeological Society of Alberta, Medicine Hat.

2007 Insights into the Apachean Transition from the Subarctic Using Ceramic and Food Term Etymologies. Paper presented at "Ceramics, Mobility and Interactions in Late Prehistory," organized by Margaret Beck, 72nd Annual Meeting of the Society for American Archaeology, Austin.

2010 Dene-Yeniseian, Migration and Prehistory. Special issue, "The Dene-Yeniseian Hypothesis," edited by J. Kari and B. Potter. *Anthropological Papers of the University of Alaska* 5(1–2):324–334.

Ives, John W., Sally Rice, and Stephanie Heming

2002 On the Dispersal of Athapaskan Peoples in Western North America. Paper presented at ARCLING II: The Second Conference on the Archaeology and Linguistics of Australia, National Museum of Australia and the Australian Institute of Aboriginal and Torres Strait Islander Studies, October 1–4, Canberra.

Janetski, Joel

1994 Recent Transitions in the Eastern Great Basin: The Archaeological Record. In *Across the Desert West: Human Population Movement and the Expansion of the Numa*, edited by David B. Madsen and David Rhode, pp. 157–178. University of Utah Press, Salt Lake City.

Janetski, Joel, and Grant C. Smith

2007 *Hunter-Gatherer Archaeology in Utah Valley*. Occasional Paper No. 12. Museum of Peoples and Cultures, Brigham Young University, Provo.

Jennings, Jesse D.

1957 *Danger Cave*. University of Utah Anthropological Papers No. 27. University of Utah Press, Salt Lake City.

Kerns, Virginia

2003 *Scenes from the High Desert. Julian Steward's Life and Theory*. University of Illinois Press, Urbana.

Krauss, Michael E., and Victor K. Golla

1981 Northern Athapaskan Languages. In *Subarctic*, edited by June Helm, pp. 67–85. Handbook of North American Indians, Vol. 6. Smithsonian Institution Press, Washington, D.C.

Li Lanying, Moshous Despina, Zhou Yanguin, Wang Junhua, Xie Gang, Eduardo Salido, Diana Hu, Jean-Pierre de Villartay, and Morton J. Cowan

2002 A Founder Mutation in Artemis, an SNM1-Like Protein, Causes SCID in Athabascan-Speaking Native Americans. *Journal of Immunology* 168(12):6323–6329.

Li Lanying, Dennis Drayna, Diana Hu, Anthony Hayward, Sheila Gahagan, Henry Pabst, and Morton J. Cowan

1998 The Gene for Severe Combined Immunodeficiency Disease in Athabascan-Speaking Native Americans Is Located on Chromosome 10p. *American Journal of Human Genetics* 62: 136–144.

Madsen, David B.

1989 *Exploring the Fremont*. University of Utah Occasional Paper No. 8. Salt Lake City.

Magne, Martin P. R., and Michael Klassen

2002 A Possible Fluteplayer Pictograph Site near Exshaw, Alberta. *Canadian Journal of Archaeology* 26(1):1–24.

Magne, Martin P. R., and R. G. Matson

2010 Moving On: Expanding Perspectives on Athapaskan Migration. *Canadian Journal of Archaeology* 34(2):212–239.

Malhi, Ripan, Angelica Gonzalez-Oliver, Kari Britt Schroeder, Brian M. Kemp, Jonathan A. Greenberg, Solomon Z. Dobrowski, David Glenn Smith, Andres Resendez, Tatiana Karafet, Michael Hammer, Stephen Zegura, and Tatiana Brovko

2008 Distribution of Y Chromosomes Among Native North Americans: A Study of Athapaskan Population History. *American Journal of Physical Anthropology* 137:412–424.

Malhi, Ripan S., Holly M. Mortensen, Jason A. Eshleman, Brian M. Kemp, Joseph G. Lorenz, Frederika A. Kaestle, John R. Johnson, Clara Gorodezky, and David Glenn Smith

2003 Native American mtDNA Prehistory in the American Southwest. *American Journal of Physical Anthropology* 120:108–124.

Marie, Suzan, and Judy Thompson

2004 *Whadǫǫ Tehmį. Long-Ago People's Packsack. Dene Babiche Bags: Tradition and Revival*. Canadian Museum of Civilization, Mercury Series, Ethnology Paper, 141. Hull.

Marwitt, John P.

1973 *Median Village and Fremont Culture Regional Variation*. University of Utah Anthropological Papers No. 95. University of Utah Press, Salt Lake City.

Matson, R. G., and Martin P. R. Magne

2007 *Athapaskan Migrations. The Archaeology of Eagle Lake, British Columbia*. University of Arizona Press, Tucson.

Mooney, James

1898 *Calendar History of the Kiowa Indians*. 17th Annual Report of the Bureau of American Ethnology. Government Printing Office, Washington, D.C.

Ortman, S. G.

2009 Genes, Language and Culture in Tewa Ethnogenesis, AD 1150–1400. Unpublished Ph.D. dissertation, Arizona State University.

2010 Kiowa Odyssey: Evidence of a Colorado Plateau Origin of the Kiowa Speech Community. Paper presented at the 32nd Great Basin Anthropological Conference, October 20–23, Layton.

Reichard, Gladys A.

1928 *Social Life of Navajo Indians*. Columbia University Press, New York.

Reynolds, Marge

1977 *Dene Arts and Crafts*. Saskatchewan Indian Cultural College, Saskatoon.

Sapir, Edward

1936 Internal Linguistic Evidence Suggestive of the Northern Origin of the Navaho. *American Anthropologist* 38:224–235.

Schaafsma, P.

1971 *Rock Art of Utah*. Papers of the Peabody Museum of Archaeology and Ethnology Vol. 65. Harvard University, Cambridge.

Simms, Stephen R.

1986 New Evidence for Fremont Adaptive Diversity. *Journal of California and Great Basin Anthropology* 8:204–216.

2008 *Ancient Peoples of the Great Basin and Colorado Plateau*. Left Coast Press, Walnut Creek.

Simms, Stephen R., Jason R. Bright, and Andrew Ugan
1997 Plain-Ware Ceramics and Residential Mobility: A Case Study from the Great Basin. *Journal of Archaeological Science* 24: 779–792.

Smith, Grant C.
2004 Promontory Ware or Promontory Gray? Revisiting the Classification Problems of Eastern Great Basin Ceramics. Unpublished Master's thesis, Department of Anthropology, Brigham Young University.

Steward, Julian
1937 *Ancient Caves of the Great Salt Lake Region*. Bureau of American Ethnology Bulletin, 116. Washington, D.C.
1938 *Basin–Plateau Aboriginal Sociopolitical Groups*. Bureau of American Ethnology Bulletin No. 120. Washington, D.C.
1940 Native Cultures of the Intermontane (Great Basin) Area. In *Essays in Historical Anthropology of North America. Published in Honor of John R. Swanton*, edited by Julian Steward, pp. 445–502. Smithsonian Miscellaneous Collections Vol. 100. Washington, D.C.
1943 *Culture Element Distributions, XXIII: Northern and Gosiute Shoshone*. University of California Publications: Anthropological Records, 8:3. Berkeley.
1955 Review of *Archeological Survey of Western Utah* by Jack R. Rudy. *American Antiquity* 21(1):88–89.
1960 Carrier Acculturation: The Direct Historical Approach. In *Essays in Honor of Paul Radin*, edited by S. Diamond, pp. 732–744. Columbia University Press, New York.

Teit, J. A.
1956 Field Notes on the Tahltan and Kaska Indians: 1912–1915. *Anthropologica* (O.S.) 3:39–171.

Thompson, Judy
1990 *Pride of the Indian Wardrobe. Northern Athapaskan Footwear*. Bata Shoe Museum, University of Toronto Press, Toronto.
1994 *From the Land. Two Hundred Years of Dene Clothing*. Canadian Museum of Civilization, Hull.

Thompson, Randy A.
2004 Trade or Transport: Occurrence of Obsidian from the Malad, Idaho, Source in the Great Plains. Unpublished Master's thesis, Idaho State University.

Turner, Geoffrey
1976 *Hair Embroidery in Siberia and North America*. Occasional Paper on Technology, 7. Pitt Rivers Museum, University of Oxford, Oxford.

Webber, Alika Podolinsky
1989 *North American Indian and Eskimo Footwear. A Typology and Glossary*. Bata Shoe Museum, University of Toronto Press, Toronto.

Wilshusen, Richard H.
2010 The Dine at the Edge of History: Navajo Ethnogenesis in the Northern Southwest, 1500–1750. In *Across a Great Divide: Continuity and Change in Native North American Societies, 1400–1900*, edited by Laura L. Scheiber and Mark D. Mitchell, pp. 192–211. Amerind Studies in Archaeology, University of Arizona Press, Tucson.

Wilson, C. Dean
1996 Protohistoric Ceramics from Sites near Datil, New Mexico. *Pottery Southwest* 23(1):17–23.

Workman, W. B.
1979 The Significance of Volcanism in the Prehistory of Subarctic Northwest North America. In *Volcanic Activity and Human Ecology*, edited by Payson D. Sheets and Donald K. Grayson, pp. 339–371. Academic Press, New York.

13

Rock Art's Century and More

Encounters in the Great Basin and the Northern Southwest

Polly Schaafsma

A possibly little-known fact about Don Fowler is that early in his archaeological career at age 21 he was initiated into the esoteric and "epiphenomenal" world of rock art. As a student member of the University of Utah survey team in Glen Canyon, he chalked—alas!—and photographed for posterity rock art along the Colorado River and in doing so became a participant in the ground floor business of taking rock art seriously in the Southwest (Figure 13.1). It was during that era that rock art was "officially" pursued (by means of government funding) as a component of the archaeological record deemed of value as an avenue to investigating the past. Recently Don has supported rock art research as the founding president of the Nevada Rock Art Foundation board, serving for 10 years. Kay Fowler also served as a founding board member. In concert with the foundation, Don organized a public outreach lecture series promoting rock art on a worldwide scale.

Rock art is a visual legacy that embraces the symbols and metaphors of cosmologies and worldviews, expressing cultural values and social concerns. Paintings and carvings on stone communicate and reaffirm through time the conceptual universes of people who left other traces of their existence via stone tools, pottery, and the remains of their domiciles across the landscape of the American West (and indeed all over the world). Although these are not *l'art pour l'art* in a functional sense, people frequently projected their aesthetic principals into these graphic productions, and these qualities continue to move and capture us as observers, who are distant in time, with different cultural baggage. This chapter reviews how archaeologists and others have addressed rock art over the past hundred years or more and how these studies have contributed, fueled by heated debates, to our understanding (and misunderstanding) of the peoples of the Great Basin and the northern Colorado Plateau. The resulting picture is painted with the proverbial "broad brush," highlighting significant works and of necessity overlooking others worthy of consideration elsewhere.

Before the 1960s

Images in the "wild"—and often located apart from other traces of prehistoric activity—did not fail to grab the attention of a few early and perceptually adventurous scholars and residents of the Great Basin and the Colorado Plateau. Beginning in the late nineteenth century throughout eastern Utah, spectacular images of persons in heraldic garb were described by various scholars and members of exploratory and archaeological expeditions, among them Harvard's Claflin-Emerson Expedition (1928–1929). In 1893 Garrick Mallery astutely observed that, as opposed to other imagery (i.e., pictographs) he described, rock art had the unique characteristic of being fixed in place, although it was "less susceptible of interpretations" (1893:I:vii). In the late 1800s and early 1900s, methods for approaching its meaning and function had not been devised, to say nothing of a strategy for ordering the vast amount of seemingly chaotic imagery strewn across a disheveled topography. Not unexpectedly, rock art was often subject to unbridled interpretation. Julian H. Steward (1937), a pioneer in giving credibility to rock art research, devoted several pages to enumerating prevailing misconceptions.

Claflin-Emerson Expedition member Noel Morss (1931:34–42), in his landmark monograph in which he defined the Fremont culture, included summary descriptions and thoughtful reviews of the regional rock art. Morss notes that they had encountered "abundant pictographs of distinctive types" and that all the cultural remains from this part of Utah "showed consistently a degree of divergence from corresponding features of orthodox [meaning Southwestern] cultures" (1931:xviii). Morss drew no distinction between Fremont and Barrier Canyon Style rock art found in the same region. Much later, however, Gunnerson (1969:158–159) distinguished what is now known as the Barrier Canyon Style as a "second style." He (1969:159, Figure 31A) also observed that a small panel of painted and abraded human forms in an isolated location in Barrier Canyon showed a close resemblance to figurines of Fremont age, with characteristics

FIGURE 13.1. Don Fowler (right) and Richard Ross (left) chalking rock art in Glen Canyon in 1959 (photograph by W. J. Owens; courtesy of Don D. Fowler; gift of W. J. Owens).

lacking in the other paintings in the canyon. While distinctions were made, the possibility of an Archaic component to the rock art was not yet considered (see also Malouf 1941).

In the 1950s, Utah rock art was described by Foster (1954, 1958), Hunt (1953), and Wormington (1955). Meanwhile, Steward's (1929, 1937, 1941) organizational efforts on both a regional and a general basis, plotting element distributions and a preliminary ordering of rock art into style categories, set the stage for work that followed.

The 1960s Through the 1980s and Beyond—Mapping Time and Space

During the 1960s, large-scale professional rock art projects were launched. Rock art data collection, description, and classification began taking place on an unprecedented scale, the aim being to establish a solid empirical record. This research resulted in finer-grained regional assessments designed to organize huge rock art databases. The information generated raised new questions regarding more dynamic aspects of culture histories and interactions and how sites functioned. The development of religious traditions made visible via iconography and style captured the interest of professional as well as avocational archaeologists. Significantly, in demonstrating the Archaic age of some rock paintings and engravings, greater time depth for rock art was acknowledged.

Notable is the 1962 Great Basin rock art survey by Heizer and Baumhoff, who viewed their work as an initial attempt at organizing a huge volume of data (see Nissen 1995:68–69). In an effort to be objective and establish scientific credibility, they followed Steward's earlier tack of partially focusing on individual elements and plotting their distributions. Fortunately, Heizer and Baumhoff took their organizational efforts one step further to suggest broader style complexes with regional and temporal implications. In proposing dates between ca. 5000 and 3000 BCE for the distinctive complex of heavily patinated pit-and-groove boulders (Figure 13.2), they vastly expanded previous conceptions of the possible age for Great Basin rock art.

The postulation of these early dates may be viewed as a breakthrough because this was the first time rock art in North America was considered to be older than a couple of thousand years. In addition, Heizer and Baumhoff proposed that designs scratched over older petroglyphs were added by Numic immigrants, an observation that introduced the consideration of culture history and questions about the nature of the social interaction these superimpositions imply. Twenty years later, these social issues were further addressed by Bettinger and Baumhoff (1982:493–495) and more recently by Quinlan and Woody (2003). Heizer and Baumhoff's work in the Great Basin was followed by Von Werlhof (1965), Grant (1968), Heizer and Clewlow (1973), Hedges (1982a), and Nissen (1982; see also Schaafsma 1986 for a synthesis).

Meanwhile on the Colorado Plateau, the government-sponsored Glen Canyon and Navajo Reservoir archaeological "salvage" projects in the San Juan/Colorado river system of the

FIGURE 13.2. Pit-and-groove boulder, Grimes Point, Churchill County, Nevada.

1950s and early 1960s also included rock art notations (Fowler 1959a, 1959b) as well as two monographs synthesizing the collected rock art data (Schaafsma 1963; Turner 1963). At this point in the history of Southwestern archaeology, rock art documentation was suddenly deemed important, perhaps because of an increased awareness of the enormity of the record and the loss that was about to ensue. In regard to Glen Canyon, however, Turner's monograph deals only with the Museum of Northern Arizona's survey area within the Glen Canyon regions, while the University of Utah's rock art records were never the subject of an integrated study. In Glen Canyon, the close association of rock art and other cultural remains in the canyon alcoves facilitated the organization and temporal sequencing of rock art styles, a strategy utilized previously on a much more limited scale in Basketmaker caves by Kidder and Guernsey (1919:192–199). Initially Turner (1963:5–10) described five style categories evident in Glen Canyon and neighboring regions. His extension of these categories into geographically wider areas as horizon styles, however, has been of dubious value. His failure to identify a Basketmaker component in his study area is not necessarily due to its absence but, rather, a lack of recognition (see Turner 1963:Figures 23 and 73). San Juan Basketmaker rock paintings were recorded in the Moqui Canyon drainage by the University of Utah group (sites 42Sa736 and 42Sa383, photo records on file, Utah Museum of Natural History, University of Utah, Salt Lake City). Turner's (1963:7–8) highly significant contribution was identifying Archaic rock art on the Colorado Plateau, named simply "Style 5," in accordance with his Glen Canyon sequencing scheme. I later proposed the more descriptive "Glen Canyon Linear Petroglyph Style" (Schaafsma 1980:72–76). Turner's (1971) original proposed beginning dates at ca. 100 BCE were later revised to ca. 6000–2000 BCE.

Much earlier, the aforementioned Claflin-Emerson Expedition in eastern Utah had photographed a significant number of rock art sites and amassed a photographic collection that contributed substantially to the Donald Scott Rock Art Files at Harvard's Peabody Museum. Over the years, notable additions to the Utah portion of these archives were made by Albert B. Reagan and Jesse Nusbaum, Frank Beckwith, and Dean Brimhall, among others. By 1968 these documents provided the basis for the first overall classification of Utah's rock art (Schaafsma 1971). At the time (1968–1969) the Scott collection was a welcome assemblage of rock art data on Utah. Although by today's standards it was limited (see Spangler 2004:125), it provided sufficient means to describe and initially classify Utah rock art on a statewide basis. The Barrier Canyon Style was distinguished from the Fremont, again opening the door to a much more in-depth perception of the Archaic period. Recently a related but regionally distinct Archaic style, the Grand Canyon Polychrome/Esplanade Style, has been described (Allen 1991; Cole 2004:44–48, 2009:91–96; Schaafsma 1990). Overall, the Archaic rock art on the Colorado Plateau is often spectacular, outstanding in its complexity and detail. The time and effort represented in these productions raise further questions about the social and religious roles of visual imagery within these hunter-gatherer societies.

Throughout the twentieth century, archaeologists have grappled with the cultural/historical questions of Fremont identity and origins (Aikens 1972; Gunnerson 1969:170; Jennings and Norbeck 1955; Marwitt 1986:161–163; Schaafsma 1971:137–144; Wormington 1955). Fremont rock art plays a role in this debate, for a diagnostic of Fremont culture is the distinctive broad-shouldered anthropomorphic figure, featured in rock art from western Colorado to eastern Nevada. This shared icon indicates that a widespread ideology prevailed among populations engaged in regionally diverse economic strategies. With rock art's suggestive ties both to Barrier Canyon and more impressively to Basketmaker art, its roles in Fremont origin issues have been explored by Cole (2004) and me (Schaafsma 1971, 1980, 2008). I propose that the Barrier Canyon, San Juan Basketmaker, and Fremont rock art styles together constitute the Northern Colorado Plateau Tradition, based in changing but loosely linked regional shamanic practices.

As mid-twentieth-century research progressed, terminology issues arose, and even the term *rock art* was periodically questioned as to its appropriateness. A perhaps related issue is whether or not "style" is a useful conceptual tool for categorizing rock art. While not engaging further here in these unresolved (and probably unresolvable) discussions, I can observe that the unabashed art-historical use of style as a tool to classify these graphic data has been indispensable, especially in regard to representational complexes (see Cole 2004; Schaafsma 1980; Turner 1963). Although the use of style categories has been challenged in recent years (Francis 2001; Francis and Loendorf 2002:39–47), even to the point of being called "Euro-American centric" (Francis 2005: 192), the critics *continue* to use similar groupings as organizational principles in their dialogues. In regard to terminology and this conceptual issue, Conkey's general admonishment applies:

> While we may like to think that, with each new approach or paradigm, we have gone beyond what we perceive as failings, weaknesses, and inadequacies in our previous approaches; it is rare if not impossible to start completely anew, to be detached from prior research [2001:273].

While stylistic categories are subject to challenges and adaptations to specific imagery groups, they nevertheless have been and continue to be a very useful method of classifying rock art and assigning temporal order and cultural affinities, the structural underpinnings upon which further questions can be posed.

Familiar among problems in rock art research, of course, is the old bugaboo of chronology. While various strategies exist for determining relative chronologies or associations between rock art styles and datable cultural configurations, some progress is under way in the direct dating of rock paintings (Rowe 2001:150–151). At the same time, efforts to date petroglyphs directly have not been significant. Dorn (2001) cautions that all proposed techniques for dating petroglyphs should be regarded as experimental. As rock art dating bears upon the general considerations of culture histories, including stability, change, and social interactions, as well as issues pertaining to primary and secondary functions of rock art sites, until direct dating is possible, many questions will remain unresolved.

The Interpretation Game: Hunter, Shaman, Mind, and Metaphor

Rock art, multivalent in regard to meaning and function, demands a diversity of explanatory approaches. Approaches to interpreting content or how rock art sites functioned have been (and still are) influenced by the climate of the discipline at any moment. Nevertheless, in the history of rock art research in the Great Basin and on the northern Colorado Plateau, hunting magic and shamanism have predominated as the interpretive models.

At the height of the processual era, when Binford's theoretical vision of an economic base for all human behavior was very much in vogue, a hunting magic function for Great Basin petroglyphs was posited on the basis of their alleged distribution along game trails and near hunting blinds and other points of ambush (Bettinger and Baumhoff 1982:493–495; Grant 1968: 29–42; Heizer and Baumhoff 1959, 1962:210–225; Heizer and Clewlow 1973:4–5; Von Werlhof 1965). In addition, bighorn hunting scenes are described, including those in which animals are being herded into V-shaped blinds (Nissen 1995:71–73). On the Colorado Plateau, a detailed analysis of Fremont mountain sheep hunt scenes with estimated dates between 750 and 1200 CE led Ray Matheny and his collaborators (2004) to propose a hunting narrative interpretation of these depictions. From a Eurocentric, or Western, perspective, these petroglyph scenes are often viewed as celebratory documents of a successful hunt. Although the possibility of simple disguises without any implication of shamanic powers cannot be ruled out (C. Fowler 1986:82), the horned hunters in these renderings, bolstered by much later ethnographic practices in the Great Basin, suggest the possibility of hunt shamans attempting to influence the outcome of a hunt rather than celebrating success (see Keyser and Whitley 2006: 10–15 for parallel examples on the Columbia Plateau). There is the complicating likelihood that hunt scenes represent sympathetic magic—the thesis being that the depiction of a hunt ensures success, that is, picturing the mountain sheep exerts control over its spirit, thus inducing it to comply with being killed. In the latter case, the idea that imagery is invested with power is implicit (see also D'Azevedo 1986:489–491; Fowler and Liljeblad 1986: 452; Liljeblad 1986:645–646; Nissen 1995:72).

More recently, rock art interpretation has been addressed via the lens of the postprocessual framework of cognitive archaeology. Cognitive archaeology, defined as "past ways of thought as inferred from material remains" (Renfrew 1994:3), is applicable here, rock art being the material of interest. In concert with an effort to broaden an understanding of past behavior and thought processes, one goal has been "to show that people had preferences independent of economic necessity" (Zubrow 1994:108; see also Postgate 1994). Accordingly, the hunting/sympathetic magic model has been criticized; authors cite problems of re-

FIGURE 13.3. Hunt scene, Clark County, Nevada.

ducing rock art production to subsistence needs (Quinlan and Woody 2001), a position that recalls Robert Hall's (1977) critique of "econothink." In countering the econothink of the New Archaeology, Hall stated: "Cognitive archaeology begins with the assumption that we cannot really interpret prehistory without making a conscious attempt to understand the nature of humans as symbol-using social animals affectively involved in a perceived world that they have helped to create" (1977:515, in Preucel 2006:149–150). Hall further observes that by compressing our views of the past into an economic model, we are overlooking an array of concerns of interest to anthropology.

Indeed, the postprocessual era has injected a quality of disquieting flexibility and uncomfortable ambiguity into what were previously perceived as straightforward interpretive endeavors. Rock art is a direct expression of conceptual systems and metaphors that are foreign to Euro-American thinkers. Since humans have an innate tendency to think metaphorically (Tilley 1999, in Preucel 2006:143), they communicate metaphors pictorially (Schaafsma 2009; Sekaquaptewa and Washburn 2004), demanding that the archaeologist/interpreter learn to recognize unfamiliar sets of symbolic texts that render literal interpretations suspect (Figure 13.3).

The bighorn sheep itself may have held a metaphorical role in the past as it seems to have in recent ethnographic times (Bettinger 2008:89; Nissen 1995:72–73). According to Whitley (2000:91), in Great Basin hunt scenes, the killed bighorn sheep, or the act of killing, is the metaphor for trance or entering into a trance state. Liljeblad (1986:652) observes that among Western Numic speakers a recurrent tale tells of a wounded animal leading the hunter into an adventure in the lower world. Whether this ethnographic narrative provides a shamanic interpretive model for ancient Great Basin hunting scenes or is a mneumonic device for storytelling can be neither accepted nor discarded at this point. The shamanistic view is espoused by Whitley (1994a, 1994b, 2000; Whitley and Clottes 2005), who draws comparative models from Lewis-Williams's (1986, 1995) analyses of southern San rock art in Africa. Whitley (1994a, 1994b:13–14, 2000: 90–91) states that mountain sheep hunting scenes depicted over millennia were assertions of male dominance and metaphors for vision quest experiences involving identification between a "rain doctor" and his mountain sheep spirit helper.

In addition, a small amount of ethnographic information implies that special curing powers are attributed to mountain sheep, in which case they would have been of singular value to curing shamans. Bettinger (2008:89) mentions that scarce but valued mountain sheep horns and fat are sought for their magical or medicinal purposes in historic times, opening the door to possible associations with shamanic curing practices even earlier. Mountain sheep would come to people in songs along with other animals used in doctoring (Stoffle et al. 2009:38).

FIGURE 13.4. Barrier Canyon Style ritualist holding a snake, as birds and unidentifiable objects fly toward the figure and birds fly about his or her head, Emery County, Utah.

FIGURE 13.5. Basketmaker figures with ducks as or on their heads, San Juan County, Utah.

On the northern Colorado Plateau, lacking any ethnographic connections to Fremont or Archaic rock art, the metaphorical potentials of mountain sheep have not been investigated in great detail. Their oft-repeated role as tutelary spirits (with snakes, birds, and insects) pictured around the heads or at the sides of ethereal anthropomorphic figures in the Barrier Canyon Style exceeds natural models and confirms their role in the spiritual dimension of the world of these hunter-gatherers (Figure 13.4).

Birds and snakes, all featured prominently in Barrier Canyon Style paintings, are liminal creatures that transcend the layered spheres of the natural world (Eliade 1964:65; Schaafsma 1994: 53). Worldwide, the bird-like flight of the soul is one of the core beliefs of shamanism (Furst 1977:2) and has been examined at length as a flight metaphor in the Archaic Pecos River paintings also viewed as having their origins in hunter-gatherer shamanic practices (Turpin 1994). Similarly, I have described flight metaphors in Barrier Canyon Style and Basketmaker rock art where the unnatural associations of birds and anthropomorhic figures suggest travel to the spirit realm (Figure 13.5). The representational content, which includes proposed trance states, spirit helpers, transformational figures, elaborate costuming, and skeletal symbolism in the rock art of the Northern Colorado Plateau Tradition, is broadly characteristic of shamanic ritual and art elsewhere (Furst 1977; Vastokas 1977:99–104). These factors are the bases for hypothesizing shamanic origins for the rock art in this tradition (Schaafsma 1994). Widespread shamanic practices throughout ethnographic North America with probable roots in Asia (Eliade 1964:297–336; Furst 1977; Kelly 1936; Park 1934, 1938; see especially Tedlock 1982:47–53), which involve direct communication with the spirit realm via dreams, visions, or possession, lend a broad canopy of support for the notion that shamanism in American prehistory accounts for a great deal of rock art imagery.

A second argument for ascribing shamanic origins to Great Basin rock art is the widely prevalent abstract imagery thought to depict near-universal neuropsychological experiences of persons in altered states of consciousness (Figure 13.6). First proposed by Reichel-Dolmotoff (1972, 1975) on the basis of ethnographic art of the Colombian Tukano, it was quickly adopted as a facile explanation to account for abstract rock art in general (Blackburn 1977; Hedges 1976, 1982a, 1982b, 1985, 1994; Lewis-Williams 1986, 1995, 1997; Lewis-Williams and Dowson 1988, 1990). Quinlan and Woody (2001:214) point out that the popularity of this proposal in the United States owes much to Whitley's (1992, 1994b, 1998) research in California and the Great Basin. The assumption that all abstract rock art in the Great Basin can be accounted for as pictures of neuropsychological hallucinatory phenomena has been criticized for ignoring the complexities of prehistoric societies, their worldviews, and the multitudinous reasons for rock art production. More direct interpretations must also not be forgotten; modern Washoe see basket designs among the Lagomarsino petroglyphs (Figure 13.7; Quinlan and Woody 2001:214). But then, is this an off-the-cuff response, or are basket designs themselves neuropsychological in origin? According to Kelley Hays-Gilpin (personal communication 2012), it is likely that basket designs *are* concerned with spirit helpers

FIGURE 13.6. Abstract petroglyphs viewed by some researchers as depicting neuropsychological imagery, Lagomarsino, Storey County, Nevada.

FIGURE 13.7. Abstract petroglyphs interpreted by modern Washoe consultants as referring to baskets, Lagomarsino, Storey County, Nevada.

and ritual protections connected with learning basketry techniques during girls' puberty rites. Without further information, the meaning(s) of these petroglyphs remains in the realm of speculation and open to reinterpretation.

Unidimensional shamanic interpretations for rock art in the Great Basin and eastern Utah have recently been challenged (Kitchell 2010; Quinlan 2000), and shamanism as generally operative in North America, denied (Kehoe 2000). A recent discussion about Eurocentric perspectives regarding visionary experiences, mobility between cosmological realms, and a lack of boundaries between waking and dreamed worlds is an important component of this debate. It is observed that Americans are uncomfortable thinking about these aspects of Native American religions "in part because our culture perceives it [them] as irrational" (Francis 2005:194). Thus enters the Eurocentric bias.

Zubrow emphasizes that we must recognize how the cognitive processes of the archaeologist, products of a specific cultural context, influence or limit his or her research:

> Knowledge is culturally processed information, and it is both represented and the basis of action. Prehistoric natives represent knowledge according to a set of cultural rules when making material objects. Similarly, archaeologists represent knowledge according to a modern set of cultural norms and process the information according to another set of cultural rules when they interpret the material objects [1994:107].

As a result, nonshamanic interpretive approaches (see Kitchell 2010:838) potentially bowdlerize or expurgate the meaning of the art, as they reduce it to palatable, simplified, and sanitized explanations grounded in myth, narrative, group rituals, and social niceties and practices devoid of ecstatic trance experiences regarded negatively by outsiders. Meanwhile, citing shamanic roots for this imagery does not exclude narrative and mythic content, nor does it deny rock its function in promoting social cohesion and group identity, alternative functions offered by critics. While recognizing that no approach for interpreting ancient rock art in the Great Basin or on the Colorado Plateau can ever be "proven to be correct" in an absolute sense, the goal is to offer approaches that can be tested against expectations, and shamanism is one likely model.

In sum, I propose that the rock art making up the Northern Colorado Plateau Tradition, based in the complex belief systems of societies in which shamanism played a significant role, communicated esoteric knowledge, thereby promoting a sense of having a modicum of control over a fickle universe. Simultaneously the imagery may have served as a vehicle for documenting and communicating the spiritual journey, verifying group values, and in turn, fostering social stability. This work, created within the boundaries of culturally defined styles, also left the stamp of social identity upon the landscape. It remains to be asked: Were these images created over the course of centuries, or were they made during times of stress when a sense of control was needed to bring the natural and supernatural worlds in line (see Turpin 2011:3)? Down the road, improved dating methods correlated with climatological studies will help rock art researchers tackle these questions.

Socializing the Landscape

As compelling as they may be, hunting and shamanism are only limited approaches to understanding rock art. It is a truism that rock art changes and thereby socializes the sense of place simply by its presence, and the fast-growing awareness of the cultural landscape's role has broadened the field of questions that rock art poses (Christie 2009; Quinlan and Woody 2003:382). Recently researchers have explored the multitudinous ways in which imagery is perceived, its ongoing effects through time, and how it promotes behavioral responses according to cultural dictates.

Contextual site data, including evidence of campsites and indications of other activity in the vicinity of rock art sites, as well as neighboring topographic features come into play in considering the social and ritual roles of landscape imagery (Quinlan and Woody 2001, 2003:374; Rector 1977). Petroglyphs are notably present along established trails and near water holes in the Eastern Mohave. In a primary or secondary social function, Great Basin rock art may have served pragmatically to designate territories, rights to springs, or subsistence resources. For authoring groups it established an identity with place and possibly the resident supernaturals, with whom interaction was deemed to be beneficial (Quinlan and Woody 2003:382). Some of the difficulties faced by Great Basin researchers addressing how rock art functioned are exemplified by Quinlan and Woody (2001, 2003), as they have struggled to suggest its probable roles in the business of everyday living. Assuming contemporaneity between rock art production and habitation sites, they argue that the evidence of domestic activities at rock art sites indicates that the potential audience was nonexclusive and that this rock art was associated with mundane concerns such as promoting identity and social values.

Among the issues pertaining to cognition is how rock art already in place may have been perceived by later peoples. The latter is highly significant in the Great Basin, where rock art created over millennia would have acquired multiple social dimensions and been subject to changing interpretations, as it impacted groups moving into areas previously inhabited by others. In a sense we are dealing with what has been described in the context of cognitive archaeology as the cultural biography of things, and these things—in this case rock art—have agency by virtue of the fact that they affect people (Preucel 2006:15). M. Jane Young (1985, 1988) has examined how Zunis perceive power in rock art, and her findings are not exclusive to the Zuni and have much wider cultural implications. The presence of existing rock art raises a variety of questions pertaining to social relationships with other groups, ancestors perceived or actual, and the perceived conflation of time and place (Young 1988:145–158). Evidence of former inhabitants, including the highly visible rock art, would have contributed to the values ascribed to a place by newcomers, even when knowledge of its intended meaning was lost.

The Use of Ethnography for Understanding the Past

In regard to the value of fragmented ethnographic records and memories (D. Fowler 1986:29; Fowler 2009) to interpret ancient rock art, although helpful, the use of these data is subject to methodological problems, not the least of which are time discrepancies. During the last few decades, some of the interpretive research for the entire chronological sequence of Great Basin rock art has been substantially grounded in references to ethnographic information based on the assumption of an unchanging cultural milieu (Whitley 1992, 1994a, 1994b, 2000). Citing ethnographic support, Whitley states: "Throughout the Mohave Desert (and the remainder of the Great Basin outside California) this rock art was made exclusively by shamans and was intended to illustrate the supernatural events and experiences of their vision quests" (2000:89). The methodologies underlying Whitley's exegesis are properly challenged by Hedges (2001:128–135), who concludes that Whitley's reading of the ethnographic documents "give the appearance of stronger support of the interpretation than really exists" (Hedges 2001:127).

As well stated by Quinlan and Woody: "It is sufficient to note that the available ethnographies and ethnohistories will, and should, continue to provide an important *source of inspiration* for a wide range of divergent theories regarding rock art functions and symbolism" (2003:374; italics mine). They also note that ethnographic support is not likely to represent the full range of rock arts' past cultural contexts.

Strategies for using ethnographic data for the interpretation of ancient rock art need to be clearly supported, and their applicability in every case, evaluated. At stake in the Great Basin is evidence for the longevity of traditions vs. changes over time and across regions. In addition the quality of the ethnographic information needs to be assessed, and ethnographic models often only suggest approaches to interpretation or possibilities.

Ethnographic studies in the Great Basin and elsewhere reveal that among the potential roles of rock art imagery is to evoke the presence of supernatural power or to invoke oral traditions and histories (Liljeblad 1986:644–645; Quinlan and Woody 2003:377; Schaafsma and Tsosie 2009; Young 1988). Rock art production is often attributed to supernatural beings (Liljeblad 1986:Figures 1–2). In several instances contemporary Native Americans living in the Great Basin attribute rock art to Coyote or other supernaturals (Zigmond 1986:409), thus effectively denying any knowledge of its origins by human beings and associating it with otherworldly powers. Whitley (2000:90) argues that these supernatural entities, including the pervasive and powerful Water Babies, were shamans' helpers (see also Park 1934, 1938), thus fitting their role and the rock art into shamanic practices prevalent in the ethnohistoric period. Shoshone curing shamans are said to have visited rock art sites during their vision quests (Lowie 1924:295–296), but it would appear that these were after-the-fact places of power. No rock art was made in these connections, and the use of preexisting sites does not explain the original purpose or the social contexts in which rock art was created.

Similarly on the Colorado Plateau, early eighteenth-century images of Navajo *ye'ii* pictured on cliffs in New Mexico, regardless of their original function, are now viewed by many Navajo as having been produced "like a Xerox" by the Holy People themselves. Accordingly after the world was created and before the Holy People departed to an ethereal realm, they left their likenesses on the rocks so that they would not be forgotten (Schaafsma and Tsosie 2009:18). For the Navajo, these images continue to empower the landscapes where they are found and charge them with a supernatural presence.

Finally, one of the responses to perceived power in rock art, social or supernatural, was (is) to manipulate existing imagery. This may have been done for a variety of reasons including removing perceived malevolent forces, establishing cultural dominance, or even disrupting current activities, destroying the identity of groups still using these sites (Bernardini 2007). Such are the proposed motivations for the obliteration of presumed pre-Numic rock art by later—also presumed—Numic immigrants (Bettinger and Baumhoff 1982:494). In turn, the additions (abrasions, scratches, or new imagery) would have established social prerogatives and a visible sense of "ownership." In an alternative scenario, Basketmaker figures along the San Juan River were destroyed in the mid–twentieth century by neighboring Navajos. This action stripped the rock art images of their perceived power, thought to have been appropriated for use toward malevolent ends (Schaafsma and Tsosie 2009:28–29). Generally on the Colorado Plateau various kinds of manipulation of ancient imagery involved enhancement and continued use, as well as the extraction of parts of images to procure the positive power ascribed to them (Cole 2004:62–65).

Time, Change, and Creative Flux: Rock Art, Revitalization, and Reinvention

Landscapes and routes of travel are increasingly recognized as critical aspects of Native cosmologies (Fowler 2009; Snead et al. 2009), and dialogue with the landscape is a significant rock art function. Taking the available ethnographic material into account, Christensen and Dickey (2001:195–197) relate the abstract Grapevine Style in the southern Mohave Desert to the Patayan ancestors of modern Yuma speakers. They propose that the rock art may be linked to the song cycles that recount specific symbolic landscape features interlacing ideology with place. Stoffle et al. (2009) describe the cultural landscape of the Southern Paiute as a latticework of places linked by travel and song into a synergistic whole.

Rock art sites have a signifiant role in revitalization movements. Currently the Southern Paiute and Chemehuevi are incorporating preexisiting rock art locations into the reconstruction of the Salt Trail as they reestablish their relationships with their traditional landscapes. Beyond the area of concern here but closely related conceptually is the rock art along O'odham trails in the adjacent desert in southern Arizona. Songscapes or landscapes remembered through song are vital to the O'odham and include mention of rock art locations that may or may not be ancestral to them. Rock art images mentioned in song itineraries are referred to as *o'odagah*, or "song marks," signifying the spiritual presence of songs (Darling 2009:74; Darling and Lewis 2007:136–137). Locations marked with petroglyphs infused with the spiritual presence of songs are a vital part of the O'odham cognitive map and cultural landcapes synthesizing space and mental travel.

The reuse and incorporation of ancient sites in current revitalization efforts serve as a model for what was undoubtedly a process enacted again and again through time and throughout the Great Basin, as rock art sites were ascribed new meanings and new roles in an ongoing narrative that linked people to their landscapes and their movement through space. Rock art thus finds a contemporary role in the increasing awareness of Native landscapes and the networks of interrelationships among all of the features therein (Christensen and Dickey 2001:194–196; Stoffle et al. 2009; see also Darling 2009). Today Native peoples are sharing this knowledge in order to retain their identity and stewardship of their cultural heritage.

A Summing Up

As archaeologists we go to great lengths and make admirable endeavors to devise strategies for understanding the past. Exploration, speculation, documentation, and interpretation, none of which are mutually exclusive, characterize the Euro-American interface with rock art in the American West. Over the last century, research has moved from description and classification of archaeological data to ever more sophisticated approaches to understanding the many ways in which imagery functions in the communication of cultural knowledge and establishing identities. Currently postprocessual approaches and synergistic collaborations between archaeologists and Native peoples are redefining or blurring traditional boundaries in Euro-American paradigmatic thinking. As a result, we come to greater insights into the rock art. The years during Don's encounter in the mid-twentieth century with rock art and the "epiphenomenal" mark the unleashing of a critical segment of the archaeological record. Today it is better understood as the material legacy of cognitive processes fundamental to many facets of past behavior and cultural practices. Magnetic in its attraction, elusive in its meaning, little by little, reluctantly, rock art continues to reveal the complexities of the beliefs and social institutions fundamental to the lives and motivations of the ancient people of the Great Basin and the northern Colorado Plateau.

Acknowledgments

Sincere thanks go to Nancy Parezo, Joel Janetski, and James Snead for inviting me to participate in this celebratory volume in Don Fowler's honor. Allison Colburne of the Laboratory of Anthropology Library in Santa Fe was of invaluable assistance in securing all the necessary documents in preparing this chapter. I am most grateful to Kelley Hays-Gilpin and Solveig Turpin for their helpful reviews and suggestions that contributed to a better manuscript. With the exception of Figure 13.1, all photographs are by me.

References Cited

Aikens, C. Melvin
1972 Fremont Culture: Restatement of Some Problems. *American Antiquity* 37(1):61–66.

Allen, Mary K.
1991 Grand Canyon Polychrome Pictographs. *Utah Rock Art* 8:1–16. Salt Lake City.

Bernardini, Wesley
2007 *Hopi History in Stone: The Tutuveni Petroglyph Site.* Arizona State Museum Archaeological Series No. 200. University of Arizona Press, Tucson.

Bettinger, Robert L.
2008 High Altitude Sites in the Great Basin. In *The Great Basin: People and Place in Ancient Times*, edited by Catherine S. Fowler and Don D. Fowler, pp. 87–93. School for Advanced Research Press, Santa Fe, New Mexico.

Bettinger, Robert L., and M. A. Baumhoff
1982 The Numic Spread: Great Basin Cultures in Competition. *American Antiquity* 47(3):485–503.

Blackburn, T. C.
1977 Biopsychological Aspects of Chumash Rock Art. *Journal of California and Great Basin Anthropology* 4:88–94.

Christensen, Don D., and Jerry Dickey
2001 The Grapevine Style of the Eastern Mohave Desert of California and Nevada. *American Indian Rock Art* 27:185–200. Tucson.

Christie, Jessica Joyce (editor)
2009 *Landscapes of Origin in the Americas: Creation Narratives Linking Ancient Places and Present Communities.* University of Alabama Press, Tuscaloosa.

Cole, Sally J.
2004 Origins, Continuities, and Meanings in Barrier Canyon Style Rock Art. In *New Dimensions in Rock Art Studies*, edited by Ray T. Matheny, pp. 7–78. Occasional Paper Series, 9. Museum of Peoples and Cultures, Brigham Young University, Provo.
2009 [1990] *Legacy on Stone.* 2nd ed. Johnson Publishing, Boulder.

Conkey, Margaret W.
2001 Structural and Semiotic Approaches. In *Handbook of Rock Art Research*, edited by David S. Whitley, pp. 273–310. AltaMira Press, New York.

Darling, J. Andrew
2009 O'odham Trails and the Archaeology of Space. In *Landscapes of Movement: Trails, Paths, and Roads in Anthropological Perspective*, edited by James E. Snead, Clark L. Erickson, and J. Andrew Darling, pp. 61–83. University of Pennsylvania Museum of Archaeology and Anthropology, Philadelphia.

Darling, J. Andrew, and Barnaby V. Lewis
2007 Songscapes and Calendar Sticks. In *The Hohokam Millennium*, edited by Suzanne K. Fish and Paul R. Fish, pp. 131–140. School of Advanced Research, Santa Fe, New Mexico.

D'Azevedo, Warren L.
1986 Washoe. In *Handbook of North American Indians, Vol. 11: Great Basin*, edited by Warren L. D'Azevedo, pp. 466–498. Smithsonian Institution, Washington, D.C.

Dorn, Ronald I.
2001 Chronometric Techniques: Engravings. In *Handbook of Rock Art Research*, edited by David S. Whitley, pp. 167–189. AltaMira Press, New York.

Eliade, Mircea
1964 *Shamanism: Archaic Techniques of Ecstasy*. Bollingen Foundation, Princeton University Press, Princeton.

Foster, Gene
1954 Petrographic Art in Glen Canyon. *Plateau* 27(1):6–18. Flagstaff.
1958 Glen Canyon Archaeology: An Informal Reconnaissance. Museum of Northern Arizona No. 287. Manuscript on file, Flagstaff.

Fowler, Catherine S.
1986 Subsistence. In *Handbook of North American Indians, Vol. 11: Great Basin*, edited by Warren L. D'Azevedo, pp. 64–97. Smithsonian Institution, Washington, D.C.
2009 Reconstructing Southern Paiute–Chemehuevi Trails in the Mohave Desert of Southern Nevada and California: Ethnographic Perspectives from the 1930s. In *Landscapes of Movement: Trails, Paths, and Roads in Anthropological Perspective*, edited by James E. Snead, Clark L. Erickson, and J. Andrew Darling, pp. 84–105. University of Pennsylvania Museum of Archaeology and Anthropology, Philadelphia.

Fowler, Catherine S., and Sven Liljeblad
1986 Northern Paiute. In *Handbook of North American Indians, Vol. 11: Great Basin*, edited by Warren L. D'Azevedo, pp. 435–465. Smithsonian Institution, Washington, D.C.

Fowler, Don D.
1959a The Glen Canyon Archaeological Survey. In *The Glen Canyon Survey, Pt. III*, pp. 1–93. University of Utah Papers in Anthropology, 39; Glen Canyon Series, 6. U.S. National Park Service and University of Utah, Salt Lake City.
1959b Glen Canyon Main Stem Survey. In *The Glen Canyon Survey, Pt. II*, pp. 474–542. University of Utah Papers in Anthropology, 39; Glen Canyon Series, 6. U.S. National Park Service and University of Utah, Salt Lake City.
1986 History of Research. In *Handbook of North American Indians, Vol. 11: Great Basin*, edited by Warren L. D'Azevedo, pp. 15–30. Smithsonian Institution, Washington, D.C.

Francis, Julie E.
2001 Style and Classification. In *Handbook of Rock Art Research*, edited by David S. Whitley, pp. 221–244. AltaMira Press, New York.
2005 Pictographs, Petroglyphs, and Paradigms: Rock Art in North American Archaeology. In *Discovering North American Rock Art*, edited by Lawrence L. Loendorf, Christopher Chippindale, and David S. Whitley, pp. 181–195. University of Arizona Press, Tucson.

Francis, Julie E., and Lawrence L. Loendorf
2002 *Ancient Visions: Petroglyphs and Pictographs of the Wind River and Bighorn Country, Wyoming and Montana*. University of Utah Press, Salt Lake City.

Furst, Peter T.
1977 The Roots and Continuities of Shamanism. In *Stones, Bones and Skin: Ritual and Shamanic Art*, edited by Anne Trueblood Brodzky, Rose Danesewich, and Nick Johnson, pp. 1–28. An Artscanada Book, Society for Art Publications, Toronto.

Grant, Campbell
1968 *Rock Drawings of the Coso Range*. Maturango Museum Publications, 4. China Lake, California.

Gunnerson, James H.
1969 *The Fremont Culture: A Study of Culture Dynamics on the Northern Anasazi Frontier*. Papers of the Peabody Museum of American Archaeology and Ethnology, 59(2). Harvard University, Cambridge.

Hall, Robert L.
1977 An Anthropocentric Position for Eastern United States Prehistory. *American Antiquity* 42:499–518.

Hedges, Ken
1976 Southern California Rock Art as Shamanic Art. *American Indian Rock Art* 2:126–138. El Paso.
1982a Great Basin Rock Art Styles: A Revisionist View. In *American Indian Rock Art*, Vols. VII–VIII, edited by Frank G. Bock, pp. 205–211. American Rock Art Research Association, El Toro, California.
1982b Phosphenes in the Context of Native American Rock Art. In *American Indian Rock Art*, Vols. VII–VIII, edited by Frank G. Bock, pp. 1–10. American Rock Art Research Association, El Toro, California.
1985 Rock Art Portrayals of Shamanic Transformation and Magical Flight. *Rock Art Papers* 2:83–94. San Diego.
1994 Pipette Dreams and the Primordial Snake-Canoe: Analysis of an Hallucinatory Form Constant. In *Shamanism and Rock Art in North America*, edited by Solveig A. Turpin, pp. 103–124. Special Publication No. 1. Rock Art Foundation, San Antonio.
2001 Traversing the Great Gray Middle Ground: An Examination of Shamanistic Interpretation of Rock Art. *American Indian Rock Art* 27:123–136. Tucson.

Heizer, Robert F., and Martin A. Baumhoff
1959 Great Basin Petroglyphs and Prehistoric Game Trails. *Science* 129:904–905.
1962 *Prehistoric Rock Art of Nevada and Eastern California*. University of California Press, Berkeley.

Heizer, Robert F., and C. W. Clewlow, Jr.
1973 *Prehistoric Rock Art of California*, 2 vols. Ballena Press, Ramona, California.

Hunt, Alice P.
1953 *Archeological Survey of the La Sal Mountain Area, Utah*. University of Utah Anthropological Papers, 14. Salt Lake City.

Jennings, Jesse D., and E. Norbeck
1954 Great Basin Prehistory: A Review. *American Antiquity* 21(1): 1–11.

Kehoe, Alice Beck
2000 *Shamans and Religion: An Anthropological Exploration in Critical Thinking*. Waveland Press, Prospect Heights, Illinois.

Kelly, Isabel T.
1936 Chemehuevi Shamanism. In *Essays in Anthropology Presented to A. L. Kroeber in Celebration of His Sixtieth Birthday*, edited

by Robert E. Lowie, pp. 129–142. University of California Press, Berkeley.

Keyser, James D., and David S. Whitley
2006 Sympathetic Magic in Western North American Rock Art. *American Antiquity* 71(1):1–26.

Kidder, Alfred Vincent, and Samuel J. Guernsey
1919 *Archaeological Explorations in Northeastern Arizona.* Bureau of American Ethnology Bulletin, 65. Government Printing Office, Washington, D.C.

Kitchell, Jennifer A.
2010 Basketmaker and Archaic Rock Art on the Colorado Plateau. *American Antiquity* 75(4):819–840.

Lewis-Williams, J. David
1986 Cognitive and Optical Illusions in San Rock Art Research. *Current Anthropology* 23:429–449.
1995 Seeing and Construing: The Making and "Meaning" of a South African Rock Art Motif. *Cambridge Archaeological Journal* 5:3–23.
1997 Harnessing the Brain: Vision and Shamanism in Upper Paleolithic Western Europe. In *Beyond Art: Pleistocene Image and Symbol*, edited by M. W. Conkey, O. Soffer, D. Stratmann, and N. G. Jablonski, pp. 321–342. California Academy of Sciences, San Francisco.

Lewis-Williams, J. D., and T. A. Dowson
1988 The Signs of All Times: Entoptic Phenomena in Upper Palaeolithic Art. *Current Anthropology* 29:201–245.
1990 On Palaeolithic Art and the Neuropsychological Model. *Current Anthropology* 31:407–408.

Liljeblad, Sven
1986 Oral Tradition: Content and Style of Verbal Arts. In *Handbook of North American Indians, Vol. 11: Great Basin*, edited by Warren L. D'Azevedo, pp. 641–659. Smithsonian Institution, Washington, D.C.

Lowie, Robert H.
1924 Notes on Shoshonean Ethnography. *Anthropological Papers of the American Museum of Natural History* 20, Pt. 3: 185–314. New York.

Mallery, Garrick
1893 *Picture-Writing of the American Indians.* Tenth Annual Report of the Bureau of American Ethnology. Government Printing Office, Washington, D.C.

Malouf, Carling
1941 Notes on the Archaeology of the Barrier Canyon Region. *Masterkey* 15(4):150–153.

Marwitt, John P.
1986 Fremont Cultures. In *Handbook of North American Indians, Vol. 11: Great Basin*, edited by Warren L. D'Azevedo, pp. 161–172. Smithsonian Institution, Washington, D.C.

Matheny, Ray T., Deanne G. Matheny, Pamela W. Miller, and Blaine Miller
2004 Hunting Strategies and Winter Economy of the Fremont as Revealed in Rock Art of Nine Mile Canyon. In *New Dimensions in Rock Art Studies*, edited by Ray T. Matheny, pp. 145–194. Museum of Peoples and Cultures, Brigham Young University, Occasional Paper Series No. 9. Salt Lake City.

Morss, Noel
1931 *The Ancient Culture of the Fremont River in Utah.* Papers of the Peabody Museum of Archaeology and Ethnology, 12(3). Cambridge, Massachusetts.

Nissen, Karen M.
1982 Images from the Past: An Analysis of Six Western Great Basin Petroglyph Sites. Unpublished Ph.D. dissertation, Anthropology, University of California, Berkeley.
1995 Pray for Signs? Petroglyph Research in the Western Great Basin, North America. In *Rock Art Studies in the Americas*, edited by Jack Steinbring, pp. 67–76. Oxbow Monograph, 45. Short Run Press, Exeter.

Park, Willard Z.
1934 Paviotso Shamanism. *American Anthropologist* 36(1):98–113.
1938 *Shamanism in Western North America: A Study in Cultural Relationships.* Northwestern University Studies in the Social Sciences, 2. Evanston.

Postgate, J. N.
1994 Text and Figure in Ancient Mesopotamia: Match and Mismatch. In *The Ancient Mind: Elements of Cognitive Archaeology*, edited by Colin Renfrew and Ezra B. Zubrow, pp. 176–184. Cambridge University Press, Cambridge.

Preucel, Robert W.
2006 *Archaeological Semiotics.* Blackwell Publishing, Malden, Massachusetts.

Quinlan, Angus R.
2000 The Ventriloquist's Dummy: A Critical Review of Shamanism in Rock Art of Far Western North America. *California Journal of Great Basin Anthropology* 22(1):92–108.

Quinlan, Angus R., and Alanah Woody
2001 Marking Time at Lagomarsino: An Exploration of the Competing Narratives of Rock Art Studies. *American Indian Rock Art* 27:211–220. Tucson.
2003 Marks of Distinction: Rock Art and Ethnic Identification in the Great Basin. *American Antiquity* 68(2):372–390.

Rector, Carol Huber
1977 The Function of East Mohave Rock Art. In *American Indian Rock Art III*, edited by A. J. Bock, Frank Bock, and John Cawley, pp. 151–156. American Rock Art Research Association, Whittier.

Reichel-Dolmotoff, Gerald
1972 Rock Paintings of the Vaupes: An Essay of Interpretation. *Folklore Americas* 27:107–113.
1975 *The Shaman and the Jaguar: A Study of Narcotic Drugs Among the Indians of Colombia.* Temple University Press, Philadelphia.

Renfrew, Colin
1994 Toward a Cognitive Archaeology. In *The Ancient Mind: Elements of Cognitive Archaeology*, edited by Colin Renfrew and Ezra B. W. Zubrow, pp. 3–12. Cambridge University Press, Cambridge.

Rowe, Marvin W.
2001 Dating by AMS Radiocarbon Analysis. In *Handbook of Rock Art Research*, edited by David S. Whitley, pp. 139–166. AltaMira Press, New York.

Schaafsma, Polly
1963 *Rock Art in the Navajo Reservoir District.* Museum of New Mexico Papers in Anthropology No. 7. Museum of New Mexico Press, Santa Fe.
1971 *The Rock Art of Utah.* Peabody Museum of Archaeology and Ethnology, 65. Harvard University, Cambridge.
1980 *Indian Rock Art of the Southwest.* School of American Research, Santa Fe, New Mexico; and University of New Mexico Press, Albuquerque.

1986 Rock Art. In *Handbook of North American Indians, Vol. 11: Great Basin*, edited by Warren L. D'Azevedo, pp. 215–226. Smithsonian Institution, Washington, D.C.

1990 Shamans' Gallery. *Kiva* 55(3):213–234.

1994 Trance and Transformation in the Canyons: Shamanism and Early Rock Art on the Colorado Plateau. In *Shamanism and Rock Art in North America*, edited by Solveig A. Turpin, pp. 45–72. Special Publication, 1. Rock Art Foundation, Inc., San Antonio.

2008 Shamans, Shields, and Stories on Stone. In *The Great Basin: People and Places of Ancient Times*, edited by Catherine S. Fowler and Don D. Fowler, pp. 145–152. School for Advanced Research Press, Santa Fe, New Mexico.

2009 Cave in the Kiva: The Kiva Niche and Painted Walls in the Rio Grande Valley. *American Antiquity* 74(4):664–690.

Schaafsma, Polly, and William B. Tsosie

2009 Xeroxed on Stone: Times of Origin and the Navajo Holy People in Canyon Landscapes. In *Landscapes of Origin in the Americas*, edited by Jessica Joyce Christie, pp. 15–31. University of Alabama Press, Tuscaloosa.

Sekaquaptewa, Emory, and Dorothy Washburn

2004 *They Go Along Singing*: Reconstructing the Hopi Past from Ritual Metaphors in Song and Image. *American Antiquity* 69(3):457–486.

Snead, James E., Clark L. Erikson, and J. Andrew Darling (editors)

2009 *Landscapes of Movement: Trails, Paths, and Roads in Anthropological Perspective*. University of Pennsylvania Museum of Archaeology and Anthropology, Philadelphia.

Spangler, Jerry D.

2004 Categories and Conundrums: The Rock Art of Lower Nine Mile Canyon. In *New Dimensions in Rock Art Studies*, edited by Ray T. Matheny, pp. 119–144. Museum of Peoples and Cultures, Brigham Young University, Occasional Paper Series No. 9. Salt Lake City.

Steward, Julian H.

1929 *Petroglyphs of California and Adjoining States*. University of California Publications in Archaeology and Ethnology, 24(2). Berkeley.

1937 Petroglyphs of the United States. In *Smithsonian Annual Report for 1936*, pp. 405–425. Publication 3437. Washington, D.C.

1941 *Archaeological Reconnaissance of Southern Utah*. Bureau of American Ethnology Bulletin, 128. Smithsonian Institution, Washington, D.C.

Stoffle, Richard, Richard Arnold, Kathleen Van Vlack, Larry Eddy, and Betty Cornelius

2009 Nuvagantu, "Where Snow Sits": Origin Mountains of the Southern Paiutes. In *Landscapes of Origin in the Americas*, edited by Jessica Joyce Christie, pp. 32–44. University of Alabama Press, Tuscaloosa.

Tedlock, Barbara

1982 *Time and the Highland Maya*. University of New Mexico Press, Albuquerque.

Tilley, Christopher

1999 *Metaphor and Material Culture*. Blackwell, Oxford.

Turner, Christy G., II

1963 *Petrographs of the Glen Canyon Region*. Museum of Northern Arizona Bulletin No. 38; Glen Canyon Series No. 4. Flagstaff.

1971 Revised Dating for Early Rock Art of the Glen Canyon Region. *American Antiquity* 36:469–471.

Turpin, Solveig A.

1994 On a Wing and a Prayer: Flight Metaphors in Pecos River Art. In *Shamanism and Rock Art in North America*, edited by Solveig A. Turpin, pp. 73–104. Special Publication No. 1. Rock Art Foundation, Inc., San Antonio.

2011 Size Matters: The Transition from Religious to Secular Art in the Lower Pecos Region. *American Indian Rock Art* 37:1–15. Glendale, Arizona.

Vastokas, Joan M.

1977 The Shamanic Tree of Life. In *Stones, Bones and Skin: Ritual and Shamanic Art*, edited by Anne Trueblood Brodzky, Rose Danesewich, and Nick Johnson, pp. 93–117. An Artscanada Book, Society for Art Publications, Toronto.

Von Werlhof, J. C.

1965 *Rock Art of Owens Valley, California*. University of California Archaeological Survey Report, 65. Berkeley.

Whitley, David S.

1992 Shamanism and Rock Art in Western North America. *Cambridge Archaeological Journal* 2(1):89–113.

1994a By the Hunter, for the Gatherer. Art, Social Relations and Subsistence Change in the Prehistoric Great Basin. *World Archaeology* 25(3):356–373.

1994b Shamanism, Natural Modeling and the Rock Art of Far Western North American Hunter-Gatherers. In *Shamanism and Rock Art in North America*, edited by Solveig A. Turpin, pp. 1–44. Special Publication, 1. Rock Art Foundation, Inc., San Antonio.

1998 Cognitive Neuroscience, Shamanism and the Rock Art of Native America. *Anthropology of Consciousness* 9:22–37.

2000 *The Art of the Shaman: Rock Art of California*. University of Utah Press, Salt Lake City.

Whitley, David S., and Jean Clottes

2005 In Steward's Shadow: Histories of Research in the Far West and Western Europe. In *Discovering North American Rock Art*, edited by L. L. Loendorf, C. Chippindale, and D. S. Whitley, pp. 161–177. University of Arizona Press, Tucson.

Wormington, H. M.

1955 *A Reappraisal of the Fremont Culture*. Proceedings No. 1. Denver Museum of Natural History, Denver.

Young, M. Jane

1985 Images of Power and the Power of Images. *Journal of American Folklore* 98:3–48.

1988 *Signs from the Ancestors*. University of New Mexico Press, Albuquerque.

Zigmond, Maurice

1986 Kawaiisu. In *Handbook of North American Indians, Vol. 11: Great Basin*, edited by Warren L. D'Azevedo, pp. 398–411. Smithsonian Institution, Washington, D.C.

Zubrow, Ezra B. W.

1994 Knowledge Representation and Archaeology: A Cognitive Example Using GIS. In *The Ancient Mind: Elements of Cognitive Archaeology*, edited by Colin Renfrew and Ezra B. W. Zubrow, pp. 107–118. Cambridge University Press, Cambridge.

14

Some Thoughts on Evolution, Ecology, and Archaeology in the Great Basin

Steven R. Simms, James F. O'Connell, and Kevin T. Jones

Some 30 years ago, we opined that culture history and descriptive ecology, the two analytic frameworks then being used to *explore* Great Basin prehistory, could not in the end *explain* it (O'Connell et al. 1982). We agreed that both were important: culture history as the approach best suited to basic description of the archaeological record; descriptive ecology as the simplest means of documenting the relationship between certain aspects of that record and the nonhuman environment in which it was situated. Missing from the enterprise in our view was a reliable way of addressing the underlying "why" questions: *why* the record took shape as it did, *why* it articulated with its environment as it did, and *why* the past human behavior inferred from those lines of evidence varied as it did.

Like many archaeologists of that time, we thought that a materialist approach, one that paid little attention to speculation about the motives, ideas, or agency of past human actors, was the best way of tackling these questions. We were inspired by the work of Julian Steward but recognized the limits of cultural ecology.

We argued that the explanatory framework of behavioral ecology provides the tools to move beyond culture-historical description and mechanistic responses of culture to an externalized natural environment. The emerging discipline of behavioral ecology offered a way of transcending these limits, one that we thought would allow us not only to test Steward's model and other ethnographically grounded formulations like it but also to develop similar arguments about human behavior in environmental settings significantly different from those of the nineteenth-century Great Basin.

We wanted to know why culture was at times plastic and at other times resistant and why cultures could be behaviorally homogeneous or fonts of behavioral diversity. We were, and remain, well aware of the forces in anthropology and broadly across our culture that forbid any quest to know human behavior in a scientific sense and especially in a deterministic sense. We decided to treat the matter as an empirical issue.

Looking back, we see that the essay reflects a certain missionary zeal that probably accounts for the mixed reaction it received among some of our colleagues, notably some of our distinguished elders. We are less inclined toward proselytizing now, but our passion for the approach remains intact.

Here we offer "further thoughts" on the topic in honor of Don D. Fowler, a true historian of anthropology. Our retrospective places evolutionary ecology and its subset behavioral ecology in intellectual context, and we share a glimpse of how we arrived at the position we took in 1982. We selectively review progress made over the last three decades but note that more thorough reviews are available elsewhere (e.g., Bird and O'Connell 2006; Zeanah and Simms 1999). The next iteration of behavioral ecology in Great Basin archaeology is already upon us, as archaeologists investigate the late Holocene sea change of intensification and cultural complexity. The debate over "prestige hunting" is one element of this investigation, and while we find it a productive line of research, we also see some familiar pitfalls. We employ the prestige debate to offer some reminders about key concepts in behavioral ecology that may help to resolve some perceived differences of interpretation and move the research forward.

In Pursuit of a Great Basin Past

Great Basin archaeology, as we learned it, was dominated by the culture-historical approach to data collection and analysis. Broadly speaking, the exercise involved excavating sites containing rich arrays of material remains; describing certain of those remains in terms of formal artifact types; tracing the distribution of those types through time and space; identifying readily bounded, co-occurring sets of types as archaeological "cultures"; and accounting for changes in their composition and distribution by reference to past movements of people, ideas, or both. Typical Great Basin examples include Marwitt 1970 on the Fremont, Jennings 1964 on the Desert West, and Heizer 1956 on the Lower Humboldt Valley. The approach was unabashedly inductive; its results, narrowly historical.

Lewis Binford (1962) and other proponents of the New (later, processual) Archaeology argued that the discipline could do much better than this. They reckoned that the material record represented a far more complete body of information on past human behavior than the culture historians had imagined; that it could be tapped most effectively through systematic, comprehensive approaches to data collection and analysis; and that properly tackled it offered the best available basis for developing and testing explanations for long-term changes in the human condition. Walter Taylor (1948) presented a similar argument 14 years earlier, but the spirit of the times was against him. Binford, writing in the 1960s, found a more receptive audience, at least among the younger set. Some of his students and others farther afield pursued these leads in a series of influential case studies. Based on fieldwork in the central Great Basin, David Hurst Thomas's (1973) archaeological evaluation of Steward's model of seasonal transhumance was among the very best of these efforts.

As phrased initially (and as the subsequent shift in title to "processual" implies), the New Archaeology's goals were more than merely methodological. Binford himself was a protégé of the archmaterialist Leslie White; many of his archaeological followers found similar inspiration in the works of Steward and Marvin Harris. Countering the established Boasian tradition in American anthropology, all denied the proposition that an accounting of culture history was in any sense an explanation of that history but, instead, saw history as a phenomenon that itself demanded explanation.

Despite the rhetoric, their attempts to achieve this goal foundered on the prior problem of reconstructing those aspects of past behavior reflected in archaeological remains. Absent a relevant ethnographic model of the sort that made Thomas's exercise so successful, that basic difficulty soon became the primary focus of attention. "Middle-range" research on site-formation processes and their behavioral implications preoccupied the field (Binford 1977; Schiffer 1987). Concern with the ultimate goal of explaining variation in past human behavior faded accordingly. As Barbara Price trenchantly observed,

> What is surprising...is that the "new archaeology" begins its downward deductions at so resolutely middle a level, precluding significant generalization and producing a corpus of work remarkable (at least in retrospect and given its initially revolutionary program) for its intellectual conservatism [1982:714].

By the late 1970s, we saw this as a significant problem and were ready to embrace a theoretical framework that would help regain purchase on broader questions about cultural variability. We were of course not alone in this.

Growing Points: Behavioral Ecology and Human Behavior

Darwin's theory of natural selection sought to explain the emergence of morphological variation without reference to a Creator. Beginning in the 1950s, ethologists Niko Tinbergen, Konrad Lorenz, and others extended this "selectionist" thinking into the realm of behavior. The disciplines now called evolutionary and (its subset) behavioral ecology were among the results (Krebs and Davies 1997). Tinbergen (1963) in particular drew a crucial distinction between "proximate" and "ultimate" causation in evolution. Proximate explanations are concerned with *how* behaviors work, and the concept is recognizable to anthropologists as functionalism. Ultimate explanations focus on *why* behaviors arise in the first place—questions that echo anthropology's interest in explaining the development of cultural form and variability in general (that is to say, nomothetic) terms.

One of our sources of inspiration, evolutionary biologist Eric Charnov, often illustrated the difference between proximate and ultimate causation with the question, "Why do birds fly south for the winter?" As he said, proximate explanations speak to physiological changes in birds during the fall season, the mechanisms of bird navigation, and so forth. They show how migration works. None of them explains why some birds evolved to migrate seasonally while others did not. "Who was the first bird to fly south?" Charnov would ask. Ultimate explanations focus on the circumstances that select for migration from among the array of behaviors present in an existing population.

Anthropologists can apply the proximate/ultimate distinction to many of their own questions. For instance, archaeologists generally describe the origins of agriculture in largely proximate terms: as a historical process and as a system that functions to achieve certain purposes. Ultimate explanations aim at why agriculture was developed, adopted, or in some cases rejected when and where it was. Perhaps surprisingly, attempts at such explanations remain few and far between (Kennett and Winterhalder 2006).

Our excitement about evolutionary and behavioral ecology was heightened by a 1979 visit to Utah by biologist George Williams, author of the landmark book *Adaptation and Natural Selection: A Critique of Some Current Evolutionary Thought* (1966). Williams critiqued the progressive view of adaptation and was one of a cadre of evolutionary biologists, including John Maynard Smith, John Krebs, Robert MacArthur, Robert Trivers, William Hamilton, and others, who pioneered the application of selectionist thinking to the study of animal behavior. They argued that selection operates on the level of the individual organism, not on whole species. They saw adaptation as a process that favors the persistence and spread of certain behaviors at the expense of others, not as the product of wholesale transformations toward "better" species. They recognized that virtually all organisms (especially members of the same species) deal with conflicts of interest, regardless of whether they are sentient or not. Most important for anthropology, they saw adaptation in Darwinian terms, rather than in the tautological, progress-laden dictums of Herbert Spencer that are still so pervasive among social scientists.

Nicholas Blurton Jones, a former student of Tinbergen's, was among those who carried this discussion into the human arena. In an edited volume with the telling title *Growing Points in Ethology*, Blurton Jones (1976) drew attention to anthropology's purported interest in nomothetic explanations for variation in human behavior and to the fact that it was repeatedly thwarted in pursuit of that interest by fears that are deeply rooted in Western thought, particularly the fear of explanations that eschew reference to human intention in favor of attention to "mindless" material circumstance.

The same fear existed in the mind of Darwin, who was alarmed by his own early notebooks and sketches (1838–1844) where he subscribed to philosophical materialism, which he saw as a more heretical notion than evolution. Darwin even saw his materialism informing "the citadel itself—the human mind." Though Darwin felt that natural selection was a key to explanation, for human affairs he could only allow that "light will be thrown on the origin of man and his history" (Gould 1977:25). It is not the theory of evolution that bedevils Darwin in our culture but, rather, his materialism.

The tenacity of this cultural bias was evident in the visceral reaction to Leslie White half a century ago because he was a "materialist," who did not acknowledge that "it is people who make history" (Peace 2004:185–186). This cultural preconception continues: witness the widespread appeal of such phenomena as postmodern anthropology, postprocessual archaeology, agency theory, historical process, and the recent eclectic spasm dubbed "processual-plus" archaeology.

Blurton Jones wondered if an integration of behavioral ecology and ecological anthropology might break this impasse. He noted that work done under the banner of ecological anthropology had shown that adaptation is a concept relevant to the study of human affairs, and he speculated about the ultimate explanations that might lie behind that finding. His provocative observation caught our attention: "Surely we are not here dealing with the directing effects of natural selection? Or are we?" (Blurton Jones 1976:439).

Behavioral Ecology in Great Basin Archaeology

More than half a century ago, W. D. Billings (1951) drew attention to a characteristic common to many Great Basin scholars: their attraction to (some might say infatuation with) the region itself–the dry white playas and great salt lakes, the vast sagebrush oceans and rugged montane islands. For anthropologists, that appeal has additional, discipline-specific dimensions. Steward's cultural ecology was shaped both by his youthful experience of the land and its indigenous inhabitants (Kerns 2009, 2010) and by a deep interest in fundamental questions about the determinants of human behavior. For archaeologists, the unusually well-preserved records derived from dry cave deposits spoke not only to the Native experience of local environments and the changes they sustained over time but also to developing ideas about the basic nature of hunter-gatherer lifestyles and the proposition that they represented what many thought of as the fundamental human condition. For us, the intersection of austere landscape, rich archaeological record, detailed ethnohistory, and broad disciplinary relevance combined with the appeal of a newly emerging theoretical perspective to create an irresistible opportunity. Thirty years ago, the obvious point of entry was through foraging theory. Charnov and Orians (1973) had shown that simple mathematical models allowed one to explain key aspects of animal subsistence behavior in organisms as distantly related as fish and birds. By the time we drafted our 1982 essay, provocative ethnographic applications of these models had already been reported. Bruce Winterhalder (1977, 1981) had explored the utility of formal models of prey and patch choice among the sub-Arctic Cree. O'Connell and Kristen Hawkes (1981) had used the prey model as the framework for a hypothesis about the recent elimination of formerly important seed resources from the diets of central Australian Alyawara. Eric Alden Smith (1980, 1981) had employed the notion of foraging efficiency as a basis for predictions about the size of foraging groups among the Inuit.

Archaeological applications had appeared even earlier. Edwin Wilmsen (1973) appealed to Henry Horn's (1968) model of blackbird territoriality in speculating about group size and settlement location among Paleoindian populations on the Great Plains. John Beaton (1973) proposed that widely recognized but poorly understood changes in the composition of coastal California shell middens could be explained by reference to long-term, predation-driven declines in the availability of economically high-ranked prey and the consequently increased appeal of lower-ranked taxa. Frank Bayham (1977, 1979) employed a diet breadth model to understand changes in hunting patterns at the famed Ventana Cave, Arizona, and showed that the same model helped to account for similarities in Archaic patterns of faunal procurement in the Southeast, in the Midwest, and at Hogup Cave in the Great Basin.

In a widely read review essay in the Michael Schiffer–edited *Advances in Archaeological Method and Theory*, Great Basin archaeologist Robert Bettinger (1980) summarized these and other early applications of models from behavioral ecology to problems in anthropology in general and archaeology in particular. In a subsequent piece written with California archaeologist Martin Baumhoff (Bettinger and Baumhoff 1982), Bettinger used the concept of alternative subsistence strategies and competing "adaptive peaks" to propose a novel explanation for the displacement of resident Basin populations by migrating Numic speakers. In short, our polemic was drafted during a period of substantive exploration of behavioral ecology as a framework for the systematic study of human behavior.

Early archaeological applications of foraging models commonly foundered on the paucity of quantitative data regarding the costs of acquiring various food resources and processing them for consumption. Once the potential of the approach had been illustrated by the case studies noted above, it was clear that ethnographic and experimental work designed to provide the necessary data was essential. We gathered some of those data and shared the results at conferences and in publications in the early 1980s (e.g., Jones 1981; Jones and Simms 1980; Simms 1982). These data served as the basis for tests of Steward's model of ethnographic diet breadth (Simms 1984, 1987; Zeanah and Simms 1999). The surprising result: even when differences in men's vs. women's foraging goals were considered in the analysis, the diet breadth model indicated that small seeds should *not* have been part of the ethnographic diet. Only when one considered the storability of seeds, to be consumed in winter when other options were unavailable, did they enter the optimal diet.

Far from marking a "failure of optimal foraging theory," as some critics suggested, the exercise illustrated the capacity of the approach to move inquiry in productive directions. Indeed, further studies adding complexity to the modeling process followed in short order. For example, transport costs were calculated (Jones and Madsen 1989), and the differential transportability of resources was seen to hold implications for mobile vs. logistic settlement strategies (Rhode 1990).

Settlement patterns became a target of investigation, and this required the development of prey choice models that take resource abundance into account in order to model the proportional contribution of resources to the diet. The signal examples were studies in the Carson Desert of western Nevada by Christopher Raven and Robert Elston (1989), Robert Kelly (2001), and David Zeanah (2004). These investigators plotted the regional distribution of resource patches over the last two millennia, quantified return rates available from potential prey in each, assessed patch rank by reference to men's vs. women's foraging goals, and predicted the resulting distribution of archaeological sites and the character of associated assemblages.

As anticipated, subsequent analyses showed that late prehistoric residential site location on the desert floor was determined by women's foraging choices while special-purpose sites used mainly by men were more widely distributed across the surrounding terrain. Analysis of human skeletal remains exposed by flooding of the Carson Desert in the 1980s revealed differences in lifetime workloads consistent with the inferred settlement patterns. CT scans of humeri and femora indicated that women were significantly less mobile than men but engaged in substantial upper body work. Men's remains showed the effect of repeated long-distance movement over steep terrain (Larson and Kelly 1995).

Elston and Zeanah (2002) carried this line of research further by using the prey choice model to predict the sexual division of labor and its patch choice implications at various Great Basin locations in Paleoindian times, a period well beyond the reach of standard ethnographic analogies. The impact of prey choice on processing and transport strategies and its implications for archaeological assemblage composition were further explored in two studies by Duncan Metcalfe and Renee Barlow. Theoretical modeling indicated that high-ranked prey, defined as such by the fact that they have relatively low handling costs, should be processed and their low-utility parts discarded at the point of acquisition, mainly because that practice allows foragers to maximize the overall utility of loads carried back to residential bases (Metcalfe and Barlow 1992).

Treating lower-ranked items in similar fashion also improves load utility, but the gain is more than offset by the consequent loss in time available for foraging. Low-ranked items should more often be returned to base for processing. The implication: debris produced from handling high-ranked prey is likely to be underrepresented at residential sites, with debris from low-ranked prey overrepresented, a finding crucial for analysts interested in the reconstruction of past diets.

A second study illustrated the role of handling costs as determinants of residential site location, the key message being that foragers should position base camps in or near patches containing economically important but relatively hard-to-handle prey (Barlow and Metcalfe 1996). This finding provides additional support for the findings of the Carson Desert studies noted above.

Building on a lead initially offered by Hawkes and O'Connell (1992), Jason Bright, Andrew Ugan, and Lori Hunsaker (2002) extended the concept of handling costs to include investment in related technology. The basic argument: increasing diet breadth by definition entails greater investment in processing, which in turn favors increased investment in processing technology. The greater the diversity of low-ranked prey added to the diet, the greater the payoff for developing tools that, despite their higher cost to manufacture, increase processing efficiency for specific resources. Thus, as diet breadth increases, technological diversity and the associated costs of making and maintaining the technology should increase as well.

Ugan et al. (2003) and Bettinger et al. (2006) subsequently extended the argument in a discussion of factors that determine the geographic spread of more expensive technologies at the expense of less costly ones; the high-cost bow and arrow vs. the low-cost atlatl and dart being the provocative case in point. Counterintuitively, the argument contends that broad-based foraging economies and technologies will generally displace those focused on the exploitation of a narrower range of high-ranked prey, despite the fact that they are in a fundamental sense more expensive.

INTENSIFICATION: NEW FRONTIERS?

Anthropologists will recognize the replacement of less costly technologies with more expensive ones as "intensification." Greater investments in grinding stones, specialized basketry, pronghorn traps, snares, seed beaters, rabbit nets, fishing technology, and the bow and arrow all exemplify the process. The path toward intensification began after 4,000 years ago in the western Great Basin (Bettinger 1999) but is most apparent between 1500 and 650 BP, when there were larger populations of foragers, changes in social organization, sustained occupation of places, increased storage, increased investment in technology such as the above-mentioned adoption of the bow and arrow, and in some locales even an expensive ceramic technology.

The most dramatic example of intensification in the region is the Fremont in the eastern Great Basin and northern Colorado Plateau. The adoption of farming by indigenous peoples in the face of demographic change associated with immigration from the Southwest after 2000 BP produced villages of hundreds of people, ceramics, large-scale storage, irrigation, architectural variability, public spaces, and a sophisticated rock art tradition distinct from that of the preceding Archaic foragers (Simms 2008).

The Fremont and the foragers of the western Great Basin mark a sea change in the trajectory of cultural evolution in the Basin–Plateau: increased investment of human labor, increased productivity, and declining efficiency. What circumstances would produce the culture histories and consequent archaeological records of these two regions, one a case of foragers and the other a case of foragers becoming farmers? Kelly McGuire and William Hildebrandt (2005:705–707) hint at such a comparison. The culture histories are unique, but they exhibit similarities of structure and process, and the two cases are coeval. An explanation that unifies these geographically and culturally distinct histories is of obvious intellectual value, just as the theory of natural selection enables us to synthesize the distinct histories of organisms as seemingly different as birds and fish. Could we, as Blurton Jones wondered over 35 years ago, be dealing with selection? Considering selection as process, and as a tool for investigation, we answer in the affirmative.

We advocate research on intensification in the late Holocene western Great Basin and its counterpart in the adoption of agriculture in the eastern Great Basin and northern Colorado Plateau. Such an exploration would bring new variables to the modeling process: population growth in response to increased production, inequality among people in their access to resources, inequality in the sexual division of labor, competition among social groups, altruism, and the evolution of leadership.

The Late Archaic of the western Great Basin represents the murmurs of complexity in a place long held to be an archetype of egalitarian forager society. Investigation of the ultimate, evolutionary causes of intensification and cultural complexity are best accomplished by examining their development in hunter-gatherer contexts, not cases where complexity is already manifest.

The Fremont holds a similar position. Long marginalized as egalitarian foragers who practiced some farming, the Fremont are in fact a laboratory for the investigation of the emergence of cultural complexity. We have argued that our 1982 advocacy was merely one voice in an emerging chorus, and our role here is no different. The first steps toward an investigation of the circumstances selecting for Fremont farming and for complexity in the Late Archaic western Great Basin have already been taken

Renee Barlow (2002, 2006) has quantified the costs of Fremont farming using ethnographic, historical, and experimental data and shows that prehistoric maize farming was competitive with many wild plant foods. She documents significant variation in the costs and benefits of different types of farming and in the process reveals a key feature of intensification: increasing productivity per unit area correlates with declining rates of return. The decision to adopt maize farming was driven by subcontinental demographic realities (Simms 2008) but was subject to the effects of these realities on local ecological considerations, primarily the trade-offs between farming and exploiting wild resources. Barlow's model predicts various degrees of commitment to farming and to residential stability, with alternative adaptive strategies occurring in varying mixes over time. The fit with the archaeological record of the Fremont is dramatic, and the extension of this line of investigation into the realm of inequality, group size, leadership, resource depression, competition, architecture, and other trappings of cultural complexity is the next logical step. The tools of behavioral ecology would bring hypothesis testing and an analysis of evolutionary processes that would only build on and synthesize post hoc historical descriptions.

In the western Great Basin changes in the organization of societies are evident in the shift from public to private goods (Eerkens 2004) and the evolution of social inequality (Eerkens 2009). Climatic patterns favored increases in the abundance of large game (Broughton et al. 2008), and the amelioration of food resources in general at this time holds implications for human demography. In the late Holocene, changes in hunting behavior to some degree reflect declining efficiency and a role for prestige in the adaptive mix (McGuire and Hildebrandt 2005).

These forays into the evolution of late Holocene behavior provoke healthy debate, some polemics, and some contention; all are familiar to those of us who explored the application of behavioral ecology to Great Basin archaeology in the late 1970s and early 1980s. We urge this research on, but our vantage also stirs some reminders about basic principles of behavioral ecology and rouses "some thoughts" about Great Basin archaeology. We employ the prestige hunting debate as a vehicle for those thoughts.

Transcending the Prestige Hunting Debate

The lively debate over costly signaling in the form of "prestige hunting" is an extension of pioneering research on late Holocene intensification and cultural complexity in California (e.g., Broughton 1994; Erlandson 1991; Hildebrandt and Jones 1992; Hildebrandt and McGuire 2002, 2003; Kennett 2005; Raab 1992, 1996; Wohlgemuth 1996). Kelly McGuire and William Hildebrandt (2005) propose that Late Archaic intensification in the western Great Basin is reflected in rising human populations that increase hunting pressure on large game. They argue that instead of depressing the number of large game and their representation in the archaeological record as predicted by a diet breadth model, there is a proportional increase in large game in archaeological assemblages after 4000 BP. They propose that large game hunting continued despite rising costs because in a context of increasing cultural complexity, prestige became more valuable. A corollary of their argument is that diets remained broad at this time, and they present evidence that expensive resources, such as seeds, indeed remain in the Late Archaic diet. Their zooarchaeological evidence comes from two sites in northern and central Nevada (Pie Creek and Gatecliff shelters), but McGuire and Hildebrandt assemble other evidence for intensification from the western Great Basin: increases in the costs of technology, the bow and arrow after about 2000 BP, the costly movement of toolstone over long distances, the construction and maintenance of costly hunting facilities such as game drives, and the Late Archaic elaboration of rock art.

Jack Broughton, Frank Bayham, and David Byers (Broughton and Bayham 2003; Byers and Broughton 2004) and more recently Broughton et al. (2008; Broughton et al. 2011) employ data from the western United States to show that the increases in large game after 4000 BP coincide with climatic amelioration favorable to large-game populations. Human populations in the western Great Basin at that time were in fact depressed in the wake of mid-Holocene desiccation (Louderback et al. 2011) but subsequently increased, likely in response to the increasing productivity of the environment after 4000 BP (and demographic expansions in the Southwest and California). These researchers argue that human predation eventually depressed large game abundance in archaeological assemblages after 3000–2500 BP and that prestige hunting either is unlikely to have had an effect or is unnecessary to invoke as a cause of the changes in the archaeological record.

Hildebrandt and McGuire (2002:231) initially cast the argument for prestige hunting as a refutation of optimal foraging, implying that if prestige becomes a relevant currency in hunter decision making, then efficiency becomes irrelevant. Broughton and Bayham acknowledged that hunting is "motivated by multiple fitness-enhancing goals," but they dismissed prestige as a possible "rationale" (2003:785). The discussion became polarized into two camps, each advocating for an *essentialist* type—optimal foragers *or* prestige hunters—and these positions colored subsequent investigation. The situation presents an opportunity to refer to underlying issues regarding costly signaling theory but, more importantly, to offer some reminders of basic tenets of behavioral ecology relevant to this issue.

McGuire and Hildebrandt appeal to costly signaling theory as a framework for understanding prestige hunting. *Costly signaling* (see Bliege Bird and Smith 2005) is a contemporary term for a rich intellectual tradition regarding the mysteries of reciprocity in the sociological investigations of Thorstein Veblen (1931 [1899]) and Marcel Mauss (1924), the economic anthropological inquiries of Marshall Sahlins (1972), and the practice theory of Pierre Bourdieu (1977). Human reciprocity is a form of signaling and raises a conundrum because at times seemingly wasteful efforts at reciprocity and altruism may bring prestige and power to individuals or benefits to groups. Biologists too have a long history of evaluating animal communication systems that bring costs and benefits to both signalers and receivers (Krebs and Davies 1997; Trivers 1971). The study of signaling in biology weighs the selection pressures for signaling against the underlying tendency of selection to favor lower risk and lower energetic costs.

Evolutionary studies of signaling in human cases reveal a wide range of reciprocity, from extensive food sharing based on reciprocal altruism to sharing that seems to be unconditionally generous but which in fact yields benefits to providers. The concept of prestige hunting as applied to the Great Basin is of the latter variety and is a form of symbolic capital wherein successful hunters benefit from their efforts and their generosity in ways that extend beyond caloric return (e.g., Bliege Bird and Smith 2005; Hawkes 1993).

McGuire and Hildebrandt have good reason to investigate prestige hunting. The application of foraging models in ethnographic cases shows that in general, energy maximization drives human hunting, but it also shows that men's hunting does not *inevitably* maximize energy and minimize time (e.g., Bliege Bird et al. 2001; Hawkes et al. 1991; Hill et al. 1987; Wiessner 2002). Of course, the relevant question is what circumstances will favor one or another behavioral alternative in an adaptive mix, not whether a particular culture or time period is all one way or another.

Brian Codding and Terry Jones (2007) highlight the key problem: payoffs associated with signaling are likely to be highly situational in both absolute and relative terms. The selective pressures for signaling must be consistently present to reinforce the behavior, or the alternative behavior of energy maximization and nonsignaling will overcome the inefficient "costly" behavior of prestige seekers. Costly signaling will thus represent some fraction of the possible behaviors that make up an evolutionarily stable strategy (ESS), a situation where the behavioral mix resists invasion by other behaviors.

Since the pressures for costly signaling are not constantly present, other behaviors such as energy maximization will always be part of the invading strategy and, hence, the adaptive mix. The only way prestige hunting could constitute an ESS would be if it provided a payoff so great that energy maximization was rendered inconsequential. Ethnographic studies have thus far not found such a case.

This is not a death knell for prestige hunting in the late Holocene Great Basin but, rather, an indication that the issue needs to be reframed. The question is not whether representatives of an entire culture or an entire archaeological period are "prestige hunters" but, rather, a matter of which circumstances select for an increased frequency of prestige hunting relative to energetically efficient foraging.

On the other side, Broughton et al. (2008) present substantial evidence that climatically and ecologically induced fluctuations in the abundance of large game play a significant role in shaping archaeological faunal assemblages during the middle and late Holocene. We agree but suspect that the abundance of large game is not what is driving human population growth and the trend toward intensification. These trends reflect increased investment of human labor, increased productivity, and declining efficiency. It is unlikely that large game were ever the *primary* component of any diet in the region.

Broughton et al. (2011) employ evidence from Hogup Cave, Utah, and the Little Boulder Basin in northeastern Nevada to propose that at least in those places, late Holocene faunal assemblages take their form from climatically driven increases in large-game populations. They also argue that diet narrowed in these places, implying that people increasingly turned to inexpensive large game instead of costlier resources.

The analysis of Broughton et al. (2011) is sophisticated but narrowly archaeological. Their conclusion that the late Holocene eastern Great Basin was a place of contracting diets as people feasted off inexpensively procured large game is strangely out of context. Late Holocene North America in general was a time of increasing human populations, accompanied by increases in residential stability, investment in new technologies and infrastructure, and increases in cultural complexity. This was true of western Great Basin foragers and eastern Basin Fremont farmers as well. As Barlow clearly showed, heavy investment in the cultivation of plant domesticates is a high-cost/relatively low-return strategy—the epitome of a broad diet. Large Fremont farming villages and a dense human population were located along the Wasatch Front, a few days' walk from Hogup Cave.

It is more likely that the increases of large game in archaeological assemblages such as Hogup Cave reflect increasing human populations and the intensification of labor. Ethnographic evidence shows that while big game hunting may produce high returns upon encounter and successful pursuit, the high costs of travel and search, the problem of failed search and pursuit sequences (Bird et al. 2009), and the sheer difficulty of large game hunting ensure that it will remain a highly variable and often a relatively small fraction of the overall diet.

Both parties in the prestige hunting debate bring evidence to the problem that begs for synthesis: a model that accommodates the evidence for variability in the frequencies of alternative adaptive strategies and trends over time, rather than normative characterizations of coarse-grained chronological categories such as "Late Archaic" or "late Holocene." Both parties in the debate advocate for one or another alternative adaptive strategy, rather than conceptualizing and pursuing an investigation of the circumstances that would select for trends in the mix of behaviors over time.

The tendency of archaeologists to cast the past in normative terms is remarkably persistent. Optimal foraging theory and costly signaling theory are not essentialist categories that characterize even the behavior of a single individual, let alone an entire group, culture, or period. This was a flaw of the traveler–processor model 30 years ago (Bettinger and Baumhoff 1982), and it is a problem here.

Efficient hunting and prestige hunting constitute an evolutionarily stable strategy. The concept is germane to framing the trade-offs between prestige hunting and efficient hunting. Efficiency will always experience selection because foragers must eat, and one's own effort is the best available means of getting enough. On the other hand, male hunters, depending on their life history stage, experience the need for allies and supporters and compete for mates. The larger and more entwined the social setting, the greater the potential payoffs associated with signaling to aid the creation and maintenance of these relationships. Ethnographic accounts convey a sense of this; for instance, Codding et al. report:

> When offspring provisioning benefits are high and opportunity costs low, men should shift their focus to low-variance resources when and where they become available. For example, turtle hunting among Meriam is associated with moderate variance and is most frequently undertaken by unmarried men; turtle collecting during the nesting season is more reliable and is undertaken more by married men.... Similarly, Hadza men switch from targeting large unreliable prey to smaller reliable prey when their wives are pregnant..., and Martu men switch from hunting kangaroo to hunting monitor lizards when older.... Larger social networks provide a forager with a larger pool of potential recipients and a larger audience, leading to higher payoffs for returning with large quantities of food to distribute widely, such as gaining higher status, deference in decision-making and perhaps greater social support...; these in turn may provide indirect benefits to existing offspring, including increased offspring survivorship [2011:6].

Despite these trade-offs, prestige hunting will always be a fraction of the behavioral set because energy maximization will always be the invading strategy. By framing the question in terms of an ESS, archaeology may be able to muster the evidence for the circumstances where a higher frequency of prestige hunting may be expected. Single sites, however, will never prove or disprove such questions.

Thus far the prestige hunting debate has used ethnographic evidence only in a post hoc manner. A better approach might be to marry theory with arguments about process based on ethnographic cases to model/predict variation in costly behaviors relative to efficient behaviors. Ethnographic analysis exemplified by the quote above can help archaeologists take an important step in this direction. The general understanding of the late Holocene Great Basin, intensification, and the attendant behaviors is unlikely to be resolved if approached only in a narrowly empirical and strictly archaeological manner.

Looking Forward

Prestige hunting is part of the larger investigation of intensification and cultural complexity in the western Great Basin, and to their credit, McGuire and Hildebrandt frame their argument in these terms. Larger geographic scales are also appropriate for this issue, and Simms (2008) provides a general synthesis that considers the effects of surrounding regions on the ancient history of the Great Basin—especially the Southwest and California.

When larger scales of analysis are employed, the findings from individual sites can be placed in context, restraining the unrealistic expectation that site-by-site comparisons of assemblages will reveal prestige hunting vs. efficient hunting or broad diets vs. narrow diets. Site-specific circumstances and the resulting variability will cumulatively reveal patterning as the sample grows, and it is in these larger patterns and trends that matters of regional demographics, technological investment, shifts in storage strategy, residential and logistic mobility, inequality, leadership, and prestige will be identified.

The late Holocene western Great Basin and the eastern Great Basin/northern Colorado Plateau are contexts wherein we should expect behaviors associated with intensification, including but not limited to prestige hunting. Radiocarbon frequencies from multiple studies show that there were more people in the eastern and the western Great Basin between 1500 and 650 BP than at any other time in antiquity (Lindsay 2005; Louderback et al. 2011; Massimino and Metcalfe 1999). These trends fly in the face of an argument that foragers lived the good life by avoiding high-cost resources because large game was so plentiful.

Research aimed at identifying trends may be productive. For example, Jacob Fisher (2010) employs faunal analysis and strontium isotopes from large-mammal assemblages at the Fremont village of Five Finger Ridge in central Utah to test for change over time in the travel and transport costs of large game hunting. Fisher finds change in faunal exploitation during the life of the village that is inconsistent with a least-cost prey choice model. The preliminary nature of his conclusions is surely due in part to the paucity of baseline data on strontium isotope levels in large game, but his results certainly suggest the potential utility of this line of research.

Deanna Grimstead (2010) attempts to model how far a hunter can travel before the efficiency of large game hunting declines to the point where it is costly. She proposes that hunting remains efficient at distances of 150–200 km. Her model only measures the energetic expenditure of a human walking and carrying a load, rather than the crucial currency of time that is essential to the power of foraging models. Further, she models humans as single-prey loaders, rather than employing patch choice and the marginal value theorem, which would predict how far a hunter would go before stopping at a profitable patch. We suspect that the distances hunters can travel before the costs of large game hunting become costly are much shorter.

McGuire et al. (2007) model travel costs from the Owens Valley to high-altitude hunting camps in the White Mountains. They find that return rates for such ventures are well below 1,000 kcal/hour, return rates that make such hunting expensive. Whitaker and Carpenter (2012) appropriately return to the variables of time and energy, as well as patch choice and opportunity costs. They find that the distance at which large game hunting becomes costly is highly variable, but under many circumstances hunting trips become costly beyond only a few tens of kilometers.

We propose that the circumstances of prestige hunting are subject to modeling among contrasting Great Basin situations ranging from village base camps in wetlands, to fall pinyon camps, to quarrying and lithic reduction locales, to high-altitude hunting expeditions, to large Fremont villages and dispersed Fremont hamlets. Archaeological contexts such as these may be compared and framed with those known ethnographically to generate expectations of the alternative adaptive strategies that could compose an ESS under various circumstances such as those above. For instance, Hadza hunters of all ages rarely miss an opportunity to show off (Hawkes et al. 1991), and their efforts are widely noted and comparatively evaluated (Blurton Jones et al. 1997). Martu hunters are equally opportunistic (Bird et al. 2009), as are Meriam men in Torres Strait (Bliege Bird et al. 2001; Smith et al. 2003). Nunamiut hunters appear to be provisioners (Binford 1978; see Codding et al. 2011 for a comparative review). Young adult Ache hunters pursue prestige because they have the best chance of success due to their physical abilities and the benefit of prestige may translate into mating opportunities. Middle-aged Ache men with families to feed favor a risk-minimization strategy that aims at consistency in provisioning. Older men whose physical capabilities have become diminished may tend to focus on resources with lower pursuit costs and perhaps greater processing/handling costs (Hill and Hurtado 1996).

We will, of course, never see all of these individual behaviors in the archaeological record, but behavioral ecology never proposed to model behavior on a moment-to-moment basis, even in ethnographic situations. The goal is to provide explanations of the forces that produce a behavioral mix and changes in frequencies of alternative behaviors over time. After all, it is this sort of change that we recognize retrospectively as "history." We do not presume to speak to all aspects of this issue here, and we do see the investigation of prestige hunting only as an example of the broader exploration of intensification and cultural complexity. We applaud the efforts to tackle the many faces of intensification using evolutionary modeling that are in play among archaeologists working in the western Great Basin. We suggest that Fremont archaeology has much to gain from further work along these lines. Indeed, as McGuire and Hildebrandt (2005) note, the processes on the opposite sides of the Basin are similar. A synthesis enriches the descriptive histories but does not challenge them, because history is always part of evolution and adaptation—the outcome of organisms dealing with the problems of life.

The goal of academic debate is understanding. The Great Basin past is better understood now than it was 30 years ago, and the principles of behavioral ecology have helped inform that effort. We find much to be enthusiastic about and think that Basin archaeologists are among the leaders in practicing scientific archaeology. Many of the criticisms we made in 1982 are no longer valid, and to us, the evolution that has taken place in our field is gratifying and healthy.

References Cited

Barlow, K. Renee

2002 Predicting Maize Agriculture Among the Fremont: An Economic Comparison of Farming and Foraging in the American Southwest. *American Antiquity* 67:65–88.

2006 A Formal Model for Predicting Agriculture Among the Fremont. In *Behavioral Ecology and the Transition to Agriculture*, edited by B. Winterhalder and D. Kennett, pp. 87–102. University of California Press, Berkeley.

Barlow, K. Renee, and Duncan Metcalfe

1996 Plant Utility Indices: Two Great Basin Examples. *Journal of Archaeological Science* 23:351–371.

Bayham, Frank E.

1977 A Diachronic Analysis of Prehistoric Animal Exploitation at Ventana Cave. Unpublished Ph.D. dissertation, Department of Anthropology, Arizona State University, Tempe.

1979 Factors Influencing the Archaic Pattern of Animal Exploitation. *Kiva* 44:219–235.

Beaton, John M.

1973 The Nature of Aboriginal Exploitation of Mollusk Populations in Southern California. Unpublished Master's thesis, University of California, Los Angeles.

Bettinger, Robert L.

1980 Explanatory/Predictive Models of Hunter-Gatherer Adaptation. *Advances in Archaeological Method and Theory* 3:189–255.

1999 What Happened in the Medithermal? In *Models for the Millennium: Great Basin Anthropology Today*, edited by C. Beck, pp. 62–74. University of Utah Press, Salt Lake City.

Bettinger, Robert L., and Martin A. Baumhoff

1982 The Numic Spread: Great Basin Cultures in Competition. *American Antiquity* 47:485–503.

Bettinger, Robert L., Bruce Winterhalder, and Richard McElreath

2006 A Simple Model of Technological Intensification. *Journal of Archaeological Science* 33:538–545.

Billings, William D.

1951 Vegetational Zonation in the Great Basin of Western North America. In *Les Bases Écologiques de la Régénération de la Végétation de Zones Arides*, pp. 101–122. International Union of Biological Sciences, Series B, No. 9. Paris.

Binford, Lewis R.

1962 Archaeology as Anthropology. *American Antiquity* 28:217–225.

1977 *For Theory Building in Archaeology*. Academic Press, New York.

1978 *Nunamiut Ethnoarchaeology*. Academic Press, New York.

Bird, Douglas W., Rebecca Bliege Bird, and Brian F. Codding

2009 In Pursuit of Mobile Prey: Martu Hunting Strategies and Archaeofaunal Interpretation. *American Antiquity* 74:3–29.

Bird, Douglas W., and James F. O'Connell

2006 Behavioral Ecology and Archaeology. *Journal of Archaeological Research* 14:143–188.

Bliege Bird, Rebecca, and Eric Alden Smith

2005 Signaling Theory, Strategic Interaction, and Symbolic Capital. *Current Anthropology* 46:221–248.

Bliege Bird, Rebecca, Eric Alden Smith, and Douglas W. Bird

2001 The Hunting Handicap: Costly Signaling in Male Foraging Strategies. *Behavioral Ecology and Sociobiology* 50:9–19.

Blurton Jones, Nicholas

1976 Growing Points in Human Ethology: Another Link Between Ethology and the Social Sciences? In *Growing Points in Ethology*, edited by P. P. A. Bateson and R. A. Hinde, pp. 427–450. Cambridge University Press, Cambridge.

Blurton Jones, Nicholas G., Kristen Hawkes, and James F. O'Connell

1997 Why Do Hadza Children Forage? In *Uniting Psychology and Biology: Integrative Perspectives on Human Development*, edited by N. Segal, G. E. Weisfeld, and C. C. Weisfeld, pp. 279–314. American Psychological Association, Washington, D.C.

Bourdieu, Pierre

1977 *Outline of a Theory of Practice*. Cambridge University Press, Cambridge.

Bright, Jason, Andrew Ugan, and Lori Hunsaker

2002 The Effect of Handling Time on Subsistence Technology. *World Archaeology* 34:164–181.

Broughton, Jack

1994 Declines in Foraging Efficiency During the Late Holocene: The Archaeological Mammal Evidence from San Francisco Bay, California. *Journal of Anthropological Archaeology* 13:371–401.

Broughton, Jack M., and Frank E. Bayham

2003 Showing Off, Foraging Models, and the Ascendance of Large-Game Hunting in the California Middle Archaic. *American Antiquity* 68:783–789.

Broughton, Jack M., David A. Byers, Reid Bryson, William Eckerle, and David B. Madsen

2008 Did Climatic Seasonality Control Late Quaternary Artiodactyl Densities in Western North America? *Quaternary Science Reviews* 37:1916–1937.

Broughton, Jack M., Michael D. Cannon, Frank E. Bayham, and David A. Byers

2011 Prey Body Size and Ranking in Zooarchaeology: Theory, Empirical Evidence, and Applications from the Northern Great Basin. *American Antiquity* 76:403–428.

Byers, David, and Jack M. Broughton

2004 Holocene Environmental Change, Artiodactyl Abundances, and Human Hunting Strategies in the Great Basin. *American Antiquity* 69:235–255.

Charnov, Eric L., and Gordon Orians

1973 *Optimal Foraging: Some Theoretical Explorations*. University of Washington, Seattle.

Codding, Brian F., Rebecca Bliege Bird, and Douglas W. Bird
2011 Provisioning Offspring and Others: Risk–Energy Trade-Offs and Gender Differences in Hunter-Gatherer Foraging Strategies. *Proceedings of the Royal Society B* 278. Electronic document, DOI: 10.1098/rspb.2010.2403.

Codding, Brian F., and Terry L. Jones
2007 Man the Showoff? Or the Ascendance of a Just-So-Story: A Comment on Recent Applications of Costly Signaling Theory in American Archaeology. *American Antiquity* 72:349–357.

Eerkens, Jelmer
2004 Privatization, Small-Seed Intensification, and the Origins of Pottery in the Western Great Basin. *American Antiquity* 69:653–670.
2009 Privatization of Resources and the Evolution of Prehistoric Leadership Strategies. In *The Evolution of Leadership: Transitions in Decision Making from Small-Scale to Middle-Range Societies*, edited by K. J. Vaughn, J. W. Eerkens, and J. Kantner, pp. 73–94. School for Advanced Research Press, Santa Fe, New Mexico.

Elston, Robert G., and David W. Zeanah
2002 Thinking Outside the Box: A New Perspective on Diet Breadth and Sexual Division of Labor in the Pre-Archaic Great Basin. *World Archaeology* 34:103–130.

Erlandson, Jon M.
1991 Shellfish and Seeds as Optimal Resources: Early Holocene Subsistence on the Santa Barbara Coast. In *Hunter-Gatherers of Early Holocene Coastal California*, edited by J. M. Erlandson and R. H. Colton, pp. 101–111. Institute of Archaeology, University of California, Los Angeles.

Fisher, Jacob L.
2010 Costly Signaling and Changing Faunal Abundances at Five Finger Ridge, Utah. Unpublished Ph.D. dissertation, University of Washington, Seattle.

Gould, Stephen Jay
1977 *Ever Since Darwin: Reflections in Natural History*. W. W. Norton, New York.

Grimstead, Deanna N.
2010 Ethnographic and Modeled Costs of Long-Distance, Big-Game Hunting. *American Antiquity* 75:61–80.

Hawkes, Kristen
1993 Why Hunter-Gatherers Work: An Ancient Version of the Problem of Public Goods. *Current Anthropology* 34:341–361.

Hawkes, Kristen, and James F. O'Connell
1992 On Optimal Foraging Models and Subsistence Transitions. *Current Anthropology* 33:63–65.

Hawkes, Kristen, James F. O'Connell, and Nicholas Blurton Jones
1991 Hunting Income Patterns Among the Hadza: Big Game, Common Goods, Foraging Goals, and the Evolution of the Human Diet. *Philosophical Transactions of the Royal Society, London, Series B* 334:243–251.

Heizer, Robert F.
1956 Recent Cave Explorations in the Lower Humboldt Valley, Nevada. Papers on California Archaeology No. 42. *Reports of the University of California Archaeological Survey* 33:50–57. Berkeley.

Hildebrandt, William R., and Terry L. Jones
1992 Evolution of Marine Mammal Hunting: A View from the California and Oregon Coasts. *Journal of Anthropological Archaeology* 11:360–401.

Hildebrandt, William R., and Kelly R. McGuire
2002 The Ascendance of Hunting During the California Middle Archaic: An Evolutionary Perspective. *American Antiquity* 67:231–256.
2003 Large-Game Hunting, Gender-Differentiated Work Organization, and the Role of Evolutionary Ecology in California and Great Basin Prehistory. *American Antiquity* 68:790–792.

Hill, Kim, and Anna Magdalena Hurtado
1996 *Ache Life History: The Ecology and Demography of a Foraging People*. Aldine de Gruyter, Hawthorne, New York.

Hill, Kim, Hillard Kaplan, Kristen Hawkes, and Anna Magdalena Hurtado
1987 Foraging Decisions Among Ache Hunter-Gatherers: New Data and Implications for Optimal Foraging Theory. *Ethology and Sociobiology* 8:1–36.

Horn, Henry S.
1968 The Adaptive Significance of Colonial Nesting in the Brewer's Blackbird (*Euphagus cyanocephalus*). *Ecology* 49:682–694.

Jennings, Jesse D.
1964 The Desert West. In *Prehistoric Man in the New World*, edited by J. D. Jennings and E. Norbeck, pp. 149–174. University of Chicago Press, Chicago.

Jones, Kevin T.
1981 Optimal Foragers: Aboriginal Resource Choice in the Great Basin. Manuscript in possession of the author.

Jones, Kevin T., and David B. Madsen
1989 Calculating the Cost of Resource Transportation: A Great Basin Example. *Current Anthropology* 30:529–534.

Jones, Kevin T., and Steven R. Simms
1980 Models of Optimal Foraging and Aboriginal Great Basin Subsistence. Paper presented at the 17th Biennial Great Basin Anthropological Conference, Salt Lake City.

Kelly, Robert L.
2001 *Prehistory of the Carson Desert and Stillwater Mountains: Environment, Mobility, and Subsistence in a Great Basin Wetland*. Anthropological Papers, 123. University of Utah, Salt Lake City.

Kennett, Douglas J.
2005 *The Island Chumash: Behavioral Ecology of a Maritime Society*. University of California Press, Berkeley.

Kennett, Douglas, and Bruce Winterhalder (editors)
2006 *Behavioral Ecology and the Transition to Agriculture*. University of California Press, Berkeley.

Kerns, Virginia
2009 *Scenes from the High Desert: Julian Steward's Life and Theory*. University of Illinois Press, Champaign.
2010 *Journeys West: Jane and Julian Steward and Their Guides*. University of Nebraska Press, Lincoln.

Krebs, John, and Nicolas Davies
1997 *An Introduction to Behavioural Ecology*. 4th ed. Blackwell Scientific, Oxford.

Larson, Clark S., and Robert L. Kelly
1995 *Bioarchaeology of the Stillwater Marsh: Prehistoric Human Adaptation in the Western Great Basin*. American Museum of Natural History Anthropological Papers No. 77. New York.

Lindsay, Clint
2005 Late Prehistoric/Protohistoric Demography. In *Kern River 2003 Expansion Project*, Vol. IV, edited by A. D. Reed, M. T. Seddon, and H. K. Stettler, pp. 381–392. Alpine Archaeological

Consultants, Montrose, Colorado; and SWCA Environmental Consultants, Salt Lake City.

Louderback, Lisbeth A., Donald K. Grayson, and Marcos Llobera
2011 Middle-Holocene Climates and Human Population Densities in the Great Basin, Western USA. *The Holocene* 21:366–373.

Marwitt, John C.
1970 *Median Village and Fremont Culture Regional Variation.* Anthropological Papers No. 95. University of Utah Press, Salt Lake City.

Massimino, Jacquelyn, and Duncan Metcalfe
1999 New Form for the Formative. *Utah Archaeology* 12:1–16.

Mauss, Marcel
1924 *The Gift: Forms and Functions of Exchange in Archaic Societies.* Cohen and West, London.

McGuire, Kelly R., and William R. Hildebrandt
2005 Re-Thinking Great Basin Foragers: Prestige Hunting and Costly Signaling During the Middle Archaic Period. *American Antiquity* 70:695–712.

McGuire, Kelly R., William R. Hildebrandt, and Kimberly L. Carpenter
2007 Costly Signaling and the Ascendance of No-Can-Do Archaeology: A Reply to Codding and Jones. *American Antiquity* 72:358–365.

Metcalfe, Duncan, and K. Renee Barlow
1992 A Model for Exploring the Optimal Trade-Off Between Field Processing and Transport. *American Anthropologist* 94: 340–356.

O'Connell, James F., and Kristen Hawkes
1981 Alyawara Plant Use and Optimal Foraging Theory. In *Hunter-Gatherer Foraging Strategies: Ethnographic and Archaeological Analyses*, edited by B. Winterhalder and E. A. Smith, pp. 99–125. University of Chicago Press, Chicago.

O'Connell, James F., Kevin T. Jones, and Steven R. Simms
1982 Some Thoughts on Prehistoric Archaeology in the Great Basin. In *Man and Environment in the Great Basin*, edited by D. B. Madsen and J. F. O'Connell, pp. 227–240. SAA Papers, 2. Society for American Archaeology, Washington, D.C.

Peace, William J.
2004 *Leslie A. White: Evolution and Revolution in Anthropology.* University of Nebraska Press, Lincoln.

Price, Barbara
1982 Cultural Materialism: A Theoretical Review. *American Antiquity* 47:709–741.

Raab, L. Mark
1992 An Optimal Foraging Analysis of Prehistoric Shellfish Collecting on San Clemente Island, California. *Journal of Ethnobiology* 12:63–80.
1996 Debating Prehistory in Coastal Southern California: Resource Intensification Versus Political Economy. *Journal of California and Great Basin Anthropology* 18:64–80.

Raven, Christopher R., and Robert G. Elston
1989 *Prehistoric Human Geography in the Carson Desert, Pt. I: A Predictive Model of Land Use in the Stillwater Wildlife Management Area.* Cultural Resource Series No. 3. U.S. Department of the Interior, U.S. Fish and Wildlife Service, Region 1, Portland, Oregon.

Rhode, David
1990 On Transportation Costs of Great Basin Resources: An Assessment of the Jones–Madsen Model. *Current Anthropology* 31: 413–419.

Sahlins, Marshall D.
1972 *Stone Age Economics.* Aldine, Chicago.

Schiffer, Michael B.
1987 *Formation Processes of the Archaeological Record.* University of New Mexico Press, Albuquerque.

Simms, Steven. R.
1982 Experimentally Derived Cost-Benefit Data for Use in Models of Optimal Foraging. Paper presented at the 18th Biennial Great Basin Anthropological Conference, Reno.
1984 Aboriginal Great Basin Foraging Strategies: An Evolutionary Analysis. Unpublished Ph.D. dissertation, Department of Anthropology, University of Utah.
1987 *Behavioral Ecology and Hunter-Gatherer Foraging: An Example from the Great Basin.* BAR International Series, 381. British Archaeological Reports, Oxford.
2008 *Ancient Peoples of the Great Basin and Colorado Plateau.* Left Coast Press, Walnut Creek.

Smith, Eric A.
1980 Evolutionary Ecology and the Analysis of Human Foraging Behavior: An Inuit Example from the East Coast of Hudson Bay. Unpublished Ph.D. dissertation, Department of Anthropology, Cornell University.
1981 The Application of Optimal Foraging Theory to the Analysis of Hunter-Gatherer Group Size. In *Hunter-Gatherer Foraging Strategies: Ethnographic and Archaeological Analyses*, edited by B. Winterhalder and E. A. Smith, pp. 36–65. University of Chicago Press, Chicago.

Smith, Eric A., Rebecca Bliege Bird, and Douglas W. Bird
2003 The Benefits of Costly Signaling: Meriam Turtle Hunters. *Behavioral Ecology* 14:116–126.

Taylor, Walter W.
1948 *A Study of Archeology.* Memoirs No. 69. American Anthropological Association, Washington, D.C.

Thomas, David H.
1973 An Empirical Test for Steward's Model of Great Basin Settlement Patterns. *American Antiquity* 38:155–176.

Tinbergen, Niko
1963 On Aims and Methods of Ethology. *Zeitschrift fur Tierpsychologie* 20:404–433.

Trivers, Robert L.
1971 The Evolution of Reciprocal Altruism. *Quarterly Review of Biology* 46:35–57.

Ugan, Andrew, Jason Bright, and Alan Rogers
2003 When Is Technology Worth the Trouble? *Journal of Archaeological Science* 30:1315–1329.

Veblen, Thorstein
1931 [1899] *The Theory of the Leisure Class.* Viking Press, New York.

Whitaker, Adrian R., and Kimberley L. Carpenter
2012 Economic Foraging at a Distance Is Not a Question of If but When: A Response to Grimstead. *American Antiquity* 77: 160–167.

Wiessner, Polly
2002 Hunting, Healing and Hxaro Exchange: A Long-Term Perspective on !Kung (Ju/'hoansi) Large Game Hunting. *Evolution and Human Behavior* 23:407–436.

Williams, George C.
1966 *Adaptation and Natural Selection: A Critique of Some Current Evolutionary Thought.* Princeton University Press, Princeton.

Wilmsen, Edwin N.

1973 Interaction, Spacing Behavior, and the Organization of Hunting Bands. *Journal of Anthropological Research* 29:1–31.

Winterhalder, Bruce

1977 Foraging Strategy Adaptations of the Boreal Forest Cree: An Evaluation of Theory and Models from Evolutionary Ecology. Unpublished Ph.D. dissertation, Department of Anthropology, Cornell University.

1981 Foraging Strategies in the Boreal Forest: An Analysis of Cree Hunting and Gathering. In *Hunter-Gatherer Foraging Strategies: Ethnographic and Archaeological Analyses*, edited by B. Winterhalder and E. A. Smith, pp. 66–98. University of Chicago Press, Chicago.

Wohlgemuth, Eric

1996 Resource Intensification in Prehistoric Central California: Evidence from Archaeobotanical Data. *Journal of California and Great Basin Anthropology* 18:81–103.

Zeanah, David W.

2004 Sexual Division of Labor and Central Place Foraging: A Model for the Carson Desert of Western Nevada. *Journal of Anthropological Archaeology* 23:1–32.

Zeanah, David W., and Steven R. Simms

1999 Modeling the Gastric: Great Basin Subsistence Studies Since 1982 and the Evolution of General Theory. In *Models for the Millennium: Great Basin Anthropology Today*, edited by C. Beck, pp. 118–140. University of Utah Press, Salt Lake City.

PART III

Specialty Studies in Social and Historical Contexts

15

Eight Decades Eating Dust

A Short History of Archaeological Research at Danger Cave

David B. Madsen

A major aspect of Don Fowler's career has been a focus on the history of archaeology and, in particular, the history of archaeological research at the University of Utah, particularly in the Glen Canyon area of southeastern Utah during the late 1950s and early 1960s. While these studies constituted a major segment of the university's mid-twentieth-century archaeological research, the history of another equally important area of study within the Archeological Survey's overall research program remains largely anecdotal. This research focus involved the excavation of numerous caves and rockshelters in the Bonneville Basin of northwestern Utah, the most important and best known of which is Danger Cave. Here, I want to honor Don's career by reviewing the long history of archaeological work at Danger Cave and by trying to place that research in the general context of larger research trends in American archaeology.

Danger Cave

Danger Cave is located in an outcrop of the Silver Island Range on the Utah/Nevada border adjacent to the western margin of the Great Salt Lake Desert (Figure 15.1). The Silver Island Range consists of low, largely treeless and poorly vegetated mountains reaching 2,300 m above sea level, with most areas well below 2,000 m. The range extends northeast from near Wendover, Utah/Nevada, about 40 km into the playa of the Great Salt Lake Desert. It formed a narrow peninsula in Lake Bonneville during the last glacial period. The lower mountain slopes are sparsely vegetated with low sagebrush (*Artemisia* spp.), saltbush (*Atriplex canescens*), and greasewood (*Sarcobatus vermiculatus*), while scattered juniper (*Juniperus osteosperma*) woodlands are restricted to the uppermost margins of the highest peaks. The nearest major pinyon (*Pinus monophylla*) forests are found ~35 km to the north on the Pilot Range and ~25 km west in the Toano Range. The playa margins are covered by salt-tolerant plants, such as the prolific pickleweed plant (*Allenrolphea occidentalis*), which produces thousands of tiny edible seeds.[1] There are a number of small spring-fed marshes where a variety of plant and animal resources are available. One of the larger of these marsh systems lies outside Danger Cave.

Danger Cave sits at an elevation of 1,314 m, with the cave's base lying ~20 m above the modern playa and ~15 m above the Gilbert level of Lake Bonneville. The large single-chambered cave is about 18 m wide at its mouth and ~36 m deep, with a maximum interior height of ~12 m. The cave's mouth is triangular in shape, with a maximum height of ~5 m above lacustrine gravel deposits laid down during the regression of Lake Bonneville. Cultural deposits occur primarily at the cave mouth; when the cave was originally discovered, they choked off access to the cave interior. These cultural deposits were originally up to ~4.5 m deep, sloped toward the rear, and confined to the front two-thirds of the cave.

Ancient Caves of the Great Salt Lake: Human Antiquity in the Great Basin

Initial research at Danger Cave, beginning in the late 1930s, was a product of a burgeoning Great Basin–wide interest in excavating dry caves during the previous decade. This early work in Basin caves was a product of three factors. First, unlike a number of other areas in North America, the Great Basin was largely unknown, archaeologically speaking, particularly with regard to the chronological depth of human occupation. Second, there was a growing recognition, based largely on previous work in American Southwest dry caves, that dry caves' preservation and stratigraphy could produce a wealth of artifacts in a definable sequence. A research goal became the creation of a long and detailed culture history of the region. Finally, but no less fundamental, a small but growing cadre of professionally trained anthropologists at the region's universities saw the development of a history of modern Native Americans as critical to their anthropological studies.

One of the first of these was Llewellyn L. Loud of the Museum of Anthropology, University of California–Berkeley. Loud worked under the direction of Alfred L. Kroeber and, at the

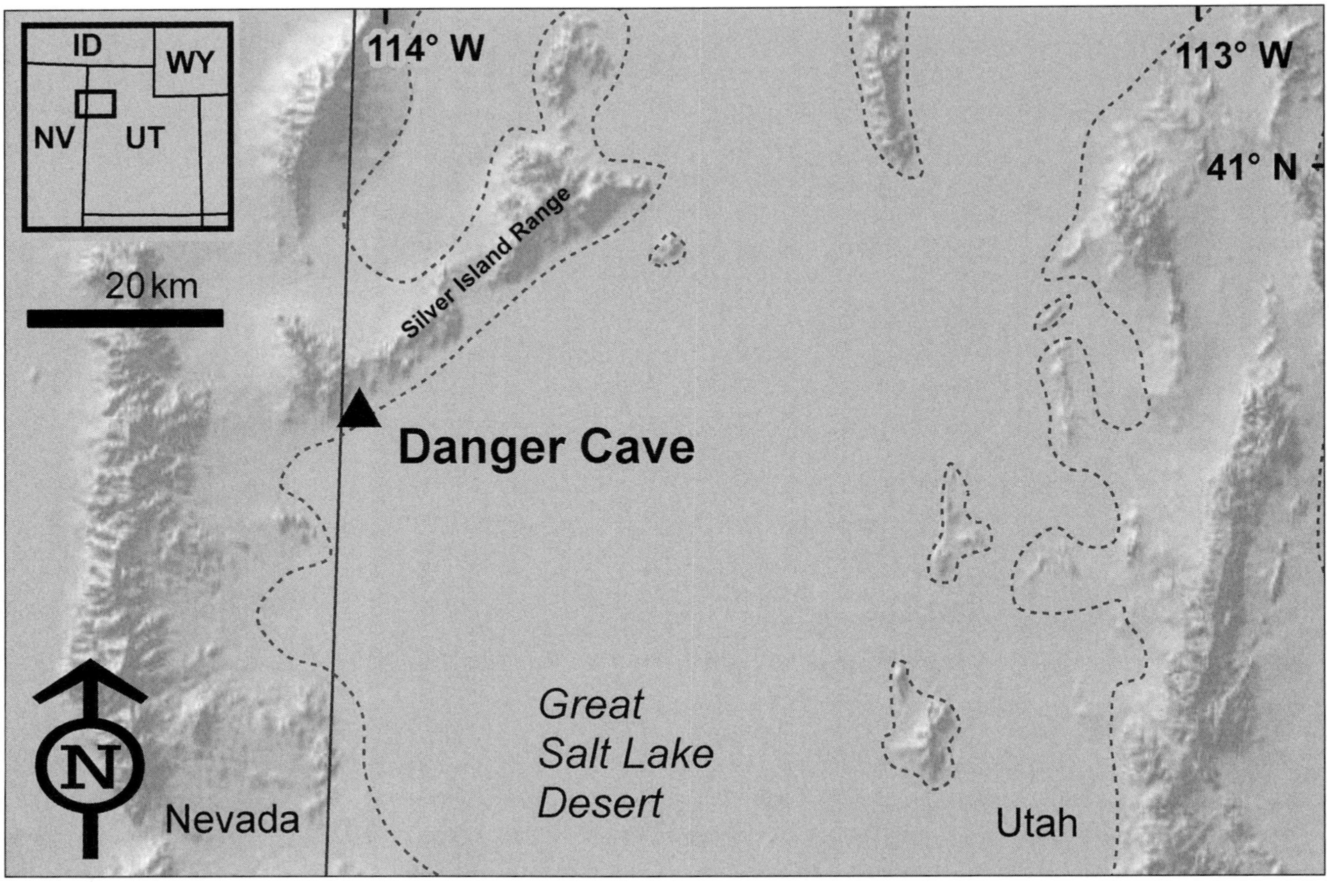

FIGURE 15.1. Map of the western Bonneville Basin area showing the location of Danger Cave on the Utah/Nevada border. The Silver Island Range extends northeastward from Danger Cave into the Great Salt Lake Desert (modified from Rhode et al. 2006).

latter's suggestion, undertook a solo excavation of Lovelock Cave in western Nevada. While no published report resulted from this work, it did lead to further excavations in 1924, headed by Mark H. Harrington of the Heye Foundation of the American Indian. With Loud's assistance, Harrington excavated the cave and recovered an astounding array of well-preserved artifacts including feathered duck decoys that produced a wave of excitement within the small Great Basin anthropological community (Loud and Harrington 1929). Harrington next shifted to the southern Great Basin and in 1930–1931 excavated Gypsum Cave (see Harrington 1933). Work there suggested that early Great Basin peoples were contemporaneous with extinct Ice Age mammals, in particular the giant ground sloth. Although this interpretation was later shown to be incorrect (e.g., Heizer and Berger 1970), at the time it generated a growing sense that dry Great Basin caves could provide a stratified record spanning the entire postglacial history of the region.

Simultaneously Julian H. Steward arrived at the University of Utah. Steward was trained primarily as an ethnologist and claimed that he was mostly self-taught as an archaeologist (Kerns 2003). Nevertheless, he spent a year at Berkeley when Loud's initial work at Lovelock Cave was generating interest, before finishing his undergraduate work at Cornell. Steward returned to Berkeley for his graduate studies while Harrington and Loud were conducting the second phase of Lovelock Cave excavation and laboratory analysis for their 1929 monograph. With a conception of what dry Great Basin caves might contain when he arrived at Utah in 1930, Steward was fully prepared to take over an archaeology program that had primarily focused on Anasazi ruins in Utah's southern canyonlands and now the excavation of dry caves around Great Salt Lake.

As Joel Janetski (1999) notes, Steward's contract with the university contained an explicit mandate to create a formal archaeological research program. This he did immediately and energetically, focusing on numerous caves around the Great Salt Lake and excavating Fremont mounds in central Utah. Steward's Utah cave research was short-lived, with field seasons only in 1930 and 1931, but it had an enormous impact on Utah archaeology and, in particular, on the excavation of Danger Cave. While Steward's research involved the first professional excavation of cave sites in Utah, more importantly, it was based on a research design that explicitly focused on chronology and the establishment of a regional occupational sequence. Steward's intention was to provide a detailed culture history "which could be dated by reference to the chronology of the lake" (1937a:1). Karl Gilbert's (1890) and others' geological analyses had made the history of Pleistocene Lake Bonneville and the Holocene Great Salt Lake reasonably well known and reasonably accurate chronologically. By focusing on caves formed by past lake high stands, Steward hoped to establish the antiquity of human occupation in the Great Salt Lake area.

Steward excavated three cave sites, Promontory Caves #1 and #2 and Black Rock Cave #1, and briefly tested eight others, mostly in the Promontory area. While he excavated the sites in arbitrary levels, his (1937a) published report includes stratigraphic profiles of the natural stratigraphy. Unfortunately, while he was able to excavate down to lacustrine gravels that he knew to be associated with Pleistocene high stands of Lake Bonneville, Steward could define no early materials on these lake gravels. He could only posit a preliminary cultural-historical sequence for the Bonneville Basin.

Steward left the University of Utah rather precipitously in 1933 and was never able to complete his cave studies in Utah. After obtaining an appointment at the Smithsonian Institution he did manage to get his *Ancient Caves of the Great Salt Lake Region* published by that institution and also produced a number of additional essays summarizing his views of the regional cultural-historical sequence (e.g., Steward 1940). In this later work he reiterated his earlier culture-history sequence, but despite his recognition that earlier cultural complexes probably existed in the Bonneville Basin, he was only able to describe materials older than the mid- to late Archaic "Black Rock Culture" as "Miscellaneous." For anything that might be associated with the even earlier regressive stages of Lake Bonneville he simply inserted a big question mark.

Concurrently with Steward's work in the eastern Great Basin, cave work was also expanding in the northern Great Basin, with the arrival of Luther S. Cressman at the University of Oregon in 1929. Cressman's work at a number of different caves in the Great Basin areas of southeastern Oregon during the mid- to late 1930s, including Fort Rock and Catlow caves, was groundbreaking in that it involved interdisciplinary research that included paleobotanists, geologists, and zoologists (Grayson 2011). Such a multifaceted research approach was later to be applied at Danger Cave and is now standard procedure in most large-scale archaeological research projects. More important at the time, however, was Cressman's discovery of well-preserved sandals below a volcanic ash at Fort Rock Cave and an association of cultural materials with the bones of extinct fauna, including horses, at Paisley Caves. This led Cressman to speculate that the antiquity of human occupation in the Great Basin exceeded 10,000 years (Cressman et al. 1942) and, along with Harrington's Gypsum Cave work, made it clear that other cave sites in the Great Basin would likely also contain deposits of great antiquity (Cressman 1988).

Hands and Knees Cave: Defining a Culture History for the Eastern Great Basin

Despite this recognition that there was considerable time depth to the human occupation of the region, exactly how early was still unknown and therefore of great interest. Perhaps of even more concern to the small archaeological community at the time was that no one had any notion of the spatial or chronological limits of many of the artifact types they were finding. Reading the letters of Great Basin archaeologists, one is struck by just how many questions there were about what kinds of artifacts were found where. In short, a perceived goal of the archaeological community of the time was to create regional culture histories that would include recognition of the age and distribution of named, diagnostic artifact types, which, in turn, would allow a definition of a series of archaeologically defined "cultures" that had evolved in the region. While people like Steward and Cressman had made a start in this direction, it was obvious to all that the cultural-historical record was very incomplete.

Somewhat surprisingly, the first actual archaeological work at Danger Cave was conducted not by a local archaeologist but by a graduate student at the University of California–Berkeley by the name of Robert F. Heizer, who was to become one of the Great Basin's leading anthropological archaeologists. Heizer spent much of his childhood in Lovelock, Nevada, and it was during his formative years that the work of Loud and Harrington at Lovelock Cave was stirring so much excitement among both the general public and the nascent professional community. This childhood interest in archaeology led Heizer eventually to Berkeley, where he completed his undergraduate studies in anthropology in 1936. In 1937, as a 21-year-old first-year graduate student, he was named as the titular leader of a group of fellow students (including Joe Ben Wheat) who initiated an archaeological survey in eastern Nevada and western Utah looking for dry caves like Fort Rock, Gypsum, and Lovelock.

Early that year, Heizer had written to Julian Steward for advice that may have led him to survey near the town of Wendover, on the Utah/Nevada border. In May 1937, Heizer wrote a long letter to Steward from "Wendover, Utah (or it may be Nevada)," thanking Steward for his "tips on survey," detailing the initial results of his research, and reporting on sites he called "Wendover #1" and "Wendover #2."[2] The Heizer group had only been in the Wendover area "several days" when he wrote Steward and planned on staying only "a few days more," but in that brief period he and his fellow students located and tested 10 dry caves and rockshelters in the area. One was called "Hands and Knees Cave," and it appears that Heizer was guided to the site by a local informant, as he was aware of the name even then: "Entrance is all choked—crawl in on hands and knees, hence the local name."[3]

According to the field notes kept by Heizer and other crew members, they worked in the Wendover area from May 15 to June 15 recording and testing sites. For some unknown reason, Heizer never pursued more in-depth research or reported the results of these brief test excavations. However, in later years he did send both his field notes and the collected artifacts to the University of Utah, and Jack Rudy described the sites briefly in a 1953 monograph, *An Archeological Survey of Western Utah*. Rudy gives brief descriptions of Heizer's 10 sites and artifactual collection. Only two sites were revisited by the Utah Archeology Survey team and given new Smithsonian trinomial numbers—Heizer's "site #4," which came to be known as Danger Cave (42To13), and "site #5," now called Juke Box Cave (42To20). There are artifacts listed for all but one of the 10 sites, indicating that Heizer conducted test excavations or made surface collections at each. For example, from Juke Box Cave Heizer collected chipped-stone tools such as projectile points, scrapers, and drills; Fremont pottery; Promontory pegs; worked bone tools; gaming sticks; and a variety of other artifacts. The size of the collections at these sites, combined with the rather limited time Heizer spent in the Wendover area, suggests that he was conducting rather hurried shovel tests rather than controlled excavations. The exception to this list of sites associated with artifacts is "site #4," but why Rudy listed no artifacts for that site is unclear, since it is apparent from Heizer's field notes that he collected "a number of manos, broken mutates [*sic*] and a few animal bones" from the interior surface of the cave. It may be that the artifacts Heizer collected from Hands and Knees Cave had already been sent to a fellow graduate student who subsequently worked at the site, Elmer R. Smith.

Elmer R. Smith received his undergraduate degree in 1931 from the University of Utah and obtained a master's degree a year later. It was during this time that he became interested in archaeology, working with and/or taking classes from John Gillin, Andrew Kerr, and Julian Steward (Jennings 1969). It appears that Steward took Smith under his wing and involved him extensively in his cave work. It was under Steward that Smith got his basic training as an archaeologist, and it was Steward who seems to have steered him toward the excavation of dry caves in the Bonneville Basin. When Steward left the University of Utah, Smith coincidentally did as well. After a stint teaching at Snow College in central Utah, however, Smith returned to the university when he was offered a position in the Department of Sociology and Anthropology in April 1937, replacing John Gillen. As a condition of that offer George Thomas, president of the university, required that Smith take a heavy course load of graduate classes at the University of California–Berkeley before the appointment would become effective. This, of course, was where his mentor Julian Steward had received his Ph.D. and where he came in contact with Robert Heizer. Smith arrived at Berkeley around the middle of April and was there at least eight months before returning to Utah.[4] Given that there were very few archaeology students at Berkeley at the time (Kroeber 1981), particularly ones interested in the dry caves of the Great Basin, it seems likely that upon his return Heizer would have told Smith about his Wendover test excavations and would have enlisted his aid in understanding how the artifacts he recovered compared with those Julian Steward and Smith had found in caves around the Great Salt Lake.

After his return to Utah, Elmer Smith immediately refocused his attention on the dry caves of the Bonneville Basin, excavating Black Rock Cave #2 and initiating the Dead Man's Cave excavations in 1938 (see Smith 1941). In 1939, while continuing to work at Dead Man's Cave, Smith started excavating cave sites in the Wendover area, although when exactly he started work at Hands and Knees Cave is not entirely clear (Figure 15.2). "Hands and Knees Cave" was, as Heizer noted, the local name for his Wendover #4, and Smith chose to continue to use that name in addition to giving the cave a catalog number of U-144 in the state site record files.

FIGURE 15.2. Elmer Smith at Danger Cave, early 1940s (courtesy of Don Fowler).

Unfortunately, most of Smith's notes and photographs for these Wendover cave excavations during the years 1939–1941 were lost over the course of World War II, and what work Smith did at Hands and Knees Cave, and exactly when, must be reconstructed from other sources. According to Jennings (1957), Smith only worked at Hands and Knees Cave in 1940 and 1941, but the accession catalog at the Utah Museum of Natural History clearly indicates that artifacts from the site were collected in 1939. Smith apparently excavated the site in arbitrary 6-inch levels, and during those first 1939 excavations he reached a depth of 65 inches in his test pits at the mouth of the cave. Jennings (1957) gives a specific description of where Smith's excavations were; it appears that during the three years of intermittent excavation Smith excavated a roughly 5-×-8-m area at the north side of the

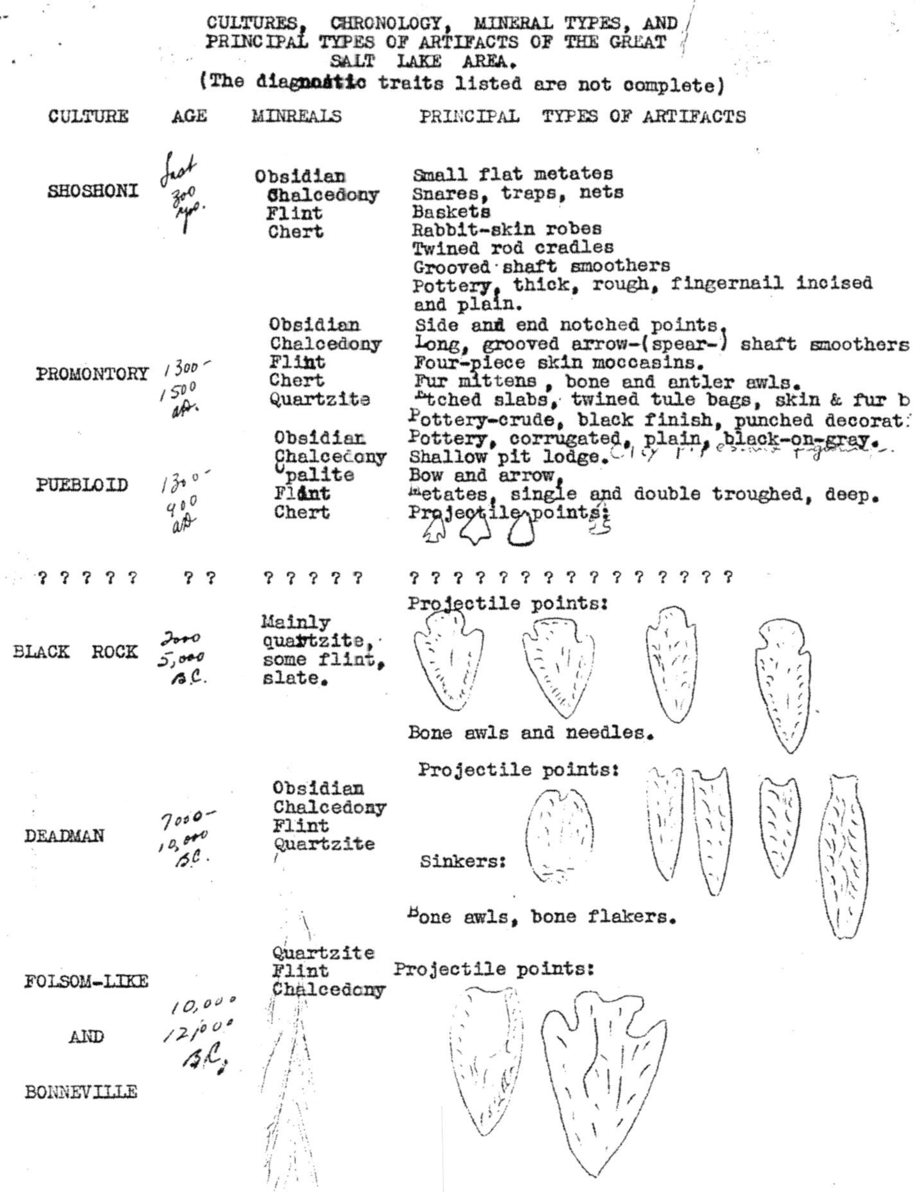
CULTURES, CHRONOLOGY, MINERAL TYPES, AND PRINCIPAL TYPES OF ARTIFACTS OF THE GREAT SALT LAKE AREA.
(The diagnostic traits listed are not complete)

CULTURE	AGE	MINREALS	PRINCIPAL TYPES OF ARTIFACTS
SHOSHONI	last 300 yrs.	Obsidian, Chalcedony, Flint, Chert	Small flat metates; Snares, traps, nets; Baskets; Rabbit-skin robes; Twined rod cradles; Grooved shaft smoothers; Pottery, thick, rough, fingernail incised and plain.
PROMONTORY	1300–1500 AD.	Obsidian, Chalcedony, Flint, Chert, Quartzite	Side and end notched points. Long, grooved arrow-(spear-) shaft smoothers; Four-piece skin moccasins. Fur mittens, bone and antler awls. Etched slabs, twined tule bags, skin & fur b; Pottery-crude, black finish, punched decorat
PUEBLOID	1300–900 AD	Obsidian, Chalcedony, Opalite, Flint, Chert	Pottery, corrugated, plain, black-on-gray. Shallow pit lodge. Bow and arrow. Metates, single and double troughed, deep. Projectile points:
? ? ? ? ?	? ?	? ? ? ? ?	? ? ? ? ? ? ? ? ? ? ? ? ? ? ? ? ?
BLACK ROCK	3000–5,000 B.C.	Mainly quartzite, some flint, slate.	Projectile points: Bone awls and needles.
DEADMAN	7000–10,000 B.C.	Obsidian, Chalcedony, Flint, Quartzite	Projectile points: Sinkers: Bone awls, bone flakers.
FOLSOM-LIKE AND BONNEVILLE	10,000–12,000 B.C.	Quartzite, Flint, Chalcedony	Projectile points:

FIGURE 15.3. Summary diagram prepared for, but never published in, Elmer R. Smith's "Early Man in the Great Salt Lake Area" (1942). Smith's handwritten notations on chronology, written well before the advent of radiocarbon dating, are amazingly close to the sequence recognized at the present time. Note the line of question marks suggesting a possible hiatus between the late Archaic and Fremont periods (courtesy of the University of Utah Archives).

cave mouth and extended these excavations down to a depth of at least "level 30, 133"–136"."

As early as 1939 Smith was using these cave excavations to construct a culture-history profile for the Bonneville Basin area. In a 1939 report to the president of the University of Utah detailing the results of the summer's research, Smith describes finding and photographing "five (5) different firepits resting on or within two (2) inches of the Lake Bonneville gravels" at site U-145.[5] By combining this older record with the cultural-historical reconstruction of Steward for later intervals, Smith was able to describe an occupational sequence for the region spanning at least 7,000–10,000 years. While this sequence is not well defined in this simple report to the president, Smith did refine it substantially for a 1942 publication (Figure 15.3). In it he not only constructs a chronological and material culture framework for the Bonneville Basin region that would still be relatively accurate today but also provides the only written record we have of his Danger Cave excavations. For that reason alone it is worth quoting at length:

> The earliest evidence we have of man's existence in the region immediately in the vicinity of the Great Salt Lake comes from a number of caves in the Wendover area.... The cave yielding the oldest culture is located about eighty feet above

the Stansbury level of Lake Bonneville.[6] The cave faces east, thus it overlooked the ancient lake, and is some quarter of a mile from an old spring that used to flow from the base of the Desert Mountains. The cave itself has been filled with human debris to a depth of nearly fifteen feet; the bottom layer of the cave is composed of light colored pebbles deposited by Lake Bonneville. Fire pits are found directly on the Bonneville gravels, showing that man moved into the cave soon after the water had receded enough to allow him to gain entrance to the cave.

The deepest twenty-six inches above the Bonneville gravels contained evidences of chipped flint flakes as well as a very distinctive type of projectile point. The point was formed by roughly chipping a flint nearly the size of the palm of the hand into a triangle, then the notches were chipped in from each corner making a wide stem and base; the base was notched in the center.[7] This culture has been tentatively named the Bonneville Culture and it possibly represents the oldest culture in the Great Salt Lake Valley.

The level above the Bonneville culture (80–112 inches below the surface of the cave floor) shows a mixture of cultures, but the most characteristic projectile point seems to be a Folsom-like artifact made from light flint and finely chipped.... This seems to correspond to the Folsom-like points found in another part of the Great Basin by the Campbells while working for the Southwest Museum of Los Angeles.... Two partly cremated burials were found associated with the Folsom-like points.[8] [The Bonneville Culture and this Folsom-like culture were combined in Smith's chronology at 12,000–10,000 BC]...

The Deadman type of culture was found directly above the Folsom-like layer (60–86 inches below the surface). This type of culture was first identified and carefully studied in Deadman Cave near Garfield, Utah. The Deadman Culture is characterized by projectile points having a pronounced concave base, a straight or convex edge, and a symmetrical form showing definite chipping of long slender flakes across each face.... A projectile closely related to the previous type, and found in the same level, is characterized by having a concave base or nearly straight base, rounded shoulders appearing about one-fourth of the way from the base and giving the upper part of the point a "swallow-tail" appearance.[9] Also associated with this culture were a number of metates or "grinding stones" which were usually roughly shaped, thin and in the majority of cases had a pecked, flat surface. The manos, associated with the metates were usually pecked into a rounded form from water worn stones.[10] [This was 10,000–7000 BC in Smith's chronology.]...

The next type of culture represented in the Wendover cave as well as in three other caves of the Great Salt Lake region located near Black Rock Beach, is given the name Black Rock Culture. It is located 49 to 60 inches below the surface of the Wendover Cave, and at nearly the same depths in the other caves excavated. The most outstanding characteristic of the Black Rock culture seems to be a specific type of projectile point with wide bases which are either straight or very slightly convex; the edges are straight or slightly convex while the barbs tend to be fairly uniform in width as well as in length. The notches extend in from the corners and the widths are fairly uniform. [This was 5000–2000 BC in Smith's chronology.]

At the Wendover site at a depth of 45–49 inches and directly above the Black Rock cultural level, a very hard greyish layer was found.... Above this hard layer the Puebloid culture was encountered, and above that the Promontory and finally the modern Shoshoni. [These were AD 900–1300, AD 1300–1500, and the last 300 years, respectively, in Smith's chronology.]

In 1942, Smith visited the Wendover caves with geologist and paleoclimatologist Ernst Antevs and, based on Antevs estimates for the ages of Lake Bonneville shorelines, revised the cultural chronology he first constructed in his 1939 report to the president of the university. This chronology is listed in tabular form in Smith's 1942 essay, but a summary in the manuscript for that article that did not ultimately get included is perhaps more instructive because it includes drawings of projectile point forms.[11]

Smith's work at Hands and Knees Cave was abruptly halted during the 1941 field season when a large secton of the cliff face above the cave mouth suddently broke free and crashed down on a spot at the mouth of the cave where the crew had been working only minutes before stopping for lunch. Smith then renamed the site "Danger Cave" to emphasize that event, a name by which the site has been known ever since (Jennings 1957). The large boulder remains there today, possibly protecting some of the fire pits on Bonneville gravels that Smith identified during his excavations. With the advent of World War II, Smith was unable to continue work and was only able to visit sporadically with other scientists such as Ernst Antevs.

During the war, Smith was asked by the U.S. government to be involved in what we would today call applied anthropology, and Smith's interests seem to have changed dramatically. With the exception of rewriting and republishing some of his earlier archaeological research, most of his subsequent research focused primarily on issues of ethnicity and racism (e.g., Jennings 1961). After the war another dynamic and charismatic archaeologist, Jesse D. Jennings, was added to the Department of Anthropology, and one might be tempted to speculate exactly how much of this shift was of Smith's own volition. According to Don Fowler (personal communication 2011), however, who was a student of both Smith and Jennings during the late 1950s, the pair got along with a great deal of respect for one another. It appears that Smith was instrumental in getting Jennings to continue his work in the dry caves around Wendover, leaving him free to pursue his new interest in applied anthropology.

The Desert Culture: Culture History and the Transition to Cultural Ecology

The cultural history of the Bonneville Basin, initially outlined by Julian Steward and expanded by Elmer Smith, Carling Malouf, and others, remained rather broadly and poorly defined at the time Jesse Jennings began his cave excavation in the Wendover area. At the outset of the project it was Jennings's intention to identify a fine-grained stratigraphic record for the region that contained as complete a list as possible of the material culture traits that distinguished each sequent "culture," a type of approach he (1934) had advocated as early as his graduate student days. That is, what he hoped to produce was a much more detailed culture history of the Bonneville Basin (indeed the Great Basin) than was currently available. To this end he employed natural stratigraphy, often identified at a rather small scale, to control his excavations and ½-inch and ¼-inch mesh screens to provide a greater emphasis on collecting bones, plant remains, and other items than had traditionally existed in the Great Basin.[12] He largely succeeded at creating a far more detailed regional artifact sequence than was previously available, and while endless refinements have been, and probably are still to be, made in that sequence, the chronology of major artifact groups in the Bonneville Basin had been largely established by the end of the Danger Cave excavations and analyses (although a named projectile point sequence would not come until later). This attention to greater detail was a phenomenon that was being repeated across the Great Basin (indeed throughout North America) as other well-trained archaeologists, such as Robert Heizer in the western Basin, sought also to provide more specificity to the prehistoric record. This aspect of Jennings's Danger Cave work was more representative than transformative of much of the research that was going on at the time.

As these excavations and analyses proceeded, however, and as he became more familiar with Julian Steward's (1937b, 1938) Great Basin ethnographic work, Jennings also began to hope that he could incorporate a more interpretive understanding of prehistoric lifeways into the Danger Cave report. Steward's major thesis was that Great Basin cultures (indeed, cultures generally) were a product of people coming to grips with the environment within which they lived and that the tools they employ, the residence patterns they follow, and the subsistance practices they utilize can all be seen as a reaction to the environmental constraints surrounding them. That is, ethnographic (or prehistoric) cultures had to be viewed within the environmental setting where they were found, an approach that came to be known as cultural ecology. This was an approach Jennings explicity sought to employ, although he somewhat disingenuously claimed in his Danger Cave monograph that "it had been the hope in the beginning of this study that a thoroughgoing ecological orientation of these data would be feasible. This idea has been abandoned because I find myself inadequately prepared for the task" (1957:276). However, he continues, "there is no reasonable way to escape the conclusion that the culture represented by the artifacts described in this report was one completely adapted to a special environment" (1957:276), and his definition of the "Desert Culture" in the Danger Cave report and elsewhere (e.g., Jennings and Norbeck 1955) has an explicity cultural-ecological foundation. While not as fully formed, detailed, or complete as later cultural ecology work, Jennings's study was nonetheless a move from culture history alone as a principal research goal to research that included more interpretive analyses and conclusions. In this regard it can be considered a transformative work that bridged the gap between two major eras of archaeological study in the American West.

Jesse D. Jennings (1994) was born in Oklahoma but was raised principally in New Mexico. Following initial undergraduate work at Montezuma College in New Mexico, he enrolled at the University of Chicago in 1929. After receiving his Ph.D. in 1946, Jennings worked briefly for the National Park Service before joining the anthropology department of the University of Utah in 1948. When he arrived at Utah, with training in the Southeast and experience on the Plains, he did not know much of the extant literature, research trends, or problems then fomenting in the Great Basin and had initially to rely on Elmer Smith's guidance on local issues. Smith immediately led Jennings to the dry caves of the Wendover area.

One of Jennings's first steps was to create what came to be called the Utah Statewide Archaeological Survey, with an explicit goal of exploring, documenting, and reporting the state's archaeological resources. For this, Jennings was able to obtain ongoing annual funding from both the university and the state legislature. The initial work of the survey was done in conjunction with a summer archaeological field school that Jennings started in 1949. The survey initially consisted largely of revisiting and rerecording sites Elmer Smith had first documented and expanding the investigated area from the immediate vicinity of Wendover to much of the western Bonneville Basin. This focus on the caves in the Wendover area seems to have been the result of the same research goal that initially led Smith to the sites: to find the earliest evidence of human occupation in the state. From the first, a major goal of the whole program was to uncover "data which will contribute materially toward the solution of problems regarding man's antiquity in North America" (Jennings 1957:vi).

The field school proper focused at first on the excavation of Juke Box Cave in 1949 (Figure 15.4). The initial work at Danger Cave that year consisted, for the most part, only in exposing Smith's old profiles and cleaning out the damage left by relic hunters during World War II (a problem that was to plague work at Danger Cave for the next 60 years). Jennings chose Juke Box initially because (1) it was a large, dry cave site with sufficient deposits unlikely to have been damaged extensively by relic hunters; (2) it contained rock art potentially linked to a historic Native American occupation; and (3) it was located high enough on a hillside to have been open to occupation relatively early in the regressive sequence of Lake Bonneville. Thus, Jennings felt that Juke Box might contain a long and complete record of human

FIGURE 15.4. Field school students excavating, while Jesse Jennings contemplates the Juke Box Cave stratigraphy, 1949 (courtesy of the University of Utah Archives).

antiquity in the region. As it turned out, Juke Box did not contain the kind of record that Jennings envisioned, and the field school operation shifted to Danger Cave in 1950. This was largely because Smith (1942) had reported that he had recovered two fluted points from the site, and Jennings felt that, as a result, Danger might contain the long record he had hoped to find at Juke Box Cave.[13] This 1950 field school at Danger Cave continued in 1951, and most of the excavation work at the site dates to these two years, with some limited additional follow-up work conducted in 1953.

The nature of this excavation work can be gleaned from Jennings's description of working conditions in the cave:

> There was nothing except layer after layer of fill lying smoothly upon one another. The very formlessness and monotony of the debris made for difficulty in understanding.

> Dry for millennia, the colloidally fine particles of dust and ash which comprised the fill were quite unstable. In a waste heap or exposed in a face, the gray or buff fill ran in rivulets when touched or disturbed by the transmitted shock of digging anywhere in the cave. Once disturbed all the fill materials flowed like water downward and outward until a precarious stability was reached. As the dust eddied in the restless air, a gray pall settled on all exposed cuts dulling the already subdued colors and obscuring contrasts between layers. By the same token, slight contrasts in color or texture which might be visible in vertical section or trench walls could not be detected with precision in any peeling or stripping operation because of the lack of firm texture or of hardened surfaces or because of the lack of strong color contrasts. Added to these handicaps, and probably the greatest problem of all, were the suffocating clouds of dust which hampered visibility during work and rendered breathing without respirators impossible. Work was sometimes done as much by touch as vision. Close observation of the working face was impossible [1957:9].

Despite these enormous handicaps, Jennings was able to maintain stratigraphic control, defining 70 minor stratigraphic units or features, which he combined into 14 major stratigraphic units during fieldwork. He eventually collapsed these major stratigraphic units into five "Cultural Strata" (DI–DV) for analytic purposes, but it is still possible to reconstruct a finer stratigraphy using the field designations for the major units, combined with the notes and profile drawings. By the end of Jennings's work at Danger Cave in 1953, it could be said that at the time Danger Cave was the best cave excavation ever conducted in the Great Basin. By 1957, it was also one of the best reported. It was a landmark work during the middle of the twentieth century and remains a landmark to the present. Jennings was enormously proud of this work and justifiably so.

While Jennings's Danger Cave work is a benchmark in the definition of Great Basin culture history, it is also historically important because of the role Danger Cave played in the development of the radiocarbon dating technique. Developed by W. F. Libby during the immediate postwar years (Taylor 1987), radiocarbon techniques were first employed to date archaeological sites in 1949 (e.g., Libby et al. 1949). Jennings was initially suspicious of radiocarbon dating, and he was not the first to apply the technique in the Great Basin. Samples from Fort Rock and Lovelock caves were dated earlier than anything from Danger Cave, for example (Cressman 1951). He eventually warmed to the potential that radiocarbon dating had for defining a viable chronological sequence in the Great Basin and with the fervor of a convert tried to apply the technique to the Danger Cave analysis and interpretation. The use of the new radiocarbon technique at Danger Cave set it apart from other early dated sites in three important ways. First, dating was incorporated directly into the analysis and interpretation of the site. Previous dates on materials from dry western North American caves had been run in a post hoc fashion on individual samples from curated materials and were not directly related to the overall cultural-historical sequence at the site, and Jennings made sure that the dates he obtained were related to understanding the entire sequence of deposition of the site. Second, radiocarbon dating at Danger Cave involved both solid carbon and gas techniques, and the results were instrumental in resolving which of the two methods was most reliable (i.e., gas). Finally, with age determinations of more than 11,000 (plus or minus) radiocarbon years on charcoal from the lowest hearths at the site, Danger Cave proved to be one of the most critical sites in demonstrating the antiquity of people in the Great Basin and, indeed, in the New World.

Jennings's work at Danger Cave epitomizes his approach to archaeology and how he understood scientific investigation generally. As Aikens points out, Jennings's work and how he trained students contained "a stress on order, cleanliness, and thoughtfulness in excavation, with serious attention to tracking and recording structural and contextual details" (Aikens 1999:4). Jennings's methodology is also characterized by what he considered to be an atheoretical, inductive approach to archaeological research. He was opposed to the use of "theory," stressing that excavations should be conducted descriptively, without interpretation until both fieldwork and analyses were complete. So strong were his views on this topic that he devoted the last chapter of his 1994 autobiography, entitled "Archaeology Without Theory: An Innocent at Work," to denigrating modern archaeologists who employ a more deductive approach in their research. Jennings professed "no scientific goals, having wearied during the 1950s of attempting to follow the sterility or the speculative dead-end paths or the convoluted mazes that lie within the tangled forest of theory upon which 'scientific' archaeology is based" (1994:264).

Yet, despite this claim, Jennings's work at Danger Cave was implicitly theoretical and colored both his analyses of the artifactual material he recovered and his interpretation of the data. His description of a "Desert Culture" is, as I noted, cultural ecological in form, stressing as it does an interpretation based on environmental constraints and reference to the ethnographic record of local modern foragers. However, his focus on continuity in the Danger Cave record led him to ignore important archaeological evidence of change. The same data that led Elmer Smith to define seven sequent prehistoric "cultures" in the Bonneville Basin led Jennings to define a single monolithic Desert Culture, which he described as remaining largely unaltered from earliest antiquity to modern times. Moreover, Jennings's theoretical views also led him to ignore change in the environmental constraints that were so important in the way the Desert Culture was defined. While Jennings suggested that he abandoned "a thoroughgoing ecological orientation" of the Danger Cave data because he found himself "inadequately prepared for the task," he was well aware of work by Ernst Antevs (e.g., 1948, 1955) and others showing that there had been dramatic environmental change in the Great

Basin during the Holocene.[14] Apparently he chose to abandon a thoroughgoing ecological orientation, or downplay it, not because he was inadequately prepared but because it did not fit his theoretical model. This difference between an overtly inductive/descriptive, but implicitly theoretical, research framework and an approach based on the examination of ideas derived deductively from an explicit overarching theoretical framework is the major difference separating Jennings's mid-twentiety-century work from later research work at Danger Cave.

Hogup Cave: Danger Cave as an Archive and as a Continuing Source of Data

Danger Cave was largely abandoned after Jennings completed his excavaton work in 1953 and was again left to the relic hunters and vandals of the region. Jennings had opened up the cave using a dragline to expose a pathway into the cave, and this led, along with his open excavation areas and the cave's location next to a major east–west highway, to what seemed like the almost complete destruction of the remaining deposits at the site. Within only a few years, the cave looked more like a World War I battlefield than an archaeological site. This went largely unnoticed, as the attention of Jennings and the Utah Archeological Survey shifted away from the dry caves of the Bonneville Basin to salvage efforts associated with the construction of large reservoirs on the Colorado and Green rivers. After nearly 15 years of salvage work, however, Jennings's interest in the long depositional histories to be found in these caves was revived, and he, along with his former student C. Melvin Aikens, resolved to excavate another Danger Cave–like site in as much or greater detail. To this end, they chose to work at Hogup Cave, located in the Hogup Mountains on the northwestern margin of the Great Salt Lake.

The history of that research and its impetus is available elsewhere (Aikens 1970) and is not relevant here. What is relevant is that this led Aikens, and several of Jennings's graduate students who were involved in the research, to reexamine much of the Danger Cave material in comparison to data that were being retrieved from Hogup. In particular, the analysis of projectile point types and their stratigraphic distribution at Hogup led Aikens to reassess Jennings's interpretation of the Danger Cave stratigraphy. During the intervening decades a number of people had questioned both the validity of the stratigraphic sequence at Danger Cave and Jennings's use of that sequence as the basis for his definition of the Desert Culture (e.g., Baumhoff and Heizer 1965; Cressman 1966; Davis 1964; Heizer 1956; Napton 1969). Aikens sought to resolve those questions by comparing the Danger Cave projectile point sequence to the much finer-grained Hogup Cave stratigraphic sequence. Based on that reanalysis, he suggested that, for the most part, there was "no intermixing of strata below DV" (1970:198) but that DV probably should have been subdivided into two separate units: DV and DVI. Aikens went on to speculate that this missing DVI level at Danger Cave was not the result of faulty excavation by Jennings but, rather, was due to Jennings incorporating artifacts collected by Elmer Smith from the rockshelter area of the site into the overall analysis.

With this reanalysis in hand, Aikens went on to examine the larger question of the validity of a relatively continuous "Desert Culture." As might be expected from a report that was "initiated and supported by [Jesse D. Jennings] and was carried out under his cognizance" (1970:v), Aikens walked a rather delicate path in stating his conclusions:

> Both Hogup and Danger contain artifacts referable to the post-Christian-era Fremont and Shosoni cultures, each of which introduced new cultural traits and perhaps new peoples into the region. The parallel records of the two sites combine to firmly demonstrate (1) that very long periods of cultural stability in the Great Salt Lake region are actual, not spurious, and (2) that change nevertheless did occur at intervals, as marked by the three cultural transitions just noted (not including the possible cultural differences that might exist between the scanty manifestations of Danger Cave layer DI and the subsequent, much richer layer DII [1970:198].

In short, Aikens returned largely to the cultural-historical sequence originally defined by Elmer Smith in 1942, confining the Desert Culture essentially to the Archaic period. Aikens abandoned even this nod to the idea of cultural continuity only a short time later when he and I divided the Archaic of the Bonneville Basin into the sequent "Wendover" (9500–6000 rcy BP) and "Black Rock" (6000–1500 rcy BP) periods (Aikens and Madsen 1986),[15] leaving a sequence almost exactly like that described by Smith 40 years earlier.

The Hogup Cave excavations were carried out during the summer months of 1967 and 1968. One of the graduate students involved in the first year of excavation was Gary F. Fry. Fry had become enamoured of the possibility that the dried human fecal remains that he and the rest of the crew were recovering by the hundreds from Hogup could tell more of a story than they had when the Danger Cave materials were first analyzed, and he resolved to make the analysis of the Hogup coprolites and a reanalysis of the Danger Cave coprolites the topic of his dissertation research. To this end, Fry and a small crew returned to Danger Cave during spring 1968 to determine if any intact deposits remained at Danger Cave and, if so, to excavate a small area in the same kind of stratigraphic detail that was being employed at Hogup Cave and retrieve as many coprolites as possible in a more fine-grained sequence than was possible using the curated Danger Cave specimens (Figure 15.5).

I was a member of that small crew, involved in what was only my second field experience and my first in a dry cave. What I remember most about that experience, beyond the choking dust, was the realization that Danger Cave, one of the most well-known sites in North America, had become an unmitigated disaster. The entire floor of the large cave was covered with huge potholes and piles of backdirt from relic-hunting. It was almost

FIGURE 15.5. Gary Fry at Hogup Cave, 1967 (courtesy of the University of Utah Archives).

impossible to see where Jennings's original excavations had occurred, and none of the deposits seemed to be intact. Shovel testing in various areas revealed only piles of disturbed fill, with younger potholes dug into the backdirt of older ones. It was as if the entire fill of the cave had been put into a giant blender and dumped back onto the cave floor. Our attempt to relocate and excavate from the 1953 profiles was a failure, but we did manage to locate a small area at the rear of the cultural depositions where some intact materials remained.

Fry excavated a ~2-×-6-m area at the extreme interior tail end of the cultural deposits that tapered from the mouth of the cave, eventually exposing a sequence that was a maximum of ~1.3-m thick. These deposits consisted almost entirely of very thin layers of pickleweed chaff and saltbush twigs, which it was assumed, represented the entire sequence originally defined by Jennings. Unfortunately, at this extreme margin of the main occupational area there was little in the way of the artifactual materials that had characterized the deposits in Jennings's excavations. Particularly disappointing was the lack of coprolites Fry hoped to find and study.

The primary focus of the 1968 excavations, however, was the collection of bulk samples for the identification of floral and faunal changes in the stratigraphic sequence (Harper and Alder 1972).[16] The bulk samples were collected at 15-cm intervals from four profiles spaced across Fry's excavation area by using a coffee can. The can, which Harper and Alder (1972) describe as a "sharpened steel cylinder," was driven into the face of the profile in order to collect samples of equal volume. The weight of each sample varied considerably, however, due to varation in the amount of rock, pickleweed chaff, twigs, and fecal matter each sample contained. The eight radiocarbon samples from two profiles, with a single exception, seemed to produce a consistent sequence of age estimates spanning a period ~10–5 ^{14}C ka. From what they thought was a valid chronological sequence, and from the plants and animals in the bulk samples, Harper and Alder (1972) attempted to reconstruct Holocene climate change in the Bonneville Basin, with the most surprising aspect of their reconstruction (to them as well as later researchers) being the identification of a significant dry period dating to about 10,000 radiocarbon years ago.

One of the problems with this sampling technique, of course, was that it combined multiple depositional layers into a single sample, a problem that was particularly acute at the rear of Danger Cave, where an 8,000- to 10,000-year sequence was compressed into little over a meter of deposits. Given that accelerator mass spectrometry dating was not available at the time and that a relatively large sample of unburned organic material was required to obtain a radiocarbon date, a subsample for dating drawn from each coffee can sample was necessarily composed of a mix of several stratigraphic units. This rather obvious problem went unrecognized at the time, and age estimates in excess of 10,000 radiocarbon years on samples containing pickleweed chaff were taken to accurately date the age of seed processing at Danger Cave, despite the radiocarbon analyst's note that the samples were "dated on selected twigs, dungs, etc." rather than on pickleweed chaff directly (Harper and Alder 1972:15). Only a single sample was run on the entire bulk sample, and it produced what was thought to be an anomalous date of ~7 ^{14}C ka because, as the analyst noted, it therefore "may have a little reason to show younger date than the true age" (Harper and Alder 1972:15).

This problem was exacerbated by Fry's coporolite studies. Since insufficent numbers of new coprolites were discovered in the 1968 excavations, Fry necessarily had to rely on curated materials collected by Jennings. While Fry's detailed analyses of these dried fecal remains produced astonishing evidence of both prehistoric disease (e.g., Fry and Moore 1969; Moore et al. 1969) and prehistoric diet (Fry 1976, 1978), he was forced to rely on the provenience assignments originally employed by Jennings (1957). More important, since he did not directly date any of the specimens (again because of the need for large samples of unburned organic material), he was forced to rely on the radiocarbon dating done in the 1950s and on Jennings's application of these age estimates to the relatively coarse DI–DV cave sequence. As a result, six paleofecal samples thought to be older than 10,000 radiocarbon years appeared to suggest that extensive seed processing was part of the diet from the earliest human occupation of the cave.

While the implications of Fry's work for the age of early seed processing were later to be challenged (Rhode et al. 2006), his use of curated specimens from Danger Cave did help illustrate the ongoing value of Jennings's original collections as an archive of data that could be mined for new and valuable insights into the life of prehistoric foragers in the Bonneville Basin. In addition to Aikens's (1970) reanalysis of the Danger Cave projectile points and Fry's analyses of the Danger Cave coprolites, James Adovasio (e.g., 1970) conducted an extensive analysis of Danger Cave textiles, and Donald Grayson (1988) reworked the faunal collections from the site. These and other continuing applications of new ideas and techniques to the material originally collected by Jennings reflect what is perhaps the most valuable ongoing aspect of that research. Jennings's theoretical speculations about the Desert Culture, while extremely valuable as a spur to other work in the Great Basin, have largely fallen out of favor. Jennings (1973) himself eventually abandoned the notion of the Desert Culture but noted the great extent to which it had stimulated archaeological research in the American West. While the notion of a "Desert Culture" may fade, the descriptive detail available in Jennings's work and his collection of a relatively complete array of material in sequence will always make the Danger Cave report a valuable resource.

The Silver Island Expedition: The Application of Foraging Theory to the Excavation and Analyses of Bonneville Basin Caves

Danger Cave was again abandoned to the relic collectors after Fry's expedition revealed that there were still deposits to be vandalized, and in the ensuing years the floor of the cave again began to look as if it had been churned up by some kind of Pleistocene megagopher (Figure 15.6). By 1981, when Jack Rudy revisited Danger Cave as part of an effort to update information about this National Historic Landmark, there did not seem to be many intact deposits left in the cave. By the time the report was completed and submitted, the National Park Service suggested that "it is doubtful that enough of the original fill is still present to warrant any further scientific investigations" (Weiss 1984).

Yet, while most of the continuing vandalism at the cave consisted of digging through the backdirt of previous relic hunters, some of it was revealing. In spring 1985, when Don Grayson, Jim O'Connell, Steve Simms, and I revisited Danger Cave, fresh vandalism had exposed intact deposits at the southern margin of the cave mouth. While limited in area to little more than a square meter, the exposure consisted of an almost complete vertical column of the depositional sequence at the site, including the most recent deposits that Aikens (1970) had suggested represented DVI. Upon close inspection of this column, we discovered that pine nut hulls were scattered throughout much of the depositional sequence in the column. In the decades after Jennings's, Aikens's, and Fry's work, the chronology and direction of the postglacial migration of pinyon pine from refugia in the southern Great Basin had become an important biogeographical issue (e.g., Thompson and Mead 1982), as had the timing of human use of what was one of the principal plant resources used ethnographically in the Great Basin (e.g., Madsen 1986). As a result, we thought it important to salvage what information we could from the limited exposure, and I sought and received funding from the National Science Foundation to recover what we thought were the last intact deposits at Danger Cave (Figure 15.7).

In 1986, we returned to the site, isolated the column, and removed it in very fine-grained stratigraphic units. Depositional units in such caves range from a basket load of pickleweed chaff laid down in only a moment over a very small area to thick layers of roof spall laid down over several centuries, and it is not always possible to excavate individual stratigraphic layers. Doing so only results in spurious accuracy when finer-grained sediments, such as pickleweed chaff, are deposited above and sift down into coarser-grained sediments, such as ebouli (roof fall rocks) and saltbush twigs. In the case of the removed column, we were able to identify 106 "mappable" depositional units but could separately and confidently remove only 37 "excavatable" strata (Figure 15.8).

The fill from each of these units was placed in its entirety in large plastic garbage bags that were removed to the laboratory and sorted. Nothing was discarded, and everything, dust, rocks, twigs, twine, coprolites, and so on, was separated and analyzed.[17] This allowed us to identify even the smallest fragments of pine nut shells and cone fragments, and David Rhode and I were able to find the remains of pine nut processing in virtually every one of the excavated units in the dry upper two-thirds of the column (preservation was minimal in the lower third). We identified these pine fragments as pinyon and suggested that, dating to ~7,900 radiocarbon years ago, the oldest of these shell fragments represented the earliest records of both the advent of pinyon

FIGURE 15.6. Backhoe removing spoil dirt from Jesse Jennings's excavation area inside Danger Cave, 1986: David Rhode (left), David Madsen (center), and Jay Hall (right; courtesy of the Utah Division of State History).

FIGURE 15.7. David Madsen (left) and David Rhode exposing what was thought to be the last intact vertical column of cultural deposits at Danger Cave, 1986 (courtesy of the Utah Division of State History).

FIGURE 15.8. Jim Adovasio, Stephanie Livingston, and Don Grayson screening at Danger Cave, 1986. A list of those who have worked at Danger Cave would make a great start on a Who's Who of Great Basin archaeology (courtesy of the Utah Division of State History).

forests in the northern Great Basin and the earliest human use of the resource in the area (Madsen and Rhode 1990). The chronological and stratigraphic controls were sufficient to convince one reviewer that the "work is fantastic and proof without doubt," a quote I now keep over my desk—not for reasons one might think but to remind me of unwarranted hubris. We had misidentified some of the smaller fragments, forcing us to write a follow-up article correcting this error (Rhode and Madsen 1998). This new identification proved to be even more interesting, as the earliest shell fragments (those dating to ~7.4 ^{14}C ka and stratigraphically older) turned out to be limber pine (*Pinus flexilus*). This suggested that foragers in the region were initially collecting limber pine nuts but turned to the higher-return (more calories/hour) pinyon pine nuts almost immediately once they became locally available.

Our work at Danger Cave in the mid-1980s was explicitly conducted to explore archaeological implications of foraging theory. We could take this approach because of a fortunate coincidence involving a rise of the Great Salt Lake to flood levels, a scheme to pump these high lake waters into the Bonneville Salt Flats, and federal regulations requiring the excavation of a cave that would be impacted by the project. This cave, known as Floating Island Cave, is located on the opposite end of the Silver Island Range from Danger Cave, on its northeastern margin. The Floating Island outcrop is completely surrounded by the mudflats of the Great Salt Lake Desert, and unlike the much larger Danger Cave, the small cave is more than 25 km from the nearest available water. It was obvious from the start that the use of Danger and Floating Island caves by prehistoric foragers must have been considerably different, and we hoped to test predictions made from foraging theory about exactly what that difference might have been. We therefore designed the excavation plan at Floating Island Cave to match the one employed simultaneously at Danger Cave so that the data from the two caves were sufficiently comparable that tests of our theoretically derived expectations would be reliable.

This approach to excavation is obviously very different from that espoused by Jennings, and it was this view of anthropological archaeology as "science" rather than as "history" that he was eventually to rail against in his 1994 autobiography. However, at the time we returned to the cave in the mid-1980s, this archaeology as science approach was dominated by attempts to apply "midrange" theory to the investigation of Great Basin caves and rockshelters (e.g., Thomas 1983). Midrange theory primarily involves the identification of taphonomic processes (e.g., Binford 1977; Raab and Goodyear 1984)—a laudable goal, but hardly one related to general biological and anthropological theories about why people do what they do. We considered using this approach as our primary research focus but sought a more comprehensive theoretical orientation that might better help explain the history of human behavior at Danger Cave. We found that in a theoretical approach, now loosely encompassed under the rubric of "behavioral ecology," that was also beginning to be applied in Great Basin archaeological studies (e.g., O'Connell et al. 1982). Of the two approaches, it seemed to us that the latter was likely to produce the more viable results, and it was an approach we chose to try at Danger Cave.

Using models derived from foraging theory we constructed testable predictions about the differential use of the caves. These included such predictions as, for example, foragers would be likely to more completely process pickleweed seeds at Danger Cave than at Floating Island Cave. These predictions then led us to collect and examine data in ways we otherwise would not have. Again using the pickleweed example, when we examined dried fecal boluses from similar sample columns at the two caves, we were interested in determining the relative proportion of chaff to seeds, to examine transport models rather than simply measuring the total weight of pickleweed in each bolus. We compared foraging behavior at the caves in terms of ground stone, lithic technology, resource processing, transport costs, and a whole array of other things not previously examined at dry caves in the Bonneville Basin.

Unfortunately, much of this work remains available only in manuscript form (but see Barlow and Metcalfe 1996; Jones and Madsen 1989; Rhode and Madsen 1998) for a number of reasons. Mostly this has been due to the enormous amount of time it takes to process and analyze deposits removed in their entirety from the two caves and to the fact that the analyses have been performed by a very wide variety of specialists working independently without remuneration. In large part, however, it has also been due to continuous and surprising revelations that Danger Cave still contains a remarkable amount of undisturbed archaeological deposits.

After we completed the removal of what we thought was the last remaining vertical column of intact deposits in the cave, and with no means to close the wide mouth of the cave, we left it open as had others before us. This meant that the cave continued to attract relic hunters and other vandals, who concluded that if the cave was still attractive to professional archaeologists, it must still contain material attractive to them. Finally, by the mid-1990s the appearance of the cave was so bad that a decision was reached to do something about it. Danger Cave, together with Juke Box Cave, had been made a state park in the mid-1960s, about the same time it had been nominated as a National Historic Landmark. The park had been undeveloped for decades (and remains so), but in 1998 the Utah Division of State Parks was finally able to put together a combination of state, federal, and private funds and enclose the site to prevent further vandalism. As part of this enclosure process, a small Bobcat front-end loader was brought in to smooth out the potholes and mounds of backdirt and to create a berm across which a gated entry could be installed. In so doing, the Bobcat exposed a small, roughly 50-cm diameter, area in the approximate center of the site that appeared to still have intact deposits. At the time the gate was installed these intact deposits were not recognized, and it was not until we returned to inspect the enclosure in 2000 that we realized it might be possible to expand our vertical column sample to these lower and better-preserved deposits farther back in the cave.

In 2001, in 2002, and again in 2004 David Rhode, Kevin Jones, and I, together with several dozen professional and amateur volunteers, were able to explore and expose these remaining intact deposits (Figure 15.9). What we found was astonishing, at least to me. It turned out that approximately the bottom half of Jennings's last profile, the one he had left when he finally finished his excavations in 1953, and the deposits behind that profile, remained largely undisturbed. Apparently much of the ongoing vandalism at the cave, spanning nearly 5 decades, had consisted of turning over old backdirt again and again. By actually leaving the inglorious mounds of spoil dirt in place, the lowest and oldest deposits were protected and remained intact.

We were able to expose about a 4-m-wide span of Jennings's (1957) Feature 143 profile face, consisting of strata in DI, DII, and the lower section of DIII (Rhode et al. 2006). In so doing, we were also able to identify a DI hearth in that profile resting atop eolian sands and lake gravels that Jennings had dated to 10,270 ± 600 ^{14}C BP. We ran two charcoal samples from that hearth and an adjacent one and received age estimates of 10,270 ± 50 and 10,310 ± 40 ^{14}C BP, a rather remarkable similarity given the experimental era of radiocarbon dating that existed when Jennings's dates were run. We were also able to relocate and expose the area at the rear of the cultural deposits excavated by Fry in 1968. These profiles too were almost completely intact, and we were able to remap both Jennings's and Fry's profiles, correlate their stratigraphic descriptions and interpretations with our own, and obtain additional radiocarbon age estimates for several of these stratigraphic units (Rhode et al. 2006). Other than

FIGURE 15.9. Kevin Jones contemplating what was left of Jesse Jennings's 143 profile face as it was being exposed in 2002 (courtesy of David Rhode).

the extraction of samples for dating from these cleaned profiles, we have conducted no further excavations at the cave. This work did, however, allow us to correlate a large suite of dates, obtained over the course of more than five decades, with the depositional sequence in the cave and, among other things, demonstrate that seed grinding at the site did not begin until ~8.6 ^{14}C ka, 1,500–2,000 radiocarbon years later than previously thought. However, Danger Cave does, for now, still remain the site of the earliest directly dated seed processing in the Americas.[18]

Danger Cave and the Future of Archaeological Research

From what we have been able to determine from our exposure of portions of Jennings's and Fry's excavation areas, nearly 150 m^2 of intact cultural deposits remain at the rear of Danger Cave. Only the basal section of the sequence remains, but these represent the earliest deposits at the site, ranging in age from ~5 ^{14}C ka to well over 10 ^{14}C ka. The amount of disturbance to this relatively large area is unclear, but undisturbed cultural deposits remain to be investigated. What future research in these deposits will consist of and what that research will tell us about the human condition are unknown, of course, but it is possible to at least speculate on what research in the foreseeable future might tell us.

Recent advances in the extraction and analysis of DNA from ancient human remains suggest that a number of such studies are likely to be carried out at Danger Cave in the near future. Some of this work is already under way. Steve Simms and Brian Kemp are currently involved in a project investigating the possible continuity of Fremont to Late Prehistoric populations in the Bonneville Basin by using DNA extracted from quids. Quids are the roots of (primarily) bulrush plants (*Scirpus* spp.) that foragers at Danger Cave and other similar dry caves situated near marsh systems chewed to extract the starches they contain. The wads of the remaining well-masticated fibers, what Jennings called "these unlovely specimens" (1957:224), were then simply spit out. Danger Cave contains (or contained) literally thousands of such unlovely specimens, and Kemp and Simms are using curated materials collected during previous excavations in their investigations.

While the remaining intact deposits at Danger Cave likely contain hundreds more of these quids, they are not the only unlovely product of human consumption that contain ancient DNA. Boluses of dried human fecal material were also quite common in the upper, drier deposits Jennings excavated toward the mouth of the cave and are likely to be found in the earliest deposits toward the rear of the cave, where preservation is good even down to the levels dating to 12,000 calendar years ago and older. The remains of bulrush appear to be restricted to the middle Holocene deposits and later, so it may be that these dried boluses represent the only chance to extract DNA left by the earliest foragers in the Bonneville Basin. DNA has already been extracted from even older human boluses elsewhere in the Great Basin (e.g., Gilbert et al. 2008), and it seems likely that a project aimed at excavating and studying the very oldest human fecal material from Danger Cave will be undertaken in the near future.

Such studies will likely be biologically oriented and directed at understanding the population dynamics of the earliest foragers in North America, but the study of ancient DNA from dung boluses and quids at Danger Cave may also have more behavioral implications. During the parallel excavations and analyses of Danger and Floating Island caves, my colleague Jim Adovasio noted that some of the textiles from the two caves were so similar that they were likely to have been made by the same woman or her daughter. This raises the possibility that, at least at times, the same group of foragers was using the two sites. As there are a number of dry caves and rockshelters in the vicinity of Danger Cave (e.g., Bonneville Estates Rockshelter [Goebel et al. 2007]), it seems likely that some attempt will be made to try to trace the actual seasonal movement of a group of prehistoric foragers, as opposed to speculating on what mobility patterns may have existed.

What other research projects might yet be carried out at Danger Cave is more speculative. Certainly, we still know little about the Great Basin's earliest foragers since the very large majority of Paleoarchaic sites in the Great Basin are open sites preserving little more than lithic material. It seems likely that the well-preserved Paleoarchaic materials still extant in the rear of Danger Cave could provide a rare window into the lifestyles of some of the Great Basin's earliest peoples, and I suspect that a large-scale project geared toward the recovery of Paleoarchaic textiles, food remains, and other artifacts susceptible to degradation will eventually take place at the site. Whether or not such a large-scale project actually does take place, or merely a series of smaller projects with more specific research goals are conducted, it seems likely that Danger Cave will be the focus of continuing archaeological research. I think that someone in the future will be writing a history of a century or more of study at Danger Cave, rather than just that of the last eight decades. As in the past, such future research will likely be representative of the then current trends in American anthropological archaeology.

Acknowledgments

David Rhode and Joel Janetski allowed me to utilize some of their own archival research, for which I am grateful. Billy Clewlow was kind enough to spend time at the Bancroft Library at the University of California, Berkeley, going through Robert Heizer's 1937 field notes. Kirk Baddley at the University of Utah Archives and Renae Weder at the Utah Division of State History were of great help in locating old photographs. I am indebted to Don Fowler for the photograph of Elmer Smith and for his insight into the relationship between Smith and Jesse Jennings. Glenna Nielsen at the Utah Museum of Natural History helped me with the accession notes that resolved some temporal conflicts. I am grateful to Don Grayson, Joel Janetski, Kevin Jones, David Rhode, and Evelyn Seelinger for their useful comments on an initial draft. Finally, I want to extend my gratitude to all the professional archaeologists, students, and amateurs who spent so much of their time, efforts, and mental acuity eating dust at Danger Cave over the last eight decades. They have largely gone unrecognized here, but without them none of the research described above would ever have been accomplished.

Notes

1. The more correct common name for *Allenrolphea* spp. is "iodine bush," but the term *pickleweed* is used in every previous publication on Danger Cave, and I continue to use the term here to reduce confusion.
2. Robert Heizer to Julian Steward, May 30, 1937, Julian H. Steward Collection, University of Illinois–Urbana Archives.
3. "Nevada Survey" 1937 field notes, Robert Fleming Heizer Papers, BANC FILM 2106 (Originals: BANC MSS 78/17 c), Bancroft Library, University of California, Berkeley.
4. Elmer Smith to Arthur L. Beeley, chairman of the University of Utah Department of Sociology and Anthropology, November 30, 1937, Elmer R. Smith's Faculty Historical File, University of Utah Archives, Salt Lake City, Accession 526.
5. Elmer Smith, Report on Accomplishments of University of Utah Museum of Anthropology Archaeological Expedition for Summer of 1939, Special Report to President George Thomas, Presidential Papers, University of Utah Archives, Salt Lake City.

Smith (1939) also briefly describes his work around Wendover in several paragraphs published in the *Museum News*. The most interesting aspect of the brief report is his description of structures built on the surface of several cave sites. Whether one of these sites was Danger Cave is unclear. Site U-145 is now listed as 42To30 in the state archaeological record files. It is a shallow cave/rockshelter immediately adjacent the main thoroughfare on the east edge of the town of Wendover, Utah.

6. This is a source of possible confusion, as Danger Cave is not located 80 ft above the Stansbury level. However, the description fits Danger Cave, and the only other possible cave site located a quarter mile from the dry spring is Juke Box Cave, which Jennings (1957) identifies as U-149. Also, Juke Box is actually at the Stansbury level, not 80 ft above it. Smith may have been confusing the Stansbury level with the Gilbert level of Lake Bonneville/Great Salt Lake, which actually is about 80 ft below the mouth of Danger Cave. The Gilbert level of the lake was not defined at the time, and Smith may have associated it with the higher Stansbury level.
7. This may be the hafted biface illustrated by Jennings in figure 156 of his Danger Cave monograph (1957).
8. Jennings (1957) claims that a little less than 25 percent of the artifacts he analyzed and described in his Danger Cave monograph came from Elmer Smith's 1939–1941 excavations. This suggests that most of the material Smith collected survived World War II, yet there is no mention of these two burials in Jennings's monograph. It may be that Smith confused another site containing burials, likely U-145 (42To30), with Hands and Knees Cave.
9. These represent what we now refer to as Pinto and Humboldt projectile points.
10. It took more than 60 years for archaeologists to recognize that ground stone and the grinding of seeds only appear at Danger Cave during the early Archaic, in association with such Archaic projectile points as the Pinto and Humboldt varieties (Rhode et al. 2006). During the interval, and based on the work of Jennings (1957) and Fry (1970), many regarded Danger Cave as the only site in the Great Basin where it could be demonstrated that the earliest Paleoarchaic foragers were grinding seeds. Smith seems to have had it right all along.
11. In this figure, as well as in the tabular summary in the published version, readers will note that Smith suggests there is some kind of hiatus between the Black Rock (Archaic) and Puebloid (Fremont) cultures in the cave records from around the Great Salt Lake. This is something a colleague and I recognized more than 30 years later (Madsen and Berry 1975), but we failed to give Smith proper credit as the originator of the idea.
12. According to Grayson (1988), Jennings told him that no more than 80 percent of the deposits were screened and that the screens varied from ⅓ to ½ inch when they were used.
13. These two projectile points were lost during World War II, and Jennings had only Smith's report to go on. Nearly 30 years later the points were relocated and, as Smith later suspected, proved not be fluted points at all (Holmer 1986).
14. Antevs visited Danger and Juke Box caves a number of times with Elmer Smith and in 1949 and 1950 gave lectures to the field school students, with Jennings in attendance. After the 1949 visit Jennings wrote extensively in the Juke Box Cave field notes about how Antevs's visit helped him understand the history of the cave. After the 1950 visit to Danger Cave, however, Jennings only noted that "E. Antevs and E. R. Smith visited the site in P.M. Antevs no great help" (July 28, 1950, F1 field notes, University of Utah Archives, Salt Lake City).
15. Aikens and Madsen 1986 was published in 1986 but written in manuscript form in the early 1970s.
16. In Fry's field notes he states that Danger Cave is "being reexcavated at this time to obtain constant volume samples of the deposits for analysis by K. T. Harper of the U of Utah dept. of Botany and for pollen analysis" (March 20, 1968, F1 field notes, University of Utah Archives, Salt Lake City). While that was Fry's appointed task, I remember Fry mostly talking about his hope of obtaining coprolites with greater stratigraphic control.
17. This rather tedious task was aided by "volunteers" from the local court system, condemned to perform public service as part of their sentence. One woman, after picking through a tray of dust, rocks, and sheep fecal pellets for an hour or two, suddenly jumped to her feet, threw down her tweezers, and stormed out, exclaiming as she went, "I would rather be in jail than do this #&*%."
18. There are any number of sites in western North America, including Danger Cave, that contain ground stone in deposits dating to older than 9,000 ^{14}C years ago (e.g., Yoder et al. 2010), but direct evidence of human consumption of ground seeds (in coprolites) is missing.

References Cited

Adovasio, James M.
1970 The Origin, Development and Distribution of Western Archaic Textiles. *Tebiwa* 13:1–40.

Aikens, C. Melvin
1970 *Hogup Cave*. University of Utah Anthropological Papers, 93. Salt Lake City.
1999 Jesse D. Jennings: A Biographical Memoir. *Biographical Memoirs* 77:1–20. Washington, D.C.

Aikens, C. Melvin, and David B. Madsen
1986 Prehistory of the Eastern Area. In *Great Basin*, edited by Warren L. d'Azevedo, pp. 149–160. Handbook of North American Indians, Vol. 11, William C. Sturtevant, general editor, Smithsonian Institution, Washington, D.C.

Antevs, Ernst
1948 Climate Changes and Pre-White Man. In *The Great Basin with Emphasis on Glacial and Postglacial Times*, pp. 168–191. Bulletin of the University of Utah, 38(20). Salt Lake City.
1955 Geologic-Climatic Dating in the West. *American Antiquity* 20:317–335.

Barlow, K. Renee, and Duncan Metcalfe
1996 Plant Utility Indices: Two Great Basin Examples. *Journal of Archaeological Science* 23:351–371.

Baumhoff, Martin A., and Robert F. Heizer
1965 Postglacial Climate and Archaeology in the Desert West. In *The Quaternary of the United States*, edited by H. E. Wright, Jr., and David G. Frey, pp. 697–707. Princeton University Press, Princeton.

Binford, Lewis R.
1977 General Introduction. In *For Theory Building in Archaeology*, edited by Lewis R. Binford, pp. 1–10. Academic Press, New York.

Cressman, Luther S.
1951 Western Prehistory in the Light of Carbon 14 Dating. *Southwest Journal of Anthropology* 7:289–313.
1966 Man in Association with Extinct Fauna in the Great Basin. *American Antiquity* 31:866–867.

1988 *A Golden Journey: Memoirs of an Archaeologist*. University of Utah Press, Salt Lake City.

Cressman, Luther S., Frank C. Baker, Paul S. Conger, Henry P. Hansen, and Robert F. Heizer

1942 *Archaeological Researches in the Northern Great Basin*. Carnegie Institution of Washington Publication, 538. Washington, D.C.

Davis, Wilbur A.

1964 Theoretical Problems in Western Prehistory. In *Current Status of Anthropological Research in the Great Basin*, edited by Warren d'Azevedo, Wilber A. Davis, Donald D. Fowler, and W. Suttles, pp. 147–165. University of Nevada, Desert Research Institute Social Sciences and Humanities Publication, 1. Reno.

Fry, Gary F.

1970 Prehistoric Human Ecology in Utah: Based on the Analysis of Coprolites. Unpublished Ph.D. dissertation, Department of Anthropology, University of Utah, Salt Lake City.

1976 *Analysis of Prehistoric Coprolites from Utah*. University of Utah Anthropological Papers, 97. Salt Lake City.

1978 *Prehistoric Diet at Danger Cave, Utah as Determined by the Analysis of Coprolites*. Miscellaneous Paper, 23; University of Utah Anthropological Papers, 99. Salt Lake City.

Fry, Gary F., and John G. Moore

1969 *Enterobius vermicularis*: 10,000-Year-Old Human Infection. *Science* 166:1620.

Gilbert, Grove Karl

1890 *Lake Bonneville*. U.S. Geological Survey Monograph, 1. Washington, D.C.

Gilbert, M. Thomas P., Dennis L. Jenkins, Anders Götherstrom, Nuria Naveran, Juan J. Sanchez, Michael Hofreiter, Philip Francis Thomsen, Jonas Binladen, Thomas F. G. Higham, Robert M. Yohe, II, Robert Parr, Linda Scott Cummings, and Eske Willerslev

2008 DNA from Pre-Clovis Human Coprolites in Oregon, North America. *Science* 320:786–789.

Goebel, Ted, Kelly Graf, Bryan Hocket, and David Rhode

2007 The Paleoindian Occupations at Bonneville Estates Rockshelter, Danger Cave, and Smith Creek Cave (Eastern Great Basin, U.S.A.): Interpreting Their Radiocarbon Chronologies. In *On Shelter's Ledge: Histories, Theories and Methods of Rockshelter Research*, edited by Marcel Kornfeld, Sergey Vasil'ev, and Laura Miotti, pp. 147–162. BAR International Series, 1655. Oxford.

Grayson, Donald K.

1988 *Danger Cave, Last Supper Cave, and Hanging Rock Shelter: The Faunas*. Anthropological Papers of the American Museum of Natural History, 66. New York.

2011 *The Great Basin: A Natural Prehistory*. University of California Press, Berkeley.

Harper, K. T., and G. M. Alder

1972 Paleoclimatic Inferences Concerning the Last 10,000 Years from a Resampling of Danger Cave, Utah. In *Great Basin Cultural Ecology: A Symposium*, edited by Donald D. Fowler, pp. 13–23. Desert Research Institute Publications in the Social Sciences, 8. Reno.

Harrington, Mark R.

1933 *Gypsum Cave, Nevada*. Southwest Museum Papers No. 8. Los Angeles.

Heizer, Robert F.

1956 Recent Cave Explorations in the Lower Humboldt Valley, Nevada. *University of California Archaeological Survey Reports* 33:50–57.

Heizer, Robert F., and C. Rainer Berger

1970 *Radiocarbon Age of the Gypsum Cave Culture*. Contributions of the University of California Archaeological Research Facility, 7. Berkeley.

Holmer, Richard N.

1986 Common Projectile Points of the Intermountain West. In *Anthropology of the Desert West: Essays in Honor of Jesse D. Jennings*, edited by Carole J. Condie and Donald D. Fowler, pp. 89–115. University of Utah Anthropological Papers, 110. Salt Lake City.

Janetski, Joel C.

1999 Julian Steward and Utah Archaeology. In *Julian Steward and the Great Basin: The Making of an Anthropologist*, edited by Richard O. Clemmer, L. Daniel Myers, and Mary Elizabeth Rudden, pp. 19–34. University of Utah Press, Salt Lake City.

Jennings, Jesse D.

1934 The Importance of Scientific Method in Excavation. *Bulletin of the Archeological Society of North Carolina* 1:13–15.

1957 *Danger Cave*. University of Utah Anthropological Papers, 27. Salt Lake City.

1961 Elmer Richard Smith, 1909–1960. *American Antiquity* 26: 535–536.

1973 The Short Useful Life of a Simple Hypothesis. *Tebiwa* 16:1–9.

1994 *Accidental Archaeologist*. University of Utah Press, Salt Lake City.

Jennings, Jesse D., and Edward Norbeck

1955 Great Basin Prehistory: A Review. *American Antiquity* 21:1–11.

Jones, Kevin T., and David B. Madsen

1989 Calculating the Cost of Resource Transportation: A Great Basin Example. *Current Anthropology* 30:529–534.

Kerns, Virginia

2003 *Scenes from the High Desert: Julian Steward's Life and Theory*. University of Illinois Press, Urbana.

Kroeber, C. B.

1981 A Dedication to the Memory of Robert F. Heizer 1915–1979. *Arizona and the West* 23:208–212.

Libby, W. F., E. C. Anderson, and J. R. Arnold

1949 Age Determination by Radiocarbon Content: World-Wide Assay of Natural Radiocarbon. *Science* 109:227–228.

Loud, Llewellyn L., and Mark R. Harrington

1929 *Lovelock Cave*. University of California Publications in American Archeology and Ethnology, 25. Berkeley.

Madsen, David B.

1986 Great Basin Nuts: A Short Treatise on the Distribution, Productivity, and Use of Pinyon. In *Anthropology of the Desert West: Essays in Honor of Jesse D. Jennings*, edited by Carole J. Condie and Donald D. Fowler, pp. 21–41. University of Utah Anthropological Papers, 110. Salt Lake City.

Madsen, David B., and Michael S. Berry

1975 A Reassessment of Northeastern Great Basin Prehistory. *American Antiquity* 40:391–405.

Madsen, David B., and David Rhode

1990 Early Holocene Pinyon (*Pinus monophylla*) in the Northeastern Great Basin. *Quaternary Research* 33:94–101.

Moore, John G., Gary F. Fry, and Edwin Englert, Jr.

1969 Thorny-Headed Worm Infection in North American Prehistoric Man. *Science* 163:1324–1325.

Napton, Lewis K.

1969 Lacustrine Subsistence Pattern in the Desert West. *Kroeber*

Anthropological Society Papers Special Publication 2:29–98. Berkeley.

O'Connell, James F., Kevin T. Jones, and Steven R. Simms

1982 Some Thoughts on Prehistoric Archaeology in the Great Basin. In *Man and Environment in the Great Basin*, edited by David B. Madsen and James F. O'Connell, pp. 227–240. Society for American Archaeology Papers, 2. Washington, D.C.

Raab, L. M., and A. C. Goodyear

1984 Middle-Range Theory in Archaeology: A Critical Review of Origins and Applications. *American Antiquity* 49:255–256.

Rhode, David, and David B. Madsen

1998 Pine Nut Use in the Early Holocene and Beyond: The Danger Cave Archaeobotanical Record. *Journal of Archaeological Science* 25:1199–1210.

Rhode, David, David B. Madsen, and Kevin T. Jones

2006 Antiquity of Early Holocene Small-Seed Consumption and Processing at Danger Cave. *Antiquity* 80:328–339.

Rudy, Jack R.

1953 *An Archeological Survey of Western Utah*. University of Utah Anthropological Papers, 12. Salt Lake City.

Smith, Elmer R.

1939 Fieldwork: Utah. *Museum News* 17(10):3.

1941 The Archaeology of Deadman Cave, Utah. *University of Utah Bulletin* 32(4):1–43. Salt Lake City.

1942 Early Man in the Great Salt Lake Area. *Mineralogical Society of Utah* 3:27–32.

Steward, Julian H.

1937a *Ancient Caves of the Great Salt Lake Region*. Bureau of American Ethnology Bulletin, 116. Washington, D.C.

1937b Ecological Aspects of Southwestern Society. *Anthropos* 32: 87–104.

1938 *Basin–Plateau Aboriginal Sociopolitical Groups*. Bureau of American Ethnology Bulletin, 120. Washington, D.C.

1940 Native Cultures of the Intermontane (Great Basin) Area. In *Essays in Historical Anthropology of North America, Published in Honor of John R. Swanton*, edited by Julian H. Steward, pp. 445–502. Smithsonian Miscellaneous Collections, 100. Washington, D.C.

Taylor, Robert E.

1987 *Radiocarbon Dating: An Archaeological Perspective*. Wiley, New York.

Thomas, David H.

1983 *The Archaeology of Monitor Valley 1: Epistemology*. Anthropological Papers of the American Museum of Natural History, 58(1). New York.

Thompson, Robert S., and James I. Mead

1982 Late Quaternary Environments and Biogeography in the Great Basin. *Quaternary Research* 17:39–55.

Weiss, Frances D.

1984 National Register of Historic Places Inventory—Nomination Form: Danger Cave. On file, Utah Division of State History, Salt Lake City.

Yoder, David T., Mark L. Bodily, Sara Hill, Joel C. Janetski, and Bradley A. Newbold

2010 The Onset of Small Seed Processing on the Colorado Plateau. *Kiva* 75:425–426.

16

Long-Term Continuity and Change in Obsidian Conveyance at Danger Cave, Utah

Richard E. Hughes

Danger Cave holds a special place in the prehistory of the Great Basin because it was excavations at this site that prompted Jesse Jennings (1953, 1957, 1964; Jennings and Norbeck 1955) to advance one of the most enduring and pervasive concepts in Great Basin prehistory—the concept of the Desert Culture. Stripped to its essence, the Desert Culture concept posited a long-term stable relationship between humans and a harsh environment for over 10,000 years, during which "a desert way of life fundamentally like that of historic times was established" (Jennings and Norbeck 1955:3). In the years since its introduction, the Desert Culture concept has drawn both support and criticism. Some have argued that archaeological evidence offers strong support for long-term stability in settlement and subsistence throughout much of the Great Basin (Aikens 1978), while others emphasize that the Basin contains a host of distinctive microenvironments (lakes, rivers, and marshes) that supported specialized adaptations (Baumhoff and Heizer 1965; Heizer 1956; Heizer et al. 1968) more elaborate than posited by Jennings (see Aikens 1983; Aikens and Madsen 1986; Fowler and Jennings 1982; Janetski and Madsen 1990).[1]

While the specific details of arguments about the usefulness of the Desert Culture concept are tangential to the purpose of this chapter, the implications are not. If a long-term stable adaptation to local resources was characteristic of the entire prehistory of Danger Cave, then we would anticipate that the range of lithic source materials introduced when the site was first occupied might persist, in basically the same frequencies, throughout the time the site was occupied. If directional changes were observed through time in the use of such resources, this might signal shifts in foraging radius and/or external social ties. One way to monitor this is to identify the geologic source(s) of obsidian projectile points used at Danger Cave and to use typological and stratigraphic evidence to determine whether or not directional changes appear.

This study is not the first to examine obsidian from Danger Cave. In 1970 Condie and Blaxland published a short essay that, to my knowledge, was the first of its kind to apply trace element obsidian geochemistry to Great Basin archaeology. On the basis of trace element analysis of a small number of specimens, they concluded that only one primary source was represented among the artifacts examined from Danger Cave but were unable to link the trace element data generated from artifacts with any known geologic obsidian source. They speculated, however, that "the obsidian came from flows and perhaps welded tuff in northwestern Utah and adjacent parts of Nevada and Idaho" (1970:281).

That same year Fry and Adovasio (1970) repeated Condie and Blaxland's (1970) single-source conclusion for Danger Cave artifacts. Justice takes it a bit further, stating that "obsidians used for tools at the two sites [Danger Cave and Hogup Cave] are from different sources. Trade or exchange in raw materials and obsidian tools [between the two sites] was apparently not taking place" (2002:11). Most recently, Simms has written that at "Danger Cave...the obsidian from Topaz and other Sevier Desert sources to the south were favored" (2008:166).

Dating Background for the Present Study

Before proceeding, a short digression is in order about projectile point dating because the present study focuses exclusively on typologically distinct forms from Danger Cave. All students of Great Basin prehistory are familiar with the lack of congruence between projectile point chronologies in the eastern and western Great Basin. Based on observed stratigraphic relations, though a small number of radiocarbon dates, Clewlow (1967), Heizer and Baumhoff (1961), Lanning (1963), and O'Connell (1967) proposed a chronologically sensitive sequence of projectile point types for the western and central Great Basin (see also Heizer and Hester 1978; Hester 1973). But as this chronology was applied farther away from the western and central Basin incongruities began to appear.[2] The discrepancy was addressed head on by Aikens (1970), who mustered stratigraphic and radiocarbon evidence from Hogup Cave, in the eastern Great Basin,

TABLE 16.1. Obsidian sources for all typologically distinct projectile points from Danger Cave.

	Obsidian Source (Chemical Type)						
Point Type	Brown's Bench	Brown's Bench Area	Topaz Mountain	Black Rock Area	Wild Horse Canyon	Malad	Total
Desert Side-Notched	2	0	0	0	0	0	2
Rosegate Series	8	1	3	1	1	1	15
Elko Series	29	3	1	0	1	1	35
Gatecliff Series	6	2	0	0	0	0	8
Northern Side-Notched	14	5	1	0	0	0	21
Total	59	12	5	1	2	2	81[a]

[a] Excludes one untypable corner-notched point (23142.4) from an unknown obsidian source.

to argue for a much longer time span for many projectile point forms than indicated by the western and central Basin evidence. This was to pit the "short" (western and central Basin) against the "long" (eastern Basin) chronology, and for some time disagreements abounded about which chronology would prevail. Thomas's (1981) metric analysis and stratigraphic evidence from Gatecliff Shelter in the central Great Basin refined the dating scheme for points in that area, but as this chronology was applied farther away from the region where it was explicitly designed, dating inconsistencies appeared. Based on an extensive metric analysis of a large number of projectile points from stratigraphic and radiocarbon-dated contexts in the eastern Great Basin, Holmer (1986) came to the same general conclusion as had Aikens (1970): many projectile point types were, indeed, introduced earlier—and persisted later—in the eastern Great Basin than in the west and central area. This latter conclusion is generally accepted today, with scholars applying differing chronological age ranges to points in the eastern and western parts of the Great Basin (Beck 1999; Grayson 1993, 2011; Thomas 1982).

This sketch provides context for understanding the Danger Cave sourcing results and their implications for dating. Aikens (1970:45–55) reclassified the Danger Cave points to accord with terminology employed in his Hogup Cave monograph, but the catalog numbers for each reclassified specimen were not published. Hence, there may, or may not, be concordance between the typological assignments I make (in Table 16.2) and the assignments made by Aikens. But as will be discussed below, any potential disagreements in classification carry little significance in the present study.

Laboratory Analysis

I conducted nondestructive trace element analysis of Danger Cave obsidian projectile points using a QuanX-EC (Thermo Electron Corporation) energy-dispersive X-ray fluorescence spectrometer equipped with a silver (Ag) X-ray tube, a 50-kV X-ray generator, a digital pulse processor with automated energy calibration, and a Peltier cooled solid state detector with 145-eV resolution (FWHM) at 5.9 keV. The X-ray tube was operated at differing voltage and current settings to optimize excitation of the elements selected for analysis. In this case analyses were conducted for the elements rubidium (Rb Kα), strontium (Sr Kα), yttrium (Y Kα), zirconium (Zr Kα), and niobium (Nb Kα). Barium (Ba Kα), titanium (Ti Kα), manganese (Mn Kα), iron ($Fe_2O_3^T$), and iron vs. manganese (Fe Kα/Mn Kα) ratios also were generated for certain artifacts. The analyses were conducted at 120–240 dead time–corrected seconds, with tube current scaled to the physical size of the specimen. Other details involving laboratory analysis protocol, including information on calibration and element-specific measurement resolution, appear elsewhere (Hughes 1988, 1994, 2005:249–250; Hughes and Pavesic 2005).

Results

Ninety obsidian projectile points were analyzed from Danger Cave. The Appendix presents trace element data for each specimen, along with stratigraphic provenance, typological attribution, and artifact-to-source (chemical type) assignment.[3] The points were classified following the criteria proposed by Thomas (1981), but as noted above, the temporal implications of these type assignments should be considered with respect to the eastern—not western—Great Basin point chronology. Several examples of each type are illustrated in Figures 16.1–16.3.

Sixty-two of 90 specimens (69 percent of the total sample) analyzed match the trace element profile of ash-flow tuff obsidian of the Brown's Bench chemical type (Hughes 1990:Table 1; Nelson 1984:Table 5, source #34), located perhaps as near as 90 km north of the cave (see Figure 16.4). Since the areal extent of artifact-quality Brown's Bench obsidian is still poorly known, it is possible that toolstone-caliber material occurs even closer than 90 km. Another 15 specimens (17 percent of the sample) conform to the fingerprint of a chemical variant of Brown's Bench ash-flow tuff obsidian provisionally named Brown's Bench area (see Hughes and Smith 1993:87–88, Figure 8, for discussion). Together, these two "sources" (actually, chemical variants) account for over 85 percent of the obsidian projectile point assemblage. Minor amounts of Topaz Mountain, Black Rock area, and Wild Horse Canyon obsidian were identified (cf. Hughes 2005:Table II.2; Nelson 1984:Table 5, sources 2, 5–7, 8–11), along with a small

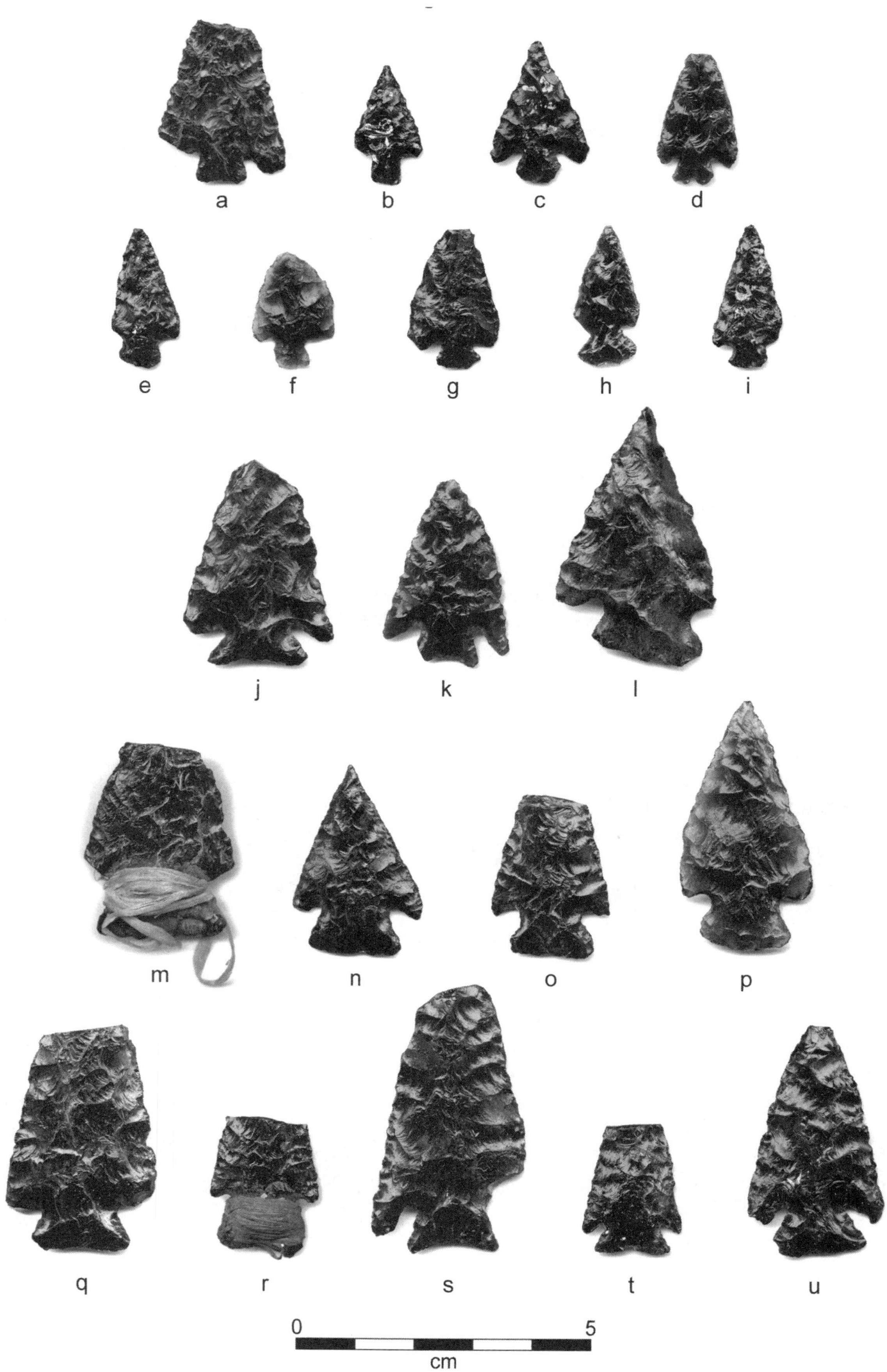

FIGURE 16.1. Obsidian Rosegate series (a–i) and Elko series (Elko Corner-notched, j–u) projectile points from Danger Cave: (a) 19518.13; (b) 17951.1; (c) 17961; (d) 17980.4; (e) 19320; (f) 23159.1; (g) 23334.27; (h) AR 870; (i) AR 904; (j) 19409.8; (k) 19845; (l) 22807.6; (m) 22993.4; (n) 23098.23; (o) 23118.7; (p) 23228.3; (q) 23334.16; (r) 23665.5; (s) 23695.25; (t) AR 870; (u) AR 873.

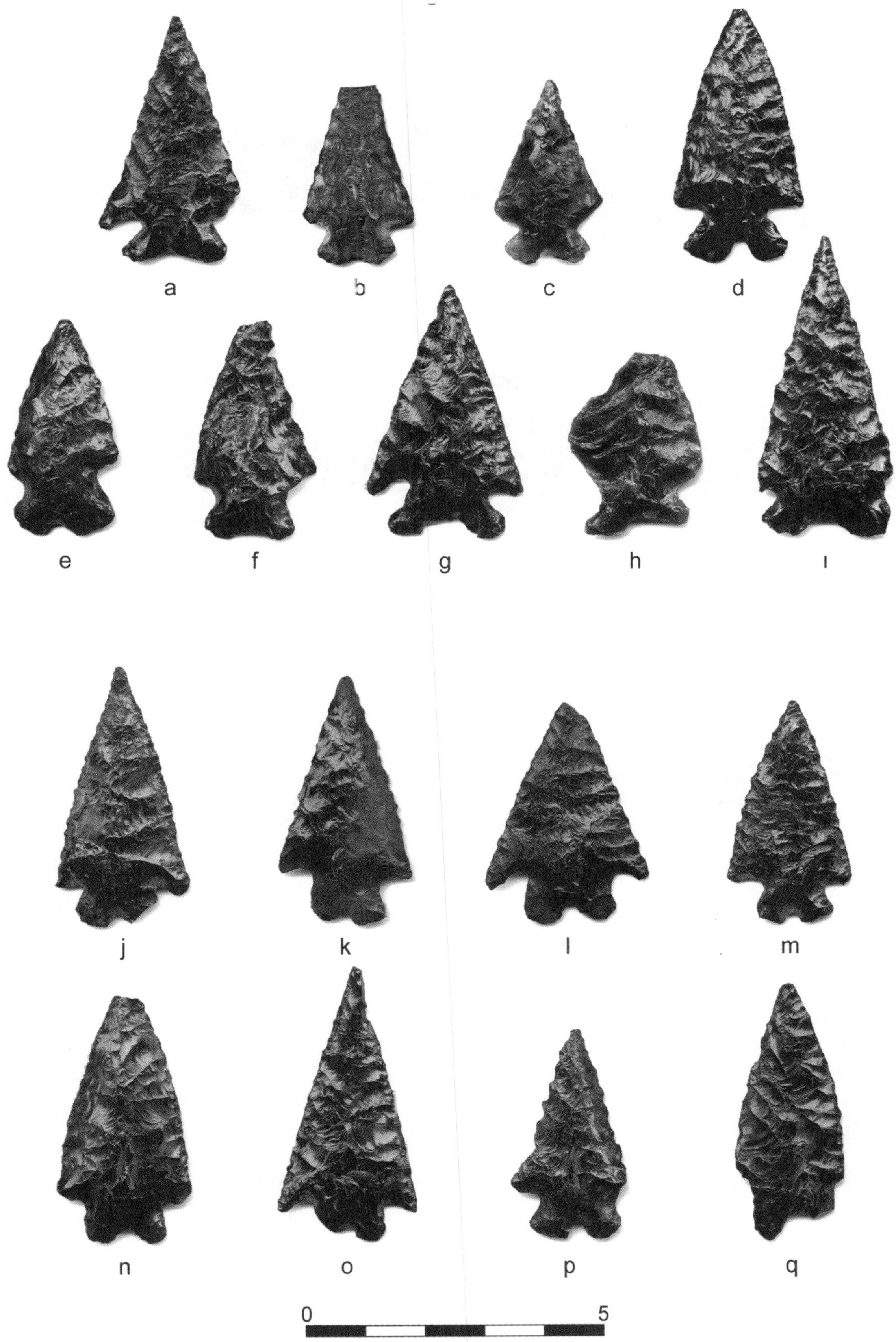

FIGURE 16.2. Obsidian Elko series (Elko Eared, a–i) and Gatecliff series (j–q) projectile points from Danger Cave: (a) 17877.4; (b) 19444.4; (c) 23038.2; (d) 23074.3; (e) 23133.2; (f) 23310.2; (g) 23318.2; (h) 23707.21; (i) 23710.4; (j) 23031.5; (k) 23069.1; (l) 23093.1; (m) 23106.3; (n) 23227.1; (o) 23372.12; (p) 23681.3; (q) AR 867.

FIGURE 16.3. Obsidian Northern Side-notched (a–g, i–l) and Desert Side-notched (h) projectile points from Danger Cave: (a) 19581; (b) 22993.3; (c) 23006.1; (d) 23061.3; (e) 23229.3; (f) 23287.1; (g) 23297.1; (h) 23300.2; (i) 23310.1; (j) 23318.3; (k) 23671; (l) 22987.21.

amount from Malad (cf. Giauque et al. 1993:Table 6; Hughes 1984:Table 3; Nelson 1984:Table 5, source #31).

Table 16.2 summarizes data from the Appendix, presenting the obsidian source attributions for all 90 specimens analyzed. Nine artifacts were not sufficiently complete to allow classification, so Table 16.1 presents the source breakdown for the 81 typologically distinct specimens.

Whether one uses stratigraphic occurrence (Table 16.2) or projectile point typology (see Table 16.1) as a measure, it is quite apparent from these data that the vast majority of obsidian (86 percent of the total sample) used to make projectile points came from ash-flow tuff obsidians of the Brown's Bench area of northwestern Utah, southern Idaho, and northeastern Nevada (see Hughes 1990; Hughes and Smith 1993).[4] Smaller frequencies of obsidian from Malad, Topaz Mountain,[5] the Black Rock area, and Wild Horse Canyon were identified, but all four of these sources combined account for <15 percent of the overall assemblage. In no case does the frequency of these obsidians approach those documented from the Brown's Bench area.[6]

However, 40 percent of obsidian used to fashion Rosegate series points (six of 15 specimens identified) came from non–Brown's Bench sources, whereas other point types range from 0 to 9 percent non–Brown's Bench (Table 16.1).[7] With the exception of a single Rosegate series specimen made from Malad volcanic glass, these data indicate that a source-use shift occurred at this time, featuring conveyance of distant obsidians from the southeast (Topaz Mountain, Black Rock area, and Wild Horse Canyon).[8]

Discussion

Brown's Bench area ash-flow tuff obsidian occurs as near as 90 km north of Danger Cave, and Figure 16.4 shows that all other identified sources are much more distant. Topaz Mountain is located ca. 125 km to the southeast, Wild Horse Canyon

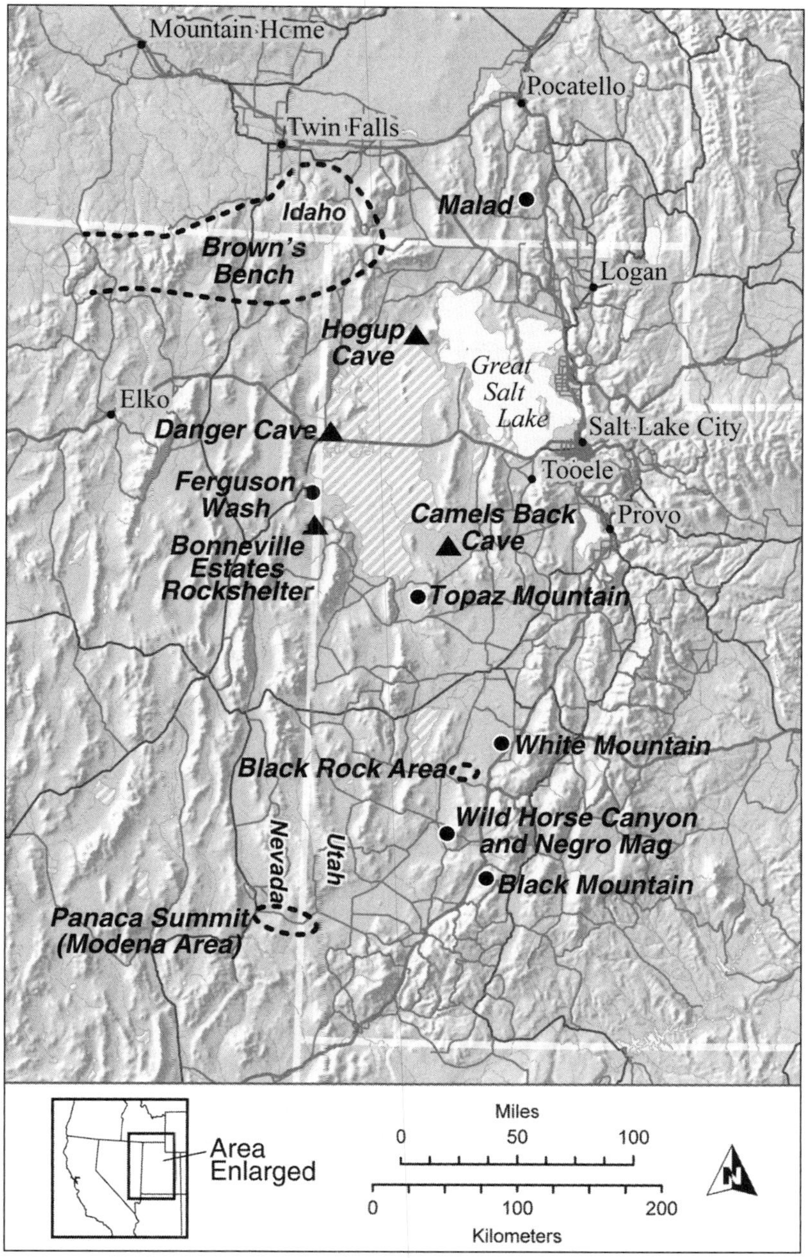

FIGURE 16.4. Map of part of the eastern Great Basin, showing the locations of archaeological sites (filled triangles) and obsidian sources (black dots) discussed in the text. The dashed line indicates the inferred distribution of Brown's Bench ash-flow tuff obsidian (from Bonnichsen 1982; Bonnichsen and Citron 1982; Coates 1964; Hughes et al. 1996; Watkins et al. 1996).

TABLE 16.2. Obsidian sources identified by stratum for all projectile points analyzed from Danger Cave.

	Obsidian Source (Chemical Type)							
Stratum	Brown's Bench	Brown's Bench Area	Topaz Mountain	Black Rock Area	Wild Horse Canyon	Malad	Unknown	Total
Surface	1	0	0	0	0	0	0	1
D-V	17	4	3	1	1	1	0	27
D-IV	2	0	0	0	0		0	2
D-III	25	5	1	0	0	0	0	31
D-II[a]	8	4	0	0	1	1	1	15
D-I	0	0	0	0	0	0	0	0
Unknown	9	2	2	1	0	0	0	14
Total	62	15	6	2	2	2	1	90

[a] Includes one specimen (23229.1) from stratum D-II/III.

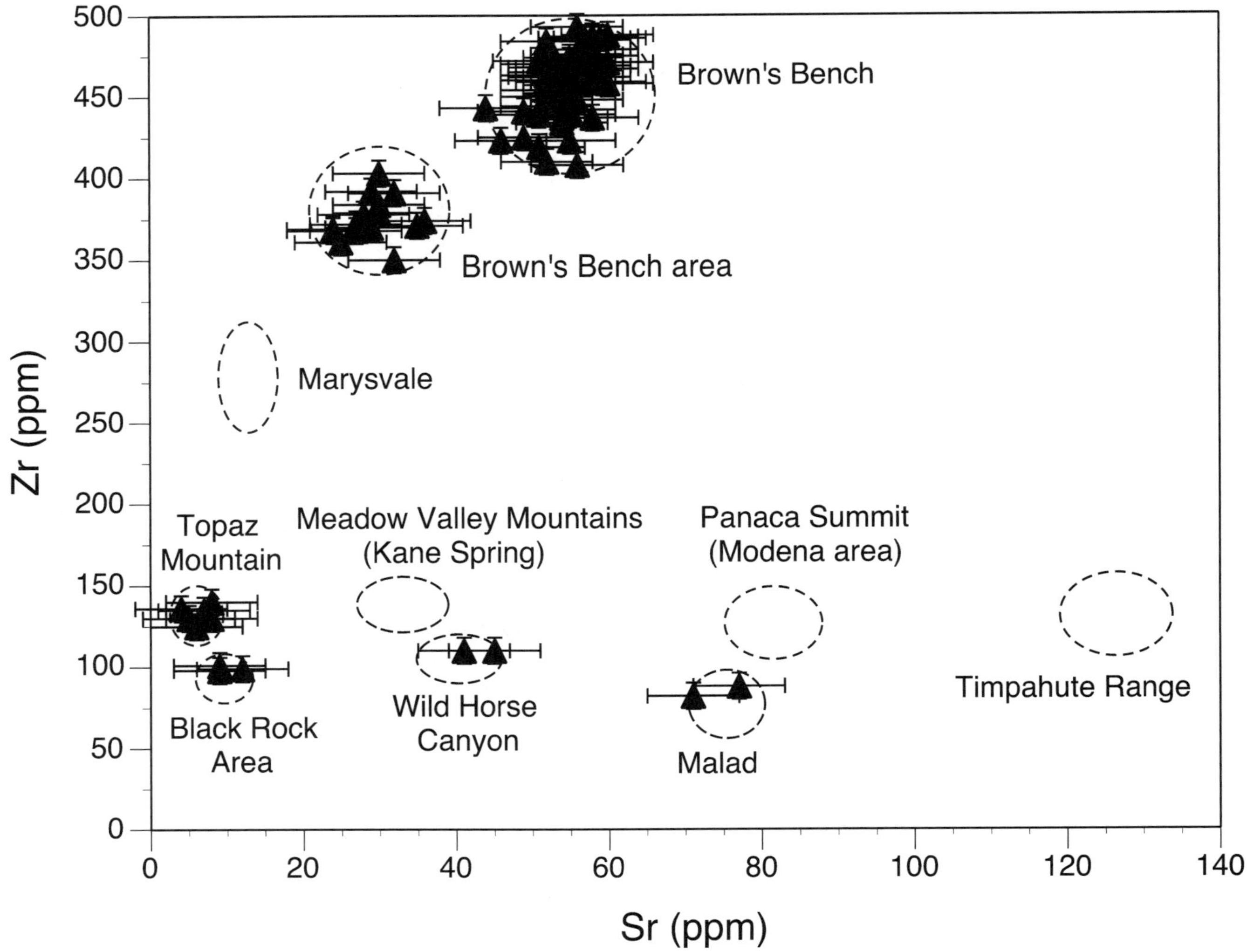

FIGURE 16.5. Zr vs. Sr composition of obsidian projectile points from Danger Cave. Dashed lines represent the range of variation measured in geologic obsidian source samples (from Hughes 1984, 2005, 2010a). Filled triangles plot artifacts listed in the appendix, summarized in Table 16.1. Error bars are two-sigma (95 percent confidence interval) composition estimates for each specimen. The number of artifact plots does not correspond exactly to the tabulations in Table 16.1 because of the convergence of data points at this scale. See note 3.

and the Black Rock area are over 225 km to the southeast of the cave, and Malad obsidian occurs ca. 210 km to the north of the cave. The sole exception is the Ferguson Wash source (Hughes 2005:Table II.2), located less than 35 km to the south of the cave. Despite proximity and the high quality of the obsidian there, energy-dispersive X-ray fluorescence data (Table 16.1 and Figure 16.5) show that not a single Danger Cave projectile point was manufactured from Ferguson Wash obsidian, providing another object lesson of the pitfalls one may encounter by assuming the overriding importance of proximity in provenance studies (Hughes and Pavesic 2005). At nearby Bonneville Estates Rockshelter, Goebel (2007) has identified a difference between Pre-Archaic and Early Archaic obsidian use, with the former period dominated by use of Brown's Bench obsidian, and the latter, by use of local Ferguson Wash material.[9] Goebel's results, however, were obtained mostly from obsidian flakes—not projectile points—so the relationship to Danger Cave is yet to be determined. By contrast, virtually all obsidian samples analyzed from Camels Back Cave, containing strata contemporaneous with Danger Cave, were from the Topaz Mountain source near Camels Back Cave (Hughes 2005).

Beyond this, long-term continuity in the sources of obsidian used to manufacture projectile points deposited at Danger Cave can be considered in relation to paleoenvironmental and paleobotanical evidence. Viewed from the standpoint of Jennings's settlement-subsistence reconstruction, things stayed pretty much the same for thousands of years (see Madsen, this volume). But Rhode et al. (2006) have documented extensive use of local small seeds at Danger Cave by ca. 8500 BP, which they argue represents an adaptation to dwindling higher-ranked resources in the vicinity of the cave. However, there are no obsidian points from the earliest level (D-I) to address the issue; but if people were using the cave as a base for processing pickleweed, one would not expect many points to have been discarded or lost therefrom. After about 8500 BP, beginning during D-II times, the numbers of obsidian projectile points increase, with

TABLE 16.3. Stratigraphic distribution of typologically distinct obsidian projectile points analyzed from Danger Cave.

	Point Type					
Stratum	Desert Side-Notched	Rosegate Series	Elko Series	Gatecliff Series	Northern Side-Notched	Total
Surface			1			1
D-V		8	9	2	4	23
D-IV			2			2
D-III	2	1	10	3	14	30
D-II[a]			9	3	1	13
D-I						0
Total	2	9	31	8	19	69[b]

[a] Includes one specimen (23229.1) from stratum D-II/III.
[b] Excludes 14 specimens with unknown stratum provenience and seven untypable obsidian points.

peak frequencies occurring during the D-III level, corresponding with peak frequencies of jackrabbit remains (*Lepus* sp.) in the deposits (Grayson 1988:Table 15). The D-III stratum, dating to ca. 7000–6500 BP (Grayson 1988:Table 1), yielded nearly one-third of all typable obsidian points recovered from the cave (see Table 16.2). This time period also coincides with the first evidence for the use of pinyon pine nuts at Danger Cave (Madsen 2000; Madsen and Rhode 1990; Rhode and Madsen 1998), and one might infer from the dominant obsidian source direction that this resource may have existed in greater abundance to the north of the cave—perhaps in the Raft River Mountains—thus positioning peoples to exploit both biotic and geologic resources in the area. Only two typable obsidian points (both made from Brown's Bench obsidian) were recovered from the D-IV layer at Danger Cave, which reflects a rather dramatic drop from the preceding D-III stratum.

Although dating of the succeeding D-V stratum is problematic (Aikens 1970:197–198), it contained the second-highest number of typable obsidian projectile points. Mixing within this stratum may blur the significance of the presence of more distant sources in the projectile point inventory, but during D-V times six of 27 (22 percent) samples analyzed were made from non–Brown's Bench area obsidians; overall this level accounted for six of the 13 (46 percent) non–Brown's Bench area artifacts identified at the site (Table 16.2).[10] The stratigraphic distribution of diagnostic obsidian projectile point types (Table 16.3) shows that, as Aikens (1970:Figure 26, 190–192) observed, Rosegate and Elko points are coeval in D-V, which he dated between 1250 BC and AD 400. Such an early date for Rosegate series points clashes dramatically with the age range advanced for similar forms in the central Great Basin (ca. AD 700–1300 [Thomas 1981:19]), but as Grayson (2011:310–311) points out, dating for many point types outside the central Basin has been significantly revised in recent years. Whereas the stratigraphic data from D-V suggest that Rosegate and Elko series points were temporally coeval (Table 16.3), the significant difference in obsidian source use seen in Brown's Bench vs. non–Brown's Bench obsidian points (Table 16.1) complicates the issue, supporting the position for a disparity between them.[11] If there was no difference, one would expect Elko series and Rosegate series points to share the same obsidian source-use profile, and they do not.

Though Madsen and Rhode (1990; Rhode and Madsen 1998) suggest that pine nut use may have commenced slightly before 7000 BP at Danger Cave, they point out that there is no paleobotanical evidence for pine trees in the immediate vicinity of Danger Cave, so they must have been brought in from a greater distance. Pine nuts were not a proximate resource, but the Danger Cave deposits show that they were important. By contrast, obsidian was a local resource. The high-quality obsidian occurring at Ferguson Wash is only a short distance south of the cave, yet this source was ignored as a raw material for fashioning Danger Cave projectile points. Taken together, the botanical evidence and the strong direction (northern) trend in the obsidian projectile point assemblage support the view that settlement-subsistence activities in which Danger Cave played a part were primarily oriented north, where pine nuts may have been the principal magnet. Brown's Bench area obsidian occurs to the north also, so obsidian could have been obtained there during visits to pine nut groves and then spent, lost, or discarded at the cave by mobile groups or individuals who used the cave as a stopover during more general subsistence pursuits. This does not negate the possibility that other social factors were at work; information exchange with peoples living to the north about the productivity cycles of pine nut groves (as well as the availability of deer, antelope, seed, and root resources) also could have resulted in the exchange of mates, visitors, and relocated relatives, who brought with them artifacts made from the glassy material abundant in their homelands. Until comparably old site collections proximate to the Brown's Bench source area are analyzed, it will not be possible to determine whether significant numbers of local obsidian projectile points (i.e., those made from Ferguson Wash glass) may have been moved north by peoples exploiting upland resources. The present evidence, meager as it is, suggests that they were not.

Another, more general, point is worth making here. As noted by numerous scholars, the Desert Culture (or Desert Archaic) is, in effect, the projection of Steward's ethnographically based observations into the past. Given this, it is somewhat ironic that the disagreements about the archaeological applicability of Steward's Basin-wide characterization, and Jennings's use of it in formulating the Desert Culture concept, have largely ignored the fact that there is *very* little archaeological evidence of cave occupation by Great Basin peoples during the "ethnographic period."[12] Granted that the Desert Culture *is* the projection of Steward's settlement and subsistence regimens into the past, and that ethnographically based reconstruction has comparatively little to say about cave use during the ethnographic time frame, how do we understand and integrate cave-based archaeological results (which, after all, made it possible to assign time depth to Steward's characterizations) with the broader picture of settlement-subsistence adaptation inferred from these cave sites? Reconciliation will take studies focused on the overall settlement-subsistence system at particular points in time and explication of the ways in which *all* archaeological sites are integrated during those time intervals.

I am reminded of Don Fowler's "linkage problem" (1977:7). Although in that essay he was referring explicitly to genetic models, he could just as well have been addressing difficulties inherent in translating conceptual schemes operating at differing levels of abstraction. While one might consider disagreements over the utility of the Desert Culture concept as an example of the generalist vs. reductionist dilemma, as Fowler (1982) and Aikens (1970) have pointed out, the issues more correctly revolve around, and are a consequence of, which set of analytical spectacles one adopts. I think that it is telling that Jennings never explicitly invoked the direct historical approach to interpret the Danger Cave materials despite a specific debt and appeal to Steward's (1938) Basin-wide reconstructions. The following is about as close as Jennings got:

> It is suggested that with such time depth as the Basin caves provide, and the near identity with historic traits exhibited by this archaeological debris, we can safely assert that a long stable culture is attested by the archaeological remains [1957:280].

This emphasis on adaptive stability—*not* ethnicity—is a far cry from the purported historic–prehistoric continuum that might have been argued for by others working during this time in California and the Great Basin (see Hughes 2011).

Summary and Conclusions

Even though Tables 16.1 and 16.2 show that there are definite periods of waxing and waning in obsidian projectile point frequencies (discussed above) and relatively few typable obsidian points were recovered, a linear regression analysis shows that the observed results are not due to sample size effects ($r = .592$; $p = .215$). The larger the sample, the more dominant Brown's Bench area obsidian is in the Danger Cave projectile point record. The earliest record of obsidian projectile point use at Danger Cave begins with the use of Brown's Bench ash-flow tuff material, and the record ends with it too. The chemical data presented herein contradict previous statements about the obsidian sources favored at Danger Cave (e.g., Holmer 1997:194; Simms 2008:166) and provide solid empirical support for Condie and Blaxland's (1970) speculation that the source for most of the Danger Cave artifacts would be found in the ash-flow tuff obsidian deposits of northwestern Nevada and southern Idaho. Their prediction was right on the mark as far as projectile points are concerned.

Regardless of how one slices the projectile point typology, the results of this research show that, at a coarse scale, the same volcanic glass source materials were used to make projectile points throughout the 10,000-year span of occupation at Danger Cave. A small number of points made from Topaz Mountain, Wild Horse Canyon, Black Rock area, and Malad are represented in the Danger Cave projectile point assemblage, but Brown's Bench ash-flow tuff obsidian, occurring perhaps <90 km to the northwest in the Goose Creek area, dominates though time. No typable projectile points from Ferguson Wash, the closest obsidian source, were identified at Danger Cave.

But a finer-scale focus reveals important change through time at Danger Cave. Just as significant temporal variation in the paleobotanical and paleoenvironmental record has been identified (Madsen and Rhode 1990; Rhode and Madsen 1998; Rhode et al. 2006), the source-use difference recognized here between obsidian Rosegate series points and other point types during D-V times at Danger Cave is noteworthy and should be explored further. Obsidian projectile point data are consistent with the inference that during D-II through D-IV times (ca. 10,000–4000 BP), foraging activities in which Danger Cave played a role appear focused predominantly to the north, whereas during D-V times greater relative frequencies of southeastern obsidians indicate a directional reorientation and widening of the foraging radius. These changes should be reflected in other elements of the Danger Cave material record, and as research continues, counterparts may be identified at other sites in the area.

Acknowledgments

I am most grateful to the Loan Committee of the Utah Museum of Natural History for approving a loan that enabled me to study the Danger Cave projectile points. Jean Hengsbaugh (former interim registrar) and Ashley Allen (former assistant registrar) were extremely helpful and made the loan process easy. Michelle Knoll (former assistant anthropology curator) patiently answered e-mails and questions about catalog proveniences, and Annie Sager provided some badly needed last-minute information. I also am indebted to Tammara Norton for drafting Figure 16.4, to Wendy Masarweh for expertly scanning the projectile points that appear in Figures 16.1–16.3, and to Ben Hughes for technical assistance. Rick Holmer informed me of, and took me to collect from, the Coal Bank Springs locality, and more recently, Russ Bevill and Elena Nilsson have provided information on their research at other Brown's Bench localities. I particularly appreciate constructive comments on the manuscript by Mel Aikens, Rick Holmer, and David Madsen, which helped me clarify some important points.

Notes

1. Two decades after he first proposed the term, Jennings (1973) also abandoned the Desert Culture concept.
2. There were early doubts about the Basin-wide applicability of the western-based chronology. For example, in attempting to account for the difference between the postulated date for his Early Rose Spring period and radiocarbon-dated associations for Elko and Pinto points at South Fork Shelter, Lanning wrote that "either my estimated date for early Rose Spring is too conservative, or... Elko points are substantially earlier in eastern Nevada than in Inyo County" (1963:280).
3. The terms *source* and *chemical type* are used to denote groups of specimens that share a distinct *chemical* signature, or profile, independent of geographic location (for discussion, see Hughes 1998:104).
4. For the sake of this discussion, I use the term *Brown's Bench area* to subsume both the Brown's Bench chemical type proper, as identified in Hughes 1990 and Nelson 1984, and the newly discovered Coal Bank Spring ash-flow tuff occurrence, located within the area where Brown's Bench obsidian also occurs. This latter location contains slightly lower concentrations of Sr and Ba, indicating its genetic relationship to the compositional gradient within the Brown's Bench ash-flow tuff obsidians (see Hughes and Smith 1993 for discussion). However, the geographic location for the Brown's Bench area obsidian with the lowest Zr, Sr, and Ba composition has not yet been found.
5. Topaz Mountain and Ferguson Wash obsidians are quite similar in Rb and Zr composition but have significantly different Y abundance—Topaz Mountain contains around 50 ppm Y, while Ferguson Wash contains Y in concentrations ≈ 100 ppm (Hughes 2005:Table II.2). Topaz Mountain source assignments for four projectile points from Danger Cave were corroborated by Y measurements (see the Appendix).
6. These results beg comparison with the earlier Danger Cave sourcing study of Condie and Blaxland (1970). Before detailing some differences, it is important to recognize that the Condie and Blaxland study was among the first in North America (certainly in the Great Basin) to focus on "sourcing" obsidian from archaeological contexts. As of 1970, there were only a few workers at Berkeley who had done much with obsidian using X-ray fluorescence, and these studies focused mainly on Mesoamerica. In part because methodological issues had yet to be brought under control (e.g., the development of matrix correction algorithms to compensate for interelement enhancement and absorption effects and the development of peak overlap and background correction subroutines) and microcomputers were not yet in use, the going was hard and tedious. Consequently, it would be expected that in the *very* early stages of obsidian sourcing research some of the results might not stand the test of time and vastly improved instrumentation.

   It is axiomatic that artifact-to-source (chemical type) assignments be supported by empirical evidence, i.e., composition measurements for various minor, trace, and rare earth elements that occur in varying abundance in obsidians (Hughes 1984, 1986). Unless there is a compelling reason for doing otherwise (see Hughes 2010b for an example), the reporting currency is typically quantitative composition estimates, expressed as parts per million and/or weight percent composition, which allow researchers at other laboratories to compare results directly. Although we did not measure the same artifacts, Condie and Blaxland (1970:280, Figures 1b and 2b) did present their Danger Cave results in parts per million, which allowed me to directly compare results with theirs. Their study was probably confined to obsidian flakes because of the destructive nature of the wavelength-dispersive X-ray fluorescence technique they employed, but the parts per million values can be commented on. Their Figure 1b shows a cluster of Rb values from 270 to 290 ppm, accompanied by Sr values from 40 to 50 ppm. Although it is not plotted, the Danger Cave samples table at Condie and Blaxland 1970:280 shows that Zr also was measured. However, the parts per million values for all three elements likely are in error. The standards (G-2 and W-1) used by Condie and Blaxland (1970) for calibration are not for obsidian—they are granite and diabase standards. Because these latter rocks typically contain <53 percent SiO_2 by weight, and obsidians typically contain >70 percent SiO_2 (Taylor 1969), there are serious matrix effects that must be taken into account before reliable quantitative composition values can be obtained. Condie and Blaxland (1970) did not present their actual measurements for G-2 and W-1 standards, so one can only speculate that the dramatic difference between the matrix of the standards and that of the obsidian artifacts accounts for the variance observed. Other evidence to help appreciate discrepancies in parts per million values between the present study and Condie and Blaxland's appears in their Figure 2a, where the composition range for Rb in Napa Valley obsidian is given as about 130–170 ppm, with Sr values around 69–70 ppm. Several studies have presented data on Napa Valley obsidian, showing that the composition for Rb in this "source" (sensu Jackson 1989:89) ranges between 180 and 210 ppm, while Sr ranges from 5 to 10 ppm (e.g., Jack 1976:Table 11.3; Jackson 1989:Table 2; Macdonald et al. 1992:134; Stross et al. 1976:Table 13.2). The geologic source standards measurements they present serve as the final illustration. In a table entitled "Milford Obsidian Flows," Condie and Blaxland (1970:280) provide Rb values for Flows A and B, located in the Mineral Mountains east of Milford. The Rb composition values they reported (269 and 256 ppm) are nearly 75 ppm greater than measured by me (Hughes 2005:Table II.2) and by Nelson (1984:Table 4, sources 1–2; Nelson and Holmes 1979:Table 3). While the Sr values they determined for Flows A and B (33 and 34 ppm) are not seriously discordant with those published by me (Hughes 2005) and by Nelson (1984), who measured values between 35 and 38 ppm, their tabled Zr values (65–70 ppm) are significantly lower than mine and Nelson's (ranging between 105 and 130 ppm). More comparisons could be made, but it is probably sufficient to underscore that the parts per million values presented in the Condie and Blaxland (1970) study are variant with measurements by others. Nonetheless, as I will discuss below, the lack of correspondence between the parts per million values they generated and those determined by others does not nullify their prescience and intuition.
7. A Fisher's Exact Test between the Rosegate series results and those for all other point types (i.e., Desert Side-notched, Elko series, Gatecliff series, and Northern Side-notched) in Table 16.3

shows that this relationship is definitely significant ($p = .001 < p_\alpha = .05$).

8. Eliminating both Malad specimens from Table 16.1 still yields a significant result using a Fisher's Exact Test ($p = .039 < p_\alpha = .05$), supporting the view that there are more non–Brown's Bench Rosegate obsidian points from southeastern sources represented than would be expected by chance.
9. Only summary results are presented in Goebel 2007. No trace element data (i.e., actual composition measurements) are presented to substantiate the source assignments, nor is there reference to a report where they may appear.
10. A 4-×-2 chi-square test between the D-V results and those for deeper levels (D-IV, D-III, and D-II, excluding D-I, which yielded no typable specimens) in Table 16.2 shows that this relationship is not statistically significant at the .05 α level ($\chi^2 = 5.47$; $df = 3$; $p = .14$).
11. A Fisher's Exact test between Brown's Bench and non–Brown's Bench Rosegate and Elko series points listed in Table 16.1 shows that these frequency differences are statistically significant ($p = .015$).
12. Although explorers documented cave use by the Northern Paiute during the middle of the 1800s (Delano 1854:170–171; Fremont 1845:216) in the western Great Basin, Grosscup noted "relatively slight use of caves for occupation in prehistoric Northern Paiute times" (1960:60), while Heizer observed that "no real success has been realized in trying to tie the later cave archaeology with the Northern Paiute or Shoshoni" (1966:241). C. Fowler (1977:26) documents specific denials of cave use by ethnographic-period Ute, Southern Paiute, and Northern and Western Shoshoni peoples.

References Cited

Aikens, C. Melvin

1970 *Hogup Cave*. University of Utah Anthropological Papers No. 93. Salt Lake City.

1978 Archaeology of the Great Basin. *Annual Review of Anthropology* 7:71–87.

1983 Environmental Archaeology in the Western United States. In *Late-Quaternary Environments of the United States, Vol. 2: The Holocene*, edited by H. E. Wright, Jr., pp. 239–251. University of Minnesota Press, Minneapolis.

Aikens, C. Melvin, and David B. Madsen

1986 Prehistory of the Eastern Area. In *Great Basin*, edited by W. L. d'Azevedo, pp. 149–160. Handbook of North American Indians, Vol. 11, W. C. Sturtevant, general editor, Smithsonian Institution Press, Washington, D.C.

Baumhoff, Martin A., and Robert F. Heizer

1965 Postglacial Climate and Archaeology in the Desert West. In *The Quaternary of the United States*, edited by H. E. Wright, Jr., and David G. Frey, pp. 697–707. Princeton University Press, Princeton.

Beck, Charlotte

1999 Dating the Archaeological Record and Modeling Chronology. In *Models for the Millennium: Great Basin Anthropology Today*, edited by C. Beck, pp. 171–181. University of Utah Press, Salt Lake City.

Bonnichsen, Bill

1982 The Bruneau-Jarbidge Eruptive Center, Southwestern Idaho. In *Cenozoic Geology of Idaho*, edited by B. Bonnichsen and R. M. Breckenridge, pp. 237–254. Idaho Bureau of Mines and Geology Bulletin, 26. Moscow.

Bonnichsen, Bill, and Gary P. Citron

1982 The Cougar Point Tuff, Southwestern Idaho and Vicinity. In *Cenozoic Geology of Idaho*, edited by B. Bonnichsen and R. M. Breckenridge, pp. 255–281. Idaho Bureau of Mines and Geology Bulletin, 26. Moscow.

Clewlow, C. William, Jr.

1967 Time and Space Relations of Some Great Basin Projectile Point Types. In *Papers on Great Basin Archaeology*, pp. 141–149. University of California Archaeological Survey Reports No. 70. Berkeley.

Coates, Robert R.

1964 *Geology of the Jarbidge Quadrangle, Nevada–Idaho*. U.S. Geological Survey Bulletin, 1141-M. Washington, D.C.

Condie, Kent C., and Alan B. Blaxland

1970 Sources of Obsidian in Hogup and Danger Caves. In *Hogup Cave*, by C. Melvin Aikens, pp. 275–281. University of Utah Anthropological Papers No. 93. Salt Lake City.

Delano, Alonzo

1854 *Life on the Plains and Among the Diggings, Being Scenes and Adventures of an Overland Journey to California*. Miller, Orton and Mulligan, Auburn, New York.

Fowler, Catherine S.

1977 Ethnography and Great Basin Prehistory. In *Models and Great Basin Prehistory: A Symposium*, edited by D. D. Fowler, pp. 11–48. Desert Research Institute Publications in the Social Sciences No. 12. Reno.

1982 Settlement Patterns and Subsistence Systems in the Great Basin: The Ethnographic Record. In *Man and Environment in the Great Basin*, edited by D. B. Madsen and J. F. O'Connell, pp. 121–138. SAA Papers No. 2. Society for American Archaeology, Washington, D.C.

Fowler, Don D.

1977 Models and Great Basin Prehistory—Introductory Remarks. In *Models and Great Basin Prehistory: A Symposium*, edited by D. D. Fowler, pp. 3–10. Desert Research Institute Publications in the Social Sciences No. 12. Reno.

Fowler, Don D., and Jesse D. Jennings

1982 Great Basin Archaeology: A Historical Overview. In *Man and Environment in the Great Basin*, edited by D. B. Madsen and J. F. O'Connell, pp. 105–120. SAA Papers No. 2. Society for American Archaeology, Washington, D.C.

Fremont, John C.

1845 *Report on the Exploring Expedition to the Rocky Mountains in the Year 1842 and to Oregon and Northern California in the Years 1843–1844*. Gales and Seaton, Washington, D.C.

Fry, Gary F., and James F. Adovasio

1970 Population Differentiation in Hogup and Danger Caves, Two Archaic Sites in the Eastern Great Basin. In *Five Papers on the Archaeology of the Desert West*, edited by D. R. Tuohy, D. L. Rendall, and P. A. Crowell, pp. 207–215. Nevada State Museum Anthropological Papers No. 15. Carson City.

Giauque, Robert D., Frank Asaro, Fred H. Stross, and Thomas R. Hester

1993 High-Precision Non-Destructive X-Ray Fluorescence Method Applicable to Establishing the Provenance of Obsidian Artifacts. *X-Ray Spectrometry* 22:44–53.

Goebel, Ted

2007 Pre-Archaic and Early Archaic Technological Activities at

Bonneville Estates Rockshelter: A First Look at the Lithic Artifact Record. In *Paleoindian or Paleoarchaic? Great Basin Human Ecology at the Pleistocene–Holocene Transition*, edited by K. E. Graf and D. N. Schmitt, pp. 156–184. University of Utah Press, Salt Lake City.

Govindaraju, K.

1994 Compilation of Working Values and Sample Description for 383 Geostandards. Special issue, *Geostandards Newsletter* 18.

Grayson, Donald K.

1988 *Danger Cave, Last Supper Cave, and Hanging Rock Shelter: The Faunas*. Anthropological Papers of the American Museum of Natural History, 66(1). New York.

1993 *The Desert's Past: A Natural Prehistory of the Great Basin*. Smithsonian Institution Press, Washington, D.C.

2011 *The Great Basin: A Natural Prehistory*. University of California Press, Berkeley and Los Angeles.

Grosscup, Gordon L.

1960 *The Culture History of Lovelock Cave, Nevada*. University of California Archaeological Survey Reports No. 52. Berkeley.

Heizer, Robert F.

1956 Recent Cave Exploration in the Lower Humboldt Valley, Nevada. *University of California Archaeological Survey Reports* 33:50–57. Berkeley.

1966 General Comments. In *The Current Status of Anthropological Research in the Great Basin: 1964*, edited by W. L. d'Azevedo, W. A. Davis, D. D. Fowler, and W. Suttles, pp. 239–247 Desert Research Institute Social Sciences and Humanities Publication, 1. Reno.

Heizer, Robert F., and Martin A. Baumhoff

1961 Wagon Jack Shelter. In *The Archaeology of Two Sites at Eastgate, Churchill County, Nevada*, pp. 119–138. University of California Anthropological Records, 20(4). Berkeley.

Heizer, Robert F., Martin A. Baumhoff, and C. William Clewlow, Jr.

1968 Archaeology of South Fork Shelter (NV-El-11), Elko County, Nevada. In *Papers on Great Basin Prehistory*, pp. 1–58. University of California Archaeological Survey Reports No. 71. Berkeley.

Heizer, Robert F., and Thomas R. Hester

1978 Great Basin. In *Chronologies in New World Archaeology*, edited by R. E. Taylor and C. W. Meighan, pp. 147–199. Academic Press, New York.

Hester, Thomas R.

1973 *Chronological Ordering of Great Basin Prehistory*. Contributions of the University of California Archaeological Research Facility No. 17. Berkeley.

Holmer, Richard N.

1986 Common Projectile Points of the Intermountain West. In *Anthropology of the Desert West: Essays in Honor of Jesse D. Jennings*, edited by C. J. Condie and D. D. Fowler, pp. 89–116. University of Utah Anthropological Papers No. 110. Salt Lake City.

1997 Volcanic Glass Utilization in Eastern Idaho. *Tebiwa* 26(2):186–204.

Hughes, Richard E.

1984 Obsidian Sourcing Studies in the Great Basin: Problems and Prospects. In *Obsidian Studies in the Great Basin*, edited by R. E. Hughes, pp. 1–19. Contributions of the University of California Archaeological Research Facility No. 45. Berkeley.

1986 *Diachronic Variability in Obsidian Procurement Patterns in Northeastern California and Southcentral Oregon*. University of California Publications in Anthropology, 17. Berkeley and Los Angeles.

1988 The Coso Volcanic Field Reexamined: Implications for Obsidian Sourcing and Hydration Dating Research. *Geoarchaeology* 3:253–265.

1990 Obsidian Sources at James Creek Shelter, and Trace Element Geochemistry of Some Northeastern Nevada Volcanic Glasses. In *The Archaeology of James Creek Shelter*, edited by R. G. Elston and E. E. Budy, pp. 297–305. University of Utah Anthropological Papers No. 115. Salt Lake City.

1994 Intrasource Chemical Variability of Artefact-Quality Obsidians from the Casa Diablo Area, California. *Journal of Archaeological Science* 21:263–271.

1998 On Reliability, Validity, and Scale in Obsidian Sourcing Research. In *Unit Issues in Archaeology: Measuring Time, Space, and Material*, edited by A. F. Ramenofsky and A. Steffen, pp. 103–114. University of Utah Press, Salt Lake City.

2005 Determination of the Geologic Sources for Obsidian Artifacts from Camels Back Cave and Trace Element Analysis of Some Western Utah and Eastern Nevada Volcanic Glasses. In *Camels Back Cave*, by D. N. Schmitt and D. B. Madsen, pp. 249–356. University of Utah Anthropological Papers No. 125. Salt Lake City.

2010a Trace Element Characterization of Archaeologically Significant Volcanic Glasses from the Southern Great Basin of North America. In *Crossing the Straits: Prehistoric Obsidian Source Exploitation in the North Pacific Rim*, edited by Y. V. Kuzmin and M. D. Glascock, pp. 165–181. British Archaeological Reports International Series, 2152. Archaeopress, Oxford.

2010b Determining the Geologic Provenance of Tiny Obsidian Flakes in Archaeology Using Nondestructive EDXRF. *American Laboratory* 42(7):27–31.

2011 Sources of Inspiration for Studies of Prehistoric Resource Acquisition and Materials Conveyance in California and the Great Basin. In *Perspectives on Prehistoric Trade and Exchange in California and the Great Basin*, edited by R. E. Hughes, pp. 1–21. University of Utah Press, Salt Lake City.

Hughes, Richard E., and Max G. Pavesic

2005 Proximity and Provenance: A Lesson from the Sterling Cache, Idaho. *Journal of California and Great Basin Anthropology* 25:221–225.

Hughes, Richard E., and Robert L. Smith

1993 Archaeology, Geology, and Geochemistry in Obsidian Provenance Studies. In *Effects of Scale on Archaeological and Geoscientific Perspectives*, edited by J. K. Stein and A. R. Linse, pp. 79–91. Geological Society of America Special Paper, 283. Boulder.

Hughes, Scott S., Jennifer L. Parker, Anni M. Watkins, and Michael McCurry

1996 Geochemical Evidence for a Magmatic Transition Along the Yellowstone Hotspot Track. In *Geology of the Crook in the Snake River Plain, Twin Falls and Vicinity, Idaho*, edited by S. S. Hughes and R. C. Thomas, pp. 63–80. Northwest Geology, 26. Montana State University, Bozeman.

Jack, Robert N.

1976 Prehistoric Obsidian in California I: Geochemical Aspects. In *Advances in Obsidian Glass Studies: Archaeological and Geochemical Perspectives*, edited by R. E. Taylor, pp. 183–217. Noyes Press, Park Ridge, New Jersey.

Jackson, Thomas L.
1989 Late Prehistoric Obsidian Production and Exchange in the North Coast Ranges, California. In *Current Directions in California Obsidian Studies*, edited by R. E. Hughes, pp. 79–94. Contributions of the University of California Archaeological Research Facility No. 48. Berkeley.

Janetski, Joel C., and David B. Madsen (editors)
1990 *Wetland Adaptations in the Great Basin*. Museum of Peoples and Cultures, Occasional Paper, 1. Brigham Young University, Provo.

Jennings, Jesse D.
1953 Danger Cave: A Progress Summary. *El Palacio* 60:179–213.
1957 *Danger Cave*. Memoirs of the Society for American Archaeology, 14. Salt Lake City.
1964 The Desert West. In *Prehistoric Man in the New World*, edited by J. D. Jennings and E. Norbeck, pp. 149–174. University of Chicago Press, Chicago.
1973 The Short Useful Life of a Simple Hypothesis. *Tebiwa* 16(1): 1–10.

Jennings, Jesse D., and Edward Norbeck
1955 Great Basin Prehistory: A Review. *American Antiquity* 21:1–11.

Justice, Noel D.
2002 *Stone Age Spear and Arrow Points of California and the Great Basin*. Indiana University Press, Bloomington.

Lanning, Edward P.
1963 *Archaeology of the Rose Spring Site, INY-372*. University of California Publications in American Archaeology and Ethnology, 49(3). Berkeley and Los Angeles.

Macdonald, Ray, Robert L. Smith, and John E. Thomas
1992 *Chemistry of the Subalkalic Silicic Obsidians*. U.S. Geological Survey Professional Paper, 1523. Washington, D.C.

Madsen, David B.
2000 Summary and Integration. In *Late Quaternary Paleoecology in the Bonneville Basin*, edited by D. B. Madsen, pp. 165–175. Utah Geological Survey Bulletin, 130. Salt Lake City.

Madsen, David B., and David Rhode
1990 Early Holocene Pinyon (*Pinus monophylla*) in the Northeastern Great Basin. *Quaternary Research* 33:94–101.

Nelson, Fred W., Jr.
1984 X-Ray Fluorescence Analysis of Some Western North American Obsidians. In *Obsidian Studies in the Great Basin*, edited by R. E. Hughes, pp. 27–62. Contributions of the University of California Archaeological Research Facility No. 45. Berkeley.

Nelson, Fred W., and Richard D. Holmes
1979 *Trace Element Analysis of Obsidian Sources and Artifacts from Western Utah*. Antiquities Section Selected Papers, 6(15). Division of State History, Utah State Historical Society, Salt Lake City.

O'Connell, James F.
1967 Elko Eared/Elko Corner-Notched Projectile Points as Time Markers in the Great Basin. In *Papers on Great Basin Archaeology*, pp. 129–140. University of California Archaeological Survey Reports No. 70. Berkeley.

Rhode, David, and David B. Madsen
1998 Pine Nut Use in the Early Holocene and Beyond: The Danger Cave Archaeobotanical Record. *Journal of Archaeological Science* 25:1199–1210.

Rhode, David, David B. Madsen, and Kevin T. Jones
2006 Antiquity of Early Holocene Small-Seed Consumption and Processing at Danger Cave. *Antiquity* 80:328–339.

Simms, Steven R.
2008 *Ancient Peoples of the Great Basin and the Colorado Plateau*. Left Coast Press, Walnut Creek.

Steward, Julian H.
1938 *Basin–Plateau Aboriginal Sociopolitical Groups*. Bureau of American Ethnology Bulletin, 120. Washington, D.C.

Stross, Fred H., Thomas R. Hester, Robert F. Heizer, and Robert N. Jack
1976 Chemical and Archaeological Studies of Mesoamerican Obsidians. In *Advances in Obsidian Glass Studies: Archaeological and Geochemical Perspectives*, edited by R. E. Taylor, pp. 240–258. Noyes Press, Park Ridge, New Jersey.

Taylor, S. R.
1969 Trace Element Chemistry of Andesites and Associated Calc-Alkaline Rocks. In *Proceedings of the Andesite Conference*, edited by A. R. McBirney, pp. 43–63. Oregon Department of Geology and Mineral Industries Bulletin, 65. Portland.

Thomas, David Hurst
1981 How to Classify the Projectile Points from Monitor Valley, Nevada. *Journal of California and Great Basin Anthropology* 3:7–43.
1982 An Overview of Central Great Basin Prehistory. In *Man and Environment in the Great Basin*, edited by D. B. Madsen and J. F. O'Connell, pp. 156–171. SAA Papers No. 2. Society for American Archaeology, Washington, D.C.

Watkins, Anni M., Mike McCurry, and Scott. S. Hughes
1996 Preliminary Report on the Stratigraphy and Geochemistry of the Tuff of Steer Basin, Cassia Mountains, Idaho. In *Geology of the Crook in the Snake River Plain, Twin Falls, Idaho*, edited by S. S. Hughes and R. C. Thomas, pp. 107–120. Northwest Geology, 26. Montana State University, Bozeman.

Appendix: Trace Element Composition, Stratigraphic Occurrence, and Obsidian Source Attributions for Danger Cave Projectile Points

Stratum	Catalog No.	Trace Element Concentrations									Fe/Mn Ratio	Obsidian Source (Chemical Type)	Point Type	Illustration
		Rb	Sr	Y	Zr	Nb	Ba	Ti	Mn	$Fe_2O_3^T$				
Surface	22807.6	206 ± 4	58 ± 3	65 ± 3	487 ± 4	43 ± 3	1,186 ± 26	Nm	Nm	Nm	Nm	Brown's Bench	ECN	Figure 16.1l
D-V	AR 867	409 ± 4	8 ± 3	47 ± 3	130 ± 4	62 ± 3	Nm	Nm	Nm	Nm	Nm	Topaz Mountain	GSS	Figure 16.2q
D-V	AR 890	273 ± 4	9 ± 3	61 ± 3	98 ± 4	30 ± 3	Nm	Nm	Nm	Nm	20	Black Rock area	SN	Figure 16.1h
D-V	AR 894	207 ± 4	29 ± 3	63 ± 3	392 ± 4	41 ± 3	654 ± 28	Nm	Nm	Nm	Nm	Brown's Bench area	SN	None
D-V	AR 897	450 ± 4	6 ± 3	49 ± 3	125 ± 4	71 ± 3	Nm	Nm	Nm	Nm	Nm	Topaz Mountain	LS	None
D-V	AR 904	193 ± 4	57 ± 3	64 ± 3	462 ± 4	42 ± 3	1,151 ± 28	Nm	Nm	Nm	Nm	Brown's Bench	RSCN	Figure 16.1i
D-V	17877.4	215 ± 4	57 ± 3	63 ± 3	469 ± 4	46 ± 3	1,202 ± 30	Nm	Nm	Nm	Nm	Brown's Bench	EE	Figure 16.2a
D-V	17931.3	207 ± 4	57 ± 3	66 ± 3	479 ± 4	46 ± 3	1,179 ± 28	Nm	Nm	Nm	Nm	Brown's Bench	LS	None
D-V	17951.1	208 ± 4	56 ± 3	66 ± 3	474 ± 4	45 ± 3	1,196 ± 28	Nm	Nm	Nm	Nm	Brown's Bench	RSCN	Figure 16.1b
D-V	17961	222 ± 4	59 ± 3	67 ± 3	459 ± 4	49 ± 3	1,250 ± 30	Nm	Nm	Nm	Nm	Brown's Bench	RS	Figure 16.1c
D-V	17972.3	192 ± 6	56 ± 3	61 ± 5	408 ± 3	40 ± 3	1,100 ± 30	Nm	Nm	Nm	Nm	Brown's Bench	EE	None
D-V	17980.4	453 ± 4	4 ± 3	48 ± 3	136 ± 4	62 ± 3	Nm	Nm	Nm	Nm	Nm	Topaz Mountain	RS	Figure 16.1d
D-V	19320	195 ± 4	52 ± 3	60 ± 3	454 ± 4	44 ± 3	1,203 ± 30	Nm	Nm	Nm	Nm	Brown's Bench	RSCN	Figure 16.1e
D-V	19360	199 ± 4	55 ± 3	61 ± 3	457 ± 4	43 ± 3	1,159 ± 30	Nm	Nm	Nm	Nm	Brown's Bench	ECN	None
D-V	19457	198 ± 4	45 ± 3	21 ± 3	110 ± 4	25 ± 3	155 ± 26	Nm	Nm	Nm	Nm	Wild Horse Canyon	RSCN	None
D-V	19581	215 ± 4	49 ± 3	68 ± 3	441 ± 4	44 ± 3	1,079 ± 30	Nm	Nm	Nm	Nm	Brown's Bench	NSN	Figure 16.3a
D-V	23059.1	240 ± 4	32 ± 3	66 ± 3	391 ± 4	45 ± 3	610 ± 28	Nm	Nm	Nm	Nm	Brown's Bench area	NSN	None
D-V	23098.23	219 ± 4	58 ± 3	67 ± 3	467 ± 4	45 ± 3	1,194 ± 32	Nm	Nm	Nm	Nm	Brown's Bench	ECN	Figure 16.1n
D-V	23118.7	221 ± 4	54 ± 3	65 ± 3	459 ± 4	44 ± 3	1,127 ± 30	Nm	Nm	Nm	Nm	Brown's Bench	ECN	Figure 16.1o
D-V	23159.1	120 ± 4	71 ± 3	33 ± 3	82 ± 4	14 ± 3	1,601 ± 28	Nm	Nm	Nm	Nm	Malad	RSCN	Figure 16.1f
D-V	23257.6	211 ± 4	56 ± 3	67 ± 3	493 ± 4	43 ± 3	1,117 ± 30	Nm	Nm	Nm	Nm	Brown's Bench	ECN	None
D-V	23287.1	211 ± 4	56 ± 3	64 ± 3	466 ± 4	45 ± 3	1,129 ± 30	Nm	Nm	Nm	Nm	Brown's Bench	NSN	Figure 16.3f
D-V	23334.16	212 ± 4	56 ± 3	65 ± 3	467 ± 4	44 ± 3	1,136 ± 30	Nm	Nm	Nm	Nm	Brown's Bench	ECN	Figure 16.1q
D-V	23334.27	213 ± 4	52 ± 3	60 ± 3	410 ± 4	45 ± 3	1,204 ± 30	Nm	Nm	Nm	Nm	Brown's Bench	RSCN	Figure 16.1g
D-V	23339	227 ± 4	25 ± 3	66 ± 3	361 ± 4	41 ± 3	591 ± 28	Nm	Nm	Nm	Nm	Brown's Bench area	NSN	None
D-V	23354.8	245 ± 4	35 ± 3	66 ± 3	371 ± 4	43 ± 3	609 ± 28	Nm	Nm	Nm	Nm	Brown's Bench area	GS	None
D-V	23691.29	206 ± 4	56 ± 3	60 ± 3	448 ± 4	43 ± 3	1,171 ± 32	Nm	Nm	Nm	Nm	Brown's Bench	ECN	None
D-V	23695.25	217 ± 4	56 ± 3	60 ± 3	458 ± 4	43 ± 3	1,105 ± 30	Nm	Nm	Nm	Nm	Brown's Bench	ECN	Figure 16.1s
D-IV	23006.1	205 ± 4	57 ± 3	63 ± 3	485 ± 4	42 ± 3	1,140 ± 30	Nm	Nm	Nm	Nm	Brown's Bench	ECN	Figure 16.3c
D-IV	23665.5	190 ± 4	60 ± 3	31 ± 3	458 ± 4	46 ± 3	1,208 ± 32	Nm	Nm	2.82 ± .04	84	Brown's Bench	ECN	Figure 16.1r
D-III	AR 873	208 ± 4	51 ± 3	64 ± 3	472 ± 4	50 ± 3	1,200 ± 36	Nm	Nm	2.6 ± .04	90	Brown's Bench	ECN	Figure 16.1u
D-III	19401.1	187 ± 4	52 ± 3	59 ± 3	444 ± 4	42 ± 3	1,203 ± 30	Nm	Nm	Nm	Nm	Brown's Bench	ECN	None
D-III	19405.22	206 ± 4	55 ± 3	62 ± 3	423 ± 4	42 ± 3	1,049 ± 30	Nm	Nm	Nm	Nm	Brown's Bench	CS with concave base	None

Stratum	Catalog No.	Trace Element Concentrations									Fe/Mn Ratio	Obsidian Source (Chemical Type)	Point Type	Illustration
		Rb	Sr	Y	Zr	Nb	Ba	Ti	Mn	$Fe_2O_3^T$				
D-III	19409.8	209 ± 4	57 ± 3	66 ± 3	486 ± 4	45 ± 3	1,137 ± 30	Nm	Nm	Nm	Nm	Brown's Bench	ECN	Figure 16.1j
D-III	19592.1	216 ± 4	54 ± 3	62 ± 3	434 ± 4	43 ± 3	1,062 ± 30	Nm	Nm	Nm	Nm	Brown's Bench	NSN	None
D-III	22993.3	196 ± 4	60 ± 3	66 ± 3	471 ± 4	50 ± 3	1,163 ± 32	Nm	Nm	Nm	Nm	Brown's Bench	NSN	Figure 16.3b
D-III	22993.4	210 ± 4	52 ± 3	64 ± 3	484 ± 4	49 ± 3	1,162 ± 36	Nm	Nm	2.81 ± .04	84	Brown's Bench	ECN	Figure 16.1m
D-III	23061.3	216 ± 4	57 ± 3	66 ± 3	469 ± 4	44 ± 3	1,120 ± 28	Nm	Nm	Nm	Nm	Brown's Bench	NSN	Figure 16.3d
D-III	23062.4	224 ± 4	24 ± 3	62 ± 3	368 ± 4	43 ± 3	585 ± 26	Nm	Nm	Nm	Nm	Brown's Bench area	NSN	None
D-III	23074.3	240 ± 4	29 ± 3	66 ± 3	370 ± 4	41 ± 3	551 ± 28	Nm	Nm	Nm	Nm	Brown's Bench area	EE	Figure 16.2d
D-III	23093.1	208 ± 4	54 ± 3	61 ± 3	437 ± 4	42 ± 3	1,109 ± 30	Nm	Nm	Nm	Nm	Brown's Bench	GS	Figure 16.2l
D-III	23372.12	202 ± 4	56 ± 3	62 ± 3	476 ± 4	44 ± 3	1,230 ± 34	Nm	Nm	Nm	Nm	Brown's Bench	GS	Figure 16.2o
D-III	23133.2	244 ± 4	32 ± 3	62 ± 3	350 ± 4	43 ± 3	535 ± 28	Nm	Nm	Nm	82	Brown's Bench area	EE	Figure 16.2e
D-III	23136.2	225 ± 4	24 ± 3	65 ± 3	369 ± 4	41 ± 3	568 ± 28	Nm	Nm	Nm	Nm	Brown's Bench area	NSN	None
D-III	23229.3	211 ± 4	55 ± 3	63 ± 3	451 ± 4	43 ± 3	1,103 ± 32	Nm	Nm	Nm	Nm	Brown's Bench	NSN	Figure 16.3e
D-III	23231.1	213 ± 4	53 ± 3	65 ± 3	465 ± 4	42 ± 3	1,095 ± 30	Nm	Nm	Nm	Nm	Brown's Bench	ECN	None
D-III	23290.1	218 ± 4	52 ± 3	65 ± 3	460 ± 4	44 ± 3	1,139 ± 30	Nm	Nm	Nm	Nm	Brown's Bench	DSN	None
D-III	23297.2	215 ± 4	51 ± 3	65 ± 3	419 ± 4	41 ± 3	1,005 ± 30	Nm	Nm	Nm	Nm	Brown's Bench	NSN	None
D-III	23297.4	216 ± 4	55 ± 3	65 ± 3	462 ± 4	45 ± 3	1,070 ± 32	Nm	Nm	Nm	Nm	Brown's Bench	NSN	None
D-III	23297.1	231 ± 4	27 ± 3	68 ± 3	368 ± 4	42 ± 3	615 ± 28	Nm	Nm	Nm	Nm	Brown's Bench area	NSN	Figure 16.3g
D-III	23300.2	224 ± 4	55 ± 3	64 ± 3	472 ± 4	47 ± 3	1,136 ± 30	Nm	Nm	Nm	Nm	Brown's Bench	DSN	Figure 16.3h
D-III	23309.?	202 ± 4	56 ± 3	63 ± 3	459 ± 4	43 ± 3	1,200 ± 30	Nm	Nm	Nm	Nm	Brown's Bench	NSN	None
D-III	23310.1	201 ± 4	56 ± 3	62 ± 3	458 ± 4	42 ± 3	1,176 ± 32	Nm	Nm	Nm	Nm	Brown's Bench	NSN	Figure 16.3i
D-III	23318.2	215 ± 4	51 ± 3	65 ± 3	439 ± 4	42 ± 3	1,043 ± 30	Nm	Nm	Nm	Nm	Brown's Bench	EE	Figure 16.2g
D-III	23318.3	461 ± 4	8 ± 3	53 ± 3	140 ± 4	68 ± 3	0 ± 15	Nm	Nm	Nm	Nm	Topaz Mountain	NSN with notched base	Figure 16.3j
D-III	23338.5	217 ± 4	54 ± 3	65 ± 3	468 ± 4	48 ± 3	1,087 ± 32	Nm	Nm	2.8 ± .02	95	Brown's Bench	RSCN	None
D-III	23364.2	214 ± 4	58 ± 3	66 ± 3	487 ± 4	47 ± 3	1,204 ± 30	Nm	Nm	Nm	Nm	Brown's Bench	NSN	None
D-III	23671	211 ± 4	59 ± 3	64 ± 3	486 ± 4	42 ± 3	1,101 ± 30	Nm	Nm	Nm	Nm	Brown's Bench	NSN	Figure 16.3k
D-III	23681.3	214 ± 4	58 ± 3	65 ± 3	479 ± 4	44 ± 3	1,199 ± 32	Nm	Nm	Nm	Nm	Brown's Bench	GS	Figure 16.2p
D-III	23707.21	236 ± 4	44 ± 3	82 ± 3	443 ± 4	49 ± 3	951 ± 30	Nm	Nm	Nm	Nm	Brown's Bench	EE	Figure 16.2h
D-III	23710.4	211 ± 4	55 ± 3	63 ± 3	474 ± 4	45 ± 3	1,235 ± 32	Nm	Nm	Nm	Nm	Brown's Bench	EE	Figure 16.2i
D-II	19431.11	194 ± 4	58 ± 3	63 ± 3	437 ± 4	45 ± 3	1,113 ± 24	Nm	Nm	Nm	85	Brown's Bench	ECN	None
D-II	19431.16	212 ± 4	54 ± 3	65 ± 3	434 ± 4	43 ± 3	1,060 ± 30	Nm	Nm	Nm	Nm	Brown's Bench	ECN	None
D-II	19444.4	224 ± 4	27 ± 3	67 ± 3	372 ± 4	42 ± 3	597 ± 28	Nm	Nm	Nm	Nm	Brown's Bench area	EE	Figure 16.2b
D-II	23031.5	241 ± 4	30 ± 3	64 ± 3	379 ± 4	44 ± 3	632 ± 28	Nm	Nm	Nm	Nm	Brown's Bench area	GS	Figure 16.2j
D-II	23038.2	125 ± 4	77 ± 3	32 ± 3	88 ± 4	15 ± 3	1,610 ± 34	Nm	Mn	Nm	Nm	Malad	EE	Figure 16.2c
D-II	23069.1	213 ± 4	57 ± 3	66 ± 3	479 ± 4	44 ± 3	1,181 ± 30	Nm	Nm	Nm	Nm	Brown's Bench	GS	Figure 16.2k
D-II	23142.4	221 ± 4	9 ± 3	24 ± 3	101 ± 4	36 ± 3	0 ± 22	Nm	Nm	Nm	16	Unknown	Untypable CN	None
D-II	23227.1	198 ± 4	55 ± 3	64 ± 3	452 ± 4	43 ± 3	1,218 ± 30	Nm	Nm	Nm	Nm	Brown's Bench	GS	Figure 16.2n
D-II (Feature 16)	23228.3	190 ± 4	41 ± 3	21 ± 3	110 ± 4	24 ± 3	136 ± 28	Nm	Nm	.86 ± .02	21	Wild Horse Canyon	ECN	Figure 16.1p

D-II/III	23229.1	217 ± 4	49 ± 3	62 ± 3	425 ± 4	42 ± 3	1,086 ± 30	Nm	Nm	Nm	Nm	Brown's Bench	ECN	None
D-II	23240.3	205 ± 4	52 ± 3	63 ± 3	463 ± 4	44 ± 3	1,189 ± 34	Nm	Nm	Nm	Nm	Brown's Bench	ECN	None
D-II	23290.4	234 ± 4	30 ± 3	70 ± 3	403 ± 4	47 ± 3	605 ± 28	Nm	Nm	Nm	Nm	Brown's Bench area	NSN	None
D-II	23343.2	216 ± 4	46 ± 3	63 ± 3	423 ± 4	47 ± 3	1,097 ± 34	Nm	Nm	2.46	86	Brown's Bench	ECN	None
D-II	23684.12	212 ± 4	56 ± 3	62 ± 3	462 ± 4	44 ± 3	1,109 ± 30	Nm	Nm	Nm	Nm	Brown's Bench	Unclassified CN	None
D-II	23722.8	244 ± 4	30 ± 3	67 ± 3	384 ± 4	42 ± 3	594 ± 28	Nm	Nm	Nm	Nm	Brown's Bench area	ECN	None
Unknown	AR 865	216 ± 4	58 ± 3	65 ± 3	475 ± 4	44 ± 3	1,191 ± 30	Nm	Nm	Nm	Nm	Brown's Bench	ECN	None
Unknown	AR 870	191 ± 4	60 ± 3	69 ± 3	488 ± 4	59 ± 3	1,262 ± 30	Nm	Nm	2.89 ± .02	71	Brown's Bench	ECN	Figure 16.1t
Unknown	AR 871	239 ± 4	28 ± 3	68 ± 3	378 ± 4	43 ± 3	567 ± 26	Nm	Nm	Nm	Nm	Brown's Bench area	NSN	None
Unknown	AR 908	242 ± 4	52 ± 3	83 ± 3	470 ± 4	58 ± 3	892 ± 15	Nm	Nm	Nm	90	Brown's Bench	LS	None
Unknown	1793	211 ± 4	55 ± 3	62 ± 3	439 ± 4	44 ± 3	1,225 ± 34	Nm	Nm	Nm	Nm	Browns Bench	RS	None
Unknown	17788	473 ± 4	5 ± 3	49 ± 3	130 ± 4	71 ± 3	0 ± 24	Nm	Nm	Nm	Nm	Topaz Mountain	RSCN	None
Unknown	19518.13	231 ± 4	36 ± 3	61 ± 3	374 ± 4	42 ± 3	652 ± 28	Nm	Nm	Nm	Nm	Brown's Bench area	RSCN	Figure 16.1a
Unknown (25–36 inches)	19845	253 ± 4	12 ± 3	53 ± 3	99 ± 4	29 ± 3	Nm	Nm	Nm	.96 ± .02	21	Black Rock area	ECN	Figure 16.1k
Unknown (25–36 inches)	19870.2	193 ± 4	53 ± 3	62 ± 3	468 ± 4	42 ± 3	1,211 ± 30	Nm	Nm	Nm	Nm	Brown's Bench	Shouldered CS	None
Unknown[a]	22987.21	193 ± 4	52 ± 3	59 ± 3	450 ± 4	42 ± 3	1,130 ± 30	Nm	Nm	Nm	Nm	Brown's Bench	NSN	Figure 16.3l
Unknown[b]	23019.1	208 ± 4	53 ± 3	64 ± 3	462 ± 4	44 ± 3	1,131 ± 30	Nm	Nm	Nm	Nm	Brown's Bench	LSN	None
Unknown[b]	23019.2	438 ± 4	7 ± 3	48 ± 3	135 ± 4	65 ± 3	0 ± 24	Nm	Nm	Nm	Nm	Topaz Mountain	RSCN	None
Unknown	23106.3	218 ± 4	55 ± 3	65 ± 3	442 ± 4	43 ± 3	1,049 ± 30	Nm	Nm	Nm	Nm	Brown's Bench	GS	Figure 16.2m
Unknown	23310.2	210 ± 4	52 ± 3	65 ± 3	450 ± 4	45 ± 3	1,240 ± 32	Nm	Nm	Nm	Nm	Brown's Bench	EE	Figure 16.2f
U.S. Geological Survey Reference Standard														
RGM-1 (measured)		149 ± 4	109 ± 3	26 ± 3	220 ± 4	9 ± 3	807 ± 28	Nm	Nm	1.87 ± .02	64	Glass Mountain, CA		
RGM-1 (recommended)		149	108	25	219	9	807	1,600	279	1.86	Nr	Glass Mountain, CA		

Note: All values (except Fe/Mn ratios) are in parts per million (ppm) or weight percent composition ($Fe_2O_3^T$); ± = 2 ∑ estimate (in parts per million or weight percent) of x-ray counting uncertainty and regression fitting error at 120–240 seconds live time. Recommended values for RGM-1 from Govindaraju 1994. CN = corner-notched; CS = contracting stem; DSN = Desert Side-notched; ECN = Elko Corner-notched; EE = Elko Eared; GS = Gatecliff series; LS = leaf-shaped; LSN = large side-notched; NSN = Northern Side-notched; SN = side-notched; RS = Rosegate series; RSCN = Rosegate series Corner-notched; Nm = not measured; Nr = not reported.

[a] Feature F80, Sec. 145, R14–22.

[b] Feature F87, Sec. 135, R15.

17

Naming the Desert Bighorn

David Rhode

Taxonomic nomenclature has always been a crucial part of natural history, and rightly so. Scientific names of organisms, first and foremost, effectively serve communication across borders of nations and languages, letting naturalists know if they are dealing with the same species of virus, amoeba, lichen, radish, or beetle or if they may have discovered a new one. Scientific names are also nuggets of information about a creature. The Linnean binomial, a koan briefer than a haiku or a tweet, rewards the reader with clues to an organism's phylogeny, its geographic distribution, its morphology and adaptations, its useful or baleful relationships to people, or the history of its discovery. On a more personal level, if a naturalist thinks highly enough of you to tie an organism's name to your own—well, that is one of the finer tributes you may be given. If upheld by the rules of priority and justification, that organism's scientific name is a small measure of immortality for both you and the namer (Bloch 1938).

This is the story of how the desert bighorn (*Ovis canadensis nelsoni*) got its scientific name and in so doing came to honor Edward William Nelson, the great American naturalist of the late nineteenth and early twentieth century. That is the main part of my story, but only the middle part. The names we give things carry potent charges of meaning, history, and our own identity. So I start with the history of popular American names of this iconic Great Basin ungulate and finish with names given by its original namers, the Native peoples who lived with it for millennia.

An American Wild Sheep

The bighorn first came to European notice as early as the 1540s, when Coronado observed "sheep as big as a horse, with very large horns and little tails": "They are used to the rough country, so that we could not catch them and had to leave them" (Winship 1896:560, 487). In 1697, the Jesuit missionary Francis Maria Piccolo published a description of the beast from southern Baja California, calling it by the native term *tajé*, referred to in later translations as the "Taye or Californian deer" (Venegas 1759:36). To European eyes this animal was an odd chimera, having a body resembling a calf, the coat and coloration of a deer, and a deer's head but a ram's horns; the most similar animal then known was the argali, the central Asian wild sheep.

Other Spanish and Mexican explorers remarked upon bighorn over the next century (Grant 1980; Manville 1980), but Piccolo's description stood as the primary account of North American wild sheep until 1800, when Duncan McGillivray of the Northwest Fur Company bagged a few animals at the Bow River near present-day Calgary, Canada. McGillivray's specimens, displayed at the Royal Society of London and a private museum in New York, aroused considerable scientific interest. In 1804 naturalists proposed three different scientific names for the bighorn, *Ovis canadensis*, *O. cervina*, and *O. montana*, highlighting three different aspects of its known existence: geographic distribution (*canadensis*), morphology (*cervina*, or "deer-like"), and habitat (*montana*). These and other competing scientific names set off a long dispute over nomenclatural primacy, which *canadensis* eventually won (Allen 1912; Biddulph 1885; Hornaday 1901; Shackleton 1985).

As the beast became better known to European naturalists and was increasingly encountered by explorers of western North America, the popular name for the American wild sheep also remained to be settled (Stewart 1935). Several names were proposed—*mountain-ram* (McGillivray's suggestion, from the Canadian *le belier des montagnes*), *my-attic* (from a Cree name meaning "ugly reindeer"), *argali* (the Asian wild sheep), *ahsata* (from a Mandan word meaning "big horn"), *ibex* (an Asian goat), *mouflon* (the French name for wild sheep of southwest Asia), and even *taye*:

> No real progress, however, was made toward a popular name, and anyone could have noted that the English language on the popular level had had no past experience with a wild sheep, and that accordingly there could be no name ready at hand. So the matter stood before the explorations of Lewis and Clark [Stewart 1935:284].

Two names, though, soon vied for popular currency in the first decades of the 1800s: "mountain sheep" and, alternatively, "bighorn sheep." Both are simple direct English, Stewart argued, and hence they were favored. Stewart himself seems to have preferred "mountain sheep":

> The great advantage of this term was that it was thoroughly English in background thus demanding not even the process of folk etymology to make it familiar. It was moreover descriptive in a very satisfying way, for the animal was obviously a sheep and was invariably found on mountains, or at least hills. Accordingly, no matter what literary men like Irving or grandiloquent travelers like Brackenridge might prefer, those straightforward speakers of American English who hunted the animal and feasted upon its delicious mutton seem to have decided almost unanimously that just as they themselves were *mountain men* so the animal was nothing more or less than *mountain sheep*. The term had an added advantage in that, when no chance for confusion offered, it could be conveniently shortened to simple sheep [1935:286; emphasis in original].

Contrary to Stewart, however, the voyageurs, mountaineers, hunters, and trappers of the 1800s–1830s did not call themselves "mountain men" (Hardee 1999): that term was only invented later on by those grandiloquent literary types and popularized in late nineteenth-century dime novels. Nor did they speak straightforward American English but, rather, a "strange medley of English, French, and Spanish [and Native American words] and as distinct from grammatical and literary propriety as it is possible to conceive" (Chittenden 1902:63). The fact that "mountain sheep" was simple plain English mattered very little in the peculiar Creolized patois of the fur hunters. Finally, as Stewart himself noted, the animal was not quite so obviously a sheep: though definitely sheep-like in many ways and recognized as such, it lacked fleece, it had a body and coat more like a deer, and its "delicious mutton" tasted like venison (see Hornaday 1901:105; Russell 1921:134).

Thus, Stewart's Anglocentric rationale for the "unanimous" adoption of the term *mountain sheep* into American speech (that it was a straightforward English reference to a wild sheep of the mountains, used by self-appointed mountain men) appears historically weak. Other reasons for this name's success may have more traction. For one thing, this form of the name was already popular in Spanish and French (Stewart 1935:283). Spanish and Mexican explorers in the desert Southwest employed the terms *borrego cimarrón* and *carnero cimarrón* (Landeros 1997; Nabhan 1993), with *cimarrón* having meanings of "wild," "maverick," "renegade," and "mountainous" (*cima* referring to "peak" or "summit"). The French Canadian term, *les belier de montagnes* (as initially reported by Shaw and adopted by the French naturalists Etienne Geoffroy St. Hilaire and Cuvier [see Allen 1912:8–11]) easily translates to "mountain sheep." Indeed, the most straightforward way to get to "mountain sheep" as a popular name is a simple translation of *Ovis montana*, the preferred scientific epithet throughout the nineteenth century and how most American naturalists would have known it (Hornaday 1901:101). Perhaps *Ovis montana* led directly to "mountain sheep" in popular English usage.

Another name was popular early on, too: "bighorn sheep" (or, more simply, "bighorn"). Stewart points out that Lewis and Clark refer several times to the "big-horned animals" (e.g., M. Lewis, May 25, 1805, and W. Clark, May 25, 1805, in Moulton 2002), and other hunters and trappers also adopted that name (Stewart 1935:286):

> It had moreover the valuable support on the frontier of the comparable French term *gros corne*.... Its hold was strengthened by the help of place names—the Big Horn Mountains, and the river with its curiously named branch of tragic memories, the Little Big Horn [Stewart 1935:286–287].

In the later nineteenth century, the term *bighorn* fed the fascination of big-game hunters, adding to its popularity (e.g., Roosevelt 1885, 1893). These well-to-do sport hunters valued a big set of curling horns mounted over the mantel over almost any other game North America offered, for the very reason that hunting them was so difficult:

> Thousands of *Ovis montana* have been hunted down and killed for their heads alone, and thousands more have met their death before the rifles of sportsmen because they are grand game. Their wariness, their strength and agility in climbing, and the rugged mountains which they inhabit combine to render them difficult to find and difficult to kill, and therefore all the more tempting to the genuine sportsman [Hornaday 1901:105–106].

Stewart saw much of value in "bighorn"—and some poetry as well:

> For the future, bighorn seems to me to have a very good chance. It is equally, perhaps more, distinctive [than "mountain sheep"]. It is the sort of name which on the whole seems more colorful to the average literary person, whether writer or reader [1935:287–288].

On this count, Stewart was absolutely right: "bighorn" has clearly won out over "mountain sheep" as the animal's most popular name. "Bighorn sheep" is today recognized by several authorities as the "official" common name for *Ovis canadensis* (Shackleton 1985; Wilson and Cole 2000). A Google search conducted in August 2011 of "bighorn sheep" resulted in 1,510,000 hits, compared with 1,180,000 hits for "mountain sheep," and an unsystematic survey suggests a rise in the use of "bighorn sheep" over "mountain sheep" in titles of natural history books and professional articles through the past century. Both names remain in common use and are synonymous in referring to North

American wild sheep, but "bighorn sheep" has the modern edge in popularity, perhaps for the reasons Stewart suggested. As far as names of the wild sheep of the desert West are concerned, there is really no contest: "desert bighorn" clearly prevails in popularity and usage over "desert mountain sheep." Here the former phrase resulted in 157,000 Google hits, compared with only 10,100 hits for the latter. *Borrego cimarrón*, or simply *cimarrón*, remains the name of choice in Mexico (Landeros 1997; Mellink 1993).

The desert bighorn, also known as Nelson's bighorn sheep (*O. c. nelsoni*), is the largest native ungulate in the rugged dry mountains of the southern half of the Great Basin, the Mojave Desert, the Transverse Ranges of California, and the southern Colorado Plateau (Monson 1980) and a widely beloved emblem of the remaining wildlands in the desert West (Landeros 1997; Nabhan 1993). Compared with the wild sheep of the Rocky Mountains to the north, the desert bighorn is typical of desert animals in being somewhat smaller in form and paler in color, with a few other morphological distinctions as well (Cowan 1940; Ramey 1993; Wehausen and Ramey 2000).

In the late nineteenth century, Nelson's desert bighorn was quickly and alarmingly being wiped out of much of its original range by ranching, the diseases of introduced domestic sheep, and rampant gun hunting (Manville 1980:6). The bighorn's increasing rarity made it immensely desirable to trophy hunters (Hornaday 1908; Mellink 1993). As late as 1890, though, this distinctive desert denizen was still not formally known to science as anything different from any other North American wild sheep. How did the desert bighorn first become recognized and named by scientists? Why is the desert-adapted sheep known as Nelson's bighorn, and who was Nelson, anyway?

Bringing the Desert Bighorn to Science

Edward William Nelson, one of the most promising and versatile young naturalists of his generation, returned to Washington, D.C., in autumn 1881, having spent the past four long years in the Arctic (Figure 17.1). At the behest of the Smithsonian Institution's Spencer Baird, Nelson had been posted as an Army Signal Service meteorologist to St. Michael, Alaska, about as far as one could get from the nation's capital and still be on American soil. There on the edge of the Bering Sea, Nelson recorded thousands of weather observations according to his duties, but he also explored widely throughout the Yukon–Kuskokwim Delta region. He (1887) collected hundreds of new Arctic animal and plant specimens for the National Museum, with detailed notes backing up the specimens. He visited dozens of Bering Strait Eskimo communities, often the first white person ever to do so, where he (1899) obtained thousands of objects of material culture and invaluable ethnological observations. In his last year there, Nelson served as naturalist on the revenue cutter *Corwin*, exploring the coast of Siberia, Wrangell Island, St. Lawrence Island, and the coast of Alaska from Point Barrow to the Bering Strait. Every year, Nelson sent crates of his Arctic treasures to the Smithsonian, awaiting his return. Now the man himself, 26 years old, was there to work up his enormous collections and report on his adventures, sparking keen interest among the Washington scientific establishment.

Nelson, though, was rapidly becoming a broken young man. A bout of pneumonia contracted in Alaska gave way to pulmonary tuberculosis, and the disease wrecked him. "I was somewhat shocked at his gaunt and sickly appearance," recalled the ornithologist and physician Albert Kenrick "AK" Fisher, on first meeting Nelson to see his unique Arctic bird specimens: "Poor food and exposure I fear had brought on tuberculosis that shortly would end his very promising career.... I feared that maybe my first visit with him would be the last" (Papers of Albert Kenrick Fisher, U.S. National Archives, Washington, D.C.). Nelson drove himself to complete his work, but with the "sudden change to a sedentary life and long hours of close application in the climate of Washington," the "great white plague" took devastating control (Goldman 1935:145):

> [Nelson's] health failed still more so that by urgent advice he went to Colorado to spend the summer. In this fine mountain air, there was some improvement in his health, so he returned to Washington to continue work. Unfortunately, however, his dread disease seemed to be on the increase so that he had to hurry away for the southwest. He told me that at Santa Fe he had five hemorrhages of the lung in one week. Two things seemed to have saved his life, the devotion of his mother and the indomitable force of [his] character [Papers of Albert Kenrick Fisher].

Over the next few years, under his mother's care, Nelson gradually recuperated but suffered permanently damaged lungs and a weakened heart—he was ever after a "one-lunger." Nelson homesteaded in Springerville, Arizona, and with his parents and brother built a successful ranch; but the spell of natural history never left him. Locals knew Nelson as "Bug," for his abiding interests, though "owing to very limited financial resources, as well as uncertain health, his natural history studies were, for a time, much restricted in scope" (Goldman 1935:145). He kept in touch with his old benefactor Spencer Baird, offering animal specimens he had caught or prehistoric artifacts from nearby pueblo sites for the Smithsonian's collections. Baird's death in 1887, though, severed Nelson's closest connection to the eastern-based natural history establishment. Far from the center of knowledge and influence in the work he most loved, Nelson knew he could not stay in the game unless he acted quickly. In 1890, he learned that his old friend and colleague Clinton Hart Merriam was planning a large biological expedition to Death Valley and the Sierra Nevada of California. Here, figured Nelson, might be his best chance to revive his naturalist calling.

C. Hart Merriam was among the most prominent naturalists of his day, like Nelson a protégé of Baird's, and a leading figure in Washington scientific circles (Osgood 1943; Sterling 1974). In 1885 Merriam had secured a tiny appropriation in the Agriculture

FIGURE 17.1. Edward William Nelson in Mexico about 1903, 12 years after the Death Valley Expedition (photo by Edward Goldman; courtesy of the U.S. National Archives).

Department to organize the "Division of Economic Ornithology and Mammalogy," which Congress intended to gather information about controlling bird and mammal pests. But Merriam had other ideas: he (1935) skillfully steered it toward his own scientific goal of establishing a nationwide biological survey, with the ultimate aim to describe and account for the distribution of the native fauna of the United States. In 1896 Merriam changed the division's name to the Biological Survey, by which it became best known (Cameron 1929).

Merriam (1890, 1898) wanted to know how native plants and animals were organized into what he called "life zones" and the physical parameters (particularly temperature) that constrained the distribution of organisms in those life zones. By learning how these zones of natural life were distributed and which zones were best suited to specific crops or fruit trees, Merriam figured that farmers could better select crops suitable to their local areas or to new parts of the country on a more efficient and economical scientific basis (his work thereby reflecting Congress's original economic intent). These life zones spanned the eastern part of the continent as broad latitudinal belts, but in the mountains of the West the different zones stacked up vertically with increasing altitude.

In the early Biological Survey years, Merriam and his staff of fieldmen set about characterizing the natural life throughout the United States, identifying the plants and animals residing in different life zones, mapping their distribution in both latitude and altitude, and collecting large series of specimens for taxonomic investigation. Merriam's study of life zones and their physical causes influenced the developing sciences of biogeography and modern ecology (Kohler 2006; Lomolino et al. 2004; Worster 1994), and he is widely considered the founding "grandfather" of American mammalogy (Osgood 1943; Storer 1969:786–787).

In 1890, Merriam sought to expand his pioneering surveys to cover the greatest span of altitudinal relief the nation offered—from the base of Death Valley (the lowest point in the United States) to Mt. Whitney in the Sierra Nevada (the highest), separated by only 85 linear miles. The proposed Death Valley Expedition would delineate a sequence of life zones on the broadest altitudinal transect available, link the zones of the eastern United States with those found in the western mountains and deserts, and showcase Merriam's methods for the scientific community and the interested general public.

Nelson badly wanted to be part of this expedition, and he traveled to Washington to plead his case. Given the expedition's broad scope, an accomplished naturalist like Nelson would be a great addition to Merriam's small crew. But Merriam's budget was minuscule, and he demurred about bringing Nelson on. Finally AK Fisher, Merriam's second-in-command, prevailed on Merriam to bring Nelson on in the hopes that Congress would give more support (Papers of Albert Kenrick Fisher). Congress did come up with a little more money, provided that a Kansas congressman's son was included as an assistant. With this favor given, both Nelson and the congressman's son, Fred Funston, became members of the party. (Nelson stayed on with the Biological Survey for nearly 40 years, eventually succeeding Merriam as chief. Funston went on to his own illustrious career, mostly military.)

Thus in December 1890 Nelson found himself in Keeler, California, with Merriam's assistant, Vernon Bailey, a self-taught young man whom Merriam considered one of the nation's finest collectors. Nelson learned the names of the local biota, tricks for trapping gophers, and Merriam's methodical ways of doing things while he and Bailey waited to meet the rest of the expedition in Death Valley in January. Merriam himself was working Congress for his hoped-for annual appropriation, so he would not make it out until spring; in his place he had tapped Theodore Palmer, a young naturalist just graduated from Berkeley, to lead the party. Rounding out the expedition were the young botanist Frederick Coville and his unbotanical field assistant, Fred Funston; the party's cook, Tie Sing, on assignment from the U.S. Geological Survey; assorted mappers, teamsters, packers, and hostlers; and the expedition's master prankster, AK Fisher, Nelson's benefactor and, along with Nelson, one of the group's "old-timers":

> During this whole trip, Nelson and I were thrown together a good deal, and we became well acquainted and deep friendship was formed. As I knew his lungs were not in good working order, so far as possible I took details in the high country so that he might work at lower levels [Papers of Albert Kenrick Fisher].

The Death Valley Expedition was the largest biological collecting survey undertaken in the United States up to that time. From January to September expedition members explored and collected biological specimens throughout the Death Valley region, across southern Nevada, and up into the southern High Sierra. The research the expedition produced greatly expanded our knowledge of the natural history of the Mojave Desert and Sierra Nevada (Pavlik 2008), and its many biological collections remain valuable today. Here I dwell on just one of those collections: the type specimen of desert bighorn.

By the time May 1891 rolled around, the expedition's men had become deeply familiar with Death Valley—its broad contours, rough features, and many discontents. They knew well the varieties of creatures that scampered or slithered or hid or flew here and there, and they had seen the valley's blush of wildflowers come and go as springtime temperatures rose and rose. They were ready for a change, and when Merriam arrived they made plans to cover new territory. Merriam gave Nelson charge of a small party—Funston, Tie Sing and his dog, Hat, and a packer—to work in Saline Valley, northern Death Valley, and the dry highlands surrounding them.

And as May turned to June, Nelson's thoughts turned toward sheep—wild sheep. He suspected that the wild sheep living in the nearby mountains were likely nondescripts—that is, they had never been technically described or classified for science. Years before, Nelson had brought in the first specimens known to science of the Alaskan white wild sheep (*Ovis dalli*), and it was he (1884) who first described them and named them in honor of William Dall, the pioneering Arctic naturalist. Now Nelson wanted to be the one to get these local desert sheep and bring them to scientific recognition. He knew how to get them, and his daily journal tells how he did it:

> Thurs. May 28th. I went down to the Indian camp about half a mile below [our camp] and arranged with several of them to go with me to the Grapevine Mts. hunting mountain sheep. I am to pay them $10.00 each for at least three specimens [field journal, Death Valley Expedition, Archives of the Smithsonian Institution, Washington, D.C.].

The camp in Cottonwood Canyon (called Navadü, "Big canyon" [Steward 1938], or Napatün [Dayley 1989]) contained "two or three families, except during the grass-seed or piñon-nut gathering seasons, when many of the Saline Valley people go over there for a time" (Nelson 1891:372). Their home range centered on the highlands separating Saline, Panamint, and northern Death Valley, known as Sigai (Steward 1938:80); they regularly participated in subsistence activities, festivals, and social life with other families living in the broader region (Grosscup 1977; Nelson 1891; Steward 1938). Julian Steward's (1938:80) consultant Bill Dock recollected that the families of Pete Sam, Johnny Sam, and Jackass Sam lived there about 1890. Nelson's hunters were probably men of the Sam family.

> Friday, May 29th. One of the Indians going on the mt. sheep hunt with us said that five Indians were going along and wished me to camp tonight at the last grass found in lower Cottonwood Cañon. I agreed to this and when we left camp one of our hunters volunteered to go with us to show us the place.... The canon is narrow with high steep slopes and the bottom is grown up luxuriantly with willows, cottonwoods, equisetum, grapevines and other plants so that our guide was very useful in showing us the route through the tangled thickets as this trail is not used very often.... It is only about 5

or 6 miles back from starting point—but is a very bad road—we camped at the lower end of the high ridges beyond which we can see a series of foothills extending on toward Mesquite Valley.

Saturday, May 30th. Six pah ute Indians turned up last evening to go on the sheep hunt with us. They broke camp very early in the morning to go to Mesquite Valley leaving us to follow their trail to the watering palace. We got off about 8 am and traveled for about 10 miles down Cottonwood canon to its mouth and then about as much further across Mesquite Valley and about 3 miles beyond camped at Salt Wells [now known as Surveyor's Well]. During the evening the wind arose and filled the air with sand and powdery alkaline earth so that the mountains on each side were hidden [Field Journal].

Nelson's hunting party did not stay to hunt around Cottonwood Canyon but, instead, went east to the Grapevine Mountains. Presumably they could easily hunt there on the basis of kin relations. Pete and Johnny Sam's parents lived at Ohyu, a village located at Salt Wells. Cold Mountain Jack, a resident of Grapevine Canyon, frequently hunted for mountain sheep in the Grapevines (Steward 1938:90); perhaps Nelson's party included hunters from Ohyu and Grapevine Canyon as well.

Sunday, May 31st. Early in the morning four of the utes started out on foot to look over the mts along the front of the range. We broke camp and moved up Boundary Cañon about 8 or 9 miles to a spring and made camp [Hole in the Rock Spring?].... From Salt Wells to our camp at the spring 3000 ft above in Boundary Cañon the country is excessively barren. Stunted *Larrea* and *Franseria dumosa* and *Atriplex hymenelytra* being the prevailing vegetation.... The Utes caught about a dozen chuckwallies during the day and had a fine mess in the evening. They draw the entrails and after pressing out the excrement the entrails are replaced in the animal and it is roasted in the hot ashes and then eaten entire. The hunters came in and reported seeing numerous tracks of Big-Horns but none very fresh. I put out a set of traps in the afternoon.

Monday, June 1st. Yesterday after we broke camp when moving up the slope toward the cañon a fierce dust storm covered the bottom of the valley in a dense yellow cloud. At the same time a rain storm seemed to be moving down from the north. We had barely made camp when a brisk shower struck us and a heavy rain followed during a large part of the night. The hunters were exposed to the heavy rain for hours last night but were up early in the morning laughing and as talkative as ever. About 7:30 am they all went into the hills and I had to remain in camp to be on hand in case any of them get a Big Horn as I have arranged that if one is killed they are to come for me at once so that I can measure and skin it properly. In the evening the hunters came in and reported no fresh signs and it was decided to move camp tomorrow.

Tuesday, June 2nd. Broke camp early in the morning and followed up Boundary Cañon nearly to its head [Daylight Pass]. There we moved to the left up a short branch cañon and over a divide several hundred feet high [Red Pass?] and thence down into the head of the large cañon extending from the middle of Grapevine Range down into Mesquite Valley [Titus Canyon]. We followed one of the southern tributaries of this cañon down to its mouth at the upper end of the box cañon then we turned up a small cañon coming in from the north and going over a little ridge came to a trickling water supply coming out from the base of a large sandstone bluff facing west [probably at 36.87°N, 117.06°W]. The water comes out upon a layer of conglomerate and is a very scanty supply. In the vicinity is grass enough for 8 or 10 head of horses.

Wednesday, June 3. Rode several miles northerly from camp up a cañon leading down from the main part of the range to the north [Wahguyhe Peak area]. The top of the mts are very well supplied with *Pinus monophylla* to all appearances. Set out some traps and returned to camp. In the evening the hunters came in and one party of two reported that they found a bunch of 16 does [= ewes] and fawns of which they killed seven. Three other hunters came in and reported seeing a small bunch of sheep and getting a young buck. Making eight in all. I made arrangements to go out to the place where they had left them in the morning [field journal].

This flock would have been large for the Grapevine Mountains, as most herds tend to be family groups of three–five individuals. In the 1950s, Welles and Welles (1961) estimated that about 150 sheep occupied the Grapevines, living in several groups around various springs. That number has since decreased to an estimated 25–50 sheep living in the Grapevines today (Wehausen 1999).

Thursday June 4th. Started for the sheep about sunrise. Found a rough trail for our animals to the bottom of the deep canyon on the side of which the sheep were killed. There we left the horses and taking a supply of ropes and sacks on our backs with our cook and Funston as volunteer, we climbed up the rocky wall with the Indians. It was single file up extremely steep broken slopes and along narrow shelves around high cliffs up to 1300 ft above the starting point. It took a little over an hour to make it and reach the rocky shelf where the game lay. While I was going about to see the sheep with one of the Indians, I glanced up to the top of the cliffs above us and just caught sight of a mt sheep as it came out in view. The Indian made a wide detour and got a long shot at it hitting it in the paunch. The sheep at once started and ran from rock to rock down the slope and when nearly opposite and about 125 yards from the rest of us it stopped and looked about. I took one of the Indians rifles and shot it just back of the shoulder. It ran a few steps and stopped and an Indian fired hitting the ground below the animal. The sheep ran about 10 yards further, turned and fell. The Indian who fired last excused his bad shot by saying that he was not used to the gun.

I measured the sheep and after their skins were taken off one of the Indians trailed a sheep they wounded yesterday and found it dead about half a mile away. This brought the number in hand to 10. Nine of them on the canon wall and one below which had been brought to where our horses were by the Indians. We loaded ourselves with skins and meat and returned to the canon after a hard climb—getting there just at sundown.

As soon as we could get the packs on we started to return to camp but missed the trail and had to sleep on the cobblestones in bottom of the canon without a thing to eat no bed but our saddle blankets.

The sheep were killed at an altitude of about 4500 ft above Salt Wells on a black limestone ridge on E side of Mesquite Valley near Grapevine Mt. [field journal].

The most likely locale of the hunt appears to be on a side of Titus Canyon just above Klare Spring (~36.84°N, 117.09°W); at this spring, interestingly enough, is a prominent boulder covered with sheep petroglyphs. In all, six ewes, one buck, and four fawns (one female and three male) were killed. Merriam insisted that his men obtain multiple individuals of a species from each collecting locality, if possible, to best sample local variation in species morphology. Nelson and his hunters surely accomplished this aim in securing the type specimens of the desert bighorn.

> Friday June 5th. Reached camp and had breakfast at 9 am. Funston and the cook seemed thoroughly used up by the trip and I was very tired but managed to put in a full day's work on the sheep skins and got them cleaned. In the afternoon the cook helped me. Yesterday I sent one of the Indians after salt for the skins and he went to some deposit near the head of Boundary Canyon and procured a supply that answers the purpose for salting skins.
>
> Saturday, June 6th. Spent the day in cleaning skulls, salting sheep skins, etc., and put out some traps in the afternoon—Also prepared to go up to Grapevine Peak for a few days early in the morning. The Indians have "jerked" their sheep meat and started back for Cottonwood today [field journal].

Nelson's account is amazing for the remarkable tenacity he showed in reaching the sheep to measure and prepare them. Climbing the rough walls of Titus Canyon laden with bags and ropes and sheep carcasses would be heavy work for anyone: Nelson had bad lungs and a balky heart—when it sometimes threatened to stop beating, he would eat a little raw strychnine off the tip of his knife (Corey 1924). That Nelson accomplished this climb is an indication of his fearsome force of will and unflinching courage; he simply would not quit once he set his sights on a goal.

Sixty dollars lighter (about half a month's wages) and with the skins, skulls, and measurements of 10 wild sheep in hand, Nelson spent the next couple of weeks exploring northern Death Valley and Saline Valley, before finally meeting up with Merriam and his party at Lone Pine on June 16. Merriam was of course thrilled with the specimens, the first ever captured for science.

In 1897, Merriam formally described them in the *Proceedings of the Biological Society of Washington*. He noted that "in the absence of necessary material for comparison it seems best to treat the new form as a full species" (1897:217). Merriam loved to name new species. He was a notorious "splitter," calling nearly every morphological variant he came across new and often dividing existing species on grounds of geographic separation. Merriam named the Grapevine Mountains specimens *Ovis nelsoni*, to honor his friend who brought them in:

> It is a noteworthy coincidence that Mr. Nelson, who in northern Alaska discovered and named the northernmost American sheep (*Ovis dalli*), should also secure, in the Sonoran deserts of California, the southernmost representative of the group. In view of these facts, it seems peculiarly appropriate that the new sheep should perpetuate Mr. Nelson's name, which I take pleasure in bestowing upon it [1897:218].

The hunt in Death Valley was not the last to involve Nelson and wild desert sheep. After the Death Valley Expedition ended, Merriam assigned Nelson to go to Colima, western Mexico, for a three-month reconnaissance survey. From this humble beginning, Nelson and his field assistant, Edward Goldman, explored and collected in Mexico for *the next 14 years*, "visiting every state and territory in the republic—some of them a number of times—in their efforts to get a comprehensive picture of its vertebrate fauna and biogeographic regions" (Sterling 1991:40). On one of their collecting campaigns, in Chihuahua during September 1899, Nelson and Goldman secured eight desert bighorn specimens that Merriam (1901) considered to be yet another species, which he named *Ovis mexicana*.

Time and additional study have not been kind to many of Merriam's species designations, and so it is with both *Ovis nelsoni* and *O. mexicana*. Within only a few years the desert bighorn species were demoted to the subspecies level within the broader Rocky Mountain bighorn sheep group (*O. canadensis*). As Joel Asaph Allen put it,

> The numerous "subspecies" of this group are all closely related to the sheep of the central Rocky Mountains, they differing only slightly in coloration, in size, or in any other characters, although the southern forms have long been

restricted to isolated areas. It is to this fact [of geographic isolation] as much as to any marked evidences of differentiation that appears to have led to their recent recognition as nameable forms [1912:21].

Since Allen's assessment of a century ago, recent detailed morphological and genetic studies do support a significant division between the Rocky Mountain bighorn and the desert-adapted subspecies (Cowan 1940; Gutiérrez-Espeleta et al. 2000; Ramey 1993, 1995), with a broad zone of intergradation between the two in the northern Great Basin (Wehausen and Ramey 2000). The desert forms (four have been recognized) all appear to be part of a single polytypic subspecies, with local genetic and morphological differences within the range of variability expected in a geographically widespread and naturally fragmented metapopulation (Bleich et al. 1990; Bleich et al. 1996; Boyce et al. 1999; Epps 2004; Gutiérrez-Espeleta et al. 2000; Wehausen and Ramey 1993). The appropriate scientific name of that desert-adapted subspecies is *Ovis canadensis nelsoni*, Nelson's desert bighorn.

The Bighorn's First Namers

Nelson could not have captured his first specimens without the skill, knowledge, and effort of the Cottonwood Creek Timbisha hunters he hired for the job. These men grew up in a tradition where hunting bighorn was part of the way of life, in a land where pecked images of bighorn graced the rocks all around. What names did these people give the bighorn, and what do these names tell us about the bighorn's relationship to them?

Native terms for bighorn sheep typically reflect habitat, morphology, or function, much like species names in Western binomial nomenclature. For example, the Navajo *tsétah dibé*, "among rocks sheep" (Young and Morgan 1987), refers to the bighorn's preferred habitat; likewise does the Blackfoot term *miistaksoomahkihkinaa*, "mountain sheep" (Frantz and Russell 1995). The bighorn's massive headgear is highlighted in the Pawnee *arikucuuɔ*, literally "big horn" (Parks and Pratt 2008), while the Lakota people call the animal *héčhįškayapi*, "they make spoons from the horns" (Rood and Taylor 1996).

Among the Numic languages in the Great Basin, most names signify the bighorn's status as the region's premier large game animal and a valuable source of meat. The lexical threads linking bighorn names with words for killing, hunting, cooking, eating, and meat are deeply interwoven throughout the northern Uto-Aztecan languages (Numic, Takic, Tübatulabalic, and Hopic [Fowler 1972a; Miller 1967]).

Consider, for example, the main Shoshoni name for bighorn, *wásipi*. This name is derived from *wasi-*, the Shoshoni plural form of the verb "to kill" (Dayley 1989; Fowler 1972a:257), and is tied to **waʔi*, one of the primary Proto-Uto-Aztecan (PUA) root terms for "meat" (Miller 1967: cognate #280). Likewise, the Shoshoni name for a bighorn ram is *tuku* or *dukwa* (Steward 1938: 278, 282), derived from *tukku*, "meat or flesh" (Fowler 1972a:257; Miller 1996), and the verb *ti kkà* ~ *tukkua*, "to eat" (Fowler and Fowler 1971; Miller 1996), which both ultimately derive from **tuhku*, the other primary PUA root term for "meat" (Miller 1967: cognate #279). Thus the bighorn's identity in Shoshoni is directly linked semantically to killing, to meat, and to the very act of eating itself. (The Shoshoni name for the bighorn ewe, *müzambia* [Steward 1938] or *mican pia*, "lamb's mother" [Miller 1996], does not appear to follow this semantic connection; see also the Timbisha *mütsa*, "yearling lamb" [Dayley 1989:114].)

Other Numic languages also connect the bighorn's name with words for killing and food. The Northern Paiute bighorn name is *kóipa* (Fowler 1972a, 1972b, 1989:19; Fowler and Fowler 1971:211; Steward 1938:274). (Koip Peak, a nearly 13,000-ft-high eminence overlooking the Mono Basin near Yosemite, honors this Northern Paiute name; presumably sheep once lived on it.) This name derives from *koʔi-* (also *koi-*), meaning "those we kill" (Fowler 1972a:257), and ultimately from the PUA root **koya*, "to kill (plural)" (Voegelin et al. 1962:139, cognate # 45), and perhaps **kwa/kwi*, "eat/food" (Miller 1967: cognate #152). The Northern Paiute name *kóipa* differs in form from the Shoshoni names *wásipi* and *tuku*, but the words share the same extended web of meanings. (Interestingly, the Northern Paiute term for the bighorn ewe, *mutsa'* [Stewart 1941], is cognate with the Shoshoni name.)

Southern Paiute and Ute have a third distinctive bighorn name, *nagá* (Fowler 1972a; Fowler and Fowler 1971; Sapir 1931). Catherine Fowler suggests a connection to "**na-ko/na-ko'(i) y(a)* 'fight, hit/kill each other', which would relate it to the NP [Northern Paiute] term (*koipa*)" (personal communication 2011; cf. Stubbs 2008). It might also be related to the PUA reconstructed root **mak*, "to hit" (Miller 1967: cognate #233). I personally like the resemblance to the PUA root **na$_n$ka*, "ear" (Voegelin et al. 1962:139, cognate #47), in possible reference to the bighorn's headgear, but whether that linguistic correspondence stands up technically I cannot say. (The Chemehuevi term for "lamb" is *mintcatsi* [Laird 1976], another likely cognate with the Shoshoni and Northern Paiute terms for "ewe" and "yearling lamb.")

Thus, as Catherine Fowler (1972a, 1972b, 1983, 1986) has noted, the different Numic languages each have different noncognate names for the bighorn (though perhaps the *mutsa* form, for the ewe/lamb, is such a cognate). Fowler (1972a, 1972b) suggests that word taboos and respect names may have played a role in the diversity of Numic terms: "In nearly all the Numic languages, names for game animals appear to derive from what may be older respect names" (1986:95), especially those relating to the hunt and its bounty.

The major names for bighorn differ not only between each Numic language group but also from the name found in other northern Uto-Aztecan languages. Bighorn is *paʔa* in the Takic languages of southern California, *paʔat* in Tübatulabal, and *pangwi* in Hopi (Albert and Shaul 1985; Fowler 1972a; Voegelin 1958). All derive from **pa:ʔa-t*, "mountain sheep"

(Hill 2008:176–177; cf. Miller 1967: cognate #369). This name apparently derives from the PUA **paka ~ paki*, "to kill, to hit" (Miller 1967: cognate #244); again, a deep connection between the bighorn and the kill is evident. Though the various names for bighorn differ in form among the northern Uto-Aztecan languages, they hold together semantically in a web of meaning that combines hunting, killing, and eating meat (Fowler 1972a, 1986). (Southern Uto-Aztecan languages apparently lack cognate terms for the bighorn [Hill 2008].)

Additional hunting connections to bighorns are found in the spirit world. In Ute cosmology, the supernatural Sacred Mountain Sheep, mythological "boss of the Artiodactyls," is called *kwuu=pi=ci* (Goss 1972), a name that resembles the Northern Paiute *kóipa*. The constellation we know as Orion fits into tales of sheep hunting on a celestial scale (Fowler 1995). Orion's bright stars were called *nagau* by the Southern Paiute (Isabel T. Kelly, unpublished field notes from Southern Paiute and Chemehuevi, 1932–1934, University Archives, Bancroft Library, University of California, Berkeley); *nagawi* by the Chemehuevi (Laird 1976:91); *ah-mo* or *ʔmuw* by the Mohave, Kiliwa, and other Yuman-speaking peoples (Fowler 1995; Merriam 1979; Mixco 1983); *wasüppin* by the Timbisha (Dayley 1989:379); and *mojet* by the Seri (Marlett 2008)—all referring to "bighorn sheep." The mountain sheep is sometimes featured in stories highlighting hunting (e.g., Fowler and Fowler 1971:223). Most tellingly of all, the bighorn figures prominently in rock art, religious iconography, and ceremonial gear throughout western North America (Grant 1980; Janetski 2006). The bighorn's image, as much as its name, served as a powerful invocation for good luck in the hunt.

By the Names We Give, So We Shall Be Known

My purpose here has been twofold. First, I want to highlight Edward Nelson's contribution to the taxonomy of the desert bighorn and, through his own field notes, help to narrow down the location where he obtained the type specimens. Second, I reiterate the well-known truth that the names we give to things are a rich lode of meaning and history that can tell as much about the namers as they do about the named.

Don Fowler's historical studies illustrate how the history of our cultural institutions—exploring expeditions, museums, world's fairs, and anthropological research programs—can shine a bright light on who we were as a people, what we value, how we relate to the world, and how we became who we now are (e.g., Fowler 2010; Fowler et al. 2003; Parezo and Fowler 2009). I hope to have shown that the names we give to creatures—such as Nelson's desert bighorn—can do the same.

Acknowledgments

As is obvious, I am deeply influenced by Don Fowler's studies of nineteenth-century American science and anthropology and equally by Kay Fowler's remarkable insights into the history of western North American Native cultures and languages. My thanks and appreciation go to both for their many kindnesses. Thanks also go to the patient and extremely helpful archivists at the Smithsonian Institution, the National Archives, the Library of Congress Manuscripts Division, the Bancroft Library, and the Death Valley National Park Archives and to Catherine Fowler, Donald Grayson, and Joel Janetski for their sage advice on this chapter.

References Cited

Albert, Roy, and David Leedom Shaul
1985 *A Concise Hopi and English Lexicon*. John Benjamins, Philadelphia.

Allen, Joel Asaph
1912 Historical and Nomenclatural Notes on North American Sheep. *American Museum of Natural History Bulletin* 31:1–29.

Biddulph, J.
1885 On the Geographic Races of the Rocky-Mountain Bighorn. *Proceedings of the Zoological Society of London*, 1885: 678–684.

Bleich, Vernon C., John D. Wehausen, and S. A. Holl
1990 Desert-Dwelling Mountain Sheep: Conservation Implications of a Naturally Fragmented Distribution. *Conservation Biology* 4:91–98.

Bleich, Vernon C., John D. Wehausen, Rob Roy Ramey, II, and Jennifer L. Rechel
1996 Metapopulation Theory and Mountain Sheep: Implications for Conservation. In *Metapopulations and Wildlife Conservation*, edited by D. R. McCullough, pp. 353–374. Island Press, Covelo, California.

Bloch, Don
1938 Men Who Have Given Their Names. *Nature Magazine*, May: 280–283.

Boyce, W. M., R. R. Ramey, II, T. C. Rodwell, E. S. Rubin, and R. S. Singer
1999 Population Subdivision Among Desert Bighorn Sheep (*Ovis canadensis*) Ewes Revealed by Mitochondrial DNA Analysis. *Molecular Ecology* 8:99–106.

Cameron, Jenks
1929 *The Bureau of Biological Survey: Its History, Activities, and Organization*. Johns Hopkins University Press, Baltimore.

Chittenden, Hiram M.
1902 *The American Fur Trade of the Far West*, Vol. 1. Francis P. Harper, New York.

Corey, Herbert
1924 This Man Lives on Courage. *Collier's, the National Weekly*, 12 April: 12.

Cowan, Ian McTaggart
1940 The Distribution and Variation in the Native Sheep of North America. *Wildlife Monographs* 4:1–174.

Dayley, Jon P.
1989 *Tümpisa (Panamint) Shoshone Dictionary*. University of California Publications in Linguistics, 116. University of California Press, Berkeley.

Epps, Clinton W.
2004 Population Processes in a Changing Climate: Extinction,

Dispersal, and Metapopulation Dynamics of Desert Bighorn Sheep in California. Unpublished Ph.D. dissertation, University of California, Berkeley.

Fowler, Catherine S.

1972a Comparative Numic Ethnobiology. Unpublished Ph.D. dissertation, Department of Anthropology, University of Pittsburgh, Pittsburgh.

1972b Some Ecological Clues to Proto-Numic Homelands. In *Great Basin Cultural Ecology: A Symposium*, edited by Don D. Fowler, pp. 105–122. Desert Research Institute Publications in the Social Sciences, 8. Reno.

1983 Some Lexical Clues to Uto-Aztecan Prehistory. *International Journal of American Linguistics* 49(3):224–257.

1986 Subsistence. In *Great Basin*, edited by Warren L. d'Azevedo, pp. 64–97. Handbook of North American Indians, Vol. 11, William C. Sturtevant, general editor, Smithsonian Institution, Washington, D.C.

1995 Mountain Sheep in the Sky: Orion's Belt in Great Basin Mythology. *Journal of California and Great Basin Anthropology* 17(2):146–152.

Fowler, Catherine S. (compiler and editor)

1989 *Willard Z. Park's Ethnographic Notes on the Northern Paiute of Western Nevada, 1933–1944*, Vol. 1. University of Utah Anthropological Papers, 114. Salt Lake City.

Fowler, Don D.

2010 *A Laboratory for Anthropology: Science and Romanticism in the American Southwest, 1846–1930*. University of Utah Press, Salt Lake City.

Fowler, Don D., and Catherine S. Fowler (editors)

1971 *Anthropology of the Numa: John Wesley Powell's Manuscripts on the Numic Peoples of Western North America, 1868–1880*. Smithsonian Contributions to Anthropology, 14. Smithsonian Institution, Washington, D.C.

Fowler, Don D., David R. Wilcox, Jeremy A. Sabloff, and Lawrence E. Aten

2003 *Philadelphia and the Development of Americanist Archaeology*. University of Alabama Press, Tuscaloosa.

Frantz, Donald G., and Norma Jean Russell

1995 *The Blackfoot Dictionary of Stems, Roots, and Affixes*. University of Toronto Press, Toronto.

Goldman, Edward Alphonso

1935 Edward William Nelson, Naturalist. *Auk* 52:135–148.

Goss, James A.

1972 A Basin–Plateau Shoshonean Ecological Model. In *Great Basin Cultural Ecology: A Symposium*, edited by Don D. Fowler, pp. 123–128. Desert Research Institute Publications in the Social Sciences, 8. Reno.

Grant, Campbell

1980 The Desert Bighorn and Aboriginal Man. In *The Desert Bighorn: Its Life History, Ecology, and Management*, edited by Gale Monson and Lowell Sumner, pp. 7–39. University of Arizona Press, Tucson.

Grosscup, Gordon L.

1977 Notes on Boundaries and Culture of the Panamint Shoshone and Owens Valley Paiute. *University of California Archaeological Research Facility Contributions* 35:109–150. Berkeley.

Gutiérrez-Espeleta, Gustavo A., Steven T. Kalinowski, Walter M. Boyce, and Philip W. Hedrick

2000 Genetic Variation and Population Structure in Desert Bighorn Sheep: Implications for Conservation. *Conservation Genetics* 1:3–15.

Hardee, Jim

1999 Historical Use of the Term "Mountain Man." *Trapline: Quarterly Newsletter of the Fur Trade Research Center* 2(3):1–3, 9.

Hill, Jane H.

2008 Northern Uto-Aztecan and Kiowa-Tanoan: Evidence of Contact Between the Proto-Languages? *International Journal of American Linguistics* 74(2):155–188.

Hornaday, William T.

1901 *Notes on the Mountain Sheep of North America, with a Description of a New Species*. Fifth Annual Report of the New York Zoological Society. New York.

1908 *Camp-Fires of Desert and Lava*. Scribner's, New York.

Janetski, Joel C.

2006 Great Basin Animals. In *Environment, Origins, and Population*, edited by Douglas H. Ubelaker, pp. 351–364. Handbook of North American Indians, Vol. 3, William C. Sturtevant, general editor, Smithsonian Institution, Washington, D.C.

Kohler, Robert E.

2006 *All Creatures: Naturalists, Collectors, and Biodiversity, 1850–1950*. Princeton University Press, Princeton.

Laird, Carobeth

1976 *The Chemehuevis*. Malki Museum Press, Banning.

Landeros, Alberto Tapia

1997 *Cimarrón: Del Culto a la Cultura del Borrego*. Universidad Autónoma de Baja California, Mexicali.

Lomolino, Mark V., Dov F. Sax, and James H. Brown (editors)

2004 *Foundations of Biogeography: Classic Papers with Commentaries*. University of Chicago Press, Chicago.

Manville, Richard H.

1980 The Origin and Relationships of American Wild Sheep. In *The Desert Bighorn: Its Life History, Ecology, and Management*, edited by Gale Monson and Lowell Sumner, pp. 1–6. University of Arizona Press, Tucson.

Marlett, Stephen A.

2008 The Forms and Use of Names in Seri. *International Journal of American Linguistics* 74:47–81.

Mellink, Eric

1993 The President Spoke. In *Counting Sheep*, edited by Gary Paul Nabhan, pp. 201–220. University of Arizona Press, Tucson.

Merriam, Clinton Hart

1890 *Results of a Biological Survey of the San Francisco Mountain Region and Desert of the Little Colorado, Arizona*. North American Fauna, 3. U.S. Department of Agriculture, Division of Economic Ornithology and Mammalogy, Washington, D.C.

1897 *Ovis nelsoni*, a New Mountain Sheep from the Desert Region of Southern California. *Proceedings of the Biological Society of Washington* 11:217–218.

1898 *Life Zones and Crop Zones of the United States*. U.S. Department of Agriculture, Division of Biological Survey, Bulletin 10. U.S. Government Printing Office, Washington, D.C.

1901 Two New Bighorns and a New Antelope from Mexico and the United States. *Proceedings of the Biological Society of Washington* 14:29–32.

1935 The Biological Survey—Origin and Early Days—A Retrospect. *Survey* 16(3):39–43. Washington, D.C.

1979 *Indian Names for Plants and Animals Among Californian and Other Western North American Tribes*. Assembled and annotated by Robert F. Heizer. Ballena Press Publications in Archaeology, Ethnology, and History, 14. Socorro, New Mexico.

Miller, Wick R.

1967 *Uto-Aztecan Cognate Sets*. University of California Publications in Linguistics, 48. University of California Press, Berkeley.

1996 Sketch of Shoshone, an Uto-Aztecan Language. In *Languages*, edited by Ives Goddard, pp. 693–720. Handbook of North American Indians, Vol. 17, William C. Sturtevant, general editor, Smithsonian Institution, Washington, D.C.

Mixco, Mauricio J.

1983 *Kiliwa Texts*. University of Utah Anthropological Papers, 107. Salt Lake City.

Monson, Gale

1980 Distribution and Abundance. In *The Desert Bighorn: Its Life History, Ecology, and Management*, edited by Gale Monson and Lowell Sumner, pp. 40–51. University of Arizona Press, Tucson.

Moulton, Gary (editor)

2002 *The Journals of the Lewis and Clark Expedition*. University of Nebraska Press, Lincoln, and University of Nebraska–Lincoln Libraries–Electronic Text Center, Lincoln. Electronic document, http://lewisandclarkjournals.unl.edu.

Nabhan, Gary Paul (editor)

1993 *Counting Sheep: Twenty Ways of Seeing Desert Bighorn*. University of Arizona Press, Tucson.

Nelson, Edward William

1884 A New Geographical Race of the Mountain Sheep (*Ovis montana dalli* var. nov.) from Alaska. *Proceedings of the United States National Museum* 7:12–13. Washington, D.C.

1887 *Report upon Natural History Collections Made in Alaska Between the Years 1877 and 1881 by Edward W. Nelson*. Edited by Henry W. Henshaw. U.S. Senate, 49th Congress, 1st Session. Miscellaneous Document 156: Arctic Series of Publications Issued in Connection with the U.S. Army Signal Service No. 3. U.S. Government Printing Office, Washington, D.C.

1891 The Panamint and Saline Valley (Col. [*sic*]) Indians. *American Anthropologist* 4:371–372.

1899 The Eskimo About Bering Strait. In *Eighteenth Annual Report of the Bureau of American Ethnology*, pp. 19–518. U.S. Government Printing Office, Washington, D.C.

Osgood, Wilfred

1943 Clinton Hart Merriam, 1855–1942. *Journal of Mammalogy* 24:421–436.

Parezo, Nancy J., and Don D. Fowler

2009 *Anthropology Goes to the Fair: The 1904 Louisiana Purchase Exposition*. University of Nebraska Press, Lincoln.

Parks, Douglas R., and Lula Nora Pratt

2008 *A Dictionary of Skiri Pawnee*. University of Nebraska Press, Lincoln.

Pavlik, Bruce

2008 *The California Deserts: An Ecological Rediscovery*. University of California Press, Berkeley.

Ramey, Rob Roy, II

1993 Evolutionary Genetics and Systematics of North American Mountain Sheep. Unpublished Ph.D. dissertation, Cornell University, Ithaca.

1995 Mitochondrial DNA Variation, Population Structure, and Evolution of Mountain Sheep in the Southwestern United States and Mexico. *Molecular Ecology* 4:429–439.

Rood, David S., and Allan R. Taylor

1996 Sketch of Lakhota, a Siouan Language. In *Languages*, edited by Ives Goddard, pp. 440–482. Handbook of North American Indians, Vol. 17, William C. Sturtevant, general editor, Smithsonian Institution, Washington, D.C.

Roosevelt, Theodore

1885 *Hunting Trips of a Ranchman*. G. P. Putnam's Sons, New York.

1893 *The Wilderness Hunter*. G. P. Putnam's Sons, New York.

Russell, Osborne

1921 *Journal of a Trapper, or, Nine Years in the Rocky Mountains 1834–1843*. Syms-York Company, Boise.

Sapir, Edward

1931 Southern Paiute Dictionary. *Proceedings of the American Academy of Arts and Sciences* 65(3):539–730. Philadelphia.

Shackleton, David M.

1985 *Ovis canadensis*. *Mammalian Species* 230:1–9.

Sterling, Keir B.

1974 *Last of the Naturalists: The Career of C. Hart Merriam*. Arno Press, New York.

1991 Two Pioneering American Mammalogists in Mexico: The Field Investigations of Edward William Nelson and Edward Alphonso Goldman, 1892–1906. In *Latin American Mammalogy: History, Biodiversity, and Conservation*, edited by Michael A. Mares and David J. Schmidly, pp. 33–47. University of Oklahoma Press, Norman.

Steward, Julian H.

1938 *Basin–Plateau Aboriginal Sociopolitical Groups*. Bureau of American Ethnology Bulletin, 120. U.S. Department of the Interior, Washington, D.C.

Stewart, George R.

1935 Popular Names for the Mountain Sheep. *American Speech* 10:283–288.

Stewart, Omer C.

1941 *Culture Element Distributions, XIV: Northern Paiute*. Anthropological Records 4:3. University of California Press, Berkeley.

Storer, Tracy I.

1969 Mammalogy and the American Society of Mammalogists, 1919–1969. *Journal of Mammalogy* 50(4):785–793.

Stubbs, Brian D.

2008 *Uto-Aztecan: A Comparative Vocabulary*. Shumway, Yorba Linda.

Venegas, Miguel

1759 *A Natural and Civil History of California*. James Rivington and James Fletcher, London.

Voegelin, Charles F.

1958 A Working Dictionary of Tübatulabal. *International Journal of American Linguistics* 24(3):221–228.

Voegelin, C. F., F. M. Voegelin, and Kenneth L. Hale

1962 *Typological and Comparative Grammar of Uto-Aztecan: I (Phonology)*. Indiana University Publications in Anthropology and Linguistics Memoir, 17. Supplement to *International Journal of American Linguistics* 28(1). Waverly Press, Baltimore.

Wehausen, John D.

1999 Rapid Extinction of Mountain Sheep Populations Revisited. *Conservation Biology* 13(2):378–384.

Wehausen, John D., and Rob Roy Ramey, II

1993 A Morphological Reevaluation of the Peninsular Bighorn Subspecies. *Desert Bighorn Council Transactions* 37:1–10.

2000 Cranial Morphometric and Evolutionary Relationships in the

Northern Range of *Ovis canadensis*. *Journal of Mammalogy* 81(1):145–161.

Welles, Ralph E., and Florence B. Welles

1961 *The Bighorn of Death Valley*. Fauna of the National Parks of the United States, Fauna Series No. 6. National Park Service, U.S. Department of the Interior, Washington, D.C.

Wilson, Don E., and F. Russell Cole

2000 *Common Names of Mammals of the World*. Smithsonian Institution Press, Washington, D.C.

Winship, George Parker

1896 The Coronado Expedition 1540–1542. In *Fourteenth Annual Report of the Bureau of American Ethnology*, pp. 329–637. U.S. Government Printing Office, Washington, D.C.

Worster, Donald

1994 *Nature's Economy: A History of Ecological Ideas*. 2nd ed. Cambridge University Press, New York.

Young, Robert W., and William Morgan, Sr.

1987 *The Navajo Language: A Grammar and Colloquial Dictionary*. University of New Mexico Press, Albuquerque.

18

When the Elders Speak, Just Listen

Heidi Roberts

In 2009 my company, HRA, Inc., Conservation Archaeology, was hired by the Kane County Water Conservancy District to manage a large data-recovery project for the Jackson Flat Reservoir located just south of Kanab in Kane County, Utah. During the excavation of the most extensive habitation of the nine prehistoric sites investigated (42Ka6165) we discovered and excavated 29 burial features containing 54 individuals.

42Ka6165 is a large habitation site that was occupied between AD 200 and 1050. The portion of the site excavated contained over 30 habitations and dozens of storage pits, hearths, and special-use spaces concentrated in three main areas. All of the human remains were recovered from the southeastern area of the site. Sixteen burials, containing 36 individuals, were concentrated between two habitation areas on the site's eastern ridge.

The Kaibab Band of Paiutes and the Hopi were concerned that the remains would be removed from the site or maybe analyzed using destructive methods. To discuss these issues about 30 agency representatives (both state and federal), tribal claimants, landowners, and attorneys gathered in Kanab in April 2010. Army Corps of Engineers matching funding for the project kicked in the 106 process, yet the burials were located on lands that were privately owned, and as a result they fell under Utah rather than federal reburial laws. Under Utah law it fell to the Kane County Water Conservancy to hire an osteologist to examine the remains and make a cultural affiliation recommendation in compliance with the state of Utah's Native American Graves Protection and Repatriation Act (*Utah Code Ann.* Title 9, Chapter 9, Part 4) and its implementing rules (*Utah Admin. Code* R230-1). This process is in contrast to national laws, which place responsibility on the federal land management agency.

The Kaibab wanted to rebury the remains immediately, without the benefit of the state's comprehensive analysis process, which typically included inventory, measurements, observations, and destructive methods such as radiocarbon dating, carbon isotope ratio, and DNA analysis. The Hopi representative and the other Southern Paiute bands supported the Kaibab's claim and their request that no scientific studies be performed.

As director of the data-recovery project and a trained osteologist, I saw my role in this meeting as a facilitator rather than a decision maker. My job was to remove the remains, ensure their safety, and conduct whatever analyses were needed to satisfy the law without compromising the wishes of the claimants. I felt that it was the tribe's and agency's responsibility to tell me what treatment protocol I should follow.

The meeting opened with a recap of Utah's repatriation process, and then discussions drifted to relevant laws and the wishes of the claimants. The Kaibab were insistent that the remains should be returned to the earth immediately. They wanted no analysis, no measurements, no radiocarbon dating, and no DNA studies. After hours of discussion no one seemed willing to compromise, and the meeting steered toward a stalemate. The state archaeologists felt that destructive analyses were needed to determine affiliation, while the Kaibab believed that these studies would be a desecration and a waste of time. The 1,000-year-old skeletons were their ancestors, period.

To convince the tribal representatives of the scientific value of the skeletal analyses two of the archaeologists provided some examples of cases where important insights had been gained using scientific methods. Proudly they explained that the skeletal remains they had recently studied confirmed Ute stories of Indian massacres by Euro-American settlers. The room was silent as one of the archaeologists turned to the tribal representatives and asked in a pleading voice: "Don't you want to know their story? Scientific analyses can tell you so much about the lives of these people."

A heavy silence fell over the room until one of the Paiute participants, a small elderly woman who was confined to a wheelchair, raised her hand and slapped it down hard on the table. Thwack! All eyes turned her way. Her hard stare bored into the archaeologist, and then she looked at each of us, one by one. When it was my turn I sensed her frustration, and after a heavy pause she shook her head and spat.

"You just don't get it, do you? We already know their story."

After another long pause she began instructing us. I wish I had a clearer memory of exactly what she said, but the gist of it was that we should not disturb the dead. There can be serious consequences. She told us that her tribe already knew the stories of these burials and furthermore it was none of our business. Then she asked, "How do you expect me to trust you to care for my ancestors when your people don't even take care of the living?"

While she spoke I happened to gaze down at the note pad that the archaeologist sitting next to me was busy scribbling on. My eyes went wide as I read what he was writing: "Old lady in wheelchair goes on a rant."

What? Didn't he have any idea what was happening here? Wasn't he listening to her at all? His comment was not just rude, it was culturally insensitive. Didn't this archaeologist understand that this woman was a respected Elder who had attended this meeting to instruct us?

The archaeologist never did get it, but a compromise was reached. The agencies agreed that no destructive studies would be done, the remains would be stored on-site, and a minimum of analyses would be performed to determine age at death, sex, race, stature, and observations on morphological traits that could yield clues of affinity.

The meeting had given me a lot to think about. What would it be like to walk in that Elder's shoes? What if archaeologists excavated one of my ancestors, for example, my great-great-grandfather, and I had no written claim except for my family's oral history. What would the osteologist be able to tell me about him that I did not already know?

From listening to my grandmother's stories I knew that my great-great-great-grandfather was named Captain Henry Clinton Davis. He had been a school principal until he joined the 18th Connecticut Volunteers to fight in the Civil War. In June 1863 he was captured during the Battle of Winchester, and he served out the remainder of the war in Libby Prison and other detention facilities. Much of what my grandmother knew about him came from beautiful love letters that he had exchanged with his young wife throughout the war. What could science tell me about him that could equal what I had learned from his prose-filled letters?

Perhaps the osteologist might be able to verify that Captain Davis returned from war sick and broken? He contracted tuberculosis in the camps and eventually died from the disease. Sometimes tuberculosis can leave traces on skeletal remains that an osteologist can recognize. The osteologist would also be able to determine his stature, sex, and age at death, but then I already knew most of that. DNA would verify that we are related, wouldn't it? What if the captain did not father his youngest daughter, who was my great-grandmother? After all she was born when he was away in the war. What if the osteologist learned that we were not genetically related at all? Would that mean that he was not my ancestor?

My family's oral history for the past 150 years was quite detailed, but what did I know about my family 500 or even 1,000 years ago? My mother's ancestry can be traced to George Soule, who settled in Plymouth after sailing across the ocean on the *Mayflower*, and we all know that story—or at least the Pilgrims' side of it.

My father's ancestors 1,000 years ago lived in Sweden and were Vikings, spreading their genetic material throughout Europe, Asia, and maybe even North America the old-fashioned way—by rape, pillage, and plunder. Thanks to the Norse oral tradition we now know that the Vikings beat Columbus to North America. No one believed that oral history until it was archaeologically verified in Nova Scotia.

If the Viking sagas contain grains of truth, why do we dismiss the Kaibab's oral tradition? The Kaibab tell us that their ancestors are the Virgin Puebloans, yet archaeologists refuse to believe them until there is tangible "proof." The coroner agreed that the burials are clearly Native American, and they were recovered from Kaibab traditional lands. So why don't archaeologists take the Kaibab's claim at face value and hand the remains over for reburial? Why must we study the remains at all? Why do we place the Kaibab in the position of having to fight for their ancestors?

Many archaeologists insist that the Virgin Puebloans are not the ancestors of the Southern Paiute people because it is generally believed that the Southern Paiute people entered the region around AD 1200 or after the region's abandonment by Fremont and Virgin Puebloan groups. However, after decades of intensive scientific research, this model remains controversial and unverified (Madsen and Rhode 1994). If there is no clear consensus, why do archaeologists cling to the Numic Spread idea so fiercely? Perhaps an answer to this question could be found in the intellectual history of Southwestern archaeology. What insights on this question can be gleaned from Don Fowler's long list of relevant publications and his magnum opus—*A Laboratory for Anthropology* (2010)?

About halfway through *A Laboratory for Anthropology* it occurred to me why the archaeologists in the repatriation meeting had so little respect for the Kaibab Elders' certainty that the Virgin Puebloans were their relatives. At the risk of sounding presentist, it became evident to me that Southwestern archaeologists have had a long tradition of not consulting Native Americans *before* excavating their ancestors' graves and sending the artifacts and human remains to museums. With a few exceptions, the Southwest's first archaeologists went about their business amassing huge collections of artifacts and burials without asking permission of possible descendants; without caring what the tribes thought about their excavations—except when those tribes threatened them with bodily harm for desecrating sites; and without respect for the dead. To many archaeologists, Indians were cheap labor, sometimes skilled labor, but more often than not sources for interpretation. Science always trumped sacred; our bad reputation developed early and still lingers today. One could say that contemporary archaeologists are following in the traditions of their ancestors.

Yet most of us are painfully aware of that chapter of our past, so let us not dwell on it. The key question is: Why do archaeologists dismiss the possibility that the Southern Paiute people are the descendants of the Virgin Puebloans? After some additional research I discovered that the answer to this question is in Don's publications, too, and it is a two-part story. First, cultural evolution is still viewed as unidirectional (D. Fowler 2010), and second, the reconstruction of the past is often done to legitimize a political agenda (Fowler 1987).

Pioneer archaeologists conceived of cultural evolution as a one-way ticket; once you climbed aboard Morgan's and John Wesley Powell's (or V. G. Child's or Leslie White's) journey from savagery, to barbarism, to civilization, there was no going back. The unidirectionality of cultural evolution seems to be one of the immutable laws of American anthropology: when a culture embraces the benefits of a higher level of development, it can never regress. Why would it? Cultures that make it up the next rung of the ladder and cannot sustain that level in a given environment usually die out, or they move around, but they do not regress. Just saying the word *devolution* makes anthropologists uncomfortable.

In 1962 James Gunnerson hypothesized that the Virgin-branch Puebloans were the Proto-Plateau Shoshoneans and that the Fremont and Sevier peoples (now considered the Fremont) were represented historically by the Ute–Southern Paiute and Shoshone-Comanche, respectively (1962:41). Gunnerson used linguistic and archaeological data to argue that the Virgin-branch region was the ancestral homeland of the Shoshone, Comanche, Northern Paiute, Southern Paiute, and Ute tribes. He (1962) suggested that worsening climatic conditions in the AD 1200s forced the Virgin and Fremont people to abandon farming and return to hunting and gathering.

Soon after Gunnerson's article appeared his ideas were attacked by Albert Schroeder (1963) and a year later by Robert Euler (1964), primarily because

> there was no common denominator between cultural patterns.... [I]f the changes came about by cultural recession, we should expect to find definite links in techniques, pottery, and other items that survived the supposed change, not just an occasional trait similarity [Schroeder 1963:559].

Table 18.1 contains a list of trait differences that Schroeder used to refute Gunnerson's ideas. On the basis of what most archaeologists considered overwhelming evidence for population replacement, Gunnerson's hypothesis was dismissed in favor of the Numic Spread model.

In 1958 linguist Sydney Lamb calculated that "the Numic languages had spread across the Great Basin from a homeland beginning about AD 1000" (Sutton and Rhode 1994:8). Linguistic research following Lamb's publication lent support to his hypothesis and identified the southwestern Great Basin as the Numic homeland (Fowler 1983). Regional archaeologists quickly and often uncritically embraced the hypothesis (Sutton and Rhode 1994:11), easily equating archaeological data to linguistic and ethic units. The migration of a new ethnic group into the region explained the drastic changes that occurred around AD 1200 in those areas of the Great Basin where the economy shifted from a focus on horticulture to hunting and gathering.

TABLE 18.1. Differences between Numic and Puebloan/Fremont groups.

FREMONT/VIRGIN PUEBLOANS	NUMIC GROUPS
Scraped, thinned, decorated, and corrugated pottery	Paddle-and-anvil brownware pottery
Rose Springs and Parowan Basal-notched points	Desert Side-notched points
Sedentary masonry habitations in villages	Ephemeral brush shelters
Farming of corn, beans, and squash	Hunting and gathering of wild plants
Coiled basketry and distinctive Fremont types	Dominantly twined basketry

As part of the Glen Canyon project Robert Euler worked closely with Southern Paiutes to identify their ancestral archaeological sites, and he also examined the ethnohistoric literature. Given the evidence, he (1964, 1966) concluded that the Numic migration model was the best explanation for the changes in the archaeological record. Using the direct historical approach he (1964:381) compared ceramics, milling stones, and projectile points plus individual sites to conclude that the Southern Paiute occupied the region after AD 1150 and their lifeways were not disrupted until the nineteenth century. In 1975 when David Madsen published his *American Antiquity* article on the timing of the Numic migration, it was a done deal; Numic groups moved into the region *after* the Fremont and Virgin Puebloans disappeared between AD 1150 and 1300. The only loose ends that needed to be tied up involved the mechanisms for the abandonment and migration. Discussions on these topics continue, as new linguistics (Hill 2002; Merrill et al. 2009), genetic (Cabana 2002; Kaestle and Smith 2001), ethnographic (C. Fowler 2010), and archaeological data (Perry 2003; Roberts 2002) continue to provide fodder for debate.

About 50 years after Schroeder published his article refuting Gunnerson's hypothesis, some of these new data provide compelling evidence—both archaeological and linguistic—in support of cultural continuity. Here I will examine each of Schroeder's main points.

SUBSISTENCE STRATEGIES

The historical and archaeological evidence demonstrates that horticulture played a greater role in Southern Paiute economies than either Euler or Schroeder suspected (Allison et al. 2008; Fowler and Fowler 1981; Roberts 2002; Stoffle and Dobyns 1983). Catherine Fowler's (2010) research into Isabel Kelly's ethnographic materials for the bands in southern Nevada demonstrates that the Las Vegas, Pahrump, and Moapa bands practiced farming around springs and other water sources. The extent of gardening activities varied from band to band, but the historic evidence of farming, and even the use of irrigation, is overwhelming, particularly in the St. George Basin of southwestern Utah and the Moapa Valley. Did Julian Steward downplay the importance of farming among the Paiute bands that occupied the Virgin Puebloan culture area on purpose because it did not fit his culture ecology model for the Great Basin? If so, could we categorize this as an instance of scientific-sociopolitical consideration, which has affected the theory and what is considered data, unsystematic information, or noise? At the very least it demonstrates that Steward's model is normative and not tested by actual behavior—what is really happening on the ground.

Pottery

Research by Margaret Lyneis (1994, 1998, 2007, 2010) and Laureen Perry (2003) has shed light on the differences between Virgin Puebloan and Southern Paiute pottery technology known as Great Basin Brown Ware. By studying brownware from archaeological sites in the Las Vegas Valley, the Moapa Valley, Ash Meadows, and the St. George Basin, they have learned that this pottery was made with coil-and-scrape methods rather than paddle and anvil as Schroeder claimed.

In fact, Perry (2003) identifies some Great Basin Brown Ware recovered from sites in Utah that is corrugated. Could this be considered an intermediate type? The shapes of the vessels are also not as different as once thought. In southwest Utah vessel shapes include globular jars and bowls, in addition to the jars with conical-shaped bases; some vessels had handles and had been mended. Richard Thompson, who worked throughout the region, also identified corrugated Great Basin Brown Ware (Walling et al. 1986) and believed that the ceramic traditions were similar enough to suggest continuity (Barbara Frank, personal communication 2006).

What about the color, temper, and thickness differences? Lyneis (1998) and Perry (2003) have found that temper used in Great Basin Brown Ware came from the adjacent mountains rather than from the valley bottomlands. In the 1970s archaeologists working west of St. George in the Beaver Dam Mountains identified what they thought might be transitional types between gray- and brownwares. Moffitt et al. (1978:107) had difficulties distinguishing between Southern Paiute Utility ware, Moapa Brown ware, and Shinarump Brown ware (Virgin series) in ceramic assemblages recovered from sites, like this one, that spanned the occupations. They concluded that

> as a result of the project ceramic analysis, including stratigraphic studies of several sites...it is apparent that the entire realm of Virgin–Paiute relationships needs to be reexamined in light of the possible mixing or blending of groups in certain areas rather than migration and total abandonment [Moffitt 1978:107].

The mixing of Virgin Puebloan, Fremont, and Southern Paiute ceramics within a 1-m-thick deposit of cultural fill from O'Malley Shelter (Rhode 1994:126) perplexed archaeologists (Fowler et al. 1973) and led to further research (Pippin 1986; Rhode 1994:126–127). In an effort to solve the puzzle, Rhode obtained thermoluminescence dates on a Great Basin Brown Ware sherd and a Fremont sherd from the mixed component at O'Malley Shelter. While the brownware sherd submitted was too thin to date, the date on the Fremont sherd was surprisingly late—AD 1512 ± 41. A second analysis, involving a Fremont sherd and a Paiute sherd from the same cultural level at Conaway Shelter, produced a date of AD 1066 ± 74 on the former and AD 822 ± 105 on the latter. Rhode (1994:127) concluded that the dates from Conaway Shelter support the contemporaneity of Fremont and brownware ceramics by at least AD 1000 in southeastern Nevada.

There is one additional data set that is worth mentioning in this context. In 2005 HRA, Inc., excavated a small rockshelter in the Moapa Valley that had been occupied by Southern Paiute people in the 1800s (Harper 2005). Harper recovered six sherds from one stratum inside the shelter; most were Great Basin Brown Ware, and a few were Virgin Puebloan. Harper sent two of the brownware sherds and two of the Puebloan grayware sherds for thermoluminescence dating. The two brownware sherds dated to AD 1820 ± 52 and AD 1749 ± 42, and the two Puebloan sherds dated to AD 1793 ± 22 and AD 1250 ± 38. The older piece was a North Creek Gray sherd with strong rim eversion, suggesting a Puebloan II date. The North Creek Gray sherd that dated to AD 1793 was a Black-on-gray bowl fragment. Could gray pottery have continued to be made after architectural sites were abandoned? Perhaps the single pottery vessel that John Wesley Powell collected from the Kaibab Paiute, which was a Virgin grayware jar and is thought to have been a curated pot (Fowler and Fowler 1981), was actually Paiute manufactured.

Projectile Point Styles

Are changes in projectile point types during these periods even relevant? Desert Side-notched points replaced the earlier varieties across the entire Great Basin and Southwest and into the Plains areas (Justice 2002a, 2002b). The point style was used by all late-historic groups including the Apache, Navajo, Shoshone, Paiute, Ute, Tohono O'odham, and even Sobaipuri. Desert Side-notched points are a time marker, not an ethnic marker, and their origin and spread are linked to the point type's technological advantages rather than to an ethnic migration.

Architecture

To argue the next point about architecture, I appeal to Steadman Upham's (1988) article on the issue of visibility and the underclass of archaeological sites and what Linda Cordell and Fred Plog (1979) called the problems of normative archaeology. They argue that when mobility increases, site visibility decreases, so that populations that appear to have vanished, such as the Virgin

Puebloans, may have just become more mobile and more difficult to identify in the archaeological record.

The lack of permanent architecture at Southern Paiute sites is often seen as a major cultural difference between the Paiute and Pueblo periods. Virgin Anasazi architectural features consisted of formal habitation structures, which were generally pithouses or surface structures, and storage features consisting of slab-lined cists and slab-lined rectangular rooms. In the Pueblo II period, and possibly earlier (Schroeder 1955), these storage rooms were linked into rows forming circular or C-shaped alignments (Lyneis 1995).

In contrast, Southern Paiute sites consist of clusters of hearth features, roasting pits, and shallow structural remains consistent with wickiups reported in the ethnohistoric literature (Moffitt et al. 1978:12–14; Roberts and Eskenazi 2005; Talbot and Richens 2002:438). Paiute houses, as described by the Mormon settlers, were fairly impermanent brush structures, although later ethnographers noted that some of the winter lodges were covered with dirt (Kelly and Fowler 1986).

The archaeological record in southwestern Utah suggests that formal architecture was more gradually phased out than has been previously thought. This fact is often obscured, in part, because many sites and features were reused and remodeled, which tends to make such a trend difficult to identify. A close examination of the architectural record in the Quail Creek area north of St. George, Utah, shows that architecture becomes less formal during the Late Pueblo II and Pueblo III periods than it was during the Basketmaker III and Pueblo I periods (Walling et al. 1986).

Schroeder (1955) may have been one of the first to record this pattern, in his report on his archaeological investigations in Zion National Park in southwestern Utah. Schroeder's (1955) figure 22 summarizes the history of Virgin Puebloan architectural change in the park area. The figure suggests that the earliest sites, without corrugated ceramics, consisted of pithouses and slab-lined cists. Later sites had pithouses and storerooms. The storerooms were subsequently linked into arcs or circles around pithouses or kivas. Architectural complexity decreased once corrugated ceramics were added to the assemblage. Schroeder's figure suggests that sites with corrugated ceramics contained fewer storage rooms and were situated in rockshelters.

Site NA11,405, excavated during the Navajo–McCullough project, in the mountainous regions of Washington County, Utah, is an important example of how a discontinuity bias can affect our interpretation of the archaeological record (Moffitt et al. 1978). The site contained four ephemeral habitation structures (labeled wickiups), roasting pits, and a small slab-lined cist. A single radiocarbon date of AD 1755 was obtained from Roasting Pit 4, located more than 10 m from the habitation features. No stratigraphic relationships were observed among the four structures; however, the artifact assemblages suggested to the excavators that two of the structures—Wickiups 1 and 2—were occupied during the Southern Paiute period and that one—Wickiup 3—was occupied during the Virgin Anasazi period. That feature was associated with decorated Virgin Anasazi ceramics and consisted of a "vague depression" (Moffitt et al. 1978:12) that was located in the center of the other three habitation structures. Because the feature had a well-defined floor and contained decorated Virgin Puebloan ceramics, the excavators concluded that it may have been a Puebloan pithouse, brush structure, or activity area. A fourth structure, Wickiup Depression 4, contained a mixed assemblage of Virgin Puebloan and Great Basin Brown Ware pottery. This feature, consisting of a poorly defined floor and a roughly circular unlined hearth located near the center, was interpreted to have been primarily Southern Paiute. Isn't it just as possible that this feature, with its mixed Southern Paiute and Virgin Puebloan assemblage, is transitional between Virgin Puebloan and Southern Paiute occupations?

After AD 1050 there is an explosion of Kayenta, Mesa Verde, and other trade wares at Virgin Puebloan II sites, suggesting links to adjacent regions. In southern Nevada, buff wares from the Colorado River region make an appearance about this same time, and over the next 200 years Virgin Puebloan settlements move from the valley bottoms to hilltops and rockshelters. In the St. George Basin and Moapa Valley slab-lined architecture, which is the hallmark of Virgin Puebloan architecture, was never replaced by large masonry pueblos like those found to the east.

In southwestern Utah (Walling et al. 1986) and the Moapa Valley area of Nevada (Hayden 1930; Shutler 1961) late sites do seem to have been relocated to more defensive settings. In the Las Vegas area settlements become less permanent, and they move to small rockshelters in the foothills surrounding the valley (Ahlstrom and Roberts 2001). Slab-lined heaths continued to be used at sites containing Great Basin Brown Ware, but formal pit structures are replaced by more ephemeral habitations.

Linguistics

Uto-Aztecan is one of the most widespread Native American language families, extending from Central America to the Great Basin (Miller 1983). Lamb's idea that the Numic peoples entered the Great Basin from the south about 1,000 years ago no longer finds support among linguists (Grayson 1994; Hill 2001). However, Lamb's and later C. Fowler's (1983) placement of the homeland range in southern California, New Mexico, and northern Mexico continues to find favor, although Merrill et al. (2009) have recently proposed a central Nevada origin.

Recent linguistic research by Bellwood (1997) and Hill (2001) questions the mechanism and timing of the spread of the Uto-Aztecan languages. Lexical evidence supports a model in which the original Proto-Uto-Aztecan (PUA) speakers were farmers who carried their technology northward with them into the Southwest between 4500 and 3000 BP. Bellwood proposed that the PUA community was located in Mesoamerica, where maize was first domesticated. The large-scale geographical spread and "rake-like" composition of the language branches suggest an association with a major technological innovation, such as cultivation (Hill 2001). Supporting this argument is the fact that few foragers adopt cultivation and maintain their ethnic identity, and primary cultivators are unlikely to replace one another (Hill 2001).

Hill's (2001) study of linguistic evidence suggests that biogeographic data do not rule out a Mesoamerican homeland, and the "rake-like" structure of Uto-Aztecan suggests rapid expansion. The vocabulary associated with maize cultivation and water management reconstructs to the PUA period, and the archaeological data support the spread of maize cultivators from Mesoamerica into the Southwest between 4000 and 3000 BP. This was followed by the introduction of squash around 2900 BP and beans about 2500 BP. In support of this point, Hill argues that the Uto-Aztecan words for cultivation are not loanwords; rather, recent studies "make a case for autochthonous Uto-Aztecan origin of much of the maize-cultivation vocabulary" (Hill 2001: 924). Hill proposes that northward expansion occurred through demic diffusion and "leapfrogging," in which the cultivators moved northward from river valley to river valley in search of arable land. Last, Hill suggests that ancestral Numic groups that spread north into Utah and the southern Great Basin were farmers who shifted to foraging with climatic change and as their range extended beyond the arable regions.

Genetics

Genetic data from skeletal remains collected from prehistoric sites in the Great Basin and Southwest have been reported by Shearin et al. (1989), O'Rourke et al. (1996), Parr et al. (1996), Carlyle et al. (2000), Kaestle and Smith (2001), and Cabana (2002). The pattern that is emerging from mitochondrial DNA shows that Puebloan groups have a different haplogroup frequency distribution than Athapaskan or Great Basin groups. Puebloan groups have a pattern of high frequencies of B, moderate to low C, and an absence of A and D. Athapaskans have high frequencies of haplogroup A and low frequencies of the other groups. A study on ancient remains from the Great Basin suggests that Archaic populations from Nevada were similar to ancient Californians, the Fremont are grouped with the Southwest, and the modern Great Basin group is intermediate (Kaestle and Smith 2001). No remains from Virgin Puebloan sites have been compared with modern Southern Paiute or other populations.

Discussion

Beginning around AD 1250 the Southwest and Great Basin regions underwent dramatic changes and turmoil that culminated in exploration and colonization by Europeans in the 1500s. In the Four Corners region we have evidence of migrations, population aggregation (Gregory and Wilcox 2009), and intensive violence (LeBlanc 1999; Turner and Turner 1999) that extended as far west as the Fremont culture area (Novak and Kollmann 2000). A drought placed additional strain on the region just as Athapaskan groups entered from the north and the Colorado River tribes moved up the Colorado River as far north as the Utah border (McGuire et al. 2010; Roberts et al. 2011). In the Four Corners area populations moved east and south, aggregating into large pueblos (Cordell and Gumerman 1989; Gregory and Wilcox 2009; Lekson 2008).

In the Moapa Valley Virgin Puebloans may have attempted aggregation at sheltered locations, such as Mesa House, and it is possible that the deteriorating environmental conditions combined with the collapse of the Puebloan system made defense against populations encroaching from the north and south unfeasible. Perhaps some Virgin Puebloans moved east to join larger Puebloan groups (Roberts et al. 2011), while others scattered to the upland regions, where they merged with Great Basin groups. Mobility increased, and site visibility decreased. The region's occupants continued to farm when conditions allowed; perhaps they even reused Virgin Puebloan sites, as Margaret Lyneis (2010) thinks occurred at the Yamashita sites in the Moapa Valley. Over time local populations formed new alliances; they adapted and became the Southern Paiute people whom Dominguez and Escalante observed farming along the Virgin River in 1776.

A few years ago Richard Ahlstrom and I (2001) developed hypotheses to explain why small rockshelters were the focus of occupation in the Las Vegas Valley between AD 1300 and 1600. One day I was discussing my ideas with the Paiute Elders, when one of them looked at me, smiled, and said, "Heidi, when our enemies came we hid in the mountains." Her comment slashed through all my arguments with the precision of Occam's razor. Is that what happened to the Virgin Puebloans? They decreased the visibility of their habitations and relocated to rockshelters to evade their enemies. It made sense, the kind of common sense and clear appraisal that an Elder would see.

This elegant, culturally based reconstruction of Southern Paiute and Virgin Puebloan has led me in new directions and encouraged me to examine the archaeological record from a new perspective. I have used the Elder's suggestion to reevaluate the data from southern Nevada's post–Puebloan period sites and found support for these ideas in the regions' excavated archaeological sites.

The main point I make here is that if you listen to the Elders, you may hear knowledge that could send you in new directions, provide more intellectually satisfying paradigms and theories, and yield hypotheses for future research. The past that we Great Basin archaeologists study is not only ours; it belongs to the descendants of people who lived here, and they have a deeper understanding of it than we ever may. So when the Elders speak, sit quietly, show respect, and just listen.

References Cited

Ahlstrom, Richard V. N., and Heidi Roberts (editors)

2001 *Archaeology at the Apex: Excavations in the Apex Project Area, Southern Nevada*. HRA Papers in Archaeology No. 2. Distributed by the University of Utah Press, Salt Lake City.

Allison, James R., Cathryn M. Meegan, and Shawn Sabrina Murray

2008 Archaeology and Archaeobotany of Southern Paiute Horticulture in the Saint George Basin, Southwestern Utah. *Kiva* 73(4):417–448.

Bellwood, P.

1997 Prehistoric Cultural Explanations for Widespread Linguistic Families. In *Archaeology and Linguistics: Aboriginal Australia in Global Perspective*, edited by P. McConvell and N. Evans, pp. 123–134. Oxford University Press, Melbourne.

Cabana, Graciela Susana

2002 A Demographic Simulation Model to Assess Prehistoric Migrations. Unpublished Ph.D. dissertation, University of Michigan, Ann Arbor.

Carlyle, Shawn W., Ryan L. Parr, M. Geoffrey Hayes, and Dennis O'Rourke

2000 Context of Maternal Lineages in the Great Southwest. *American Journal of Physical Anthropology* 113:85–101.

Cordell, Linda S., and George J. Gumerman

1989 *Dynamic of Southwest Prehistory*. Smithsonian Institution Press, Washington, D.C.

Cordell, Linda S., and Fred Plog

1979 Escaping the Confines of Normative Thought: A Reevaluation of Puebloan Prehistory. *American Antiquity* 44(3):405–429.

Euler, Robert C.

1964 Southern Paiute Archaeology. *American Antiquity* 29(3):379–381.

1966 *Southern Paiute Ethnohistory*. University of Utah Anthropology Papers No. 78. Salt Lake City.

Fowler, Catherine S.

1983 Lexical Clues to Uto-Aztecan Prehistory. *International Journal of American Linguistics* 49:224–257.

2010 *Facing Snow Mountain: Las Vegas–Pahrump–Desert Southern Paiute Culture in the Late 19th Century*. HRA, Inc. Archaeological Report No. 07-28. HRA, Inc., Conservation Archaeology, Las Vegas.

Fowler, Catherine S., and Don D. Fowler

1981 The Southern Paiute: AD 1400–1776. In *The Protohistoric Period in the North American Southwest, AD 1450–1700*, edited by David R. Wilcox and W. Bruce Masse, pp. 129–162. Anthropological Research Papers No. 24. Arizona State University, Tempe.

Fowler, Don D.

1987 Uses of the Past: Archaeology in the Service of the State. *American Antiquity* 52(2):229–248.

2010 *A Laboratory for Anthropology*. University of Utah Press, Salt Lake City.

Fowler, Don D., David B. Madsen, and Eugene M. Hattori

1973 *Prehistory of Southeastern Nevada*. Publication in the Social Sciences No. 6. Desert Research Institute, Reno.

Grayson, Donald K.

1994 Chronology, Glottochronology, and Numic Expansion. In *Across the West: Human Population Movement and the Expansion of the Numa*, edited by David B. Madsen and David Rhode, pp. 20–23. University of Utah Press, Salt Lake City.

Gregory, David A., and David R. Wilcox (editors)

2007 *Zuni Origins: Toward a Synthesis of Southwestern Archaeology*. University of Arizona Press, Tucson.

Gunnerson, James H.

1962 Plateau Shoshonean Prehistory: A Suggested Reconstruction. *American Antiquity* 28(1):41–45.

Harper, Christopher

2005 *A Room with a View: Data Recovery of an Early Historical Rockshelter Site Located in the Upper Moapa Valley, Clark County, Nevada*. BLM Report, 5-2510; HRA Papers in Archaeology No. 5. HRA, Inc., Conservation Archaeology, Las Vegas.

Hayden, Irwin

1930 Mesa House. In *Archaeological Explorations in Southern Nevada*, pp. 26–92. Paper No. 4. Southwest Museum, Los Angeles.

Hill, Jane H.

2001 Proto-Uto-Aztecan: A Community of Cultivators in Central Mexico? *American Anthropologist* 103(4):913–934.

2002 Toward a Linguistic Prehistory of the Southwest: "Azteco-Tanoan" and the Arrival of Maize Cultivation. *Journal of Anthropological Research* 58:457–475.

Justice, Noel

2002a *Stone Age Spear and Arrow Points of California and the Great Basin*. Indiana University Press, Bloomington.

2002b *Stone Age Spear and Arrow Points of the Southwestern United States*. Indiana University Press, Bloomington.

Kaestle, Frederika A., and David Glenn Smith

2001 Ancient Mitochondrial DNA Evidence for Prehistoric Population Movement: The Numic Expansion. *American Journal of Physical Anthropology* 115:1–12.

Kelly, Isabel T., and Catherine S. Fowler

1986 Southern Paiute. In *Handbook of North American Indians, Vol. 11: Great Basin*, edited by Warren L. D'Azevedo, pp. 368–397. Smithsonian Institution, Washington, D.C.

LeBlanc, Steven A.

1999 *Prehistoric Warfare in the American Southwest*. University of Utah Press, Salt Lake City.

Lekson, Stephen H.

2008 *A History of the Ancient Southwest*. School for Advanced Research Press, Santa Fe, New Mexico.

Lyneis, Margaret M.

1994 East and onto the Plateaus? An Archaeological Examination of the Numic Expansion in Southern Nevada, Northern Arizona, and Southern Utah. In *Across the West: Human Population Movement and the Expansion of the Numa*, edited by David B. Madsen and David Rhode, pp. 141–149. University of Utah Press, Salt Lake City.

1995 The Virgin Anasazi, Far Western Puebloans. *Journal of World Prehistory* 9(2):199–241.

1998 A Transported Brown Ware Assemblage from Southern Nevada. Paper presented at the 26th Great Basin Anthropological Conference, on file with the author at the University of Nevada, Las Vegas.

2007 Ceramic Artifacts. In *Shared Place: An Archaeological Survey of the Ash Meadows National Wildlife Refuge, Nye County, Nevada*, by Jerry Lyon, Heidi Roberts, Richard V. N. Ahlstrom, Christopher Harper, Suzanne Eskenazi, Robert Davide, Catherine Fowler, and Elizabeth von Till Warren, pp. 293–306.

HRA, Inc. Archaeological Report No. 07-24. HRA, Inc., Conservation Archaeology, Las Vegas.

2010 The Role of Materials Availability in Pottery Production at Corn Creek and Ash Meadows in Southern Nevada. Paper presented at the Nevada Archaeological Association Meeting, Las Vegas.

Madsen, David B.

1975 Dating Paiute-Shoshoni Expansion in the Great Basin. *American Antiquity* 40:82–86.

Madsen, David B., and David Rhode (editors)

1994 *Across the West: Human Population Movement and the Expansion of the Numa.* University of Utah Press, Salt Lake City.

McGuire, Kelly, William Hildebrandt, Amy Gilreath, Jerome King, and John Berg

2010 *Final Research Results for the Gold Butte Study Area, Clark County, Nevada.* BLM Report, 5-2617. On file, Las Vegas Field Office, Las Vegas.

Merrill, William L., Robert J. Hard, Jonathan B. Mabry, Gayle J. Fritz, Karen R. Adams, John R. Ronery, and A. C. MacWilliams

2009 The Diffusion of Maize to the Southwestern United States and Its Impact. Electronic document, http://www.pnas.org/content/106/50/21019.full.pdf.

Miller, Wick R.

1983 Uto-Aztecan Languages. In *Handbook of North American Indians*, Vol. 10, edited by Alfonso Ortiz, pp. 113–124. Smithsonian Institution, Washington, D.C.

Moffitt, Kathleen, Sandra Rayl, and Michael Metcalf

1978 *Archaeological Investigations Along the Navajo McCullough Transmission Line Southern Utah and Northern Arizona.* Museum of Northern Arizona Research Report No. 10. Flagstaff.

Novak, Shannon A., and Dana D. Kollmann

2000 Perimortem Processing of Human Remains Among the Great Basin Fremont. *International Journal of Osteoarchaeology* 10: 65–75.

O'Rourke, Dennis H., Shawn W. Carlyle, and Ryan L. Parr

1996 Ancient DNA: Methods, Progress, and Perspectives. *American Journal of Human Biology* 9:557–571.

Parr, Ryan L., Shawn W. Carlyle, and Dennis H. O'Rourke

1996 Ancient DNA Analysis of Fremont Amerindians of the Great Salt Lake Wetlands. *American Journal of Physical Anthropology* 99:507–518.

Perry, Laureen M.

2003 Ceramic Analysis. In *The Coral Canyon Project: Archaeological Investigations in the St. George Basin, Southwestern Utah*, edited by Heidi Roberts and Richard V. N. Ahlstrom, pp. 201–212. HRA Papers in Archaeology No. 3. HRA, Inc., Conservation Archaeology, Las Vegas.

Pippin, Lonnie C. (editor)

1986 *An Overview of Cultural Resources on Pahute and Rainier Mesas on the Nevada Test Site, Nye County, Nevada.* Desert Research Institute, Quaternary Sciences Center, Technical Report No. 45. Reno.

Rhode, David

1994 Direct Dating of Brown Ware Ceramics Using Thermoluminescence and Its Relation to the Numic Spread. In *Across the West: Human Population Movement and the Expansion of the Numa*, edited by David B. Madsen and David Rhode, pp. 124–132. University of Utah Press, Salt Lake City.

Roberts, Heidi

2002 Settlement and Subsistence Strategies of the Southern Paiute in the St. George Basin, Southern Utah. *Spanish Traces* 3:19–25.

Roberts, Heidi, Richard V. N. Ahlstrom, and Samantha Rubinson

2011 *A Prehistoric Context for Southern Nevada.* HRA, Inc. Archaeological Report No. 011-05. HRA, Inc., Conservation Archaeology, Las Vegas.

Roberts, Heidi, and Suzanne Eskenazi (editors)

2005 *The Coral Canyon II Project: Archaeological Investigations in the St. George Basin, Southwestern Utah.* HRA, Inc. Archaeological Report No. 02-09. HRA, Inc., Conservation Archaeology, Las Vegas.

Schroeder, Albert H.

1955 *Archaeology of Zion Park.* University of Utah Anthropological Papers No. 22. University of Utah Press, Salt Lake City.

1963 Comment on Gunnerson's "Plateau Shoshonean Prehistory." *American Antiquity* 28(4):559–560.

Shearin, N. L., E. J. King, and Dennis H. O'Rourke

1989 DNA Preservation in Pre-Columbian Remains from the American Southwest. *Human Evolution* 4:263–270.

Shutler, Richard, Jr.

1961 *Lost City: Pueblo Grande de Nevada.* Anthropological Papers No. 5. Nevada State Museum, Carson City.

Stoffle, Richard W., and Henry F. Dobyns

1983 *Nuvagantu: Nevada Indians Comment on the Intermountain Power Project.* Bureau of Land Management Cultural Resource Series No. 7. Reno.

Sutton, Mark Q., and David Rhode

1994 Background to the Numic Problem. In *Across the West: Human Population Movement and the Expansion of the Numa*, edited by David B. Madsen and David Rhode, pp. 6–15. University of Utah Press, Salt Lake City.

Talbot, Richard K., and Lane D. Richens

2002 *Shifting Sands: The Archaeology of Sand Hollow.* Office of Public Archaeology, Brigham Young University, Provo.

Turner, Christy G., II, and Jacqueline A. Turner

1999 *Man Corn: Cannibalism and Violence in the Prehistoric American Southwest.* University of Utah Press, Salt Lake City.

Upham, Steadman

1988 Archaeological Visibility and the Underclass of Southwestern Prehistory. *American Antiquity* 53:245–261.

Walling, Barbara A., Richard A. Thompson, Gardiner F. Dalley, and Dennis G. Weder

1986 *Excavations at Quail Creek.* Cultural Resources Series No. 20. U.S. Department of the Interior, Bureau of Land Management, Utah State Office, Salt Lake City.

19

Journeys of Rediscovery

Archaeology, Territory, and Legitimacy in Contemporary Native Nevada

María Nieves Zedeño

Understanding the relationship between past peoples and present power is one of Don Fowler's enduring legacies. Throughout his career as a field archaeologist and historian of anthropology he furthered the view that archaeology is a powerful resource, a symbol of America's intellect, and a political weapon. Don Fowler (1987) has taken every opportunity to remind his colleagues that we walk a fine ethical line, particularly when our practice may be co-opted and used to disenfranchise the people whose ancestral records we handle. In this chapter I integrate three of Don and Catherine "Kay" Fowler's areas of interest—Nevada archaeology, anthropology's history, and ethnography—to illustrate how historic preservation law has helped Nevada's Native American communities to strengthen or restore their territorial identities and to rewrite key aspects of their traditional history in their own terms. Concomitantly, these communities have also influenced substantive anthropological views of the past.

Specifically, I am concerned with presenting two distinct but interrelated end results of long-term, legally mandated consultation and research involving Native Americans and archaeology. First is the rediscovery of ancestral territorial connections by contemporary tribal members who, through treaty and national security land withdrawal, lost rights of access and use over a vast portion of central and southern Nevada; nonetheless, they kept in their individual and social memories a clear understanding of the lay of the land and the ontology and practices that modified it. Second is the intellectual and practical impact that participation in this process has had on the anthropological scholarship of those who were parties to it, particularly on the selection of research themes, formulation of frameworks, and interpretation of results.

I address research that took place over a decade (1995–2005) of my professional involvement in applied research with Shoshone and Paiute tribes whose ancestral sites in Nevada are currently managed by the U.S. Department of Energy (DOE-NV), the U.S. Air Force, the National Park Service, and U.S. Fish and Wildlife (Figure 19.1). It is through this long-term collaboration that I was able to expand my rudimentary, "urbanite" understanding of human–land interaction and thus learn how to better convey Native American views and concerns over heritage resources to land managers, archaeologists, and the public. Many scholars, federal officials, and tribal representatives were involved in the success of this long-term research and consultation program (Beck et al. 2000; Stoffle et al. 2001), but I can only speak from the perspective of the impact it had on my own intellectual growth and research direction—namely, the integration of Native American ontology and practical knowledge into research design that focuses on human landscapes, territories, and complex objects among North American hunter-gatherers, past and present.

After a brief introduction to the history and environment surrounding the development of the DOE-NV's research and consultation program and its ramifications, I examine three scales at which Numic worldviews held by participant Native Americans impacted the interpretation of archaeological remains. I also discuss the theoretical and methodological implications of these interactions for contemporary archaeology, especially on research design and the formulation of testable hypotheses.

Applied Anthropology and Descendant Communities

In a recent commentary about Zuni origins, Don Fowler (2008: 431) points out that ethnicity, ethnogenesis, and heritage are processes that aim at taking control of the past by present groups. His comments explicitly focus on contemporary political and legal conflicts and realities that archaeologists and descendant communities face when attempting to reconcile the past and the present from two vastly different worldviews. Western science, which has dominated explanations of the origin and development of ancient cultures and societies since archaeology became a formal discipline in North America (Fowler 2000; Thomas 2000), has slowly made room for alternative perspectives that take into consideration Native or indigenous histories and which attempt

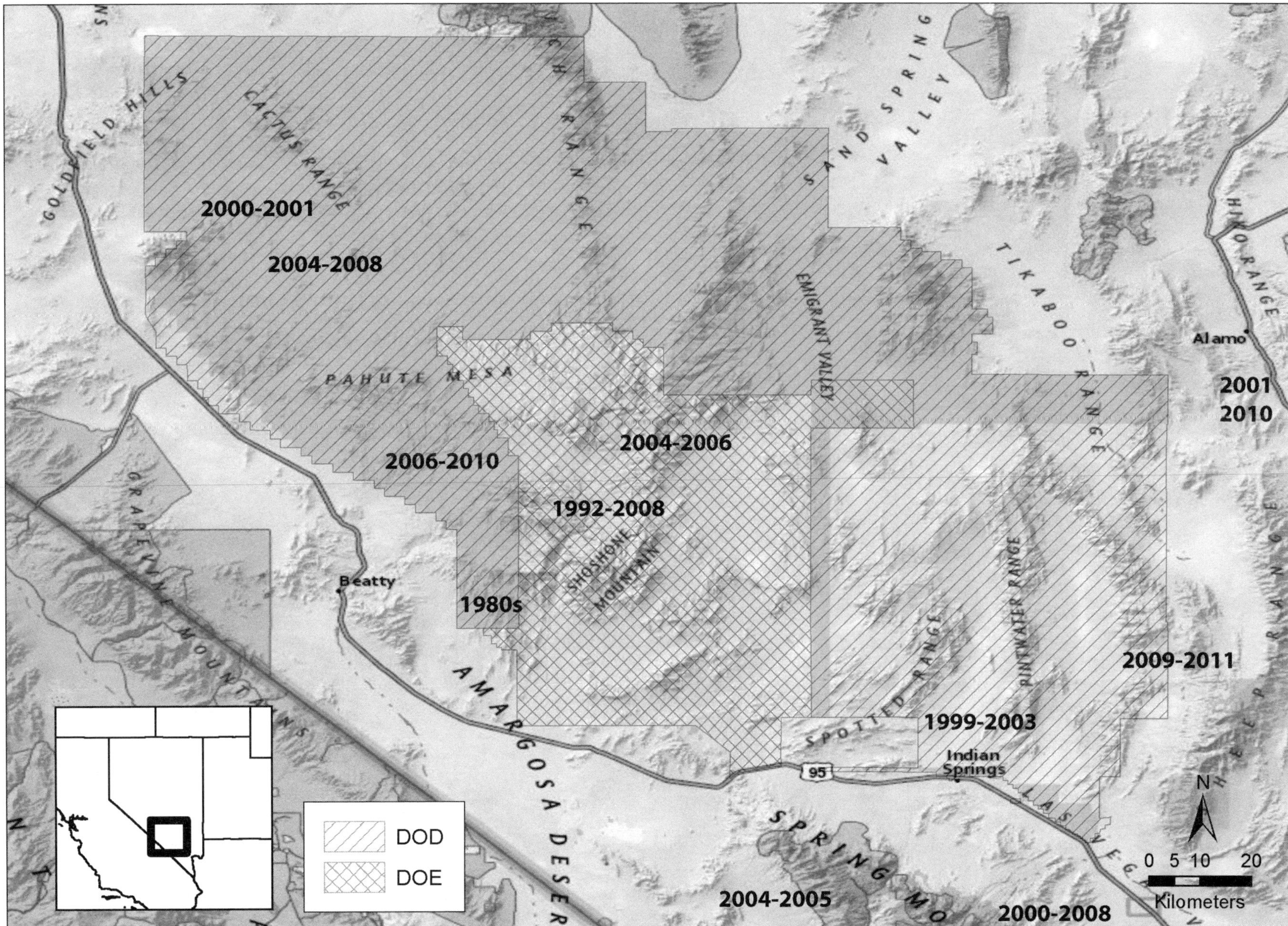

FIGURE 19.1. Federal lands covered by the long-term research and consultation program (cartography by Shane Miller, University of Arizona).

to reconcile both worldviews in archaeological interpretation (e.g., Ferguson and Colwell-Chanthaphonh 2006; Kluth 2000; Spector 1993). This shift is largely the result of lessons learned through the implementation of cultural resource preservation legislation (Adler and Bruning 2008; Colwell-Chanthaphonh 2010:4; Roberts, this volume; Zedeño 2000:102).

Given the profusion of debates in the discipline about the validity of Native American traditional history in archaeological research (e.g., Clark 2003; Mason 2000; McGhee 2008; Milo 2002; Silliman 2010; Watkins 2000), I will not add to them here. Rather, I will focus on exploring the impacts of collaborative research with Nevada's descendant communities—Paiutes and Western Shoshones specifically—on both heritage and theory building. My arguments center on the archaeology and ethnography of human–land interaction, with particular emphasis on territorial identity as well as multiscalar relationships among objects, places, and people.

The DOE-NV Research and Consultation Program

Rights to land are foremost in the minds and hearts of Native Americans nationwide, directing contemporary indigenous scholasticism to pursue practical territorial goals (e.g., Crum 1994; Yellowhorn 2002). However, for displaced communities, the geographical and substantive distance between ancestral territories and modern reservations has often resulted in the loss of important knowledge about land and identity. Culturally significant resources in and near reservations are known and experienced in the course of a person's life, whereas off-reservation places and events may only be acknowledged historically but never seen or personally experienced. Distant or inaccessible places and resources are often the subject of stories and songs, but they lie outside the realm of everyday practice. Consequently, tribes generally welcome opportunities to explore and reconnect with withdrawn and ceded land and recapture its cultural vitality.

In Nevada, tribal opportunities to reconnect with heritage resources and territory materialized in the 1980s with involvement in ethnographic site assessments for the nuclear waste repository at Yucca Mountain (Stoffle et al. 1990). Thereafter, the U.S. Department of Energy funded a 15-year government-to-government consultation program aimed at the systematic inventory of tribal resources in the Nevada Test Site and neighboring facilities in central Nevada (Stoffle et al. 2001). In 1999, the program expanded into Nellis Air Force Base and Bombing Range (Stoffle et al. 2000c; Stoffle et al. 2002; Toupal et al. 2001; Zedeño et al. 2006), and it continues today in land managed by U.S. Fish and Wildlife, the Bureau of Land Management, and the U.S. Forest Service (see Figure 19.1; Stoffle et al. 2002; Stoffle et al. 2004a; SWCA Environmental Consultants and the Bureau of Applied Research in Anthropology 2011).

The land encompassed by energy and defense facilities was withdrawn from public use during World War II; it included the southern half of Western Shoshone territory and the northernmost portion of Southern Paiute territory. Although at least two generations have passed since members of these ethnic groups used or lived on this land, strong federal support for multiyear consultation programs in Nevada has contributed greatly to restoring a sense of territorial identity in a highly contested area. Likewise, social and kinship networks among Southern Paiute, Western Shoshone, and the more distant Owens Valley Paiute that, as noted by Steward (1933, 1970 [1938]), were a driving force in the movement of people across the Basin–Plateau, were rebuilt and strengthened through opportunities for interaction afforded by this program. The multiple and sometimes unexpected impacts of long-term consultation have been felt by federal officials, tribes, and anthropologists; the chronology of these impacts reflects both strengthening political and social ties and theoretical and methodological growth.

Multiyear interaction among representatives of 16 Western Shoshone, Southern Paiute, and Owens Valley Paiute tribes and organizations working toward a common goal while becoming reacquainted with one another resulted in the rise of a self-defined consolidated decision-making group (Beck et al. 2000; Halmo 1994). First, this group became recognized by tribal governments and federal agencies as a legitimate government-to-government consultation entity that would work on multiple projects, from repatriation to mitigation of adverse effects over cultural resources and from systematic ethnographic resource inventories to archaeological site assessments. Second, because the group prioritized consensus over ethnic diversity and tribal political differences, consultation over time gave rise to a new process, wherein both tribes and anthropologists integrated everyone's knowledge and experience into a single pool of observations, interpretations, and explanations of the past. And third, working as a corporate group provided tribes a sense of empowerment while allowing them to formulate coherent arguments about land use and history that reveal the relevance of Numic ontology in the dynamics of ancestral land use.

Somebody in the future will have to pass judgment on the positive and negative aspects of this contemporary phenomenon; from the experience of program officers and Native American participants (American Indian Writers Subgroup 2001; Furlow 2001), it is clear that the Consolidated Group of Tribes and Organizations has fulfilled important political and cultural roles. From the perspective of scholars and students who were involved in a multifaceted endeavor entailing the identification of natural landmarks, archaeological sites, resource locales, and trail networks, interaction with tribal members led to the reevaluation of conventional views of Shoshone and Paiute culture and society. Subsequently, they became engaged in developing a conceptual framework and explicit methodology for undertaking field-based studies of place, cultural landscape, and territory formation. This framework has contributed substantively to the understanding of indigenous relationships with the landscape not only in the Basin–Plateau but also in other regions of North

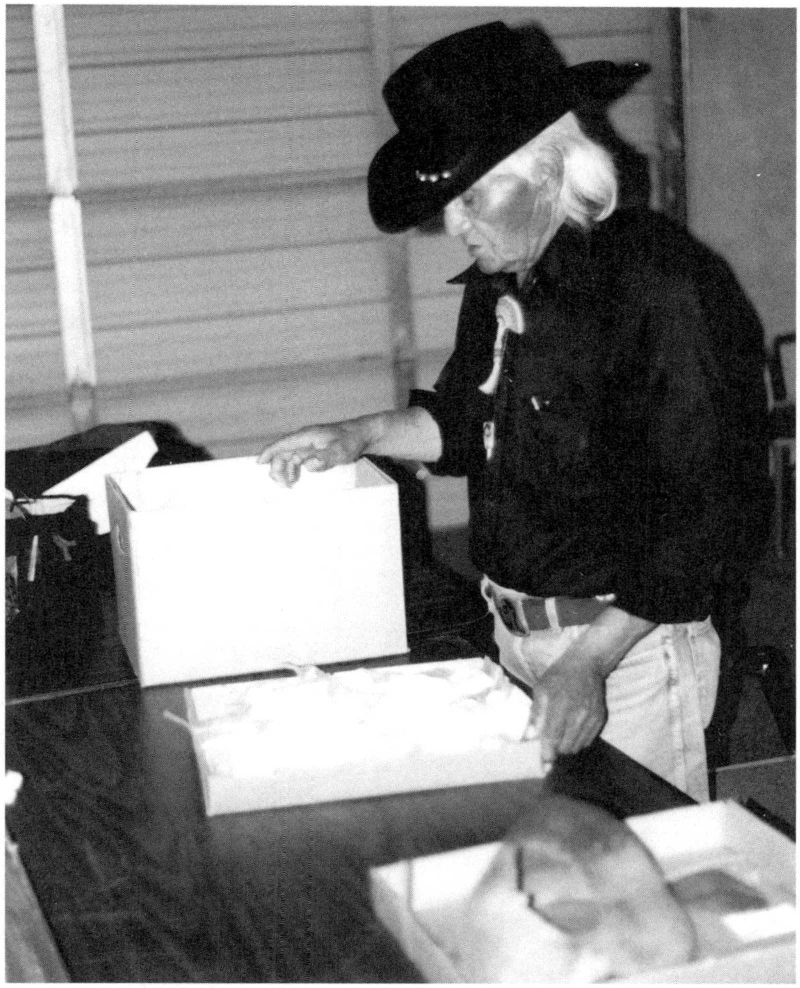

FIGURE 19.2. Southern Paiute elder examining artifacts during Native American Graves Protection and Repatriation Act consultation, 1994 (photo by Richard Stoffle, Bureau of Applied Research in Anthropology Archives, University of Arizona).

America (Carroll 2007; Carroll et al. 2004; Murray et al. 2011; Ruuska 2009; Stoffle and Arnold 2003; Stoffle and Zedeño 2001a, 2001b; Stoffle et al. 1997; Stoffle et al. 2000a; Toupal et al. 2001; Van Vlack 2012; Zedeño 1997, 2000, 2008a, 2008b, 2013a, 2013b; Zedeño and Bowser 2009; Zedeño and Stoffle 2003; Zedeño et al. 2009).

Resources, Objects, and Places

While archaeological remains have been the overwhelming focus of cultural resource legislation across the country, since its inception the DOE-NV research and consultation program placed equal effort on the evaluation of sacred sites and ethnographic resources, particularly plants. This effort was guided by Native Americans for whom the vegetation growing around archaeological sites held tremendous value and often attracted more attention than most other resources (not surprisingly, considering that the Numa are consummate plant foragers [Bye 1972; Fowler 1992; Thomas 2013]). The development of a detailed field methodology for recovering ethnobotanical data and Numic plant names was strongly encouraged by tribes involved with Yucca Mountain (Stoffle et al. 1990, 1999). At Paiute and Rainier mesas, applied studies in archaeology, ethnobotany, and ethnobiology were conducted in the mid-1990s. A rock art assessment in Fortymile Canyon and other areas of the Nevada Test Site was completed in 1999, as were other site-specific assessments in central and southern Nevada (Stoffle et al. 2001; Stoffle et al. 2004a; Stoffle et al. 2004b).

Concomitantly with resource inventories and site assessments it became necessary to undergo Native American Graves Protection and Repatriation Act (NAGPRA) consultation on the large (450,000+ artifacts) archaeological collection recovered from DOE-NV facilities and curated by Desert Research Institute (Figure 19.2). Without a doubt, this was a painful and often contentious affair that required multiple visits to the artifact repository and to sites where the artifacts were collected. Fortunately, it culminated in a reburial ceremony at Gold Meadows that strengthened relations between the Consolidated Group of Tribes and Organizations and the DOE-NV (Furlow 2001). As far as anthropological lessons are concerned, what eventually became the focus of theory building was not the process of individual resource assessments or NAGPRA consultation per se but, rather, what transpired from the connections Native Americans made among places, objects, and resources.

Relational Ontology and Cultural Significance

For scholars who are trained to classify things by their observable properties and then explain sources of variation in individual classes, the idea that objects may be related to one another by reasons other than space, time, or form—that they are capable of social interaction—is preposterous (Foucault 1994:xv; Gell 1998). Yet agency and communication in material culture are commonplace in non-Western societies—so much so that they have generated a flurry of important and provocative literature in archaeology (e.g., Meskell 2004; Miller 2005; Mills and Walker 2008; Schiffer and Miller 1999; Watts 2013). In North America, Numic ontology has been the focus of ethnology since John Wesley Powell entered the Basin–Plateau in the late nineteenth century; the ontological concept of "power" (*puha*), which guides Numic ordering of the world, has been, in fact, described in detail by Kay Fowler and others (Fowler 1992; Fowler and Liljeblad 1986; Liljeblad 1986; Miller 1983). The notion that power animates the world and connects all things and beings permeates Numic thought and practice today just as it did in the distant and recent past. For example, in her book entitled *In the Shadow of Fox Peak*, Catherine Fowler writes,

> One of the most basic beliefs that guided the interactions of people with the land and its resources was the concept that the Earth was a living being, just as were the Sun and Moon, the Stars, and natural forces such as Water, Wind, and Fire. The life force within all of these, as well as particular geographic features and classes of spirit beings, was power (puha).... [A]lthough power potentially resides anywhere, its association with mountains, caves, springs or other water sources, and the results of past activities by Immortals or humans, was particularly apparent [1992:170–172].

This paragraph precisely describes the interactive experience that my colleagues and I had when working with Numic people in the field. Throughout the years spent assessing countless sites and resources, it became increasingly clear not only that the concept *puha* influenced tribal representatives' ascriptions of cultural significance to seemingly ordinary things but that it also organized their logic behind inferences of place use and significance as well as explanations of past and present relationships between them.

Indicator Objects

Place logic loomed large during the NAGPRA consultation for the Nevada Test Site when, faced with thousands of artifacts, tribal elders demanded to be taken to each of the sites represented in the collection so that they could better identify sacred objects, items of cultural patrimony, and funerary offerings. Because in Numic culture ordinary objects are routinely used in individual rituals, group ceremonies, and memorial rites, a subgroup of representatives deemed it necessary to combine information on site location and recovery context with artifact type and condition (e.g., painted, broken, or burnt) to create a list of "indicator items," or objects that have intrinsic value across Numic tribes (e.g., red paint, crystals, pipes, beads, and pendants). From this list, tribal representatives used their own logic to derive a series of relational criteria for identifying sacred objects and assemblages by virtue of intrinsic properties, association between indicator items and ordinary artifacts, and the particularities of archaeological discard deposits. Also considered was the proximity of artifacts to powerful natural features such as caves and rockshelters, rock crevices, canyon constrictions, natural holes in rock faces, and springs (Stoffle et al. 2000b).

In view of this mounting knowledge about place in indigenous culture, which had suddenly jumped to the forefront of anthropology after the publication in 1996 of Keith Basso's celebrated book, *Wisdom Sits in Places*, DOE-NV's research and consultation program quickly shifted in focus from single resource classes to interactions among objects, places, and landscapes (Stoffle et al. 1997; Zedeño et al. 1997). For the anthropologists involved this was a career-changing decision, as it completely altered the conceptual frameworks we had hitherto followed in archaeological and applied research, and it carried on into other regions and other Native American and immigrant groups in North America (e.g., Murray 2011; Ruuska 2009; Toupal et al. 2001; Zedeño 2008a, 2008b) and the Caribbean Islands (Stoffle and Minnis 2007). Just recently, for example, I reformulated the original Numic concept of "indicator item" (index object) and integrated it with principles of Algonquian and Siouan ontology to make it applicable to a broad range of modified and unmodified objects found in archaeological and ethnographic collections across much of the United States. This update included the outline of a relational taxonomy that captures indigenous ontological principles of classification better than do conventional artifact systematics (Zedeño 2009, 2013a).

Rock Art as Place

An important theoretical and methodological contribution of this program to Basin–Plateau anthropology is the evaluation of rock art that was developed for the Nevada Test Site. Rock art is at the core of Numic cultural landscapes. Everyone familiar with the Basin–Plateau knows that rock art has historically been an essential element in regional archaeology; yet until recently its study was generally limited to relative chronology, formal variation, and ethnic association. In contrast, the contribution of our long-term program, which complements well David Whitley's (2000) perspectives on the topic, was to situate rock art within the sacred geography of the Numic tribes and incorporate contextual and relational properties in the interpretation of design (Zedeño et al. 1999; Zedeño et al. 2001). Rock art research led

FIGURE 19.3. Western Shoshone elder interpreting a petroglyph panel, Pahranagat Valley, Nevada (photo by Richard Stoffle, Bureau of Applied Research in Anthropology Archives, University of Arizona).

to the reconceptualization of connections between consecrated places and ritual performance among the Numa and Yuma (Carroll 2007; Carroll et al. 2004; Van Vlack 2012).

This was a heritage study in Lowenthal's (1996) and Fowler's (2008) sense—founded upon the contemporary Numic premise that rock art is a permanent feature that both modifies and becomes integrated with the natural environment. Once placed on the landscape, it will be used and referred to by people regardless of its age, literal meaning, and original purpose. The cultural significance ascribed to rock art ranges from political and territorial marking to healing and from vision seeking to spiritual protection and magic. It is also closely associated with the nineteenth-century Ghost Dance religion and its contemporary revival (Carroll 2007; Carroll et al. 2004; Stoffle et al. 2000a; Vander 1997).

Current research by David Whitley (2000) demonstrates that the placement of petroglyphs and pictographs is patterned across Arizona, Nevada, and California. My colleagues and I, too, found that its most conspicuous pattern is the clustering of rock art in box canyons or constricted rock formations that may also contain ceremonial items such as red paint sources, crystals, native tobacco, and hallucinogenic plants as well as certain features such as springs or natural holes in the rock (e.g., Carroll et al. 2004; Stoffle et al. 2000c; also Monteleone 1994).

In the process of visiting and interpreting rock art sites in various locations and facilities, tribal members progressively identified connections among origin stories, traditional land uses, ecology, and personal history and experience. For example, in the Pahranagat and Delamar valleys, where Don Fowler and his colleagues conducted archaeological surveys in the 1960s (Fowler and Sharrock 1973), Southern Paiute and Western Shoshone elders drew associations between ancient petroglyph designs and origin stories. Associations were made between fishnet petroglyph designs and Ocean Woman, between "water baby" depictions and shamanistic practices associated with nearby springs and with the Ghost Dance (Figure 19.3), and between the geology of a particular landform and the sacred story of the Hawk (Carroll et al. 2004; Fowler and Fowler 1971; Stoffle et al. 2002; SWCA Environmental Consultants and the Bureau of Applied Research in Anthropology 2011). The resulting cultural landscape of the Pahranagat–Delamar area is especially significant for restoring territorial identities given its proximity to the boundary between Southern Paiute and Virgin Anasazi areas and to known trail systems that connected the Pahrump, Moapa, and Las Vegas bands of Southern Paiutes with Shoshone bands to the north (Kelly and Fowler 1986).

Although the creators of rock art may never be known, and their original reasons for making it may be only tenuously understood, rethinking rock art as a place rather than simply as a mode of expression allows one to better ascertain its relationship with topography, resources, and other cultural remains; its distribution may also help to characterize land-use patterns. For example, certain performance characteristics of petroglyphs and pictographs vary according to visibility, seclusion, and elevation.

FIGURE 19.4. Tribal representatives surveying petroglyphs and geoglyphs in Upper Fortymile Canyon, Nevada (photo by Richard Stoffle, Bureau of Applied Research in Anthropology Archives, University of Arizona).

There are, as well, gender-specific uses of rock art sites that depend on location and sources of flaking or grinding stone, sand, and water (Zedeño et al. 2001). Appropriately named *tumpitu-winap* or "storied rock," rock art sites also provide clues to how people attach themselves to the land, name it, and inscribe their activities in place.

Trail Systems and Territorial Identity

Since land use is at the center of political processes of identity formation, archaeology plays an incredibly important role in restoring *ontological security*—that sense of well-being and stability associated with continuity and tenure of place (Hiscock et al. 2001; Hollenback 2010)—to Native communities. Owning the past is an effective means of demonstrating presence and long-term continuity in situ, which in turn reaffirms the right to possess land and to dispose of it at will. When, for instance, a Native American asks, "How old is this site?" he or she is not simply expressing intellectual curiosity. The person really wants to know, "How long have I been here?" It is a very personal quest for legitimacy and belonging. Unfortunately, the contest for human remains and objects that dominated political discourse in American archaeology for decades has overshadowed the crucial meaning that landscapes, sites, burials, and artifacts bring to the pursuit of territorial identity, or as Welch and Ferguson (2005) call it, the *patria* of repatriation.

Perhaps the most significant, substantive contribution of the DOE-NV research and consultation program to Basin–Plateau cultural history is the reconstruction of landscapes of movement. Across the area occupied by the Department of Energy and U.S. Air Force, from Red Spring in central Nevada to Cane Spring near Las Vegas, west to Beatty and east to Delamar Valley and beyond into the Mohave Desert and the Grand Canyon (Figure 19.4), ancient trails were first noted by groups of 49ers who used them to find food and water (Koenig 1984:67). Because of this connection, Indian trails were essential to miners and explorers in the nineteenth century just as they had been for Native Americans whose lifeways and worldviews were largely defined by movement (Wheeler 1875:24).

In 1905, members of the U.S. Geological Survey traversed southern Nevada to map its topography and mineral resources; they produced the Kawich Quadrangle (Chapman and Douglas 1908), which contained a detailed map of Indian trails. This was the map that guided Julian Steward (1970 [1938]), who expanded and completed it with his ethnographic research. Among the most valuable observations of the surveyors, notably Sidney Ball (Nevada Reconnaissance Notebook, 1905, Department of the Interior, United States Geological Survey, Geologic Records, Notebooks 740–742, Nevada Historical Society Archives, Reno), is the connection among trails, water, and "Indian hieroglyphs," which he thought were made specifically to mark remote water sources along the Eleana, Kawich, and Belted ranges and west to Obsidian Butte. Many more archaeological sites and features associated with these trails were located in the early decades of the twentieth century (McLane 1991; Winslow 1996), as were other trails mapped by the Automobile Club of Southern California in 1919 (Lingenfelter 1986:402). Yet another trail system originally

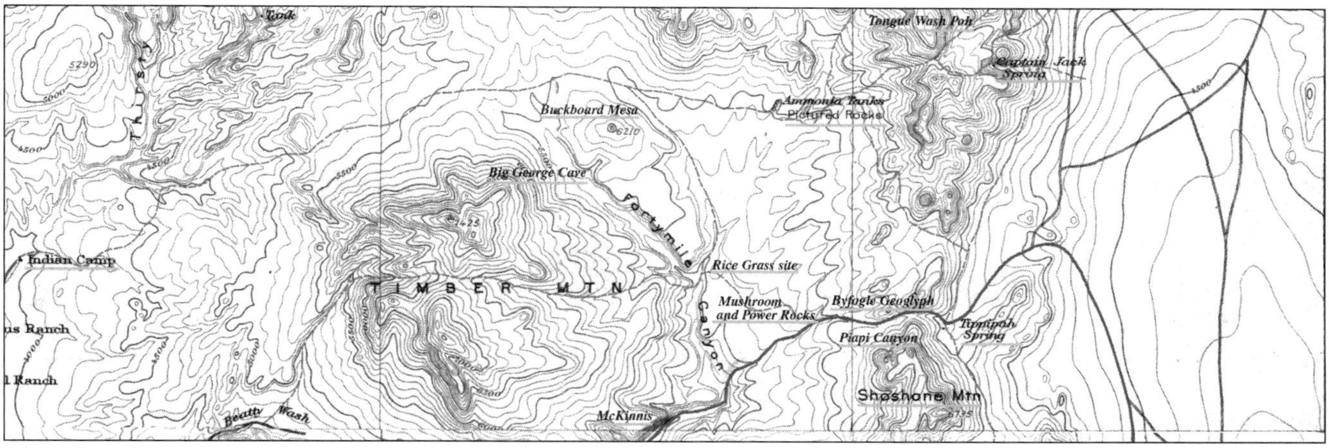

FIGURE 19.5. Detail of archaeological sites connected by Indian trails (middle trail junctions), many of which were mapped in the Kawich Quadrangle of 1908 (after Zedeño et al. 2006:Figure 25).

recorded by Isabel Kelly in the 1930s, which Kay Fowler studied and published in 2009, was created by the Southern Paiute and Chemehuevi groups across the Mohave Desert.

Retracing the trail systems across energy and defense facilities was incremental and initially focused on specific locations such as Paiute Mesa, Buckboard Mesa, and Fortymile Canyon, where more than 300 petroglyph panels made on basalt boulders had been recorded by Desert Research Institute (Drollinger et al. 2000). Research in Nevada progressively incorporated dozens of localities with pilgrimage sites, landforms, traditional camps, painted and inhabited caves, geoglyph and petroglyph sites, springs, historic cabins, and natural resource locales into at least three trail systems (Figure 19.5; Carroll et al. 2006; Stoffle et al. 2002; Van Vlack 2012; Zedeño et al. 2006). The resulting body of research not only contributed to the development of a cultural landscape model for the region under discussion but also provided a bird's-eye view of Numic territory, with multiple lines of evidence that had hitherto been uncovered and discussed in isolation from one another but which together became more than the sum of the parts.

A fascinating revelation of this research, one that escaped Steward but was captured by J. W. Powell and others, is that movement was, in and of itself, the source of Numic place logic, territorial identity, and notions of permanence and ownership. As Jay Miller notes, human movement is ontologically linked to the spread of power in a web-like design:

> People in the Basin were most successful when their movements and the arrangements of their lives duplicated those of power. Without recognizing its full significance, many scholars have noted this web- or net-like character. The attraction of power for life is such that any gathering...will concentrate it, while a closed dance circle contains it for some time.... After such a concentration, power apportions itself among the participants, going along with them as each takes separate trails radiating away from the central location. For this reason, trails in the Basin are sacred [1983:80].

Not surprisingly, movement across ancient trails resulted in enduring attachments to the land. Of these trails John Wesley Powell wrote:

> It is curious to notice with what tenacity an Indian clings to a trail; a path which has been followed by his forefathers is sacred to him, and though in the constant and rapid erosion of the gulches and sides of the hills and mountains these trails have become very difficult yet he never abandons them when they can by any possibility be followed, even though a shorter and better road is very perceptible [in Fowler and Fowler 1971:39].

Fowler (2009:84, 91) states that attachment to trail systems derives from the memories of events and beings encountered along trails. Every detail of a trail, even small stone piles, may be imbued with power as well as with songs, dreams, and experiences recorded in complex systems of nomenclature, which all together contribute to the development of a sense of land-based identity. After studying Numic landscapes and then moving on to explore indigenous movement in the western Great Lakes and northern Plains, my own conclusion is that the more routinely people move across the landscape, regardless of the reason for travel, the more ingrained the notions of possession, belonging, and territorial sentiment become. But because modern concepts of territory and territoriality are founded upon Western geopolitical notions of permanent and bounded space, the relationship between movement and territory formation has been seldom, if at all, viewed as causal (Zedeño 1997, 2008c; Zedeño and Anderson 2010; Zedeño et al. 2009).

A big part of the Western worldviews that inform archaeology has to do with isolating different aspects of human–land interaction and interpreting them in their own terms. This is most evident in the arbitrary separation of sacred and mundane forms of land use, which in turn ignores the cultural and political roles that religion plays in territory formation. In the Basin–Plateau region there are two very important models of Native land use.

The first model, found in John Wesley Powell's writings, which the Fowlers edited and published under the title *Anthropology of the Numa* (Fowler and Fowler 1971), emphasizes territoriality, permanence, and profound attachments to land expressed in names, origin stories, and songs, as Powell observed and understood them in the late nineteenth century:

> An Indian will never ask to what nation or tribe or body of people another Indian belongs but to "what land do you belong and how are your lands [—] named?" Thus the very name of the Indian is his title deed to his home and thus it is that these Indians have contended so fiercely for the possession of the soil, for a tribe to yield the district which it inhabits they must lose their nationality and become incorporated in other tribes and perhaps to do so it becomes necessary for them to fight for a recognition [in Fowler and Fowler 1971:38].

Powell was mainly concerned with discovering the land and its inhabitants; it was perhaps his keen interest in the landscape that lent his observations about the Natives, particularly the Southern Paiute, a clear sense of connection between people and land. Stories about landforms and their relationship to politics and ritual, place-names, and musical lyrics abound in his notes. Powell and Steward, the two great scholars of the Basin–Plateau, whose deep knowledge of land and people continues to influence anthropology within and beyond the region, nevertheless understood Numic land use and territory very differently from one another.

Julian Steward's view, which was partially based on Powell's original research and no doubt influenced by the impact of Anglo-American settlement and concomitant Native "deculturation" of the communities Steward studied in the 1930s, focused almost exclusively on aboriginal subsistence, settlement patterns, and social organization. Steward (1970:248 [1938]) was convinced that the Numa, for the most part, lacked territorial attachments to any swath of land and had a simplistic autochthonous body of religious beliefs. Indeed, he wrote, the Numa had a practical, "gastric" approach to life, augmented only by their strong kinship networks (1970:46 [1938]; see Clemmer 1999). Even though other ethnographers of his time, including Isabel Kelly (1965 [1932]), Carobeth Laird (1976), and Omer Stewart (1941, 1966), produced more holistic ethnographic overviews of Numic culture and society, Steward's powerful but narrowly conceived model of Basin–Plateau sociopolitical organization came to completely dominate archaeological analysis of prehistoric populations in the Great Basin.

In her second biography of Steward, Virginia Kerns (2010:46) notes not only that he struggled to frame his Numic informants' explanations of the sociopolitics of land use and boundaries within his own anthropological perspective but that, intriguingly enough, Steward never made use of his mentor Alfred Kroeber's ideas about aboriginal territory formation. This struggle led him to reject Indian claims of land ownership in the Basin–Plateau (Kerns 2010:161–167). In a letter to Omer Stewart regarding the nature of indigenous territorial boundaries and how to frame this research, Kroeber explained: "Their whole point of view was the opposite of ours. We begin by delimiting a state by such and such surveyed lines; then we survey some more lines, and whatever is inside a set of four becomes a county." Instead of beginning in this manner, with an outside frame, an Indian "begins with the spot where he was born," Kroeber said:

> Around this is the territory where he habitually wandered over and got his food from. Farther up the creek, or in the hills, is territory where he might occasionally hunt. His mind works outward from a spot, or a group of spots; the edges are hazy [in Kerns 2010:20–21].

In the elegant simplicity of Kroeber's note to his graduate student one may find movement as the conceptual foundation of territory formation among mobile hunter-gatherers and the Numa in particular. This very foundation insinuated itself once a place-centered view of archaeological and ethnographic resources was adopted by the DOE-NV research and consultation program. And yet, it took the better part of two decades, and many journeys after my colleagues and I had begun research on Native American land use in the Basin–Plateau region, to formulate an explicitly political, movement-centered model of hunter-gatherer territory formation (Zedeño and Anderson 2010; Zedeño et al. 2009). Echoing Kroeber, this model focuses on core places (homesites, resource locales, sacred sites), on the pathways or trails that connect them, and on flexible boundaries that represent the confines of a people's experiential knowledge of the land.

Anthropology and Native Americans: Areas of Impact

As American anthropologists involved in cultural resource preservation and legal compliance revisit the problem of the cultural affiliation, ethnogenesis, and territorial identity of prehistoric and historic groups, and piece together the fragmentary evidence needed to rebuild the difficult paths Indian groups followed to the present day, we face an opportunity for tremendous intellectual growth—so long, that is, as we are willing to reconcile the apparent contradiction between the normative definition of origin and development and the requirement of a dynamic and flexible understanding of ethnogenesis and territorial identity. It is often easy to forget that "tribes" are arbitrary political entities created by the U.S. government. Cases such as the Colorado River Indian Tribes in California, where traditional enemies that share neither language nor history, society nor culture, were placed together and required to live on the same land and agree on the terms of its management, remind everyone that, in our country today, identity and territory are complex, multilayered entities that defy the anthropological norm. Contemporary tribes that engage in consultation about human remains, sacred objects, or heritage sites and resources must reconcile past and present trajectories through alternative, "indigenous" forms of archaeological, historical, and ethnographic research. This process, however painful it may be, carries important corollary benefits for tribes as well as for scholars with an open mind.

First, for the tribes, cultural affiliation studies bring together disparate and previously inaccessible information into a coherent story line that can be examined and debated by the tribal members; often, these studies foster the rediscovery of events and places that had been hitherto forgotten by the community. They also open up access to evidence of other tribal histories and their common or contested connections to one another and to aboriginal territories. For archaeologists, cultural affiliation research has furnished the opportunity to critically and constructively examine Native worldviews and traditional histories as well as documents and to review and reinterpret existing data in light of this knowledge.

Second, Native Americans are experiencing the recovery and expansion of ecological knowledge, which has been brought about by tribal assessments of sites and areas with multiple cultural resources as well as by the repatriation of archaeological and ethnographic collections. The past 150 years of assimilation and interference with traditional cultural practices and human–land interactions have had a strong negative impact on American Indian knowledge about nature and the appropriation of natural resources for cultural practices. Knowledge lost is slowly resurfacing due to the partial restoration of connections among people, nature, and objects. Archaeology can contribute immensely to the revitalization of knowledge by incorporating Native views of the past and embracing non-Western ideas as points of departure for scientific research.

And third, artifact collections play a critical role in the restoration of ecological and ritual knowledge. John Wesley Powell's ethnographic collection of the Numa (Fowler and Matley 1979), for example, contains basketry, nets, clothing, headdresses, cradleboards, pottery, and a wide assortment of items made of tortoise shell, horn, feathers, wood, leather, and stone. Complementing the ethnographic collections are, of course, documents and photographs that explain more or less the time and place where the collections were made as well as classical ethnographies that describe the manufacturing process and context of use of these items (Fowler and Fowler 1995).

All this information helps descendant communities identify natural resources once available in their traditional territories while stimulating curiosity about past technologies and culturally appropriate artifact uses. Archaeological and ethnographic collections refer tribal members not only to nature and technology but also to origin stories, spiritual beings, songs, values, and places that, together, embody miniature versions of the aboriginal territory. Native Americans are further empowered by taking responsibility for the curation of artifact collections and the return of ceremonial objects to their traditional use contexts.

Across the Basin–Plateau region (and the rest of Native North America, for that matter) one may find instances of widespread religious practices involving "ordinary" objects that do not follow any archaeological conventions that make them fit neatly into any NAGPRA category except for culturally bound meanings intrinsic to certain things (Zedeño 2009) and the context where they were retired (Walker 1995). Hence the importance of considering place and object life histories in discussions of repatriation. Beyond NAGPRA, cultural resource management legislation now requires consultation and monitoring of archaeological survey and excavation. Additionally, federal land managers engage tribes in research projects that focus on traditional resource uses, including traditional cultural properties, ethnobotany, ethnozoology, ethnomineralogy, and cultural geography. In more advanced collaborations, tribal members are engaged in formulating research questions of mutual relevance and contributing to research design. Ultimately, partnerships are the ideal, and in many cases, the real reward of this historical process is Native American cultural revitalization and reacquaintance with land and archaeology.

In conclusion, since the time Meriwether Lewis and William Clark undertook their journey of continental discovery, American Indian land-use history in the American West has been permeated by systematic dispossession and ontological insecurity (Hollenback 2010). While disease, poverty, emigration, knowledge loss, and apostasy have since eroded traditional institutions, the Native *sense of place* has been somehow spared from obliteration (Basso 1996). As a student of landscapes and territories I have come to realize that attachment to place often lies beneath the surface of social memory and individual experience regardless of the time elapsed since land cessions, relocation, and confinement dispossessed Indian communities. Sense of place can also regenerate and evolve as opportunities for acquiring new knowledge, self-awareness, and cultural and economic independence arise and interact with contemporary practice (Giddens 1991).

Through involvement in traditional land-use studies and ethnographic resource assessments, Native Americans may reestablish contact with natural resources and habitats that were previously inaccessible and thus revisit or restore ancient knowledge. Demonstrating depth of ecological knowledge and familiarity with particular environments further reasserts land rights and strengthens territorial identities. Indian tribes may never recover lost land, but certainly they have slowly asserted the right to tell their own origin story and to determine whether and how their past should be investigated and shared with the public. Legislative and judicial decisions largely stand behind the tribal power to sanction research in ancestral lands now managed by federal agencies, to veto projects that go against their cultural principles, to influence public opinion regarding the reburial of human remains and the repatriation of sacred objects, and to reserve the use rights of sacred places. They have garnered the support of powerful allies to help them restore their spiritual and physical connection with aboriginal territories and write interpretations of the archaeological record that best reflect these connections. The next logical step is to engage Basin–Plateau tribes in the framing of research that both expands archaeological knowledge and contributes to the preservation of their territorial legitimacy.

References Cited

Adler, Michael, and Susan Bruning

2008 Navigating the Fluidity of Social Identity: Collaborative Research into Cultural Affiliation in the American Southwest. In *Collaboration in Archaeological Practice: Engaging Descendant Communities*, edited by C. Colwell-Chanthaphonh and T. J. Ferguson, pp. 35–54. AltaMira Press, Walnut Creek.

American Indian Writers Subgroup

2001 Preface to Part 1. In *American Indians and the Nevada Test Site: A Model of Research and Consultation*, edited by R. W. Stoffle, M. N. Zedeño, and D. B. Halmo, pp. 1–2. U.S. Government Printing Office, Washington, D.C.

Basso, Keith

1996 *Wisdom Sits in Places: Landscape and Language Among the Western Apache*. University of New Mexico Press, Albuquerque.

Beck, Colleen M., N. Zedeño, and R. Furlow

2000 Time, Trust, and the Measure of Success: The Nevada Test Site Cultural Resources Program. In *Working Together: Native Americans and Archaeologists*, edited by K. Dongoske, M. Aldenderfer, and K. Doehner, pp. 165–171. Society for American Archaeology, Washington, D.C.

Bye, Robert A., Jr.

1972 Ethnobotany of the Southern Paiute Indians in the 1870s, with a Note on the Early Botanical Contributions of Dr. Edward D. Palmer. In *Great Basin Cultural Ecology: A Symposium*, edited by Don D. Fowler, pp. 87–104. University of Nevada Desert Research Institute Publications in the Social Sciences, Reno.

Carroll, Alex K., Richard W. Stoffle, Kathleen Van Vlack, Richard Arnold, Rebecca Toupal, Heather Fauland, and Arin Haverland

2006 *Black Mountain: Traditional Uses of a Volcanic Landscape*. Report prepared for the U.S. Air Force—Air Combat Command, Nevada Test and Training Range, and URS Group, Inc. Bureau of Applied Research in Anthropology, University of Arizona, Tucson.

Carroll, Alex K., Maria. N. Zedeño, and Richard W. Stoffle

2004 Landscapes of the Ghost Dance: A Cartography of Numic Ritual. *Journal of Archaeological Method and Theory* 11(2):127–155.

Carroll, K.

2007 Place, Performance, and Social Memory in the 1890s Ghost Dance. Unpublished Ph.D. dissertation, Department of Anthropology, University of Arizona, Tucson.

Chapman, R. H., and S. Douglas

1908 Map of Kawich Quadrangle, Nye County, Nevada, June 1908, Side 2. U.S. Geological Survey. Electronic document, http://digital.library.unlv.edu/u?/LV_Maps,851.

Clark, G. A.

2003 American Archaeology's Uncertain Future. In *Archaeology Is Anthropology*, edited by S. Gillespie and D. Nichols, pp. 51–68. Archaeological Papers of the American Anthropological Association No. 13. Arlington, Virginia.

Clemmer, Richard

1999 Steward's Gap: Why Steward Did Not Use His Theory of Culture Change to Explain Shoshoni Culture Change. In *Julian Steward and the Great Basin: The Making of an Anthropologist*, edited by Richard O. Clemmer, L. Daniel Myers, and Mary Elizabeth Rudden, pp. 144–163. University of Utah Press, Salt Lake City.

Colwell-Chanthaphonh, C.

2010 *Living Histories: Native Americans and Southwestern Archaeology*. AltaMira Press, Walnut Creek.

Crum, Stephen

1994 *The Road on Which We Came: A History of the Western Shoshone*. University of Utah Press, Salt Lake City.

Drollinger, H., C. Beck, and R. Jones

2000 *The Petroglyphs of Fortymile Canyon, Nevada Test Site, Nye County, Nevada*. Cultural Resources Technical Report No. 96. Desert Research Institute, University and Community College System of Nevada, Las Vegas.

Ferguson, T. J., and C. Colwell-Chanthaphonh

2006 *History Is in the Land: Multivocal Tribal Traditions in Arizona's San Pedro Valley*. University of Arizona Press, Tucson.

Foucault, Michel

1994 *The Order of Things: An Archaeology of the Human Sciences*. Vintage Books, Random House Inc., New York.

Fowler, Catherine S.

1992 *In the Shadow of Fox Peak: An Ethnography of the Cat-Tail Eater Northern Paiute of Stillwater Marsh*. Cultural Resource Series No. 5. U.S. Department of Interior, Fish and Wildlife Service Region 1, Still Water National Wildlife Refuge, Fallon, Nevada.

2009 Reconstructing the Southern Paiute–Chemehuevi Trails in the Mojave Desert of Southern Nevada and California: Ethnographic Perspectives from the 1930s. In *Landscapes of Movement: Trails, Paths, and Roads in Anthropological Perspective*, edited by J. Snead, C. Erickson, and A. Darling, pp. 84–105. University of Pennsylvania Museum of Archaeology and Anthropology and University of Pennsylvania Press, Philadelphia.

Fowler, Catherine S., and Don D. Fowler

1995 Formation Processes of Ethnographic Collections. Examples from the Great Basin of Western North America. In *Learning from Things*, edited by David Kingery, pp. 129–144. Smithsonian Institution Press, Washington, D.C.

Fowler, Catherine S., and S. Liljeblad

1986 Northern Paiute. In *Handbook of North American Indians, Vol. 11: Great Basin*, edited by W. L. D'Azevedo, pp. 412–434. Smithsonian Institution Press, Washington, D.C.

Fowler, Don D.

1987 Uses of the Past: Archaeology in the Service of the State. *American Antiquity* 52:229–248.

2000 *A Laboratory for Anthropology: Science and Romanticism in the*

American Southwest, 1846–1930. University of New Mexico Press, Albuquerque.
2008 Comments on Zuni Origins: Toward a New Synthesis of Southwestern Archaeology. In *Zuni Origins*, edited by D. A. Gregory and D. R. Wilcox, pp. 424–433. University of Arizona Press, Tucson.

Fowler, Don D., and Catherine Fowler (editors)
1971 *Anthropology of the Numa: John Wesley Powell's Manuscripts on the Numic Peoples of Western North America, 1868–1880*. Smithsonian Contributions to Anthropology No. 14. Smithsonian Institution Press, Washington, D.C.

Fowler, Don D., and John F. Matley
1979 *Material Culture of the Numa: The John Wesley Powell Collection 1867–1889*. Smithsonian Contributions to Anthropology, 26. Washington, D.C.

Fowler, Don D., and Floyd Sharrock
1973 Appendix A. In *Prehistory of Southeastern Nevada*, by Don D. Fowler, David B. Madsen, and Eugene H. Hattori, pp. 97–136. Desert Research Institute Publications in the Social Sciences No. 6. Reno.

Furlow, Robert
2001 Foreword. In *American Indians and the Nevada Test Site: A Model of Research and Consultation*, edited by R. W. Stoffle, M. N. Zedeño, and D. B. Halmo, pp. xiv–xvii. U.S. Government Printing Office, Washington, D.C.

Gell, Alfred
1998 *Art and Agency: An Anthropological Theory*. Oxford University Press, Oxford.

Giddens, Anthony
1991 *Modernity and Self-Identity. Self and Society in the Late Modern Age*. Polity Press, Cambridge.

Halmo, David B.
1994 With One Voice: Collective Action in Cultural Impact Assessment. *Practicing Anthropology* 16(3):14–16.

Hiscock, R., A. Kearns, S. Macintyre, and A. Ellaway
2001 Ontological Security and Psychosocial Benefits from the Home: Qualitative Evidence on Issues of Tenure. *Housing, Theory, and Society* 18(1–2):50–66.

Hollenback, Kacy L.
2010 Social Memory of Disaster: Exploring Historic Smallpox Epidemics Among the Mandan and Hidatsa. Graduate Student Award winner, paper presented at the 68th Annual Plains Anthropological Conference, October 6–9, Bismarck.

Kelly, Isabel T.
1965 [1932] Ethnography of the Surprise Valley Paiute. Reprint. Krauss Reprint, New York (originally *University of California Publications in American Archaeology and Ethnology* 31[3]:67–210, Berkeley).

Kelly, Isabel T., and Catherine S. Fowler
1986 Southern Paiute. In *Handbook of North American Indians, Vol. 11: Great Basin*, edited by Warren L. D'Azevedo, pp. 368–397. Smithsonian Institution, Washington, D.C.

Kerns, Virginia
2010 *Journeys West: Jane and Julian Steward and Their Guides*. University of Nebraska Press, Lincoln.

Kluth, Rose
2000 The Integration of Traditional and Scientific Knowledge on Leech Lake Reservation, Cass Lake, Minnesota. In *Working Together: Native Americans and Archaeologists*, edited by K. Dongoske, M. Aldenderfer, and K. Doehner, pp. 139–145. Society for American Archaeology, Washington, D.C.

Koenig, George
1984 *Beyond This Place There Be Dragons*. Arthur Clark Co., Chicago.

Laird, Carobeth
1976 *The Chemehuevis*. Malki Museum, Banning.

Liljeblad, Sven
1986 Oral Tradition: Content and Style of Verbal Arts. In *Handbook of North American Indians, Vol. 11: Great Basin*, edited by W. L. D'Azevedo, pp. 641–659. Smithsonian Institution Press, Washington, D.C.

Lingenfelter, Richard
1986 *Death Valley and the Amargosa: Land of Illusion*. University of California Press, Berkeley and Los Angeles.

Lowenthal, David
1996 *The Heritage Crusade and the Spoils of History*. Free Press, New York.

Mason, R. J.
2000 Archaeology and Native North American Oral Traditions. *American Antiquity* 65:239–266.

McGhee, Robert
2008 Aboriginalism and the Problem of Indigenous Archaeology. *American Antiquity* 73:579–597.

McLane, A. R.
1991 History of Buckboard Mesa Region. In *Archaeological Investigations on the Buckboard Mesa Road Project*, edited by D. Amick, G. Henton, and L. Pipping, pp. 13–15. DRI Technical Report, 69. Las Vegas.

Meskell, Lynn
2004 *Object Worlds in Ancient Egypt: Material Biographies Past and Present*. Berg, London.

Miller, Daniel
2005 *Materiality (Politics, History, and Culture)*. Duke University Press, Durham.

Miller, Jay
1983 Basin Religion and Theology: A Comparative Study of Power (Puha). *Journal of California and Great Basin Anthropology* 15(1–2):66–86.

Mills, Barbara, and William Walker (editors)
2008 *Memory Work: The Archaeology of Material Practices*. SAR Press, Santa Fe, New Mexico.

Milo, Richard G.
2002 Review of *Indigenous Archaeology*, by J. Watkins. *South African Archaeological Bulletin* 57(175):42–47.

Monteleone, S. A.
1994 Rock Art in Context: The Pictographs of the Eleana Range, Southern Nevada. Unpublished Master's thesis, Department of Anthropology, University of Nevada, Reno.

Murray, W. F.
2011 Feathers, Fasting, and the Eagle Complex: A Contemporary Analysis of the Eagle as a Cultural Resource in the Northern Plains. *Plains Anthropologist* 56(218):143–154.

Murray, W. F., M. N. Zedeño, K. Hollenback, C. Grinnell, and E. Crows Breast
2011 The Remaking of Lake Sakakawea: Locating Cultural Viability in Negative Heritage on the Missouri River. *American Ethnologist* 38:468–483.

Ruuska, A. K.
2009 Anishnabe Migration Trail Through Pictured Rocks National

Lakeshore, Michigan. Anthropology Department, Northern Arizona University, Marquette, Michigan. Electronic document, http://www.nmuanthro.net.

Schiffer, M. B., and A. Miller

1999 *The Material Life of Human Beings: Artifacts, Behavior, and Communication*. Routledge, London.

Silliman, S. W.

2010 The Value and Diversity of Indigenous Archaeology: A Response to McGhee. *American Antiquity* 75:217–220.

Spector, Janet

1993 *What This Awl Means: Feminist Archaeology at a Wahpeton Village*. Minnesota Historical Society Press, St. Paul.

Steward, Julian

1933 Ethnography of the Owens Valley Paiute. *University of California Publications in Anthropology* 33(3):233–250.

1970 [1938] *Basin–Plateau Aboriginal Sociopolitical Groups*. Reprint. University of Utah Press, Salt Lake City (originally Bureau of American Ethnology Bulletin, 120, Washington, D.C.).

Stewart, Omer C.

1941 Culture Element Distributions, XVIII: Ute–Southern Paiute. *Anthropological Records* 6(4):315. Berkeley.

1966 Tribal Distributions and Boundaries in the Great Basin. In *The Current Status of Anthropological Research in the Great Basin, 1964*, edited by Warren L. d'Azevedo, Wilbur H. Davis, Don D. Fowler, and Wayne Suttles, pp. 167–238. Desert Research Institute Social Sciences and Humanity Publications No. 1. University of Nevada, Reno.

Stoffle, R. W., and R. Arnold

2003 Confronting the Angry Rock: American Indian's Situated Risk from Radioactivity. *Ethnos* 68(2):230–248.

Stoffle, Richard W., Fletcher P. Chmara-Huff, Kathleen A. Van Vlack, and Rebecca S. Toupal

2004a *Puha Flows from It: The Cultural Landscape Study of the Spring Mountains*. Bureau of Applied Research in Anthropology, University of Arizona, Tucson.

Stoffle, Richard W., David Halmo, and Diane Austin

1997 Cultural Landscapes and Traditional Cultural Properties: A Southern Paiute View of the Grand Canyon and Colorado River. *American Indian Quarterly* 21(2):229–249.

Stoffle, Richard W., David B. Halmo, John E. Olmstead, and Michael J. Evans

1990 *Native American Cultural Resource Studies at Yucca Mountain, Nevada*. Institute for Social Research, University of Michigan, Ann Arbor.

1999 *Puchuxwavaats Uapi* (To Know About Plants): Traditional Knowledge and the Cultural Significance of Southern Paiute Plants. *Human Organization* 58:416–429.

Stoffle, R. W., L. Loendorf, D. Austin, D. Halmo, and A. Bullets

2000a Ghost-Dancing the Grand Canyon: Southern Paiute Rock Art, Ceremony, and Cultural Landscapes. *Current Anthropology* 41:11–38.

Stoffle, R., and J. Minnis

2007 Marine Protected Areas and the Traditional Settlements of the Exumas, Bahamas. *Coral Reefs* 26(4):1023–1032.

Stoffle, Richard W., Rebecca S. Toupal, and María Nieves Zedeño

2002 *East of Nellis: Cultural Landscapes of the Sheep and Pahranagat Mountain Ranges*. Bureau of Applied Research in Anthropology, University of Arizona, Tucson.

Stoffle, Richard W., and M. N. Zedeño

2001a American Indian Worldviews I: The Concept "Power" and Its Connection to People, Places, and Resources. In *American Indians and the Nevada Test Site: A Model of Research and Consultation*, edited by R. W. Stoffle, M. N. Zedeño, and D. B. Halmo, pp. 58–76. U.S. Government Printing Office, Washington, D.C.

2001b American Indian Worldviews II: Power and Cultural Landscapes. In *American Indians and the Nevada Test Site: A Model of Research and Consultation*, edited by R. W. Stoffle, M. N. Zedeño, and D. B. Halmo, pp. 139–152. U.S. Government Printing Office, Washington, D.C.

Stoffle, Richard W., M. N. Zedeño, and A. K. Carroll

2000b *From Place to Object: NAGPRA Consultation for the Hot Creek Valley Collection, Central Nevada Test Area*. Bureau of Applied Research in Anthropology, University of Arizona, Tucson.

Stoffle, Richard W., María Nieves Zedeño, Amy Eisenberg, Rebecca Toupal, and Alex Carroll

2004b Shifting Risks: Hoover Dam Bridge Impacts on American Indian Sacred Landscapes. In *Facility Siting: Risk, Power, and Identity in Land Use Planning*, edited by Åsa Boholm and Ragnar Löfstedt, pp. 127–143. Earthscan, London.

Stoffle, Richard W., María Nieves Zedeño, Jaime K. Eyrich, and Patrick Barabe

2000c *The Wellington Canyon Ethnographic Study at Pintwater Range, Nevada*. Bureau of Applied Research in Anthropology, University of Arizona, Tucson.

Stoffle, Richard W., María Nieves Zedeño, and David B. Halmo (editors)

2001 *American Indians and the Nevada Test Site: A Model of Research and Consultation*. U.S. Government Printing Office, Washington, D.C.

SWCA Environmental Consultants and the Bureau of Applied Research in Anthropology

2011 *University of Arizona Ethnographic and Class I Records Searches for Proposed Solar Energy Zones in California, Nevada, and Utah for the Bureau of Land Management's Solar Programmatic Environmental Impact Statement*. Prepared for the Bureau of Land Management, National Operations Center. SWCA Environmental Consultants, Albuquerque.

Thomas, David H.

2000 *Skull Wars: Kennewick Man, Archaeology, and the Battle for American Indian Identity*. Basic Books, New York.

2013 Engineering Alta Toquima: Social Investments and Dividends at 11,000 Feet. In *Engineering Mountain Landscapes: An Archaeology of Social Investment*, edited by L. Scheiber and M. N. Zedeño. University of Utah Press, Salt Lake City, in preparation.

Toupal, R., R. W. Stoffle, and M. N. Zedeño

2001 Cultural Landscapes and Ethnographic Cartographies: Scandinavian-American and American Indian Knowledge of the Land. *Environmental Science and Policy* 4(4–5):171–184.

Vander, Judith

1997 *Shoshone Ghost Dance Religion: Poetry Songs and Great Basin Context*. University of Illinois Press, Champaign.

Van Vlack, Kathleen A.

2012 Puaxant Tuvip: "Powerlands" Southern Paiute Cultural Landscapes and Pilgrimage Trails. Unpublished Ph.D. dissertation, American Indian Studies Department, University of Arizona, Tucson.

Walker, W. H.

1995 Ceremonial Trash. In *Expanding Archaeology*, edited by

J. Skibo, W. Walker, and A. Nielsen, pp. 100–115. University of Utah Press, Salt Lake City.

Watkins, Joe

2000 *Indigenous Archaeology: American Indian and Scientific Practice*. AltaMira Press, Walnut Creek.

Watts, Christopher (editor)

2013 *Relational Archaeologies: Humans, Animals, Things*. Routledge, London, forthcoming.

Welch, John R., and T. J. Ferguson

2005 Putting *Patria* Back into Repatriation. *Journal of Social Archaeology* 7:171–198.

Wheeler, Geo M.

1875 *Report upon the Geological and Geographical Surveys West of the One Hundredth Meridian*. U.S. Government Printing Office, Washington, D.C.

Whitley, David S.

2000 *The Art of the Shaman: Rock Art in California*. University of Utah Press, Salt Lake City.

Winslow, Diane

1996 *Restricted Reconnaissance: The History and Archaeology of S. M. Wheeler in Nye County, Nevada*. Master's thesis, Department of Anthropology, University of Nevada, Las Vegas. University Microfilms, Ann Arbor.

Yellowhorn, Eldon

2002 Awakening Internalist Archaeology in the Aboriginal World. Unpublished Ph.D. dissertation, Department of Anthropology, McGill University, Montreal.

Zedeño, M. N.

1997 Landscapes, Land Use, and the History of Territory Formation: An Example from the Puebloan Southwest. *Journal of Archaeological Method and Theory* 4(1):67–103.

2000 On What People Make of Places: A Behavioral Cartography. In *Social Theory in Archaeology*, edited by M. B. Schiffer, pp. 97–111. University of Utah Press, Salt Lake City.

2008a Bundled Worlds: The Roles and Interactions of Complex Objects from the North American Plains. *Journal of Archaeological Method and Theory* 15(4):362–378.

2008b Traditional Knowledge, Ritual Behavior, and Contemporary Interpretations of the Archaeological Record. In *Belief in the Past: Theoretical Approaches to the Archaeology of Religion*, edited by D. S. Whitley and K. Hays-Gilpin, pp. 259–274. Left Coast Press, Walnut Creek.

2008c The Archaeology of Territory and Territoriality. In *The Handbook of Landscape Archaeology*, edited by B. David and J. Thomas, pp. 210–217. Left Coast Press, Walnut Creek.

2009 Animating by Association: Index Objects and Relational Taxonomies. *Cambridge Archaeological Journal* 19(3):407–417.

2013a Methodological Challenges in the Practice of Relational Archaeologies: A View from the Hunting Ground. In *Relational Archaeologies: Humans, Animals, Things*, edited by Christopher Watts, pp. 117–134. Routledge, London.

2013b To Become a Mountain Hunter: Flexible Core Values and Subsistence Hunting Among Reservation-Era Blackfeet. In *The Historical Ecology of Small-Scale Societies*, edited by V. Thompson and J. Waggoner, Jr., pp. 141–163. University Press of Florida, Gainesville.

Zedeño, M. N., and D. Anderson

2010 Agency and Politics in Hunter-Gatherer Territory Formation. *Revista de Arqueologia* 23(1):10–29.

Zedeño, M. N., Diane Austin, and Richard W. Stoffle

1997 Landmark and Landscape: A Conceptual Approach to the Management of American Indian Resources. *Culture and Agriculture* 19(3):123–129.

Zedeño, M. N., and B. Bowser

2009 The Archaeology of Meaningful Places. In *The Archaeology of Meaningful Places*, edited by B. Bowser and M. N. Zedeño, pp. 1–14. University of Utah Press, Salt Lake City.

Zedeño, M. N., K. Hollenback, and C. Grinnell

2009 From Path to Myth: Journeys and the Naturalization of Territorial Identity Along the Missouri River. In *Landscapes of Movement: Trails, Paths, and Roads in Anthropological Perspective*, edited by J. Snead, C. Erickson, and A. Darling, pp. 106–133. University of Pennsylvania Press, Philadelphia.

Zedeño, M. N., F. Schmara-Huff, A. K. Carroll, and R. Toupal

2006 *From Red Spring to Cane Spring: Landscapes of Movement Along the Greater Belted Range*. Bureau of Applied Research in Anthropology, University of Arizona, Tucson.

Zedeño, M. N., and R. Stoffle

2003 Tracking the Role of Pathways in the Evolution of a Human Landscape: The St. Croix Riverway in Ethnohistorical Perspective. In *Colonization of Unfamiliar Landscapes: The Archaeology of Human Adaptation*, edited by M. Rockman and J. Steele, pp. 59–80. Routledge, London.

Zedeño, M. N., R. Stoffle, G. Dewey-Hefley, and D. Shaul

1999 *Storied Rocks: American Indian Inventory and Interpretation of Rock Art on the Nevada Test Site*. Desert Research Institute Technical Report, 93. Bureau of Applied Research in Anthropology, University of Arizona, Tucson.

Zedeño, M. N., R. W. Stoffle, and D. L. Shaul

2001 Storied Rocks: American Indian Assessment of Rock Art Sites. In *American Indians and the Nevada Test Site: A Model of Research and Consultation*, edited by R. W. Stoffle, M. N. Zedeño, and D. B. Halmo, pp. 122–138. U.S. Government Printing Office, Washington, D.C.

20

Microcosm and Macrocosm in Southwestern Archaeology

David R. Wilcox

For any social system one can look inward to explicate the processes that structure its microcosm and affect its trajectory, or one can look at it from the outside to understand the macrocosm that shapes it and affects its trajectory. Better yet, one can do both, examining the interaction of microcosm and macrocosm, on multiple scales of internal/external interactions (Neitzel 1999). The history of archaeology in the American Southwest reveals a long preoccupation with a presumption of local autonomy (Bandelier 1892) or self-sufficiency by social groups (microcosms) and an explanatory conviction that at the macrocosm level "the environment made them do it" (Colton 1918; Dean et al. 1985; Doyel and Dean 2006; Gumerman 1988). The clear implication of these perspectives is the assumption that American Indians are part of nature. The common narratives of Southwestern archaeology are in fact derivative from a general trope in Anglo-American history in which, since first contact with European civilization, "primitive" Indians are viewed as part of a great "wilderness" that can be legitimately appropriated for more productive uses (Kagan 2007). This is part of the "cant of conquest" or the "doctrine of discovery," European perspectives that have long affected Euro-American interactions with American Indians—in the law, in how the U.S. government can consider American Indian nations "wards of the government" that need to be placed in a trust status, and in the plethora of stereotypes in the news and in movies that depict Indians as beings who impede development or the civilizing of the wilderness (Williams 1990). It is to be expected that archaeology, as part of American culture, has incorporated this imaging and worldview. Unfortunately, as Zedeño and Roberts reflect in their chapters, old habits of thought and embedded classification systems die hard. Speaking of the Office of Anthropological Research at the Smithsonian Institution, Richard Woodbury and Nathalie Woodbury mordantly noted that "the Department is now listed as residing in the National Museum of Natural History/National Museum of Man. This recent change represents a century-late recognition that human cultural material is distinct from the non-human part of natural history" (1999:293). Is it not now time to construct a new narrative about the archaeology of American Indians, one that recognizes that they had brains in their heads and have always been capable of interacting with their natural and cultural environments in ways more complex than those of insects (Kohler and Van West 1996: 190 n. 9) helplessly subject to the whims of temperature and precipitation (see Andrewartha and Birch 1970)—or, as used to be stated in the nineteenth century, ground squirrels who dug their homes in the ground (Parezo and Fowler 2007)?

When hominids first peopled the New World (Fiedel 2002; Meltzer 2009), their ancestors had been talking to one another and living in sophisticated societies for tens of thousands of years: they no doubt arrived here with ideas in their heads about the cosmos and their role in it. They may, for example, have already developed evolutionary concepts of a dichotomous upperworld and an underworld and the importance of celestial events such as solstices and equinoxes in the movements of the sun, moon, and stars (Wilcox 1991a:101–102).[1] The domestication of New World plants clearly led to the emergent concept of a maize god and other ideas (Millbrath 1999), which may have diffused from central or west Mexico northward. It should be noted that whether it was both people and plants or only plants that moved with such ideas remains controversial and the subject of ongoing debates (Bellwood 2005; Golla 2010; Hill 2001; Kohler et al. 2007; Merrill et al. 2009; Wilcox et al. 2008)—just like the Numic spread arguments that others in this book discuss. Early maize, beans, and squash may *not* have provided populations that had them (possibly as early as 8700 BP at Xihuatoxtla Shelter [see Figure 20.1] in Guerrero [Piperno et al. 2009; Ranere et al. 2009]) with an exceptional adaptive advantage (cf. Bellwood 2005; Hill 2001; see Fuller 2010) until several millennia later: Widespread evidence for the spread of maize currently dates from about 5500 BP (Staller et al. 2006), and the appearance of complex (Olmec) civilization, to about 3750 BP (Pool 2007)—just after the time maize is now well attested as present in the American Southwest (Diehl et al. 2005; Gregory 2001; Gregory and Diehl 2002; Mabry 1999). While the use of clay in simple figurines and pinch pots is also well documented during

FIGURE 20.1. Xihuatoxtla Shelter (Ranere et al. 2009).

the Southwestern "Early Agricultural period" (Huckell 1995) in the Southwest, true "container technology" is not found until the early centuries CE (Heidke et al. 2002), over two millennia later than its appearance on the Pacific coast of Chiapas (Pool 2007:9).

A. V. Kidder (1924) famously argued that once cultigens and pottery were introduced to the Southwest from Mexico, Southwestern populations thereafter were "autochthonous" in their subsequent evolution, thus denying that these populations were later influenced by a larger macrocosm we now call "Mesoamerica" (see also Kidder 1936). Debate about this issue has been persistent, controversial, important, and unresolved to the present day (e.g., Di Peso 1974; Fowler 2000; Kelley and Kelley 1975; Mathien and McGuire 1986; Mathiowetz 2011; McGuire 1980; Riley 2005; Weigand and Weigand 2001; Wilcox and Fowler 2002; Wilcox et al. 2008, 2009)—although there is no doubt that certain preciosities (pseudocloisonné mirrors, copper bells, scarlet macaws—and now chocolate [Crown and Hurst 2009]) did come into the Southwest from west Mexico (Vokes and Gregory 2007; Wilcox 1986a, 1986b, 2002; Wilcox et al. 2008, 2009).

To engage in "population thinking" about the archaeological history of American Indians necessitates a methodological pivot from the logic of an entity and its qualities (a labeling game) to the logic of relations (Wilcox 2005a), in which it is the interaction of individuals and social groups defined on multiple spatial scales that is to be measured. By redefining the Hohokam culture as a regional system, for example (Wilcox 1979, 1980, 1987; Wilcox and Sternberg 1983), the interaction of neighboring populations sharing the use of red-on-buff pottery became a focus of attention, and how their social, economic, and political relations evolved became the subject of inquiry. This methodological perspective was soon extended to an examination of and comparison with the Chacoan (Crown and Judge 1991) and Casas Grandes (Schaafsma and Riley 1999) "worlds," to a comparison of the American Southwest and Southeast (Neitzel 1999), and, more recently, to Mogollon populations (Gregory and Wilcox 2007). Today, the book *Crucible of Pueblos* (Wilshusen et al. 2012) applies the logic of relations to the emergence of true villages of 100+ people in the northern Southwest in ways that fundamentally contribute to world archaeology and set a new standard for social archaeology in the Southwest.[2]

Earlier, in the Hohokam case, studies of the microcosms of individual buildings such as the Casa Grande (Wilcox and Shenk 1977) and individual settlements such as Snaketown (Haury 1976; Wilcox et al. 1981; Figure 20.2) and the Valencia Vieja site (Wallace 2003) led to a recognition of repetitive patterns of central plazas with extralarge houses oriented to them (see also Cable and Doyel 1987; Figure 20.3) and the identification of the domains of households now called "courtyard groups" (Howard 1985) and spatial aggregates of them forming suprahousehold groups and residential precincts within Hohokam settlements (Wilcox 1991b; Wilcox et al. 1990). On a regional scale, the distribution of the public ritual features once thought to be "ball courts" (Haury 1937; but see Wilcox et al. 2008) is inferred to indicate networks of intra- and intervillage interactions (Figure 20.4) that modern "transactional" ceramic studies are showing had profound economic implications throughout the Phoenix Basin core area of the system (Abbott 2000, 2012; Abbott et al. 2007).

David Doyel's (1981) concept of Hohokam "irrigation communities" soon led to the recognition that multiple villages often were linked together in such communities (Gregory and Nials 1985; cf. Fish 1999; see also Turney 1929). Furthermore, the clustering of large Hohokam villages along the Lower Verde River in the 1000s CE, centered on the extralarge site of Azatlan, led Doyel and Crary (1996) to infer that these villages were politically integrated into a common polity. The abrupt

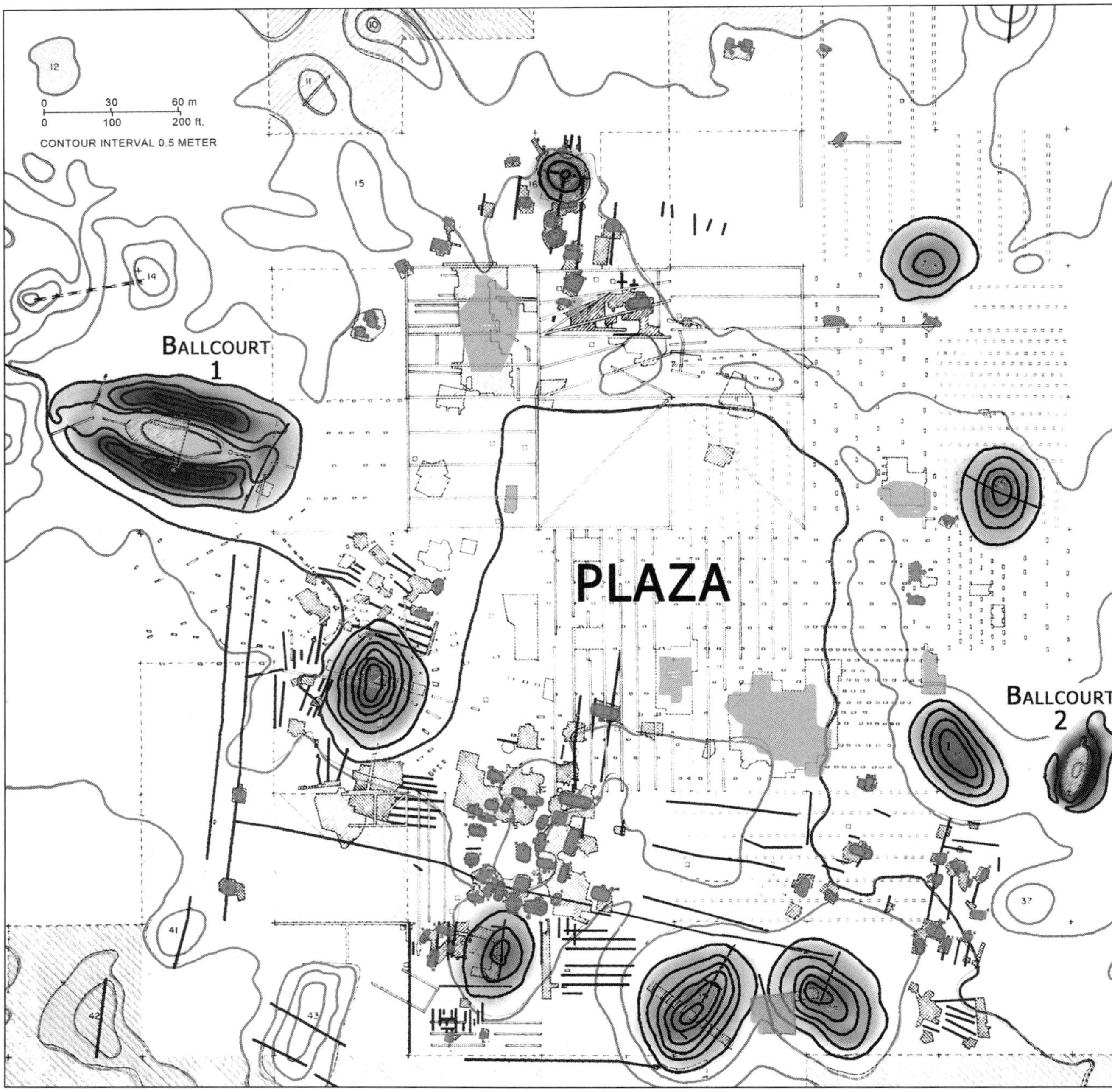

FIGURE 20.2. Snaketown site structure (after Haury 1976; Wilcox et al. 1981).

depopulation of these villages by about 1100 CE (Canouts 1975) and the sharp increase of population in the upper part of the Lower Salt River valley at that time, together with the marked clustering of villages along that river during the Classic period of 1100–1380 CE and the clear size hierarchy in the investment in civic-ceremonial features called "platform mounds" (Doelle et al. 1995; Gregory 1988), support a hypothesis that the whole Lower Salt Valley during the Classic period was politically integrated into a common polity (Figure 20.5), which, at its height, served an estimated 12,000–15,000 people (Wilcox et al. 2008, 2009). A wide buffer zone that emerged by 1100 CE, differentiating the Phoenix Basin Hohokam from their neighbors (Figure 20.6), is cited as further support for this inference.

The Hohokam political system in the Phoenix Basin was arguably ideologically structured by a dual organization marked by turquoise-encrusted emblems of office (Wilcox 2003): raptorial bird (sky/sun) and toad (earth/moon) symbols (Figure 20.7; see also Millbrath 1999 for the connection between toads and the moon). The fact that the two by-far largest platform mounds (Pueblo Grande and Mesa Grande [Howard 2006]) are located at the head of the two macrocanal systems in the valley and are only 8 air miles apart appears to support these inferences (Wilcox et al. 2008, 2009).[3]

A brief consideration of one other example further illustrates the application of the logic of relations to the study of Southwestern archaeology. By "drilling down" to the facts now in

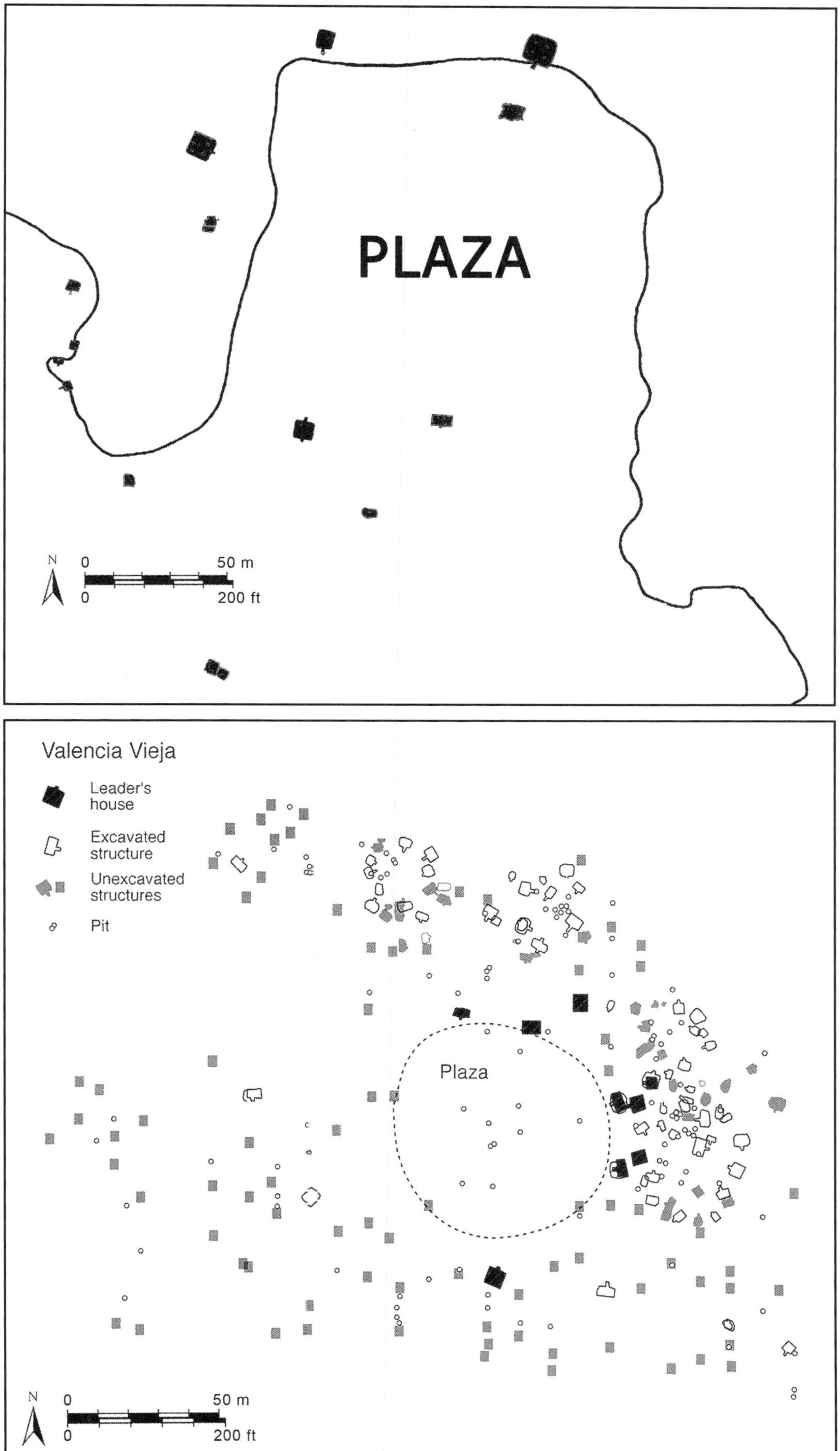

FIGURE 20.3. (a) Snaketown central plaza, with Vahki houses (after Haury 1976; Wilcox et al. 1981); (b) Valencia Vieja site, with early large houses around a central plaza (after Wallace 2003).

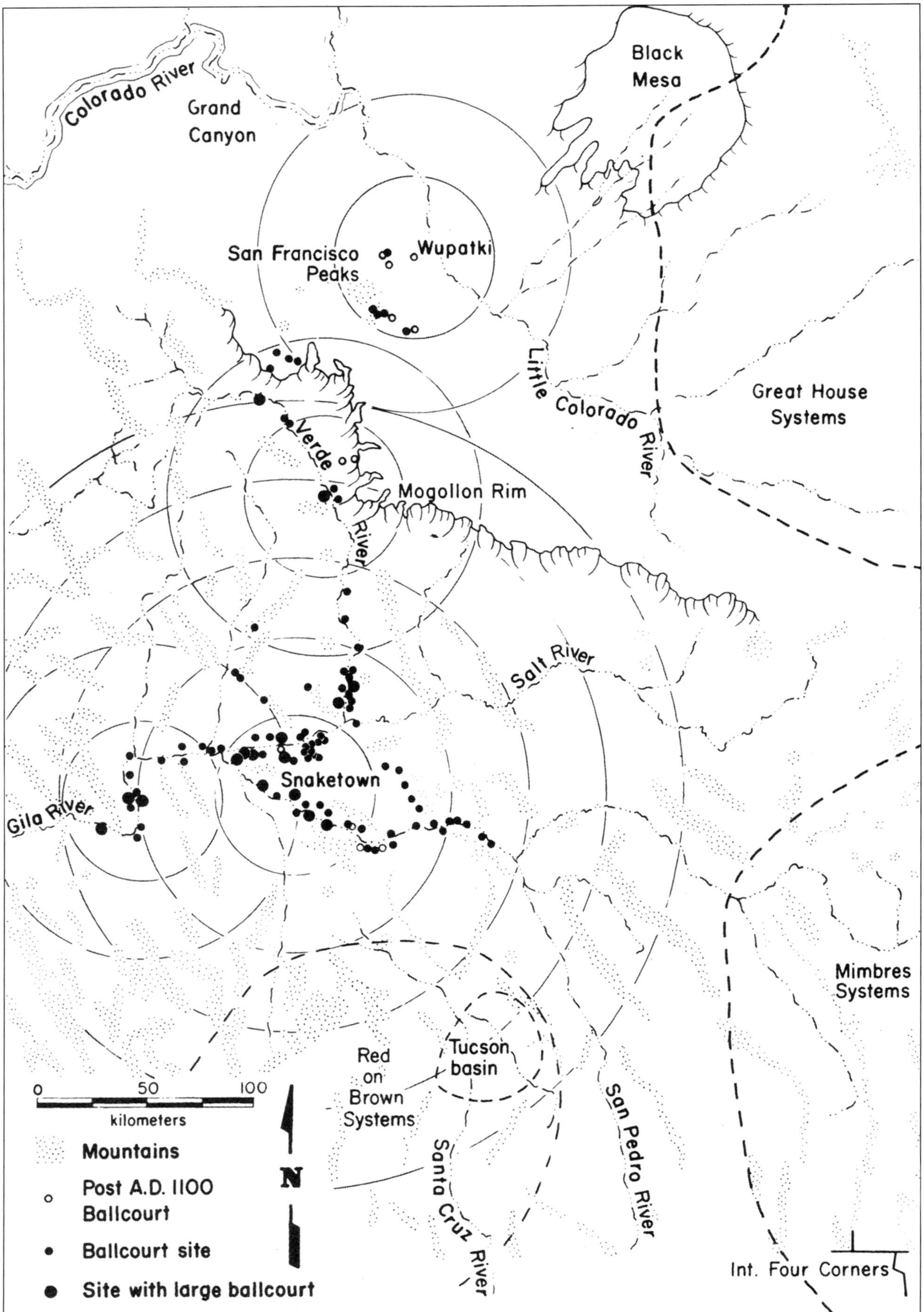

FIGURE 20.4. Hohokam ball court network ca. 1000–1150 CE (after Wilcox 1999).

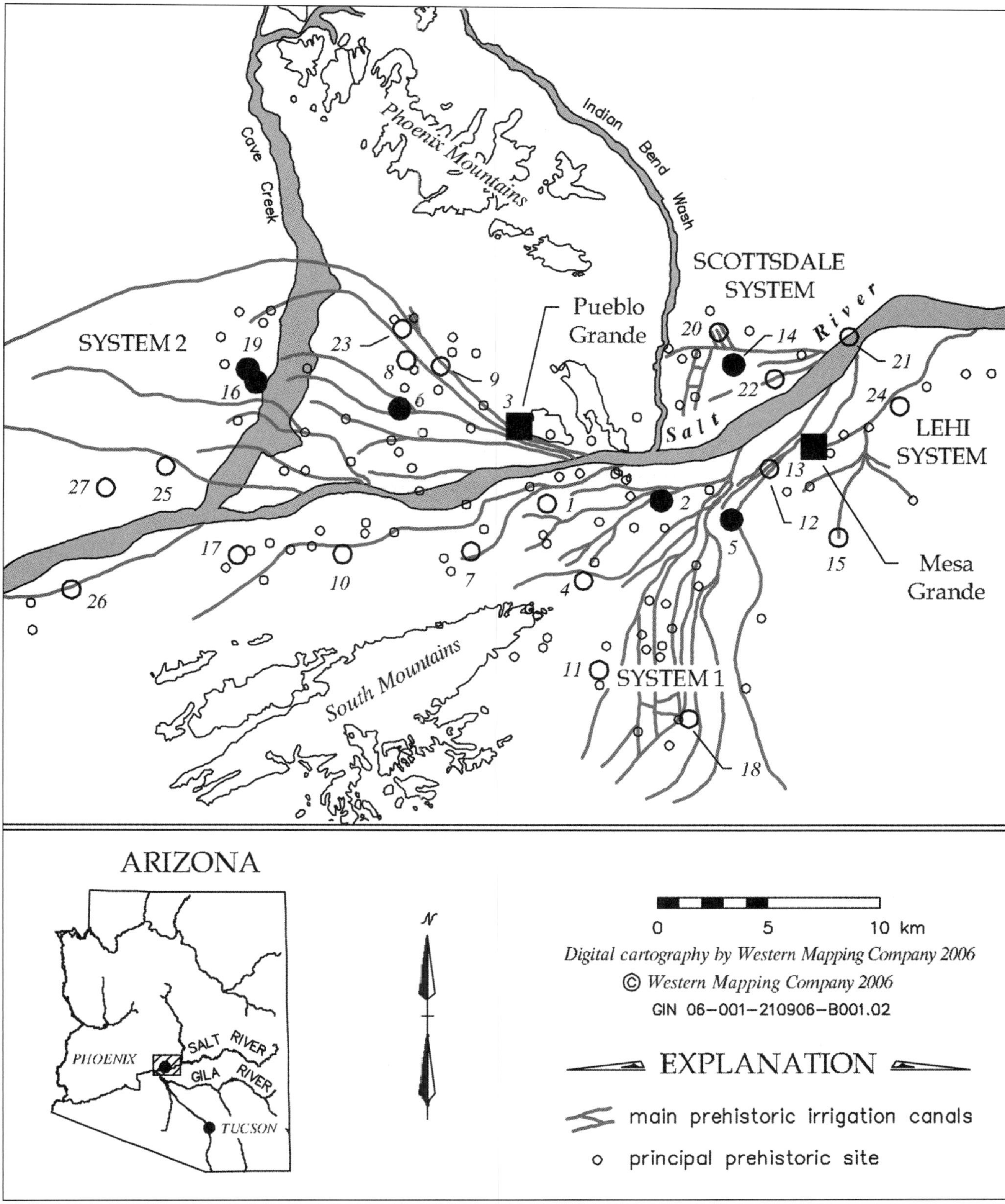

FIGURE 20.5. Classic period Hohokam canal systems and sites ca. 1300 CE (after Wilcox et al. 2008).

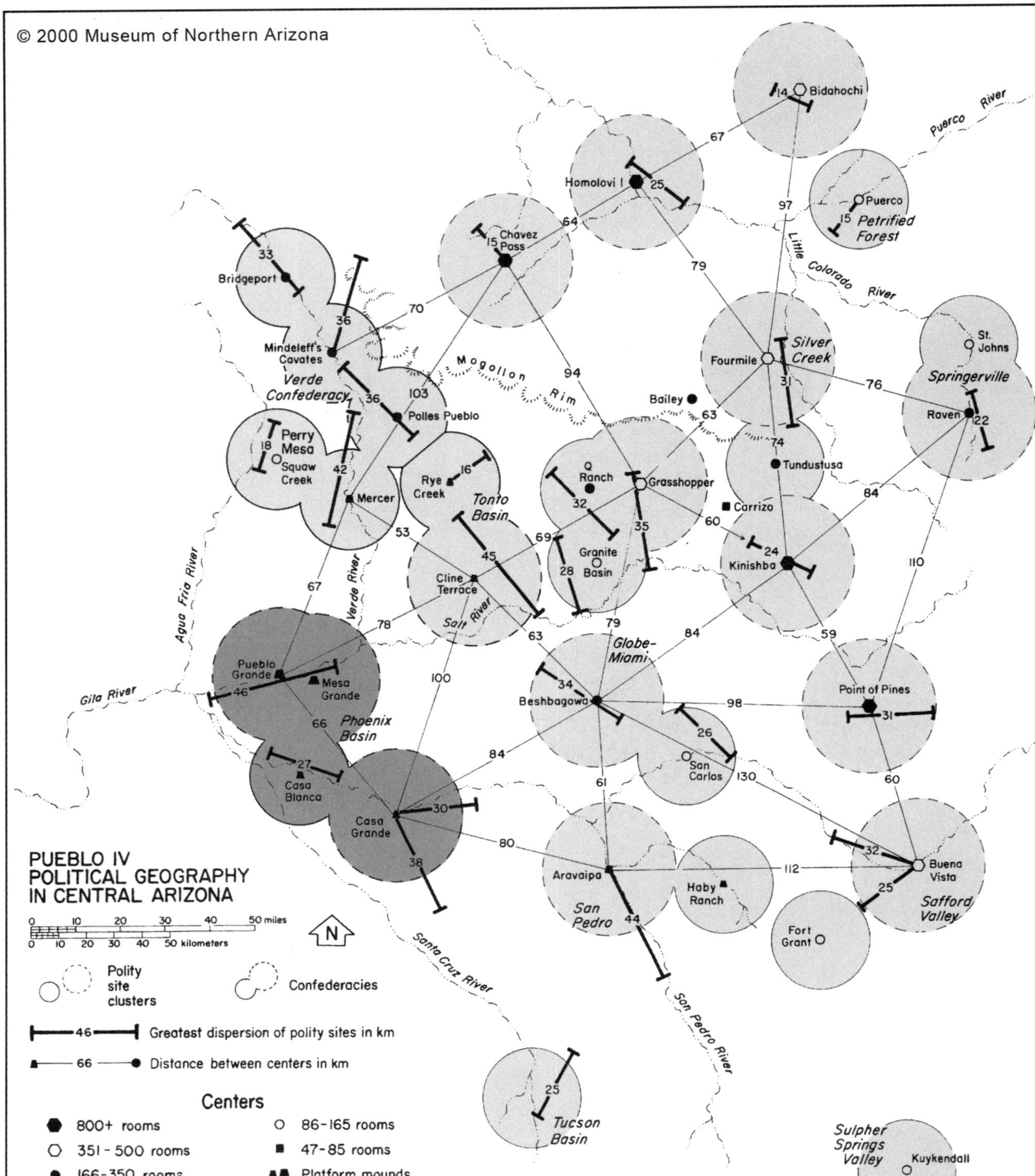

FIGURE 20.6. Site clusters in central and southern Arizona ca. 1300–1350 CE (after Wilcox et al. 2001).

evidence about the age and size of Chacoan "great houses" and their distribution, a computerized geographic information system can be constructed that produces many significant patterns (Wilcox 2005b), eight of which are mentioned here:

1. A regional system emerged in the early 900s CE that became more widespread and internally complex over the next 300 years (Figure 20.8).
2. The distinct cluster of great houses in and immediately around Chaco Canyon (the "Chaco Core Community") continued throughout to have the greatest "investment" in great house construction as measured by floor area (Figure 20.9).
3. The expansion of this regional system into the Totah area of the Animas–La Plata–San Juan drainages was sudden, late,

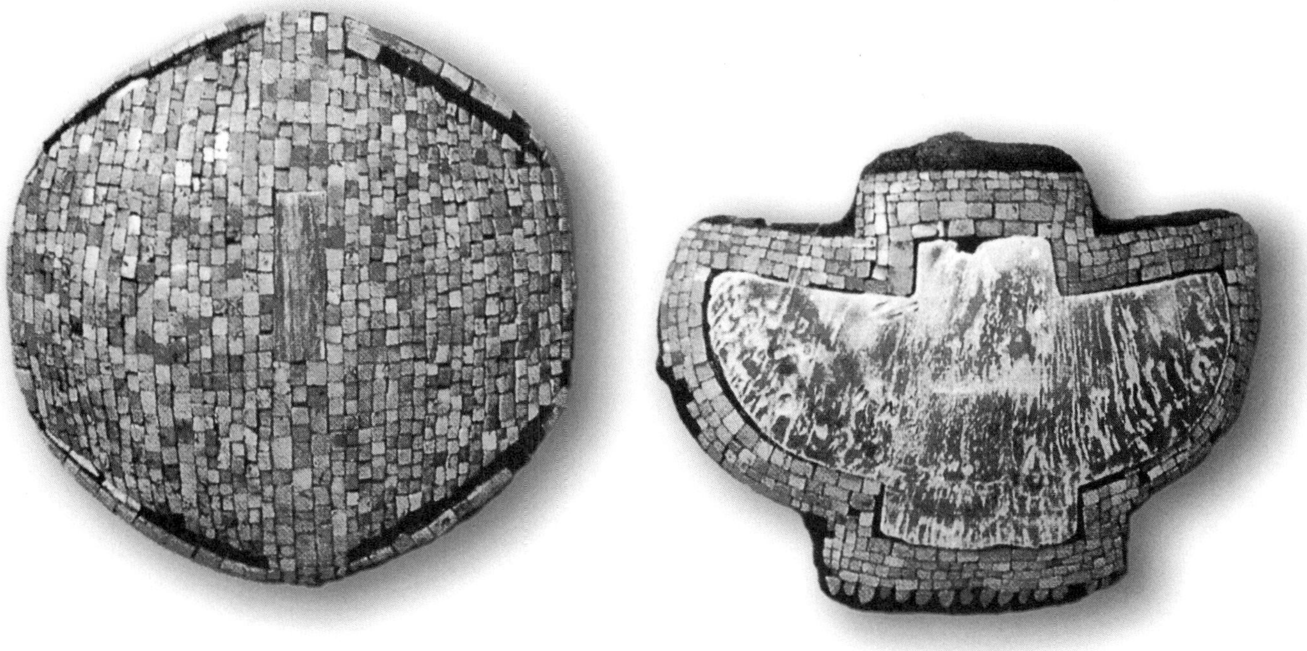

FIGURE 20.7. Turquoise-encrusted toad and raptorial bird (after Wilcox et al. 2008).

and marked by the construction of several of the largest great houses, whose total investment was immediately larger than the total investment of the earlier Puerco of the West or Red Rock Valley subsystems (Figures 20.8c–d and 20.9).

4. Only one great house (Chimney Rock) was built in the highlands east of the San Juan Basin (Malville 2004; Malville and Matlock 1993), and a wide buffer zone intervened between it and its allied Largo-Gallina populations (see Simpson 2008; Figure 20.10) and the Chaco Core Community (Dew 2003).
5. The establishment of the Salmon Great House in the Totah in 1088–1094 CE (Figures 20.8c and 20.10a) placed it on the western edge of the buffer zone with the Largo-Gallina highlanders, protecting the La Plata and San Juan great houses to the west from incursion.
6. Salmon, when it was first built, was the fifth-largest great house (the first large one outside of Chaco Canyon), and its moment of construction occurred during a lull of construction in the Chaco Core Community (Figure 20.11).
7. The construction of the Aztec complex in the Totah (Figure 20.8d) correlates with a second surge of construction in Chaco Canyon (Wilcox 1999; Figure 20.11) and the depopulation of Chimney Rock and its Largo-Gallina populations north of the San Juan River by about 1125 CE (Eddy 1977; Figure 20.10b).
8. Bis sa'ani, constructed as a likely fortress (Figure 20.12) on the northeastern edge of the Chaco Core Community, ca. 1130–1140 CE (Doyel et al. 1984), faced the enduring Largo-Gallina highlanders, just as Pueblo Pintado had since 1060 CE.

These findings support a model of Chacoan political evolution (Wilcox 1999, 2005b, 2010a) in which the Chaco Core Community became an integrated polity that exacted tribute from its neighbors, deliberately expanded into the well-watered Totah region as a political act, drove out the Chimney Rock upstart and forced the redeployment of its Largo-Gallina allies by about 1125 CE, and expanded internally again in the early 1100s CE. This lasted until its encirclement by smaller but similarly organized polities (Figure 20.13) forced its collapse by 1200–1225 CE, resulting in the general dispersion of the old Chacoan-world populations into emergent centers to the southwest (Hopi), south (Zuni), and east (Puerco of the East and Rio Grande [see Boyer et al. 2010]; Figure 20.14). The construction of the "Coalescent Communities Database" (Wilcox et al. 2007) has allowed us to pursue the demographic and political questions of what happened after the Chacoan demise (Gregory and Wilcox 2007; Wilcox 2007; Wilcox et al. 2006), but further elaboration of that story must be left to another time. *Leaving Mesa Verde* (Kohler et al. 2010) provides an excellent place to begin such an inquiry.

For now, I simply suggest that behavioral inferences based on observed relationships in the archaeological record are sufficiently robust to allow us to construct testable models of human social systems in the American Southwest on multiple scales of interaction that define a new narrative of American Indian history. "Onward!" as Don Fowler would say.

a

b

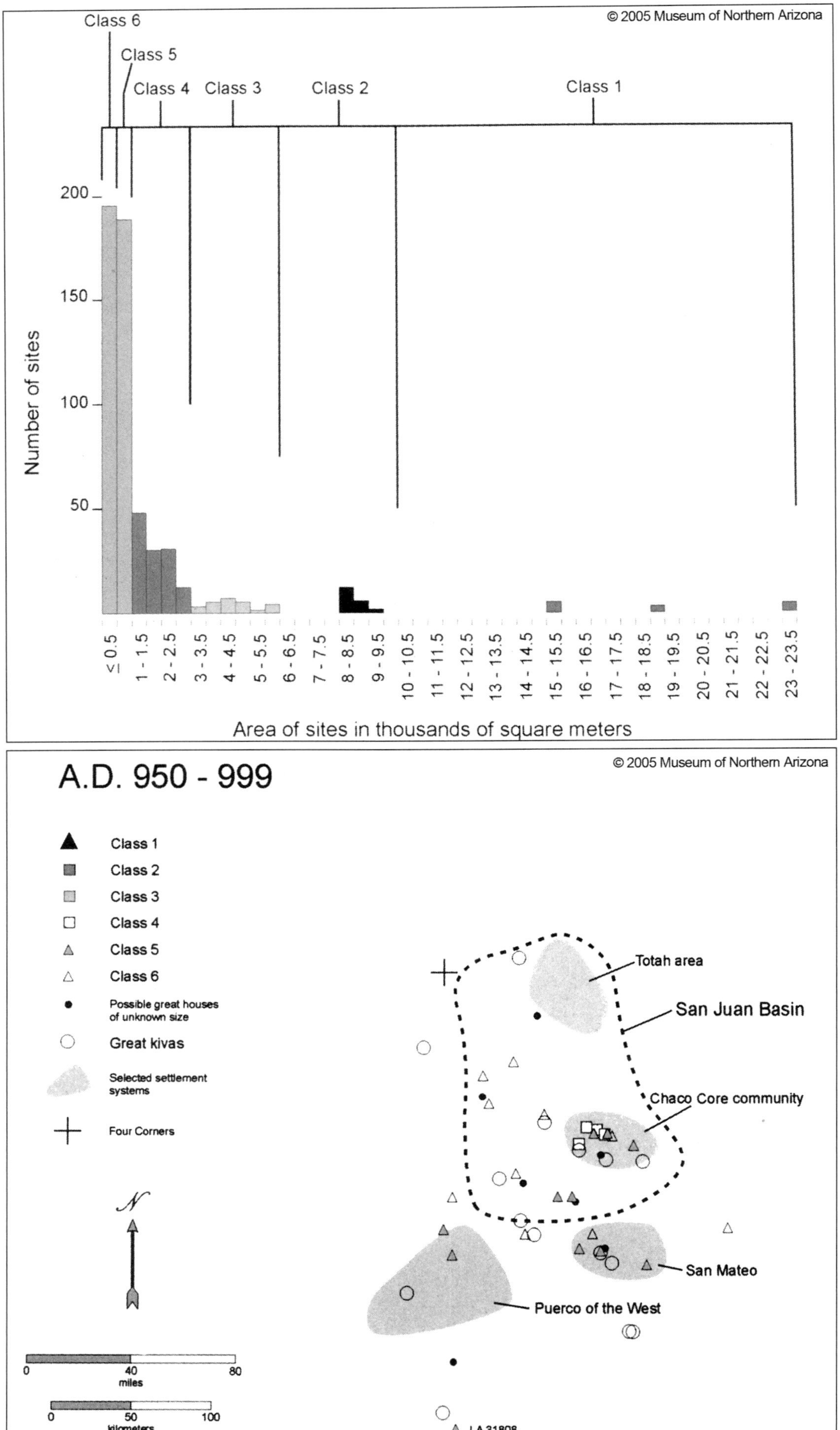

FIGURE 20.8. (a) Histogram of Chacoan great house floor areas; (b) Chacoan world, 950–999 CE; (c) Chacoan world, 1050–1074 CE; (d) Chacoan world, 1100–1149 CE (after Wilcox 2005).

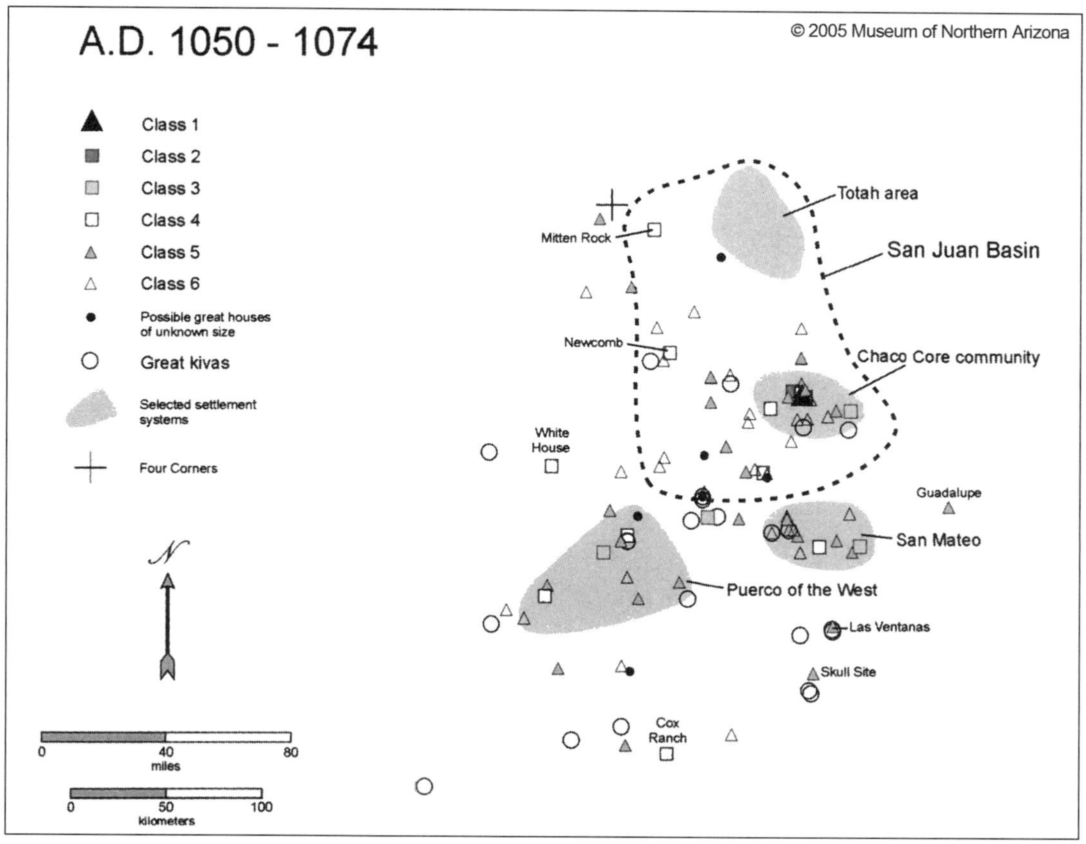
A.D. 1050 - 1074
© 2005 Museum of Northern Arizona
Class 1
Class 2
Class 3
Class 4
Class 5
Class 6
Possible great houses of unknown size
Great kivas
Selected settlement systems
Four Corners
N
0
40
80
miles
0
50
100
kilometers
Totah area
San Juan Basin
Mitten Rock
Newcomb
Chaco Core community
White House
Guadalupe
San Mateo
Puerco of the West
Las Ventanas
Skull Site
Cox Ranch

c

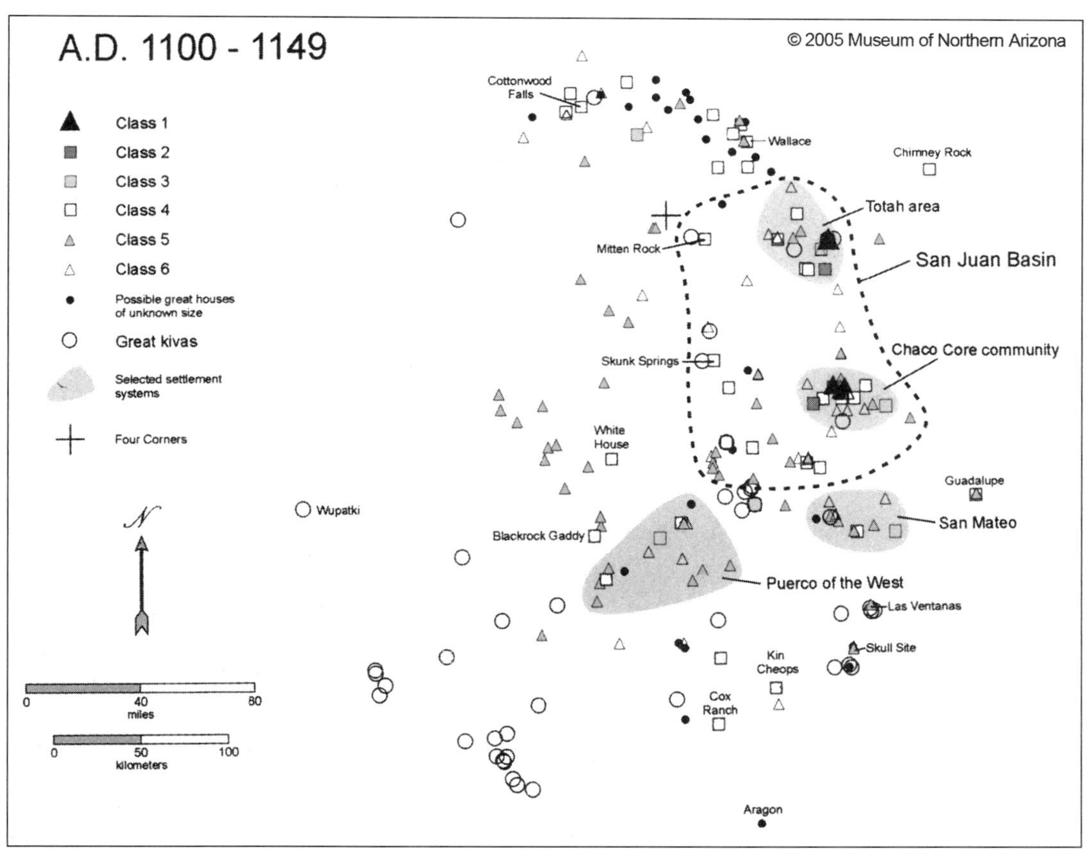
A.D. 1100 - 1149
© 2005 Museum of Northern Arizona
Class 1
Class 2
Class 3
Class 4
Class 5
Class 6
Possible great houses of unknown size
Great kivas
Selected settlement systems
Four Corners
N
0
40
80
miles
0
50
100
kilometers
Cottonwood Falls
Wallace
Chimney Rock
Totah area
Mitten Rock
San Juan Basin
Skunk Springs
Chaco Core community
White House
Wupatki
Guadalupe
San Mateo
Blackrock Gaddy
Puerco of the West
Las Ventanas
Skull Site
Kin Cheops
Cox Ranch
Aragon

d

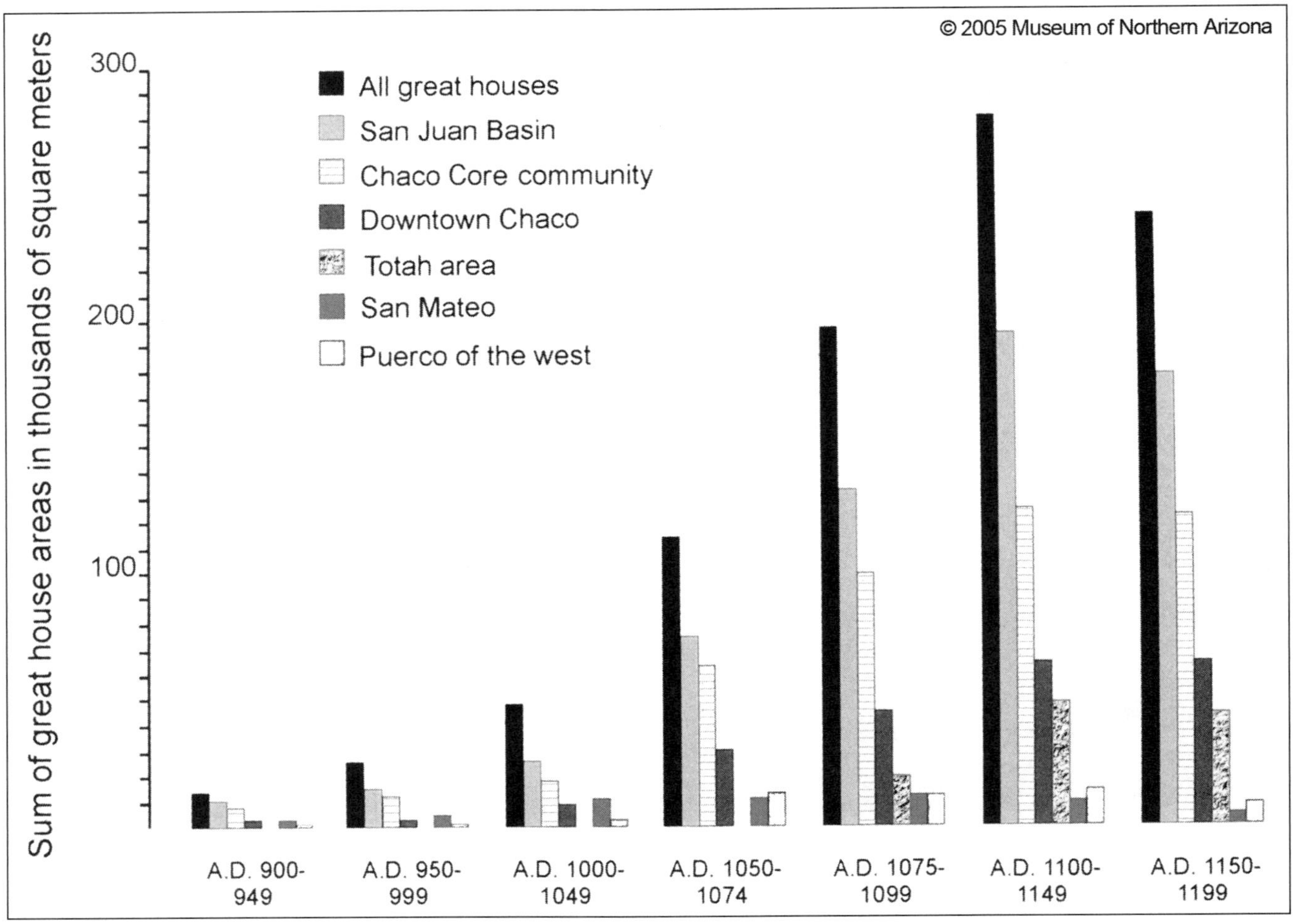

FIGURE 20.9. Histogram of selected subregions of the Chacoan world, with cumulative floor areas.

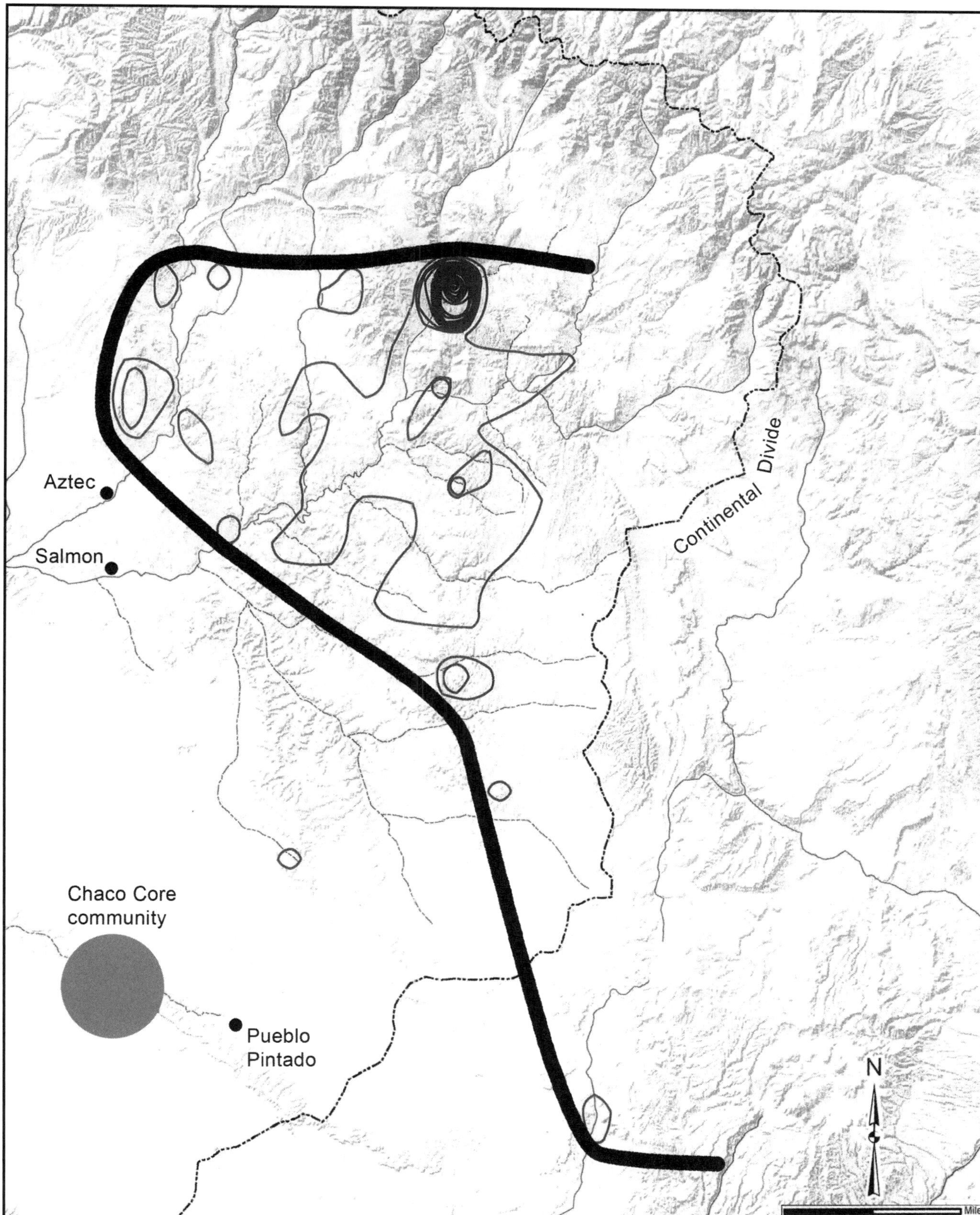

FIGURE 20.10a. Largo-Gallina populations and boundary with the Chacoan world: (a) ca. 1095–1125 CE; (b) ca. 1125–1200 CE (after Simpson 2010; Wilcox 2010).

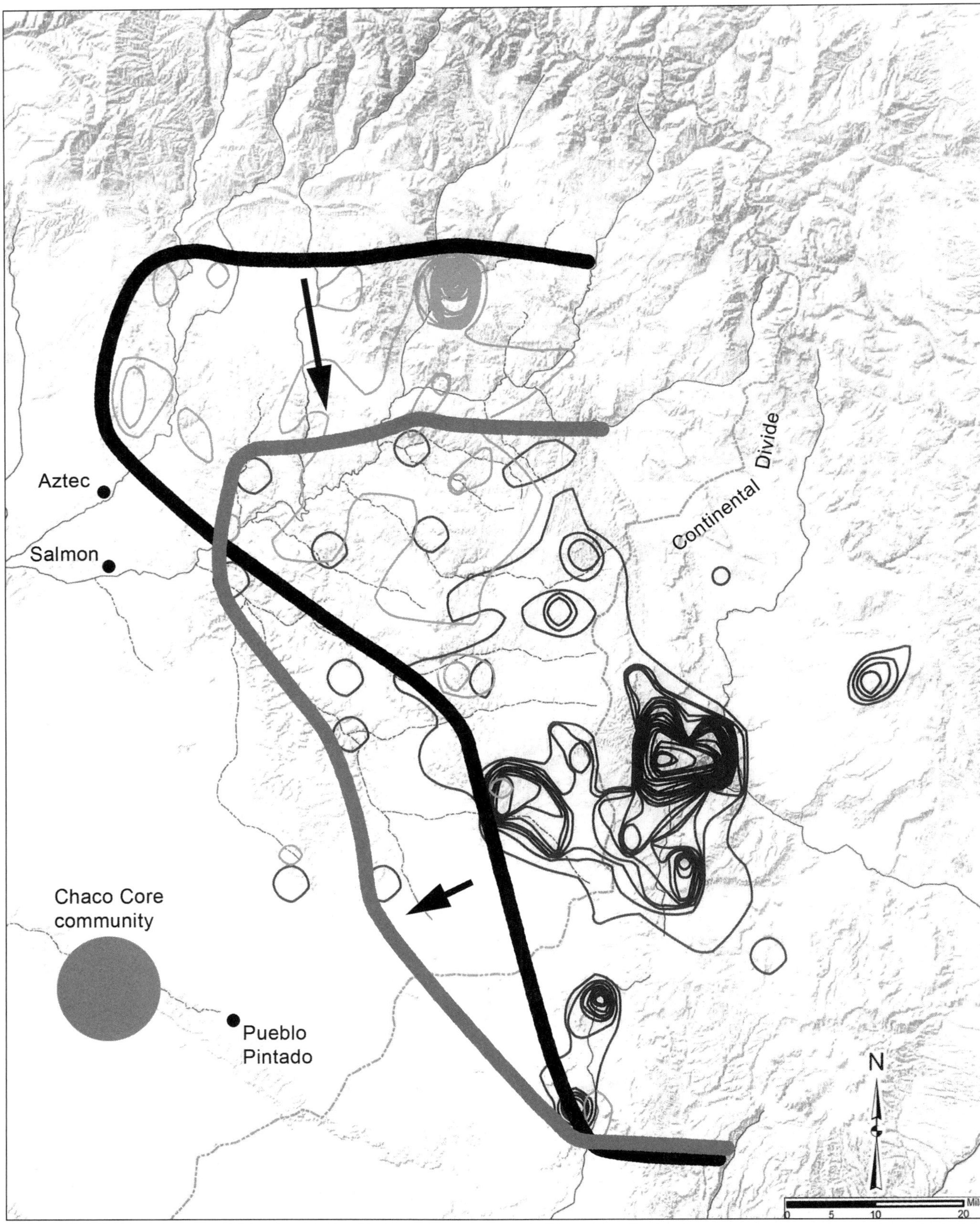

FIGURE 20.10b. Largo-Gallina populations and boundary with the Chacoan world: (a) ca. 1095–1125 CE; (b) ca. 1125–1200 CE (after Simpson 2010; Wilcox 2010).

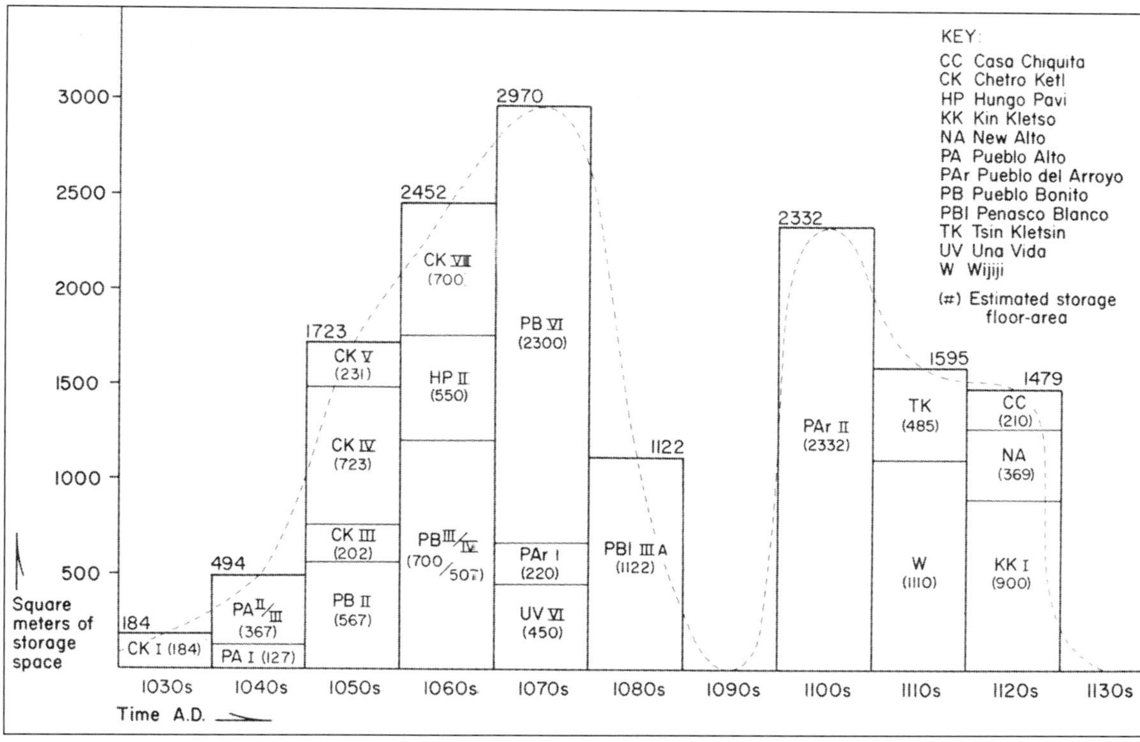

FIGURE 20.11. Histogram of major construction events in Chaco Canyon, ca. 1030–1130 CE (after Wilcox 1999).

FIGURE 20.12. Pueblo Bis sa'ani (photo by David R. Wilcox).

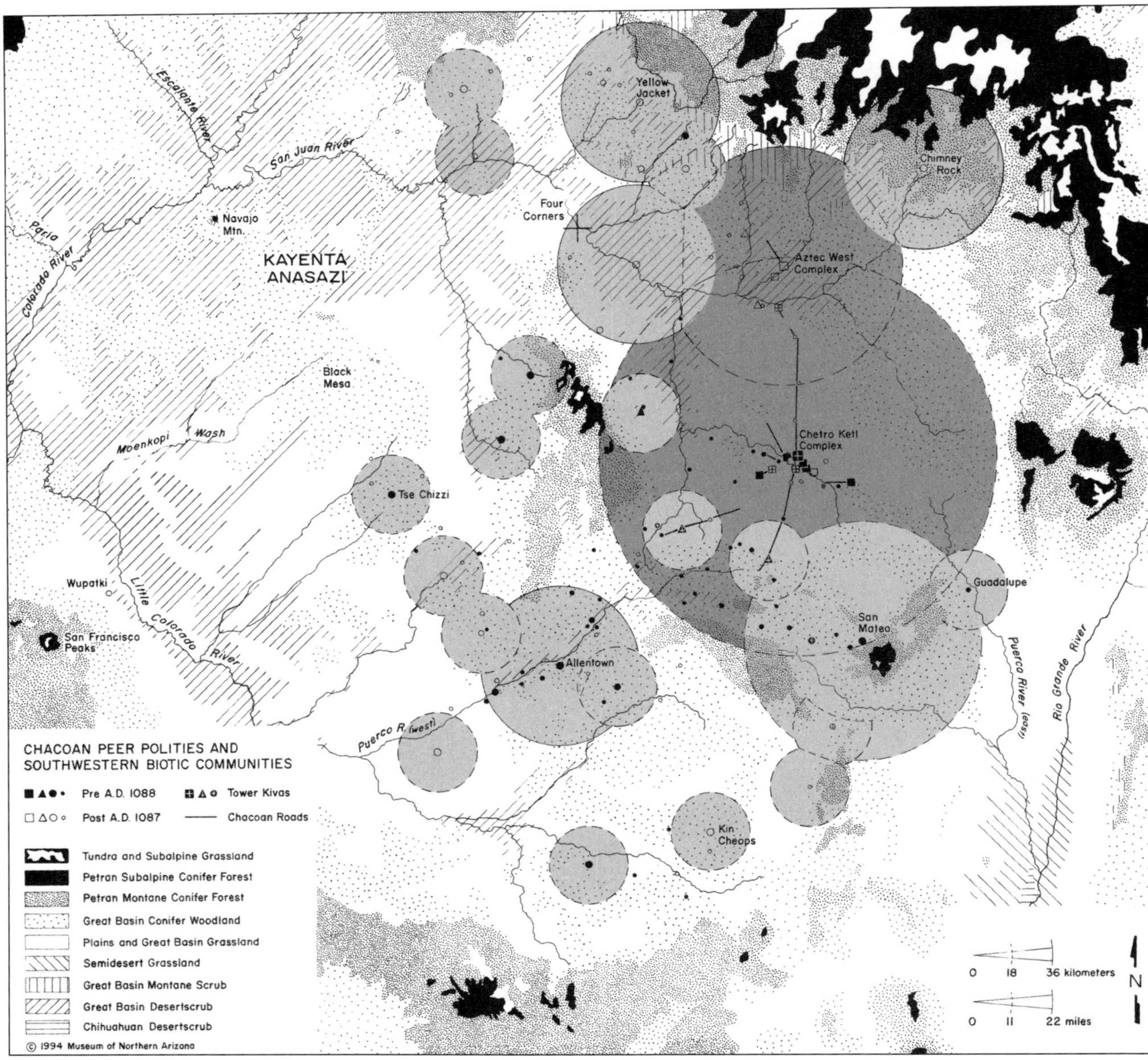

FIGURE 20.13. Chacoan world in relation to major biotic zones (after Wilcox).

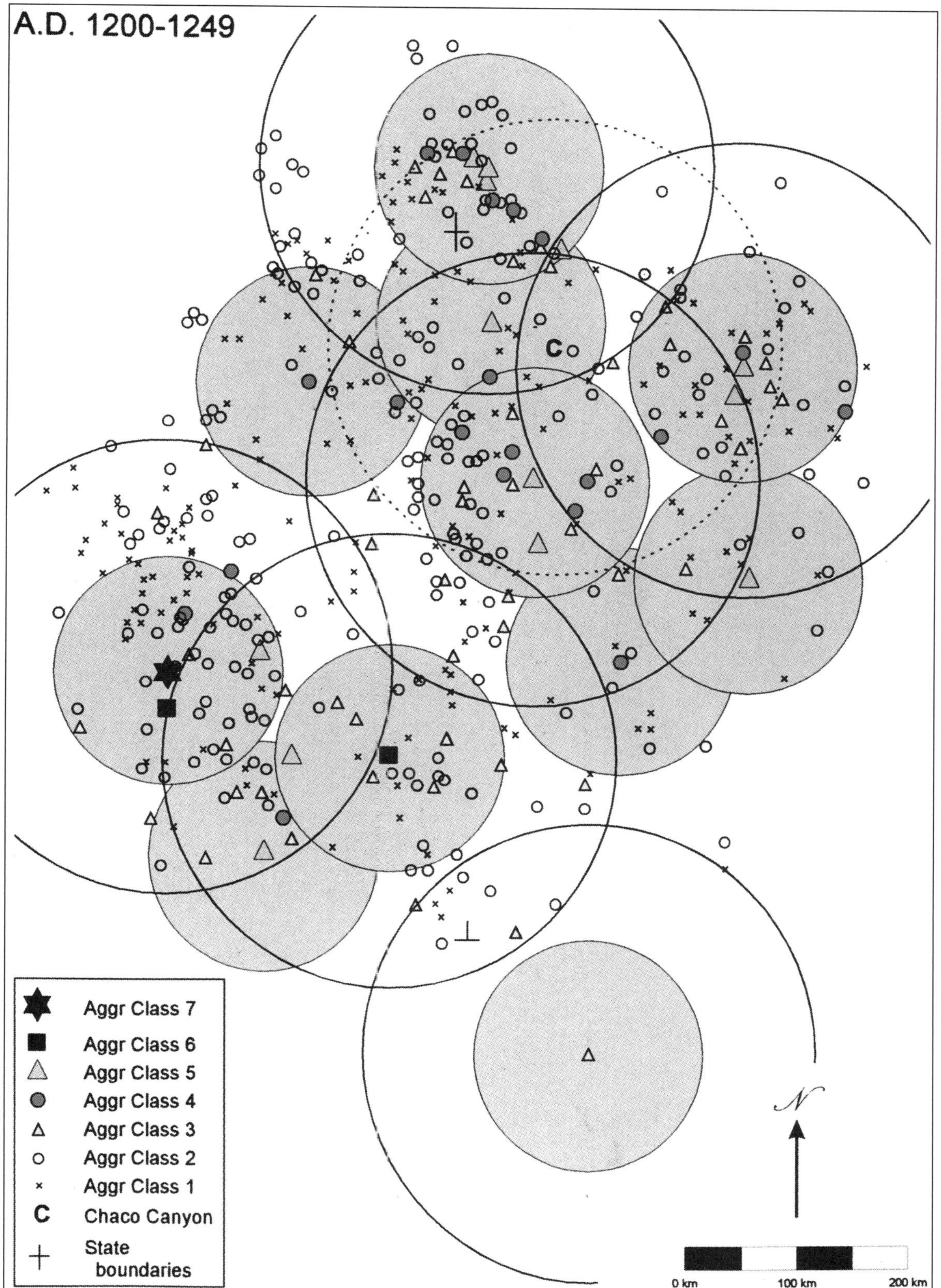

FIGURE 20.14. Distribution of "catchment commun t es" in the North American Southwest ca. 1200–1249 CE (after Wilcox et al. 2007).

Acknowledgments

Thanks go to James Snead, Joel Janetski, and Nancy Parezo for inviting me to participate in the Fowler festschrift. I have enjoyed many collaborative projects with Don Fowler and greatly appreciate his ever present generosity and good cheer. For preparation of the figures, thanks go to Jodi Griffith, Museum of Northern Arizona, and both Daniel Boone and Ryan Belnap, Bilby Research Center, Northern Arizona University. I want to thank my old friend Anthony Ranere for calling my attention to his important work at the Xihuatoxtla Shelter in Guerrero, Mexico. Dennis Gilpin added greatly to the database on which the Chaco maps are based. Special thanks go to Michael Bremer for spending memorable days showing both me and members of the Verde Valley Archaeology Society large Jemez sites and the Largo-Gallina sites in the Llaves Valley. I am grateful to Donna Massouh for inviting me to be a discussant at the symposium "The Largo-Gallina: Prehistoric Inhabitants of the American Southwest," which she organized at the 75th Annual Meeting of the Society for American Archaeology, St. Louis, Missouri, April 16, 2010; I learned much from her and all of the participants. For any errors of fact or interpretation, I alone am responsible.

Notes

1. If true, this would mean that the populations that ended up in today's American Southwest already knew these cosmological verities from the beginning and did not have to learn them by diffusion from the emergent high civilizations to the south—indeed, they knew enough already to be skeptical of newfangled ideas coming their way from that source.
2. The long-standing and all-too-widespread practice of many Southwestern archaeologists of calling any settlement, from those with only two pithouses to ones with more than 1,000 rooms, a "village" has prevented them from effectively contributing to social archaeology. The minority view (e.g., Wilcox 1978, 2010b; Wilcox et al. 2007; Wilshusen 1990) of distinguishing among farmsteads or homesteads, hamlets, and villages, so often seen elsewhere in the Americas, now seems to be gaining ground at long last in the Southwest.
3. What has not been adequately explained, as Charles Redman aptly pointed out in 2006 at the dissertation defense of Jerry Howard at Arizona State University, Tempe, is what changes happened organizationally during the 300 years between 1100 and 1400 CE, during all of which time the Salt River Hohokam may have been politically integrated in some way.

References Cited

Abbott, David R.

2000 *Ceramics and Community Organization Among the Hohokam.* University of Arizona Press, Tucson.

2012 Advances in Hohokam Ceramic Research. http://www.youtube.com/watch?v=mHOaH_z1ZMQ.

Abbott, David R., Alexa M. Smith, and Emiliano Gallaga

2007 Ballcourts and Ceramics: The Case for Hohokam Marketplaces in the Arizona Desert. *American Antiquity* 72(3):461–484.

Andrewartha, H. G., and L. C. Birch

1970 *Distribution and Abundance of Animals.* University of Chicago Press, Chicago.

Bandelier, Adolph F.

1892 *Final Report of Investigations Among the Indians of the Southwestern United States, Pt. II.* Papers of the Archaeological Institute of America, American Series Vol. 4. Cambridge.

Bellwood, Peter

2005 *The First Farmers, the Origins of Agricultural Societies.* Blackwell Publishing, Malden, Massachusetts.

Boyer, Jeffrey L., James L. Moore, Steven A. Lakatos, Nancy J. Aiken, C. Dean Wilson, and Eric Blinman

2010 Remodeling Immigration: A Northern Rio Grande Perspective on Depopulation, Migration, and Donation-Side Models. In *Leaving Mesa Verde: Peril and Change in the Thirteenth-Century Southwest*, edited by Timothy A. Kohler, Mark D. Varien, and Aaron M. Wright, pp. 285–323. Amerind Studies in Archaeology Vol. 5. University of Arizona Press, Tucson.

Cable, John S., and David E. Doyel

1987 Pioneer Period Village Structure and Settlement Pattern in the Phoenix Basin. In *The Hohokam Village: Site Structure and Organization*, edited by David E. Doyel, pp. 21–70. American Association for the Advancement of Science, Glenwood Springs, Colorado.

Canouts, Veletta (assembler)

1975 *An Archaeological Survey of the Orme Reservoir.* Arizona State Museum Archaeological Series No. 92. University of Arizona, Tucson.

Colton, Harold S.

1918 Geography of Certain Ruins near the San Francisco Mountains, Arizona. *Geographical Society of Philadelphia Bulletin* 16(2):37–60.

Crown, Patricia L., and W. Jeffrey Hurst

2009 Evidence of Cacao Use in the Prehispanic American Southwest. *Proceedings of the National Academy of Sciences* 106:2110–2113.

Crown, Patricia L., and James Judge (editors)

1991 *Chaco and Hohokam: Prehistoric Regional Systems in the American Southwest.* School of American Research Press, Santa Fe, New Mexico.

Dean, Jeffrey S., Robert C. Euler, George J. Gumerman, Fred Plog, Richard H. Hevly, and Thor N. V. Karlstrom

1985 Human Behavior, Demography, and Paleoenvironment on the Colorado Plateau. *American Antiquity* 50:537–554.

Dew, Margaret A.

2003 A Pueblo II and III Buffer Zone Between the Chaco and Gallina Areas of Northwest New Mexico. *Artifact* 41:65–78.

Diehl, Michael W. (editor)

2005 *Subsistence and Resource Use Strategies of Early Agricultural Communities in Southern Arizona.* Anthropological Papers No. 34. Center for Desert Archaeology, Tucson.

Di Peso, Charles C.

1974 *Casas Grandes: A Fallen Trading Center of the Gran Chichimeca*, Vols. 1–3. Amerind Foundation No. 9. Dragoon, Arizona.

Doelle, William H., David A. Gregory, and Henry D. Wallace

1995 Classic Period Platform Mound Systems in Southern Arizona. In *The Roosevelt Community Development Study: New Perspectives on Tonto Basin Prehistory*, edited by Mark D. Elson, Miriam T. Stark, and David A. Gregory, pp. 385–440. Anthropological Papers No. 15. Center for Desert Archaeology, Tucson.

Doyel, David E.

1981 *Late Hohokam Prehistory in Southern Arizona.* Contributions in Archaeology No. 2. Gila Press, Scottsdale.

Doyel, David E., Cory D. Breternitz, and Michael P. Marshall

1984 Chacoan Community Structure: Bis sa'ani Pueblo and the

Chaco Halo. In *Recent Research on Chaco Prehistory*, edited by W. James Judge and John D. Schelberg, pp. 37–54. Reports of the Chaco Center No. 8. Division of Cultural Research, National Park Service, Albuquerque.

Doyel, David E., and Jeffrey S. Dean (editors)

2006 *Environmental Change and Human Adaptation in the Ancient American Southwest*. University of Utah Press, Salt Lake City.

Eddy, Frank

1977 *Archaeological Investigations at Chimney Rock Mesa: 1970–1972*. Memoirs of the Colorado Archaeological Society No. 1. Boulder.

Fiedel, Stuart J.

2002 Initial Human Colonization of the Americas: An Overview of the Issues and the Evidence. *Radiocarbon* 44:407–436.

Fish, Suzanne K.

1999 How Complex Were the Southwestern Great Towns' Polities. In *Great Towns and Regional Polities in the American Southwest and Southeast*, edited by Jill E. Neitzel, pp. 45–58. University of New Mexico Press, Albuquerque.

Fowler, Don D.

2000 *A Laboratory for Anthropology. Science and Romanticism in the North American Southwest, 1846–1930*. University of New Mexico Press, Albuquerque.

Fuller, Dorian Q.

2010 An Emerging Paradigm Shift in the Origins of Agriculture. *General Anthropology* 17(2):1, 8–12.

Golla, Victor

2010 Comment [on Heggarty and Beresford-Jones]. *Current Anthropology* 51(2):184–185.

Gregory, David A. (editor)

1988 *The 1982–1984 Excavations at Las Colinas: The Mound 8 Precinct*. Arizona State Museum Archaeological Series, 162(3). University of Arizona, Tucson.

2001 *Excavations in the Santa Cruz River Floodplain: The Early Agricultural Period Component at Los Pozos*. Anthropological Papers No. 21. Center for Desert Archaeology, Tucson.

Gregory, David A., and Michael W. Diehl

2002 Duration, Continuity, and Intensity of Occupation at a Late Cienega Phase Settlement in the Santa Cruz River Floodplain. In *Traditions, Transitions, and Technologies: Themes in Southwestern Archaeology*, edited by Sarah H. Schlanger, pp. 200–223. University Press of Colorado, Boulder.

Gregory, David A., and Thomas R. McGuire

1982 *Research Design for the Testing of Interstate 10 Corridor Prehistoric and Historic Archaeological Remains Between Interstate 17 and 30th Drive (Group II, Las Colinas)*. Arizona State Museum Archaeological Series, 157. University of Arizona, Tucson.

Gregory, David A., and Fred L. Nials

1985 Observations Concerning the Distribution of Classic Period Platform Mounds. In *Proceedings of the 1983 Hohokam Conference*, edited by Alfred E. Dittert, Jr., and Donald E. Dove, pp. 373–388. Occasional Paper No. 2. Phoenix Chapter, Arizona Archaeological Society, Phoenix.

Gregory, David A., and David R. Wilcox (editors)

2007 *Zuni Origins: Toward a New Synthesis of Southwestern Archaeology*. University of Arizona Press, Tucson.

Gumerman, George J. (editor)

1988 *The Anasazi in a Changing Environment*. School of American Research, Santa Fe, New Mexico.

Haury, Emil W.

1937 Ballcourts. In *Excavations at Snaketown: Material Culture*, by Harold S. Gladwin, Emil W. Haury, E. B. Sayles, and Nora Gladwin, pp. 36–39. Medallion Papers No. XXV. Gila Pueblo, Globe, Arizona.

1976 *The Hohokam: Desert Farmers and Craftsmen*. University of Arizona Press, Tucson.

Heidke, James M., Elizabeth J. Miksa, and Henry D. Wallace

2002 A Petrographic Approach to Sand-Tempered Pottery Provenance Studies: Examples from Two Hohokam Local Systems. In *Ceramic Production and Circulation in the Greater Southwest: Source Determination by INAA and Complementary Mineralogical Investigations*, edited by D. M. Glowacki and H. Neff, pp. 152–178. Monograph No. 44. Cotsen Institute of Archaeology, University of California, Los Angeles.

Hill, Jane

2001 Proto-Uto-Aztecan: A Community of Cultivators in Central Mexico? *American Anthropologist* 103:913–934.

Howard, Jerry B.

1985 Courtyard Groups and Domestic Cycling: A Hypothetical Model of Growth. In *Proceedings of the 1983 Hohokam Symposium, Pt. I*, edited by Alfred E. Dittert, Jr., and Donald E. Dove, pp. 311–326. Phoenix Chapter, Arizona Archaeological Society, Phoenix.

2006 Hohokam Irrigation Communities: A Study of Internal Structure, External Relationships and Sociopolitical Complexity. Unpublished Ph.D. dissertation, Arizona State University, Tempe.

Huckell, Bruce B.

1995 *Of Marshes and Maize: Preceramic Agricultural Settlements in the Cienega Valley, Southeastern Arizona*. Anthropological Papers of the University of Arizona No. 59. University of Arizona Press, Tucson.

Kagan, Robert

2007 *Dangerous Nation: America's Foreign Policy from Its Earliest Days to the Dawn of the Twentieth Century*. Vintage Books, New York.

Kelley, J. Charles, and Ellen Abbott Kelley

1975 An Alternative Hypothesis for the Explanation of Anasazi Culture History. In *Collected Papers in Honor of Florence Hawley Ellis*, edited by Theodore Frisbie, pp. 178–223. Papers of the Archaeological Society of New Mexico No. 2. Albuquerque.

Kidder, Alfred Vincent

1924 *An Introduction to the Study of Southwestern Archaeology*. Papers of the Southwestern Expedition No. 1. Department of Archaeology, Phillips Academy, Andover, Massachusetts.

1936 Speculations on New World Prehistory. In *Essays in Anthropology: Presented to A. L. Kroeber in Celebration of His Sixtieth Birthday, June 11, 1936*, edited by Robert H. Lowie, pp. 143–151. University of California Press, Berkeley.

Kohler, Timothy A., Matt Pier-Glaude, Jean-Pierre Bacquet-Appel, and Brian M. Kemp

2007 The Neolithic Demographic Transition in the U.S. Southwest. *American Antiquity* 73(4):645–669.

Kohler, Timothy A., and Carla Van West

1996 The Calculus of Self-Interest in the Development of Cooperation: Sociopolitical Development and Risk Among the Northern Anasazi. In *Evolving Complexity and Environmental Risk in the Prehistoric Southwest*, edited by Joseph A. Tainter and Bonnie Bagley Tainter, pp. 169–196. Addison-Wesley, New York.

Kohler, Timothy A., Mark D. Varien, and Aaron M. Wright (editors)
2010 *Leaving Mesa Verde: Peril and Change in the Thirteenth-Century Southwest.* University of Arizona Press, Tucson.

Mabry, Jonathan B.
1999 Las Capas and Early Irrigation Farming. *Archaeology Southwest* 13(1):14.

Malville, J. McKim (editor)
2004 *Chimney Rock: The Ultimate Outlier.* Lexington Books, Lanham, Maryland.

Malville, J. McKim, and Gary Matlock (editors)
1993 *The Chimney Rock Archaeological Symposium.* General Technical Report, RM-227. Rocky Mountain Range and Forest Experiment Station, U.S. Department of Agriculture Forest Service, Fort Collins.

Mathien, Frances Joan, and Randall H. McGuire (editors)
1986 *Ripples in the Chichimec Sea.* Southern Illinois University Press, Carbondale.

Mathiowetz, Michael Dean
2011 The Diurnal Path of the Sun: Ideology and Interregional Interaction in Ancient Northwest Mesoamerica and the American Southwest. Unpublished Ph.D. dissertation, Department of Anthropology, University of California, Riverside.

McGuire, Randall H.
1980 The Mesoamerican Connection in the Southwest. *Kiva* 46(1–2):3–38.

Meltzer, David J.
2009 *First Peoples in a New World: Colonizing Ice Age America.* University of California Press, Berkeley.

Merrill, William L., Robert J. Hard, Jonathan B. Mabry, Gayle J. Fritz, Karen R. Adams, John R. Roney, and A. C. MacWilliams
2009 The Diffusion of Maize the Southwestern United States and Its Impact. *Proceedings of the National Academy of Sciences* 106(50), December 15: 21019–21026.

Millbrath, Susan
1999 *Star Gods of the Maya: Astronomy in Art, Folklore and Calendars.* University of Texas Press, Austin.

Neitzel, Jill (editor)
1999 *Great Towns and Regional Polities.* University of New Mexico Press, Albuquerque.

Parezo, Nancy J., and Don D. Fowler
2007 *Anthropology Goes to the Fair: The 1904 Louisiana Purchase Exposition.* University of Nebraska Press, Lincoln.

Piperno, Dolores R., Anthony J. Ranere, Irene Holst, Jose Iriarte, and Ruth Dickau
2009 Starch Grain and Phytolith Evidence for Early Ninth Millennium BP Maize from the Central Balsas River Valley, Mexico. *Proceedings of the National Academy of Sciences* 106(13), March 13: 5019–5024.

Pool, Christopher A.
2007 *Olmec Archaeology and Early Mesoamerica.* Cambridge University Press, Cambridge.

Ranere, Anthony J., Dolores R. Piperno, Irene Holst, Ruth Dickau, and José Iriarte
2009 The Cultural and Chronological Context of Early Holocene Maize and Squash Domestication in the Central Balsas River Valley, Mexico. *Proceedings of the National Academy of Sciences* 106(13), March 13: 5014–5018.

Riley, Carroll L.
2005 *Becoming Aztlan: Mesoamerican Influence in the Greater Southwest, AD 1200–1500.* University of Utah Press, Salt Lake City.

Schaafsma, Curtis F., and Carroll L. Riley (editors)
1999 *The Casas Grandes World.* University of Utah Press, Salt Lake City.

Simpson, David Erik
2008 Architectural Patterning in Residential Structures of the Gallina Phase from Northwestern New Mexico. Unpublished Master's thesis, Department of Anthropology, Prescott College, Prescott.
2010 A Settlement Pattern Analysis of Adaptation and Continuity in the Upper San Juan and Gallina Highlands. Paper presented at "The Largo-Gallina: Prehistoric Inhabitants of the American Southwest" Symposium, 75th Annual Meeting of the Society for American Archaeology, St. Louis, April 16.

Staller, John E., Robert H. Tykot, and Bruce F. Benz
2006 *Histories of Maize: Multi-Disciplinary Approaches to the Prehistory, Linguistics, Biogeography, Domestication, and Evolution of Maize.* Academic Press, New York.

Turney, Omar
1929 *Prehistoric Irrigation in Arizona.* Arizona Historian, Phoenix.

Vokes, Arthur H., and David A. Gregory
2007 Trade and Exchange Networks for Exotic Goods in the American Southwest and Northwest Mexico. In *Zuni Origins: Toward a New Synthesis in Southwestern Archaeology,* edited by David A. Gregory and David R. Wilcox, pp. 318–360. University of Arizona Press, Tucson.

Wallace, Henry D. (editor)
2003 *Roots of Sedentism: Archaeological Excavations at Valencia Vieja, a Founding Village in the Tucson Basin of Southern Arizona.* Anthropological Papers No. 29. Center for Desert Archaeology, Tucson.

Weigand, Phil C., and Acelia García de Weigand
2001 A Macroregional Study of the Relationships Between the Ancient Cultures of the American Southwest and Mesoamerica. In *The Road to Aztlan: Art from a Mythic Homeland,* edited by Virginia Fields and Victor Zamudio-Taylor, pp. 184–195. Los Angeles County Museum of Art, Los Angeles.

Wilcox, David R.
1978 The Theoretical Implications of Fieldhouses. In *Limited Activity and Occupation Sites: A Collection of Conference Papers,* edited by Albert E. Ward, pp. 25–34. Occasional Papers of the Center for Anthropological Studies No. l. Albuquerque.
1979 The Hohokam Regional System. In *An Archaeological Test of Sites in the Gila Butte–Santan Region,* by Glen Rice, David Wilcox, Kevin Rafferty, and James Schoenwetter, pp. 77–116. Arizona State University Anthropological Research Papers No. 18. Tempe.
1980 The Current Status of the Hohokam Concept. In *Current Issues in Hohokam Prehistory: Proceedings of a Conference,* edited by David Doyel and Fred Plog, pp. 236–242. Arizona State University Anthropological Research Papers No. 23. Tempe.
1986a A Historical Analysis of the Problem of Southwestern–Mesoamerican Connections. In *Ripples in the Chichimec Sea,* edited by F. Joan Mathien and Randall H. McGuire, pp. 9–44. Southern Illinois University Press, Carbondale.
1986b The Tepiman Connection: A Model of Southwestern–

Mesoamerican Interactions. In *Ripples in the Chichimec Sea*, edited by F. Joan Mathien and Randall H. McGuire, pp. 135–153. Southern Illinois University Press, Carbondale.

1987 The Evolution of Hohokam Ceremonial Systems. In *Astronomy and Ceremony in the Prehistoric Southwest*, edited by John Carlson and W. James Judge, pp. 149–168. Papers of the Maxwell Museum of Anthropology No. 2. Albuquerque.

1988 Rethinking the Mogollon Concept. *Kiva* 53(2):205–209.

1991a The Mesoamerican Ballgame in the American Southwest. In *The Mesoamerican Ballgame*, edited by Vernon Scarborough and David R. Wilcox, pp. 101–125. University of Arizona Press, Tucson.

1991b Hohokam Social Complexity. In *Chaco and Hohokam: Prehistoric Regional Systems in the American Southwest*, edited by Patricia L. Crown and W. James Judge, pp. 253–276. School of American Research, Santa Fe, New Mexico.

1999 A Peregrine View of Macroregional Systems in the North American Southwest, AD 750–1250. In *Great Towns and Regional Polities*, edited by Jill E. Neitzel, pp. 115–142. University of New Mexico Press, Albuquerque.

2002 The Wupatki Nexus: Chaco–Hohokam–Chumash Connectivity, AD 1150–1225. In *The Archaeology of Contact: Processes and Consequences. Proceedings of the Twenty-Fifth Annual Conference of the Archaeological Association of the University of Calgary*, edited by Kurtis Lesick, Barbara Kulle, Christine Cluney, and Meaghan Peuramaki-Brown, pp. 218–234. Archaeological Association of the University of Calgary, Calgary.

2003 Appendix: Turquoise Encrusted Toads and Raptorial Birds in the North American Southwest. In *Philadelphia and the Development of Americanist Archaeology*, edited by Don D Fowler and David R. Wilcox, pp. 189–193. University of Alabama Press, Tuscaloosa.

2005a Big Issues, New Syntheses. Theme issue, "Big Picture Archaeology," *Plateau* 2(1):8–21.

2005b Things Chaco, a Peregrine Perspective. Theme issue, "Big Picture Archaeology," *Plateau* 2(1):36–55.

2007 Discussion of the Pottery Mound Essays and Some Alternative Proposals. In *New Perspectives on Pottery Mound Pueblo*, edited by Polly Schaafsma, pp. 229–250. University of New Mexico Press, Albuquerque.

2010a Discussion of "The Largo-Gallina: Prehistoric Inhabitants of the American Southwest" Symposium, 75th Annual Meeting of the Society for American Archaeology, St. Louis, April 16.

2010b Previous Research and Culture History Relevant to the Walnut Canyon Study Area and Its National Significance. In *An Assessment of the National Significance of Cultural Resources for the Walnut Canyon Special Resource Study*, by Theodore Neff, Tim Givvs, Kimberly Spur, Kirk C. Anderson, Jason Nez, Bern Carey, and David R. Wilcox, pp. 50–108. Museum of Northern Arizona, Flagstaff.

Wilcox, David R., and Don D. Fowler

2002 The Beginnings of Anthropological Archaeology in the North American Southwest: From Thomas Jefferson to the Pecos Conference. *Journal of the Southwest*, Summer: 121–234.

Wilcox, David R., David A. Gregory, and J. Brett Hill

2007 Zuni in the Puebloan and Southwestern Worlds. In *Zuni Origins: Toward a New Synthesis of Southwestern Archaeology*, edited by David A. Gregory and David R. Wilcox, pp. 165–209. University of Arizona Press, Tucson.

Wilcox, David R., David A. Gregory, J. Brett Hill, and Gary Funkhouser

2006 The Changing Contexts for Warfare in the North American Southwest, AD 1200–1700. In *Papers of the New Mexico Archaeological Society in Honor of Charlotte J. and Theodore R. Frisbie*, edited by Regge N. Wiseman, Thomas C. O'Laughlin, and Cordelia T. Snow, pp. 203–232. Archaeological Society of New Mexico Papers No. 32. Albuquerque.

Wilcox, David R., Jerry B. Howard, and Rueben Nelson

1990 *One Hundred Years of Archaeology at La Ciudad de los Hornos*. Soil Systems Publications in Archaeology No. 16. Phoenix.

Wilcox, David R., Thomas R. McGuire, and Charles Sternberg

1981 *Snaketown Revisited*. Arizona State Museum Archaeological Series No. 155. University of Arizona, Tucson.

Wilcox, David R., Gerald Robertson, Jr., and J. Scott Wood

2001 Organized for War: The Perry Mesa Settlement System and Its Central Arizona Neighbors. In *Deadly Landscapes: Case Studies in Prehistoric Southwestern Warfare*, edited by Glen E. Rice and Steven A. LeBlanc, pp. 141–194. University of Utah Press, Salt Lake City.

Wilcox, David R., and Lynette O. Shenk

1977 *The Architecture of the Casa Grande and Its Interpretation*. Arizona State Museum Archaeological Series No. 115. University of Arizona, Tucson.

Wilcox, David R., and Charles Sternberg

1983 *Hohokam Ballcourts and Their Interpretation*. Arizona State Museum Archaeological Series No. 160. University of Arizona, Tucson.

Wilcox, David R., Phil C. Weigand, J. Scott Wood, and Jerry B. Howard

2008 Cultural Interplay of the American Southwest in the Mexican Northwest. *Journal of the Southwest* 50(2), Summer: 103–206.

2009 *Interactión Cultural Antigua del suroeste americano en el noroeste mexicano*. El Colegio de Michoacán, Zamora.

Williams, Robert A., Jr.

1990 *The American Indian in Western Legal Thought: The Discourses of Conquest*. Oxford University Press, New York.

Wilshusen, Richard H.

1990 Early Villages in the American Southwest: Cross-Cultural and Archaeological Perspectives. Unpublished Ph.D. dissertation, Department of Anthropology, University of Colorado, Boulder.

Wilshusen, Richard H., Gregson Schachner, and James R. Allison (editors)

2012 *Crucible of Pueblos: The Early Pueblo Period in the Northern Southwest*. Monograph No. 71. Cotsen Institute of Archaeology Press, University of California, Los Angeles.

Woodbury, Richard B., and Nathalie F. S. Woodbury

1999 The Rise and Fall of the Bureau of American Ethnology. *Journal of the Southwest* 41(3):283–296.

21

The Role of Nonprofit Organizations in the History of Southwest Archaeology

William H. Doelle

Nonprofit institutions have played major roles in the history of Southwestern archaeology. They were innovators present at the inception of key legal initiatives, they have engaged in substantive research for over a century, and they have helped make the protection of archaeological sites a core archaeological value. Nonprofits have played diverse roles over time, and in recent years increased specialization in nonprofit missions is evident. This chapter explores the early history of nonprofits and traces the entrepreneurial paths that have been taken by nonprofit institutions over time.

Many Southwestern nonprofits are not considered here. One criterion used in selection was that the organization had at least some direct involvement in research. A second criterion was size. For nonprofits that are still in existence at this writing, minimum gross revenue for 2008 of $150,000 was a cutoff. This was established by consulting the publicly accessible Form 990s that nonprofits file with the Internal Revenue Service. This minimum size is large enough to ensure that the organization has permanent professional staff members who pursue the nonprofit's mission. The focus is on organizations actually located in the Southwest, thus major nonprofits such as the American Museum of Natural History (New York City) and the Field Museum (Chicago) that carried out research expeditions in the Southwest are not discussed here. In addition, small nonprofits that implement their missions through volunteers and various state or local archaeological societies are not considered in this review. It is recognized that such organizations play important roles in their respective local, regional, or state contexts. However, the goal here is to consider Southwest-based organizations that have social, cultural, and intellectual impacts on the level of the Southwest as a region and often nationally or globally.

The time depth of private-sector organizations is impressive. It is useful to break nonprofits into three temporal groups. The pioneering nonprofit, the Archaeological Institute of America (AIA), stands alone. It was founded at the end of the 1870s and has persisted to the present as a national organization with regional chapters that focus on knowledge dissemination as well as sponsor research. A second group of nonprofits was established early in the twentieth century, and their local presence and large-scale surveys and excavations greatly advanced the knowledge base about Southwest archaeology. The third group of nonprofits began in the late 1960s, and they all have strong entrepreneurial attributes. Though it is important to note that the surviving early nonprofits all had to go through one or more reinvention phases, they too are now very entrepreneurial. With time there has been a trend toward specialization of function in nonprofits. In this chapter I provide historical overviews of these three groups of organizations, and then I consider five themes: research, funding, public outreach, site protection, and advocacy.

Prelude to America's Antiquities Act

Actions by a tubercular Swede that were interpreted by Americans as a "theft" of the nation's antiquities stimulated initial efforts by both the AIA and academics to develop federal protections for archaeological sites and artifacts. The early exploration of the cliff dwellings in the Mesa Verde area by the Wetherill brothers in the 1880s is well documented (Blackburn 2006; Blackburn and Williamson 1997). Gustaf Nordenskiöld, son of a Swedish baron, excavated at Mesa Verde in 1891 (see Nordenskiöld 1979 [1893]), with assistance from the Wetherills. When finished, he packed up the artifacts and shipped them overseas. The southwestern Colorado community was outraged that these local resources were being taken from them. Nordenskiöld was arrested and held briefly in a Durango, Colorado, jail, but ultimately it was realized that there was no legal basis for controlling what happened to these antiquities (Reynolds and Reynolds 2006:82–85). Despite the attempted intervention, these collections went to Sweden and were later transferred to the National Museum of Finland, where they remain today. What started as a local "theft" soon developed into an effort to pass a federal Antiquities Act, which finally succeeded in 1906.

The AIA: An Early Pioneer in Policy and Research

The pioneer nonprofit in this country was the Archaeological Institute of America. It was founded in 1879 by Harvard University professor Charles Eliot Norton, with 108 people attending its first meeting. While it has transformed dramatically over its existence, the AIA is still an important nonprofit today. The AIA was built on a core philosophical premise that the cultural values of the United States derived from the traditions of ancient Greece and Rome. Thus, the membership promoted direct participation in excavations in the ancient Mediterranean region and provided access to classical archaeology through public lectures they sponsored in the United States. From the outset, there was a professed interest in the archaeology of this country, and from 1880 through 1885 the AIA funded Adolph Bandelier's explorations in the Southwest. The results of that work were published by the AIA in 1892 (Bandelier 1892).

Beyond Bandelier's early research efforts, however, in the United States the AIA focused mostly on national policy issues. Edgar Lee Hewett, a man of remarkable energy, had become a self-trained archaeologist, largely based on summer visits to ruins in the Southwest during his five-year tenure as president of New Mexico Normal College in Las Vegas, New Mexico. When his contract at the college was not renewed, Hewett spent a year at the University of Geneva in Switzerland, where he ultimately earned a doctorate. In fall 1904, Hewett returned to the United States and was employed by the Government Land Office to prepare an important memorandum that summarized the condition of the archaeological sites in the Southwest (Hewett 1904). In 1905, Hewett received the Bowditch Fellowship of the AIA and used both previous and new contacts to play the central role in an archaeological conservation alliance that helped to move a congressional bill forward (Thompson 2000). The Antiquities Act passed Congress and was signed into law by President Theodore Roosevelt on June 8, 1906.

The Antiquities Act was an important step in professionalizing archaeology in the United States. It authorized fines up to $500, imprisonment of no more than 90 days, or both for individuals who excavated or destroyed sites or objects of antiquity on federal lands without a permit. Furthermore, permits would be granted only to qualified institutions, excavating and making collections had to be for the purpose of increasing knowledge, and the results of such work had to go ultimately for permanent preservation in a public museum. It took 15 years to develop an effective response to Nordenskiöld carrying off artifacts from Mesa Verde.

Another key element of the act was the broad language giving the president the authority to proclaim national monuments. Teddy Roosevelt began using that authority, and by the end of his term in January 1909 he had designated 18 national monuments in nine states.

The permitting and penalties elements of the Antiquities Act were largely superseded by the Archaeological Resources Protection Act of 1979, but that act elaborated upon the basic principles outlined in the original Antiquities Act. The ability to proclaim national monuments has been utilized by nearly all subsequent presidents regardless of political affiliation (Harmon et al. 2006; Leshy 1998:83). The effort of the pioneering nonprofit, the AIA, and of Edgar Lee Hewett, in particular, was very much at the heart of creating this basic national policy. As will be considered further below, these early events helped shape the subsequent actions of nonprofit organizations and continue to affect the archaeology of the Southwest.

The Legal Basis for Modern Nonprofits

The Sixteenth Amendment to the U.S. Constitution was ratified in 1913, giving Congress the authority to levy a federal income tax. In the Revenue Act of 1913, Congress exempted from taxation entities "organized and operated exclusively for religious, charitable, scientific or educational purposes." In 1917, U.S. tax law introduced the opportunity for individuals who contribute to charitable institutions to deduct a portion of those donations from their income taxes. In 1934 Congress put limits on the extent to which nonprofit organizations can engage in "lobbying" and prohibited them from engaging in direct political activity. These elements of U.S. law are relevant to the nonprofit institutions involved in Southwest archaeology that are reviewed here. These laws and subsequent laws and regulations establish the criteria for achieving and maintaining tax-exempt status, provide incentives for donors to support these organizations, and establish the guidelines for engaging in public policy and advocacy work.

The First Wave of Modern Nonprofits in the Southwest

There have been two waves of nonprofit establishment, and they have distinctly different trajectories (see Figure 21.1). Between 1907 and 1937, five new private institutions were established in Arizona and New Mexico, and they had a major impact on the course of archaeological research, as these brief highlights show. As head of today's School for Advanced Research (SAR)—named the School of American Archaeology when it was established in 1907—Edgar Lee Hewett conducted research at Puyé, Chaco, and Bandelier. The Laboratory of Anthropology, initially funded by John D. Rockefeller and directed by Kenneth Chapman, supported H. P. Mera's important mapping of precontact pueblos in New Mexico. Harold Gladwin's Gila Pueblo launched very large-scale surveys and funded key excavations at sites such as Roosevelt 9:6 and Snaketown that defined the Hohokam culture (Gladwin et al. 1937; Haury 1932), and Harold Colton's Museum of Northern Arizona undertook extensive surveys, defined regional pottery types, and conducted important excavations at Sunset Crater and Wupatki (Colton 1932, 1946). In southeastern Arizona, the Amerind Foundation began with small-scale

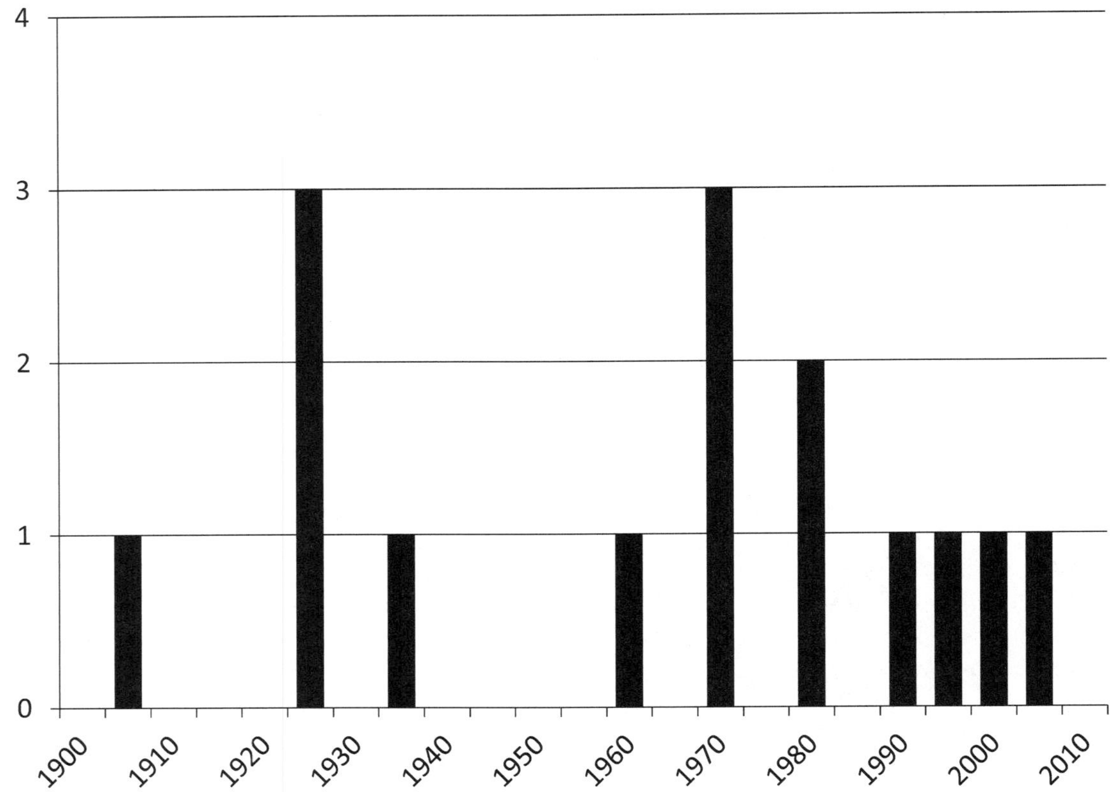

FIGURE 21.1. Founding dates of Southwest nonprofits over the past century by half decade.

excavations in the late 1920s and gradually built a museum (Fenner 1977) and implemented major excavations at San Pedro River sites (Di Peso 1951, 1953, 1958; Tuthill 1947), then at the huge site of Paquimé in Mexico (Di Peso 1974), and finally in the Mimbres area (Woosley and McIntyre 1996). The impact of the research by these early nonprofit organizations is still notable today, as exemplified by this quotation from Reid and Whittlesey:

> During seven critical years in southwestern prehistory between 1930 and 1937, Haury and his colleagues at Gila Pueblo Archaeological Foundation defined the Hohokam, Mogollon, and Salado cultures and laid the groundwork for the later definition of the Cochise culture, the preceramic culture of southeastern Arizona [2005:47].

The financial underpinnings of four of these early institutions came directly from the wealth of Gladwin, Colton, Fulton, and Rockefeller and thus derived from the eastern United States. Their establishment as local institutions was in part a reaction to the large-scale exporting of antiquities from the Southwest to museums in the American East. Hewett's School of American Archaeology was launched with eastern wealth by eastern intellectuals, but Hewett rapidly showed remarkable entrepreneurial talent and energy. He built a public audience, launched preservation as a core element of the institutional mission, and taught many new professional archaeologists through annual field schools.

Interestingly, despite the wealth that the founders of the early twentieth-century institutions brought to the establishment and initial operations phases, none of them left huge endowments to carry these institutions forward. As a result, all of the successful institutions have had to develop their own financial underpinnings under subsequent entrepreneurial leaders.

Not all of these early nonprofits survived. Gila Pueblo had flourished in the 1930s, but the departure of Emil Haury in 1937 was a serious loss. Harold Gladwin was not able to sustain the productive research environment that had been characteristic of earlier times. Ultimately the organization closed altogether, and its collections were incorporated into the Arizona State Museum in 1951 (Haury 1988). The Laboratory of Anthropology received funds for a building and five years of operations from John D. Rockefeller (Munson 2007:119). Unfortunately, the impact of the Great Depression on Rockefeller's priorities resulted in a failure to provide an endowment that would have helped secure the future of the organization. It was ultimately transferred to the state of New Mexico in 1959. Thus, changing conditions are a constant challenge to nonprofits and can result in new directions, decline, or even closure.

The Second Wave of Nonprofits

While the first wave of nonprofits was led by displaced Easterners, the second wave is predominantly "homegrown." These organizations derive from archaeological entrepreneurship and grassroots community activism rather than established individ-

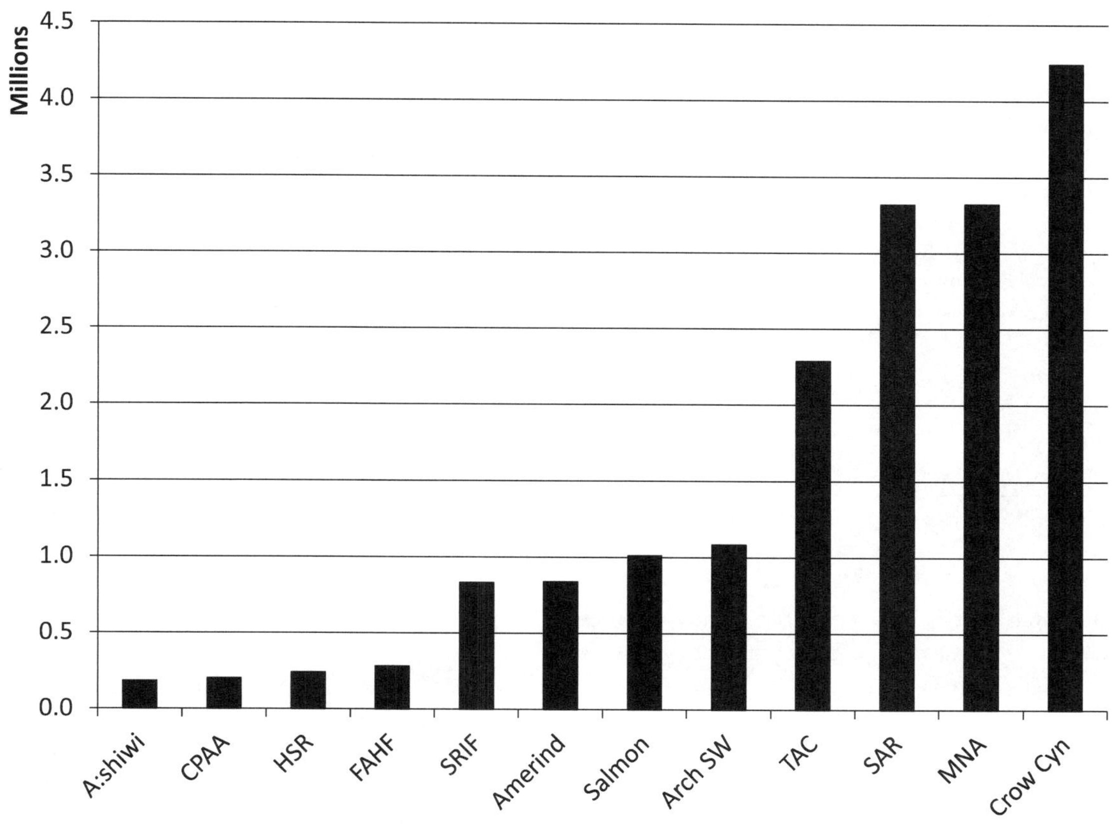

FIGURE 21.2. Twelve Southwest nonprofits in 2008: their total annual budgets equal $17.8 million. A:shiwi = A:shiwi A:wan Museum; CPAA = Colorado Plateau Archaeological Alliance; HSR = Human Systems Research; FAHF = Fort Apache Heritage Foundation; SRIF = SRI Foundation; Amerind = Amerind Foundation; Salmon = Salmon Ruins; Arch SW = Archaeology Southwest; TAC = the Archaeological Conservancy; SAR = School for Advanced Research; MNA = Museum of Northern Arizona; Crow Cyn = Crow Canyon Archaeological Center.

ual wealth and patronage. Each story is slightly different, and they are summarized in chronological order:

- Beginning in 1964, a remarkable community-based effort resulted in the purchase of a major Chacoan outlier, Salmon Ruins, and then secured funding to build a museum. The community also recruited the dynamic archaeologist Cynthia Irwin-Williams to run the initial research program, and the long-term program has been underwritten in part by cultural resource management (CRM) contracts.
- Human Systems Research was founded in 1972 by two graduate students from the University of New Mexico. CRM funding enabled organizational growth and stability over the years and was supplemented by grants and fund-raising.
- Crow Canyon Archaeological Center was founded in 1973 by Stuart Struever, who moved his public archaeology model established in Illinois to southwestern Colorado to carry out regional research and public education programs.
- The Mimbres Foundation was established in 1974 by Steven LeBlanc, who brought in private donations and other funds to carry out a major research and site protection program in the Mimbres Valley of southern New Mexico.
- The Archaeological Conservancy was established in 1980 by lawyer Mark Michel, Steven LeBlanc, and California businessman Jay Last. It had initial funding from the Ford and Rockefeller foundations and built a national-level organization through membership, private donations, and grants.
- The Center for Desert Archaeology, now Archaeology Southwest, was founded in 1982 and derived support initially from compliance-related contracts and later from the for-profit CRM firm I founded and own.
- The A:shiwi A:wan Museum at Zuni was established in 1992 to serve the local tribal community. It is an independent nonprofit, not directly reporting to the tribal government.
- Fort Apache Heritage Foundation was chartered in 1998 by the White Mountain Apache Tribe to provide assistance in the tribe's historic preservation, cultural and language perpetuation, and other heritage efforts.
- The SRI Foundation was incorporated in 2001 by Jeffrey Altschul with resources from a for-profit CRM firm he established in 1983.
- The Colorado Plateau Archaeological Alliance was established in late 2005 by a group of professionals with a strong concern for site protection issues on public lands.

Figure 21.2 depicts the 2008 budgets of the 12 institutions that were still active in that year. The total of $17.8 million was

TABLE 21.1. Major elements of the missions of 12 Southwest nonprofits.

Nonprofit	Year Founded	Regional Synthesis	Field Research	Public Outreach	Site Protection	Publication	Public Policy
School for Advanced Research	1907	X	X*	X	X*	X	
Museum of Northern Arizona	1928	x	x, X*	X		X	
Amerind Foundation	1937	X	X*	X		X	
Salmon Ruins	1964	x	X	X	+		
Human Systems Research	1972	x	X	X	x		
Archaeological Conservancy	1980			X	X		x
Archaeology Southwest	1982	x	X	X	X	X	x
Crow Canyon Archaeological Center	1983	x	X	X	x	x	
A:shiwi A:wan Museum	1992			X			
Fort Apache Heritage Foundation	1998			X	x		
SRI Foundation	2001			X			X
Colorado Plateau Archaeological Alliance	2005		X	X			X

Note: Table does not consider compliance-related contracts. X = major element; x = minor element; X* = historically important; + = reason for establishment.

not all spent on archaeology, but it conveys that these are institutions of substance. The key components of their missions are summarized in Table 21.1.

Theme 1: Research

It is notable that a degree of specialization has emerged in the nonprofit sector. For example, it is clear that two of our older institutions—SAR and the Amerind Foundation—have ceased to be primary generators of archaeological data. Instead, they create a high-quality environment within which researchers already laden with data and ideas are brought into direct interaction with similarly prepared scholars. Time of residence within this advanced seminar or resident scholar environment varies from two days to a year, but it is definitely not long-term.

Six institutions—Crow Canyon, Archaeology Southwest, Salmon Ruins, Human Systems Research, the Museum of Northern Arizona, and the Colorado Plateau Archaeological Alliance—do actively pursue archaeological fieldwork to meet their research goals, the latter four with significant support from contracts. The extent of this work is not on the grand scale of previous excavations by nonprofits at Chaco, Snaketown, or Paquimé. Especially for nonthreatened sites, excavation and analysis costs, curation costs, concerns of Native Americans, and the fact that our discipline exploits a nonrenewable resource are major factors limiting the scale of excavations (Lipe 1974):

- Crow Canyon is undertaking the most extensive excavations of any nonprofit, but it employs sampling strategies and a very long-term regional research program as a means to achieve the scale of data to meet its research goals. Over 15 years of its research in the Middle Mesa Verde region of southwestern Colorado are synthesized in a recent publication (Varien and Wilshusen 2002), and field reports and associated data are available on the Internet.
- Archaeology Southwest is also pursuing research on a large regional scale, but excavations are limited and are supplemented to the maximum extent possible by new analyses of existing collections. A recent publication on Zuni origins (Gregory and Wilcox 2007) was a partnership with the Museum of Northern Arizona to synthesize existing information on a broad regional scale, and two decades of field and laboratory research along the Lower San Pedro River are reported in a current book (Clark and Lyons 2012).
- Salmon Ruins conducts contract-funded research and has a partnership with Archaeology Southwest carrying out research on Chaco and post-Chaco developments in the Middle San Juan area (Reed 2006, 2008).
- Human Systems Research has a long history of contract-funded research primarily in southern New Mexico and is currently completing a research project in partnership with a private landowner along Cañada Alamosa, a tributary of the Rio Grande with a rich archaeological record (Laumbach 2004).
- The Colorado Plateau Archaeological Alliance has focused its research on compiling the background data to help land managers do a better job of protecting archaeological sites. For example, conducting research on the effects of back-country roads, which cause both direct and indirect impacts, on archaeological sites facilitates a science-based approach to off-highway vehicle policies for an agency such as the Bureau of Land Management.
- The Museum of Northern Arizona (MNA) has a long history of field research since its inception (Downum 1990; Miller 1991; Wilcox 2010). Research related to defining the Sinagua (Colton 1946) and examining past cultural boundaries in the area involved significant surveys and excavations. MNA carried out most of the highway salvage archaeology in northern Arizona during the 1950s and 1960s (Wasley 1957), and it developed a larger-scale contract-funded program in the 1970s and 1980s. David Wilcox (now retired) has carried out a significant program of survey and site mapping in the

Perry Mesa and Verde River areas (Wilcox 2010; Wilcox and Holmlund 2007). Most recently, Ted Neff has led a major contract-funded research effort in the Grand Canyon. MNA recently completed a state-of-the-art curation facility and encourages new research using the materials in its extensive collections.

As this brief summary indicates, the "great excavations" of the past are no longer taking place in private nonprofit environments. Larger projects, when they do occur in the Southwest, are funded by contracts.

Four other organizations are highly specialized:

- The Archaeological Conservancy's primary mission is to protect archaeological sites for the future. It is not directly involved with research but encourages qualified researchers to conduct focused research on sites it owns or manages.
- The SRI Foundation conducts student training through a Summer Institute in Cultural Resource Management in partnership with the University of Maryland, short continuing education courses, public policy and compliance consulting, and some synthetic research.
- A:shiwi A:wan Museum conducts research that is defined and implemented primarily by and for the local tribal community.
- Fort Apache Heritage Foundation conducts research that is primarily for the preservation and interpretation of key prehistoric and historic cultural resources that it makes available to the community and the broader public.

Theme 2: Funding

A central challenge for every nonprofit is sustainable funding for staff, facilities, and programs. In the early days of the AIA, which was dependent on private rather than government funding, it was always financially challenging to mount large excavations. Exacerbating the problem, the field expeditions from European countries received generous government support (Allen 2002: 11–12). Thus, concern with funding is not a new issue.

Data from the Giving USA Foundation for 2009 show that charitable giving in the United States was just over $300 billion. Breaking that information down by source, 75 percent comes from individuals, 13 percent from foundations, 8 percent as bequests, and only 4 percent from corporations (http://nccs.urban.org/FAQ/index.cfm). The specific nonprofits considered here vary widely in their funding sources. A detailed analysis was not carried out, but at least half of the Southwest nonprofits receive significant support from individual members and donors.

Government grants and compliance contracts are another potential source of funding for nonprofits. Research grants from the National Science Foundation or National Endowment for the Humanities are the largest sources for the Southwest nonprofits. Contracts for legal compliance are significant income sources only for Salmon and Human Systems Research.

The economic downturn since 2008 has shown the degree to which all potential sources of nonprofit funding are subject to fluctuation. While endowments are one source of insulation against declines in outside income, endowments were hard hit by the economic decline as well. SAR, Crow Canyon, and Amerind have endowments greater than $10 million that contribute substantially to their annual operations; MNA, the Archaeological Conservancy, Archaeology Southwest, and A:shiwi A:wan have endowments in the $1 million–5 million range; and the others have small or no endowments.

While nonprofits are officially governed by boards of directors, the role of the executive director (or the president and CEO) is at the core of success for nonprofits. Executive directors take the lead in guiding the development of endowments, cultivation of donors, writing of grants, creation of networks, outreach to public audiences, management of staff, and compliance with increasingly complex federal laws. Thus, it is important to underscore the degree to which nonprofits depend on creative and energized leadership. If nonprofit leaders perform well, their organizations can be much more agile than large institutions such as universities that are subject to legislative whims. The actions of exceptional executive directors are often transformative for the organization. Edgar Lee Hewett built complex personal and institutional networks to build the SAR, though it had declined and was in a highly weakened state following his death in 1946. Douglas Schwartz subsequently stepped in and built SAR into a very different organization over his 34-year term at its head. Most recently, Robert Breunig stepped into the leadership role at MNA and brought it back from near financial collapse. The stories and means are different in each case, but the power of individual leadership is underscored by each example.

Theme 3: Public Outreach

As noted earlier, Nordenskiöld's excavations at Mesa Verde drew a strong negative response from the local community. As population increased in the American West, the AIA expanded its membership base by chartering affiliated societies across the country (Snead 2001, 2002). In 1903, the Southwest Society, based in Los Angeles, became an affiliate. The founder, Charles F. Lummis, promoted a much stronger form of public outreach than the AIA had traditionally undertaken through its program of public lectures. Lummis sought to build local community identity through cultural heritage by promoting local research and the establishment of local museums. In 1906, the AIA sent Edgar Lee Hewett to Los Angeles as an emissary to evaluate the fieldwork standards on a planned project by the Southwest Society. That trip introduced Hewett to the workings of the western AIA affiliates and brought Hewett and Lummis into an association that continued in subsequent years. In 1907, Hewett was appointed director of American studies for the AIA. Lacking financial support from the AIA, however, Hewett tapped several of the western affiliated societies, which provided the funding for fieldwork sessions such as the major excavation he directed at the New Mexican Pueblo of Puyé. Snead points out that these local programs were focused almost exclusively on the short-term goals of excavation and the procurement of artifacts for museums. There was little support for analyses, scientific reporting, and long-term research programs. What they did establish was an audience for archaeology. That such audiences were growing was an important context for the new institutions that came into existence in the early 1900s.

Throughout his career at SAR Edgar Lee Hewett continued to expand the audience for archaeology as a discipline. Within six years of the founding of the School of American Archaeology, Hewett, the Museum of New Mexico, and the New Mexico Archaeological Society were publishing the journal *El Palacio*. Hewett placed great emphasis on experiential learning; thus SAR's early offering of field schools in conjunction with the University of New Mexico was meant to expose students to archaeology. And while Hewett's scientific publication record is thin, his published works geared toward a general audience were numerous (e.g., Hewett 1936, 1953; Hewett and Fisher 1943). Looking at today's nonprofits, general-audience publications, tours, lectures, and hands-on opportunities are widely practiced.

Every nonprofit that is still operating has a significant public outreach element of its mission. This is not surprising given that these organizations have a legal obligation to provide a public benefit. As the discipline of archaeology has developed, increasing amounts of public funding are expended through compliance projects. While the nonprofits considered here play a very minor role in that aspect of the discipline, they do play a substantial role in bringing archaeology and the outcomes of research to the public. Crow Canyon has the most extensive public education program. Its 2010 annual report cites nearly 2,000 students in its school programs and 161 participants in its cultural exploration travels. The Museum of Northern Arizona offers tours from its base in Flagstaff, and the Archaeological Conservancy regularly conducts week-long tours within, and more often beyond, the Southwest. This format of scholar-led tours has proved to be a remarkable learning experience for participants and generally has financial benefits for the nonprofit.

Publications are another form of public outreach. SAR has a major press operation and publishes both scholarly and general-interest books. In recent years it has initiated a very successful series that assembles a synthetic volume on the prehistory of a specific region that is written by scholars for a general audience. Archaeology Southwest's quarterly, *Archaeology Southwest Magazine*, is its primary publication for a general audience, and MNA's *Plateau* is a full-color magazine for its members. In addition, reflecting new technologies, the majority of the Southwest nonprofits invest substantial resources in their Web sites to share information easily and widely.

The role of nonprofits organized by federally recognized tribes is a new and interesting development. The A:shiwi A:wan Museum serves primarily the Zuni community through educational and other community-based activities. The Fort Apache Heritage Foundation has a strong educational role in the local community and promotes heritage tourism.

Theme 4: Site Protection

Edgar Lee Hewett placed heavy emphasis on the idea of preservation in his early writings (e.g., Hewett 1904, 1905a, 1905b, 1905c, 1906, 1907). He (1905a:590) advanced a notion of two kinds of preservation: permanent and temporary. He called for permanent preservation "in cases where the condition and historic or ethnic significance of the ruins give them special educational value," and for ruins that did not meet those conditions, he called for their protection "until all data of importance to science have been investigated and all artifacts in connection therewith removed to museums for permanent preservation" (1905a:589–591). At the time of Hewett's writing, only the Casa Grande Ruins had been set aside via a presidential proclamation by Benjamin Harrison in 1892 (Taylor 2009). After the passage of the Antiquities Act, Hewett played a role in getting other important prehistoric monuments into government ownership: Gran Quivira (proclaimed a National Monument by President Taft in 1909) and Quarai and Abo (obtained by the University of New Mexico in 1928 and 1937, respectively). Hewett helped to preserve additional archaeological sites through direct ownership by SAR. Most significant were nearly 1,300 acres at Chaco Canyon that were ultimately incorporated into the National Park (Lewis 2007:47).

Local community members in Farmington and Bloomfield, New Mexico, organized to purchase Salmon Ruins in 1964 (James 2002), but preservation through direct purchase of private land took hold in a systematic way through the Mimbres Foundation's work in the 1970s. Steve LeBlanc notes that archaeologists could never keep up with the pace at which the looters were destroying Mimbres sites. He states: "We found that sites in the Mimbres area could be purchased for a fraction of the cost of excavating them. Thus, with the same resources we could acquire and preserve many more sites than we could excavate" (1983:167). They did indeed purchase several sites and took conservation easements on several others. In 1980, LeBlanc, Mark Michel, and Jay Last founded the Archaeological Conservancy, which has expanded to cover the entire United States and owns more than 400 archaeological sites at present. Site protection is one of the core elements of Archaeology Southwest's mission as well, and its staff places a high priority on developing conservation easements due to their lower initial cost. Also, Archaeology Southwest limits its geographic focus to the Southwest so that sites with easements can be monitored regularly with limited staff. Collaboration with large private conservation organizations such as the Nature Conservancy (TNC) has also proved productive. Proximity to water in the arid Southwest is a key to both natural and cultural resources, and often the two classes of resources co-occur or are in close proximity. While cultural resources are not part of the mission of an organization such as

TNC, it has generally welcomed input, and in some cases approaching landowners from a cultural resource perspective has been more effective than TNC's natural resource focus.

Theme 5: Advocacy

The original nonprofit advocacy role goes back to Hewett and the AIA in getting the Antiquities Act passed, and then significant effort was invested in moving important archaeological properties into the protective ownership of the federal government. New laws and regulations over time have created new options for protection. The Bureau of Land Management's National Landscape Conservation System contains some 27 million acres of prime landscapes including wilderness areas, national conservation areas, and national monuments. In a multiuse management framework pursued by both the Bureau of Land Management and the Forest Service, it is helpful, perhaps essential, to have outside professionals who are willing to take on the issues of how such lands are being managed. The Colorado Plateau Archaeological Alliance has a major focus on ensuring that

> development projects on public lands have adequately complied with cultural resource protection laws, analyzing the potential for unknown and unstudied archaeological sites that could be lost through development, and conducting quality research into site degradation that can assist land managers and public officials to determine appropriate strategies to protect threatened resources [2013].

Archaeology Southwest is expanding its investment in monitoring projects that have the potential to affect cultural resources on a large spatial scale as well as programmatic agreements by agencies when they may have a broad regional impact. Many projects required to comply with Section 106 of the National Historic Preservation Act do little up front to plan for the avoidance of impacts to cultural resources. Instead, archaeology is programmed in as the cost of doing a data-recovery program. Archaeology Southwest and the Colorado Plateau Archaeological Alliance see advance planning as the key to achieving the preservation of archaeological sites in place rather than just preserving a sample of the artifacts and information through excavation.

The laws and regulations that serve to protect cultural resources have increased and have become more complex over time. The SRI Foundation invests significant effort in training archaeologists and in the development and promotion of best practices in historic preservation for various government agencies.

A Powerful Collaboration

A recent exhibit at the Museum of Northern Arizona represents an encouraging collaboration between two nonprofit museums with very different histories and missions. The A:shiwi A:wan Museum and Heritage Center of the Pueblo of Zuni, under Executive Director Jim Enote, created an exhibit for the tribal community preparing and presenting what he calls "Zuni map art." It brought Zuni artists and cultural advisers together for discussions and field trips, with a goal of having the artists make maps "that would serve as learning tools for the Zuni community." After nearly a year of conversations, a round of mapmaking was embarked upon at the level of the village, the reservation, and the Zuni region. Other areas were added based on the success of the first efforts. Enote says: "These maps are intended for a Zuni audience, but . . . the maps are also strategic and therefore can serve a powerful role to inspire non-Zuni audiences" (2011:8). Thus through an exhibit and a substantial color catalog and essays this view of the Zuni cultural landscape is being shared outside of the tribal community. This is a powerful message. The creative act of rediscovering a cultural landscape that has diminished in size and clarity since the time of the initial Spanish entrada in 1540 is taking place within the Zuni community through the leadership of their nonprofit museum. Sharing the results with the broader academic and public world was accomplished through partnerships with another Southwestern nonprofit, the Museum of Northern Arizona.

The Future

As it has matured as a profession, archaeology has come to be practiced in an increasing diversity of institutional contexts. Private, nonprofit organizations have a long history, and some of the key early roles of nonprofits have been explored. Nonprofits are mission-driven organizations. While they are shaped by their environment, if they are effective, their missions are focused on directing change within that environment. The nonprofits reviewed here in some cases measure their existence in years, others count by decades, and two are in their second centuries. There have been major positive contributions by all of these organizations, and the nonprofit sector has the potential to continue to be a significant force in the development of the archaeological discipline.

In closing, I make some observations regarding the future:

- Most, if not all, institutions have working relationships with Native American communities, a process that is likely to continue.
- Emphasis on effective communication with the public is widespread. These efforts will continue to grow, and the necessity for more sophisticated approaches by the archaeological community to meet that need will also grow.
- The higher-level synthetic efforts that are already being carried out through advanced seminars at SAR and Amerind are expected to continue and expand.
- Preservation issues must be carefully addressed prior to any field excavation effort.
- Collections-based research should be prioritized by nonprofits. There are shocking quantities of insufficiently analyzed collections out there. In addition, many large and small collections generated from contract-funded projects have

not had their research potential exhausted. Such collections will continue to accumulate in regional repositories.

- There are many reasons why new fieldwork will continue to be both appropriate and necessary for the advancement of the field. The fiscal constraints and concerns over long-term preservation identified above will likely limit the scope of such fieldwork. This will place additional importance on the development of high-quality research designs prior to field-work in order to maximize results when the archaeological record is consumed.
- The role of partnerships and collaboration in the success of nonprofit organizations is great, and both are widespread among all in this set of nonprofits.

Acknowledgments

An early version of this chapter with coauthor John Kantner was presented previously (Doelle and Kantner 2010). John's contributions to that paper and additional comments on this much expanded chapter are gratefully acknowledged.

References Cited

Allen, Susan Heuck
2002 The Archaeology of the AIA: An Introduction. In *Excavating Our Past: Perspectives on the History of the Archaeological Institute of America*, edited by Susan Hueck Allen, pp. 1–28. Colloquia and Conference Papers, 5. Archaeological Institute of America, Boston.

Bandelier, Adolph F.
1892 *Final Report of Investigations Among the Indians of the Southwestern United States Carried on Mainly in the Years 1880 to 1885*, Pt. II. Papers of the Archaeological Institute of America, American Series, Vol. 4. John Wilson and Son, Cambridge.

Blackburn, Fred M.
2006 *The Wetherills: Friends of Mesa Verde*. Durango Herald Small Press, Durango, Colorado.

Blackburn, Fred M., and Ray A. Williamson
1997 *Cowboys and Cave Dwellers: Basketmaker Archaeology in Utah's Grand Gulch*. SAR Press, Santa Fe, New Mexico.

Clark, Jeffery J., and Patrick D. Lyons (editors)
2012 *Migrants and Mounds: Classic Period Archaeology of the San Pedro Valley*. Anthropological Papers No. 45. Archaeology Southwest, Tucson.

Colorado Plateau Archaeological Alliance
2013 Frequently Asked Questions: What Does CPAA Do? Electronic document, http://www.cparch.org/27.html, accessed June 15, 2013.

Colton, Harold S.
1932 Sunset Crater: The Effect of a Volcanic Eruption on the Ancient Pueblo People. *Geographical Review* 22:582–590.
1946 *The Sinagua: A Summary of the Archaeology of the Region of Flagstaff, Arizona*. Bulletin No. 22. Museum of Northern Arizona and the Northern Arizona Society of Science and Art, Flagstaff.

Di Peso, Charles C.
1951 *The Babocomari Village Site on the Babocomari River, Southeastern Arizona*. Archaeology Series No. 5. Amerind Foundation, Dragoon, Arizona.
1953 *The Sobaipuri Indians of the Upper San Pedro River Valley, Southeastern Arizona*. Archaeology Series No. 6. Amerind Foundation, Dragoon, Arizona.
1958 *The Reeve Ruin of Southeastern Arizona: A Study of Prehistoric Western Pueblo Migration into the Middle San Pedro Valley*. Archaeology Series No. 8. Amerind Foundation, Dragoon, Arizona.
1974 *Casas Grandes: A Fallen Trading Center of the Gran Chichimeca: Vols. 1–9*. Amerind Foundation Archaeology Series No. 9. Northland Press, Flagstaff.

Doelle, William H., and John Kantner
2010 The Nonprofit "Pentagon" of the Southwest. Paper presented at the 75th Annual Meeting of the Society for American Archaeology, St. Louis.

Downum, Christian E.
1990 From Myths to Methods: Intellectual Transitions in Flagstaff Archaeology. In *Perspectives on Southwestern Prehistory*, edited by Paul E. Minnis and Charles L. Redman, pp. 351–366. Westview Press, Boulder.

Enote, Jim
2011 *A:shiwi A:wan Ulohnanne—The Zuni World*. A:shiwi A:wan Museum and Heritage Center, Zuni, New Mexico; and Museum of Northern Arizona, Flagstaff.

Fenner, Gloria J.
1977 History and Scope of the Amerind Foundation. *Kiva* 42:317–329.

Gladwin, Harold S., Emil W. Haury, E. B. Sayles, and Nora Gladwin
1937 *Excavations at Snaketown: Material Culture*. Medallion Papers No. 25. Gila Pueblo, Globe, Arizona.

Gregory, David A., and David R. Wilcox (editors)
2007 *Zuni Origins: Toward a New Synthesis of Southwestern Archaeology*. University of Arizona Press, Tucson.

Harmon, David, Francis P. McManamon, and Dwight T. Pitcaithley
2006 The Antiquities Act: A Cornerstone of Archaeology, Historic Preservation, and Conservation. In *The Antiquities Act: A Century of American Archaeology, Historic Preservation, and Nature Conservation*, edited by David Harmon, Francis P. McManamon, and Dwight T. Pitcaithley, pp. 267–285. University of Arizona Press, Tucson.

Haury, Emil W.
1932 *Roosevelt 9:6: A Hohokam Site of the Colonial Period*. Medallion Papers No. 1. Gila Pueblo, Globe, Arizona.
1988 Gila Pueblo Archaeological Foundation: A History and Some Personal Notes. *Kiva* 54:1–77.

Hewett, Edgar L.
1904 *Circular Relating to Historic and Prehistoric Ruins of the Southwest and Their Preservation*. Department of the Interior, General Land Office. U.S. Government Printing Office, Washington, D.C.
1905a *A General View of the Archeology of the Pueblo Region*. Annual Report of the Board of Regents of the Smithsonian Institution for the Year Ending June 30, 1904. U.S. Government Printing Office, Washington, D.C.

1905b Preservation of Antiquities. *American Anthropologist* 7:164–166.
1905c Preservation of Antiquities. *American Anthropologist* 7:569–570.
1906 Preservation of American Antiquities: Progress During the Last Year; Needed Legislation. *American Anthropologist* 8:109–114.
1907 Preservation of American Antiquities. *American Anthropologist* 9:233–234.
1936 *The Chaco Canyon and Its Monuments*. Handbooks of Archaeological History. University of New Mexico Press, Albuquerque.
1953 *Pajarito Plateau and Its Ancient People*. 2nd ed. School of American Research, Santa Fe, New Mexico; and University of New Mexico Press, Albuquerque.

Hewett, Edgar L., and Reginald Fisher
1943 *Mission Monuments of New Mexico*. University of New Mexico Press, Albuquerque.

James, Alton
2002 A Brief History of the San Juan County Museum Association and Salmon Ruins. *Archaeology Southwest* 16(2):4.

Laumbach, Karl W.
2004 The Cañada Alamosa Project: Investigations of a Prehistoric Frontier. *Archaeology Southwest* 18(2):4.

LeBlanc, Steven A.
1983 *The Mimbres People: Ancient Painters of the American Southwest*. Thames and Hudson, London.

Leshy, John D.
1998 Putting the Antiquities Act in Perspective. In *Visions of the Grand Staircase–Escalante: Examining Utah's Newest National Monument*, edited by Robert B. Keiter, Sarah B. George, and Joro Walker, pp. 83–88. Utah Museum of Natural History and Wallace Stegner Center, Salt Lake City.

Lewis, Nancy Owen
2007 Creating a School for American Research, 1907–1966. In *A Peculiar Alchemy: A Centennial History of SAR, 1907–2007*, by Nancy Owen Lewis and Kay Leigh Hagen, pp. 3–77. SAR Press, Santa Fe, New Mexico.

Lipe, William D.
1974 A Conservation Model for American Archaeology. *Kiva* 39: 213–245.

Miller, Jimmy
1991 *The Life of Harold Sellers Colton: A Philadelphia Brahmin in Flagstaff*. Navajo Community College Press, Tsaile, Arizona.

Munson, Marit K. (editor)
2007 *Kenneth Chapman's Santa Fe: Artists and Archaeologists, 1907–1931*. SAR Press, Santa Fe, New Mexico.

Nordenskiöld, Gustaf
1979 [1893] *The Cliff Dwellers of the Mesa Verde, Southwestern Colorado: Their Pottery and Implements*. Reprint. Rio Grande Press, Glorieta, New Mexico.

Reed, Paul F. (editor)
2006 *Thirty-Five Years of Archaeological Research at Salmon Ruins, New Mexico*. 3 vols. Center for Desert Archaeology, Tucson.
2008 *Chaco's Northern Prodigies: Salmon, Aztec, and the Ascendancy of the Middle San Juan Region After AD 1100*. University of Utah Press, Salt Lake City.

Reid, J. Jefferson, and Stephanie M. Whittlesey
2005 *Thirty Years into Yesterday: A History of Archaeology at Grasshopper Pueblo*. University of Arizona Press, Tucson.

Reynolds, Judith L., and David Reynolds
2006 *Nordenskiöld of Mesa Verde: A Biography*. Xlibris Corporation, Bloomington, Indiana.

Snead, James E.
2001 *Ruins and Rivals: The Making of Southwest Archaeology*. University of Arizona Press, Tucson.
2002 The "Western Idea": Local Societies and American Archaeology. In *Excavating Our Past: Perspectives on the History of the Archaeological Institute of America*, edited by Susan Hueck Allen, pp. 123–140. Colloquia and Conference Papers, 5. Archaeological Institute of America, Boston.

Taylor, Toby Lopez
2009 The Nation's First Federally Protected Archaeological Site. *Archaeology Southwest* 23(4):5.

Thompson, Raymond H.
2000 An Old and Reliable Authority: An Act for the Preservation of American Antiquities. *Journal of the Southwest* 42:191–381.

Tuthill, Carr
1947 *The Tres Alamos Site on the San Pedro River, Southeastern Arizona*. Archaeology Series No. 4. Amerind Foundation, Dragoon, Arizona.

Varien, Mark D., and Richard H. Wilshusen (editors)
2002 *Seeking the Center Place: Archaeology and Ancient Communities in the Mesa Verde Region*. University of Utah Press, Salt Lake City.

Wasley, William W.
1957 Highway Salvage Archaeology in Arizona. *Kiva* 23(2):4–7.

Wilcox, David R.
2010 Seizing the Moment: Collaboration and Cooperation in the Founding and Growth of the Museum of Northern Arizona, 1928–2008. *Journal of the Southwest* 52:435–537.

Wilcox, David R., and James P. Holmlund
2007 *The Archaeology of Perry Mesa and Its World*. Bilby Research Center Occasional Papers No. 3. Northern Arizona University, Flagstaff.

Woosley, Anne I., and Allan J. McIntyre
1996 *Mimbres Mogollon Archaeology: Charles C. Di Peso's Excavations at Wind Mountain*. Amerind Foundation Archaeology Series No. 10. University of New Mexico Press, Albuquerque.

22

The Evolution of Historical Archaeology in the American West

Donald L. Hardesty and Eugene M. Hattori

The evolution of historical archaeology in the American West has been a "thing of shreds and patches" tied together with serendipity. Ad hoc and site-specific rather than regional research strategies have dominated the region. In the early years of the historical archaeology of the American West, the paradigm of the "Mythic and Monolithic West," filled with the archaeology of such popular events in the West of the American imagination as the Pony Express and the Donner Party tragedy, dominated the thinking of archaeologists and historians alike. Certainly these sites would not have been selected for archaeological study if they had not played such a role. The Pony Express is a case in point. Archaeological studies of Pony Express station sites in central Nevada began in 1976 as a by-product of the efforts by federal land-managing agencies to celebrate the American Bicentennial. Among other things, they selected the Pony Express as a symbol of the "opening" of the West and westward expansion of the American state.

Archaeological research offered a way of documenting and gathering information to help interpret Pony Express stations to visitors. At the same time, the archaeological research that was done in the service of the "Mythic West" opened up new pathways to alternative, local, and diverse histories, real lives, and new perceptions of the past that helped to create a new paradigm of the "counter-Mythic West" in the same genre as the new western historians such as Patricia Limerick and Richard White.

Research Pathways in Western Historical Archaeology

Several themes in this new paradigm emerged and characterized the historical archaeology of the American West during the 1980s and the 1990s. First of all is the archaeology of identity, memory, and commemoration of a wide variety of social and cultural groups defined by, among other things, power structures, ethnicity, and gender. The archaeology of the Ludlow Massacre, working-class identity, and the commemoration of labor history (Larkin and McGuire 2009; Saitta 2007) illustrate this theme, as do battlefield sites such as Wounded Knee (Brown 2001) and concentration camps such as Manzanar (Dubel 2001). William Lees's (2004) study of military conflict sites in Indian Territory in Oklahoma is another excellent example of this same theme. Lees clearly shows the importance of diverse social and cultural identities in understanding armed conflict taking place in this region, and the American West in general, during the time period of the Civil War. Native American traditions of conflict and historical tribal conflicts played important roles in the origin and conduct of battlefield events that had nothing to do with the Civil War as visualized east of the Mississippi. Mark Warner and Daryl Baldwin's (2004) research on the Miami Indians of Oklahoma also illustrates the archaeology of identity by focusing upon how the consumer behavior of this tribal group reflects a negotiated material culture with both commonalities with and differences from that of white society.

The time scales of historical archaeology in the American West began to change in the 1990s, when research strategies were being developed that recognized more than a post-Columbian archaeology. Elizabeth Pauls (2006) views the American grasslands as a repeated series of similar patterns of connections, settlements, and travel over the last 800 years that involved Native Americans, colonizers, and settlers alike both before and after AD 1492. Research strategies in the historical archaeology of the American West began to consider multiple scales of time and space, taking into account the approach taken by the Annales school of social history, which interprets the past with a set of time-linked historical structures or organizational schemes. Historical structures are interconnected events, places, things, and relations that are formed at different time scales ranging from centuries and millennia to years and days. At one end of the time scale are historical structures formed over very long periods of time. They include biogeophysical processes such as the geological structures associated with the formation and spatial arrangement of ore bodies. In the middle of the time scale are historical structures linking together social and cultural entities, relations, and processes that play a key role in social reproduction and change. They include social structures grounded in the ideologies of class, ethnicity, and gender. Historical structures created in short-term time link together the actions, social relations, and perceptions of individuals or specific social units such as domestic households or companies. They are, in effect, historical biographies or life histories and may be expressed in landscapes as networks or mosaics of microenvironments.

Cross-cultural comparison as a research strategy in the historical archaeology of the American West is another theme in the "new" paradigm. For the grasslands, Elizabeth Pauls (2006) suggests a cross-cultural research agenda to explore the landscape experience of indigenes, colonizers, and settlers in similar environments around the world, such as the South American pampas, the African savanna, and the central Asian steppe. This, of course, brings to mind the multilinear evolution and cross-cultural types of Julian Steward. The late Robert Netting (1993) illustrates the continued usefulness of this approach with his study of smallholder farmers as a cross-cultural type. James Delgado (2009) also suggests the usefulness of a cross-cultural comparison of urban places in the Pacific Rim maritime frontier, such as San Francisco, Sydney, Auckland, Valparaiso, and Hong Kong.

The archaeology of ethnogenesis and other new social formations defines another research theme in the historical archaeology of the American West (Hardesty 1999). In contrast to the social and cultural homogenization long predicted to be the consequence of globalization, the modern world continues diversifying at an increasing rate. New ethnic and other culturally defined social groups often emerge as new places are incorporated into expanding world systems. Thomas Hall argues that the expansion of the American state in New Mexico transformed indigenous Hispanic groups into "an enclaved ethnic group with a distinctive culture and a distinct class position within a larger structure" (1989:210). Barbara Voss's *The Archaeology of Ethnogenesis: Race and Sexuality in Colonial San Francisco* (2008) illustrates the same theme.

The historical archaeology of the American West is well positioned to shed light on the emergence of new social groups organized on cultural principles other than ethnicity. Of all the changes brought about by the industrialization of the American West, none is quite as dramatic as the creation of a distinctive class of wageworkers. As in ethnogenesis and community formation, historical archaeology is well positioned to interpret western wageworkers as a new class-based social group that emerged during the industrialization of the American West. Karin Larkin and Randall McGuire's *The Archaeology of Class War: The Colorado Coalfield Strike of 1913–1914* (2009) illustrates this theme.

The modern world is marked by accelerating global population movements and more effective technologies of transportation and communication, all bringing about increasing contact with others. How "others know others" is a critical issue in the historical archaeology of the American West (Hardesty 1999). The archaeological remains of colonies offer glimpses into how the immigrants and indigenous peoples viewed one another, how both dealt with the exotic. Related to such colonies are industrial places such as settlements of immigrant workers in and around company towns, which introduced views of the exotic both to the immigrant workers and to indigenous peoples (Hardesty 1998). Other places playing an important role in our understanding of others knowing others are the displaced persons resettlement camps around missions and forts, concentration camps, and internment camps such as the Japanese American relocation centers during World War II (Dubel 2001). Battlefields and other places of conflict give yet another perspective. Richard Fox's (1997) study of the Custer battlefield shows how archaeological remains can be used to interpret how the warring parties viewed and responded to one another during the short but famous conflict. Michael Wilcox's *The Pueblo Revolt and the Mythology of Conquest* (2009) illustrates an indigenous archaeology of contact. Kent Lightfoot's *Indians, Missionaries, and Merchants* (2005) also elucidates the theme of the archaeology of colonial encounters.

Landscape is another key concept in the evolution of historical archaeology in the American West that has emerged within the last few years. Landscapes reflect the cumulative history of human–environmental interactions. Elizabeth Pauls (2006) explores the grasslands as a regional cultural tradition in the best sense of what the new western historians and geographers might consider a geographical place with a distinctive past. As a physical and cultural place, the grasslands crosscut and interplay with such concepts as frontier and world system periphery. Considering the grasslands as a place reflects the phenomenological approach in geography and landscape archaeology advocated by Christopher Tilley in his book *A Phenomenology of Landscape* (1994). The landscape theme is also expressed in James Delgado's (2009) study of the Pacific Rim maritime frontier. Commemorative landscapes, of course, such as Ludlow in Colorado, Civil War battlefields in Oklahoma, and the Manzanar Japanese American relocation camp in California, recall the theme of identity and commemoration.

Landscapes can be viewed as a physical expression of social networks that reflect the creative and active agency of human individuals and social groups (Hardesty 1998). From this perspective, social systems can be viewed as overlapping networks of social power that may be ideological, economic, political, or military in origin. Social systems are organized around power networks that are hierarchical or heterarchical, in which interactions among individuals and groups are situational, changing, flexible, and constantly being negotiated (Crumley 1994). Sex/gender systems are among the most distinctive of the social and cultural constructions expressed in landscapes and played a significant role in transforming landscapes during the colonization of and establishment of frontiers in the American West (Hardesty 2010). Landscapes reflect and evoke interactions between gender and ethnicity, class, and occupation and the organization of space within settlements and settlement systems (Sunseri 2010). Sex/gender systems are expressed in the architectural and other material remains of households, local settlements, regional settlement systems, and global interactions such as population migrations and world systems.

CASE STUDY: LANDSCAPES AND MINING FRONTIERS IN THE AMERICAN WEST

Consider, for example, how mining landscapes in the American West are linked to current research issues in historical archaeology (Hardesty 2011). Several mining rushes including California's 1849 gold rush, the Comstock silver strike in 1859, and Alaska's 1898 Klondike Stampede transformed the American West in the nineteenth and early twentieth centuries. The rushes brought about new social and cultural frontiers, with distinctive communities and landscapes marked by rapid economic, demographic, and environmental change. These frontier societies, cultures, and landscapes constitute a "cross-cultural type" as originally conceptualized by Julian Steward (1955). They serve as a model for contemporary mining frontier communities around the world and are analogous to the "smallholder intensive farming" cross-cultural type defined by Robert Netting (1993).

The key component of frontier mining as a cross-cultural type involves flexible and shifting networks of social power as a principle of community organization (Hardesty 1998). Individuals and groups negotiate power within the networks, using methods that vary from violence to ideology to politics as a way of controlling mining resources such as capital or ore deposits or water or labor. Lipman-Blumen defines social power is "a set of processes whereby one party gains the capacity to impose its will on another by its potential to contribute or to withhold critical resources and rewards or by threatening or inflicting punishment" (1994:110). From this perspective, social systems may also be viewed as networks of social power within which individuals and groups negotiate relationships (Mann 1986:1–2). Frontier mining social networks ranged from informal and ephemeral cooperative organizations to households, local settlements, regional settlement systems, and global interactions. Such networks may be hierarchical, as in company towns, but often are flexible, situational, and changing (Hardesty 1998:82), networks that Crumley (1994:186–187) refers to as heterarchies. Household, settlement, and sociotechnical heterarchies typically underlie the organization of frontier mining communities.

Frontier mining households are organized around shifting social networks for purposes of mutual protection or to take advantage of resource opportunities. Flexibility in household morphology and activities was advantageous on a rapidly changing mining frontier. Single-person households, coresidential groups such as partners and families, and cooperative households consisting of nonresidential groups sharing activities of resource production, distribution, and consumption are common adaptations to mining frontiers (Hardesty 1992).

Settlements constitute another type of heterarchy underlying the organization of mining frontiers in the American West. In much the same way as households, local mining settlements typically interacted within larger settlement networks that formed regional communities. Mining districts often defined the boundaries of the networks. Regional settlement networks changed rapidly over time, both in terms of the local settlements that participated and in terms of the economic and political position of settlements within the networks.

But perhaps the key component of frontier mining as a cross-cultural type is rapid change and organizational flexibility in sociotechnical systems, networks of social interactions that link mining resources, techniques, tools, and work culture to the social coordination of labor (Hughes 1983; Pfaffenberger 1992). Mining landscapes express the sociotechnical heterarchies of frontier mining communities as shifting networks of microenvironments. The Cortez mining district in central Nevada is illustrative (Hardesty 2006). Prospectors organized the mining district in 1863 after finding silver in what became known as the Nevada Giant Ledge in the Cortez Mountains. Mining in the ledge created the first microenvironment. Another microenvironment emerged the following year with the construction of a Washoe process pan amalgamation mill in Mill Canyon a few miles away, leading to the exploitation of the surrounding pinyon-juniper forests for wood and charcoal needed to fuel steam boilers and furnaces. Finally, salt used in the mill's amalgamation technology led to the creation of yet another microenvironment, a saltworks on the shores of Pleistocene Lake Gilbert in nearby Grass Valley. In 1869, the pan amalgamation mill closed, and the Mill Canyon and Lake Gilbert microenvironments dropped out of the landscape network, along with their associated settlements.

This network of microenvironments changed substantially about 15 years later with the construction of an innovative Russell leaching process mill at the mouth of Arctic Canyon in 1886. Lime used in the leaching process led to the connection of a new limestone microenvironment nearby with an outcrop that could be quarried and processed into lime with kilns. Water for the mill came by pipeline from an aquifer 7 mi away at the other side of Grass Valley. And as the demand for wood for fuel greatly increased, the clear-cutting and thinning of the pinyon-juniper woodlands intensified. The mill closed in 1892.

The next mining episode began in 1908 when a new mining company refitted the abandoned mill with cyanide technology, bringing about the extraction of low-grade ores, the reworking of old mill wastes, and a distinctive change in landform patterns. New landforms originating in cyanide technology continued to transform the landscape after the mill burned in 1915. The Consolidated Cortez Silver Mines Company built and operated another cyanide and flotation mill farther up Arctic Canyon from 1923 until 1929. Tailings from the mill eventually formed a large tailings flow downslope about a mile to the valley floor. Afterward, small-scale mining continued sporadically in the Cortez district until the 1980s, when high gold and silver prices once again reestablished large-scale industrial mining, this time as an open-pit operation, which still continues.

Historical Archaeology in the Public

Another characteristic of the evolution of historical archaeology in the American West and elsewhere was the beginning of what has become known as "public archaeology" in the late twentieth century. Through legal mandates, public grants, and tourism, the public increasingly supported the practice of historical archaeology, making its public persona a key component of the profession for the first time. The public persona of historical archaeology was characterized by public visibility and perception, political action, and presentation. Clearly, the emergence of public archaeology in the late twentieth century increased public visibility. The media played an important role, and many historical archaeologists became very media savvy. Flashy newspaper, radio, and television accounts were commonplace. Historical archaeology came to appear in *Archaeology Magazine* and in places such as *Dig*, a children's magazine published by the Smithsonian Institution. The U.S. Forest Service began to sponsor Passport in Time projects every summer for volunteers, and historical archaeologists continue to play a major part in this endeavor. Field schools and research projects began to commonly include volunteers. Political action is another late twentieth-century development in the historical archaeology of the American West. The Abandoned Shipwreck Act of 1987 is perhaps the best-known and most successful example of the fruits of the lobbying efforts engaged in by historical archaeologists during this period. Public archaeology perhaps first and foremost is characterized by efforts to interpret the past through presentation to the public. *Presentation* involves communication, education, marketing, and visitor management. Asking local communities what they are interested in, for example, is becoming an important part of interpretation in public archaeology. The interplay between preservation and presentation, however, is the key issue. The presentation of archaeological sites and monuments to the public, as we all know, can be destructive.

Historical Archaeology and Cultural Resource Management

A major factor affecting historical archaeology's development in the West was Section 106 of the National Historic Preservation Act of 1966, as amended, and subsequent state and local legislation. Historical archaeological sites, typically older than 50 years in age, were assessed against significance criteria in order to determine their eligibility for listing on the National Register of Historic Places. Following the publication of 36 CFR 800 regulations, state and federal agencies began hiring archaeologists as cultural resource specialists to review federal undertakings on behalf of the agency or state historic preservation offices.

In the early days of cultural resource management (CRM), and up through the 1980s and later, many historical archaeological sites were overlooked by both archaeologists and agency reviewers, who received their technical archaeological training in prehistory. Likewise, many anthropology departments lacked faculty during CRM's formative period to teach courses in historical archaeology or historic preservation law, especially in the West. In some instances students formed the nucleus of university CRM historical practitioners. For example, Bill Adams's (1977) Silcott townsite study on the Snake River, Washington, was largely a Washington State University student-based historical archaeology study. Frank Leonhardy, a prehistorian, served as the encompassing Alpowa Project's principal investigator, but Adams directed the site excavations and write-up for his dissertation. Ric Sprague at the nearby University of Idaho served as a capable adviser for Washington State's historical archaeologists.

University- and museum-based cultural resource management units conducted many of the early cultural resource inventories and data-recovery projects due to the paucity of private CRM firms. Among the notable surviving university CRM units with expertise in historical archaeology is Sonoma State University's Anthropological Studies Center; other programs, such as Washington State University's Washington Archaeological Research Center, were dropped due to a variety of factors, including CRM's scheduling demands on faculty and a lack of institutional or state support. Surviving university programs have faculty dedicated to conducting CRM projects, and students can use the programs' historical archaeological CRM projects as the basis of their theses and dissertations.

Of great importance to large numbers of archaeologists, agency Section 106 compliance spawned private CRM consulting firms that responded to CRM demand in the West and the project proponents' construction schedules, while creating a much needed job market for anthropology students and graduates. Among the early historical archaeological projects by private firms was Bobby Greenwood's San Buenaventura project, which was also an early study of overseas Chinese historical archaeology.

Some early historical archaeological projects employed historians as a means to bridge the gap between the archaeologists (prehistorians) and historic archaeological sites within a project area. Some of these experiments worked, and some did not. Some consulting historians were disinterested in daily lifeways, related material culture, and archaeological features. Instead, they were more interested in specific individuals, historical events not directly represented in the archaeological record, and historic minutiae akin to some of our own material culture studies. Many historical archaeological curricula now require course work through history departments. We are also still striking a balance in attempting to recognize the data considered important by each discipline, but most historical archaeologists have moved beyond catalogs of basic to excessive artifact and feature description in our reports and have moved on to presenting our findings within "meaningful" contexts. Agencies, including state historic preservation offices, provide some guidance through various historic preservation planning documents.

Another CRM-related development arising from the West was archaeological investigations of overseas Chinese. Artifact assemblages representing large numbers of utilitarian, Chinese ceramic tablewares and containers represented overseas Chinese enclaves within Euro-American communities studied in 1970s CRM projects (Greenwood 1976; Hattori et al. 1979). Our early focus was largely descriptive and typically concluded with determining proportions of Chinese vs. Euro-American material culture and related cultural practices. Couched within the term *acculturation*, we hypothesized that the pattern revealed a minimal adoption of Euro-American culture because we were dealing with a sojourner population.

From its beginnings and at various points in its development, CRM progressed a great deal through the years. There has been an effort by some notable private CRM firms and agency personnel alike to go the extra step and produce reports that contribute to our knowledge of the historic period and to do so within current research paradigms. Some firms provide support for reworking and publishing CRM results in *Historical Archaeology* or through other publications, including books. Now, we realize that site treatments should include sharing our findings with others, including the public and interested parties, especially descendant communities, and should include these interested parties during site excavation and write-up when schedules permit. Additional forms of treatment include public presentations and site tours, popular publications, museum exhibits, signage and plaques, media coverage, and Web-based presentations. It is unlikely that poorer-quality gray literature will disappear, despite attempts to improve quality by stricter agency review. However, we hope that trends toward higher-quality reports by a few CRM firms and innovative treatment plans through public outreach spread to other firms.

Conclusions

Over the past couple of decades, historical archaeology in the American West has come into its own with substantial theoretical underpinnings and literature. Its most distinctive features originated in the unique historical, cultural, and environmental characteristics of the region. Adaptations to an arid environment and the formation of hydraulic societies organized around the control of water underlie one research theme that uniquely characterizes the conduct and future direction of historical archaeology in the region. Another distinctive theme in the historical archaeology of the American West lies in the historical pattern of a regional economic system organized around high-risk and uncertain enterprises such as mining and ranching.

Yet another characteristic of historical archaeology in the region is a research focus upon the legacy of conquest, the distinctive social and cultural institutions that emerged from the Anglo-American invasion and conquest of the American West. The region's historical dependency upon the federal government is perhaps the most distinctive theme in the historical archaeology of the American West. Thus, because of the vast amount of public lands in the region, public lands archaeology supported by the federal government has been the key to archaeological research in the American West since the 1960s and will continue to be so into the future.

Finally, the archaeological research of historically underrepresented or misrepresented immigrant ethnic groups in the West has extended beyond overseas Chinese to include immigrant European and ethnic North American groups. Descendant group participation in historic archaeological projects is also becoming a more common part of outreach and primary research. Likewise, archaeologists are refining the context of so-called ethnic markers and documenting their adoption outside the immigrant communities.

References Cited

Adams, William H.
1977 *Silcott, Washington: Ethnoarchaeology of a Rural American Community*. Reports of Investigations, 54. Laboratory of Anthropology, Washington State University, Pullman.

Brown, Gail
2001 Wounded Knee: The Conflict of Interpretation. In *Myth, Memory, and the Making of the American Landscape*, edited by Paul A. Shackel, pp. 103–118. University Press of Florida, Gainesville.

Crumley, Carole L. (editor)
1994 *Historical Ecology: Cultural Knowledge and Changing Landscapes*. School of American Research Press, Santa Fe, New Mexico.

Delgado, James
2009 *Gold Rush Port: The Maritime Archaeology of San Francisco's Waterfront*. University of California Press, Berkeley.

Dubel, Janice L.
2001 Remembering a Japanese-American Concentration Camp at Manzanar National Historic Site. In *Myth, Memory, and the Making of the American Landscape*, edited by Paul A. Shackel, pp. 85–102. University Press of Florida, Gainesville.

Fox, Richard
1997 *Archaeology, History, and Custer's Last Battle: The Little Big Horn Re-Examined*. University of Oklahoma Press, Norman.

Greenwood, Roberta S.
1976 *The Changing Faces of Main Street*. Report to the Redevelopment Agency, City of San Buenaventura from Greenwood and Associates, Pacific Palisades, California.

Hall, Thomas D.
1989 *Social Change in the Southwest, 1350–1880*. University Press of Kansas, Lawrence.

Hardesty, Donald L.
1992 The Miner's Domestic Household: Perspectives from the American West. In *Sozialgeschichte des Bergbau im 19. und 20. Jahrundert*, edited by Klaus Tenfeldt, pp. 180–196. Verlag C. H. Beck, Munich.

1998 Power and the Industrial Mining Community in the American West. In *Social Approaches to an Industrial Past: The Archaeology and Anthropology of Mining*, edited by A. Bernard Knapp, Vincent C. Pigott, and Eugenia W. Herbert, pp. 81–96. Routledge Press, London.

1999 Historical Archaeology in the New Millennium: A Forum. *Historical Archaeology* 33(2):51–58.

2006 Industrial Archaeology, Landscapes, and Historical Knowledge. In *Monitoring Science and Technology Symposium: Unifying Knowledge for Sustainability in the Western Hemisphere*, edited by Celedonio Aguirre-Bravo, pp. 514–517. Proceedings RMRS-P-42CD. U.S. Department of Agriculture, Forest Service, Rocky Mountain Research Station, Fort Collins.

2010 Gendering Mining Landscapes. In *Archaeology and the Preservation of Gendered Landscapes*, edited by Sherene Baugher and Suzanne M. Spencer-Wood, pp. 293–312. Springer, New York.

2011 Theoretical Perspectives on the Frontier Mining Pattern. In *Eldorado! The Archaeology of Gold Mining in the Far North*, edited by Catherine Holder Spude, Robin O. Mills, Karl Gurcke, and Roderick Sprague, pp. 25–33. University of Nebraska Press, Lincoln.

Hattori, Eugene M., Mary K. Rusco, and Donald R. Tuohy (editors)

1979 *Archaeological and Historical Studies at Ninth and Amherst, Lovelock, Nevada*. Nevada State Museum Archaeological Services Report Vols. 1–2. Carson City.

Hughes, Thomas

1983 *Networks of Power*. Johns Hopkins University Press, Baltimore.

Larkin, Karen, and Randall McGuire (editors)

2009 *The Archaeology of Class War: The Colorado Coalfield Strike of 1913–1914*. University Press of Colorado, Boulder.

Lees, William

2004 Confronting the Stereotype: A Proper Context for the Study of the Civil War (and Other Military Conflicts) in the West. Paper presented at the Society for Historical Archaeology Conference, St. Louis, Missouri.

Lightfoot, Kent

2005 *Indians, Missionaries, and Merchants: The Legacy of Colonial Encounters on the California Frontiers*. University of California Press, Berkeley.

Lipman-Blumen, Jean

1994 The Existential Basis of Power Relationships: The Gender Role Case. In *Power/Gender: Social Relations in Theory and Practice*, edited by H. L. Radtke and H. J. Stam, pp. 108–135. Sage, London.

Mann, Michael

1986 *The Sources of Social Power, Vol. I: A History of Power from the Beginning to AD 1760*. Cambridge University Press, Cambridge.

Netting, Robert M.

1993 *Smallholders, Householders: Farm Families and the Ecology of Intensive, Sustainable Agriculture*. Stanford University Press, Stanford.

Pauls, Elizabeth

2006 The Place of Space: Architecture, Landscape, and Social Life. In *Historical Archaeology*, edited by M. Hall and S. W. Sillman, pp. 65–83. Blackwell, Malden, Massachusetts.

Pfaffenberger, Brian

1992 The Social Anthropology of Technology. *Annual Review of Anthropology* 21:491–516.

Saitta, Dean J.

2007 *The Archaeology of Collective Action*. University Press of Florida, Gainesville.

Steward, Julian H.

1955 *Theory of Culture Change*. University of Illinois Press, Urbana.

Sunseri, Jun U.

2010 (Re)Constructing la Tierra de la Guerra: An Indo-Hispano Gendered Landscape on the Rito Colorado Frontier of Spanish Colonial New Mexico. In *Archaeology and the Preservation of Gendered Landscapes*, edited by Sherene Baugher and Suzanne M. Spencer-Wood, pp. 141–164. Springer, New York.

Tilley, Christopher

1994 *A Phenomenology of Landscape: Places, Paths, and Monuments*. Berg, Oxford.

Voss, Barbara

2008 *The Archaeology of Ethnogenesis: Race and Sexuality in Colonial San Francisco*. University of California Press, Berkeley.

Warner, Mark, and Daryl Baldwin

2004 Building Ties: The Collaboration Between the Miami Nation and Archaeology. In *Places in Mind: Archaeology as Applied Anthropology*, edited by Paul A. Shackel and Erve Chambers, pp. 137–152. Routledge, London.

Wilcox, Michael V.

2009 *The Pueblo Revolt and the Mythology of Conquest: An Indigenous Archaeology of Contact*. University of California Press, Berkeley.

23

Origins of an Archaeological Tree-Ring Data Set

Flagstaff Area, Northeastern Arizona

Richard V. N. Ahlstrom and Christian E. Downum

From 1960 to 1975, the Laboratory of Tree-Ring Research at the University of Arizona reanalyzed its collection of tree-ring samples recovered from prehistoric archaeological sites in the vicinity of Flagstaff, Arizona. This study resulted in the publication of two monographs, or "quadrangle reports" (Bannister et al. 1966; Robinson et al. 1975), that were part of the Tree-Ring Laboratory's (TRL) larger undertaking to reexamine and redate all of the samples in its possession that had been obtained from archaeological contexts throughout the American Southwest. This larger effort resulted in the publication, between 1966 and 1975, of 16 quadrangle reports containing thousands of tree-ring dates from hundreds of archaeological sites (Robinson 1976:16; Robinson et al. 1975:ii). Since the completion of the quadrangle series, the TRL has dated thousands of additional samples: as of 1990 (and the latest full inventory available), the count exceeded 27,000 dates from more than 1,300 prehistoric and historical-period Native American sites (Robinson and Cameron 1991).

The TRL's "reanalysis project" was important for two reasons. First, it resulted in a substantial increase in the number of dates from sites that had been excavated over the preceding decades. In the Flagstaff case, this involved an increase from the 265 dates from 46 sites that were available in 1946 when Harold Colton published his archaeological synthesis, *The Sinagua*, to the 670 or so dates from the same inventory of sites that were included in the relevant quadrangle report (Robinson et al. 1975). Second, the project systematized one of the most coherent and significant bodies of data produced by American and, indeed, world archaeology. This panregional data set is as coherent as it is, first, because all of the included dates have been derived by a single method of analysis that was developed by the founder of American dendrochronology, A. E. Douglass, and his associates at the TRL; second, because all of the dating analyses were conducted at that one institution; and third, because the resulting tree-ring dates have been reported according to a single standardized format that indicates the key features of the individual dates (Ahlstrom 1985:30–39; Robinson et al. 1975).

The significance of the data set lies in the fact that it has supported the high-resolution dating of thousands of events, relating most directly to the procurement of timbers and the construction of buildings, at hundreds of archaeological sites. These events can be assigned with confidence to intervals of time ranging in length from several years to as little as the growing or nongrowing season of a single year (Ahlstrom 1985; Dean 1978a). Combined with time-sensitive change in ceramic decoration, the tree-ring record has made possible the definition of cultural phases that are 100 years, 50 years, or even 20 years in length (as in the case of the Winona phase, discussed below). Tree-ring dates have also been summed or aggregated over multiple sites within and across regions to produce proxy records of temporal variation in construction activity, population size and movement, and degrees of settlement mobility (Ahlstrom 1998a; Benson and Berry 2009; Berry 1982; Lipe 1995; Lipe and Varien 1999; Plog 1984, 1989; Potter et al. 2012; Windes and McKenna 2001).

For all of these kinds of analysis, but especially for those that make use of data from multiple sites, an understanding of the nature of the sample of tree-ring-dated events is crucial (Ahlstrom 1997, 1998a, 1998b; Nash and Rogers, this volume). This conclusion follows from a most basic principle of archaeological chronology, that it is rarely possible to directly date more than a small fraction of the past events that are relevant to any research agenda (Ahlstrom 1985, 1997, 1998a, 1998b, 2008). The factors that determine the characteristics of a multisite sample of tree-ring dates can be grouped into four categories. They include (1) the distribution of datable tree species in the area of interest; (2) the ways in which the people whose archaeological remains are being investigated made use of the wood that they obtained from both datable *and* nondatable tree species; (3) archaeological site formation processes (Dean 1978b; Schiffer 1987) that have led to the preservation of wood or charcoal that has the potential to be tree-ring dated; and (4) the decisions of archaeologists in selecting sites to be excavated or, in select cases, to be sampled directly for tree-ring specimens that have resulted

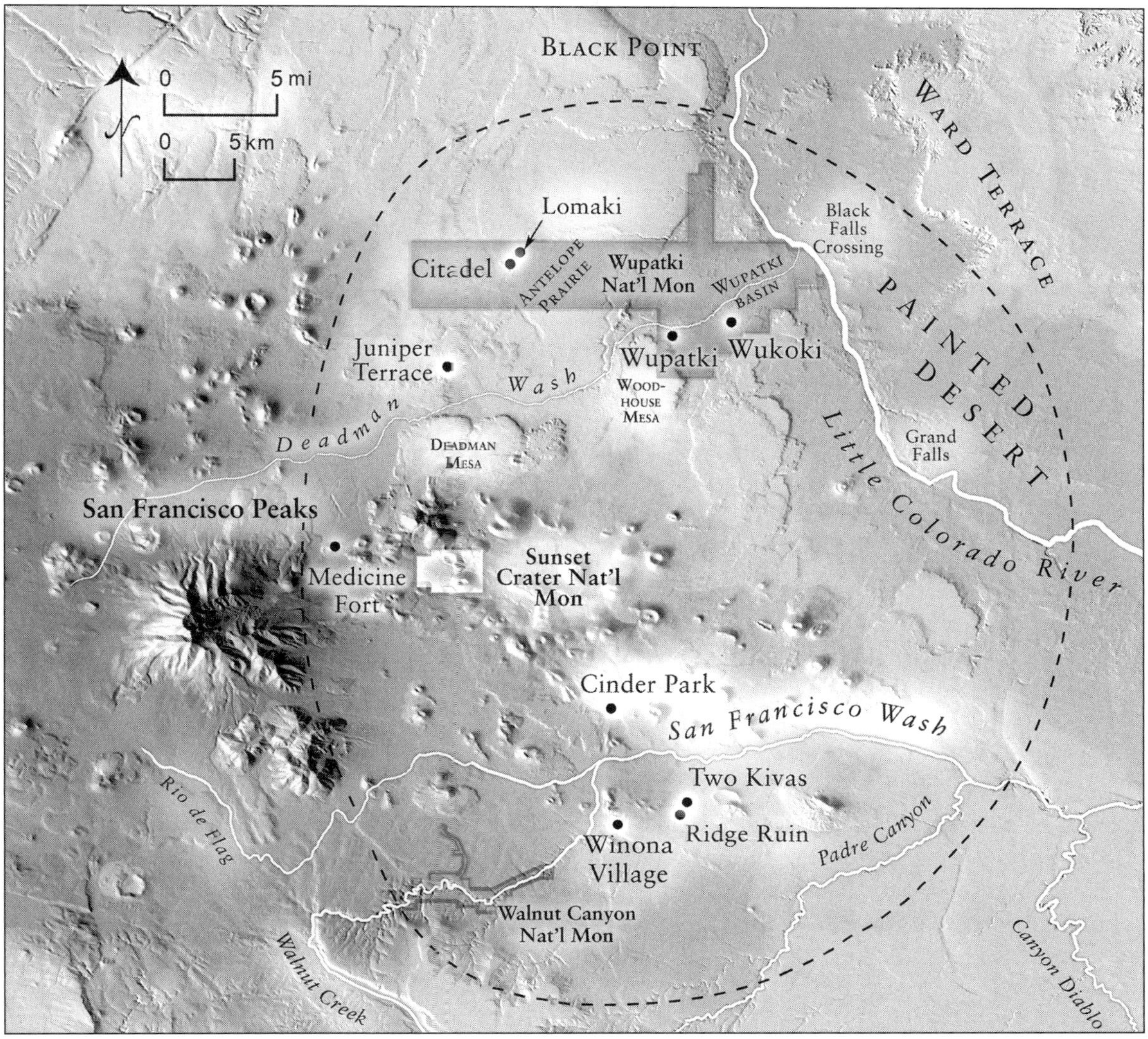

FIGURE 23.1. Map of the area east of the San Francisco Peaks, showing the extent of the Sunset Crater ash (dashed line) and the locations of major sites mentioned in the text.

in the collection of wood or charcoal samples suitable for tree-ring analysis. (As elsewhere in the Southwest, the vast majority of Flagstaff-area tree-ring dates appear to come from wood that was used in construction rather than for other purposes for example, as fuelwood or in the making of tools or other implements [Ahlstrom 1985:455–478].)

Previous research has shown that there is variability over time and space in the operation of these "sources of variation" in the archaeological tree-ring record (Ahlstrom 1997; Nash and Rogers, this volume). The Flagstaff area provides a valuable case study for understanding how the action and interaction of these factors can affect the interpretive potential of a body of tree-ring data.

The Flagstaff Tree-Ring Data Set

The archaeological sites that produced the Flagstaff area's tree-ring dates are located in the TRL's Arizona Quadrangles I and O. They lie primarily to the east of the San Francisco Peaks in an area that extends from the flanks of these mountains for a distance of 15 mi to the northeast in the direction of the Little Colorado River, 5 mi to the east toward Sunset Crater, and 35 mi to the southeast to Anderson Mesa (Figure 23.1). The data set discussed here includes the 993 tree-ring dates listed in the two cited quadrangle reports as well as an additional 119 dates determined since those reports were published. These 1,112 tree-ring dates come from 86 sites.

Behavior of Archaeologists

Due to the profound effect that the behavior of archaeologists has had on the character of the Flagstaff area's tree-ring data set, we begin our discussion with this "source of variation" in the tree-ring record. More than half of the Flagstaff-area dates come from samples collected by the Museum of Northern Arizona (MNA) before World War II. Specifically, as of 1988

> about 72% (105 of 145) of the contexts [in Arizona I] that [had] produced tree-ring dates were excavated or sampled prior to World War II.... Of the total number of [dated]

> tree-ring samples from these contexts (980), nearly 70% (680) were obtained from pre-war investigations [Downum 1988:142].

It follows that MNA's archaeological agenda during this interval had a profound influence on the tree-ring data set that exists today (Nash 1999:143–184).

A significant source of bias can be identified in MNA's procedures for selecting sites that were to be investigated during this prewar period. In the course of the museum's 1930 field expedition, "four separate observations were made that demonstrated conclusively that Sunset Crater, a cinder cone volcano about 15 miles northeast of Flagstaff, had erupted during the prehistoric pueblo occupation" (Downum 1988:107). MNA's archaeologists came to believe that the ash expelled from this volcano acted as a natural mulch that increased the agricultural potential of the land and, as a result, inspired a land rush to the area northeast of the San Francisco Peaks where the ash had been deposited (Elson et al. 2006:26–30; Pilles 1979; Waring 2007:59–60). Because of this event's importance to local prehistory, the dating of Sunset Crater's eruption became a primary focus of MNA's field expeditions from 1931 to 1935. Considerable excavation effort was expended, for example, in the Bonito Park/Bonito Terrace area,

> where Pueblo I and early Pueblo II sherds—now known to be pre-eruptive in age—had been seen at the surface. It was hoped that these "sherd areas" would mark the locations of ash-covered pithouses, and that they would provide specimens suitable for dating [Downum 1988:112].

MNA's archaeologists employed a testing procedure to locate and evaluate pithouses that were hidden under the surface deposit of Sunset Crater ash. When evidence of a structure was identified, the testing was continued to determine if it had burned. If it had, it was excavated; if not, the investigation was ended, and the test unit was filled in. The explicit goal of this procedure was to recover tree-ring-datable samples of charcoal that could assist in the building of tree-ring chronologies and, by extension, in the dating of Sunset Crater's eruption (Colton 1946:126; Downum 1988:112, 115; Hargrave 1933:16, 22–24). This strategy could bias the sample of excavated structures, particularly if there was variation over time in the intentional burning of structures. This could occur, for example, if structures were burned during periods of conflict or in ritual abandonment (Ahlstrom 1985; Wilshusen 1986). MNA's sampling strategy is also of note because it shows that "problem-oriented" research (Lipe 1974:231–234) is not a recent invention but, in fact, has deep roots in Southwestern archaeology.

The desire on the part of MNA's archaeologists to date the eruption of Sunset Crater is the primary reason why a map showing the distribution of volcanic ash from that event is so similar to one showing the distribution of sites in Arizona I that have produced tree-ring dates (Colton 1946:Figure 144; Pilles 1979: Figure 15.1; Robinson et al 1975:Figure 2). Along with the excavated sites that are within the ash-fall zone, many others are located not far from it. In all likelihood, the desire to study the effects of the volcanic ash on prehistoric settlement played a role in the selection of these sites for investigation as well. Whatever the precise selection criteria, MNA excavated sites mostly to the east and northeast of the San Francisco Peaks. Numerous sites have also, however, been identified in other parts of the Sinagua domain and in other directions from these mountains (Pilles 1988). Except for several sites excavated on Anderson Mesa (Bannister et al. 1966; McGregor 1973), located well to the southeast of the San Francisco Peaks, prehistoric settlement in these other areas is not reflected in the regional sample of tree-ring-dated events. This is an important source of bias in the tree-ring record, particularly considering the extent to which shifts in Sinagua population are known to have occurred over time (Pilles 1979, 1988).

Environmental Setting

The sites with tree-ring dates located to the northeast and east of the San Francisco Peaks lie along an elevational and environmental gradient that includes a series of four biotic communities. These "biomes" include, from southwest to northeast and from highest elevation to lowest, (1) Rocky Mountain montane conifer forest, (2) Great Basin conifer woodland, (3) Great Basin grassland, and (4) Great Basin desert scrub (Brown 1982; Brown and Lowe 1980). The four communities are characterized by different tree-ring-datable tree species, and they vary as well with respect to the frequency of archaeological sites that have produced dated tree-ring samples. Spruce and fir (whose wood and charcoal can be difficult to distinguish when recovered from archaeological contexts) and Douglas fir occur high on the slopes of the San Francisco Peaks, in the upper elevational range of the montane conifer forest. Douglas fir can also be found growing at lower elevations in protected canyon settings. Ponderosa pines cover the lower slopes of the mountains as well as the surrounding plateaus, within the lower elevational range of the montane conifer forest. Sites with tree-ring dates are absent from the higher-elevation portion of the conifer forest that is dominated by spruce and fir trees but quite abundant within the lower-elevation ponderosa pine forest. The next biome along the transect, conifer woodland, is characterized by two datable tree species, pinyon and juniper. Some sites excavated in this zone have produced tree-ring dates. The two lowest biomes in the series, grassland and desert scrub, do not support the growth of datable tree species. Sites with dates do, however, occur in the grassland biome but, with few exceptions, are absent from the desert scrub biome. We will return to the spatial relationship between each of the four biomes and its record of archaeological tree-ring dates shortly.

Elevation is not the only variable affecting the distribution of tree-ring-datable tree species along the environmental gradient. A second factor concerns the distribution of volcanic ash, or cinders, ejected by the many small volcanoes and, in particular, small cinder cones that cluster within 15–20 mi north and east of the San Francisco Peaks:

> The cinders have been found to retain moisture for long periods of time. This promotes tree growth…and allows ponderosa and juniper to grow 300 m (1000 ft) lower in elevation than their normal range of occurrence [Pilles 1979:467–468; see also Brown and Lowe 1980; Colton 1946:Figure 144].

Environmental Setting and Prehistoric Behavior Interaction

Several dozen semisubterranean earth lodge–style pithouses (Colton 1933:5) dating from the ninth through the eleventh centuries have been excavated in the ponderosa pine forest immediately northeast and east of the San Francisco Peaks (Colton 1946; Elson 2006). Not surprisingly, the majority of tree-ring dates obtained from these structures come from samples of ponderosa pine. In other biomes, the relationship between the species of local trees and those of dated tree-ring samples is more complex. A number of pithouses dating between the AD 1080s and 1130s have been excavated at Winona Village (Figure 23.1), located southeast of the mountains in conifer woodland. In keeping with this setting, the site has produced numerous tree-ring dates from samples of pinyon and juniper. It has also, however, provided dates from samples of ponderosa pine and Douglas fir. Ponderosa pine trees can be found today within about 5 mi west of Winona Village, and both ponderosa pine and Douglas fir grow within 5 to 10 mi southwest of the site in Walnut Canyon.

The disjunction between the species represented by local trees and those represented by dated tree-ring samples is even greater at Wupatki, a masonry pueblo with about 80 ground-floor rooms and an additional 20 upper-story rooms (Figure 23.1; Brennan and Downum 2001; Downum et al. 1999). The site has produced 171 tree-ring dates, which fall mostly between AD 1110 and 1215, with three late dates in the 1250s–1260s. In spite of its location in the grassland biome, Wupatki's inventory of tree-ring dates comes primarily from samples of ponderosa pine ($n = 66$), spruce or fir ($n = 77$), and Douglas fir ($n = 21$). Today, ponderosa pine grows 8 mi and more from Wupatki (Douglass 1935:47), and Douglas firs may occur in localized settings at comparable distances. One must travel substantially farther up the slopes of the San Francisco Peaks—to a distance of 20 mi or more from the site—to encounter substantial stands of spruce or fir.

A. E. Douglass interpreted the abundance of ponderosa pine at Wupatki as evidence of environmental change:

> There is no doubt that the large number of these Wupatki timbers indicate a nearby forest. Judging by our investigations at other points, one would conclude that the pine forest…extended in the twelfth century to the mesa immediately above the ruin [1935:47, quoted in Downum 1988:184].

A similar argument was applied to explain the presence of Douglas fir beams at Winona Village (discussed above) and Ridge Ruin, which lie today within the conifer woodland biome. In the case of all three of these sites, the use of nonlocal species was taken as evidence of environmental change, specifically in support of the hypothesis that the Sunset Crater ash had acted as moisture-retaining mulch that allowed the tree species in question to grow at lower-than-normal elevations.

From today's perspective, the presence of substantial numbers of ponderosa pine, spruce/fir, and Douglas fir beams at Wupatki is likely a function of prehistoric behavior, specifically involving the long-distance transport of construction wood, rather than a result of change in the distribution of the relevant tree species. The same is true of smaller assemblages of analyzed beams at sites in the vicinity of Wupatki, including Wukoki, Citadel, Nalakihu, Lomaki, Heiser Springs, and Three Courts pueblos. Two lines of evidence, involving the size of Wupatki and the presence of a ball court nearby (Colton 1946), indicate that the site was home to a community that was significantly larger and more socially complex than the households that constructed the previously mentioned ninth- to eleventh-century pithouses that are located in the ponderosa pine forest. Those pithouses were generally built one at a time with locally available materials. The effort expended in the construction of one of these structures, including the transport of materials, would have been influenced by the knowledge that the structure would probably survive for no more than 15–20 years before needing to be rebuilt or replaced (Ahlstrom 1985:633–639; Cameron 1990; Schlanger 1987).

At the opposite end of the prehistoric Southwestern social scale are Chaco Canyon's large pueblos, whose construction presumably involved the coordinated effort of village-sized communities. That effort included the procurement of thousands of timbers from the Chuska Mountains, up to 50 mi from Chaco Canyon (Betancourt et al. 1986; Dean and Warren 1983). Windes and McKenna (2001) have suggested that this task was performed by groups that specialized in this activity. The product of this coordinated effort consisted of buildings that, with proper maintenance, could be expected to remain in use for decades. Wupatki and the contemporaneous pueblos in its vicinity did not operate at a social scale as complex as that inferred for the Chacoan system. The Chaco example does, however, provide a context for arguing that the long-distance transport of timbers, though costly in terms of labor investment, could have been well within the means of the communities that built and occupied Wupatki and the neighboring pueblos. The effort required to procure the beams from distant sources would, however, have been substantial: the 171 dated samples from Wupatki represent only an estimated 10–15 percent of the pueblo's original complement of wooden construction elements (Downum et al. 2013).

It is important to note that the arguments inferring environmental change on the basis of beam species data from the Wupatki and Winona sites were introduced at a time when it

```
A.D.
 800    80|0*
        81|1*
        82|                         KEY:  0  = noncutting date
        83|                               0i = cutting date, from sample with
        84|                                    incomplete outer growth ring
 850    85|                               2c = cutting date, from sample with
        86|                                    complete outer growth ring
        87|2                              2v = probable cutting date
        88|                               0* = dated sample from roof-support post
        89|3*
 900    90|
        91|3
        92|
        93|
        94|1  7*
 950    95|9
        96|2  6
        97|3
        98|
        99|7
1000   100|
       101|
       102|
       103|
       104|
1050   105|
       106|                                        106|4
       107|0i 2  6  8                              107|3  4  4  5  6  6  7  9
       108|4  6                                    108|0  0  2  2  3v 4  4v 4v 4v 5v 5v 5c 6  6  6v
       109|1  2  2  2  2v 2i 2c 3v 3v 3i 3i        109|5                    6i 6c 6c 6c 6c 6c 7
1100   110|

                 a) NA 1625C                          b) Winona Village (NA 2133A)
```

FIGURE 23.2. Stem-and-leaf diagrams of tree-ring dates from pithouses at (a) Site NA 1625C and (b) Winona Village (NA 2133A).

was thought that the eruption of Sunset Crater had occurred by around AD 900 (Downum 1988:150–153). This might have provided sufficient time for the lower forest border to have advanced downslope closer to Wupatki and Winona Village before those sites were occupied. This interval would have been 150–200 years in the case of Winona Village and 200–300 years in the case of Wupatki. Subsequent redating of Sunset Crater's initial eruption to the AD 1060s (Smiley 1958; also Colton 1946:258; Pilles 1979) and, more recently, of this volcano's entire eruption episode to the AD 1040s–1090s (Ort et al. 2007) has, however, reduced this potential "response interval" for the tree species in question, eliminating it in the case of Winona Village and cutting it to about a century for Wupatki.

The downslope shift in the distribution of ponderosa pines to the northeast of the San Francisco Peaks that was described earlier appears to have been made possible, at least in part, by the presence of volcanic ash in this area. The ash in question was not, however, produced primarily by Sunset Crater but, rather, by a sequence of eruptions in the Sunset Crater volcanic field that extends tens if not hundreds of thousands of years into the past and which simply includes the creation of Sunset Crater as its latest episode.

Prehistoric Behavior

Data from earth lodge–style pithouses in the Flagstaff area suggest that the degree of stability vs. mobility in local settlement systems can have an effect on the collections of tree-ring dates obtained from individual structures and, by extension, on multisite date distributions. This evidence involves the contrasting shapes of date distributions from structures located within the ponderosa pine forest immediately east of the San Francisco Peaks and of structures at Winona Village, located southeast of the mountains in the conifer woodland biome. Tree-ring dates from structures in the former area tend to be spread over intervals of a century or more, whereas those from Winona Village typically fall in intervals of 50 years or fewer (Figure 23.2; Ahlstrom 1985: 455–483). One implication of these data is that the inhabitants of the earth lodges located near the mountains tended to relocate to new homes over distances that were short enough to encourage the salvaging, transport, and reuse of beams from their previous residences. (Some of the spread in tree-ring date distributions from these structures is also no doubt a function of the erosion of outer rings from the sampled beams—though even the scale of that effect may relate indirectly to the extended use lives of reused timbers.) Both ceramic evidence and tree-ring dates do in fact indicate that the area near the mountains was inhabited more or less continuously over the relevant interval of AD 900–1100 (Ahlstrom 1985; Robinson et al. 1975).

The founders of Winona Village, on the other hand, appear to have relocated to this spot over distances that made the reuse of beams from their former homes impractical. Regional settlement data indicate that there may have been a population shift to the conifer woodland biome, where Winona Village is located, during the corresponding Angell/Winona phase. The designs of pithouses at Winona Village differed from those of earlier periods, and it is also possible that the "old" timbers were poorly suited for use in the new structures.

There is an additional set of tree-ring evidence that documents the reuse of a particular, valued category of timbers by the pithouse dwellers of the ponderosa forest. An analysis of date distributions from earth lodge–style pithouses near the San Francisco Peaks shows that the dates from upright roof-support posts generally fall in the first or second quartiles of their respective date distributions (Figure 23.2; Ahlstrom 1985:473–478). These data point to the preferential reuse of these posts, even within the context of the high overall rate of beam reuse identified for these structures. John McGregor reported more traditional archaeological evidence for the reuse of support posts (and other construction elements) from the area's "timber" pithouses (i.e., those with wood-lined house pits):

> The lack of any of the larger support poles in almost all of the sites in Bonito Terrace would argue that these sites were habitually robbed of the main beams before abandonment, and later the small amount of wooden material left [was] burned. For if these houses had been burned with the entire wooden inner structure intact it is only logical to suppose that at least the bases of the beams near the floor level would have been preserved [1936:14].

The large size of the postholes in some structures could have resulted from "the rocking back and forth of the posts to loosen them, or the digging away of the clay around them" to facilitate their removal for reuse elsewhere (McGregor 1936:14).

Site Formation Processes and Postdepositional Events

An aspect of prehistoric behavior that has a major impact on the preservation of datable tree-ring samples is the decision on the part of the prehistoric actors to locate their homes in open vs. sheltered settings (Ahlstrom 1997). All but 17 of the 1,112 tree-ring dates included in the Flagstaff data set are from open sites. In considering how datable samples are preserved at sites in open settings, it is useful to distinguish between semisubterranean earth lodges, or pithouses, and surface masonry rooms. Three factors contribute to the often successful tree-ring dating of Southwestern pithouses. They include (1) the large amounts of wood that were incorporated in these buildings' superstructures; (2) the frequency with which these structures were burned, either on purpose or accidentally; and (3) conditions in the burning structures, involving in particular the collapse of the heavy, earthen-covered superstructure into the house pit, that led to the preservation of charred segments of wooden beams. Up to the AD 1130s, burned earth lodge–style pithouses are responsible for the majority of Flagstaff-area tree-ring dates.

It is unusual for a burned pithouse to produce a collection of charred tree-ring samples that approaches a full inventory of the wooden beams incorporated in its superstructure (Figure 23.2). One reason for this shortfall is the previously discussed removal of reusable beams prior to the structure's having been set on fire (Ahlstrom 1985:82–90; McGregor 1936:14). A second factor involves the incomplete burning of structures. Lyndon Hargrave made several observations about patterning in the burning of Flagstaff-area pithouses that are worth repeating here. He refers to

> the usual absence of charcoal in the center of the room, the high roof seldom burning thus serving as a fire extinguisher by smothering the fire when the roof supports collapse.... Amount of charcoal encountered along the sides [of the structure] and the condition of the corner posts fairly accurately determine the extent of burning, experience having shown that the rear of the structure is often burned while the wood at the front is decayed.... The use of a ventilating system would create a draft sufficient to keep the ventilator from burning [1933:22–23].

Somewhat different "rules" can be identified for the preservation of datable samples from surface masonry rooms. There are two circumstances under which a surface masonry pueblo in an open or unsheltered setting is most likely to produce a large number of tree-ring dates: the Flagstaff area has produced one good example of each of these situations. Wooden beams or beam segments can be preserved in relatively massive and typically multistory masonry pueblos where the presence of standing walls, combined with the collapse of upper and outer rooms, has protected wooden construction elements located in the inner portions of the structure from contact with decay-hastening moisture derived from rain or snow. Roof beams can be protected in this manner, as can wooden door lintels and other intramural construction elements. The effect is further enhanced if the local environment is especially dry, even by Southwestern standards. Such cases are relatively rare among sites in open settings. The best-known examples are located in Chaco Canyon in northwestern New Mexico (Dean and Warren 1983).

The Flagstaff-area site that best fits this scenario is Wupatki Pueblo. Almost all of the dated tree-ring samples from this site consist of wood: fewer than 10 of Wupatki's 171 dated samples consist of charred wood or charcoal. Most of the charcoal samples came from a burned structure that underlay the masonry pueblo and, thus, are not directly related to its occupation (Downum et al. 1999).

Surface structures can also produce tree-ring dates in the same manner as pit structures, that is, from beams that have burned to charcoal. Although surface structures with walls made of jacal (consisting of aligned, close-set upright poles that were generally plastered over) have produced tree-ring dates in other locations (Ahlstrom 1985, 1998a:155–157), this construction technique is unknown in the Flagstaff area. Pueblo rooms here were instead built exclusively of stone masonry. Although individual rooms in masonry pueblos did burn on occasion, evidence for the catastrophic burning of blocks of rooms is relatively rare in the Southwestern archaeological record. The masonry used in the construction of these buildings apparently created "fire walls" that retarded the spread of fire from one room to another. Rooms whose roofs were destroyed by fire could also have been cleaned out and reroofed (Icove et al. 2006), making the occurrence of fire appear less common in masonry pueblos than it actually was. In any case, there are relatively few catastrophically burned Southwestern pueblos that have produced large numbers of tree-ring dates.

The local example of this kind of preservation is Two Kivas Pueblo, located 10 mi southeast of the San Francisco Peaks (Figure 23.1; McGregor 1973; Robinson et al. 1975). This site's main room block incorporated about 15 ground-floor rooms, several of which were topped by second-story rooms. Eleven of the room spaces (including both first- and presumed upper-story rooms) produced a total of 162 tree-ring dates, all obtained from charcoal samples. The overall date distribution from Two Kivas Pueblo provides evidence of an interval of beam procurement that lasted from the AD 1160s through the first decade of the 1200s. There is also a single later date, in the AD 1240s. Ceramic evidence, including the presence of Kayenta Black-on-white and Kiet Siel Polychrome, indicates that Two Kivas Pueblo was occupied to AD 1250 or perhaps AD 1275, much later than the bulk of the site's date distribution would imply.

The important point about these data, from the perspective of interpretive methodology, is that even a large collection of tree-ring dates made possible by the catastrophic burning of a large portion of the Two Kivas site does not provide a complete temporal record of the site's occupation. This is often the case (Ahlstrom 1985). The majority of Southwestern tree-ring dates relate most directly to the construction of buildings, and some relate to their subsequent remodeling or repair. It is generally thought that these activities continued throughout most of the occupation of a typical Southwestern pueblo. The pace of new construction and, eventually, remodeling and repair would have slowed over time, however, resulting in a progressive decrease in the likelihood of obtaining tree-ring evidence of later construction events (Ahlstrom 1985, 1998a; Hantman 1983). In the case of Two Kivas Pueblo, only one of the total sample of 162 tree-ring dates provides evidence relating to the last 30–50 years of the site's occupation.

Only a fraction of excavated structures in the Southwest have yielded datable tree-ring samples, and only a fraction of these structures can be interpreted as reliably tree-ring dated (Ahlstrom 1985:Table 31). This truism can be illustrated with data from the Bonito Park/Bonito Terrace area, located several miles east of the San Francisco Peaks. MNA's pre–World War II field expeditions worked repeatedly in this locality, excavating pithouses there in 1931, 1932, and 1935 (Downum 1988:111–129). Colton (1946) provides data on 25 houses in this area that were either tested or excavated. Nine of the 25 buildings produced evidence of burning; eight of these structures provided tree-ring specimens; and seven of those produced between one and 10 tree-ring dates each. Only one of these pithouses (NA 1920B) can be characterized as "well dated" based on tree-ring evidence, though a tentative date can be suggested for a second (NA 1925B [Ahlstrom 1985:Table 2.1]).

The Flagstaff Area's Tree-Ring Record: Chronological Summary

Figure 23.3 summarizes the body of tree-ring data from prehistoric archaeological contexts in the Flagstaff area. It charts the tree-ring evidence on a decadal time scale and in terms of three variables (Ahlstrom 1997). The first of these, which consists of the total number of tree-ring dates per decade, shows variation in the quantity of available tree-ring evidence over time. The second variable, the percentage of cutting dates per decade, reflects the quality of that tree-ring evidence. (A cutting date provides a generally accurate estimate of the year during which a beam or other piece of construction wood was procured. A noncutting date, on the other hand, provides a potentially early and, in that sense, biased estimate of when this event occurred [Ahlstrom 1985; Dean 1978a; Nash 1997].) The third variable included in the figure involves the dating of individual construction events (identified in Ahlstrom 1985:278–280, 305, 457–458; Downum 1988:342–346, 382–389). It provides a degree of control over potential bias in the first variable, which places the greatest emphasis on individual sites and structures that have produced atypically large numbers of tree-ring dates. As plotted in Figure 23.3, this third variable applies mostly to pit structures, primarily semisubterranean earth lodges but also including some structures with masonry-lined house pits. A cutoff date of AD 1150 was chosen for the plotting of these dated construction events because most of the later tree-ring dates come from masonry surface rooms that are incorporated in blocks of similar rooms. In this kind of setting, individual dated room-construction events can be difficult to identify, and criteria for weighting events based on the number of rooms involved are difficult to operationalize.

Figure 23.3 also includes a sequence of archaeological phases, consisting essentially of named ceramic complexes assigned to discrete time intervals, that has been developed for the Sinagua

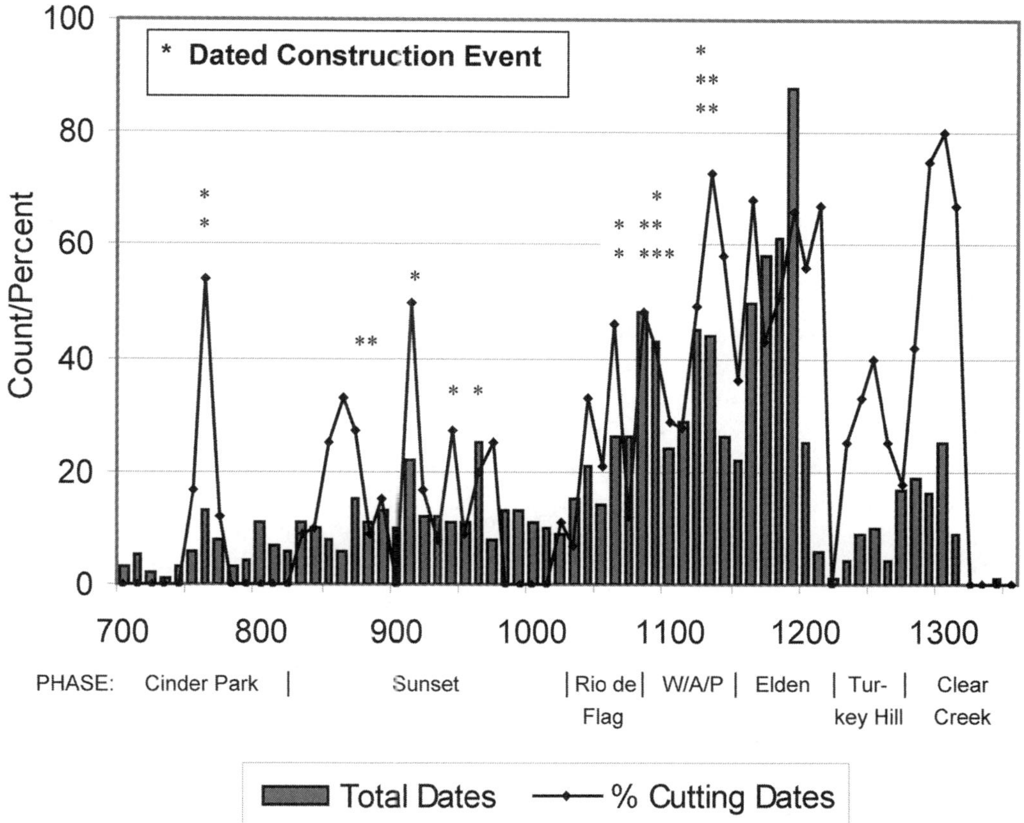

FIGURE 23.3. Summary chart of the Flagstaff-area tree-ring data, AD 700–1350, showing numbers of dates and percentages of cutting dates per decade, as well as tree-ring-dated construction events involving pithouses and other pit structures to AD 1150. Also indicated are the time intervals of the local phase sequence. W/A/P = combined Winona, Angell, and Padre phases.

archaeological culture (Colton 1946; Pilles 1988). This is one of three such cultures identified in the Flagstaff area, the others being the Cohonina and prehistoric Puebloan cultures. The phases have recently been redated by Downum, using the mean ceramic date formula developed by Andrew Christenson (1994) for use with Kayenta ceramics, and it is those new dates that are referenced here. As suggested above, most sites that have been recorded in the area lack tree-ring dates, and it is therefore necessary to refer to phases to place the sites that do have dates in the wider context of Flagstaff-area prehistory.

Cinder Park Phase (AD 550?–830)

This phase, which begins earlier than the time scale depicted in Figure 23.3, includes a small number of noncutting tree-ring dates between AD 650 and 750, many of which are probably from eroded beams that have lost a number of rings and which were, in fact, cut during the following interval. Dates from a structure in Cinder Park may, however, relate directly to beam-procurement and construction activity in the late AD 600s. The post–AD 750 portion of the phase also includes small per-decade counts of noncutting dates, as well as a modest clustering of dates centered on the AD 760s. This decade also has a high percentage of cutting dates, mostly from two pithouses whose construction can be dated to this interval based on the tree-ring evidence. The structures are located far apart, one a few miles east of the San Francisco Peaks and the other 25–30 mi to the southeast near Anderson Mesa, so the agreement in their dating is probably coincidental. The Anderson Mesa structure appears to have been built in the AD 760s but, based on a single late date, to have been repaired in the mid-770s. This pithouse is located well outside the Sunset Crater ash-fall zone and in the conifer woodland biome; consistent with that setting, its dates come predominantly from samples of pinyon.

Sunset Phase (AD 830–1030)

Most dates falling in the Sunset phase are from earth lodge–style pithouses. The phase includes peaks in the percentages of cutting dates in the AD 850s–870s, 910s, 940s, and 960s–970s. The second and fourth of these peaks are associated with increases in the total numbers of dates per decade. The four "groupings" of tree-ring evidence support the dating of five pithouses between the AD 870s and 970s. All of these structures are earth lodge–style pithouses that are located in or near the montane conifer zone and within a few miles east or northeast of the San Francisco Peaks. It is not surprising, therefore, that most of the dated samples from these pithouses are of ponderosa or, in lesser quantities, Douglas fir. The dated structures are also all located in the Sunset Crater ash-fall zone. The late portion of the Sunset phase, from AD 980 to 1030, is represented by small numbers of tree-ring dates per decade, few cutting dates, and no dated construction events.

To summarize, the pre-eruptive Cinder Park and Sunset phases (AD 550?–1030) are characterized by brief intervals with increased percentages of cutting dates and, in some cases, increased numbers of total dates that are associated with a few dated pithouse-construction events. Because so few structures contribute to the intervals with successful dating, there is no reason to place any interpretive emphasis on the intervening intervals that lack this kind of evidence. In other words, the tree-ring record provides a poor representation of variation in construction activity over the course of these two "pre-eruptive" phases.

Also worth repeating here is the earlier observation that a number of the structures dated to this interval on the basis of tree-ring dates, ceramic evidence, or both have date distributions that are spread over a century or more. The "summing" of these distributions to produce Figure 23.3 explains the occurrence of at least a few noncutting dates during every decade of the two phases. Given the earlier argument for the frequent reuse of timbers during this time, including but not limited to roof-support posts, it is almost certain that some of these nondescript dates provide shadowy evidence relating to the construction of buildings that cannot be identified "on the ground." Though tantalizing, this evidence from reused wood is insufficient in quantity or quality to provide a useful record of construction activity over any portion of the pre-eruptive phases.

Rio de Flag Phase (AD 1030–1085)

This short phase is characterized by a gradual increase in the number of dates per decade and, somewhat less consistently, by an increase in the percentage of cutting dates. It is only toward the end of the phase during the AD 1060s that the tree-ring evidence supports the dating of individual pithouse-construction events. The Rio de Flag phase has traditionally been considered "pre-eruptive" and, until recently, was generally thought to have ended by the AD 1060s, when Sunset Crater was thought to have erupted (Pilles 1988). Recent redating of both the phase (to AD 1030–1085) and the eruption (to AD 1040–1100) suggests that the temporal relationship between these two "events" needs to be reexamined.

Angell (AD 1090–1130), Winona (AD 1085–1105), and Padre (AD 1090–1150) Phases

It has long been thought that the Winona and Angell phases were largely contemporaneous though culturally distinct, with the Winona phase defined on the basis of data from one site, Winona Village. The validity of the Winona phase as separate from the Angell phase has been questioned, however (Pilles 1988). The combined Angell and Winona phases were followed by the Padre phase. Downum's redating of this portion of the Flagstaff chronology suggests, however, that there was substantial temporal overlap among all three phases.

Together, the Angell/Winona and Padre phases cover an interval lasting just under 70 years. The upward trends in the three variables depicted in Figure 23.3 that began in the Rio de Flag phase continue into this period. The last three decades of the Rio de Flag phase and the combined Angell/Winona and Padre phases, amounting to just under 100 years, are associated with 13 dated construction events. The dated structures include 10 earth lodge–style pithouses, one masonry pit structure, one four-room pueblo, and one building that combines elements of an earth lodge and a masonry pit structure (in this last case, the tree-ring dates may not relate to this structure alone but, rather, to the small site where it is located as a whole). Wupatki Pueblo begins contributing to the counts of dates and relatively high percentages of cutting dates beginning in the AD 1130s.

The 13 dated structures from this interval are in four localities. First, the pueblo and four of the pithouses are in or near Medicine Valley, within 6 mi of the San Francisco Peaks, in montane conifer forest, and within the bounds of the Sunset Crater ash-fall zone. Tree-ring dates from these structures are predominantly from samples of ponderosa pine and Douglas fir (though some spruce/fir beams are also included). This use of locally available species near the mountains continues the pattern of the preceding phases. Second, one earth lodge–style pithouse and the masonry pit structure are on Juniper Terrace, more than 6 mi from the mountains but still in the ash-fall zone. The site is in conifer woodland, though "the main forest of [ponderosa] pine lies four miles to the south of the site" (Colton 1946:147). Most of the pithouse's dates are from samples of ponderosa pine. Dates from the masonry pit structure are from pinyon, which grows in the vicinity, and spruce/fir. Today, one must travel several miles from the dated structure onto the slopes of the San Francisco Peaks to find stands of spruce or fir trees. Third, the earth lodge/masonry structure is at Heiser Spring, more than a dozen miles northeast of the mountains and near the border of the conifer woodland and grassland biomes. Most of this structure's dates are from samples of spruce/fir, which means that the builders in this case had to walk even farther to obtain beams of this kind than did those living at Juniper Terrace. Fourth, the remaining five dated pithouses are at Winona Village, located in conifer woodland and in the ash-fall zone. A variety of species are represented among the site's dated tree-ring samples, including locally available pinyon and juniper, as well as not-so-available ponderosa pine and Douglas fir.

The Angell/Winona and Padre phases and, to some extent, the preceding Rio de Flag phase have more dates, higher percentages of cutting dates, and many more dated construction events per decade than the preceding phases. The dated structures are also distributed more widely than during the earlier periods, though still within the range of Sunset Crater ash. In the case of Winona Village, the sample of dated construction events, in combination with the overall date distribution, provides a good picture of the site's occupation, which extended from the AD 1070s through the 1130s (Ahlstrom 1985).

Sites near the San Francisco Peaks that date to the combined Angell/Winona and Padre phases have produced tree-ring dates from locally available species, whereas those at a greater distance from the mountains have a mix of locally available and more distant species. With the exception of Winona Village—which possesses a ball court—the sites located away from the San Francisco Peaks appear to be only marginally larger and more complex than those near the mountains. This would suggest that factors other than social complexity played a role in creating a willingness to procure construction wood from distant sources. These might include a reduction in the quality of timbers that could be obtained from pinyon and juniper trees as one moves lower in the conifer woodland, as well as a need for larger and longer beams to roof the masonry structures that were becoming more popular by the Padre phase. Finally, the increase in tree-ring evidence "per decade" after ca. AD 1050, together with a comparable increase in the temporal sensitivity of ceramic design, makes possible a reduction in the lengths of archaeological phases, from 200 or more years before AD 1050 to no more than 75 years after that date.

Elden Phase (AD 1150–1225)

The early Elden phase, to ca. AD 1200, has high counts of dates and high percentages of cutting dates per decade. Most of these dates are from two sites in the ash-fall zone, Wupatki and Two Kivas pueblos. Wupatki lies in grassland; Two Kivas, in conifer woodland. Ridge Ruin, a third pueblo situated in the ash-fall zone near the boundary between conifer woodland and grassland, also has a number of dates in the early Elden phase. Like Wupatki, Ridge Ruin has a ball court. Most dates from these three sites are from tree species that do not occur locally, including ponderosa pine, Douglas fir, and spruce/fir. These are large sites, by Flagstaff standards, and their inventories of dated samples are drawn from populations that included hundreds if not thousands of beams. The scale of effort expended in the procurement of beams from nonlocal sources is doubtless a reflection of the size and social complexity of these communities.

Turkey Hill (AD 1225–1275) and Clear Creek (AD 1275–1400) Phases

With the exception of three "late" (i.e., post–AD 1215) dates from Wupatki, all of the dates falling in the Turkey Hill and Clear Creek phases are from three sites, Kinnikinnick Pueblo, the Pollock site, and Chavez Pass Ruin, which are located on or near Anderson Mesa, some miles to the southeast of the area with Sunset Crater ash. The interval from the AD 1210s to the 1260s, representing the end of the Elden phase and first half of the Turkey Hill phase, includes only small counts of dates per decade. It is followed by a period with higher counts of dates that lasts from the AD 1270s through the 1310s. The final decades of the Clear Creek phase, from AD 1320 to 1400, are represented by just four tree-ring dates.

Most of the dates clustering between AD 1270 and 1319 (n = 56) are from a single room at Kinnikinnick Pueblo, introducing significant bias into the regional date distribution (Figure 23.3). The majority of samples producing these and other dates from the pueblo are ponderosa pine, though a few are pinyon or juniper. Use of the latter two species is consistent with the site's location in conifer woodland. As for ponderosa pine, some trees of this kind have been observed nearby in Kinnikinnick Canyon (Conner 1943), and more extensive ponderosa pine forest can be found about 5 mi southwest of the site.

Conclusion

Archaeologists and their dendrochronologist colleagues have been collecting and dating tree-ring samples and interpreting the resulting dates and other tree-ring evidence from the Flagstaff area for more than 80 years. Two episodes stand out in that history of study: they include excavations conducted in the 1930s by MNA to date the eruption of Sunset Crater and to understand the effects of that event on local prehistory and the TRL's reanalysis of all of the area's "archived" tree-ring samples, which took place in the 1960s–1970s. This latter project not only increased the number of tree-ring dates substantially but enhanced the reliability and comparability of the tree-ring data set. This and subsequent analyses are responsible for an assemblage of 1,112 tree-ring dates from 86 sites.

The strengths and weaknesses of these data are a function of the playing out, including the interaction, of the four sources of variation in any archaeological tree-ring record. Those sources of variation depend on the natural environment, the behavior of the area's prehistoric residents, postabandonment site formation processes, and the behavior of archaeologists and dendrochronologists. Among the most important of these factors in the Flagstaff case are (1) the distribution of datable tree species among the local biotic communities (including the montane conifer forest, conifer woodland, grassland, and desert scrub biomes); (2) the use and reuse of datable wood, including that procured at a distance from the sites involved; (3) the focus of archaeological effort on the area to the east and northeast of the San Francisco Peaks within or near the Sunset Crater ash-fall zone; and (4) the concentration of that effort on sites and structures with the greatest potential of yielding datable tree-ring samples, in the form of either wood or charcoal.

The strengths of the resulting data set include its usefulness for dating individual sites and structures within sites, for dating the occurrence of architectural styles (particularly timber pithouses and masonry pueblos), for identifying patterning in beam reuse and local vs. distant beam procurement, and for dating ceramic complexes and their associated archaeological phases. The latter has made it possible for dendrochronological evidence obtained from fewer than 100 sites to be applied, indirectly, to the dating of thousands of other sites in the Flagstaff area (Downum and Sullivan 1990; Garcia 2004; Sullivan and Downum 1991).

The weaknesses in the Flagstaff tree-ring data set relate in particular to the overall distributions of dates and dated construction events depicted in Figure 23.3. This aggregated data set exhibits substantial variation over time in the quantity and quality of tree-ring evidence and in the numbers of identifiable construction events that can be dated on the basis of that evidence. Two points concerning the influences of the four sources of variation on the Flagstaff area's overall tree-ring record are paramount. First, their role changes over the interval represented by the tree-ring date distribution, and for that reason, the data set cannot be considered the result of a single sampling process. Second, the sample of tree-ring dates, as interpreted with reference to both beam-procurement and construction events, cannot be considered either a random or a generally representative sample of those events. The tree-ring record here, as in other areas of the Southwest, has been generated by a complex historical process, and its potential and limitations for analysis must be judged accordingly.

References Cited

Ahlstrom, Richard V. N.

1985 *The Interpretation of Archaeological Tree-Ring Dates*. Ph.D. dissertation, University of Arizona, Tucson. University Microfilms International, Ann Arbor.

1997 Sources of Variation in the Southwestern Tree-Ring Record. *Kiva* 62(4):321–348.

1998a Tree-Ring Models and Applications: Puebloan Chronometry on Black Mesa. In *Archaeological Chronometry: Radiocarbon and Tree-Ring Models and Applications from Black Mesa, Arizona*, by Francis E. Smiley and Richard V. N. Ahlstrom, pp. 135–214. Center for Archaeological Investigations Occasional Paper No. 16. Southern Illinois University, Carbondale.

1998b Chronological Interpretation of Tree-Ring-Dated Puebloan Sites on Black Mesa. In *Archaeological Chronometry: Radiocarbon and Tree-Ring Models and Applications from Black Mesa, Arizona*, by Francis E. Smiley and Richard V. N. Ahlstrom, pp. 237–265. Center for Archaeological Investigations Occasional Paper No. 16. Southern Illinois University, Carbondale.

2008 Beyond Tree Rings: Integrating Multiple Lines of Dating Evidence. *Kiva* 73(4):387–416.

Bannister, Bryant, Elizabeth A. M. Gell, and John W. Hannah

1966 *Tree-Ring Dates from Arizona N–Q: Verde–Showlow–St. Johns Area*. Laboratory of Tree-Ring Research, University of Arizona, Tucson.

Benson, Larry V., and Michael S. Berry

2009 Climate Change and Cultural Response in the Prehistoric American Southwest. *Kiva* 75(1):89–117.

Berry, Michael S.

1982 *Time, Space, and Transition in Anasazi Prehistory*. University of Utah Press, Salt Lake City.

Betancourt, Julio L., Jeffrey S. Dean, and Herbert M. Hull

1986 Prehistoric Long-Distance Transport of Construction Beams, Chaco Canyon, New Mexico. *American Antiquity* 51(2):370–375.

Brennan, Ellen, and Christian Downum

2001 *Report of Findings, Prestabilization Documentation for Wupatki Pueblo (NA405), Wupatki National Monument*. Northern Arizona University, Flagstaff.

Brown, David E.

1982 Biotic Communities of the American Southwest—United States and Mexico. *Desert Plants* 4(1–4).

Brown, David E., and Charles H. Lowe

1980 *Biotic Communities of the Southwest*. Map, scale 1:1,000,000. USDA Forest Service General Technical Report, RM-78. Rocky Mountain Forest and Range Experiment Station, Fort Collins.

Cameron, Catherine M.

1990 The Effect of Varying Estimates of Pit Structure Use-Life on Prehistoric Population Estimates in the American Southwest. *Kiva* 55(2):155–166.

Christenson, Andrew L.

1994 A Test of Mean Ceramic Dating Using Well-Dated Kayenta Anasazi Sites. *Kiva* 59:297–317.

Colton, Harold S.

1933 Pueblo II in the San Francisco Mountains, Arizona. *Museum of Northern Arizona Bulletin* 4:3–14.

1946 *The Sinagua: A Summary of the Archaeology of the Region of Flagstaff, Arizona*. Museum of Northern Arizona Bulletin, 22. Flagstaff.

Conner, Sydney

1943 Excavations at Kinnikinnick, Arizona. *American Antiquity* 8(4):376–379.

Dean, Jeffrey S.

1978a *Tree-Ring Dating in Archeology*. Miscellaneous Paper No. 24; University of Utah Anthropological Papers No. 99. University of Utah Press, Salt Lake City.

1978b Independent Dating in Archaeological Analysis. In *Advances in Archaeological Method and Theory*, Vol. 1, edited by Michael B. Schiffer, pp. 223–255. Academic Press, New York.

Dean, Jeffrey S., and Richard L. Warren

1983 Dendrochronology. In *The Architecture and Dendrochronology of Chetro Ketl, Chaco Canyon, New Mexico*, edited by Stephen H. Lekson, pp. 105–240. Reports of the Chaco Center No. 6. Division of Cultural Research, National Park Service, Albuquerque.

Douglass, Andrew E.

1935 *Dating Pueblo Bonito and Other Ruins of the Southwest*. National Geographic Society, Contributed Technical Papers, Pueblo Bonito Series, 1. Washington, D.C.

Downum, Christian E.

1988 "One Grand History": A Critical Review of Flagstaff Archaeology, 1851 to 1988. Unpublished Ph.D. dissertation, University of Arizona, Tucson.

Downum, Christian E., Ellen Brennan, and James P. Holmlund

1999 *An Architectural Study of Wupatki Pueblo (NA405)*. Archaeological Report, 1175. Northern Arizona University, Flagstaff.

2013 Wupatki Pueblo: Red House in Black Sand. In *Hisat'sinom: Ancient Peoples in a Land Without Water*, edited by Christian E. Downum, pp. 79–86. School for Advanced Research Press, Santa Fe, in press.

Downum, Christian E., and Alan P. Sullivan, III

1990 Description and Analysis of Prehistoric Settlement Patterns at

Wupatki National Monument. In *The Wupatki Archeological Inventory Survey Project: Final Report*, compiled by Bruce A. Anderson, pp. 5.1–5.90. U.S. National Park Service, Division of Anthropology, Southwest Cultural Resources Center, Professional Paper No. 35. National Park Service Southwest Regional Office, Santa Fe, New Mexico.

Elson, Mark D. (editor)

2006 *Sunset Crater Archaeology: The History of a Volcanic Landscape, Introduction and Site Descriptions*, Pts. 1–2. Anthropological Papers No. 30. Center for Desert Archaeology, Tucson.

Elson, Mark D., Michael H. Ort, and Bruce G. Phillips

2006 Environmental Setting. In *Sunset Crater Archaeology: The History of a Volcanic Landscape, Introduction and Site Descriptions, Pt. 1*, edited by Mark D. Elson, pp. 17–41. Anthropological Papers No. 30. Center for Desert Archaeology, Tucson.

Garcia, Daniel

2004 Prehistoric Ceramic Boundaries in the Flagstaff Region of Northern Arizona. Unpublished Master's thesis, Department of Anthropology, Northern Arizona University, Flagstaff.

Hantman, Jeffrey L.

1983 Social Networks and Stylistic Distributions in the Prehistoric Plateau Southwest. Unpublished Ph.D. dissertation, Arizona State University, Tempe.

Hargrave, Lyndon L.

1933 Pueblo II Houses of the San Francisco Mountains, Arizona. *Museum of Northern Arizona Bulletin* 4:15–75. Flagstaff.

Icove, David J., H. E. Welborn, A. J. Vonarx, E. Charles Adams, James R. Lally, and Timothy G. Huff

2006 Scientific Investigation and Modeling of Prehistoric Structural Fires at Chevelon Pueblo. In *Proceedings of the 2006 International Symposium on Fire Investigation Science and Technology*, pp. 457–467. National Association of Arson Investigators, Sarasota.

Lipe, William D.

1974 A Conservation Model for American Archaeology. *Kiva* 39(3–4):213–245.

1995 The Depopulation of the Northern San Juan: Conditions in the Turbulent 1200s. *Journal of Anthropological Anthropology* 14:143–169.

Lipe, William D., and Mark D. Varien

1999 Pueblo III (AD 1150–1300). In *Colorado Prehistory: A Context for the Southern Colorado River Basin*, edited by William D. Lipe, Mark D. Varien, and Richard H. Wilshusen, pp. 290–352. Colorado Council of Professional Archaeologists, Denver.

McGregor, John C.

1936 *Culture of Sites Which Were Occupied Shortly Before the Eruption of Sunset Crater*. Museum of Northern Arizona Bulletin, 9. Northern Arizona Society of Science and Art, Flagstaff.

1973 Three Sinagua Sites East of Flagstaff, Arizona. Unpublished manuscript in the possession of Christian E. Downum, Northern Arizona University, Flagstaff.

Nash, Stephen E.

1997 Archaeological Cutting Date Estimation and the Interpretation of Estimated Tree-Ring Dates. *American Antiquity* 62(2): 260–272.

1999 *Time, Trees, and Prehistory*. University of Utah Press, Salt Lake City.

Ort, Michael H., Mark D. Elson, and Duane E. Champion

2007 A Paleomagnetic Dating Study of Sunset Crater Volcano. In *Sunset Crater Archaeology: The History of a Volcanic Landscape, Environmental Analyses*, edited by Mark D. Elson, pp. 95–102. Anthropological Papers No. 33. Center for Desert Archaeology, Tucson.

Pilles, Peter J., Jr.

1979 Sunset Crater and the Sinagua: A New Interpretation. In *Volcanic Activity and Human Ecology*, edited by Payson D. Sheets and Donald K. Grayson, pp. 459–485. Academic Press, New York.

1988 Angell Phase; Cinder Park Phase; Elden Phase; Flagstaff Province; Padre Phase; Rio de Flag Phase; Sunset Phase; Turkey Hill Phase; Winona Focus. In *Historical Dictionary of North American Archaeology*, edited by Edward B. Jelks and Juliet C. Jelks, pp. 15–16, 99–100, 103–104, 149–150, 162–164, 357–358, 410, 472, 498–499, 533–534. Greenwood Press, New York.

Plog, Fred

1984 Exchange, Tribes and Alliances: The Northern Southwest. *American Archeology* 4:217–223.

1989 The Sinagua and Their Relations. In *Dynamics of Southwest Prehistory*, edited by Linda S. Cordell and George J. Gumerman, pp. 263–291. Smithsonian Institution Press, Washington, D.C.

Potter, James M., Jason P. Chuipka, and Jerry Fetterman

2012 The Eastern Mesa Verde Region: Migrants, Cultural Diversity, and Violence in the East. In *Crucible of Pueblos: The Early Pueblo Period in the Northern Southwest*, edited by Richard H. Wilshusen, Gregson Schachner, and James R. Allison, pp. 53–71. Monograph 71. Cotsen Institute of Archaeology, University of California, Los Angeles.

Robinson, William J.

1976 Tree-Ring Dating and Archaeology in the American Southwest. *Tree-Ring Bulletin* 36:9–20.

Robinson, William J., and Catherine M. Cameron

1991 *A Directory of Tree-Ring Dated Prehistoric Sites in the American Southwest*. Laboratory of Tree-Ring Research, University of Arizona, Tucson.

Robinson, William J., Bruce G. Harrill, and Richard L. Warren

1975 *Tree-Ring Dates from Arizona H–I: Flagstaff Area*. Laboratory of Tree-Ring Research, University of Arizona, Tucson.

Schiffer, Michael B.

1987 *Formation Processes of the Archaeological Record*. University of New Mexico Press, Albuquerque.

Schlanger, Sarah H.

1987 Population Measurement, Size, and Change, AD 600–1175. In *Dolores Archaeological Program: Supporting Studies: Settlement and Environment*, compiled by Kenneth L. Petersen and Janet D. Orcutt, pp. 569–613. U.S. Department of the Interior, Bureau of Reclamation, Denver.

Smiley, Terah L.

1958 The Geology and Dating of Sunset Crater, Flagstaff, Arizona. In *Guidebook of the Black Mesa Basin, Northeastern Arizona*, edited by R. Y. Anderson and J. W. Harshbarger, pp. 186–190. New Mexico Geological Society, Ninth Field Conference, Socorro.

Sullivan, Alan P., III, and Christian E. Downum

1991 Aridity, Activity, and Volcanic Ash Agriculture: A Study of Short Term Prehistoric Cultural-Ecological Dynamics. *World Archaeology* 22:271–287.

Waring, Gwendolyn
2007 Hopi Corn and Volcanic Cinders: A Test of the Relationship Between Tephra and Agriculture in Northern Arizona. In *Sunset Crater Archaeology: The History of a Volcanic Landscape, Environmental Analyses*, edited by Mark D. Elson, pp. 59–70. Anthropological Papers No. 33. Center for Desert Archaeology, Tucson.

Wilshusen, Richard
1986 The Relationship Between Abandonment Mode and Ritual Use in Pueblo I Anasazi Protokivas. *Journal of Field Archaeology* 13:245–254.

Windes, Thomas C., and Peter J. McKenna
2001 Going Against the Grain: Wood Production in Chacoan Society. *American Antiquity* 66(1):119–140.

24

An Embarrassment of Riches

Tree-Ring Dating, the History of Archaeology, and the Interpretation of Precolumbian History at Mesa Verde National Park

Stephen E. Nash and Christina T. Rogers

Mesa Verde National Park (MVNP) in southwestern Colorado is home to more than 4,500 documented archaeological sites. After nearly a century of archaeological tree-ring research within the park's boundaries, there are now available to archaeologists 4,389 reliable, high-quality tree-ring dates from 143 cliff and open-air sites at MVNP.[1]

In an essay entitled "Tree-Ring Dates and Demographic Change in the Southern Colorado Plateau and Rio Grande Regions," Michael S. Berry and Larry V. Benson used a large, regional database of tree-ring dates from the American Southwest to "estimate regional-scale timber-harvesting and construction activities between AD 600 and 1600" (2010:53; see also Benson and Berry 2009; Berry 1982; cf. Dean 1985). While acknowledging that sampling bias exists in their data set, they "opted to consider the likelihood that these [tree-ring] data are, in fact, representative of prehistoric reality" (2010:56). They posit specifically that their database of 6,984 dates from 413 sites across the Four Corners and northern Rio Grande regions serves as a "relative measure of construction activity" in those areas during the millennium in question (2010:56).

To test Berry and Benson's (2010:56) assertions, this chapter offers a historical and contextual analysis of the recently developed Mesa Verde tree-ring date database. In doing so, it demonstrates that even large tree-ring data sets are archaeologically and historically contingent, contain significant sampling bias, and should be considered representative of some unknown prehistoric reality only with extreme caution and after detailed analysis to empirically determine the sources of variation in the tree-ring record.

Archaeological Tree-Ring Dating

Dendrochronology, the study of tree-time, is the science of assigning solar calendar dates to the growth rings of trees (Nash 2008). Dendrochronology enjoys an astonishing array of worldwide applications in climatology, forest ecology, geomorphology, art history, archaeology, and other disciplines (Nash 2002; Towner 2002).

The basic principle underlying all tree-ring dating is cross-dating, the process by which patterns in specific aspects of ring morphology sequences (e.g., ring width, density, missing rings, double rings, frost rings, etc.) are matched and dated against some known, independent, usually solar calendar going back further and further in time (Douglass 1942; Stokes and Smiley 1996). Tree-ring dating emphatically is *not* ring counting, although ring counts may occasionally be used as part of the cross-dating process.

To accurately determine solar calendar dates for individual tree-rings on a specimen, the dendrochronologist must understand, in great detail and through the process of cross-dating, the sequence of growth rings in numerous trees of a given species in a given area. Once those sequences have been properly understood and cross-dated against one another, an actual, master tree-ring chronology can be created. The tree-ring chronology may then be extended further and further back in time by cross-dating numerous and successively older specimens against it. Once a chronology has been established that includes the area and era of archaeological interest, dates may then possibly be obtained for archaeological tree-ring specimens.

To obtain a date for an archaeological specimen, the dendrochronologist must cross-date the ring sequence on the archaeological specimen against the previously developed master chronology for that region. In so doing, the dendrochronologist must identify all missing, double, and other problematic rings on the specimen being analyzed. Once each of those problematic rings has been identified and accounted for, dates may be assigned to each ring on the sample, including the last growth ring, which hopefully possesses attributes indicating that it was the last ring grown by the tree before it died (see discussion of cutting and noncutting dates below).

There are several prerequisites to successful tree-ring dating in archaeological contexts (Dean 1996a, 1996b). The first is behavioral and requires that Precolumbian construction workers made use of tree species with cross-datable ring sequences. If inhabitants of an archaeological site in the American Southwest built their structures with cottonwood trees and cooked their food exclusively with ironwood logs, it simply would not be possible to tree-ring date those phenomena because cottonwood and ironwood do not cross-date. Precolumbian construction workers at MVNP did, in fact, use logs from cottonwood trees and other nondatable species in their work, but these construction events are thankfully small in number (see Street 2001a).

The second and third prerequisites for archaeological tree-ring dating are good specimen preservation and subsequent recovery by archaeologists. Thirteenth-century cliff dwellings in the American Southwest, like those at MVNP, tend to be well dated for two reasons. First, the wood beams with which they were constructed are often exquisitely preserved in the dry rockshelter environments of the Mesa Verde landform (Ahlstrom 1997). Second, the cliff dwellings have received a tremendous amount of archaeological attention over the last 130 years, followed by intense dendrochronological attention over the last 80 years. Tenth-century (e.g., Pueblo I period) pit structures, on the other hand, tend to be less well dated because wood does not preserve well in unburned, open-air sites and because archaeologists have spent less time and effort researching these less glamorous structures (but see below [Ahlstrom 1997]).

Finally, even under the best of circumstances, in which Precolumbian construction workers made extensive use of cross-datable species, construction wood from those species is well preserved in archaeological sites, and those sites have been properly and systematically investigated by professional archaeologists, the simple fact is that not all tree-ring samples can be dated. Although MVNP is undeniably one of the best places in the world to conduct archaeological tree-ring dating, fewer than half of all archaeological tree-ring samples collected there ever yield dates because of vagaries in tree growth, preservation, and other random and nonrandom natural and cultural formation processes that are beyond the dendrochronologist's control (Schiffer 1987).

The Interpretation of Archaeological Tree-Ring Dates

Dendrochronology is the only chronometric technique that does not have statistical uncertainty associated with the dates produced (see Nash, ed. 2000, 2009, and chapters therein). When properly cross-dated, tree-ring dates yield solar calendar dates in the strictest sense; they have no associated random or systematic error, and they are accurate and precise to that calendar year. Even in spite of their high chronometric quality, tree-ring dates still require contextual analysis and interpretation by the archaeologist. A substantial body of theory for the proper interpretation of tree-ring dates has been developed over the last eight decades (Ahlstrom 1997; Bannister 1962; Dean 1978; Haury 1935; Nash 1997; Towner 1997). Several key concepts warrant review.

Dendrochronologists distinguish between "cutting" and "noncutting" dates. Cutting dates are assigned to archaeological specimens that possess attributes, such as bark or beetle galleries, indicating that the last ring present on the specimen was the last ring grown by the tree before it died or (preferably) was intentionally killed by Precolumbian construction workers. If such attributes are present, the dendrochronologist assigns symbols (i.e., "B" for bark, "G" for beetle galleries) to the outer date indicating that it is a "cutting date." Noncutting dates are assigned to specimens for which there is no evidence that the last ring present on the specimen was the last one grown by the tree before it died or was killed. In this case, the dendrochronologist assigns symbols (e.g., "vv" for "very variable" outer ring) to the specimen's outer date indicating that it is a "noncutting date" (see Nash 1999:17). Near-cutting dates are assigned when the dendrochronologist believes that one ring (or rarely more) is missing from the extreme outer portion of a specimen's ring sequence. The dendrochronologist cannot prove the existence of the missing ring(s) and therefore cannot definitively assign a cutting date, but based on experience with tens of thousands of other tree-ring samples, he or she is confident enough to assign a "+" symbol indicating that the date is a near-cutting date.

From an interpretive standpoint, cutting and near-cutting dates are of far greater utility to the archaeologist than are noncutting dates. Because a cutting date indicates the solar calendar year in which the tree died (or was killed), it is by definition closer to the behavioral events of interest to the archaeologist (Dean 1978; Smiley and Ahlstrom 1998:7–10). The situation is more complicated with noncutting dates. Because an unknown and potentially very large number of rings are missing from the outside of the dated specimen, many more potentially mitigating circumstances must be taken into account before a noncutting date may be accepted as a reliable date for some Precolumbian behavior or archaeological phenomenon (Dean 1978). In the absence of additional, high-quality contextual data, a noncutting date merely offers a *terminus post quem*, date after which, a given event must have occurred. Despite substantive efforts to alleviate the interpretive difficulties associated with noncutting dates, they remain a serious problem for archaeological interpretation (though see Nash 1997 and references therein).

There is some interpretive safety in numbers, however. Archaeological analysis and interpretation are better served when large numbers of tree-ring dates are available (Ahlstrom et al. 1991; Nash 1997). Dendroarchaeologists typically place greater interpretive reliance on date clusters than on individual dates. Date clusters are defined as accumulations of three or more dates in the same or proximal calendar years within some spatially delineated space, such as a room or, possibly, a site (Ahlstrom 1997; Smiley and Ahlstrom 1998). If a number of tree-ring dates from a given site cluster, one can infer that some behavioral event (e.g., wood cutting, stockpiling, construction, etc.) in the past has been well dated. Thankfully, the long history of tree-ring dating at MVNP ensures that there are large numbers of dates that occur in significant clusters spanning more than 1,100 years of local wood-cutting activity, if not occupation. The question is, of course, What do these date clusters actually mean?

A Précis of Archaeological Tree-Ring Dating at Mesa Verde National Park

The history of archaeological tree-ring dating at MVNP could fill volumes; a précis is sufficient here. Oliver Ricketson and Jean Jeançon, working under the auspices of the National Geographic Society's First Beam Expedition, collected tree-ring samples from cliff dwellings at MVNP in 1923 (Nash 1999:40–42). In the December 1929 issue of *National Geographic* magazine, astronomer Andrew Ellicott Douglass of the University of Arizona published newly derived tree-ring dates for archaeological sites in the American Southwest, including eight dates from six of the classic cliff dwellings at MVNP (see Peterson 1935).

One of Douglass's first dendrochronology students, Harry T. Getty, procured a larger (but still limited) sample of tree-ring specimens at MVNP in 1932 and 1933 (Nash 1999:91). He sought to carry on that effort throughout the mid-1930s, but depression-era budget cuts precluded further work (see Getty 1935a, 1935b, 1935c). Throughout the 1940s and 1950s, a series of smaller excavation projects at MVNP, particularly on pithouse sites, allowed archaeologists to push the first well-dated occupation of the area further and further back in time (Lancaster and Watson 1943; Smiley 1947; Watson 1947).

In 1951, Terah L. Smiley of the University of Arizona published a summary synthesis of all the reliable tree-ring dates then available from the American Southwest, including 136 dates from 26 sites in MVNP. Smiley's database represented an order of magnitude improvement over the numbers of dated MVNP samples and sites that Douglass published a generation earlier. Smiley's database still did not constitute an overwhelming body of evidence, however.

With increased postwar visitation straining the National Park Service facilities and posing ever greater threats to the park's archaeological resources, in 1958 the National Park Service initiated the Wetherill Mesa Archaeological Project (WMAP), a multiyear fieldwork program that lasted until 1963. WMAP analysis and writing continued for several years thereafter (see Lister 1968; Nichols 1963; Nichols and Harlan 1967; Nichols and Smith 1965). WMAP was a comprehensive archaeological, tree-ring, and ecological project designed to mitigate the impact of opening Wetherill Mesa to greater public visitation.

WMAP reestablished a research standard for archaeological tree-ring dating set in the 1930s by actively deploying dendrochronologists on archaeological field research teams as active specimen collectors, not simply as laboratory technicians to whom samples were submitted after excavation (see Nash 1999, 2000). This is not a trivial point. Archaeological fieldworkers who are not trained in dendrochronology often erroneously assume that larger wood and charcoal specimens are more likely to yield tree-ring dates than smaller ones; smaller pieces are therefore more likely to get discarded in the field. In fact and in practice, it is not the size of the specimen that matters in the American Southwest; it is the number of rings present on the specimen and the ring width variability exhibited by those rings that matters to dendrochronologists. As a result of this emphasis on field dendrochronology, WMAP obtained large numbers of reliable new tree-ring dates from well-provenienced archaeological samples and contexts, thereby increasing the analytical and interpretive potential of MVNP tree-ring dates beyond strictly chronometric and toward behavioral variables (Lister 1968; Nichols 1963; Nichols and Harlan 1967; Nichols and Smith 1965; see also Dean 1996a, 1996b; Street 2001a, 2001b).

As part of a much larger National Science Foundation–funded project to synthesize tree-ring dates from across the American Southwest, William J. Robinson and Bruce G. Harrill (1974) published a "Quadrangle Report" for Colorado V, a rectangular cartographic region that included MVNP (see Nash 2000:77–78). Robinson and Harrill's (1974) synthesis did not include the WMAP dates, as these had been cross-dated according to modern standards and were considered reliable and not in need of reanalysis.

Between the WMAP contributions and the Quadrangle Report, archaeologists in 1974 had access to 1,717 reliable tree-ring dates from 78 sites in MVNP. These numbers constitute an order of magnitude increase in the number of dated specimens and a threefold increase in the number of dated sites over the numbers Smiley published in 1951. This marked the first time that archaeologists had access to a reliable, large, regional tree-ring date distribution, but the data were accessible only in Laboratory of Tree-Ring Research (LTRR) archives and publications, not in a comprehensive, searchable, and sortable database.

Not much archaeological tree-ring research occurred at MVNP in the late 1970s through the 1980s, but in the early 1990s researchers at the LTRR at the University of Arizona in Tucson began a series of intensive sampling projects at MVNP sites including Balcony House (Fairchild-Parks and Dean 1993; Fiero 1999), Oak Tree House (Windes 1995), Spring House (Parks and Dean 1997), 20 1/2 House (Parks and Dean 1997), Long House (Street 2001a, 2001b), Spruce Tree House, Square Tower House, and others. These efforts led to the derivation of thousands more new, well-provenienced tree-ring dates. Again, however, these data were largely accessible only in the gray literature, in reports on file at the LTRR and MVNP.

In 2008, Nash obtained a grant (2008-02-030) from the State Historic Fund of the Colorado Historical Society to conduct what amounts to a final dendrochronological mop-up operation at MVNP. The goal of this project was to ensure that all previously excavated and potentially datable tree-ring specimens from the area had been systematically analyzed by the LTRR. All archived tree-ring specimens from MVNP were sent to LTRR for one final round of analysis, which is now complete (Nash

2010). The project included a fieldwork component to collect the few remaining potentially datable specimens from cliff sites that had not been completely and intensively sampled. This effort led to the production of more than two dozen new dates and, perhaps more importantly, certainty that all curated specimens that can be dated have indeed now been dated.

In 2009, with support from Crow Canyon Archaeological Center's National Science Foundation–funded Village Ecodynamics Project (grant DEB-0816400 from the Dynamics of Coupled Natural and Human Systems program), Nash began a systematic and comprehensive examination of research and accession files at LTRR to update and refine the Village Ecodynamics Project's database of tree-ring dates from MVNP, the surrounding Four Corners region, and the northern Rio Grande region. That effort is now complete, and the resulting database contains 19,436 reliable tree-ring dates, including 5,706 cutting dates, 1,939 near-cutting dates, and 11,791 noncutting dates, all of which can be sorted and analyzed by region, site, subsite provenience, and other variables.

The new database of tree-ring dates from MVNP now includes 4,389 reliable dates from 143 archaeological sites ranging from the earliest noncutting date of AD 255 from the Soda Canyon Campground site to the latest near-cutting date of AD 1281 from a loose log in Kiva D in Spring House. These numbers constitute 258 percent and 182 percent increases, respectively, in the number of dates from and dated sites in MVNP since the publication of the Quadrangle Report (Robinson and Harrill 1974) and the WMAP archives and publications (Lister 1968; Nichols 1963; Nichols and Harlan 1967; Nichols and Smith 1965).

If and when new archaeological excavations are conducted at MVNP, the number of dated charcoal samples from pithouse structures will likely increase, and may increase significantly, because large numbers of buried but open-air sites remain to be excavated within MVNP boundaries. It is highly unlikely, however, that the number of dated wood samples will increase substantially, because the vast majority of datable wood from cliff dwellings in MVNP has now been collected and analyzed (Nash 2010). As we shall see, this may have significant implications for the interpretation of the MVNP date distribution.

Historical Analysis of the MVNP Tree-Ring Date Distributions

The purpose of this chapter is to test Berry and Benson's assertion that large, regional tree-ring data sets are "representative of prehistoric reality" (2010:56). To do so, we will conduct a historical analysis of the MVNP tree-ring date distributions available for analysis by archaeologists in 1929, 1951, 1974, and 2013.

Table 24.1 summarizes the numeric status of archaeological tree-ring dating at four critical points in the history of research at MVNP. The first is 1929, when Douglass published tree-ring dates for six MVNP sites. The second is 1951, when Smiley published his synthesis. The third is 1974, after WMAP was complete and after Robinson and Harrill published their synthesis. The fourth is 2013, when results of all recent projects were incorporated in the tabulation. For symmetry's sake, a fifth bi-decadal entry for about 1990 might have been included in Table 24.1, but there was very little archaeological tree-ring research conducted at MVNP between 1974 and the early 1990s, and such an entry is therefore superfluous.

TABLE 24.1. Tree-ring-dated sites and samples, Mesa Verde National Park, 1929–2013.

Year	Number of Dated Sites	Number of Dated Samples
1929	6	8
1951	26	136
1974	78	1,717
2013	143	4,389

Table 24.1 demonstrates that the number of dated samples increased by an order of magnitude between 1929 and 1951, increased by an order of magnitude again between 1951 and 1974, and then almost doubled between 1974 and 2013. The six sites represented in 1929 were all cliff dwellings. The 26 sites represented in 1951 include pithouses, pueblos, and cliff dwellings, as do the 78 sites represented in 1974. The total number of dated sites available today, 143, includes pithouses, pueblos, and cliff dwellings. Although 143 dated sites may sound impressive, we should not forget that this number constitutes less than 3 percent of the more than 4,500 documented archaeological sites within MVNP's boundaries and that the park itself has not yet been completely surveyed for archaeological resources.

This point alone demonstrates that there is systematic bias in the MVNP tree-ring date distribution. It follows logically that there is systematic bias in any large, regional tree-ring date distribution, as well as in large, regional data sets representing any archaeological phenomenon. That is the nature of the beast. Nevertheless, it is worthwhile to examine the MVNP tree-ring date distribution in greater detail to further understand the sources of variability therein. As we shall see, tree-ring-dated sites tend to be those that are well preserved, have been the focus of archaeological research, or happen to be located in areas where modern development, and therefore salvage archaeology, has taken place (Ahlstrom 1997; Dean 1985). This has serious implications for the interpretation of tree-ring date distributions, all of which are historically contingent.

Douglass (1929) published eight dates for six sites at MVNP: AD 1073 for Cliff Palace, AD 1112 for Oak Tree House, AD 1115 for Spring House, AD 1190 and 1206 for Balcony House, AD 1204 for Square Tower House, and AD 1216 and 1262 for Spruce Tree House. There were two notable reactions to this list at the time it was published (Nash 1999:60–67). First, the late thirteenth-century dates for the cliff dwellings came as a shock to many archaeologists, who thought, on the basis of little more than educated guesses, that the sites were going to be much older. Second, the AD 1073 Cliff Palace date proved confounding to archaeologists, dendrochronologists, and MVNP personnel, all of whom were forced to explain why Cliff Palace was apparently two centuries older than Spruce Tree House and other sites despite their architectural and artifactual similarities and proximity to one another.

Tree-ring dating theory was not well developed in 1929 (see Nash 2000). Douglass (1929) did not even differentiate between cutting and noncutting dates, much less consider the possibility that the AD 1073 Cliff Palace date might have come from a reused beam in the well-preserved dwelling. So the AD 1073 date was accepted at face value. Today, our understanding is more nuanced, and we recognize that a single tree-ring date is not enough to securely interpret the chronometric history of any site, much less one as complex as Cliff Palace. In modern parlance, the AD 1073 might be deemed "anomalous" because it was dendrochronologically reliable but otherwise did not fit well within the archaeological context from which it was recovered (Dean 1978; Nash 1997).[2]

Based on today's expanded tree-ring date list, we now know that only one of Douglass's 1929 dates—the AD 1262 date from Spruce Tree House—comes close to the primary construction and occupation of the site from which it was derived.[3] The remaining seven dates Douglass (1929) published are now recognized either as noncutting dates or as having come from reused beams. This brief example illustrates the need to (1) use cutting dates whenever possible, (2) obtain large sample sizes whenever possible, and (3) systematically analyze tree-ring dates within their archaeological contexts.

Before moving on to the 1951, 1974, and 2013 date distribution curves, three important caveats must be noted. The first caveat is that only cutting (n = 1,361) and near-cutting dates (n = 458) are considered in the rest of this analysis, following Berry and Benson (2010:56). Noncutting dates (n = 2,570) have been eliminated from consideration for reasons mentioned above. The total number of 1,819 cutting and near-cutting dates included in the analysis is nevertheless sufficient to provide us with insights regarding the strengths and potential weaknesses of regional tree-ring date distributions.

The second caveat is that the earliest portion of the MVNP tree-ring date distribution has been arbitrarily cut off at AD 600 so that the main sequence is more visible.[4] This means the loss of only seven cutting dates and six near-cutting dates from the MVNP distribution and therefore this analysis. This is a trivial number consisting of less than 1 percent of the total database. The use of this arbitrary cutoff is acceptable because we are interested in exploring the historically contingent nature of the tree-ring date distribution and the archaeological interpretation thereof, not in the absolute range of MVNP tree-ring dates across space and through time.

The third caveat is that the dates have been grouped by decade such that the histograms have visual coherence and meaning. Berry and Benson (2010:57, Figure 3.3) narrow their analysis from century-long intervals to half-century and finally decadal bins. Each of these intervals has individual merit but is variously appropriate depending on the hypotheses being tested. The decadal intervals used herein are coupled with a detailed historical and contextual analysis to specifically and precisely identify and analyze key aspects of the date distribution. In so doing, we highlight the challenges that archaeologists face when interpreting large, regional tree-ring data sets. The use of less granular groupings, such as half-century or century-length intervals, would only increase the number of dates in each cluster while diminishing the analytical resolution thereof, so they are not pursued further.

Figure 24.1 presents the distribution of the 90 cutting and near-cutting dates from MVNP that were available to archaeologists in 1951, when Smiley published his synthesis. Note that Smiley (1951:22–23, following Douglass 1929) summarized the 136 dates from 26 MVNP sites and did not list all of them individually. Rather, he provided date ranges for each site or component thereof, just as Douglass (1929) had. Although Smiley did not differentiate between cutting and noncutting dates, these data are reconstructed from the detailed analysis of accession records at the LTRR and the publication record Smiley used in compiling his synthesis (see references in Smiley 1951).

The y-axis of Figure 24.1 is important. Note that it ranges from zero to 18 dates. If date clusters are defined as three or more dates in the same or proximal calendar years within some spatially delineated space, such as a room or site, there were only nine possible date clusters available for archaeological analysis in the entire MVNP date distribution as it existed in 1951.[5] The x-axis is also important, for the cutting and near-cutting dates known in 1951 range from AD 853 to 1279. As we shall see, the x-axis will shift 250 years to the left, earlier in time, in the plots of the tree-ring date distribution as it existed in 1974 (Figure 24.2) and 2013 (Figure 24.3), both of which were created *after* MVNP emphasized pithouse excavation and development.

The largest cluster evident in Figure 24.1, in the AD 1270s, is composed of 18 dates from Cliff Palace, demonstrating the prominent role this site played in the history of tree-ring dating at MVNP prior to 1951, as well as dendrochronologists' efforts to make sense of the surprisingly early AD 1073 date that Douglass had obtained in 1929. The second-largest cluster, in the AD 890s, is composed of two AD 898 and 10 AD 899 cutting dates derived from pinyon samples Getty collected in the Far View group of sites in the 1930s. Other small clusters, such as that consisting of five AD 1059 cutting dates from Room 33 at Far View House, are present in Figure 24.1. Still others are, upon analysis, mirages.

After consulting spatial data in the MVNP database, the apparent cluster of seven dates in the AD 1260s is not actually a cluster at all, for it is composed of two dates from Kodak House, a single date from Mesa Verde Site 0013, and four dates from different subsite contexts at Cliff Palace. The point here is that while aggregate, regional tree-ring date distributions can indeed demonstrate temporal clustering, they do not provide the spatial data necessary to determine whether a cluster is "real" (as defined above) or not. The contemporaneous tree-cutting events that

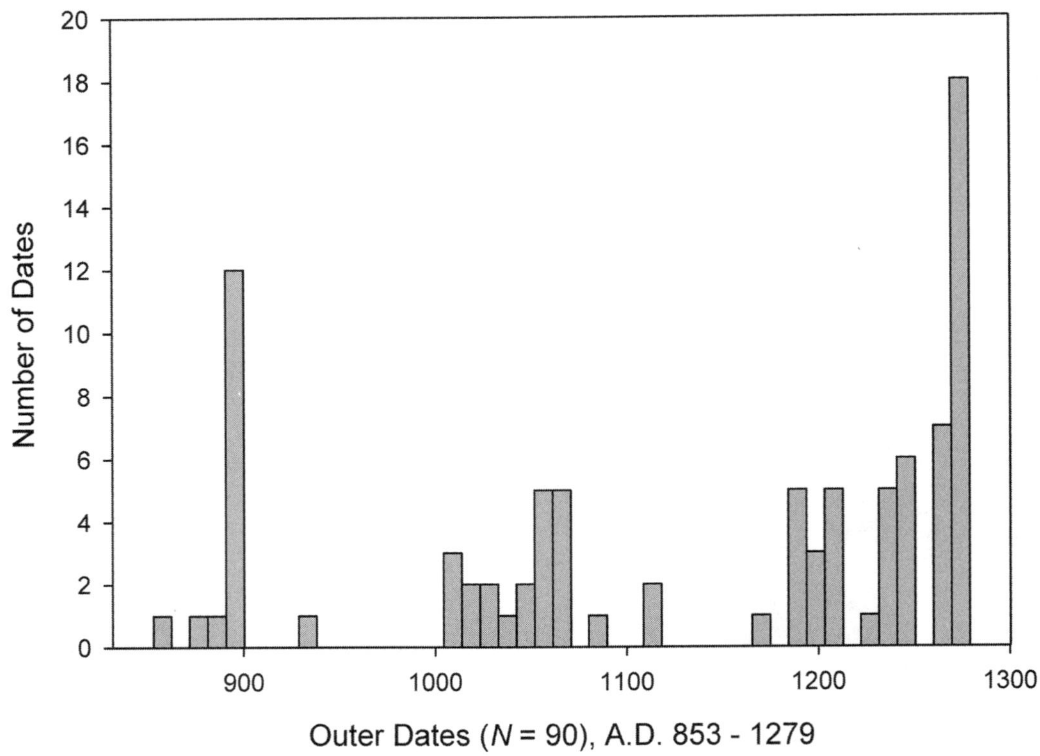

FIGURE 24.1. Distribution of 90 cutting and near-cutting dates available from Mesa Verde National Park in 1951.

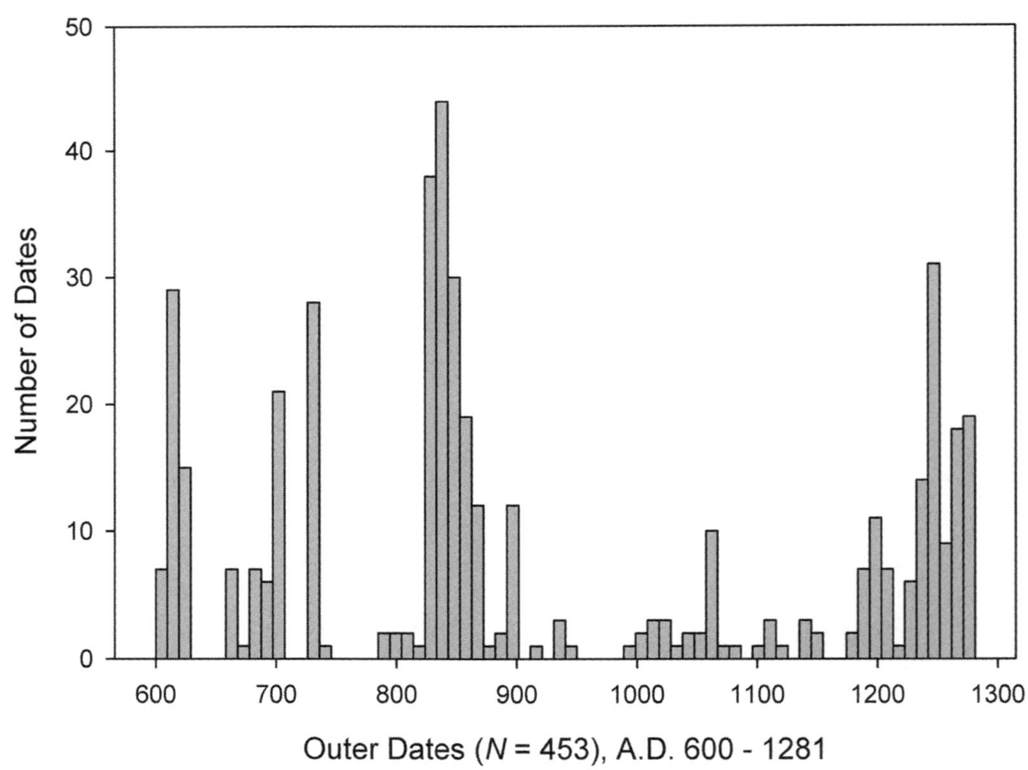

FIGURE 24.2. Distribution of 453 cutting and near-cutting dates available from Mesa Verde National Park in 1974.

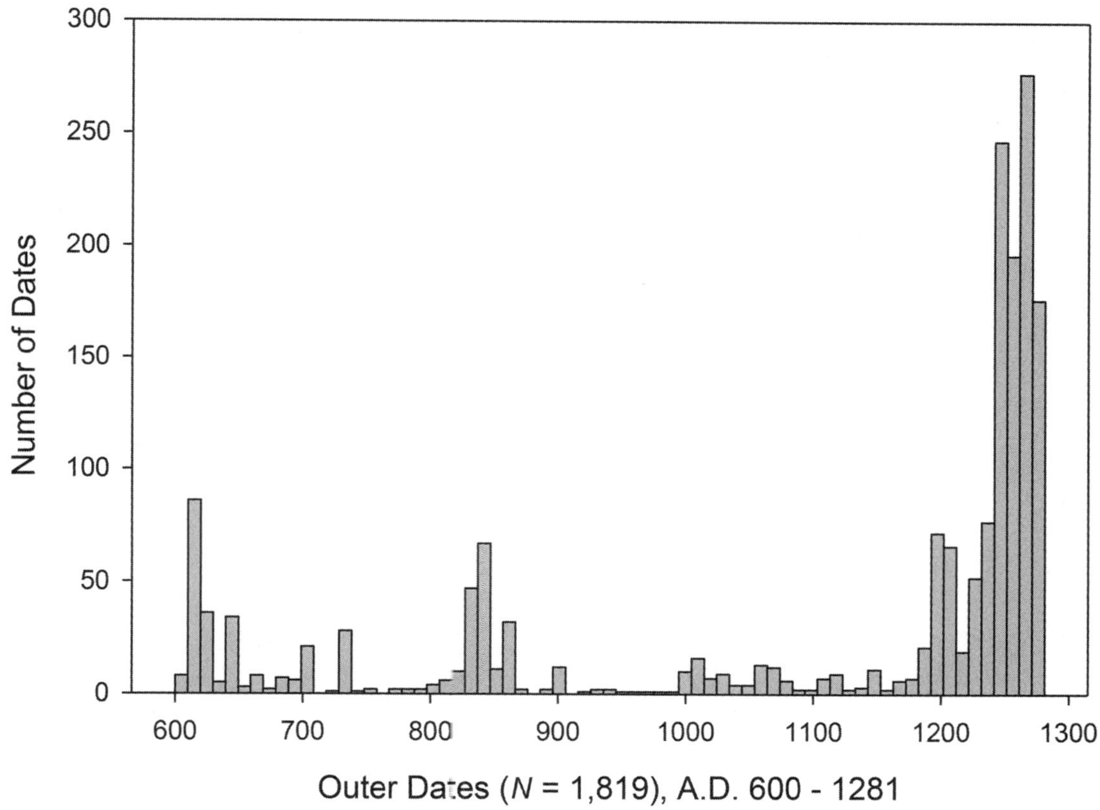

FIGURE 24.3. Distribution of 1,819 cutting and near-cutting dates available from Mesa Verde National Park in 2013.

led to these tree-ring dates *may* be behaviorally related, but then again, they may not be. Only detailed analysis of their archaeological context can help determine that answer.

Note that the 1951 cutting and near-cutting date distribution contains no dates at all from the AD 1250s (Figure 24.1). As we shall see, this is curious because the 1974 date distribution (Figure 24.2) contains 17 dates from the AD 1250s and the 2013 date distribution (Figure 24.3) contains 218 such dates. The majority of the AD 1250s dates in the 1974 date distribution, and by extension the 2013 date distribution, come from Spruce Tree House, Spring House, and Mesa Verde Ruin No. 11 (Nordenskiöld), all of which were sampled by Getty and others prior to 1951 but which for some unknown reason did not yield dates in the 1250s. This lacuna may be a function of the Synthesis Project's reanalysis in the 1960s (Robinson and Harrill 1974) and challenges associated with the tree-ring chronology in the AD 1250s. Less likely, but still possible, is sampling error, whereby none of the samples collected by Getty and others were from components of those sites built in the AD 1250s. Whatever the case may be, another significant construction period in the region's history was missing from the 1951 date distribution. The general outline of Precolumbian history at MVNP, with tree-cutting activity evident in the late AD 800s, throughout the 1000s, and peaking in the mid- to late 1200s, nevertheless seems evident in this small, regional tree-ring date distribution (Figure 24.1).

Figure 24.2 presents the distribution of MVNP cutting and near-cutting dates (n = 453) available to archaeologists in 1974. Note that the y-axis has expanded threefold. Whereas the date distribution for 1951 had at most 18 dated specimens for any given decade, the 1974 distribution has six potential clusters with 25 or more dates. Note also that the x-axis has expanded, moving 250 years earlier, and two years later, in time.

The largest concentration of dates in the 1974 date distribution consists of 143 cutting and near-cutting dates spread between AD 824 and AD 865. Of these 143 dates, 96 come from Robert Lister's University of Colorado field school excavation of the Great Kiva at Morfield Canyon Site 1930 (Robinson and Harrill 1974:110–112). Another 22 came from Deric O'Bryan's excavation of Pithouse I and Pithouse II at Mesa Verde Site 0102 on Chapin Mesa for Gila Pueblo in 1947, and 14 come from the University of Colorado's excavation of Pithouse 1 at Morfield Canyon Site 1930–1971.[6] Put another way, 92 percent (132 of 143) of the dates in the largest cluster in the 1974 date distribution stem from the excavation of only four structures. If Lister and Nusbaum had not excavated those four structures, only 8 percent (21 of 143 dates) of the AD 824–865 cluster would be present in Figure 24.2. Twenty-one dates scattered over four decades do not make a cluster. To be blunt, the cluster would be gone.

Beyond the AD 824–865 cluster, the second-largest single-decade cluster in Figure 24.2 is in the AD 1250s and was discussed above. The third-largest single-decade cluster in Figure 24.2 consists of 29 dates in the AD 620s and is composed of 23 cutting and six near-cutting dates from four sites (Mesa Verde Sites 0145, 1937, 1938, and 1824), all but one of which (Mesa Verde 0145) are

Decade	Year
38	1
::::	
43	6
::	
46	7
:	
48	4
::::	
53	0 7
54	2
:	
56	2 8
57	1
::	
60	9
61	7
62	1 **1 3**
63	7
64	2
65	2 5 6
66	57
:	
68	0 2 **6** 8
69	4 8
70	**0 0** 1 3 7 9
71	8 8 9 9
72	2 5 5 6 8 8 8 8 **8 9 9 9 9 9 9 9 9 9** **9 9 9 9 9 9 9 9 9 9 9 9 9 9 9 9 9 9**

FIGURE 24.4. Stem-and-leaf plot of 74 tree-ring dates from Mesa Verde Site 1990. The left-hand column indicates the decade (e.g., the stem), and the right-hand column lists individual tree-ring dates in chronological order by year (e.g., the leaves). To read the stem-and-leaf plot, the two-digit entry under "Decade" is combined with the single-digit entry under "Year" to make a three-digit calendar year. Cutting dates are in bold; noncutting dates are in plain text. The earliest tree-ring date from Mesa Verde Site 1990 is a noncutting date at AD 381. The latest tree-ring dates from Mesa Verde Site 1990 are a strong series of 27 cutting dates from AD 729. Note that the archaeological, historical, and other contextual data necessary to further evaluate the nature and integrity of date clusters are not presented in this summary plot.

located on Wetherill Mesa. All four of these sites were excavated by the WMAP or the University of Colorado field school.

The fourth-largest single-decade cluster in Figure 24.2 is in the AD 720s and is composed of one AD 728 cutting date and 27 AD 729 near-cutting dates from a single antechambered Basketmaker III pithouse excavated by Robert Lister's University of Colorado field school in 1969 and 1971 (Mesa Verde Site 1990 [see Robinson and Harrill 1974:157–158]). Figure 24.4 presents a stem-and-leaf plot of the Mesa Verde Site 1990 date distribution. The site itself is clearly well dated to AD 729, for only six other cutting or near-cutting dates are scattered throughout the date distribution.

The following point cannot be overstated: The largest cluster in Figure 24.2, covering four decades from AD 824 to 865, is attributable to the excavation of only four structures. The third-largest cluster in Figure 24.2 is also attributable to the excavation of only four structures. The fourth-largest cluster in Figure 24.2 is attributable to the excavation of a single structure. If Lister and his students had not excavated that single antechambered Basketmaker III pithouse (Mesa Verde Site 1990), one of the largest clusters in the 1974 date distribution (Figure 24.2) would be completely missing, period.

But Lister and his students did excavate that pithouse, and the tree-ring date cluster is therefore real and does indeed indicate that Precolumbian construction workers cut at least 28 trees in a two-year period while preparing to build the pithouse. This is indeed a record of Precolumbian reality, but can we be sure that it is representative of Precolumbian reality across the region? The simple fact is that we have no idea how many other single, unexcavated pithouses will have a similar effect on the date distribution.

The same thing holds for the larger AD 824–865 cluster. Lister and Nusbaum did excavate those four structures; that is part of our historical and archaeological reality. The data they gathered clearly indicate that a substantial amount of tree-cutting activity is well recorded, as is the construction of four structures within MVNP. That is Precolumbian reality reflected in the tree-ring date distribution. The question is, Can, or more appropriately should, archaeologists assume that these specific events evident in the tree-ring date distribution are a "relative measure of [Precolumbian] construction activity" across the region (Berry and Benson 2010:56)? Relative to what? To all Precolumbian construction activity within MVNP? We simply cannot know a priori what gaps in the tree-ring date distribution might be filled in the future, or what clusters might be embellished, by the excavation of individual structures. We can and should recognize the historically contingent nature of the data and the date distributions we have, however.

A final, notable aspect of the 1974 date distribution curve as a whole (Figure 24.2) is how generally different it looks when compared with the distributions for 1951 (Figure 24.1) and 2013 (Figure 24.3). Indeed, the 1974 date distribution does not resemble the popular conception of the occupation of MVNP, according to which we expect most of the construction activity to have occurred during the late thirteenth century, when the cliff dwellings were built and occupied. Rather, the pithouse-derived date clusters early in the sequence in Figure 24.2 dwarf all other clusters. The simple fact is that the 1974 tree-ring date distribution is demonstrably contingent upon the history of archaeological research in the park and demonstrates the administrative emphasis on the excavation of pithouse sites and visitation-related development during the middle part of the twentieth century.

Figure 24.3 presents the date distribution of 1,819 cutting and near-cutting dates at MVNP available to archaeologists today. Note that the x-axis has not changed since 1974; the earliest date is the AD 600 cutoff, and the latest date is the near-cutting date at AD 1281. More important, note that the y-axis has expanded again to include clusters of more than 250 dates in a given decade, which are derived from well-preserved cliff dwellings and stand in mute testimony to the effectiveness of the 100 percent sampling strategies implemented by the LTRR beginning in the early 1990s. The outstanding new cluster of 86 cutting and near-cutting dates in the AD 610s is attributable to the derivation of 56 new dates during the excavation of pithouses in Step House Cave.

The cluster of dates in the AD 1190s and AD 1200s is more clearly evident in the 2013 curve (Figure 24.3) than it was in 1974 (Figure 24.2) and certainly more than in 1951 (Figure 24.1). This large cluster, spanning two decades, is almost exclusively derived from intensive sampling at Square Tower House, Spring House, Long House, and other sites. Generally speaking, the 2013 curve looks like the popular conception of the region's Precolumbian history, with activity in the cliff-dwelling periods dwarfing that of earlier periods. Note, however, that the large cluster of dates between AD 824 and 865 still dominates the middle range of Figure 24.3, just as it dominated the middle range of Figure 24.2. Again, one is left to wonder how our understanding of Precolumbian history at MVNP, as documented in the tree-ring date distribution curves, would be different if those four structures (e.g., the Great Kiva at Morfield Canyon Site 1930 and pithouses at Morfield Canyon Site 1930–1971 and Mesa Verde Site 0102) had never been excavated. If they had not, Figure 24.3 would be effectively bimodal, with evidence of tree-cutting activity largely prior to about AD 750 and again after the AD 1190s.

Discussion

This brief analysis of the history and status of tree-ring dating at MVNP demonstrates that large, regional tree-ring date distributions are contingent on the history of the research from which they derived. If we were simply to assume that the date distributions were representative of Precolumbian reality and failed to account for a few select projects, such as the University of Colorado field schools, notable clusters in the date distribution might go missing. The resulting curve, and therefore our understanding of "prehistoric reality," would look radically different as a result.

If we were to neglect archaeological contexts at the regional level, we may get swept up in the fact that we have 4,389 dated samples from 143 dated sites at MVNP, but we cannot ignore the fact that 2,570 of those dates are the interpretively less reliable noncutting dates and that those 143 sites constitute but 3 percent of the total number of documented sites within MNVP's administrative boundaries. Although MVNP is widely recognized as one of the world's best places in which to conduct archaeological tree-ring research, it should now be clear that even its regional tree-ring date distribution is beset by sampling error and bias that simply must be accounted for before assuming that it is representative of anything but the history of research and development in the region.

A simple, final, thought-provoking example illuminates some additional interpretive challenges presented by the regional tree-ring date distribution from MVNP. Cliff Palace, located on Chapin Mesa and the largest cliff dwelling in MVNP, has yielded only 65 tree-ring dates (Figure 24.5). Long House, located on Wetherill Mesa and the second-largest cliff dwelling in the park, has yielded 633 dates (Figure 24.6). How are we to account for this order of magnitude difference? Could it be that more than a century of Euro-American visitation to Cliff Palace has taken a magnificent if horrible toll on the supply of datable wood from that site, some (most?) of which became firewood (McGregor 1930; Smith 2009:21)? Did the comparative isolation of Long House, located significantly farther west and south of the park entrance, across difficult terrain, protect it from the firewood-seeking hordes that plagued Cliff Palace? Is less intense historic visitation responsible for the differential preservation of construction beams, and therefore the tree-ring record, at Long House? Perhaps. There are other cultural, natural, and historical factors to consider as well, including the location of drip lines and the fact that Long House was professionally excavated, but the circumstantial evidence is difficult to refute in this case. Cliff Palace was loved to death; Long House was not. In light of the Long House data, it is clear that the tree-ring record of Cliff Palace is not representative of its Precolumbian reality. But what about Long House? Are 633 dates enough to reconstitute that reality? The intensive dendrochronological sampling of Long House (Street 2001a, 2001b) demonstrates that there are significant gaps in our chronometric and archaeological knowledge of that site as well and that even 633 dates represent a small and unknowable fraction of the total number of trees used to build

Century	Year
10	50 78
11	**08** 74 **90 91 91**
12	**06 11 13** 31 **38 40 41** 42 44 **47 48** 57 64 **64** 66 **67 67 68 68 68** 68 **69 69 70 70** 70 71 **71 71 71 71 71 71 71 71 71 71 71** 71 **72 72 72** *73* **73 73 73 73 74 74 74 75 75 75** *78* **78 79 79 80**

FIGURE 24.5. Stem-and-leaf plot of 64 tree-ring dates from Cliff Palace. The numeric entry in the first column is the century (e.g., the "stem"), and the two-digit numeric entries in the second column are individual tree-ring dates (e.g., the "leaves"). To read the stem-and-leaf plot, the two-digit entry under "Century" is combined with the two-digit entry under "Year" to make a four-digit calendar year. Cutting dates are in bold, near-cutting dates are italicized, and noncutting dates are in plain text. The earliest tree-ring date from Cliff Palace is therefore a noncutting date at AD 1050. The latest tree-ring date from Cliff Palace is a cutting date from AD 1280. Note that the contextual data necessary to further evaluate the nature and integrity of date clusters are not presented in this summary plot.

Century	Year
2	90
3	71
4	
$5^{(3)}$	39
$5^{(4)}$	41
$5^{(5)}$	
$5^{(6)}$	61 67
$5^{(7)}$	
$5^{(8)}$	81 82 85
$5^{(9)}$	96
$6^{(0)}$	03 06
$6^{(1)}$	12 13 15 16 17 18
$6^{(2)}$	20 21 22 23 23 24 25 27
$6^{(3)}$	**30** 31 31 32 32 34 35 35 36 39
$6^{(4)}$	41 41 41 42 42 *43 44* 44 46 46 *47 47* 47 47 47 48 48 48 48 48 48 48 48 48 48 48 *48* **48 48 48 48 48 48 48 48 48 48 48 48 48 48 48 48 48 48 48 48 48 48 48 48 48 48 48 48**
$6^{(5)}$	**55 55 67**
7	
8	97 99
9	14 30 39 40 50 **64** 75 80
10	00 04 05 05
$10^{(1)}$	15
$10^{(2)}$	22 24
$10^{(3)}$	
$10^{(4)}$	47
$10^{(5)}$	55
$10^{(6)}$	*67*
$10^{(7)}$	74 75 77 79
$10^{(8)}$	80 88
$10^{(9)}$	94
$11^{(0)}$	**02 04** 05 07
$11^{(1)}$	*10* 12 16 17 18 19
$11^{(2)}$	21 **22** 24 25
$11^{(3)}$	31 33 36 36 39
$11^{(4)}$	41 42 *45* **45 45 46 47** 47 49 *49*
$11^{(5)}$	50 52 53 55
$11^{(6)}$	62 63 69 *69*
$11^{(7)}$	70 71 71 71 **72** 76 77 77 78
$11^{(8)}$	80 **83** 84 **84** 85 85 88 89 **89**
$11^{(9)}$	*90* 93 96 96 96 *96* 97 *97 97 97* **97** 98 98 *98 98 98* 99 99 99 **99 99 99**
$12^{(0)}$	00 00 00 **00 00 00 00** 01 **01** 02 02 02 **03 03 03 03** 04 04 *04 04* **04** *05* **05** 09
$12^{(1)}$	10 10 11 11 12 12 13 13 14 *15* 18 18 19 19
$12^{(2)}$	21 22 **23** 24 **25 25 25 25** *26* 26 26 27 28 28
$12^{(3)}$	30 30 30 32 32 33 *33* **33** 34 34 35 36 36 37 37 *37* 38 38 38 39 39 39
$12^{(4)}$	*40* **40** 41 41 41 41 41 41 41 41 41 41 **41** 43 44 45 45 45 **45 45** 46 46 **46** 47 47 47 *47* 48 48 48 48 48 48 48 **48 48** 49 49 49 **49 49**
$12^{(5)}$	50 50 50 50 50 *50 50* **50 50** *51 51* 52 52 52 52 *52 52* **52** 53 53 53 53 53 53 *53 53 53 53 53 53 53 53 53 53 53 53* **53 53 53 53** 54 54 54 54 54 54 54 *54 54 54 54* **54 54 54 54** 55 *55 55* 55 55 55 55 **55 55 55 55 55 55 55** 56 56 56 56 56 *56 56 56* **56** 57 57 57 57 57 57 57 57 *57 57 57 57 57 57 57 57* **57** 58 **58 58 58** 59 59 59 **59 59**
$12^{(6)}$	60 60 60 60 60 *60* **60 60 60** 61 61 61 61 **61** 62 62 62 62 62 *62 62 62 62 62* **62 62** 63 *63 63 63 63 63 63 63 63* 63 63 **63 63 63** 64 64 64 64 64 64 64 64 64 *64 64 64 64 64* **64 64 64 64 64 64 64 64 64 64** 65 65 65 65 65 65 65 *65 65 65 65 65 65* **65 65 65** 66 66 66 66 *66 66 66 66 66* **66 66 66 66 66 66 66 66 66 66 66 66 66 66** 67 67 67 67 67 67 67 *67 67 67 67* **67 67 67 67 67 67 67 67 67 67 67 67 67 67 67 67 67** 68 68 68 68 **68 68 68 68** 69 69 *69 69 69* **69**
$12^{(7)}$	70 *70 70 70 70 70* **70 70 70 70 70 70 70 70 70 70 70 70 70 70 70** 71 *71* **71 71 71 71 71 71 71 71 71** 72 *72* **72 72 72 72 72 72 72 72 72** 73 **73 73** *74 74* **74** 75 75 **75 75 76** *77 77 77* **77 77 77** 77 77 78 **78** *79 79 79 79* **79 79**

FIGURE 24.6. Stem-and-leaf plot of 643 tree-ring dates from Long House. The single- or two-digit entry in the first column is the century or decade (the "stem") in question; the two-digit entries in the second column are individual tree-ring dates (the "leaves"). Given the large number of tree-ring dates from Long House, the listings under "Century" have had to be broken into decades as indicated by the superscript, such that "$12^{(7)}$" lists dates only for the AD 1270s, rather than a full century as the column title otherwise indicates. Cutting dates are in bold, near-cutting dates are italicized, and noncutting dates are in plain text. The earliest tree-ring date from Long House is therefore a noncutting date at AD 290; the latest is a cutting date at AD 1279. Note that the archaeological, historical, and other contextual data necessary to further evaluate the nature and integrity of date clusters are not presented in this summary plot.

dwellings in the Long House rockshelter over six centuries of occupation.

Even if Cliff Palace were to somehow miraculously yield 568 new tree-ring dates to achieve numeric parity with Long House, we cannot know a priori where those new dates would fall on the 2013 date distribution curve (Figure 24.3) or the stem-and-leaf plot (Figure 24.5). Might we expect them to embellish existing clusters in the seventh century? Why? In the thirteenth century? Both? Neither? Why not? Archaeological evidence will only get us so far, even in remarkable contexts like those preserved at MVNP.

The inescapable conclusion is that the large, regional tree-ring date distribution at MVNP, and by extension, elsewhere, is incomplete with respect to its original sampling universe and is systematically biased in ways that we may never fully understand. These regional tree-ring databases are demonstrably contingent on the history of research and development in their respective regions. It therefore behooves us all to well understand the origins of the data in these data sets before assuming that they are representative of Precolumbian reality.

Conclusion

The stringent ecological and behavioral prerequisites of successful archaeological tree-ring dating mean that, even under the best of archaeological circumstances, such as those at MVNP, only a fraction of all archaeological wood and charcoal samples will yield tree-ring dates. As a sampling universe, Ancestral Puebloan wood-use and construction behavior was not randomly distributed across space and through time, and it certainly is not normally distributed about some mean value. The modes in tree-ring date distributions do indeed mean something, however. Interpreting the modes in each tree-ring date distribution requires detailed analysis of the temporal and spatial contexts from which they derive. Archaeologists have to be cautious when making assumptions and inferences about the Precolumbian sampling universe (e.g., reality) from which known tree-ring dates are derived.

All would agree that larger databases are analytically more robust than small ones. Certainly, we know more about Precolumbian reality at MVNP from the analysis of 1,819 cutting and near-cutting dates than we did from the analysis of 12, 90, or 453. It does not follow, however, that a large regional database, taken from a nonrandom, nonnormal universe, is de facto representative of Precolumbian reality by sheer virtue of its size.

Archaeological tree-ring date distributions in the American Southwest therefore constitute an embarrassment of riches. On one hand, tree-ring dates provide archaeologists with the most accurate and precise chronometric data available in the absence of historic records—and often in spite of them (Towner 2000).

Tree-ring dates provide archaeologists with the ability to accurately and precisely reconstruct specific beam-procurement and construction events in the Precolumbian past. They offer archaeologists the ability to compare those behavioral events with annually resolved climate data derived from tree-rings and other sources in an effort to search for climatic drivers of these behavioral events. But they do not allow us to make sweeping generalizations about prehistoric reality.

What, then, are we to do? The light is yellow and flashing; a warning flag is out and waving. The hazards are on. Proceed with caution.

Acknowledgments

Funding for this project was provided by the State Historic Fund of the Colorado Historical Society and by the National Science Foundation through the Village Ecodynamics Project (grant DEB-0816400). I thank Mark Varien and Scott Ortman of Crow Canyon Archaeological Center and Tim Kohler of Washington State University for inviting me to participate in this important project. Field and collections-based research was conducted at Mesa Verde National Park, and thanks are due to Julie Bell, Chris McAllister, Carolyn Landis, Lynda Knowles, Scott Travis, and Tara Travis. Archival research was conducted at the Laboratory of Tree-Ring Research at the University of Arizona, and thanks are due to Jeff Dean and Ron Towner. Eric Koenig created the stem-and-leaf plots; Christina Rogers analyzed the databases, archives, and publication records to develop the date distribution curves. Rick Ahlstrom, Nancy Parezo, Ron Towner, and Jeff Dean provided useful comments on this chapter. Stephen E. Nash is grateful to Nancy Parezo, James Snead, and Joel Janetski for the opportunity to participate in the symposium honoring Don Fowler. Finally, Nash is grateful to Don for helping so many of us experience the American Southwest as a historically and contextually grounded laboratory for anthropology.

Notes

1. The database is too large to publish herein, but copies are on file at the Denver Museum of Nature and Science, the Laboratory of Tree-Ring Research, Mesa Verde National Park, and Crow Canyon Archaeological Center. Due to vagaries in how site and subsite provenience data (e.g., "Mesa Verde area") have been recorded since the first tree-ring samples were collected from Mesa Verde in 1923, the number of dated sites may actually be slightly higher or slightly lower than 143. The number of dated specimens analyzed in this chapter was current as of June 1, 2013.
2. As it turned out, the AD 1073 date was not dendrochronologically reliable and was revised according to modern standards by the Synthesis Project (Robinson and Harrill 1974:53–54). The point remains, however, that all tree-ring dates have to be evaluated in terms of their dendrochronological properties (i.e., are they cutting, near-cutting, or noncutting dates?) and within the specific archaeological contexts from which they were recovered.
3. The AD 1262 date was also revised during the Synthesis Project (Robinson and Harrill 1974:120–121). There are currently no AD 1262 dates from Spruce Tree House, but there are three near-cutting dates at AD 1263, from second-story door lintels in Room 47 (Specimen numbers MV-0258 and MV-0259) and a wall peg from the second story of Room 124 (Specimen number MV-0649).

4. Berry and Benson (2010:57) focus their analysis on the period AD 600–1600, but their Figure 3.3 presents their date distributions going back to AD 400.
5. Note, however, that Figures 24.1, 24.2, and 24.3 do not present the spatial (e.g., site, room, or feature) data necessary to determine if a mode in these distributions is actually a date cluster as defined here. Subsite provenience-level data are contained in the LTRR accession files, in various publications, and now in the MVNP tree-ring database. They are too detailed to be published in their entirety here.
6. The distinction between Morfield Canyon Site 1930 and Morfield Canyon Site 1930–1971 is not immediately evident from the LTRR accession files. They may be different structures at the same site. Robinson and Harrill's (1974:109–113) "Morfield Canyon Group" lists four Mesa Verde site numbers (1067, 1927, 1928, and 1930) and indicates that samples were collected by the University of Colorado field school in 1967 and 1971 but does not clarify the situation further.

References Cited

Ahlstrom, R. V. N.
1997 Sources of Variation in the Southwestern Archaeological Tree-Ring Record. *Kiva* 62:321–348.

Ahlstrom, R. V. N., Jeffrey S. Dean, and William J. Robinson
1991 Evaluating Tree-Ring Interpretations at Walpi Pueblo. *American Antiquity* 56(4):628–644.

Bannister, B.
1962 The Interpretation of Tree-Ring Dates. *American Antiquity* 27:508–514.

Benson, Larry V., and Michael S. Berry
2009 Climate Change and Cultural Response in the Prehistoric American Southwest. *Kiva* 75(1):89–117.

Berry, Michael S.
1982 *Time, Space, and Transition in Anasazi Prehistory*. University of Utah Press, Salt Lake City.

Berry, Michael S., and Larry V. Benson
2010 Tree-Ring Dates and Demographic Change in the Southern Colorado Plateau and Rio Grande Regions. In *Leaving Mesa Verde: Peril and Change in the Thirteenth-Century Southwest*, edited by T. Kohler, M. Varien, and A. Wright, pp. 53–74. University of Arizona Press, Tucson.

Dean, J. S.
1978 Independent Dating in Archaeological Analysis. In *Advances in Archaeological Method and Theory*, Vol. 1, edited by M. B. Schiffer, pp. 223–255. Academic Press, New York.
1985 Review of *Time, Space, and Transition in Anasazi Prehistory*, by Michael S. Berry (1982). University of Utah Press, Salt Lake City. *American Antiquity* 50(3):704–705.
1996a Behavioral Sources of Error in Archaeological Tree-Ring Dating: Navajo and Pueblo Wood-Use. In *Tree-Rings, Environment, and Humanity: Proceedings of the International Conference, Tucson, 1994*, edited by J. S. Dean, D. M. Meko, and T. W. Swetnam, pp. 497–504. Radiocarbon, Tucson.
1996b Dendrochronology and the Study of Human Behavior. In *Tree-Rings, Environment, and Humanity: Proceedings of the International Conference, Tucson, 1994*, edited by J. S. Dean, D. M. Meko, and T. W. Swetnam, pp. 461–469. Radiocarbon, Tucson.

Douglass, A. E.
1929 The Secret of the Southwest Solved by Talkative Tree-Rings. *National Geographic* 56(6):736–770.
1942 Crossdating at Mesa Verde National Park. *Journal of Forestry* 40:347–348.

Fairchild-Parks, Jim, and Jeffrey S. Dean
1993 Analysis of Tree-Ring Dates from Balcony House, Mesa Verde National Park, Colorado. Manuscript on file, Laboratory of Tree-Ring Research, University of Arizona, Tucson.

Fiero, Kathleen
1999 *Balcony House: A History of a Cliff Dwelling*. Mesa Verde National Park Archaeological Report: Archaeological Research Series, 8-A. Cortez, Colorado.

Getty, Harry T.
1935a New Dates for Spruce Tree House, Mesa Verde. *Tree-Ring Bulletin* 1(4):28–29.
1935b New Dates from Mesa Verde. *Tree-Ring Bulletin* 1(3):21–23.
1935c Tree-Ring Dates from Spruce Tree House, Mesa Verde. *Kiva* 1(1):3.

Haury, Emil W.
1935 Tree Rings: The Archaeologist's Time-Piece. *American Antiquity* 1:98–108.

Lancaster, James Allen, and D. W. Watson
1943 Excavation of Mesa Verde Pit Houses. *American Antiquity* 9(2):190–198.

Lister, Robert H.
1968 Archaeology for Layman and Scientist at Mesa Verde. *Science* 160(3827):489–496.

McGregor, John C.
1930 Tree Ring Dating. *Museum Notes* 3(4):1–4.

Nash, Stephen E.
1997 Archaeological Cutting Date Estimation and the Interpretation of Estimated Tree-Ring Dates. *American Antiquity* 62:260–272.
1999 *Time, Trees, and Prehistory: Tree-Ring Dating and the Development of North American Archaeology 1914–1950*. University of Utah Press, Salt Lake City.
2000 Seven Decades of Archaeological Tree-Ring Dating. In *It's About Time: A History of Archaeological Dating in North America*, edited by Stephen E. Nash, pp. 60–82. University of Utah Press, Salt Lake City.
2002 Archaeological Tree-Ring Dating at the Millennium. *Journal of Archaeological Research* 10:243–275.
2008 Dendrochronology. In *Encyclopedia of Archaeology*, edited by Deborah Pearsall, pp. 1083–1088. Academic Press, New York.
2010 Asymptotically Approaching Zero: Tree-Ring Dating at Mesa Verde National Park. *SAA Archaeological Record* 10(3): 38–42.

Nash, Stephen E. (editor)
2000 *It's About Time: A History of Archaeological Dating in North America*. University of Utah Press, Salt Lake City.
2009 *Readings in Chronometric Analysis: Selections from "American Antiquity" and "Latin American Antiquity" 1935–2006*. Society for American Archaeology Press, Washington, D.C.

Nichols, Robert F.
1963 Dates from the Site 1060 Pithouse, Mesa Verde National Park. *Tree-Ring Bulletin* 24(1–2):12–14.

Nichols, Robert F., and Thomas P. Harlan
1967 Archaeological Tree-Ring Dates from Wetherill Mesa. *Tree-Ring Bulletin* 28(1–4):13–27.

Nichols, Robert F., and David G. Smith
1965 Evidence of Prehistoric Cultivation of Douglas-Fir Trees at Mesa Verde. In *Contributions of the Wetherill Mesa Archaeological Project*, assembled by Douglas Osborne, pp. 57–64. Memoirs of the Society for American Archaeology, 19. Washington, D.C.

Parks, James A., and Jeffrey S. Dean
1997 Interpretation of Tree-Ring Dates from Spring House and 20-1/2 House, Mesa Verde National Park, Colorado. Manuscript on file, Laboratory of Tree-Ring Research, University of Arizona, Tucson.

Peterson, Alfred
1935 Specimens from the Pueblo Area Collected by the First Beam Expedition 1923. *Tree-Ring Bulletin* 1(3):23–24.

Robinson, William J., and Bruce G. Harrill
1974 *Tree-Ring Dates from Colorado V (Mesa Verde Area)*. Laboratory of Tree-Ring Research, University of Arizona, Tucson.

Schiffer, Michael B.
1987 *Formation Processes of the Archaeological Record*. University of New Mexico Press, Albuquerque.

Smiley, Terah L.
1947 Dates from a Surface Pueblo at Mesa Verde. *Tree-Ring Bulletin* 13(4):30–32.
1951 A Summary of Tree-Ring Dates from Some Southwestern Archaeological Sites. Laboratory of Tree-Ring Research No. 5. *University of Arizona Bulletin* 22(4). Tucson.

Smiley, Francis E., and Richard V. N. Ahlstrom
1998 *Archaeological Chronometry: Radiocarbon and Tree-Ring Models and Applications from Black Mesa, Arizona*. Southern Illinois University at Carbondale Center for Archaeological Investigations Occasional Paper No. 16. Carbondale.

Smith, Duane A.
2009 *Images of America: Mesa Verde National Park*. Arcadia Publishing, Charleston, South Carolina.

Stokes, M. A., and T. L. Smiley
1996 *An Introduction to Tree-Ring Dating*. University of Arizona Press, Tucson.

Street, David J.
2001a The Dendroarchaeology of Long House. An Anasazi Cliff Dwelling in Mesa Verde National Park, Colorado, U.S.A. Unpublished Ph.D. dissertation, Department of Archaeology, University of Bradford, Bradford, England.
2001b How Fast Is a Kiva? The Dendroarchaeology of Long House, Mesa Verde National Park. *Kiva* 67(2):137–265.

Towner, R. H.
1997 *The Dendrochronology of the Navajo Pueblitos of Dinétah*. Ph.D. dissertation, Department of Anthropology, University of Arizona, Tucson. University Microfilms, Ann Arbor.
2000 Dendrochronology and Historical Records: Concordance and Conflict in Navajo Archaeology. In *It's About Time: A History of Archaeological Dating in North America*, edited by Stephen E. Nash, pp. 168–185. University of Utah Press, Salt Lake City.
2002 Archaeological Dendrochronology in the Southwestern United States. *Evolutionary Anthropology* 11:68–84.

Watson, Don
1947 Note on the Dating of Pipe Shrine House. *Tree-Ring Bulletin* 13(4):32.

Windes, Tom
1995 Wood Sampling at Oak Tree House and Fewkes Canyon, MVNP. Manuscript on file, Mesa Verde National Park, Cortez, Colorado.

25

In Praise of Collections Research

Basketmaker Roots of Chacoan Ritual Practices

Laurie D. Webster, Linda S. Cordell, Kelley Hays-Gilpin, and Edward A. Jolie

We are pleased to report our research in this volume honoring Don Fowler. Without Don's contributions to conserving museum collections and archival information (accession records, field notes, and documentation), our work would not be possible. Don's tireless efforts on behalf of collections research may be appreciated in his publications (Fowler 1986, 1987; Fowler and Parezo 2000) and those of his colleagues and collaborators (e.g., Childs 2004; Silverman and Parezo 1995). Museums and all of us who do collections-based research have benefited enormously from Don's leadership.

Our study concerns objects from a relatively small area of the American Southwest (see Figure 25.1), but we reference collections held by nine museums in four states and the District of Columbia (Table 25.1). The collections we focus on here are typical of those made around the turn of the twentieth century, when artifacts often were divided among various institutions. In some cases, collections were partitioned because an archaeologist was supported by and made collections for multiple institutions. In others, it was because museums considered it good practice to "share" collections among sister institutions so that each might have a representative collection of a particular ancient culture or artifact class. Even today when museums are expected to (and do) maintain good electronic databases of their collections, it requires considerable ingenuity and sleuthing skills to locate artifacts excavated or collected from a particular site.

In this chapter we explore Basketmaker connections to Chacoan ritual practice. Many researchers have investigated the Mesoamerican or west Mexican origins of certain Chacoan ceremonial practices (e.g., Crown and Hurst 2009; Frisbie 1978; Judd 1954; Pepper 1920; Reyman 1978; see Nelson 2006 for an update), but few have considered more local antecedents. We contend that many aspects of Chaco ritual practice developed from local Basketmaker traditions as formerly utilitarian practices shifted to ceremonial realms. To illustrate some of these connections, we briefly address changes in certain classes of perishable material culture (burden baskets, sandals, carved wooden sticks), the use of butterfly hair whorl imagery in ceramics and rock art, and a ceremonial corn cache from Pueblo Bonito. For those unfamiliar with the Southwestern cultural sequence, the periods and approximate date ranges we discuss are Basketmaker II (1000 BC–AD 500), Basketmaker III (AD 500–700), Pueblo I (AD 700–900), Pueblo II (AD 900–1100), and Pueblo III (AD 1100–1300). The Classic Bonito phase at Chaco Canyon, which we discuss in this chapter, falls within the late Pueblo II period.

Our work with artifacts and rock art from Chaco Canyon and Basketmaker sites in the nearby Chuska–Lukachukai area suggests continuity between certain Basketmaker practices and those used in ritual, perhaps by sodalities, in Bonito phase Chaco Canyon. We define the "Chuska–Lukachukai area" as the eastern and western slopes of the Chuska and Lukachukai mountains, including the Prayer Rock District, Canyon de Chelly, and Canyon del Muerto (Figure 25.1). We do not limit the spread of these ritual practices to Chaco, nor do we deny that many of these Basketmaker traditions were practiced outside the Chuska–Lukachukai area at sites where perishables have not survived. Most likely, many of these practices and symbols were widespread beyond the Chuskas and Chaco. As important, we recognize that the people who occupied Basketmaker sites in the Chuska–Lukachukai area and Chaco Canyon may have belonged to the same highly mobile communities (Wills and Windes 1989; Wills et al. 2012).

Because many ritual practices at Chaco were expressed materially through the use of perishable artifacts, and because of the excellent preservation of perishables in the Chuska–Lukachukai area, it is here where we are able to see our strongest connections. Large assemblages of Basketmaker-era perishable artifacts were recovered from rockshelters such as Broken Flute Cave in the Prayer Rock District and Tseahatso and Mummy caves in Canyon del Muerto (Morris 1925; Morris 1980). Doubtless, many of these connections were also present at open sites where perishables were not preserved. Although more than 160 Basketmaker

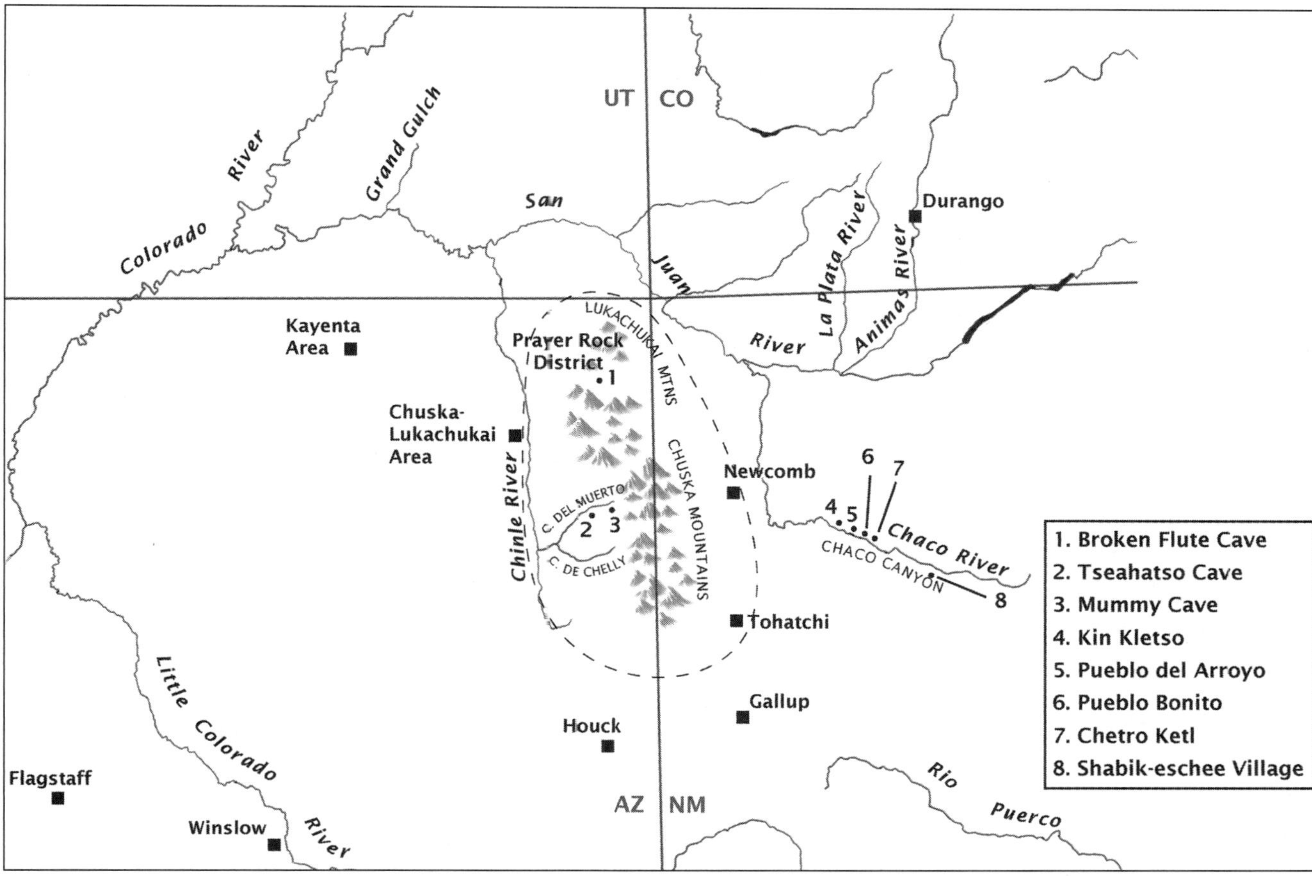

FIGURE 25.1. Location of sites and regions discussed in the chapter (map by Anthony De Luz).

TABLE 25.1. Museum collections used in this study.

Institution	Collection	Collector	Objects Referenced
American Museum of Natural History	Canyon del Muerto	Earl Morris	Burden baskets, miniature clay burden baskets, twined sandals
	Prayer Rock District	Earl Morris	Miniature clay burden baskets, twined sandals
	Pueblo Bonito	George Pepper	Burden baskets, twined sandals, sandal tablets, wooden ceremonial sticks, wooden flutes, Chuskan ceramics, corn cache
Arizona State Museum	Prayer Rock District	Earl Morris	Burden baskets, miniature clay burden baskets, twined sandals, wooden agricultural implements, wooden flutes
Museum of Northern Arizona	Interstate 40	George J. Gumerman, III	Pottery bowl fragment with figurative design
National Museum of the American Indian (Smithsonian)	Pueblo Bonito	George Pepper	Baskets, twined sandals, wooden ceremonial sticks, wooden flutes
National Museum of Natural History (Smithsonian)	Prayer Rock District	Earl Morris	Baskets, twined sandals
	Pueblo Bonito, Pueblo del Arroyo	Neil Judd	Bifurcated baskets, clay bifurcated basket effigies, sandals, sandal tablets
	Shabik'eschee Village	Frank H. H. Roberts, Jr.	Miniature clay burden basket
University of Colorado, Boulder	Canyon del Muerto	Earl Morris	Burden baskets, twined sandals
	La Plata and Durango collections	Earl Morris	Painted pottery bowls with figurative designs

III sites have been recorded in Chaco Canyon (Wills and Windes 1989:349), all are open sites. Apart from some Archaic basketry and sandals in Atlatl Cave, our earliest, well-preserved perishables from Chaco Canyon are from the early northern arc of rooms in Pueblo Bonito, where a twill plaited sandal yielded an accelerator mass spectrometry date in the early AD 800s (Jolie 2013). Although we cannot demonstrate that many of the same Chuskan perishable artifacts we emphasize here were also present in Chaco Canyon during Basketmaker times, we think that the tradition was the same or shared, based on similarities between architecture and pottery preserved at sites in both the Chuskan area, such as Broken Flute Cave, and Chaco Canyon, such as Shabik'eschee Village.

Strong economic ties between Chaco Canyon and the Chuskas have previously been demonstrated with evidence that pots, timbers, and corn from the Chuskas made their way to Chaco Canyon. Chuskan trachyte or sanidine basalt-tempered corrugated ware was identified at Pueblo Bonito, first by Anna O. Shepard (1939:280) and later by others (King 2003; Stoltman 1999; Toll 1991; Toll et al. 1980, 2006), and researchers now estimate that a third of the entire Chacoan ceramic assemblage, both utility and decorated (white) ware, was imported from the Chuska area in the eleventh century. Concomitantly, between AD 1040 and 1105, massive amounts of construction timbers were imported into Chaco, approximately half from the Chuska–Lukachukai area (Betancourt et al. 1986; Durand et al. 1999; Toll et al. 2006:125). Finally, isotope ratios show that some of the maize found at Chaco was likely grown in fields near the eastern Chuska slopes (Benson 2012; Benson et al. 2003; Benson et al. 2006).

We believe that this strong Chaco–Chuska connection dates back to Basketmaker times. Our reexamination of older artifact collections from the Chuska–Lukachukai area and Chaco Canyon suggests that Chacoan and Chuskan Basketmakers were either the same people or closely related in the AD 600s. People likely moved back and forth periodically, linking these settlements through close interaction and mobility. While we recognize and appreciate the probable multiple origins of Chaco culture (e.g., Vivian 1990), we consider influences from the Chuska–Lukachukai area to be foundational to the development of the Chaco Phenomenon.

Our evidence indicates that by the AD 1000s, if not earlier, social groups, perhaps ritual sodalities, at Chaco were making use of portable ritual artifacts derived from Basketmaker prototypes (see also Webster and Jolie 2010). We suggest that these objects were employed to express continuity with the past and to reinforce ancestral ties. Ruth Van Dyke (2007:128) has suggested a similar connection between Basketmaker and Chacoan great kivas.

The Chacoan artifacts we consider are elaborated versions of formerly utilitarian items that were used in rituals and curated when not in use. In a sense, they were special "models" of utilitarian objects not used in everyday activities. Objects that we believe to have transitioned from the utilitarian to the ceremonial realm include burden baskets, sandals, wooden crooks, staffs, and carved sticks, which we explore in greater detail below. Burden baskets and possibly some sandals apparently acquired ceremonial uses by the AD 600s–700s, or mid- to late Basketmaker III, whereas the wooden artifacts may have transitioned later. All seem to have been core components of Chacoan ritual practice by the AD 1000s, or the Pueblo II period. The use of this symbolism seems to have peaked at Chaco and elsewhere during the AD 1100s.

Burden Baskets

The idea that certain ceremonial objects found at Chaco signaled ancestral connections to Basketmaker groups was first proposed more than half a century ago by Earl Morris and Robert Burgh (1941:54–58) and Neil Judd (1954:306–320) in reference to the bifurcated baskets and ceramic bifurcated basket effigies found at Chaco and a few other sites in the Southwest. In the view of these authors, the large, decorated burden or carrying basket of the San Juan region (e.g., Guernsey and Kidder 1921:Plate 23), formerly used for gathering wild plants and transporting firewood and agricultural produce, provided at least partial inspiration for the Chacoan bifurcated basket (Figure 25.2). As the economic focus of Basketmaker societies shifted to more intensive agriculture, carrying baskets declined in the utilitarian realm and evolved into more elaborate forms with ritual functions (e.g., Morris and Burgh 1941:54, Figure 15). Miniature decorated carrying baskets were also produced that served no obvious utilitarian purpose (Morris and Burgh 1941:Figure 28).

Morris and Burgh (1941:54) hypothesized that carrying baskets began their shift to the ceremonial realm by about AD 600. However, a recent accelerator mass spectrometry date with a calibrated midpoint of AD 260 on a tumpline associated with one elaborately decorated carrying basket from Canyon de Chelly suggests that this chronology needs to be reevaluated (Morris and Burgh 1941:Frontispiece; Smiley and Robins 1997:177, Figure B.13). Morris and Burgh (1954:54–58, Figure 28, caption) considered the Basketmaker III wedge-shaped carrying basket with a basal arch the prototype for the deeply arched bifurcated baskets found earliest at Chaco Canyon and later in northeastern Arizona and southeastern Utah. In their words:

> The flaring conical carrying basket, undoubtedly utilitarian in the first place, began to be modified in Basketmaker III and by the end of that period there had developed a wedge-shaped variant of it that was the form ancestor of the bizarre ceremonial carrying basket of Pueblo III [1941:58].

Recent research by Edward Jolie (2013) suggests that the historical origins of the bifurcated basket are far more complex. Noting the lack of clear Southwestern intermediary forms of the deeply bifurcated basket, Jolie questions Morris and Burgh's local linear progression. He agrees, however, that carrying baskets, both the

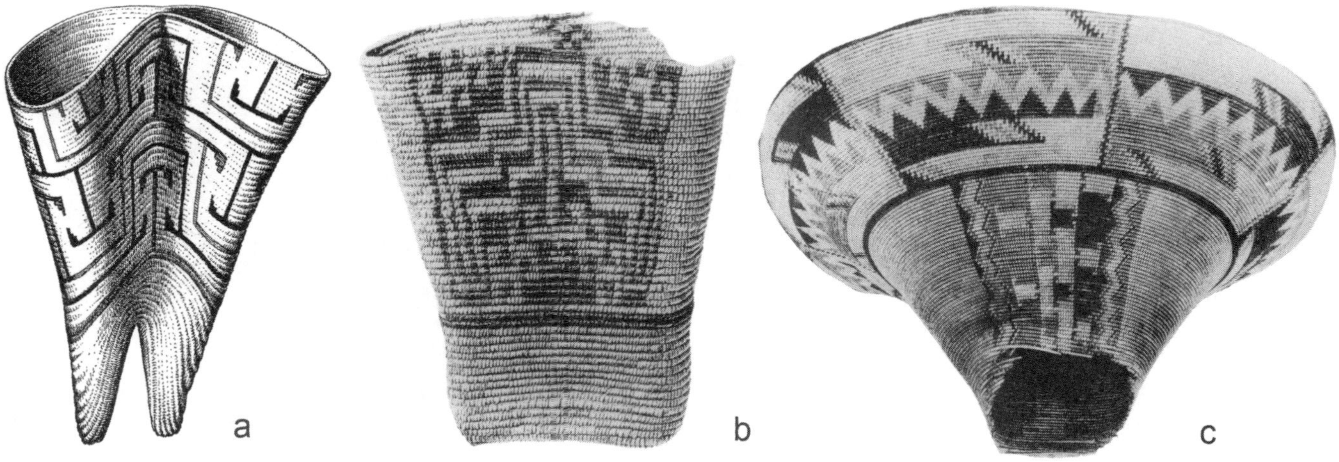

FIGURE 25.2. Pueblo period bifurcated basket and Basketmaker carrying baskets: (a) Pueblo II bifurcated basket with painted design from Room 320 in Pueblo Bonito (from Judd 1954:Figure 99); (b) Basketmaker III unfinished carrying basket with basal arch, Mummy Cave, Canyon del Muerto (adapted from Morris and Burgh 1941:Figure 28); (c) Basketmaker II or III carrying basket, Pictograph Cave, Canyon del Muerto (adapted from Morris and Burgh 1941:Frontispiece).

bifurcated form and those derived from Basketmaker nonbifurcated forms, were components of ritual practice at Chaco.

Basketmaker III miniature clay nonbifurcated carrying baskets were prevalent in Canyon del Muerto (Morris 1927:158, Figures 6f and 10–12) and the Prayer Rock District (Morris 1980: Figure 92g–i), and they also occur in the Kayenta area (Guernsey 1931:Figure 26a–b); west of the Colorado River in Utah (Morss 1931:50); and most importantly, at Shabik'eschee Village in Chaco Canyon (Roberts 1929:125, Plate 18f). The presence of a miniature clay carrying basket at Shabik'eschee suggests that carrying baskets were in use at Chaco during Basketmaker III times, even though no woven examples have survived. To the north of Chaco Canyon, small carrying baskets of fired clay are reported from Pueblo I sites in the La Plata (Morris 1939:Plate 232c–d) and Animas River drainages of southern Colorado, and the remains of a possible woven carrying basket are also reported from a Pueblo I site in the Animas drainage (Webster 2003). None of these baskets is bifurcated.

The remains of two very large coiled baskets that appear to be carrying baskets with no evidence of bifurcation were recovered from what appear to be ritual contexts in the older northern arc of rooms at Pueblo Bonito (Judd 1954:171, 234–235; Pepper 1920:68–69, 162, 234–235, Figure 100). The first, identified by Pepper as an altar painting, is a large clay-coated painted basket, which indeed could have served as an altarpiece. The other, which Pepper described as "almost a counterpart of the 'Basket Peoples' large baskets" he knew from Grand Gulch, Utah (1920: 234), was used to cover a pit filled with seemingly intentionally broken pottery and several other baskets.

The earliest reported bifurcated baskets and their related ceramic effigies in the Southwest come from late Pueblo II contexts in Chaco Canyon. At least five bifurcated baskets were recovered from the western cluster of burial rooms at Pueblo Bonito (Judd 1954:307–320), and another possible example is known from Kin Kletso (Jolie 2013). Clay effigies of bifurcated baskets are reported from Pueblo Bonito, Pueblo del Arroyo, and Kin Kletso (Judd 1954:316, Plate 88, 1959:23, 163, 317, Figure 100, Plate 35; see Jolie 2013 for the Kin Kletso effigy; Figure 25.3). These effigies may have served as altarpieces.

Morris and Burgh (1941:54) interpreted Basketmaker III carrying baskets, miniature clay carrying baskets, and clay female figurines as effigy ritual paraphernalia related to female fertility and bountiful harvests. As an alternative explanation, some if not all of these Basketmaker miniature baskets and female figurines may have functioned as toys and models for teaching gender roles (Hays-Gilpin 2000:40; Jolie 2013). In Judd's (1954:307, 320; see also Morris and Burgh 1941:56) view, the large Chaco bifurcated baskets were used to store and transport the ritual paraphernalia of a particular group, probably a women's society, descended from Basketmaker times. We agree that the ritual use of burden baskets has considerable time depth, from at least AD 600 through the 1100s, but suggest that more research is needed before they can be directly linked to sodalities of Basketmaker origin.

Sandals

Sandals, or at least the idea of sandals, seem to have acquired a ritual significance by the AD 1000s in Chaco Canyon, based on their widespread depiction in rock art (Pepper 1920:Figure 115) and the creation of portable stone, wood, and ceramic sandal forms that may have served as effigies (i.e., Judd 1954:109, Plate 81, 1959:131, Figure 29; Pepper 1920:248; Figure 25.4). The ground-stone and wood tablets, referred to in the literature as "sandal lasts," seem to us unlikely to have been used solely in sandal manufacture because of their large size (and sometimes miniature size), the presence of pigment on some stone examples, and the elaborate painted polychrome designs on some wooden and stone forms (Eaton 1991:52, Figure 6; Judd 1959:131, Figure

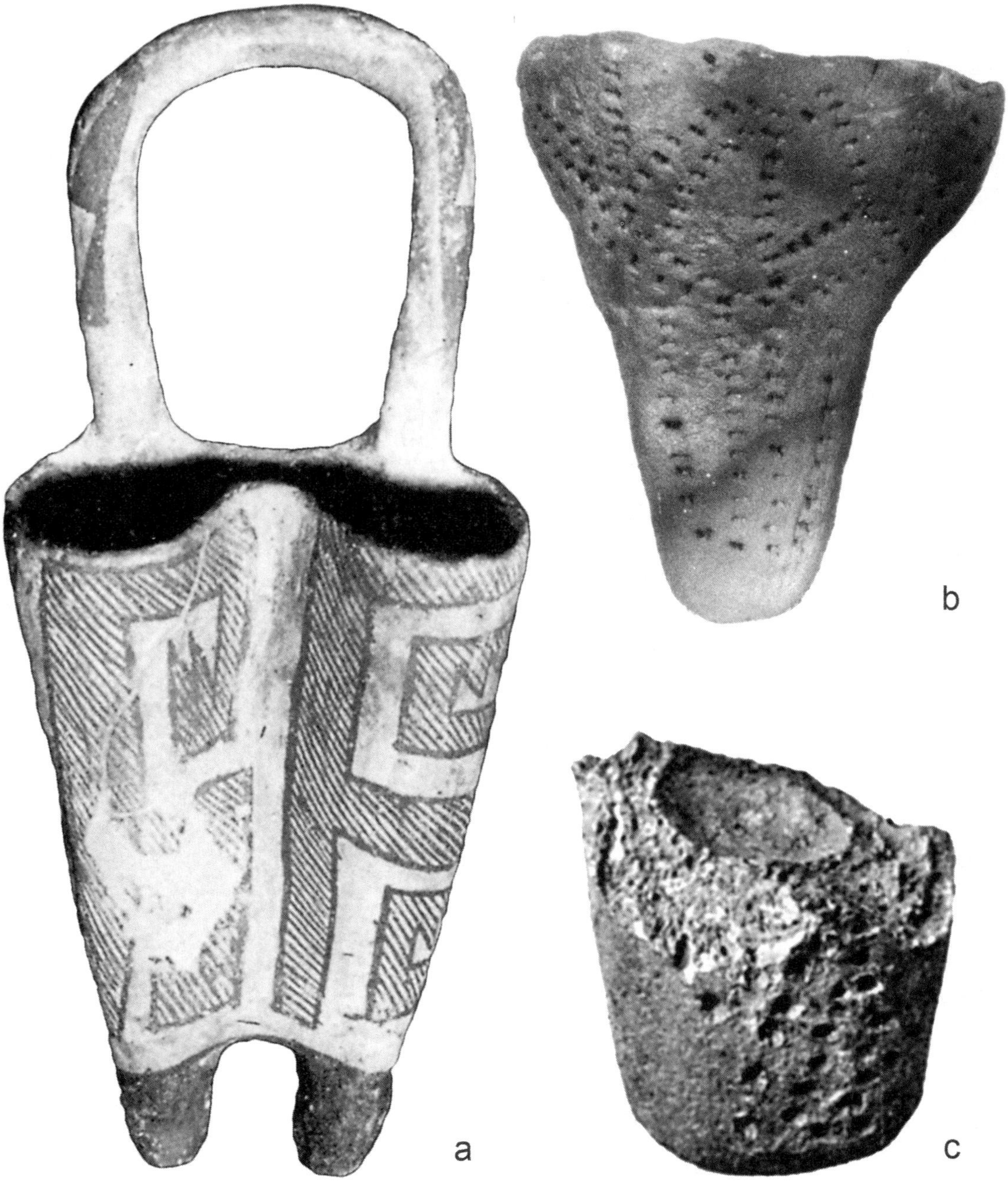

FIGURE 25.3. Pueblo period ceramic bifurcated basket effigy and Basketmaker III miniature clay carrying baskets: (a) Chaco Pueblo II–III ceramic bifurcated basket effigy, Pueblo del Arroyo (from Judd 1959:Plate 35b); (b) Basketmaker III miniature clay carrying basket, Prayer Rock District (Arizona State Museum catalog number A-13964; photo by Kelley Hays-Gilpin; courtesy of the Arizona State Museum, University of Arizona); (c) Basketmaker III base fragment of miniature clay carrying basket, Shabik'eschee Village, Chaco Canyon (from Roberts 1929:Plate 18f).

29; Morris 1928:322, 1939:Plate 145; Webster 2011). Rather, we would argue that the oversized, pigmented, or painted forms more likely served as altarpieces or other ritual paraphernalia. Indeed, sandal forms were among the components of a painted ritual wood assemblage from the West Ruin of Aztec (Webster 2011:149–152, Figure 2) and a set of painted stone figurines from a late Pueblo II period Chaco-style site near Chambers, Arizona (Eaton 1991:52, Figure 6).

If any sandal form acquired a ritual significance by the AD 1000s, it was the twined sandal, which developed sometime during the Basketmaker II period and achieved its greatest complexity during the mid- to late AD 600s (Basketmaker III [Hays-Gilpin et al. 1998; Figure 25.5]). These seventh-century Basketmaker sandals incorporate up to 14 different weave structures, are patterned with four-color geometric designs at the toe and midsole of the upper face, and have textured geometric designs on the sole (Hays-Gilpin et al. 1998). Their high message potential and the tremendous amount of labor, knowledge, and skill required to produce them suggest that twined sandals had acquired a specialized, perhaps ceremonial, use by this time

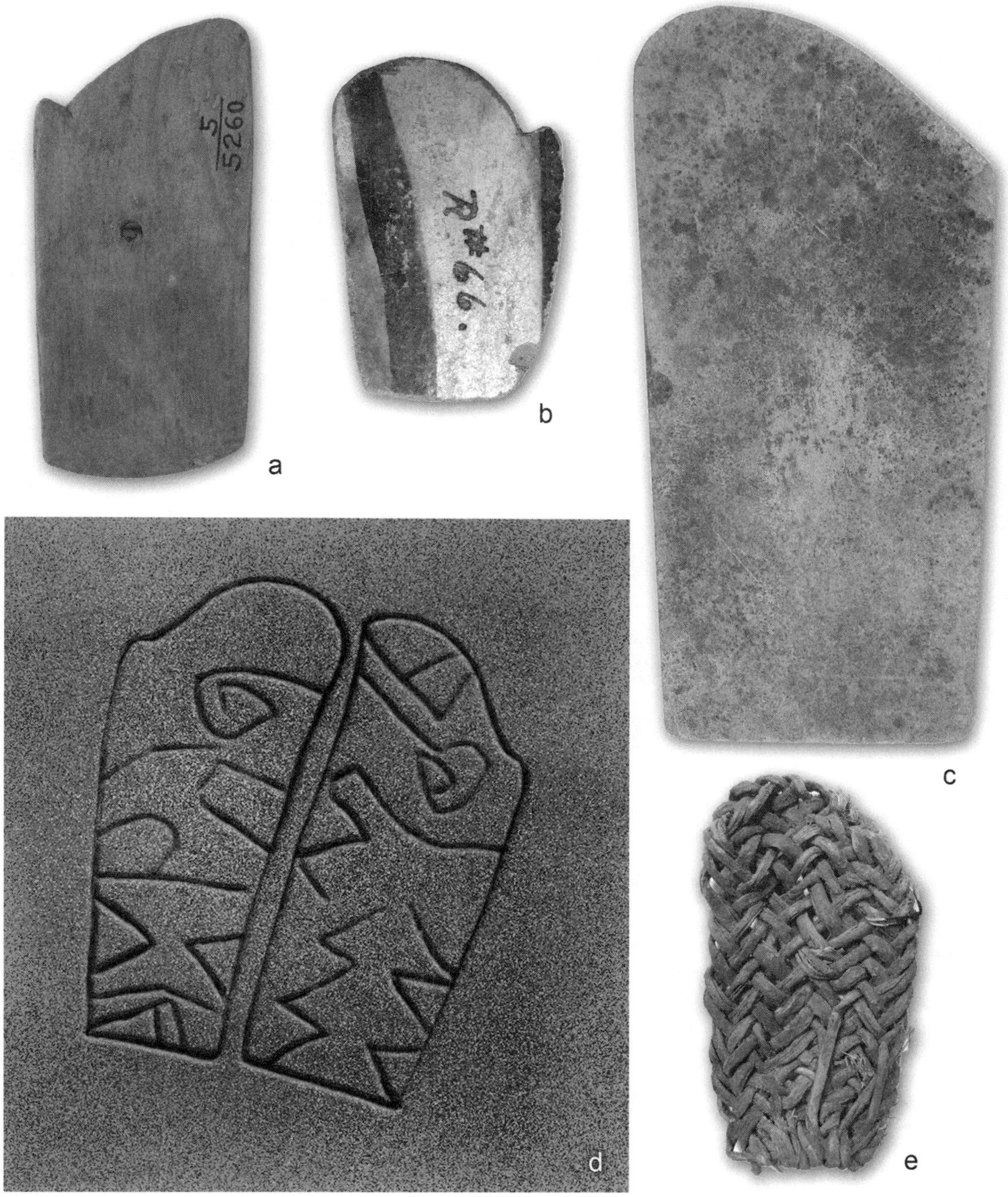

FIGURE 25.4. Pueblo period sandal forms and rock art imagery from Pueblo Bonito: (a) miniature wood sandal tablet from Room 105 (National Museum of the American Indian, Smithsonian Institution, catalog number 05/5260; photo by Laurie Webster); (b) Black-on-white potsherd in the shape of a jog-toed sandal from Room 66 (Division of Anthropology, American Museum of Natural History, catalog number H-6124; photo by Laurie Webster); (c) stone sandal slab from Room 326 (Department of Anthropology, National Museum of Natural History, Smithsonian Institution, catalog number A-335892; photo by Laurie Webster); (d) two sandal figures etched into the wall of Room 83 (drawing by Anthony De Luz; after Pepper 1920:Figure 115); (e) miniature woven sandal from Room 25 (Division of Anthropology, American Museum of Natural History, catalog number H-2923; photo by Laurie Webster).

(Webster 2008:183). The major production areas for these elaborate Basketmaker III sandals were the Chuska–Lukachukai area, the Kayenta area, and the San Juan drainage in southwestern Colorado and southeastern Utah.

Carbonized examples of these highly decorated sandals have been recovered from late Basketmaker/early Pueblo I sites on the eastern slope of the Chuska Mountains near Tohatchi, New Mexico (Webster 1999a, 1999b). If perishables had survived at Basketmaker III sites in Chaco Canyon, it seems likely that twined sandals would be among these remains. At this point, the earliest known examples from Chaco Canyon date to the late AD 800s (Judd 1924; Windes 2006). An undated decorated

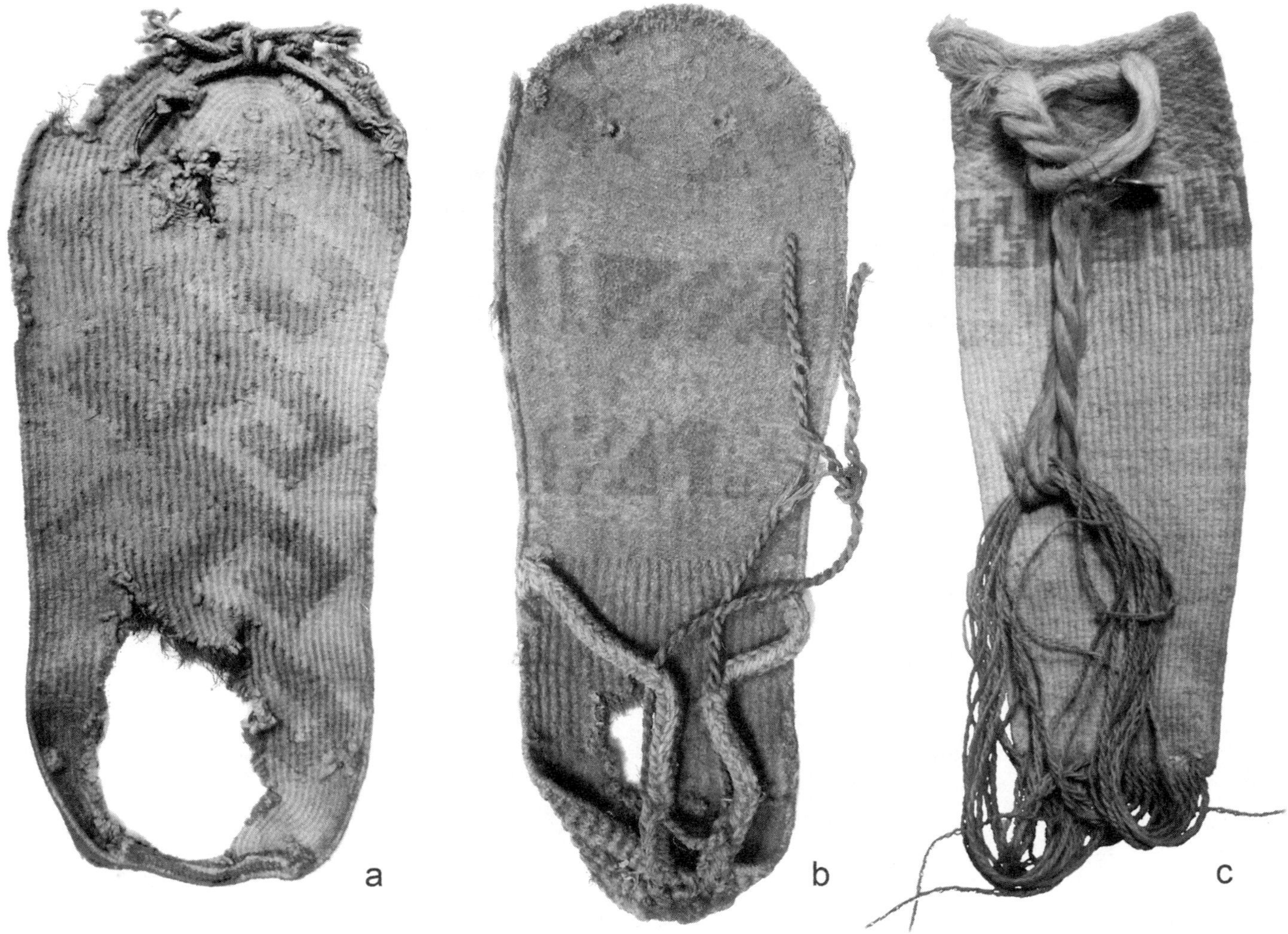

FIGURE 25.5. Pueblo period and Basketmaker III twined sandals: (a) Pueblo II twined sandal from Pueblo Bonito (American Museum of Natural History catalog number H/3942; photo by Laurie Webster); (b) probable Pueblo I twined sandal from Pueblo Bonito (American Museum of Natural History catalog number H/9183; photo by Laurie Webster); (c) Basketmaker III twined sandal, Canyon del Muerto (American Museum of Natural History catalog number 29.1/1655; photo by Kelley Hays-Gilpin; all images courtesy of the Division of Anthropology, American Museum of Natural History).

twined sandal from the northern arc of rooms at Pueblo Bonito (Figure 25.5b) likely dates to the AD 800s based on stylistic criteria and recovery from the same room as the directly dated twill plaited sandal.

Twined sandals were used at several great-house sites and at least two small-house sites in Chaco during the Classic Bonito period. Examples were found in a number of rooms in Pueblo Bonito, mostly from room fill or deposits identified as trash. Several were identified from the northern burial cluster, and western burial room 326 yielded a pair of twined sandals in an elliptical basket (Judd 1954:76). Compared with other forms of Basketmaker-style perishables at Pueblo Bonito, twined sandals are more evenly distributed and less clearly associated with ritual contexts, but their presence in Room 326 suggests that they held a special status. A stone sandal form (sandal tablet) was also found in this room (Figure 25.4c).

Twined sandals were also recovered from the great houses of Pueblo del Arroyo (Judd 1959:9, 124) and Chetro Ketl (Reiter 1933:23, 41, Plates VII, XI[1]; Vivian 1931:23–27, Figures 8–9). Carbonized fiber artifacts that may be fragments of twined sandals are present in Pueblo II collections from two small-house sites, 29SJ1360 (McKenna 1984:309, Figure 5.17, Nos. 2–3) and BC 58 (Laurie D. Webster, personal observation 2008). The wide distribution of twined sandals at both Basketmaker Chuskan and Pueblo II Chacoan sites suggests that they were not emblematic of a single sodality or kin group but were used by many community members, perhaps to mark gender or other social roles.

Wooden Crooks, Staffs, and Carved Sticks

Some forms of Basketmaker wooden implements, such as digging sticks and turkey crooks, also appear to have evolved into ritual paraphernalia in the Chaco world (Figure 25.6). Many of these same items continue to serve a ritual role among the Pueblos today. Certain ceremonial staffs from Rooms 32 and 33 at Pueblo Bonito appear to be adaptations of ancestral utilitarian objects. For example, the long ceremonial sticks with a spatulate blade at one end (Pepper's Types 3 and 4) are nearly identical to some digging sticks from Basketmaker caves in the Prayer Rock District (compare Pepper 1920:Figures 58 and 60 with Morris 1980:Figure 90d–g). The major difference is that the Chaco examples have attachments for feathers. One of Pepper's Type 2 sticks and several of his curved sticks also closely resemble Basketmaker III examples from the Prayer Rock District (compare Pepper 1920:Figures 57a and 61 with Morris 1980:Figure 84f and 84a, respectively). The simple curved crook of Basketmaker times is not reported from Chaco Canyon, but the staff with a claw-like end (Judd 1954:Figure 72; Pepper 1920:145–146, Figure 55) could be a Chaco variation. A petroglyph near Pueblo Bonito appears to depict a human holding a crook, but the image cannot be dated. The wooden flutes from Room 33 at Pueblo Bonito also have precursors at Basketmaker III sites, most notably Broken Flute Cave in the Prayer Rock District (compare Pepper 1920:Figure 67a with Morris 1959, 1980:Figure 87). Flute-player figures first appear in rock art in the Chuskas in the AD 600s and are quite common later on in Chaco Canyon, throughout the Four Corners area, and beyond.

Butterfly Hair Whorls

Chaco rock art includes depictions of figures with hair whorls (Figure 25.7). This hairstyle, consisting of round to T-shaped appendages on each side of the head, above the ears, is depicted in rock art and painted pottery in different times and places in the Ancestral Puebloan world. Today they are called "butterfly hair whorls" at Hopi and "squash blossom hair whorls" at some other pueblos. They symbolize a Pueblo "maiden" who has completed her puberty ceremony and is eligible for marriage and for initiation into important ritual roles (Hays-Gilpin 2002). To date, the earliest dated rock art image of a human figure with hair whorls appears in Canyon de Chelly. This may be another example of a ritual-related practice that began in the Chuska–Lukachukai region and spread to Chaco and beyond.

The painting of a figure with butterfly hair whorls in Canyon de Chelly is partly overlain by mud plaster containing juniper bark that has been radiocarbon dated to the AD 200s (late Basketmaker II, preceramic period [Loendorf 2010:44–45]). Therefore, the pictograph is at least that old or somewhat older. The petroglyphs in Chaco Canyon that depict figures wearing hair whorls have not been dated, but they are stylistically consistent with the figures typical of the Puebloan period. There are no known examples of hair whorls on painted pottery from Chaco, but figures with hair whorls were painted on several late Basketmaker III and early Pueblo I pottery bowls (Figures 25.8 and 25.9; Table 25.2) from Houck to Tohatchi Flats and Newcomb to Durango (Figure 25.1).

Hair whorl images, then, seem to begin in Basketmaker II contexts in Canyon de Chelly and appear later in both rock art and pottery over a broad area that includes Chaco, the northern

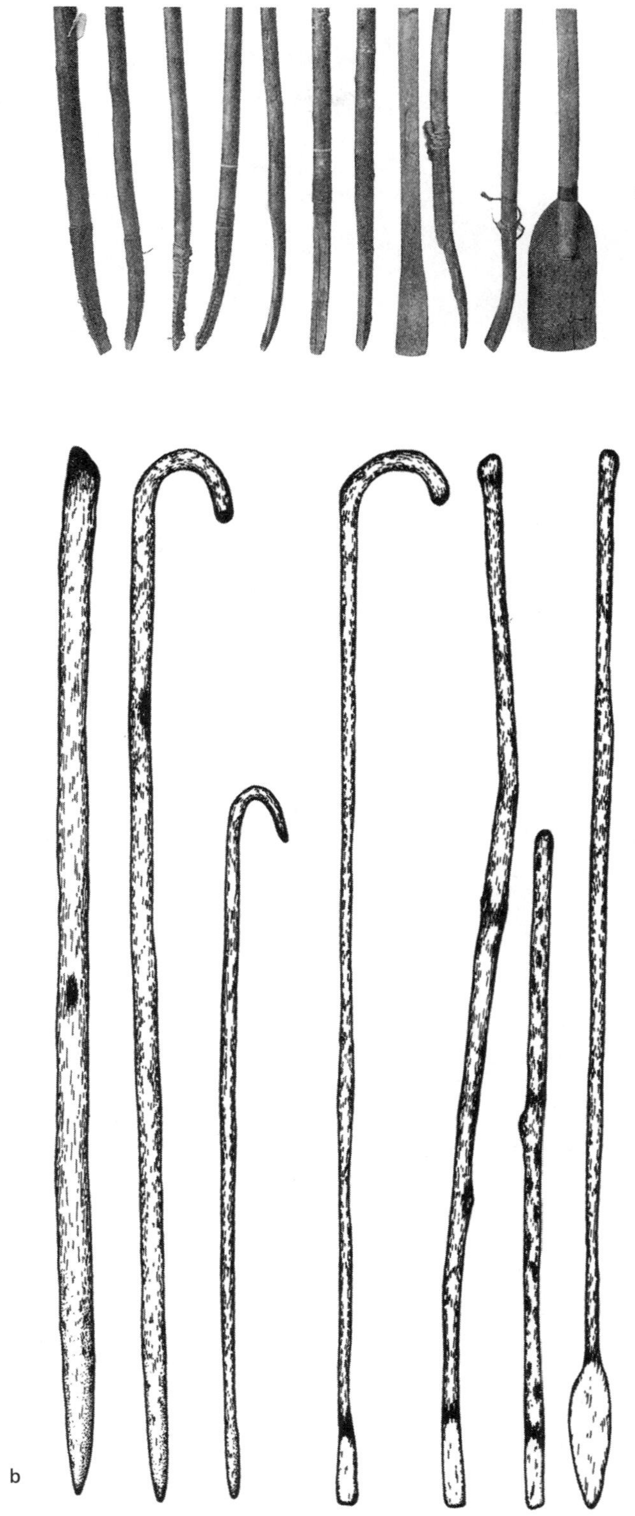

FIGURE 25.6. Pueblo period ceremonial sticks and Basketmaker agricultural sticks: (a) Pueblo II ceremonial sticks from Rooms 32 and 33, Pueblo Bonito (from Pepper 1920:Figure 58); (b) Basketmaker III agricultural digging sticks from the Prayer Rock District (adapted from Morris 1980:Figure 90).

FIGURE 25.7. Chaco Canyon petroglyphs depicting groups of figures with hair whorls (drawings by Jane Kolber).

TABLE 25.2. Basketmaker III–Pueblo I Black-on-white vessels with human figures with hair whorls.

Figure	Source	Catalog Number	Date Range	Provenience	Notes
25.8a	Museum of Northern Arizona	NA 8939.PH3.1	AD 800s dates on pithouse	Houck, AZ, NA 8939, pithouse 3	Excavated by George J. Gumerman, III, Interstate 40 project
25.8b	American Museum of Natural History	29.1/2936	Basketmaker III–Pueblo I	Captain Tom Wash near Newcomb store, NM	Excavated by Earl Morris in 1922 (Morris 1927:172)
25.8c	University of Colorado Museum of Natural History	UCM 9578	Basketmaker III–Pueblo I	Northwest edge of Durango, CO	Found by Frank Lee and given to Earl Morris by I. F. "Zeke" Flora
25.8d	University of Colorado Museum of Natural History	UCM 9509	Basketmaker III–Pueblo I	Tohatchi Flats, west of Gallup-Shiprock Highway, NM	Excavated between 1923 and 1930 by Earl Morris
25.9	University of Colorado Museum of Natural History	UCM 3849	Pueblo I	Near Mancos, CO, Morris La Plata Site 33, building III, room 3	Pitcher, excavated by Earl Morris in 1929 (Morris 1939:Plate 224-l)

Note: All vessels appear to have mineral paint but have not been positively identified.

San Juan (i.e., Durango), and modern pueblos. Today, hair whorls signify eligibility for marriage and participation in certain ritual sodalities. While we do not know the relationships among the status of the figures with hair whorls, the rituals depicted on the pottery bowls, and the figures with hair whorls in Chacoan rock art, the latter may symbolically reference Basketmaker roots in the Chuska–Lukachukai area.

Cached Corn from Pueblo Bonito

Yet another possible long-standing connection to the Chuska–Lukachukai area is illustrated by a cache of well-preserved, unburned corncobs excavated from Pueblo Bonito by Pepper in the 1890s. Six were excavated from the Room 3 series, which, based on architectural and tree-ring studies, was a single interconnecting set of rooms in one of the older (northwest) por-

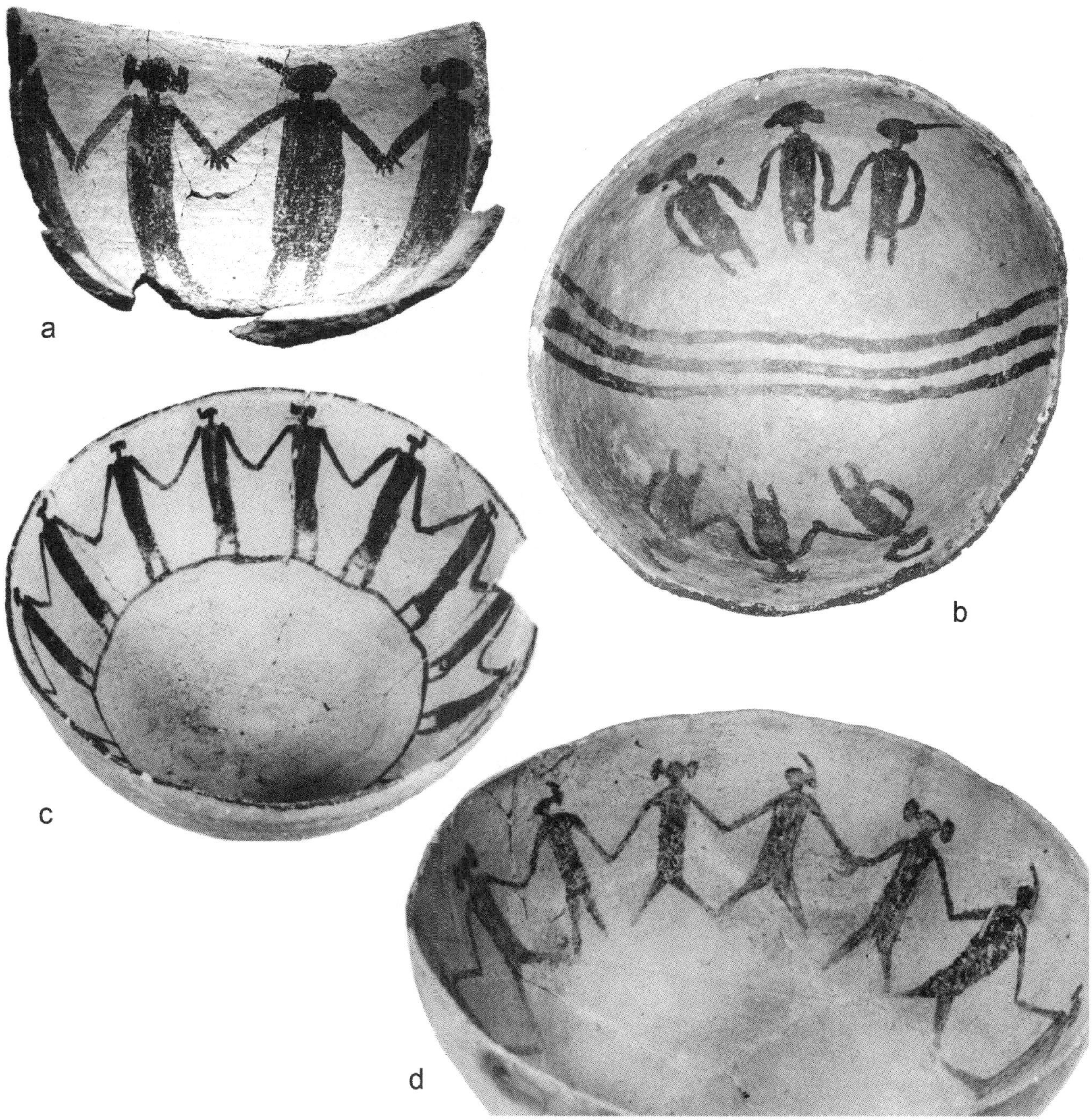

FIGURE 25.8. Pottery vessels depicting groups of figures with hair whorls: (a) Museum of Northern Arizona catalog number NA 8939.PH3.3 (photo by Kelley Hays-Gilpin); (b) Division of Anthropology, American Museum of Natural History, catalog number 29.1/2936 (photo by Laurie Webster); (c–d) University of Colorado Museum of Natural History catalog numbers UCM 9578 and UCM 9509.

tions of Pueblo Bonito (Cordell et al. 2008). The corn was recently radiocarbon dated and chemically examined to determine where the corn plants were grown. Chemical studies suggest that these cobs were grown outside Chaco Canyon near Newcomb, New Mexico, on the eastern Chuska slope (Benson et al. 2003). The intercept radiocarbon dates indicate that the corn was harvested over a 300-year period, between ca. AD 870 and 1220. Cordell and others (2008) argue either that the Room 3 series was left open so that corn could be deposited there periodically or, more likely, that this corn became part of the archaeological record when the rooms were opened periodically to place corn there. The cobs probably do not reflect the dispersal of a single bundle of corn. Rather, they seem to reflect the ritual opening of a series of rooms to deposit corn, perhaps to link those rooms to ancestral fields and communities in the Chuska–Lukachukai area.

FIGURE 25.9. Pottery pitcher with hand-holding figures wearing hair whorls (drawing by Anthony De Luz; after Morris 1939:Plate 224-l).

CONCLUSIONS

In conclusion, we posit that a significant subset of ritual artifacts and imagery documented at Classic Bonito phase Chaco Canyon originated during the Basketmaker period. These objects may have been used at Chaco to commemorate ancestral origins or the histories of particular sodalities or other social groups. Lacking perishable evidence from Basketmaker III contexts in Chaco Canyon, we cannot rule out the local development of these objects, but at this point our comparisons of Basketmaker and Chaco artifacts point to a long-standing connection with the Chuska–Lukachukai area and perhaps with the ancestral villages of the founders of some communities in Chaco Canyon. The same groups of people may have moved back and forth between these areas both during and after Basketmaker times. Certainly the evidence furnished by corn, timbers, and ceramics substantiates intensive interaction between the Chuska–Lukachukai area and Chaco Canyon. Our research suggests that objects and symbols that originated in the Chuska–Lukachukai area, perhaps as early as the Basketmaker II period, were maintained in ritual that spread to Chaco and other communities.

While some might contend that the persistence of these Basketmaker styles into the Pueblo II period simply represents cultural continuity, we argue that the uses and contexts of these artifacts changed as they moved from everyday use into the ritual realm. Their deposition in special burial clusters and ritual storerooms, their elaboration with paint or feathers, and the creation of miniature or oversized replicas or models, all reported for Chaco, suggest to us that these formerly utilitarian objects had developed ritual functions and meanings. This transition had already begun in Basketmaker III times, as suggested by miniature clay models of burden baskets. Even sandals and baskets were not necessarily or merely utilitarian during that time. It is likely that not everyone had highly decorated, elaborate sandals and baskets, and some such artifacts were deposited in "special" contexts such as mortuary assemblages. The objects and images we discuss may have been displayed and handled in sodality initiations, where novices would have learned about the origins of those who founded the rituals owned and transmitted by each group, such as practiced by modern Pueblo societies (Parsons 1939:118). Whether we are right or wrong about each specific connection, our exploration of these questions would not be possible without access to existing collections and archives. We hope to have demonstrated that collections made nearly a century ago still hold great relevance for the study of important and new anthropological questions.

Acknowledgments

Hearty thanks go to Don Fowler and to Nancy Parezo, Reba Rauch, and Joel Janetski for organizing the sessions in honor of Don. We would also like to thank everyone at the museums and archives we have mentioned for facilitating our research and caring for collections so that they will be available for future research. Special thanks go to Steve Lekson for some indispensable tidbits of data and history. Thanks go to Jana Comstock for bibliographic assistance.

References Cited

Benson, Larry V.
2012 Development and Application of Methods Used to Source Prehistoric Southwestern Maize: A Review. *Journal of Archaeological Science* 39:791–807.

Benson, Larry, Linda Cordell, Kirk Vincent, Howard Taylor, John Stein, G. Lang Farmer, and Kiyoto Futo
2003 Ancient Maize from Chacoan Great Houses: Where Was It Grown? *Proceedings of the National Academy of Sciences* 100(22):13111–13115.

Benson, Larry, John Stein, Howard Taylor, Richard Friedman and Thomas C. Windes
2006 The Agricultural Productivity of Chaco Canyon and Source(s) of Prehispanic Maize Found in Pueblo Bonito. In *Histories of Maize*, edited by J. Staller, R. H. Tycot, and B. F. Benz, pp. 289–314. Academic Press, Burlington, Massachusetts.

Betancourt, Julio A., Jeffrey S. Dean, and Herbert M. Hull
1986 Prehistoric Long-Distance Transport of Construction Beams, Chaco Canyon, New Mexico. *American Antiquity* 51(2):370–375.

Childs, S. Terry (editor)
2004 *Our Collective Responsibility: The Ethics and Practice of Archaeological Collections Stewardship*. Society for American Archaeology, Washington, D.C.

Cordell, Linda S., H. Wolcott Toll, Mollie S. Toll, and Thomas C. Windes
2008 Archaeological Corn from Pueblo Bonito, Chaco Canyon, New Mexico: Dates, Contexts, Sources. *American Antiquity* 73(3):491–513.

Crown, Patricia L., and W. Jeffrey Hurst
2009 Evidence of Cacao Use in the Prehispanic American Southwest. *Proceedings of the National Academy of Sciences* 106(7): 2110–2113.

Durand, Stephen R., Phillip H. Shelley, Ronald C. Antweiler and Howard E. Taylor
1999 Trees, Chemistry, and Prehistory in the American Southwest. *Journal of Archaeological Science* 26(2):185–203.

Eaton, Linda
1991 The Heart of the Region: The Anthropology Collections of the Museum of Northern Arizona. *American Indian Art* 16(3): 46–53.

Fowler, Don D.
1986 Conserving American Archeological Resources. In *American Archaeology Past and Future: A Celebration of Fifty Years of the Society for American Archaeology*, edited by D. Meltzer, D. Fowler, and J. Sabloff, pp. 135–162. Smithsonian Institution Press, Washington, D.C.
1987 The Uses of the Past: Archaeology in the Service of the State. *American Antiquity* 52(2):229–248.

Fowler, Don D., and Nancy J. Parezo
2000 [1995] Future Prospects. In *Ethics in American Archaeology: Challenges for the 1990s*, edited by M. Lynott and A. Wylie, pp. 50–56. Society for American Archaeology, Washington, D.C.

Frisbie, Theodore R.
1978 High Status Burials in the Greater Southwest: An Interpretive Synthesis. In *Across the Chichimec Sea: Papers in Honor of J. Charles Kelley*, edited by C. Riley and B. Hedrick, pp. 202–227. Southern Illinois University, Carbondale.

Guernsey, Samuel
1931 *Explorations in Northeastern Arizona*. Papers of the Peabody Museum of American Archaeology and Ethnology Vol. 7, No. 1. Harvard University, Cambridge.

Guernsey, Samuel J., and Alfred V. Kidder
1921 *Basket-Maker Caves of Northeastern Arizona*. Papers of the Peabody Museum of American Archaeology and Ethnology Vol. 8, No. 2. Harvard University, Cambridge.

Hays-Gilpin, Kelley
2000 Gender Constructs in the Material Culture of Seventh-Century Anasazi Farmers in North-Eastern Arizona. In *Representations of Gender from Prehistory to the Present*, edited by Moira Donald and Linda Hurcombe, pp. 31–44. Macmillan Press, Houndmills, England.
2002 Wearing a Butterfly, Coming of Age: A 1500 Year Old Puebloan Tradition. In *Children in the Prehistoric Southwest*, edited by K. Kamp, pp. 196–210. University of Utah Press, Salt Lake City.

Hays-Gilpin, Kelley A., Ann Cordy Deegan, and Elizabeth A. Morris
1998 *Prehistoric Sandals from Northeastern Arizona: The Earl H. Morris and Ann Axtell Morris Research*. Anthropological Papers of the University of Arizona No. 62. University of Arizona Press, Tucson.

Jolie, Edward A.
2013 Cultural and Social Diversity in the Prehispanic Southwest: Learning, Weaving, and Identity in the Chaco Regional System, AD 850–1150. Unpublished Ph.D. dissertation, University of New Mexico, Albuquerque.

Judd, Neil M.
1924 Two Chaco Canyon Pit Houses. In *Annual Report of the Board of Regents of the Smithsonian Institution for 1922*, pp. 399–413. Smithsonian Institution, Washington, D.C.
1954 *The Material Culture of Pueblo Bonito*. Smithsonian Miscellaneous Collections Vol. 124. Smithsonian Institution, Washington, D.C.
1959 *Pueblo del Arroyo, Chaco Canyon, New Mexico*. Smithsonian Miscellaneous Collections Vol. 138, No. 1. Smithsonian Institution, Washington, D.C.

King, Valerie Claire
2003 The Organization of Production of Chuska Gray Ware Ceramics for Distribution and Consumption in Chaco Canyon, New Mexico. Unpublished Ph.D. dissertation, University of New Mexico.

Loendorf, Lawrence L.
2010 Pigments of the Imagination: Ancestral Pueblo Painted Walls in Canyon del Muerto, Arizona. In *Painting the Cosmos: Metaphor and Worldview in Images from the Southwest Pueblos and Mexico*, edited by K. Hays-Gilpin and P. Schaafsma, pp. 41–60. Bulletin 67. Museum of Northern Arizona, Flagstaff.

McKenna, Peter J.
1984 *The Architecture and Material Culture of 29SJ1360*. Reports

of the Chaco Center No. 7. Division of Cultural Research, National Park Service, Albuquerque.

Morris, Earl H.

1925 Exploring in the Canyon of Death. *National Geographic Magazine* 48:263–300.

1927 *The Beginnings of Pottery Making in the San Juan Area: Unfired Prototypes and the Wares of the Earliest Ceramic Period.* Anthropological Papers of the American Museum of Natural History Vol. 28, No. 2. American Museum of Natural History, New York.

1928 *Notes on the Excavations in the Aztec Ruin.* Anthropological Papers, 24(5). American Museum of Natural History, New York.

1939 *Archaeological Studies in the La Plata District, Southwestern Colorado and Northwestern New Mexico.* Carnegie Institution Publication, 519. Carnegie Institution of Washington, Washington, D.C.

Morris, Earl H., and Robert F. Burgh

1941 *Anasazi Basketry: Basket Maker II Through Pueblo III: A Study Based on Specimens from the San Juan River Country.* Carnegie Institution Publication, 533. Carnegie Institution of Washington, Washington, D.C.

1954 *Basket Maker II Sites near Durango, CO.* Carnegie Institution Publication, 604. Carnegie Institution of Washington, Washington, D.C.

Morris, Elizabeth A.

1959 Basketmaker Caves in the Prayer Rock District, Northeastern Arizona. Unpublished Ph.D. dissertation, University of Arizona, Tucson.

1980 *Basketmaker Caves in the Prayer Rock District, Northeastern Arizona.* Anthropological Papers of the University of Arizona No. 35. University of Arizona Press, Tucson.

Morss, Noel

1931 *The Ancient Culture of the Fremont River in Utah. Report on the Explorations Under the Claflin-Emerson Fund, 1928–29.* Papers of the Peabody Museum of American Archaeology and Ethnology Vol. 12, No. 3. Harvard University, Cambridge.

Nelson, Ben A.

2006 Mesoamerican Objects and Symbols in Chaco Canyon Contexts. In *The Archaeology of Chaco Canyon: An Eleventh-Century Pueblo Regional Center*, edited by S. Lekson, pp. 339–371. School for Advanced Research Press, Santa Fe, New Mexico.

Parsons, Elsie C.

1939 *Pueblo Indian Religion*, Vol. 1. University of Chicago Press, Chicago.

Pepper, George H.

1920 *Pueblo Bonito.* Anthropological Papers of the American Museum of Natural History Vol. 27. American Museum of Natural History, New York.

Reiter, Winifred Stamm

1933 Personal Adornment of the Ancient Pueblo Indians. Unpublished Master's thesis, University of New Mexico, Albuquerque.

Reyman, Jonathan E.

1978 Pochteca Burials at Anasazi Sites? In *Across the Chichimec Sea: Papers in Honor of J. Charles Kelley*, edited by C. Riley and B. Hedrick, pp. 242–259. Southern Illinois University, Carbondale.

Roberts, Frank H. H., Jr.

1929 *Shabik'eschee Village. A Late Basket Maker Site in the Chaco Canyon, New Mexico.* Bureau of American Ethnology Bulletin, 92. Bureau of American Ethnology, Washington, D.C.

Shepard, Anna O.

1939 Appendix A—Technology of the La Plata Pottery. In *Archaeological Studies of the La Plata District*, edited by E. Morris, pp. 249–287. Carnegie Institution Publication, 519. Carnegie Institution of Washington, Washington, D.C.

Silverman, Sydel, and Nancy J. Parezo (editors)

1995 *Preserving the Anthropological Record.* 2nd rev. ed. Wenner-Gren Foundation, New York.

Smiley, Francis E., and Michael R. Robins (editors)

1997 *Early Farmers in the Northern Southwest: Papers on Chronometry, Social Dynamics, and Ecology.* Animas–La Plata Archaeological Project Research Paper No. 7. U.S. Department of the Interior Bureau of Reclamation, Upper Colorado Region, Salt Lake City.

Stoltman, James B.

1999 The Chaco–Chuska Connection: In Defense of Anna Shepard. In *Pottery and People, a Dynamic Interaction*, edited by J. Skibo and G. Feinman, pp. 9–24. University of Utah Press, Salt Lake City.

Toll, H. Wolcott

1991 Material Distributions and Exchange in the Chaco System. In *Chaco and Hohokam*, edited by P. Crown and W. Judge, pp. 77–107. School for Advanced Research Press, Santa Fe, New Mexico.

Toll, H. Wolcott, Thomas R. Windes, and Peter J. McKenna

1980 Late Ceramic Patterns in Chaco Canyon: The Pragmatics of Modeling Ceramic Exchange. In *Models and Methods in Regional Exchange*, edited by R. Frey, pp. 95–117. SAA Papers No. 1. Society for American Archaeology, Washington, D.C.

2006 Organization of Production. In *The Archaeology of Chaco Canyon: An Eleventh-Century Pueblo Regional Center*, edited by S. Lekson, pp. 117–152. School for Advanced Research Press, Santa Fe, New Mexico.

Van Dyke, Ruth M.

2007 *The Chaco Experience: Landscape and Ideology at the Center Place.* School of Advanced Research Press, Santa Fe, New Mexico.

Vivian, R. Gordon

1931 Basketry of Chetro Ketl. Unpublished manuscript on file at the National Park Service Chaco Archives, Albuquerque.

Vivian, R. Gwinn

1990 *The Chacoan Prehistory of the San Juan Basin.* Academic Press, San Diego.

Webster, Laurie D.

1999a Basketry and Textiles. In *Chuska Chronologies, Houses, and Hogans: Archaeological and Ethnographic Inquiry Along N30–N31 Between Mexican Springs and Navajo, McKinley County, New Mexico, Vol. III, Pt. I: Analysis*, prepared by J. Damp, pp. 185–242. Zuni Cultural Resource Enterprise Report No. 466; ZCRE Research Series No. 10. Zuni Cultural Resource Enterprise, Pueblo of Zuni.

1999b Textiles and Basketry from Basketmaker III and Pueblo II Sites in the Southern Chuska Valley. In *Pipeline Archaeology 1990–1993: The El Paso Natural Gas North System Expansion Project, New Mexico and Arizona: Vol. XII, Bk. 1, Supporting*

Studies: Nonceramic Artifacts, Subsistence and Environmental Studies, and Chronometric Studies, compiled by T. Kearns and J. McVickar, pp. 9-1–9-30. Western Cultural Resource Management, Inc., Farmington, New Mexico.

2003 *Textiles and Basketry*. Electronic document, www.woodscanyon.net/MAPL/basketry_report/index.html.

2008 An Initial Assessment of Perishable Artifact Relationships Among Salmon, Aztec, and Chaco Canyon. In *Chaco's Northern Prodigies: Salmon, Aztec, and the Ascendancy of the Middle San Juan Region After AD 1100*, edited by P. Reed, pp. 167–189. University of Utah Press, Salt Lake City.

2011 Perishable Ritual Artifacts at the West Ruin of Aztec, New Mexico: Evidence for a Chacoan Migration. *Kiva* 77(2): 139–171.

Webster, Laurie D., and Edward A. Jolie

2010 A Perishable Perspective on Chacoan Social Identity. Paper presented at "Current Issues in the Archaeology of Chaco Canyon, AD 850–1150," Amerind Foundation, Dragoon, Arizona.

Wills, W. H., and Thomas C. Windes

1989 Evidence for Population Aggregation and Dispersal During the Basketmaker III Period in Chaco Canyon, New Mexico. *American Antiquity* 54(2):347–349.

Wills, W. H., F. Scott Worman, Wetherbee Dorshow, and Heather Richards

2012 Shabik'eschee Village in Chaco Canyon: Beyond the Archetype. *American Antiquity* 77:326–350.

Windes, Thomas

2006 Early Puebloan Occupations in the Chaco Region: Excavations and Survey of Basketmaker III and Pueblo I Sites, Chaco Canyon, New Mexico, Vol. II. Unpublished draft manuscript. Reports of the Chaco Center No. 13. National Park Service, Santa Fe, New Mexico.

Contributors

Richard V. N. Ahlstrom
HRA, Inc., Conservation Archaeology

C. Melvin Aikens
Department of Anthropology, University of Oregon

Charlotte Beck
Department of Anthropology, Hamilton College

Linda S. Cordell
School for Advanced Research

William H. Doelle
Archaeology Southwest

Christian E. Downum
Department of Anthropology, Northern Arizona University

Ted Goebel
Department of Anthropology, Texas A&M University

Donald L. Hardesty
Department of Anthropology, University of Nevada–Reno

Eugene M. Hattori
Nevada State Museum

Kelley Hays-Gilpin
Department of Anthropology, Northern Arizona University

Bruce B. Huckell
Department of Anthropology and Maxwell Museum of Anthropology, University of New Mexico

Richard E. Hughes
Geochemical Research Laboratory

John W. Ives
Department of Anthropology, University of Alberta

Joel C. Janetski
Department of Anthropology, Brigham Young University

Edward A. Jolie
R. L. Andrews Center for Perishables Analysis, Mercyhurst Archaeological Institute

George T. Jones
Department of Anthropology, Hamilton College

Kevin T. Jones
Ancient Places Consulting, Salt Lake City, and Research Curator, Natural History Museum of Utah

Joshua L. Keene
Department of Anthropology, Texas A&M University

Steven H. Lekson
Department of Anthropology, University of Colorado Museum of Natural History

William D. Lipe
Department of Archaeology, Washington State University

David B. Madsen
Texas Archaeological Research Laboratory, University of Texas at Austin

Stephen E. Nash
Department of Anthropology, Denver Museum of Nature and Science

James F. O'Connell
Archaeology Center and Department of Anthropology, University of Utah

Nancy J. Parezo
American Indian Studies Program, University of Arizona

David Rhode
Desert Research Institute, University of Nevada System

Heidi Roberts
HRA, Inc., Conservation Archaeology

Christina T. Rogers
Department of Anthropology, Denver Museum of Nature and Science

Barbara J. Roth
Department of Anthropology, University of Nevada–Las Vegas

Polly Schaafsma
Laboratory of Anthropology, Museum of New Mexico

Steven R. Simms
Department of Anthropology, Utah State University

Richard K. Talbot
Office of Public Archaeology, Brigham Young University

David Hurst Thomas
Department of Anthropology, American Museum of Natural History

Laurie D. Webster
Department of Anthropology, Northern Arizona University

David R. Wilcox
Museum of Northern Arizona

D. Craig Young
Far Western Anthropological Research Group

María Nieves Zedeño
School of Anthropology, University of Arizona

Index

Numbers in *italics* indicate images.